Using WordPerfect® 5

by Charles O. Stewart III

with Elias Baumgarten
Marilyn Horn Claff
Susan Hafer
Doug Hazen, Jr.
Judy Housman
Forest Lin
Schuyler Lininger, Jr.
Hans A. Lustig
James C. McKeown
Karen Rose
Joel Shore
Anders R. Sterner

Que® Corporation
Carmel, Indiana

Dedication

To Mary

—C.O.S.

Publishing Manager
David P. Ewing

Developmental Director
Charles O. Stewart III

Editorial Director
David F. Noble

Editors
Ann Campbell Holcombe
Kathie-Jo Arnoff
Mary Bednarek
C. Beth Burch
David F. Noble
Shelley O'Hara
Barbara L. Potter
Lynn Yates

Editorial Assistant
Daniel J. Lupo

Technical Editors
Julie A. Harrison
Hans Lustig
Erin McGlyn
Mike Miller

Acquisitions Aide
Stacey Beheler

Indexer
Sharon Hilgenberg

Book Design and Production
Jennifer Matthews
Dan Armstrong
Lori A. Lyons
Carrie Torres Marshall
Diana Moore
Cindy Phipps
Joe Ramon
Dennis Sheehan
Louise Shinault
Peter Tocco

About the Authors

Charles O. Stewart III is a project director and staff writer in the Product Development Department at Que Corporation. He was instrumental in determining the emphases for this book, assembled the team of contributors, and worked closely with them through manuscript development, editing, and final review. Stewart is coauthor of *WordPerfect Tips, Tricks, and Traps*. He wrote the Introduction, Chapters 1 and 2, Appendix D, and the keyboard-command card.

Elias Baumgarten, Ph.D., is an associate professor of philosophy at the University of Michigan at Dearborn. He is the recipient of a Distinguished Teaching Award and has published articles on medical ethics and other topics in philosophy. Baumgarten was a beta tester for WordPerfect 5.0, and he has developed hundreds of macros for himself and others. He contributed Chapter 11.

Marilyn Horn Claff, director of the WordPerfect Special Interest Group of the Boston Computer Society's IBM PC Users' Group, is a WordPerfect certified instructor and independent computer consultant working in the Boston area. She is an active participant in the WordPerfect forum on CompuServe, a beta tester for WordPerfect products, and a columnist for *PC Report*, a BCS newsletter. Claff is completing a Ph.D. in Romance Languages at Harvard University. She contributed Chapters 12 and 19 and Appendixes B and C.

Susan Hafer, the microcomputer specialist for Academic Computing at Wellesley College, has been using, supporting, and teaching WordPerfect on the campus since 1986. She contributed Chapters 7, 20, and 21.

Doug Hazen, Jr., is a programmer for Intellution in Norwood, MA. Hazen, a member of the Boston Computer Society's IBM PC Users' Group and WordPerfect Special Interest Group, is an active participant in the WordPerfect forum on CompuServe. He contributed Chapter 10 and Appendix A.

Judy Housman, Ph.D., is a WordPerfect trainer and consultant who also provides microcomputer training and consulting for project management software, 1-2-3, dBASE, Reflex, and Quattro. A frequent contributor to *PC Week* and the *Boston Business Journal*, she leads the Boston Computer Society's Training and Documentation Group. Among her clients are the Commonwealth of Massachusetts, the Massachusetts Government Land Bank, and the Cambridge YMCA. She contributed Chapters 15 and 18.

Forest Lin, Ph.D., currently teaches at Tulsa Junior College. Lin, an expert on WordPerfect products, has published two books on WordPerfect, one for beginners and the other for advanced users. He is writing a book on PlanPerfect, a spreadsheet program from WordPerfect Corporation. For this book, he wrote Chapters 13 and 14.

Schuyler Lininger, Jr., an Oregon chiropractor, has been a computer consultant and writer for the last seven years. Lininger uses desktop publishing to produce a national newsletter for natural foods stores. He also serves as vice president of sales to a major food supplement company and teaches nutrition at the college level and at seminars. He contributed Chapters 3 and 5, and coauthored Chapter 9.

Hans A. Lustig is copy chief for an industrial advertising agency where he uses WordPerfect to write copy for industrial brochures and manuals. He wrote Chapter 16.

James C. McKeown, Ph.D., is a professor of accountancy at the University of Illinois at Champaign-Urbana and has worked as an expert witness and consultant. He has worked with computers of all types for 25 years and worked with WordPerfect from version 3.0 to the present. He developed Chapter 17.

Karen Rose is the owner of Write on Target, a newsletter production and management company in Santa Rosa, CA. Write on Target produces monthly, bimonthly, and quarterly newsletters using desktop-publishing technologies. Rose teaches desktop publishing courses with Aldus PageMaker, on both the PC and Macintosh, at Sonoma State University and for businesses through Ron Person & Co. She contributed Chapters 4, 6, 24, and 25.

Joel Shore is president of Documentation Systems, a Southborough, MA, private consulting firm providing microcomputer services, including software training, dBASE programming, and documentation. He teaches a range of personal computing courses at Massachusetts Bay Community College, conducts private corporate in-house seminars, and is an active participant and frequent speaker at several of the Boston Computer Society's Special Interest Groups. Shore coauthored Chapter 9 and wrote Chapters 8 and 23.

Anders R. Sterner is a partner of Tanner Propp Fersko & Sterner, a Manhattan firm where he practices law and does computer consulting for clients and other law firms using micro systems. He is a WordPerfect beta tester, having been addicted since version 3.0. Sterner is president of the Fibonacci Society of South Brooklyn, NY, and author of *Crazy Eights—South Brooklyn Rules: A Prolegomena to Any Future Exegesis*. His CompuServe I.D. number is 74076,404. He contributed Chapter 22.

Table of Contents

II Using WordPerfect's Advanced Features

14   Sorting and Selecting Data 455

15   Converting Files 479

III Using WordPerfect's Specialized Features

IV Using WordPerfect for Desktop Publishing

Trademark Acknowledgments

Que Corporation has made every attempt to supply trademarks about company names, products, and services mentioned in this book. Trademarks indicated below were derived from various sources. Que Corporation cannot attest to the accuracy of this information.

Acknowledgments

My greatest indebtedness is to the other contributors to this book. Each one brought to the project a measure of expertise, enthusiasm, professionalism, and commitment that was most gratifying to witness. Although group efforts are fraught with their own set of problems, this book is much stronger for having been a collaboration. My heartfelt thanks to all of you.

I would like to thank Dave Ewing, Publishing Manager, for making this project possible and providing direction, support, and guidance. Thanks also to Pegg Kennedy, Acquisitions Editor, who had the difficult task of communicating with thirteen contributors and overseeing the steady stream of floppy disks and printed copy.

The editors on this book deserve a sustained round of applause and special commendation for their remarkable efforts on a book that presented some unusual editorial challenges. Ann Holcombe ably organized the project meetings, coordinated the editorial effort, put in many long days over many weeks, and maintained her good cheer, support, and sanity throughout. Kathie-Jo Arnoff, Beth Burch, David Noble, Shelley O'Hara, and Barb Potter produced exceptional work despite an extremely tight schedule.

Many thanks go to Que's Production staff for their extraordinary efforts to get this book to the printer on time. Jennifer Matthews, Typesetting Supervisor, sacrificed many evenings and weekends to keep the book on schedule. Jennifer and Dan Armstrong were instrumental in determining the book's design. For their work on this project, thanks also to Dennis Sheehan and Cheryl English; typesetters Joe Ramon, Cindy Phipps, and Louise Shinault; indexer Sharon Hilgenberg; and proofreaders Lori Lyons, Carrie Torres Marshall, Diana Moore, and Peter Tocco.

I would like to thank Mike Miller, Julie Harrison, Erin McGlynn, and Hans Lustig for their technical reviews of the manuscript.

My thanks to Jeff Acerson and Rebecca Mortensen of WordPerfect Corporation for their responsiveness and cooperation throughout this book's genesis.

I want to thank friend and former colleague Noralyn Masselink, Ph.D., for the dissertation example used in Chapter 23.

Finally, I am grateful to Mary, Peter, and Molly for their love and patience.

Introduction

Q uestion: What could the following individuals possibly have in common?

- A programmer in C language

- A graduate student in Romance languages at Harvard

- A Park Avenue attorney

- A microcomputer consultant

- A professor of philosophy who specializes in ethics

- A software trainer and documentation specialist

- A chiropractor who lectures on nutrition and who is an avid organic gardener

- A desktop publisher who creates dazzling newsletters

- A professor of accounting

Answer: All of these individuals are enthusiastic users of WordPerfect®, and all of them are WordPerfect "experts." They, among other WordPerfect experts, made significant contributions to this book.

Many of the authors of this book are members of a national WordPerfect support group; many participate nightly on the WordPerfect forum on the CompuServe Information Service®. In addition, many belong to one of the country's most sophisticated, well-known user groups: the Boston Computer Society. All of them have made this book unique among books about WordPerfect, because this book is a *collaboration* in the *best* sense of that word.

But why a collaboration? Why not? Collaborative efforts are certainly not at all uncommon in academic, scientific, and business environments. In a study of writing on the job, Professor Paul Anderson reported that a survey of "265 professional people in 20 research and development institutions" revealed that around "19 percent of their writing [was] collaborative."[1] Collaborative efforts of the *best* kind have many historical precedents. When you need to accomplish a complex, tough job, and especially if time is a consideration, an excellent strategy is to pull together a team of experts, each one specializing in a particular aspect of the overall discipline.

David Macaulay, in his book *Cathedral*, uses the fictional cathedral of "Chutreaux" to detail the painstaking, difficult, *collaborative* effort that went into the making of a 13th-century Gothic cathedral. After the architect or master builder created the original design, he assembled a team of the best craftsmen he could find:

> The craftsmen were the master quarryman, the master stone cutter, the master sculptor, the master mortar maker, the master mason, the master carpenter, the master blacksmith, the master roofer, and the master glass maker.[2]

This book on WordPerfect 5, a "collaboration," pools the knowledge of a range of WordPerfect experts, all masters in *particular* areas or applications.

Some of the contributors were early testers of prototype ("beta") versions of the software. They experimented with the software, put it through its paces for a variety of applications, and made suggestions to WordPerfect Corporation on how to refine the product before its official release. WordPerfect Corporation listened, and the final result was an even better product.

I first found out about most of the experts involved in this book when I began listening in on the nightly conversations on the WordPerfect forum on CompuServe. After six to eight months of paying close attention to the discussions, I developed an accurate sense of who was most knowledgeable about WordPerfect and who might be excellent candidates for this book—a book that addresses the sweeping changes with version 5 and meets the needs of novice-to-intermediate users. Such a group of authors could both assist new users and offer expert help to 4.2 users upgrading to version 5.

As word-processing software continues to evolve rapidly and becomes feature-laden, complex, and increasingly useful to a diversity of users, the need for expertise across a *range* of experience is clear. Only a *team* of experts could adequately cover a program as advanced, complex, and versatile as WordPerfect 5. For example, now that WordPerfect allows you to mix text and graphics for desktop publishing, you need to know not only how to import an image into WordPerfect, but you need to know which graphics programs can serve as sources for images, and you need to know the basics of good page layout and overall document design.

If you add the demand for expertise to the need for a useful guide to the new version as soon as possible, you can see why a collaboration of WordPerfect experts on *Using WordPerfect 5* was an optimal solution.

Who Should Use This Book?

If you're new to WordPerfect, this book's Quick Start tutorials, complete coverage of all program features, many real-world examples, and clear instructions will help you master version 5 quickly.

If you've used an earlier version of WordPerfect, such as 4.2, this book will help you make a smooth transition from 4.2 to 5. Pete Peterson, Executive Vice President of WordPerfect Corporation, has said that version 5 represents the biggest change in the software since its inception in the early 1980s. You won't notice a radical change in the user interface, but you will find many subtle and some not-so-subtle changes throughout. Most of the changes have occurred in the areas of formatting, printing, and printer installation.

Seven of the function keys have been renamed or moved, and almost all of the submenus have changed. Some of the function keys have changed, and a number of new capabilities have been added, such as styles, a "soft" keyboard for reassigning keys, a macro command language, font attributes, and the capability of integrating text and graphics, to name just a few.

Richard Wilkes, publisher of *The WordPerfectionist*, newsletter of the WordPerfect Corporation User Support Group, has said that "WordPerfect 5.0 is the new standard. It is the platform on which all future developments will be based." If you're a 4.2 user, *Using WordPerfect 5* will help you get the most out of version 5. As a 4.2 user, you'll appreciate the references to 4.2 in the book; throughout, contributors have mentioned differences between 4.2 and 5. An entire appendix summarizes what you need to know about the differences, explains the conceptual shift from 4.2 to 5, and indicates the direction in which WordPerfect is moving. If you're an experienced WordPerfect user, you'll also appreciate the special tips, shortcuts, and macro ideas found in this book.

How To Use This Book

Using WordPerfect 5 is designed to be an excellent complement to the manual and workbook that come with version 5. Beginners will find the tutorial information in *Using WordPerfect 5* helpful; experienced users will appreciate the comprehensive coverage and expert advice. Once you become proficient with version 5, you will want to use this book as a desktop reference.

Each chapter in this book focuses on a particular operation or set of operations with WordPerfect 5. Overall, the book's movement reflects the steps typical to the creation of any document, from entering text to spell-checking and printing. Later chapters concentrate on more specialized topics, such as macros, styles, columns, file conversion, and integrating text with graphics. *Using WordPerfect 5* distills the "real-world" experience of many WordPerfect experts, so the book is applications-oriented.

Chapters 2 through 6 include Quick Start sections to give you immediate, hands-on experience with the program. If you're pressed for time and want to be creating, saving, editing, formatting, and printing documents right away, work through these Quick Starts first. Each Quick Start presents the basics of the chapter it follows, but the emphasis is strictly on "learning by doing." Later, when you want to know more about a particular program feature, you can go back and read the entire chapter.

The special "TIPS" that have been included either point out information often overlooked in the documentation or help you use WordPerfect more efficiently. You'll find many of these "tips" useful or pertinent as you become more comfortable with the software. "CAUTIONS" and "WARNINGS" alert you to potential loss of data or harm to your system.

How Is This Book Organized?

As you flip through the book, you'll notice that it has been organized to follow the natural flow of learning and using WordPerfect 5.

Using WordPerfect 5 is divided into four parts:

    I: Using WordPerfect's Basic Features
   II: Using WordPerfect's Advanced Features
 III: Using WordPerfect's Specialized Features
 IV: Using WordPerfect for Desktop Publishing

Part I describes the steps for preparing to use WordPerfect: starting the program, running the tutorial, and completing the cycle of document preparation—planning, creating, editing, formatting, spell-checking, and printing. You also learn various block operations and how to manage your files with the List Files feature.

Part II moves into the more advanced uses of the program to discuss macros, styles, merge and sort operations, converting files and importing data, and customizing program settings, including the use of alternative keyboard definitions.

Part III covers WordPerfect's specialized features, such as newspaper and parallel columns; math operations; special characters and scientific typing; footnotes and endnotes; outlining, paragraph numbering, and line numbering; creating tables of contents, lists, indexes, and tables of authority; using automatic cross-references; and creating references across files with the master document capability.

Part IV focuses on version 5's desktop publishing potential. This part of the book presents a primer on page layout, typography, design, and graphics; takes you through the mechanics of integrating text and graphics; and showcases a number of attractive documents produced with version 5.

Read the following for a chapter-by-chapter breakdown of the book's contents:

Chapter 1, "Preparing To Use WordPerfect," introduces you to WordPerfect 5, covers hardware and memory requirements, and shows you how to start the program on hard and floppy disk systems, run the tutorial, and exit the program. You learn about WordPerfect's editing screen, function key commands, cursor movement, and on-line help. WordPerfect's hidden codes are introduced.

Chapter 2, "Creating a Document," gives you the opportunity to start WordPerfect and begin entering text, moving the cursor through a document, using the function keys, selecting menu options, canceling operations, using both document windows, printing your document, and saving a file. In the first Quick Start, you create and print a one-page letter.

Chapter 3, "Editing a Document," looks at the next step in the composing process: revising and editing your document. After you learn the basics of retrieving a file saved to the disk, you explore the various methods for deleting text. This chapter also covers entering simple text enhancements (bold and underline), using search and replace as an editing tool, and editing hidden codes in WordPerfect. Finally, you learn about creating document comments and using them as an aid to revision. A second Quick Start lets you try out these editing techniques.

Chapter 4, "Working with Blocks," teaches you how to use Block to select or highlight text that you can then move, copy, delete, append, save, or print. You also learn to enhance a block of characters with features like bold, underlining, or italics, and to enlarge or reduce the size of characters in a block. A Quick Start takes you through the range of basic block operations.

Chapter 5, "Formatting and Enhancing Text," demonstrates how to alter the look of your text on the page by changing margins, tabs, and line spacing and by centering, right-justifying, and hyphenating text. This chapter also illustrates using Block to change the base font to a larger size or to choose a particular font appearance, such as italic or small caps. You learn about version 5's new capability to let you mix various fonts in one line. In a Quick Start, you have an opportunity to apply most of the line and page formatting techniques presented in this chapter.

Chapter 6, "Formatting Pages and Designing Documents," continues the topic of formatting, but goes beyond the elements of an individual page to consider overall document formatting. You learn to create headers and footers, number pages, keep certain text together, control page breaks, and choose paper and form sizes. You also find out how to establish custom settings for all your documents. A final Quick Start introduces you to some of WordPerfect 5's more powerful formatting commands.

Chapter 7, "Using the Speller and the Thesaurus," teaches you to use the Speller and Thesaurus to proofread and refine your work. This chapter demonstrates using the Speller to check the spelling of your documents and to create custom supplemental dictionaries, if you need them, and using the Thesaurus to give your writing freshness and precision.

Chapter 8, "Printing and Print Options," the first of two chapters on printing, focuses on dot-matrix printers. In this chapter, you learn to install your printer and to master the various methods of printing with WordPerfect.

Chapter 9, "Printing with Laser Printers," begins with a general discussion of laser printers and then moves to the specifics of printing with the HP LaserJet™ Series II and with printers that support PostScript®. This chapter is filled with sound advice on using built-in, cartridge, and soft fonts with your laser printer. In addition, troubleshooting tips help you solve any problems you may encounter with your laser printer.

Chapter 10, "Using List Files," completes the "basics" section and explains the principles of file and hard disk management. You practice using List Files to retrieve, delete, move, rename, print, look at, copy, and search files on disk or in a directory.

Chapter 11, "Creating Macros," provides you with an in-depth treatment of macros. This chapter teaches you to plan, create, run, store, and edit macros, from simple to complex. You can copy the macro examples provided throughout the chapter, or you can use these examples to suggest how you might create your own. The chapter includes a consideration of the macro command language, covered in Appendix C.

Chapter 12, "Using Styles," offers a clear, comprehensive explanation of the two types of styles (paired and open) and how to use them to format your documents. You learn to create, save, select, and view styles in a style library. Shortcuts—such as the use of macros with styles—and tips for working with styles are included. In addition, this chapter provides you with a library of ready-to-use style definitions.

Chapter 13, "Assembling Documents with Merge," explains the basics of merge operations; use merge operations to save time and automate many repetitive functions such as form-letter mailings. You master assembling documents from "boilerplate" text, using merge with macros to create on-screen menus, printing mailing labels, and applying merge in other creative and useful ways, such as using merge with WordPerfect's math and macro features.

Chapter 14, "Sorting and Selecting Data," teaches you about WordPerfect's sort and select features. You see how sort lets you create simple databases containing "records" that you then sort by line, paragraph, or secondary merge file. Examples used to illustrate the use of sort and select include a sales contact database and a bibliography.

Chapter 15, "Converting Files and Importing Data," which ends the section on WordPerfect's advanced features, covers converting WordPerfect files to various other file formats and importing data into WordPerfect.

Chapter 16, "Working with Text Columns," demonstrates creating attractive text columns in newspaper-style ("snaking") or parallel format. You learn to use macros and styles to make your work with columns even easier.

Chapter 17, "Using Math," is intended for those who want to include simple arithmetic calculations in their documents. This chapter shows you how to set up math columns, enter numbers, and calculate the results.

Chapter 18, "Customizing WordPerfect," explains using the Setup feature to adapt WordPerfect to your own special needs. Special emphasis is given to setting up subdirectory locations for auxiliary files, changing the default initial codes, and customizing keyboard layouts through the use of alternative keyboard definitions.

Chapter 19, "Using Special Characters and Typing Equations," examines accessing some of the 13 special character sets available with WordPerfect 5. (Whether you are able to display and print many of these characters depends on your hardware.) This chapter also shows you how to incorporate equations in your documents.

Chapter 20, "Using Footnotes and Endnotes," illustrates incorporating footnotes and endnotes in your documents. This chapter presents the steps for creating, looking at, previewing, adding, deleting, moving, customizing, and editing footnotes and endnotes.

Chapter 21, "Outlining, Paragraph Numbering, and Line Numbering," covers the steps necessary to create outlines and number paragraphs and lines. You learn to customize the defaults for footnotes and endnotes to meet the style guidelines of your particular discipline.

Chapter 22, "Assembling Document References," teaches you to mark and generate text for tables of contents, lists, indexes, and tables of authorities. This chapter demonstrates that automatic referencing, styles, macros, and document compare can be used for lengthy, structured documents.

Chapter 23, "Using the Master Document Feature for Large Projects," builds on the preceding chapter to show you how to use the master document feature to create document references across any number of subdocuments. This chapter shows how the master document simplifies the task of pulling together a project comprised of many parts. You learn to create, expand, save, and condense the master document.

Chapter 24, "Integrating Text and Graphics," the first chapter in the section on desktop publishing, explores in great detail the mechanics of integrating text and graphics with WordPerfect 5. You see how to create a box and import graphics or enter text. You learn to position a box on the page, wrap text accordingly, and edit the images that you import. You also practice using Line Draw and previewing your document in View Document mode.

Chapter 25, "Producing Publications," presents the principles of page layout and good design, introduces the various types of graphics, and showcases a number of attractive documents produced with WordPerfect 5. Each document is paired with a specification sheet explaining how the document was created.

Appendix A, "WordPerfect 5 Installation, Setup, and Start-Up," covers WordPerfect 5's installation, start-up, and setup.

Appendix B, "WordPerfect 5 for 4.2 Users," helps the 4.2 user make the transition to version 5. This appendix details the significant differences between the two versions.

Appendix C, "Macro Command Language," introduces the macro command language. The latter is presented in a reference fashion, with brief explanations of commands, syntax, and possible uses.

Appendix D, "List of WordPerfect Commands," is an alphabetical list of WordPerfect's function-key commands. When you want a quick A-Z command reference, consult this list.

At the back of the book you'll find a tear-out, color-coded, keyboard-command chart for your desktop. Keep this command chart close at hand—you'll find it an invaluable aid.

A Note on WordPerfect Upgrades

WordPerfect releases new versions of the program almost every year. You can tell the date of your release by pressing Help (F3) and noting the date at the top right corner of the screen. This book is based on the 5/5/88 release of WordPerfect 5.

Keep in mind that WordPerfect Corporation often issues unnumbered and unannounced "maintenance" releases, which are usually available at no cost or for a nominal fee ($15 to $20, depending on how many disks are involved). The best way to find out about these unofficial or interim releases is to phone WordPerfect's update number (1-800-321-4566) or subscribe to *The WordPerfectionist*.

Where To Find More Help

If you find yourself stymied at a particular point, WordPerfect's Help (F3) feature may be able to answer your questions. Using Help is explained and illustrated in Chapter 1. You can turn to WordPerfect's excellent manual and workbook, or you can turn to *this* text for help.

Should all else fail, WordPerfect Corporation provides toll-free telephone support unrivaled in the industry: 1-800-321-5906. The phone staff is helpful and knowledgeable. If they can't produce an answer on the spot, you can describe your problem to them, and they will look into the problem and get back to you soon. The help line is open 7 a.m. to 6 p.m. Mountain Standard Time, Monday through Friday.

One of the best sources of help is the WordPerfect Corporation (WPCORP) User Support Group, an independent group not affiliated with WordPerfect Corporation.

The group publishes an excellent monthly newsletter, *The WordPerfectionist*, which is a highly useful compendium of tips for getting the most out of WordPerfect and other WordPerfect Corporation products. You can subscribe to *The WordPerfectionist* for $36 a year by writing to the following address:

The WordPerfectionist
WordPerfect Support Group
P.O. Box 1577 Dept 50
Baltimore, MD 21203

The WordPerfectionist is intended for all levels of users and is filled with helpful hints, clever techniques, solid guidance, and objective reviews of books and software. You can purchase a monthly disk subscription, a communications program (TAPCIS) that you'll want if you decide to join CompuServe and participate in the support group forum, WordPerfect books, and related items from the support group.

Most if not all of the contributors to this book belong to the WordPerfect Support Group (WPSG) and subscribe to the newsletter; many participate nightly in the lively dialogue on the WPSG's special interest group on CompuServe. If you join the WPSG, you can upload useful files from the forum's many data libraries. You usually can get an answer to *any* WordPerfect question, no matter how thorny or complex, the same day or in a day or two.

Pete Peterson of WordPerfect Corporation participates nightly on the forum. As a major spokesperson and unofficial historian for the company, Pete answers questions, explains company developments and the rationale for certain decisions, and listens to suggestions for improving the entire line of WordPerfect Corporation products. If Pete can't provide an immediate answer to a question, he checks with someone else within the company. As such, he is a vital link to WordPerfect Corporation. Others, such as sysop (system operator) Joan Friedman, and the publishers of *The WordPerfectionist*, Richard and Sandy Wilkes, are usually available to field questions from forum participants.

Conventions Used in This Book

The conventions used in this book have been established to help you learn to use the program quickly and easily.

For function-key commands, the name of the command is presented first, followed by the keystrokes. Format (Shift-F8) indicates that you press and hold down the Shift key and then press the F8 key to use Format. When you must press a series of keys, the keys are separated by commas. Press and release each key. For instance to move to the top of the document, press and release Home, then Home, then ↑.

WordPerfect 5 gives you two options for selecting a menu item: you can press a letter or a number. In this book, the name of the menu option is presented first followed by the appropriate number in parentheses—for instance, Footnote (1).

Note that the letter (the "mnemonic") or number you press is presented in **bold**. WordPerfect's hidden codes are also shown in bold: **[Tab]**.

Uppercase is used to distinguish file names, DOS (disk operating system) commands, and the words "TIP" and "CAUTION." In most cases, the keys on the keyboard are represented as they appear on your keyboard. Special words or phrases defined for the first time and the text you need to type are identified by *italics*. Long passages of text that you need to type are indented, and on-screen messages appear in digital.

Charles O. Stewart III
Carmel, Indiana

[1]   Paul V. Anderson, "What Survey Research Tells Us about Writing at Work," in *Writing in Nonacademic Settings*, eds. Lee Odell and Dixie Goswami (New York: The Guilford Press, 1985), p. 50.

[2]   David Macaulay, *Cathedral: The Story of Its Construction* (Boston: Houghton Mifflin Company, 1973), p. 9.

Part
I

Using WordPerfect's
Basic Features

Includes

1

Preparing To Use WordPerfect

As project director and individual contributor, **Charles O. Stewart III** *conceived the overall structure and design for* Using WordPerfect 5. *He was instrumental in determining the particular emphases for the book, assembled the team of contributors, and worked closely with them through manuscript development, editing, and final review.* ■

This chapter acquaints you with WordPerfect 5 and prepares you for creating and printing a simple document in Chapter 2. The chapter begins with a brief introduction to WordPerfect, covers the hardware you need for operating WordPerfect, and shows you how to "boot" or start WordPerfect on your computer. You learn also about WordPerfect's "clean" editing screen, the special ways WordPerfect uses your keyboard, and the on-line Help that comes with the program. And if you're interested in taking the WordPerfect tutorial to get more comfortable with the program, this chapter provides an overview of the Tutor program and shows you how to start it.

At the end of the book are useful appendixes to help you begin to use WordPerfect. If you need to install WordPerfect on your system, turn to Appendix A, which covers everything you need to know to get WordPerfect running on your dual floppy or hard disk system.

Note: If you're eager to begin creating a document and are familiar with either word processing or WordPerfect, skim this chapter and then move to the Quick Start at the end of Chapter 2, "Creating a Document."

What Is WordPerfect?

WordPerfect is one of the world's most popular word-processing software programs, currently enjoying approximately 30% of the word-processing market. A full 27% of the readers of *PC Magazine* reported in early 1988 that they used WordPerfect as their word processor of choice. In the same survey, respondents noted that WordPerfect was number 1 where they worked.

13

Why is WordPerfect so popular? WordPerfect has all the "basic" features you would expect in a word-processing package plus a full complement of advanced features. The program is suited to your needs, whether they entail short memos or complex, lengthy documents. W. E. "Pete" Peterson, Executive Vice President of WordPerfect Corporation, put it best when he said on CompuServe that "what makes WordPerfect attractive is that it gets out of your way. It's like a well-mannered house guest who is kind enough not to disrupt your life or the way you do things." An editing screen uncluttered by menus or cryptic codes, an abundance of ever-growing features, support for a wide range of printers, and unparalleled customer assistance are just a few of the reasons why WordPerfect enjoys the preeminence it so rightly deserves.

What Is WordPerfect 5?

Released in the spring of 1988, WordPerfect 5 heralded a "quantum" leap forward for a product already enjoying ever-increasing popularity worldwide. Perhaps the most dramatic change in the program was its move toward desktop-publishing capabilities, marking an overall trend in upper-end word-processing packages in the late 1980s. Pete Peterson, Executive Vice President of WordPerfect Corporation, has said that version 5 represented the biggest change in WordPerfect since the product's inception in the early 1980s. Writing in *PC Magazine*, Jim Seymour noted that both Microsoft ® Word and WordPerfect, the two major contenders in the word-processing marketplace, had "long laundry lists of features" and "serve many kinds of users well."

With version 5, WordPerfect's list of features have become even longer:

- Integration of text and graphics, including the capability to display color graphics and edit graphics in WordPerfect

- Excellent, widespread support of laser printers, including PostScript-based printers

- Flexible font capabilities: to mix different font sizes in the same line; attach "attributes" to fonts; and use built-in, cartridge, and soft fonts

- View Document mode for previewing how a document (including facing pages and text with graphics) will print

- Styles that store formatting information for parts of a document, making quick global formatting changes easy

- A master document feature for assembling one large document from a series of subdocuments

- A built-in macro editor and macro language for sophisticated and powerful macro operations

- A soft keyboard for relocating keys or assigning macros to keys

What Hardware Do You Need To Run WordPerfect?

You can run WordPerfect on an IBM PC or 100%-compatible computer with dual floppy disk drives or a hard disk drive. WordPerfect requires DOS 2.0 or later and at least 384K of memory to run on a system. The main program file, WP.EXE, uses approximately 238K. The rest of WordPerfect's random-access memory (RAM) requirement is used by DOS and as space for editing.

Your best bet is to have at least 512K of RAM. A computer uses RAM to store temporarily your programs and data, including a portion of the disk operating system (DOS). RAM is *volatile*, which means that any programs or data in RAM are lost when you turn off the computer or a power loss occurs. How do you know how much RAM your computer has? To check your system's RAM, run the DOS CHKDSK command. CHKDSK tells you how much RAM is available on your system.

WordPerfect can take advantage of expanded memory and will immediately detect it when you install the program. Expanded memory lets you load and edit very large documents, for example, because any part of the document too large for RAM goes into the expanded memory space. WordPerfect uses overflow files to store information too large for RAM. The more RAM or extended memory you have, the more disk space you'll have.

Because WordPerfect 5 comes on 12 5 1/4-inch floppy disks or 7 3 1/2-inch disks, you frequently must swap disks in and out of your disk drives if you have a dual floppy system. To run WordPerfect with fewer interruptions, you should probably invest in a hard disk. Although WordPerfect is already a speedy program, it runs faster and performs better on a hard disk.

Monitors and Graphics Cards

WordPerfect supports a wide range of video systems, including Color Graphics Adapter (CGA), Enhanced Graphics Adapter (EGA), and Video Graphics Array (VGA). Other systems supported include the AT&T® 6300, IBM® 8514/A, Genius (full-page), and COMPAQ® Portable III/386 with plasma display.

You can run WordPerfect on a monochrome system without a graphics card, but you won't be able to see any graphics, font changes, or font attributes (superscript, subscript, italics, small caps, etc.). With a CGA card and a color or monochrome monitor, you can see graphics in View Document mode. A color monitor with this card enables you to tinker in a limited fashion with background and foreground screen colors to differentiate font attributes. EGA and VGA systems provide better resolution in graphics mode and offer more possibilities for displaying font attributes in various color combinations.

WordPerfect also supports the Hercules Graphics Card®, the Hercules Graphics Card Plus, and the Hercules InColor™ cards. If you have a Hercules Graphics Card

Plus or Hercules InColor card (color version of the Hercules Graphics Card Plus), both cards come with the Hercules RamFont™ mode, which allows you true WYSIWYG (What-You-See-Is-What-You-Get) while in editing mode. What this means is that you can see changes in font size or appearance on the screen in edit mode as they will print. For example, you can see fonts in various sizes (fine, small, large, very large, extra large), italics, small caps, underline and double underline, superscript and subscript, outline, and strikeout. In short, if you want to be able to see your document in edit mode as it will appear when printed, then by all means invest in a Hercules Plus or Hercules InColor card to take advantage of the Ramfont capability.

Printers

WordPerfect runs on a wide variety of printers, from dot-matrix to laser. Printer installation is covered in detail in Chapter 8. The printer drivers supplied on the four Printer disks are for the most common printers. WordPerfect 5 supports the same printers as 4.2, with the exception of Tandy printers in their native mode. Your printer most likely is supported by WordPerfect; if not, follow the instructions in Chapter 8 for emulating a similar printer, or call WordPerfect Corporation. If you're adventurous and technically adept, you can use the Printer program to create a custom printer driver, but this approach is *not* recommended for the novice. The list of supported printers is always being revised and increased, so, unless you have a printer manufactured in, say, Tibet, you should be able to get a printer driver that works.

Starting WordPerfect on a
Dual Floppy System

If you haven't already formatted floppy disks and made working copies of the original WordPerfect disks, turn now to Appendix A.

You can start WordPerfect in a number of ways, as explained in Appendix A, but the simplest method is to use the WP command. This section assumes that you have installed a copy of the DOS COMMAND.COM file on your working copies of the WordPerfect 1 and WordPerfect 2 disks, as explained in Appendix A.

Note: If you are using an IBM PS/2 machine, the main program files are combined on *one* 3 1/2-inch microfloppy disk labeled WordPerfect 1/WordPerfect 2.

To start WordPerfect on your computer, follow these steps:

1. Insert the working copy of your WordPerfect 1 disk in drive A:.

2. Insert a formatted data disk in drive B:.

3. Turn on your computer.

4. Respond appropriately to the operating system prompts for the date and time. (If you have an AUTOEXEC.BAT file, this step may not be necessary.)

5. At the A> prompt, type *b:* and press Enter.

   Drive B: is now the "default" drive, which means that any data you save to disk is saved to your data disk in drive B:.

6. Type *a:wp* and press Enter.

   WordPerfect will now be loaded into memory.

Unless you have an IBM PS/2 computer, the opening screen shown in figure 1.1 appears, and WordPerfect prompts you to insert the WordPerfect 2 disk. This screen contains WordPerfect copyright information, the version number of your copy, and an indication of the default directory that the system will use.

Fig. 1.1.
The WordPerfect opening screen.

```
                    WordPerfect

                    Version 5.0

                (C)Copyright 1982,1988
                  All Rights Reserved
                WordPerfect Corporation
                   Orem, Utah  USA


Insert diskette labeled "WordPerfect 2" and press any key
```

7. Remove the WordPerfect 1 disk from drive A: and insert the WordPerfect 2 disk.

8. Press any key to resume loading WordPerfect.

Starting WordPerfect on a Hard Disk System

This section assumes that you have followed the directions in Appendix A for setting up your hard disk and installing WordPerfect. If you have created an AUTOEXEC.BAT file (see Appendix A), WordPerfect loads *automatically* after you turn on the computer. (You may have to respond to the prompts for date and time, depending on how you have set up your AUTOEXEC.BAT file.)

Depending on whether your hard disk system has one or two floppy disk drives, make certain that the drive door is open for each drive.

To start WordPerfect on your hard disk system, follow these steps:

1. Turn on your computer.

2. If necessary, respond to the prompts for date and time.

    The DOS prompt C> is displayed on-screen.

3. Type *cd \wp* and press Enter.

    The current directory is now \WP, where the main WordPerfect program files are stored on your hard disk. (Note: This step assumes that you've created a \WP subdirectory for your main system files.)

4. Type *wp* and press Enter to load WordPerfect.

You should see the opening screen for just a moment, and then the editing screen is displayed.

Troubleshooting Problems with Starting WordPerfect

If you have trouble starting WordPerfect, follow these steps:

1. Check all power cords and cables to make certain that they are connected properly.

2. Make sure that your monitor is turned on and adjusted properly.

If you're using a dual floppy disk system:

1. Make certain that you formatted and copied your working and data disks properly (see Appendix A).

2. Make certain that your working copy of the WordPerfect 1 system disk (or the WordPerfect 1/WordPerfect 2 microfloppy disk if you have an IBM PS/2 computer) is in drive A:.

3. Check drive B: to make certain that you have a formatted data disk in the drive.

4. Make certain that the disks have been inserted properly and that the drive doors are closed.

If you're starting WordPerfect on a hard disk:

Make certain that you're starting the program from the proper directory (\WP or the directory to which you copied the main system files).

Restarting WordPerfect

What happens if you start WordPerfect and the power fails because of an electrical storm or an accidental pull of the plug? Or what happens if the program "freezes up" and no longer accepts any keyboard input, forcing you to turn off the computer and perform what is known as a "soft reboot" by pressing Ctrl-Alt-Del? In either instance, what results is an improper exit from WordPerfect. (You'll see at the end of this chapter how to exit the program properly.)

When you restart WordPerfect, the following prompt appears on your screen:

    Are other copies of WordPerfect currently running? Y/N

Press *N* in response to this prompt. If when you installed the program you chose to have WordPerfect perform a timed backup of your document, you'll eventually (depending on the intervals you've chosen for the timed backup) get the following error message:

    Old backup file exists 1 Rename 2 Delete

When you choose the timed backup option through the Setup menu (see Appendix A), WordPerfect creates a temporary backup file. The temporary backup file created for the document in the Doc 1 window is WP{WP}.BK1, and the file for the document in the Document 2 window is WP{WP}.BK2. In most cases, you would want to press *D* or *2* to delete the file(s). WordPerfect normally deletes such a file when you exit the program properly.

CAUTION: If you are using timed backup and a power failure causes you to lose your text on-screen (and in memory), retrieve WP{WP}.BK1 or WP{WP}.BK2 immediately when you reboot. If you don't rename or retrieve the backup file before the next timed save, whatever you have on-screen is copied to WP{WP}.BK1 or WP{WP}.BK2, writing over the backup file of your other document. Remember: after a power failure or some other program abort, retrieve the timed backup file, rename it, and save it to disk as soon as possible.

Understanding the Editing Screen

The editing screen, where you will do most of your work, appears after you start WordPerfect (see fig. 1.2).

Fig. 1.2.

The WordPerfect editing screen.

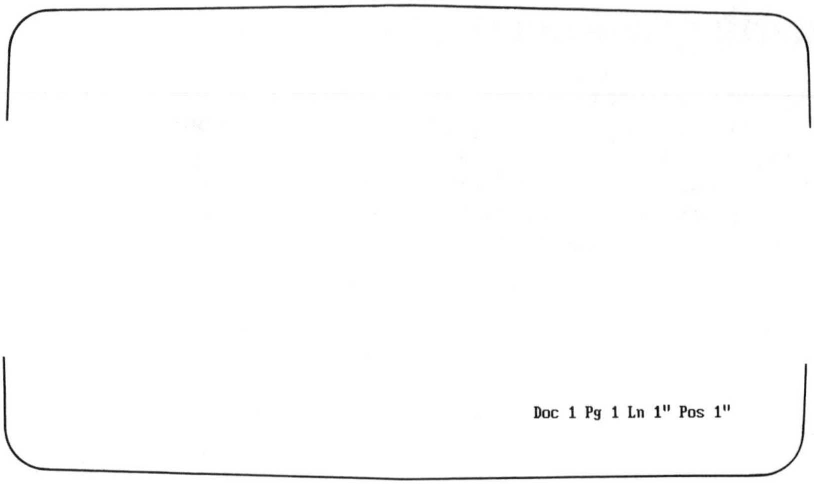

Doc 1 Pg 1 Ln 1" Pos 1"

WordPerfect's austere editing screen may seem rather intimidating at first: no menus or any other "props" are visible to help you get started. Actually, the uncluttered screen comes about as close as possible to a blank piece of paper in a typewriter. WordPerfect's beauty, to recall Pete Peterson's words, is in the way the program gets "out of your way," thereby freeing you to write and see on-screen as many of your words as possible. WordPerfect's editing screen provides you with the maximum area for viewing your work.

Until you name a document, which you must do before you can save it to disk, the only information on the screen is found in the bottom right corner (see fig. 1.2). This *status line* information tells you the position of the *cursor*—that tiny bar of blinking light on the screen. The cursor marks the point where you begin typing characters; inserting and deleting text; retrieving documents stored on disk; and embedding special "hidden" codes for formatting and text enhancements such as bold, underline, and so forth. After you name and save a document, the document's name is displayed in the lower left corner of the screen. If you don't want WordPerfect to display the file name, you can use the Setup feature to "hide" the file name (see Appendix A).

In the lower right corner of the screen, the status line indicates the cursor's position. The first item (Doc 1) shows which document window displays the cursor. You can edit in one or two separate document windows in WordPerfect, and they are referred to as Doc 1 and Doc 2. The second number is the page where the cursor is located. In figure 1.2, the cursor is on page 1. The third number indicates the cursor's vertical position, the line on which the cursor rests. The final value indicates the column in which the cursor rests—its horizontal character position.

For the default margins, WordPerfect assumes you will be using 8.5-by-11 inch paper. The flush-left position for the cursor is at 1 inch from the edge of the paper, and the status line reads Pos 1" or Pos 1i. The rightmost position is 7.5 inches—one inch from the right edge of the paper—after which the cursor is repositioned at the beginning of the next line.

In version 4.2, your only option is to indicate margins in terms of characters: the default flush-left position for the cursor is column 10, and the rightmost position is column 74. In version 5, however, you can have the position display in centimeters or points as well as inches (see Chapters 5 and 6 for more information). You use the Setup menu to choose how you want the position values to display. (For information on how to use the Setup menu, see Chapter 18 and Appendix A.)

When the Caps Lock key is depressed to allow you to enter uppercase characters, Pos displays as POS. When you depress the Num Lock key, the Pos indicator blinks on and off. Caps Lock and Num Lock work like toggle switches that you turn on and off. The number following the Pos indicator changes intensity or color in accordance with whatever text attribute you have chosen: bold, underline, double underline, italic, outline, shadow, small caps, redline, strikeout, superscript, subscript, fine, small, large, very large, or extra large (see Chapters 5 and 6 for an explanation of text attributes). But only a color monitor displays text attributes in various colors.

Using the Keyboard

Before you work with WordPerfect, you should know that computers come with several different types of keyboards. WordPerfect uses the function keys to carry out many operations, but these keys are located in one of two places, depending on the type of keyboard you have.

Skim this section to become familiar with the keys on your keyboard and their functions. This section is intended to be descriptive; in subsequent chapters, you'll have a chance to "try out" all these keys as you create, edit, revise, and print various documents.

The early Personal Computers and some PC XTs have a keyboard similar to the one shown in figure 1.3. Some Personal Computer AT keyboards are like the one shown in figure 1.4. Newer computers (the PC XT, 286 XT, and the Personal Computer AT) and PS/2 computers use a keyboard similar to that shown in figure 1.5. The keyboards function in the same manner, but the layout of some keys is different.

You should know how WordPerfect uses the three main parts of the keyboard. Note that the keyboard is similar to the keyboard of a typewriter, but there are some important differences.

Keep in mind one critical but easily overlooked difference between composing with a typewriter and composing with WordPerfect: When typing normal text, you do not need to end lines at the right margin by pressing the Enter key. When you type text in WordPerfect and reach the end of a line, the text "wraps" automatically to the next line. If you're accustomed to using a typewriter, you'll find the word wrap feature a genuine pleasure. Automatic word wrap makes it easy to create, edit, and revise your text. If you press the Enter key at the end of a line before WordPerfect has a chance to position the cursor at the beginning of the next line, you will insert

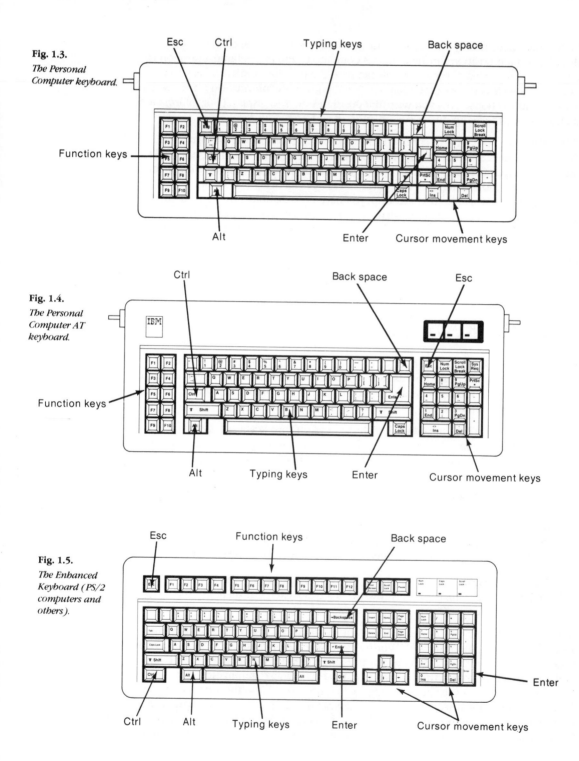

Fig. 1.3.
The Personal Computer keyboard.

Esc Ctrl Typing keys Back space

Function keys

Alt Enter Cursor movement keys

Fig. 1.4.
The Personal Computer AT keyboard.

Ctrl Back space Esc

Function keys

Alt Typing keys Enter Cursor movement keys

Fig. 1.5.
The Enhanced Keyboard (PS/2 computers and others).

Esc Function keys Back space

Ctrl Alt Typing keys Enter Cursor movement keys Enter

an unnecessary hard return (hidden code) that can wreak havoc with your text should you decide to insert or delete characters, or to reformat your text in any way.

WordPerfect uses the following three main areas of the keyboard:

- The function keys, F1 through F10, found at the left end of the keyboard on the IBM PC, XT, AT, and compatibles; or across the top of the keyboard on the Enhanced Keyboard shown in figure 1.5 (On the Enhanced Keyboard, WordPerfect uses all 12 function keys.)

- The alphanumeric or "typing" keys, located in the center of the keyboard (the keys most familiar to you from your experience with typewriter keyboards)

- The numeric and cursor keys, found at the right end of the keyboard

Using the Shift, Alt, and Control Keys

The Shift, Alt, and Control (Ctrl) keys are part of the alphanumeric keyboard. These keys are used with the function keys to carry out most of WordPerfect's commands.

The Shift key creates uppercase letters and other special characters, just as it does on a typewriter keyboard. Shift is used also with the function keys to carry out certain operations in WordPerfect.

The Alt and Ctrl keys don't do anything by themselves, but work with the function keys, number keys, or letter keys to operate various commands in WordPerfect.

Note: If you've used WordPerfect 4.2, you'll be pleased to know that WordPerfect 5 allows you to change the built-in key assignments. Chapter 18 shows you how to use the three alternative keyboard layouts supplied with version 5 or to create your own personalized keyboards. For example, you might want to move the Help key from F3 to F1 or to reassign Esc as the Cancel key. If you're new to WordPerfect, become comfortable with the built-in keyboard before experimenting with the alternative keyboards or creating your own keyboard definitions.

Using the Function Keys

Central to understanding how WordPerfect operates is knowing what the function keys are used for. Each function key has four operations, depending on whether it is used alone or in combination with the Alt, Shift, and Ctrl keys. You press a function key to have WordPerfect carry out a command. The keyboard template you received with WordPerfect is color-coded in the following manner (see fig. 1.6):

- *Black* indicates what the key does alone.

  For example, when you press Help (F3), the opening Help screen is displayed.

- *Red* indicates that you press and hold down the Ctrl key, then press also one of the function keys.

  For example, pressing Spell (Ctrl-F2) brings up the Speller menu.

- *Green* indicates that you press and hold down the Shift key, then press also one of the function keys.

  For example, pressing Retrieve (Shift-F10) produces a status-line prompt that asks you for the name of a disk file you want to retrieve to the screen.

- *Blue* indicates that you press and hold down the Alt key, then press also one of the function keys.

  For example, pressing Block (Alt-F4) turns on the Block function.

Fig. 1.6.

The WordPerfect 5 template for IBM Personal Computers and compatibles.

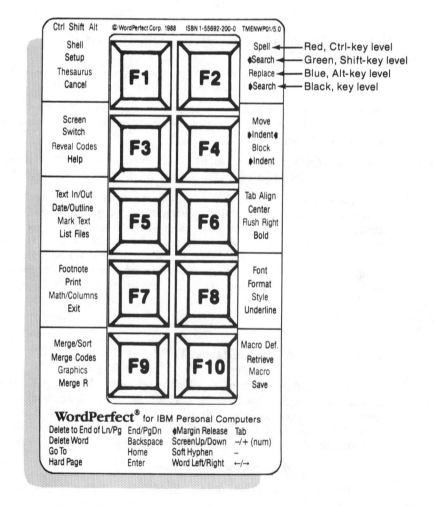

You can see an on-screen display of the function-key template if you press Help (F3) twice (see fig. 1.7). The tear-out command card at the end of this book also indicates the function-key assignments.

TIP: If you misplace your template or the tear-out command card in the back of this book, use Shift-PrtSc to print the screen shown in figure 1.7, and then use red, green, and blue highlighters to create a temporary function-key template.

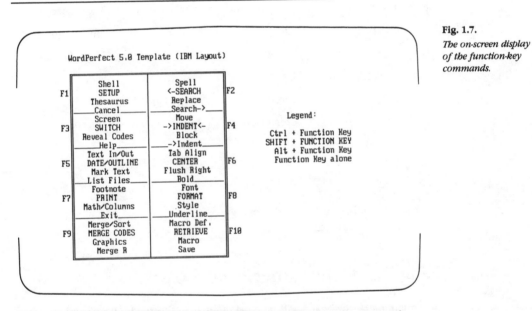

Fig. 1.7.

The on-screen display of the function-key commands.

Table 1.1 shows the function keys and what they do. If you're familiar with WordPerfect 4.2, you'll note that over 80% of the function-key assignments have remained the same in version 5, although you will find some significant additions, such as Style (Alt-F8) and Graphics (Alt-F9). Many of the menus, especially those devoted to printing and formatting, have changed dramatically. We'll get to these in subsequent chapters as you explore all the commands.

When you press some of the function keys, such as Bold (F6) or Underline (F8), a "hidden" code for bolding or underlining text, respectively, is entered in the text. To turn off bolding or underlining, you must press the appropriate key again. Pressing other function keys gives you a status-line or a full-screen menu for selecting an option.

Pressing Cancel (F1) or Esc gets you out of most menus.

Table 1.1
WordPerfect's Function-Key Commands

Key	Alone	Ctrl-Key	Shift-Key	Alt-Key
F1	Cancel or Undelete	Shell (exit to DOS)	Setup	Thesaurus
F2	Forward Search	Spell	Backward Search	Replace
F3	Help	Screen	Switch	Reveal Codes
F4	Indent	Move	L/R indent	Block
F5	List Files	Text In/Out	Date/Outline	Mark Text
F6	Bold	Tab Align	Center	Flush Right
F7	Exit	Footnote	Print	Math/Columns
F8	Underline	Font	Format	Style
F9	Merge R	Merge/Sort	Merge Codes	Graphics
F10	Save	Macro Define	Retrieve	Macro
*F11	Reveal Codes	—	—	—
*F12	Block	—	—	—

*Available only on the Enhanced Keyboard

Using the Alphanumeric Keyboard

The alphanumeric keyboard will be most familiar to those who have used typewriters or who are just now making the transition from typewriters to word processing.

The keyboard works just like a typewriter keyboard. For example, if you depress and hold down a key, the character is repeated across the screen until you release the key. You use the Shift key to uppercase letters and access special characters above the number keys at the top of the keyboard, but Shift's real power in WordPerfect is in its use with the function keys, as described previously.

The Enter key, which has been mentioned previously, is used to insert a carriage or *hard return* ([HRt]) at the end of a line when automatic word wrap is not desired. In this sense, Enter works like the Return key on a typewriter by moving the cursor down one or more lines. However, unlike the Return key on a typewriter, the Enter key inserts blank lines or breaks a line if you move the cursor into already typed text and press Enter.

Note in figure 1.5 that the IBM PS/2 keyboard comes with two Enter keys.

You press Enter also when you want to initiate some commands in WordPerfect, or when you want the system to recognize a menu option you've selected or data you've entered in a menu.

The space bar works very differently in WordPerfect. When you press the space bar, WordPerfect inserts a character space, pushing ahead any text that may follow the cursor. And if you press the Ins key on the numeric keypad (to enter Typeover mode) before pressing the space bar, the space bar wipes out any character above the cursor, inserting a blank space in place of text. Unlike what you do with the space bar on a typewriter, you cannot simply press the space bar to move through a line of text in WordPerfect. (You use the → and ← keys to do that. *Do not press the space bar to move the cursor through text.*)

Yet another key that works differently in WordPerfect than on a typewriter is the Backspace key, sometimes represented on the keyboard by a left-pointing arrow (←). When you press this key, you delete text or hidden codes to the *left* of the cursor. The Ctrl key in combination with the Backspace key (Ctrl-Backspace) deletes a word at the cursor. The Home key in combination with the Backspace key (press Home, then Backspace) deletes a word to the left of the cursor. (See Chapter 3 for an explanation of the many strategies WordPerfect provides for deleting text.)

TIP: To use Home with Backspace to delete the word immediately to the left of the cursor, you must press and release the Home key before you press the Backspace key. If you want to delete another word to the left of the cursor, you must repeat this procedure. Holding down the Home key while holding down the Backspace key or pressing it repeatedly erases text to the left only one character at a time, which is what the Backspace key can do on its own.

Another key located in the alphanumeric section of the keyboard is the Tab key, which works in part like the Tab key on a typewriter keyboard. Each time you press Tab in WordPerfect, a hidden **[Tab]** code is inserted in the text, and the cursor moves across the screen a predefined distance that depends on how you've set the tab stops (the default is a tab stop every half inch). But in WordPerfect, when you press the Ins key and then press Tab, you can tab through text without inserting a **[Tab]** code and bumping text ahead of the cursor.

On older PC keyboards, the Esc key is located at the top leftmost corner of the alphanumeric key section. On later keyboards, such as the COMPAQ 286™ keyboard or the IBM Personal Computer AT keyboard, the Esc key is positioned within the numeric keypad at the right end of the keyboard. The Enhanced Keyboard, used by IBM PS/2 computers and others, has the Esc key positioned just to the left of the 12 function keys, which run across the top of the keyboard.

Esc is used in the default keyboard configuration as the Repeat function, which allows you to repeat many actions, such as replaying a macro or putting a dash on the screen a specified number of times. When you press Esc, you see the following prompt on the status line:

```
Repeat Value = 8
```

You can change this value by entering a new value. The Repeat value can be permanently changed through the Setup menu (see Appendix A). You can use the Repeat function to repeat a macro; move the cursor a specified number of characters, words, or lines; scroll the screen; or delete characters, words, or lines. The ALTRNAT key map provided with WordPerfect 5 assigns Help to F1, Esc to F3, and Cancel (F1) to the Esc key (see Chapter 18).

Using the Numeric Keypad

The keys in the numeric keypad at the far right of the keyboard move the cursor and scroll the text on-screen. Alternately, you use some of these keys to enter numbers on-screen. When you press the Num Lock key, you can use the 1-9 keys to enter numbers; when Num Lock is off, the Home, End, PgUp, PgDn, and arrow keys move the cursor in various ways. If you are using an Enhanced Keyboard, you'll notice a second set of arrow keys. The gray minus (–) and gray plus (+) keys scroll the screen. Cursor movement is explained in detail in the following section.

Two additional keys on the numeric keypad are of critical importance: Ins and Del. When you want to switch to Typeover mode, which allows you to type *over* existing text, saving you the trouble of deleting the old text first, you press Ins and begin typing. You'll know that Ins has been toggled "on" by the Typeover prompt visible on the status line.

On the Enhanced Keyboard shown in figure 1.5, note that there are duplicate keys for Home, Page Up, Page Down, and End to allow you to use the numeric keypad to enter numbers. Duplicate Insert and Delete keys are also provided on the Enhanced Keyboard.

The Del key, which you'll have a chance to experiment and get comfortable with in Chapter 3, enables you to delete the character or hidden code on which the cursor resides. Del is also useful for deleting a highlighted block of text.

Moving the Cursor

WordPerfect comes with a number of keys or key combinations that enable you to move the cursor with precision within your file. Chief among these are the Home, PgUp, PgDn, GoTo (Ctrl-Home), and arrow keys. Precise cursor movement is especially important in positioning the cursor with respect to WordPerfect's hidden codes. (These are explained in the next section.) Learning all the ways you can move the cursor through your document saves you much time in editing.

Table 1.2 summarizes the cursor-movement keys, many of which you'll explore and use in the chapters to come. Keep in mind that you move the cursor through preexisting text or blank character spaces inserted by the space bar. Typing text or pressing Tab, Enter, or the space bar moves the cursor on a blank screen. Once you've begun your document, you can use the cursor-movement keys shown in table 1.2 to move the cursor.

Table 1.2
Cursor-Movement Keys

Key	Cursor Movement
Left(←) and right(→) arrows	One character space to the left or right
Up(↑) and down(↓) arrows	Up or down one line
Esc, *n*, up or ↓ (*n* = any number)	*n* lines up or down
Ctrl-left(←) or -right(→) arrow	Beginning of the preceding or next word
Home, ←	Left edge of the screen or the beginning of the line
Home, →	Right edge of the screen or the end of the line
Home, Home, ←	Beginning of the line, just after any hidden codes
Home, Home, Home, ←	Beginning of the line, before any hidden codes
Home, Home, → [or end]	Far right of the line
Home, ↑ [or Screen Up (gray minus key)]	Top of the current screen
Home, ↓ [or Screen Down (gray plus key)]	Bottom of the current screen
Ctrl-Home, ↑	Top of the current page
Ctrl-Home, ↓	Bottom of the current page
PgUp	Top of the preceding page
PgDn	Top of the next page
Esc, *n*, PgUp	*n* pages backward
Esc, *n*, PgDn	*n* pages forward
Home, Home, ↑	Top of the file

Key	Cursor Movement
Home, Home, ↓	Bottom of the file
Ctrl-Home, *n*	Page number *n*
Ctrl-Home, *x* (*x* = any character)	Next occurrence of *x* (if it occurs within the next 2,000 characters)
Ctrl-Home, Ctrl-Home	Original cursor location before last major motion command was issued

Note: Ctrl-Home is known as the "GoTo" command.

Understanding WordPerfect's Hidden Codes

Fundamental to understanding WordPerfect is the concept of "hidden" codes. Many times, when you press a key in WordPerfect, a hidden code is inserted into the text. Such codes can indicate tab spaces, margin settings, carriage or hard returns, indents, and a host of other information that WordPerfect needs to manage your documents. Some hidden codes contain information for headers or footers, styles, footnotes or endnotes, font changes, or document comments. Other hidden codes are used to turn on and turn off a feature, such as math or columns. Many additional hidden codes come in pairs, such as the codes for bold, underline, centering, italic, print attributes, and so forth. The first code in a pair acts as a toggle switch to turn on a feature; the second code in a pair serves to turn it off. Typical examples would include the paired codes for bolding or centering text, as shown in figure 1.8, the Reveal Codes screen for a legal document.

Note the paired codes for centering ([**Cntr**] and [**C/A/Flrt**]) and bolding ([**BOLD**] and [**bold**]) the title. Also note the [**Hrt**] (hard return) codes, which indicate each time the Enter key was pressed; the [**SRt**] (soft return) codes, which indicate word wrap; and the [**Tab**] code inserted when the Tab key was pressed to indent the first paragraph.

Don't worry too much about WordPerfect's hidden codes just yet. It's enough for now to know something about the concept of hidden codes, how these codes become a part of your document, and how you can see them in the Reveal Codes (Alt-F3, or F11) screen. In Chapter 3, when you are actively involved in editing a document, you see the full range of WordPerfect's hidden codes. You learn strategies for examining, searching for, inserting, and editing codes. You learn also how to avoid problems with codes. To recall Pete Peterson's remark about WordPerfect as akin to a "well-mannered house guest," these hidden codes stay out of your way, thereby freeing you to concentrate on your writing.

Fig. 1.8.
*A screen showing
Reveal Codes.*

```
                    LAST WILL AND TESTAMENT

                             OF

                    AMBROSE GWINETT BIERCE


         I, Ambrose Gwinett Bierce, presently domiciled and residing
    in Chihuahua, Mexico, declare this to be my Will, and in the
    execution hereof I revoke all prior Wills and Codicils.

    C:\WP5\BOOK\WILL.DOC                      Doc 1 Pg 1 Ln 1" Pos 1"
    [    ▲   ▲   ▲   ▲   ▲   ▲   ▲   ▲   ▲   ▲   }   ▲   ▲ ]
    [Cntr][BOLD]LAST WILL AND TESTAMENT[C/A/Flrt][HRt]
    [HRt]
    [Cntr]OF[C/A/Flrt][HRt]
    [HRt]
    [Cntr]AMBROSE GWINETT BIERCE[bold][C/A/Flrt][HRt]
    [HRt]
    [HRt]
    [Tab]I, Ambrose Gwinett Bierce, presently domiciled and residing[SRt]
    in Chihuahua, Mexico, declare this to be my Will, and in the[SRt]
    execution hereof I revoke all prior Wills and Codicils.[HRt]

    Press Reveal Codes to restore screen
```

WordPerfect novices seem to experience the most trouble with WordPerfect's invisible network of codes. Once you master the concept and know how to search for hidden codes, navigate the Reveal Codes screen, and learn to edit in Reveal Codes, you'll prevent many problems that incorrect or inappropriate codes can cause.

Using the Help Feature

You can get information at almost any time on many of WordPerfect's commands or cursor movements by pressing Help (F3) from the editing screen (see fig. 1.9).

Fig. 1.9.
*The opening Help
screen.*

```
    Help                                      WP 5.0   05/05/88


        Press any letter to get an alphabetical list of features.

            The list will include the features that start with that letter,
            along with the name of the key where the feature is found.  You
            can then press that key to get a description of how the feature
            works.

        Press any function key to get information about the use of the key.

            Some keys may let you choose from a menu to get more information
            about various options.  Press HELP again to display the template.

        Press Enter or Space bar to exit Help.
```

WordPerfect's two Help files, WPHELP.FIL and WPHELP2.FIL, are located on the WordPerfect 1 disk. If you get an error message indicating that WordPerfect cannot find the Help files, insert the WordPerfect 1 disk in a floppy drive, close the drive door, type the drive letter and a colon (*a:*, for example), and press Enter. Help should now be displayed properly.

With Help, you can press any letter to get a list of WordPerfect features from A to Z and the keystrokes necessary to activate those features, or you can press any function-key combination to get an explanation of that key's operation (see fig. 1.10). You must press Help (F3) first before you press any subsequent keys. Note that the Math and Columns (Alt-F7) Help screen in figure 1.10 leads to various other Help screens that provide more detail for math and text columns.

Fig. 1.10.

The Math and Columns Help screen.

```
Math and Columns

     Defines math and text columns, turns math or columns mode on and off, or
     calculates the math operations already defined and entered.

     One of the following menus will appear on the status line:

(Math on)
     1 Math Off; 2 Calculate; 3 Column On/Off; 4 Column Def

(Math off)
     1 Math On; 2 Math Def; 3 Column On/Off; 4 Column Def


               Type a menu option for more help: 0
```

You can press a key like Esc or any of the cursor-movement keys to get an explanation of what that key does in WordPerfect. If you want an alphabetical listing of WordPerfect's features, press Help (F3) and then press a letter key. For example, to view all the listings for "A," press Help (F3) and then type *a*. You soon see the screen in figure 1.11.

Fig. 1.11.

The alphabetical Help listing for "A."

```
Key           Feature                              Key Name
Ctrl-F5       Add Password                         Text In/Out,2
Shft-F7       Additional Printers                  Print,S
Shft-F8       Advance Up, Down or Line             Format,4
Ctrl-PgUp     Advanced Macros                      Macro Commands
Ctrl-F10      Advanced Macros, Help on             Macro Definition
Shft-F8       Align/Decimal Character              Format,4
Ctrl-F6       Align on Tabs                        Tab Align
Ctrl-F8       Appearance of Printed Text           Font
Ctrl-F1       Append to Shell                      Shell
Ctrl-F4       Append text to a file (Block On)     Move
Ctrl-F8       Attributes, Printed                  Font
Shft-F1       Attributes, On-Screen                Setup,3
Shift-F5      Automatic Paragraph Numbering        Date/Outline
Alt-F5        Automatic Reference                  Mark Text
Shft-F1       Automatically Format and Rewrite     Setup,3
Shft-F1       Auxiliary Files Location             Setup
```

To exit any Help screen, press Exit (F7) or the space bar.

Taking the Tutorial

WordPerfect Corporation has provided a self-paced tutorial, WordPerfect Tutor, which you can work through from beginning to end in approximately 2 1/2 hours. Even if you've had some experience with version 4.2, you should run the tutorial. You don't have to complete the lessons in any particular order, nor do you have to finish a lesson to exit the tutorial. In addition, most of the lessons range from 12 to 20 minutes.

The tutorial begins with an Introduction that explains the WordPerfect screen and use of the keyboard. The Introduction is followed by six lessons that parallel closely the first half of the "Fundamentals" section of the *WordPerfect Workbook* and use the same document examples. Because these lessons build on each other and parallel the *Workbook*, you should probably complete them in sequence.

In Lesson One, you create and print a personal note. You learn also how to clear the screen without saving the note. In Lesson Two, you type, print, and save the first draft of a letter. You learn also how to move the cursor, do some simple editing, and display a list of files in the List Files screen. In Lesson Three, you create a short memo template and learn some simple formatting and function-key commands. In Lesson Four, you retrieve and continue working on the letter you created in the second lesson. This lesson introduces you to some basic editing procedures and lets you preview the letter in View Document mode. Lesson Five resumes work on the memo created in Lesson Three. You retrieve the memo template and fill it in. In this lesson, you learn also how to underline text and edit while in the Reveal Codes screen. Lesson Six concludes the introduction to WordPerfect's fundamentals by having you complete a final draft of the letter begun in Lesson Two and then run the Speller.

After you complete the beginning lessons, you can move to the advanced lessons, which cover merge operations and creating a table of authorities. In two separate merge lessons, you learn about merge files and codes, how to run a merge, and how to deal with blank lines in merge. The second lesson concludes with a quiz on fields, records, and merge operations. If you are new to WordPerfect's merge operations, you might want to work through these two lessons. The final lesson takes you through the steps of defining, marking, and generating a table of authorities.

Unless your computer is equipped with extended memory, you must exit WordPerfect to run the Tutor. You cannot simply use the Shell key (Ctrl-F1) to exit temporarily to DOS from WordPerfect and then run the Tutor. If you do so, you are likely to get an `ERROR: Insufficient memory` message.

Running the Tutorial on a Dual Floppy Disk System

Before you can run the tutorial on a two-floppy system, make certain that the computer is on and DOS has been loaded (the DOS prompt, `A>` or `B>`, should be displayed). To run the tutorial, follow these steps:

1. Insert the WordPerfect 1 disk in drive A:.

2. Insert the Learn disk in drive B:.

3. If the current drive is not B:, change the default directory to B: by typing *b:* and pressing Enter.

4. At the B> prompt, type *tutor* to load the tutorial.

5. At the prompt, type your first name and press Enter.

The sign-on screen for the Tutor is displayed (see fig. 1.12).

Fig. 1.12.
The sign-on screen for the Tutor program.

Type your name and press Enter (◄─┘)

After you type your first name and press Enter, the Tutor's main menu is displayed (see fig. 1.13). To find out the approximate time for completing a lesson, use the up- and down-arrow (↑ and ↓) keys to move the highlight bar to a lesson; then press Help (F3).

After you complete the beginning lessons, you can move to the advanced lessons by using the arrow keys to position the highlight bar on Advanced lessons on the menu and pressing Enter. The menu of advanced lessons is shown in figure 1.14.

When you finish a session, a check mark appears on the menu next to the item you have completed. You can exit any lesson and return to the opening menu by pressing Help (F3).

To exit the Tutor, move the highlight bar to EXIT and press Enter. You are returned to the DOS prompt.

Running the Tutorial on a Hard Disk System

Before you can run the tutorial on a hard disk, make certain that the computer is on and DOS has been loaded.

Fig. 1.13.
The Tutor main menu.

```
WordPerfect Beginning Lessons

┌─────────────────────┐   ┌──────────────────────────────────────┐
│ Introduction        │   │         How to use the tutor         │
├─────────────────────┤   │                                      │
│ Lesson 1            │   │ Start                                │
├─────────────────────┤   │ Move the highlighted bar in the menu to any │
│ Lesson 2            │   │ lesson and press the Enter key (the ▊ and │
├─────────────────────┤   │ ▊ keys on the right side of the keyboard │
│ Lesson 3            │   │ move the highlighted bar).           │
├─────────────────────┤   │                                      │
│ Lesson 4            │   │ Discontinue                          │
├─────────────────────┤   │ Press ▊ anytime during a lesson to return │
│ Lesson 5            │   │ to this menu.                        │
├─────────────────────┤   │                                      │
│ Lesson 6            │   │ Exit                                 │
├─────────────────────┤   │ Highlight EXIT at the bottom of the menu │
│ Advanced Lessons    │   │ then press Enter ◀┘.                 │
├─────────────────────┤   │                                      │
│ EXIT                │   │ Lesson Summary and Estimated Time    │
└─────────────────────┘   │ Highlight a lesson and press ▊.      │
                          └──────────────────────────────────────┘
```

Fig. 1.14.
The Tutor menu of advanced lessons.

```
WordPerfect Advanced Lessons

┌─────────────────────┐   ┌──────────────────────────────────────┐
│ Mail Merge          │   │         How to use the tutor         │
├─────────────────────┤   │                                      │
│ More Mail Merge     │   │ Start                                │
├─────────────────────┤   │ Move the highlighted bar in the menu to any │
│ Table of Authorities│   │ lesson and press the Enter key (the ▊ and │
├─────────────────────┤   │ ▊ keys on the right side of the keyboard │
│ Beginning Lessons   │   │ move the highlighted bar).           │
├─────────────────────┤   │                                      │
│ EXIT                │   │ Discontinue                          │
└─────────────────────┘   │ Press ▊ anytime during a lesson to return │
                          │ to this menu.                        │
                          │                                      │
                          │ Exit                                 │
                          │ Highlight EXIT at the bottom of the menu │
                          │ then press Enter ◀┘.                 │
                          │                                      │
                          │ Lesson Summary and Estimated Time    │
                          │ Highlight a lesson and press ▊.      │
                          └──────────────────────────────────────┘
```

To run the tutorial, follow these steps:

1. If you followed the documentation's recommendation and copied the Learn files to a subdirectory you created and named \LEARN, then change directories to the \LEARN subdirectory by typing *cd \learn* and pressing Enter

   or

   If you didn't copy the Learn files to the hard disk, insert the Learn disk in drive A:, type *a:*, and press Enter.

2. At the C:\LEARN prompt, type *tutor* to load the tutorial

   or

   Type *tutor* at the A> prompt if you didn't copy the Learn files to the hard disk and want to run the Tutor from drive A:.

3. At the Tutor's sign-on screen, type your first name at the prompt and press Enter. The Tutor main menu is displayed (see fig. 1.13).

When you finish a session, a check mark appears on the menu next to the item you have completed. After you complete the beginning lessons, you can move to the advanced lessons by using the arrow keys to position the highlight bar on Advanced lessons on the menu and pressing Enter. You can exit any lesson and return to the opening menu by pressing Help (F3).

To exit the Tutor, move the highlight bar to EXIT and press Enter. You are returned to the DOS prompt.

Exiting WordPerfect

If you have WordPerfect running and want to jump immediately into creating a document, go to the Quick Start for Chapter 2 or skim Chapter 2 *first* and then work through the first Quick Start.

Follow these steps to exit WordPerfect:

1. Press Exit (F7).

   The status line displays the following prompt:

   Save document? (Y/N) Yes

2. Type *N* to exit without saving. (If you have been editing a document and want to save your changes, type *Y* to save the document and then exit.)

   The status line displays the following prompt:

   Exit WP? (Y/N) No

   Note: At this point, you can press Cancel (F1) to abort the procedure and keep WordPerfect running.

3. Type *Y* to exit WordPerfect.

WP
5 ═══ Summary

In this preparatory chapter, you've gotten a brief introduction to WordPerfect 5 and the hardware necessary to run the program.

You start or "boot" WordPerfect by typing *wp* at the DOS prompt (usually A>, B>, or C>). When starting WordPerfect, keep the following in mind:

- You cannot start WordPerfect on a dual floppy disk system unless you boot DOS first or have a copy of COMMAND.COM on both the WordPerfect 1 and WordPerfect 2 disks.

Don't panic when you see that nearly blank editing screen! The status line gives you the following information:

- Which document window contains the cursor (WordPerfect lets you edit in two document windows, Doc 1 or Doc 2.)

- The cursor's position by page, line, and column number

- A file name in the lower left corner of the screen if you have already saved the document

Although typing with WordPerfect is in some ways like using a typewriter, remember that you use the Enter key to end a paragraph, but never to end a line within a paragraph. WordPerfect "wraps" each line to the next, so you can keep on composing without worrying about ending lines. You use Enter to insert blank lines or start some commands.

WordPerfect uses the 10 (or 12, depending on your keyboard) function keys for most of its functions. You use the function-key template to give WordPerfect commands in the following manner:

- Press the function key alone.

- Press the function key in combination with the Shift, Alt, or Ctrl key.

When you press many of the function keys, hidden codes are inserted into your document, such as codes for bold, underline, margins, tabs, page numbering, and so forth. These codes tell WordPerfect what to do when your document is printed. You cannot see these codes when you type, but Reveal Codes (Alt-F3, or F11) lets you see, insert, and even edit these codes.

The cursor-movement keys are on the numeric keypad at the right end of most keyboards. You use the arrow keys, Home with the arrow keys, End, PgUp, PgDn, the gray minus key (−), and the gray plus key (+) to move the cursor to different locations in your document.

If you want more information about a particular feature or command, WordPerfect's on-line Help feature can be accessed at any time. You press Help (F3) and then press the key you would like to know more about.

An additional source of help is the WordPerfect Tutor. If you're new to WordPerfect, you would be well advised to take about 2 1/2 hours to work through the Tutor's short exercises. The Tutor introduces you to WordPerfect and leads you through the rudiments of creating, editing, revising, enhancing, printing, and managing a simple document.

Do the following steps if you want to exit WordPerfect without saving the document on-screen:

1. Press Exit (F7).

2. Press *N* to exit without saving.

3. Press *Y* to leave WordPerfect.

In the next two chapters, you'll have an opportunity to put to work many of the ideas that you've learned in this preparatory chapter. Chapters 2 and 3 cover creating, editing, saving, retrieving, and printing a simple document. If you're in a hurry, you can move now to the Quick Starts at the end of both of those chapters. Good luck!

2

Creating a Document

Charles O. Stewart III is a project director and staff writer in the Product Development Department at Que Corporation. Stewart is coauthor of WordPerfect Tips, Tricks, and Traps. ■

I f you read the preceding chapter, you already know a few WordPerfect fundamentals, such as how to start the program, what information the editing screen gives you, how to use your computer's keyboard, how to take the tutorial, and how to exit the program. With that introduction to WordPerfect, you're now ready to learn more about how to create memos, short notes, letters, reports—any kind of document—with WordPerfect.

In this chapter, you learn in much more detail how to use your computer and WordPerfect to compose the documents you need. After an introduction to writing with a word processor, you look at procedures for

- entering text
- moving the cursor through a document
- using function keys to give commands
- selecting menu options by number or letter
- using Cancel (F1) to back out of a menu or cancel a prompt
- using both document windows
- printing a document
- naming and saving a document

As a bonus, this chapter provides some advice on how you can use WordPerfect to plan and draft your writing. If you have trouble getting started or suffer from writer's block, you will see how word processing can be of tremendous assistance. This advice is based on some of the latest research on what is known about how writing habits change with word processors. If you're used to composing on a typewriter or by hand and are new to word processing, you'll find that many of these tips help you realize the benefits of word processing immediately! Even old hands at word processing will come away from this chapter with more than a few new ideas for getting started.

To learn how to create a letter or memo immediately, go to the Quick Start at the end of this chapter. In less than an hour, the Quick Start can take you through creating and printing a simple letter. You should read the chapter later, however, because the Quick Start isn't designed to cover every detail presented in the chapter.

If you read or skim the chapter first, you'll still have the opportunity to "try out" WordPerfect along the way.

Writing with a Word Processor

Writing is never easy, even for experienced writers. The good fortune for those who must write is that a word processor does indeed make writing easier. Researchers who have begun to look at what happens when people learn to write with word processors have discovered a heartening fact: that people who once dreaded writing become much more positive about it after they learn to write with a word processor.

As you read in Chapter 1, composing with a word processor is different from composing in longhand or at the typewriter. Ann Berthoff writes that "composing—putting things together—is a continuum, a process that continues without any sharp breaks."[1] WordPerfect is perfectly matched to this process, allowing you to "put things together" as well as to take them apart with ease at any stage of the writing process. Rearranging, deleting, or embellishing your words on-screen is far easier than doing so at the typewriter or in longhand.

When you enter text at the computer keyboard, words are displayed on-screen. Although you may find WordPerfect's nearly blank editing screen intimidating at first, you'll realize that putting words on the screen can be far easier than putting them on paper. WordPerfect doesn't think or plan for you, of course, but it certainly simplifies self-expression.

You use the keyboard also to tell WordPerfect to do something, such as to print a file or to save a file to disk. Until you print or save a document, your words on the screen exist in RAM and can be lost unless you save this information to a disk file, either on your hard disk or on a floppy disk. The "text files" that you name and save to disk store your words and take up little physical space.

With a word processor, you can get words on-screen as fast as you can type them, so you are freed from the frustration of not being able to record thoughts almost as fast as they occur. Researchers tell us that short-term memory lasts about five seconds—all the more reason to have a tool enabling you to record your ideas quickly. You can use a word processor across the full range of writing tasks—to create, format, revise, edit, save, retrieve, and print documents. As you will see in Chapter 4, WordPerfect lets you save text in blocks (words, sentences, paragraphs) for later retrieval and consideration.

Unlike a typewriter, the word processor lets you alter what you write with great freedom. With a word processor, it's much easier to insert new words, delete ones you don't want, or move up and down through a document to see what you wrote. Because altering what you've written can be accomplished so effortlessly, you can focus on first getting words on-screen. You can then wait until later to edit, revise, and spell-check the text. If you're a poor typist, you can leave spelling errors for WordPerfect's Speller to catch. (If you want to become more proficient at the keyboard, consider a typing tutorial program like Typing Tutor IV, published by Simon and Schuster and available in most computer software stores.)

By freeing you from much writing drudgery, WordPerfect gives you more time to be creative or to rethink your work. If poor handwriting or the sheer drudgery of recopying your work were once obstacles to writing, you'll find that WordPerfect gives you new enthusiasm for drafting, reworking, and polishing your text.

With WordPerfect's many formatting features, you can change the look of the text on the page, as you see in subsequent chapters. You can change margins, indent text, vary line spacing, control word spacing, put text in columns, create headers and footers, right-justify text, and so on. In this chapter, though, you focus on those built-in settings that WordPerfect assumes most users use (at least initially). Later you will learn how to modify these defaults to meet your needs.

Understanding WordPerfect's Built-In Settings

Before you even put fingers to keys and begin typing, WordPerfect has been at work for you. You'll recall from your experience with a typewriter that you must set margins, line spacing, and tabs, for example, before you begin composing. With WordPerfect, it isn't necessary to make any formatting decisions before you begin unless the preset values do not suit you. WordPerfect comes with a number of default settings—for margins, page numbers, tab settings, base font or basic character style, line spacing, and other features as well.

You should be familiar with the basic default settings before you begin writing. Subsequent chapters, especially those devoted to formatting, printing, and desktop publishing, explore the many ways that you can alter the look of a document. For now, though, let's assume that the default settings are acceptable.

Table 2.1 lists just a few of WordPerfect's many built-in settings. To change any of these, see Chapter 18 and Appendix A. (Don't worry if terms like "base font" and "form size" are unfamiliar to you.)

Entering Text

As you may remember from Chapter 1, WordPerfect's uncluttered editing screen resembles that blank sheet of paper you insert in a typewriter. Unlike some other word processors, though, WordPerfect doesn't require that you give your file a name before you enter an editing screen and begin typing. If fact, unless you want to save

Table 2.1
Some of WordPerfect's Built-In Settings

Setting	Preset Value
Margins	1-inch top, bottom, left, and right (left =10; right =74)
Tabs	Every 5 spaces
Base font	Depends on printer
Line spacing	Single-spaced
Page number	None
Right-justification	On
Hyphenation turned off	Both aided and automatic hyphenation
Form size	Letter-size paper (8 1/2-by-11 inches)
Date format	Month (word), day, year (all four digits). Example—July 4, 1988
Automatic backup of files	None
File name displayed on status line	On

your work to disk, you don't even need to give your text a file name. You can create and print short notes or memos— or any document that you don't want to save—and "clear" the screen for your next writing task. Once you clear the screen, you can begin typing again.

If you haven't started WordPerfect and you want to follow along in this chapter, see the steps for doing so in Chapter 1.

With the "clean" editing screen you can see as much of the text as possible. With some exceptions, what you see on-screen is what prints. In word-processing jargon, WordPerfect's editing screen comes fairly close to what is known as WYSIWYG, or What-You-See-Is-What-You-Get. To achieve true WYSIWYG with WordPerfect, your computer needs one of the Hercules graphics cards mentioned in Chapter 1.

If you have WordPerfect running and want to get started right away, type the following indented paragraph. (Remember: you don't need to press Enter at the end of each line. WordPerfect "wraps" the text to the next line as your words reach the right margin.)

Think of a place that you can either visit or remember quite clearly, a place to which you have strong reactions. Write a personal description of it, attempting to re-create for your reader the experience of seeing or entering the place you've chosen to write about.

When you type in WordPerfect, characters appear at the position of the cursor as you type, just as they do when you use a typewriter.

After you type a few words, look at the Pos indicator on the status line. This value should increase as you type and as the cursor moves horizontally across the line to the right. Unlike a typewriter, WordPerfect doesn't require that you press Enter to end a line. Wordwrap inserts what is known as a *soft return* at the end of each line and "wraps" the text to the beginning of the next line.

Inserting Blank Lines

To end a paragraph or insert blank lines in the text, use the Enter key. If you're following the preceding example, when you come to the end of the last sentence, press Enter twice and type this second paragraph:

> *Details are essential to picture what is described. Try to think of rich and suggestive words and phrases that evoke emotional responses in your readers. Appeal to the senses. Use concrete nouns and active verbs.*

Your screen should look like the one in figure 2.1. When you press Enter the first time, WordPerfect inserts a *hard return*. When you press Enter a second time, WordPerfect inserts another hard return, creating a blank line in the text.

```
    Think of a place that you can either visit or remember quite
    clearly, a place to which you have strong reactions.  Write a
    personal description of it, attempting to re-create for your
    reader the experience of seeing or entering the place you've
    chosen to write about.

    Details are essential in picturing whatever is described.  Try to
    think of rich and suggestive words and phrases that will evoke
    emotional responses in your readers.  Appeal to the senses.  Use
    concrete nouns and active verbs.




    C:\WP5\BOOK\DESCRIBE.TXT                  Doc 1 Pg 1 Ln 2.5" Pos 4.2"
```

Fig. 2.1.

Inserting a blank line with the Enter key.

Moving the Cursor

In Chapter 1 you learned that you use the keys on the numeric keypad to move the cursor through the document. The Enhanced Keyboard has a separate set of cursor movement keys that you use with the Num Lock key on so that you can type numbers at the numeric keypad. With WordPerfect you have any number of ways to move the cursor through the text or to "scroll" a document. When you think of scrolling a document, imagine a continuous sheet of paper that you can roll up or down. You can, however, view only 24 lines of this text at a time. The sections that follow illustrate the various ways to move the cursor—and thereby move around in the document.

Using Esc To Move the Cursor

Before you look at the ways to move the cursor, take a quick look at an important key: the Repeat key (Esc). Use Esc to repeat an operation *n* number of times. The default value is 8. You can use Esc to move the cursor *n* number of characters (right or left), *n* number of words (right or left), *n* number of lines (up or down), or *n* pages forward or backward.

To change the repeat value, follow these steps:

1. Press Esc.

    The prompt Repeat Value = 8 appears on the status line.

2. Type a new value, and press Enter.

To test the change, press Esc again and notice the new value, which should reflect the change. This value is in effect until you enter another value.

Keep the use of Esc in mind as you learn about the many ways that you can move the cursor in WordPerfect.

Moving from Character to Character

Moving from character to character represents the smallest increments in which you can move the cursor. When you want to make small editing changes or position the cursor with respect to WordPerfect's hidden codes, this method is quite useful. To move the cursor across the line in character increments, follow these steps:

- To move one character space left, press the left arrow (←).

- To move one character space right, press the right arrow (→).

Try moving the cursor several characters into the last word, "verbs," of the passage you just typed. Press and release the left arrow several times and notice the cursor's movement. If you hold down the arrow key, the cursor continues to move across the line. When the cursor reaches the end of a line, it moves up or down, depending on which arrow key you press, and continues to move through the text as long as the key is held down. This method is, of course, too slow if you want to move the cursor rapidly through the text.

Remember from Chapter 1 that you cannot move the cursor beyond where you stop typing. For example, with the cursor just beyond the period after "verbs," press the right-arrow key (→) and see what happens. Unless you press the Enter key or the space bar after the text you type, the cursor does not move through this "dead space."

Let's try the Repeat key (Esc) to move *n* number of characters to the right:

1. Use the arrow keys to move the cursor to the beginning of "essential" in the second paragraph.

2. Press Esc.

    The prompt `Repeat Value =8` appears on the status line.

3. Press the right arrow (→).

    The cursor moves eight characters to the right and should now be under the "l" in "essential."

Remember that you can change the repeat value for any of the cursor-movement operations that follow.

Moving from Word to Word

The arrow-key method is too slow when you want to move the cursor more quickly through text. Sometimes you want to move into a sentence quickly to edit a word, add text, enter a formatting code, or make some other sort of change. To move from word to word, use the following key combinations:

- To move from anywhere in a word to the next word (or number) to the right, press Ctrl-right arrow (→).

- To move from the beginning of a word to the beginning of the next word (or number) to the left, press Ctrl-left arrow (←).

Note an important difference between Ctrl-right arrow (→) and Ctrl-left arrow (←): when the cursor is anywhere other than under the first character in a word and you press Ctrl-left arrow (←), the cursor moves to the beginning of *that* word, *not* to the beginning of the preceding word.

To try this method of cursor movement, position the cursor somewhere on a line in the passage you typed, and press Ctrl-left arrow (←) or Ctrl-right arrow (→). Repeat this process several times and watch the cursor's movement.

Moving from Line to Line

You can also move the cursor vertically from line to line, up and down the document. With this method of scrolling, you can examine a document carefully line by line and reformat as you add or delete text.

- To move the cursor up a line, press the up arrow (↑).

- To move the cursor down a line, press the down arrow (↓).

These keys repeat if you hold them down. To move line-by-line through a document, press and release the key to move up or down a line at a time.

Try this by starting at the last line of the text example and pressing the up arrow (↑). To return to the last line, press the down arrow (↓).

Moving to the End of the Line or the Edge of the Screen

Many times you want to move the cursor from some position within a line to the end of the line or the edge of the screen. Most screens allow you to see 80 characters of text. If you're using the default left and right margins of one inch (or 10 and 74 in WordPerfect 4.2 units), the lines should extend from the left edge of the screen 65 characters across, making all of the text visible. If you widen the margins, the lines may extend beyond the right or left edges of the screen and may not be visible.

- To move the cursor to the end of the line or the right edge of the screen, whichever comes first, press Home then right arrow (→). (You can also press the End key.)

- To move the cursor to the beginning of the line or the left edge of the screen, whichever comes first, press Home then left arrow (←).

If you change margins and text "runs off" the screen,

- Press Home, Home, then left arrow (←) to move the cursor to the beginning of the line, just right of any hidden codes. (If you want to know more about hidden codes, see the section in Chapter 3 on editing hidden codes.)

- Press Home, Home, then right arrow (→) to move to the far right of the line.

The cursor's position with respect to hidden codes becomes important when you delete, enter, or examine hidden codes. To move the cursor to a position at the beginning of a line and *before* any hidden codes,

- Press Home, Home, Home, then left arrow (←).

TIP: With WordPerfect 5, you can reassign keys on the keyboard to different functions. If you're just beginning to use WordPerfect, you may be perfectly satisfied with the default or original key assignments. But if you have an Enhanced Keyboard or an IBM PS/2 machine, you may want to select the alternate keyboard ENHANCED. When you select this alternate keyboard, you can press Home and move the cursor to the beginning of the line, just before any hidden codes. The function of Home by itself is moved to the 5 key on the numeric keypad.

The ENHANCED keyboard configuration also provides keyboard shortcuts for moving the cursor up or down by sentence or paragraph. For a complete explanation of alternate keyboards, creating your keyboard definitions, and selecting these keyboard definitions, see Chapter 18.

Let's experiment with the sample text. Use the appropriate arrow keys to move the cursor to "can" in the middle of the first line of the first paragraph.

1. Press Home, then right arrow (→).

   The cursor should be at the end of the line or at the edge of the screen.

2. Press Home, then left arrow (←).

   The cursor should be at the beginning of the line, under the "T" of "Think."

   You can also use the End key to move the cursor to the end of a line. With the cursor anywhere in a line, press End. The cursor moves to the line's end.

Remember that if the margins run "off" the screen, you can press Home, Home, then left or right arrow to reach the beginning or the end, respectively, of the line.

Moving to the Top or Bottom of the Screen

You see how easy it is to move the cursor horizontally across a line of text. Here are a couple of ways to move the cursor up and down the screen, 24 lines at a time:

- To move the cursor to the top of the screen, press the Screen Up key on the numeric keypad (the gray minus sign, –).

- To move the cursor to the bottom of the screen, press the Screen Down key on the numeric keypad (the gray plus sign, +).

Notice that you cannot move the cursor to the bottom of a blank editing screen.

Moving the Cursor with GoTo

With WordPerfect's GoTo command (Ctrl-Home), you can move the cursor in great "leaps" through a document. For example, use GoTo to move the cursor

- To the top or the bottom of a page

- To a particular page number

- To the next occurrence of a particular character

You can even use GoTo to return the cursor to its starting point before you gave the GoTo command, if certain conditions are met.

You can, of course, scroll laboriously through the text by holding down the up- or down-arrow keys, but using GoTo is much quicker.

Here is how you use GoTo to scroll a page:

- To move the cursor to the top of the page, press GoTo (Ctrl-Home), then up arrow (↑).

- To move the cursor to the bottom of a page, press GoTo (Ctrl-Home), then down arrow (↓).

To move the cursor quickly to a particular character, press GoTo (Ctrl-Home) and type the letter or number to which you want to move. You're limited in how far ahead you can move the cursor; the character you type must be found in the next 2,000 characters. This command works only forward in the text. You cannot use GoTo to move backward in the document.

Perhaps the most common use of the GoTo command is to move the cursor from page to page when you work on documents longer than one page. To move from page to page, follow these steps:

1. Press GoTo (Ctrl-Home).

2. Type the page number.

3. Press Enter.

Using GoTo to move to specific pages in a long document can be a real time-saver. The only drawback to this method of moving around your document is that you have to know the page number. In addition, you cannot enter anything but Arabic numerals.

GoTo also returns the cursor to the position it occupied before what WordPerfect calls the last "major motion" command. (An example of a major motion command is using Home, Home, up arrow (↑) to position the cursor at the top of a file.) In this sense, GoTo acts as a bookmark. WordPerfect remembers the cursor location and returns you to that location when you press GoTo twice.

Moving to the Top or Bottom of a Document

WordPerfect gives you a quick way to move the cursor to the top or bottom of a file. This method is most useful for documents longer than one page, of course.

To move the cursor to the top of a document,

- Press Home, Home, up arrow (↑).

To move the cursor to the bottom of a document,

- Press Home, Home, down arrow (↓).

Moving to the Top of the Preceding Page

With the PgUp key, you can move the cursor to the first line of the preceding page. To review the flow of the text, move quickly to the first line of the preceding page and scroll the text. Pressing PgUp, then up arrow (↑) lets you check for page breaks.

Moving to the Top of the Next Page

Pressing PgDn moves the cursor quickly to the first line of the next page as you scroll through a document. You can check page breaks by pressing PgDn, then press up arrow (↑) once.

Inserting Text

One of the boons of word processing is the freedom to add text to what is already written. To add a sentence in the middle of a paragraph with a typewriter, you must retype the entire paragraph. Not so with WordPerfect. To add a word, phrase, or sentence to a document, simply position the cursor where you want to insert the text. Then type the text. With WordPerfect's Block feature, explained in detail in Chapter 4, you can cut and paste text anywhere in a document. And if you stored blocks of *boilerplate* (frequently used text) on file, you can easily insert them into a document.

Suppose that you want to add a sentence to an already typed paragraph. Let's use the example you are working with in this chapter. Move the cursor to just after the first sentence in the first paragraph. Before you start, make certain that you haven't pressed the Ins key by accident. If you have, **Typeover** is displayed on the status line. Press Ins to switch to insert mode (more on this soon).

With the cursor under the "W" in "Write," type this sentence:

> *It could be a room, a natural setting, an interesting building, the house you grew up in, King Tut's tomb—any place that interests you and that you think you can make engrossing to read about.*

Notice that as you enter new text, the existing text is pushed ahead. The text is reformatted when you press down arrow (↓) once (see fig. 2.2). If you want to insert just a word, follow the same steps as for inserting a sentence.

Using Typeover

The Insert key on your keyboard works like a toggle switch, allowing you to switch from "push ahead" mode to Typeover mode and back. When you press the

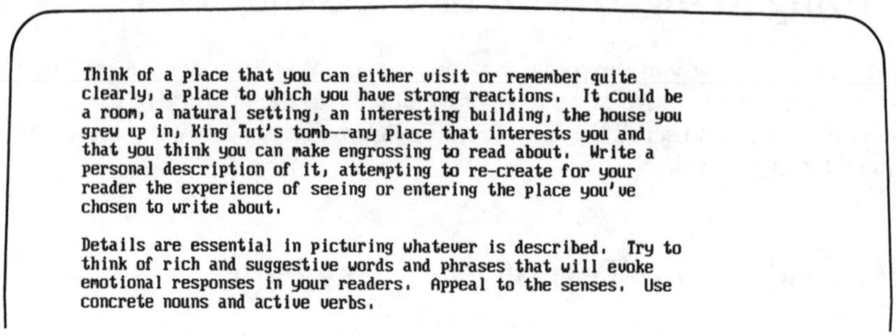

Fig. 2.2.

A new sentence inserted in the middle of a paragraph.

> Think of a place that you can either visit or remember quite clearly; a place to which you have strong reactions. It could be a room, a natural setting, an interesting building, the house you grew up in, King Tut's tomb--any place that interests you and that you think you can make engrossing to read about. Write a personal description of it, attempting to re-create for your reader the experience of seeing or entering the place you've chosen to write about.
>
> Details are essential in picturing whatever is described. Try to think of rich and suggestive words and phrases that will evoke emotional responses in your readers. Appeal to the senses. Use concrete nouns and active verbs.

Ins key, the program switches to Typeover mode and new text replaces old text. Instead of deleting a misspelled word, you can position the cursor at the appropriate position, press Ins, and type the correct characters. (For the use of Typeover during editing, see Chapter 3.)

Using Both Document Windows

Now you have done some typing and begun to get comfortable with WordPerfect's streamlined editing screen. You may recall from Chapter 1 that WordPerfect gives you two "sheets of paper," so to speak, to work on at once if you choose to do so. WordPerfect's two document "windows" give you essentially two areas within which to work. The status line tells you whether the Doc 1 or the Doc 2 window is the "active" work space. (The cursor's position determines whether the window is active.)

You can type in both windows and switch back and forth between them with ease. You can even split the screen in half to look at two documents or at different parts of the same document at once. This procedure is less complicated than it sounds. You'll find that splitting the screen is a useful feature if, for example, you're working on a long document and need to keep its beginning in mind as you work on the rest of the document.

As you see in Chapter 4, WordPerfect's two document windows make it easy to move text between two documents. You can copy text between documents, use a second document as a source of text for a first document, or use the second document window as a notepad for holding ideas that occur to you as you work on the document in the first window. If you create outlines or take notes as part of the planning process before you compose, you can display your outline or notes in one window and refer to this information as you work on your first draft in the other window. When you become more comfortable with WordPerfect, you'll find that the possibilities for using windows are manifold.

Near the end of this chapter, in the section "Using WordPerfect To Help You Develop Your Ideas," you can see how the windowing feature can help you plan and draft documents.

Switching between Document Windows

The Doc 1 window is the default window. To switch to the second document window, press Switch (Shift-F3). The status line should display Doc 2. If text is in the Doc 1 window, don't worry—it hasn't been lost. To switch back to the Doc 1 window, press Switch (Shift-F3) again.

In a typical instance, you may be working on a letter to a business contact and suddenly need to fire off a quick memo. No problem. Switch document windows (assuming, of course, that the second document window is empty), type the memo, print it using WordPerfect's "quick screen print" capability, clear the screen, and resume working on the letter. (Before you finish this chapter you'll also know how to print a document without saving it.)

Splitting the Screen

You may find it quite useful to see parts of two documents at once on-screen. Or you may want to use the second document window to keep a list of notes to yourself (see fig. 2.3). You may think it needless to split the screen when you can readily switch to the other document work space to take notes, for example, but you'll find it handy to take notes when you can see part of the primary document in the other window. You may even want to have copies of the same document in both windows, but display different parts of the document in each window. This strategy is especially useful when you work on long documents.

```
    Mr. Franklin Abbott
    Director
    Michigan Department of Commerce
    P.O. Box 30226
    Lansing, Michigan 48909

    Dear Mr. Abbott:

    Thank you for your willingness to help with our public relations
    efforts for the River Park in Indianapolis. The list of
                                      Doc 1 Pg 1 Ln 3" Pos 6.6"
    Notes re letter to F. Abbott (6/2/88):

    1.  Follow up in two weeks with phone call if we haven't
        received the list of t.v. and radio stations.
    2.  Check latest Statistical Abstract of the U.S. for data on
        park visitation rates and expenditures in Michigan.
    3.  Put him on mailing list for WaterNotes.
    4.  Send him zoo's preliminary market research (get Elizabeth
        Ferguson's OK to send him this data).

                            Doc 2 Pg 1 Ln 2.33" Pos 5.2"
```

Fig. 2.3.
The screen split for entering notes in the lower window.

The line across the middle of the screen is the tab ruler line. The downward-pointing triangles represent the tab settings for your document. In this instance, the tab ruler line shows default settings of a tab stop every half inch (or every five spaces if you choose to display the settings in WordPerfect 4.2 units). The left brace ({) represents the left margin setting; the right brace (}) represents the right margin setting. You see this ruler line when you press Reveal Codes (Alt-F3, or F11).

Before you consider the steps for splitting the screen in half, recall from Chapter 1 that you access WordPerfect's menus through the function keys: Ctrl, Alt, or Shift in combination with F1-F10—or F1-F12 if you have the Enhanced Keyboard. Up to this point, you haven't had to use any function key commands or make any menu choices. Splitting the editing screen, however, illustrates the two choices that WordPerfect gives you for making menu selections. When, for example, you press Screen (Ctrl-F3), the following menu is displayed on the status line:

0 Rewrite; **1** Window; **2** Line Draw: **0**

To make a menu selection,

- Press the number next to a menu item (default display is **bold**)

  or

- Press a letter, usually the first letter of the menu item (default display is **bold**).

To split the screen, follow these steps:

1. Press Screen (Ctrl-F3).

2. Select **Window** (**1**).

   The prompt Number of lines in this window: 24 appears on the status line.

3. Type *11*, and press Enter.

   Your screen should be split in half, with WordPerfect's tab ruler line displayed across the middle.

To switch between windows, press Switch (Shift-F3).

You may not want a 50/50 split, preferring instead to allow two-thirds of the screen for the primary document.

To resize the window to a full-screen display, follow the preceding steps, but type *24* in Step 3:

1. Press Screen (Ctrl-F3).

2. Select **Window** (**1**)

3. At the prompt asking for number of lines in the window, type *24* and press Enter.

The window is now a full-screen display.

Macros can reduce some of the keystrokes necessary for working with windows. You can read about macros in Chapter 11.

Using Cancel (F1)

To cancel any function-key command or to back out of a menu, use Cancel (F1). If, for example, you press Screen (Ctrl-F3) and then decide you do not want to split the screen, you can back out of the Screen menu by pressing Cancel (F1). Cancel (F1) gets you out of any screen menu or prompt. Esc has the same function in many other programs, such as 1-2-3® or InSet®.

In fact, if you decide that you want to try one of the alternate keyboard configurations supplied with WordPerfect 5, the ALTRNAT keyboard reassigns Cancel to the Esc key. (For details on using the "soft" keyboard feature, see Chapter 18.)

The Cancel (F1) key is also known as the Undelete key because you use it to restore up to the last three text or hidden code deletions. You learn about this use of Cancel (F1) in Chapter 3.

Printing an Unsaved Document

With WordPerfect, you can be flexible about printing. You may not want or need to save every document to disk. If you do not want to save a document, WordPerfect still lets you print it without requiring that you save it to disk first. Printing in this manner is called making a screen print, because you print what has been created and stored in temporary memory (also known as RAM).

The steps that follow assume that you installed your printer properly. If you haven't installed your printer, see Chapter 8.

To print the document on-screen, follow these steps:

1. Press Print (Shift-F7).

   The Print menu is displayed (see fig. 2.4).

2. If the text you want to print is *more* than one page, select Full Document (**1**).

   or

   If the text you want to print is a page or *less*, select **Page** (**2**).

WordPerfect flashes a * Please Wait * prompt on the status line as it prepares to print your text. If your printer is properly configured and hooked up, printing should begin almost immediately.

With WordPerfect's two document windows, you can work on a document in one window, switch to the second window and print the file in that window, then return to the first window and continue working on the file as you print the other document.

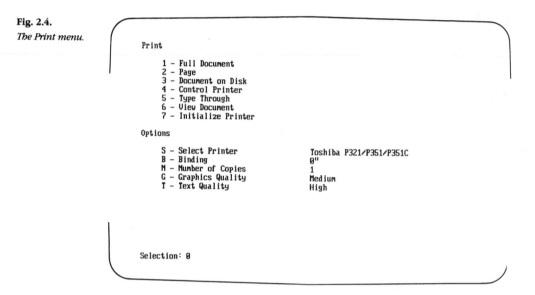

```
  Print

      1 - Full Document
      2 - Page
      3 - Document on Disk
      4 - Control Printer
      5 - Type Through
      6 - View Document
      7 - Initialize Printer

  Options

      S - Select Printer          Toshiba P321/P351/P351C
      B - Binding                 0"
      N - Number of Copies        1
      G - Graphics Quality        Medium
      T - Text Quality            High




  Selection: 0
```

Your document doesn't, however, have to be on-screen for you to print it. With WordPerfect you can print any number of documents stored on disk (floppy or hard). You can even have documents in both windows and print a document stored on disk. As you can see from the Print menu shown in figure 2.4, you can choose to print a file stored on disk. The various ways of printing and managing print jobs are treated in-depth in Chapter 8. But you know enough now to make a quick print of the text on-screen.

TIP: To review your writing, print frequent copies of your on-screen work. One limitation of composing on-screen is that you can't see more than 24 lines at a time. With such a narrow window for the text, you may lose a sense of the whole, repeat yourself, or lose a sense of the sequence of your ideas. In making the transition to word processing from typing on a typewriter or composing in longhand, you may find it hard to adjust to the lack of "global" vision that the older methods gave you.

With multi-page documents, plan to print at least several draft copies for review. Doing so helps you catch redundancies and check the flow of your work—and these matters are difficult to track when you create, revise, and edit entirely on-screen.

Saving a Document to Disk

Usually you keep copies on disk of the documents you create. WordPerfect gives you two methods of saving a file:

- With Save (F10) you save a copy of the on-screen document to disk. When you use Save, the document remains on-screen for additional work.

- With Exit (F7), you save a copy of the document to disk, but the document does *not* remain on-screen. You can keep the document on-screen by pressing Cancel when you get the Exit WP? prompt.

Use Exit to clear the screen without saving the document. This method is handy when you decide to discard what you've written.

The first time you save a document, WordPerfect prompts you for a file name. Suppose that you've created the short document example in this chapter and you now want to save the file. With your document on-screen, follow these steps:

1. Press Save (F10).

   The prompt Document to be saved: appears on the status line.

2. Type a file name for the document.

   In this instance, you can type *describe.doc*, or something that gives the file a unique name. A file name consists of two parts: a *root name* and a *suffix*. The root name can have one to eight characters. You can use the root name to describe the file's contents. The suffix, or *extension*, can have one to three characters. If you use a suffix, you must separate it from the root name by a period (.). You may omit the optional suffix if you like. When you name a file, you must observe your operating system's (MS-DOS or PC-DOS) guidelines for naming files.

3. Press Enter.

   A prompt on the status line indicates that WordPerfect is saving the file to the current directory unless you indicate otherwise. To save the file to a directory other than the current drive/directory, you must precede the file name with the drive/directory information. After you name and save a file, the file name is displayed on the status line in the left corner of the screen. (You can use Set Up to turn off the file name display if you wish. See Appendix A.)

TIP: Take advantage of WordPerfect's two backup options: timed document backup and original document backup. For steps on how to use the Set Up menu to select these backup options, see Appendix A.

WordPerfect responds a bit differently when you want to save a file that you've saved before. When you press Save (F10), WordPerfect asks you whether you want to replace the file on disk. If you press *N*, you can rename the file and save it under a different name. If you want to save the document on-screen under a *different* file name, use the right arrow (→) to move the cursor to the old file name and change it accordingly. You can change any of the information following the Document to be saved: prompt.

Clearing the Screen and Exiting WordPerfect

Use the Exit key (F7) to save the document on-screen, clear the screen, and begin working on another document if you choose. You can also use Exit to save a document, clear the screen, and exit WordPerfect. If you don't want to save your work, use Exit also to exit the file on-screen, clear the screen, and begin working on another document. Yet another use for Exit is to exit the file on-screen without saving the work—then exit the program.

To clear the screen and exit WordPerfect, follow these steps:

1. Press Exit (F7).

   WordPerfect prompts Save document? (Y/N) Yes.

2. Press *N* for No.

   WordPerfect prompts Exit WP? (Y/N) No.

3. Press *Y* for Yes.

   WordPerfect terminates, and the DOS prompt (A> , B> , or C>) appears on-screen, ending the editing session.

Using WordPerfect To Develop Ideas

This section—up to the Quick Start—is an "extra" for those who want tips on writing with a word processor. If you worked through the chapter and want some additional hands-on experience, turn now to the Quick Start. If you're new to word processing, the information in this section may help you adapt your old writing habits to this "electronic scribe." Even if you've been using a word processor—any word processor—for a while, you'll find some fresh ideas for getting those creative juices flowing.

Most writing done on the job does not require that you determine a subject or an idea for a document. Letters, memos, and reports, for example, are usually written in response to a request or a predetermined need: you respond to a customer's complaint; you write a memo recommending a certain course of action; you draw up a progress report explaining your work to date on a project.

Whether you are writing an essay at school or a memo on the job, though, you must still plan before you write. You need to determine the scope of your message and its purpose, analyze your audience, and consider how you want to present yourself. And, no matter what the writing task, you may find yourself stymied or "blocked" at certain points, sometimes right at the beginning. If you have trouble getting started, or if you're not at all sure what it is you want to say, you can use WordPerfect to generate ideas. Writing is a recursive process, one that does not proceed neatly by stages from planning to drafting to revising to final editing and polishing—and WordPerfect is a marvelous tool for assisting you through each loop of the process.

As you adapt your writing habits to the computer, keep in mind that you don't have to abandon all your old ways of doing things. If you have a penchant for jotting notes on restaurant napkins, the backs of envelopes, or in a pocket notebook, fine. You don't have to use WordPerfect for the entire composing process. But remember that WordPerfect is an ideal electronic notepad for jotting down ideas as they occur to you.

The sections that follow present tips on warming up to the writing task, discovering what you want to say, and dealing with those moments when you either can't get started or appear "blocked." You will also find tips on planning and drafting documents. Subsequent chapters on editing, formatting, spell-checking, and printing suggest ways to use WordPerfect to work through the rest of the writing cycle.

Handling Writer's Block

In *When a Writer Can't Write: Studies in Writer's Block and Other Composing Process Problems*, Mike Rose comments, "No one writes effortlessly. Our composing is marked by pauses, false starts, gnawing feelings of inadequacy, crumpled paper."[2]

WordPerfect *will* save you a mountain of "crumpled paper" (unless, of course, you simply love to hear your printer chatter and produce innumerable draft copies of your work). WordPerfect *won't* prevent those sometimes agonizing moments when the words just won't come. But by removing much of the drudgery of writing, WordPerfect does make it easier for you to record your thoughts, even to stimulate your own creativity.

If you're a halfway decent typist (if not, buy one of those typing instruction programs, such as Typing Tutor IV), you'll be amazed at how quickly you can transfer your thoughts to the screen. Researchers have found that writers talk to themselves as they compose. Many talk "out loud," rehearsing and changing phrases, clauses, sentences, and whole passages. With WordPerfect you can keep up with this running commentary and make changes and additions nearly as fast as you can speak. As an electronic scribe, WordPerfect ensures that you don't lose those evanescent thoughts.

Two strategies writers find useful for combatting writer's block are brainstorming and freewriting.

Brainstorming

When you have trouble determining a sharp focus for a document— when you aren't certain what you want to say—consider trying a semistructured writing exercise known as "brainstorming."

When you brainstorm a writing assignment on-screen, you record your ideas in list form as they occur to you. You turn off the inclination to hone each sentence before you move on to the next one. When you brainstorm, you don't worry about typos, spelling errors, or style. You can handle those matters later. Your goal is, rather, to generate as many ideas as possible about the topic (unless you're using this method to discover a topic), the purpose, or the audience. You can create and save a file for each brainstorming session.

Brainstorming can be useful before you reach the stage where a prewriting template (described subsequently) may help.

Keeping an Idea File

WordPerfect's two document windows are useful when you want to jot notes to yourself. You can keep an idea file of notes that relate to a particular project. An idea file is an extension of a brainstorming file. You can save an idea file and retrieve it when you want to add more ideas to it. Later, in the chapter on working with blocks (Chapter 4), you see how you can save a block of text to disk. You can also append a block of text to an existing file, thus adding ideas to your idea file without retrieving the file to the screen. (You will find more about file retrieval at the beginning of Chapter 3.)

Freewriting

Freewriting is less structured than brainstorming, but the two techniques are similar. Writing teacher Peter Elbow has been credited with popularizing the practice of freewriting. He defines a freewriting session as follows: "To do a freewriting exercise, simply force yourself to write without stopping for ten minutes."[3] Elbow justifies freewriting because it "separate[s] the producing process from the revising process."[4]

Begin a freewriting session with an idea or topic and, without planning or deliberation, write anything that comes into your mind about that topic. Write nonstop for at least ten minutes. Obviously, this writing is easier and less tiring with WordPerfect than with a typewriter or a pen or pencil. The most important consideration is to keep going, even if you find yourself writing nonsense or if your text begins to resemble *Finnegan's Wake*. Don't make any changes or corrections. Don't worry about typos, spelling, and other errors. Just keep up the momentum. The most important goal in freewriting—as in brainstorming—is to stimulate your thinking and get you writing.

One variation on the freewriting technique is to examine your text after each session, extract a key idea, and use this idea as the basis for the next session of on-screen freewriting. This strategy, called *looping*, forces you to find the natural coherence in the text you have produced. You can create as many *loops* as you are inclined to. Then when you have a sizeable file with a number of key ideas identified, you can delete the extraneous material and keep the "good stuff," which you can use in a prewriting template or outline.

Planning Documents

Brainstorming and freewriting at the keyboard are excellent strategies for warming up, generating ideas, and pushing your material toward a productive, critical mass. Out of chaos can come order; out of an inchoate sprawl of text on the screen—or the printout—can come the key points and direction of your message. Brainstorming and freewriting can move you closer toward that first draft, but many writers need still more preparation before formal drafting. They need interim planning.

Research into cognitive processes and the writing process suggests that experienced writers tend to have certain established mental schemas to help them in their writing tasks. That is, they have mental representations of the types of documents they need to write. They know the requirements of a particular piece of writing—whether it is a letter conveying bad news, a progress report, or a research paper—before they even begin to put fingers to keyboard. In a sense, then, they have already accomplished some planning. And experienced writers also tend to plan more: they make outlines, take notes, or make lists of ideas before they create that first draft. On the other hand, inexperienced writers often lack these internalized guidelines and therefore have trouble meeting the demands of particular writing tasks.

Interestingly enough, current research suggests that writers who use computers may do *less planning* than they did before writing with a computer.[5] The moral: beware the inclination to begin composing immediately at the keyboard. Don't let the ease with which you can put words on the screen deceive you into assuming that planning isn't necessary. Use paper to do some prewriting, or consider some of the strategies presented in this chapter. And find the best match between your writing habits and the word processor for composing. If you feel more comfortable doing some planning on paper and then transferring these notes to the screen, fine. You may even want to put notes in one of WordPerfect's document windows so that you can consult them as you create that first draft.

The seductive ease with which one composes on-screen becomes particularly problematic when writers who compose on-screen are asked to revise their work and end up merely making surface changes, shuffling words around or restating what they said without rethinking the original material.

Some researchers point out that writing on-screen makes writers unwilling to jettison poor text; in fact, the capability of frequent printouts lends yet another premature permanency to a document.[6] On the other hand, some research suggests that experienced writers eventually learn to use the editing tools of their word processor to revise, rearrange, and cut text extensively. Given the fact that research into writing with computers is still in its infancy, such seemingly contradictory evidence does not come as a surprise.

Just as experienced writers have in mind paradigms for particular documents, readers have built-in expectations for these documents. They expect documents to follow logical patterns. When these expectations are met or surpassed, readers are usually appreciative and receptive. If, for example, you ask for a refund for a damaged product, you expect a responding letter to refer to that refund request immediately and specifically. You also expect research reports to begin with a conclusion followed with supporting data, dissertations to begin with an abstract, and memos to begin with background information and a statement of the writer's purpose or recommendations.

Readers have expectations even about the sequence of elements in a paragraph or a sentence. They expect the first sentence of a paragraph to orient them to the rest of the paragraph. If you begin a sentence with new information but follow with something the reader already knows, you may force the reader to reread the sentence. The movement from new to old is unnatural and makes sentences less readable. If you don't plan your documents carefully—from sentence structure to overall design—you run the risk of violating the expectations of your readers. Frustrated readers lose confidence in the writer and may stop reading.

As part of the planning process, consider two effective tools: prewriting templates and outlines.

Using a Prewriting Template

Prewriting is everything you do up to the actual step of writing that first draft. It is very much a part of the planning stage.

A *prewriting template* is a set of prompts that force you to answer some basic questions before you begin your document. As you plan the document, you may find it helpful to use a prewriting template to refine your thinking about a particular writing task. You can ask the basic reporter's questions of "Who?" "What?" "Where?" "Why?" and "When?" Or you can simplify your planning to consider these questions:

- Who are you? What is your role in the organization? How do you want to present yourself, to be perceived?

- What is your subject? What do you need to say? What do you want to say?

- What is your purpose in writing? Why are you writing this document? What do you hope to achieve?

- Who is your audience? What do they already know? What do they need to know? What will your readers do with your message? What is your relationship to the audience? How will your audience react to your message? Can you anticipate this reaction and shape your message accordingly? Can you consider your message from your reader's point of view?

To create a prewriting template, begin with a fresh screen and enter the text you see in figure 2.5. Put each prompt in bold and leave several blank lines between each item. Name this document something like TEMPLATE and save it to disk. Then, when you need this prewriting template, retrieve it and use it again.

Speaker:

Subject:

Purpose:

Audience:

Fig. 2.5.
Prewriting template.

If you prefer to prewrite or plan on paper, you can add more lines between each prompt, print the template, and enter your responses by hand. You can then keep the written material close to the computer when you compose your first draft.

When you learn about formatting with WordPerfect, you may want to add a prompt for format or design as part of your planning strategies. Focus on matters of role, message, purpose, and audience.

Then move the cursor to the right of each prompt and begin typing notes. After you write enough notes for each category and have a clear sense of how you want to present yourself, what you need to say, why you need to say it, and who your audience is—keeping in mind that your document may have multiple audiences—you are considerably closer to creating that first draft. You can then save the prewriting template to disk, *but be sure to use another file name.*

Assuming that the second document window is empty, switch windows and begin the first draft of the letter, memo, or report. If your filled-out prewriting template isn't displayed in one of the windows, you can retrieve it and refer to it as you compose your draft in the other document window. If you're writing a report that entails research, you may want to create an outline next, based in part on the template responses in the other document window.

Use your creativity when you design prewriting templates. You may, for example, create an entire template for generating ideas about writing purpose or a template that focuses solely on audience considerations. You can list everything you know about your intended audience. Any template that helps you define a focus and structure for your document is a useful writing tool.

Using an Outline

An outline can function as a kind of template. But the overarching structure of an outline isn't easy to conceive, especially if the writing task promises to be lengthy. Besides, you may have been force-fed outlines in elementary and high school and balk at the idea of working from one.

Whether to use an outline depends, in part, on what type of writer you are. Some writers conceive elaborate plans and don't diverge much from those plans when they compose. Other writers do less planning or structuring and heavily revise their text. When you are in the middle of a writing task, however, even an informal or loose outline can give you some scaffolding on which to hang your ideas. You can use an outline as another kind of prewriting template. You don't need to follow it rigidly; you can slot ideas here and there as they occur to you. You don't need to supply all the headings and subheadings either. You can begin with a few major categories and flesh out sections here and there. You can even use brainstorming and freewriting to generate additional ideas for sections. Later, you can go back and supply transitions and add, cut, or relocate material. At some point, of course, you may need to do some research before you can flesh out an outline in preparation for that first draft.

If you have trouble getting started, try the timeworn method of creating an outline first. Successful writers have learned the importance of beginning a writing task with a roadmap to supply some sense of structure and outcome. WordPerfect's outlining feature, though not as flexible as those that allow you to collapse or expand sections of an outline, can be a helpful tool as you plan your document.

Even if you jot down just the major ideas as headings, you can go back later and develop each section. The outline is dynamic insofar as it enters the appropriate heading level numbers and updates these numbers as you add or delete sections. You can use WordPerfect's Block feature, explained in Chapter 4, to cut and paste whole sections of the outline if you need to rearrange it. For detailed coverage of the Outline feature, see Chapter 21.

For memos and short reports, you may not need an elaborate outline. Just a few headings may create a sufficient roadmap. Either way, WordPerfect makes it easy for you to jot down notes indicating your direction. As with a more elaborate or formal outline, you can keep your simple outline in the second document window for reference as you compose a draft in the other document window.

Quick Start

Creating a Short Letter

T his Quick Start guides you through creating a simple, one-page letter. You learn to start WordPerfect, enter text in the editing screen, move the cursor, cancel a command, insert blank lines in the text, print and save a letter, and exit WordPerfect.

Starting WordPerfect on a Dual Floppy System

To start WordPerfect on your dual floppy computer, make sure that DOS is on your WordPerfect disk, then follow these steps:

1. Insert the working copy of your WordPerfect 1 disk in drive A:

2. Insert a formatted data disk in drive B:

3. Turn on the computer.

4. Respond appropriately to the operating system prompts for the date and time. (If you have an AUTOEXEC.BAT file, this step may not be necessary. See Appendix A.)

5. At the A> prompt, type *b:*

6. Press Enter.

   Drive B is now the default drive, which means that any data you save to disk is saved to the data disk in drive B.

7. Type *a:wp.*

8. Press Enter.

   If you don't have an IBM PS/2™ computer, WordPerfect is now loaded into memory because all the main program files are on the WordPerfect 1/WordPerfect 2 microfloppy disk. If you are running WordPerfect on an IBM PC, XT, AT, or compatible, you must complete two additional steps:

9. Remove the WordPerfect 1 disk from drive A and insert the WordPerfect 2 disk.

10. Press any key to resume loading WordPerfect.

Starting WordPerfect on a Hard Disk System

This section assumes that you followed the directions in Appendix A for setting up your hard disk and installing WordPerfect. If you have an AUTOEXEC.BAT file (see Appendix A), WordPerfect loads *automatically* after you turn on the computer and respond to the prompts for date and time.

Depending on whether your hard-disk system has one or two floppy disk drives, make certain that the drive door is open for each drive.

To start WordPerfect on your hard-disk system, follow these steps:

1. Turn on your computer.

2. Respond to the prompts for date and time. (If you have an AUTOEXEC.BAT file, this step may not be necessary.)

   The DOS prompt C> is displayed on-screen.

3. Type *cd \wp*.

4. Press Enter.

   The current directory is now \WP, where the main WordPerfect program files are stored on the hard disk.

5. Type *wp*.

6. Press Enter.

You should see the opening screen for just a moment, after which the editing screen is displayed.

Examining the Opening Screen

Your screen should be blank except for the following information on the status line:

    Doc 1 Pg 1 Ln 1" Pos 1"

The status line tells you the cursor's location by document (either the Document 1 or Document 2 window), page, line, and column position.

If you used Set Up (Shift-F1) to change the program's defaults, your screen may not appear exactly the same as this.

Later in the Quick Start, after you name the document and save it, the document name is displayed at the left corner of the bottom of the screen.

Making Menu Choices

To practice using WordPerfect's function keys to give commands, use the Date/Outline key (Shift-F5) to enter today's date. The cursor should be at the top left corner of the screen. Follow these steps:

1. Press Date/Outline (Shift-F5).

2. Select Date **Text** (**1**).

Note that you can press either *T* or *1* to make a menu selection.

The current date is inserted in the text at the position of the cursor. (This exercise assumes that you entered the date properly when you turned on your computer.)

Using Cancel (F1)

What do you do if you press a function key and then want to back out of a menu? Use the Cancel (F1) key.

To practice using Cancel (F1), follow these steps:

1. Press Date/Outline (Shift-F5).

   Note that the menu appears across the bottom of the screen.

2. Because you don't want to insert the date again, press Cancel (F1). The menu disappears.

Inserting Blank Lines

In most letters you want several blank lines between the date and the inside address. Use the Enter key to insert blank lines in the text. Each blank line is really a "hard return" inserted in the text. To insert two blank lines between the date and the inside address, press Enter three times.

Typing Text

So far, WordPerfect has done most of the work. Now it's time for you to type the inside address, salutation, body of the letter, and closing. As you type, don't worry about typing errors. The purpose of this Quick Start is to give you a feel for the fluidity of composing with a word processor. In the next chapter's Quick Start, "Editing a Document," you'll see how to correct typing mistakes. To create a letter, follow these steps:

1. Type the following name and address, remembering to press Enter at the end of each line:

   Mr. Rudolf Steiner
   23 Goethe Street
   Chicago, Illinois 60610

2. Press Enter twice to leave two blank spaces.

3. Create the salutation by typing

   Dear Mr. Steiner:

4. Press Enter twice to enter two blank lines between the salutation and the first paragraph of the letter.

5. Type the first paragraph of the letter. Note how, as the cursor gets close to the right margin, WordPerfect wraps text down to the next line:

   Thank you for inquiring about "The Seed and the Soil: A Biodynamic Perspective," the Midwest Regional Conference of the Biodynamic Farming and Gardening Association. The conference will be held from October 7-9, 1988, in the Barn Abbey at New Harmony, Indiana. The registration packet you requested is enclosed.

6. Press Enter twice to end the paragraph and insert a blank line between paragraphs.

7. Type the second paragraph:

   This conference marks the first of its kind in the Midwest. If you're new to biodynamic gardening, you'll have a rare opportunity to learn from the experts. If you're an experienced biodynamic gardener, you'll be able to mingle and swap secrets with fellow enthusiasts.

   Your screen should now look like the one in figure 2.6.

8. Press Enter twice to end the paragraph and insert a blank line between the second and third paragraphs.

9. Type the third paragraph:

   New Harmony, once the site of two utopian and agrarian communities in the early nineteenth century, is an ideal setting for our conference. Driving time from Chicago is approximately 5 1/2 hours.

10. Press Enter twice to end the paragraph and insert a blank line between the third and final paragraphs.

11. Type the last paragraph:

    Thank you for your interest in the Midwest Regional Conference of the Biodynamic Farming and Gardening Association. We look forward to meeting and working with you in October.

12. Press Enter twice to end the paragraph and insert a blank line between the last paragraph and the closing.

```
May 13, 1988

Mr. Rudolf Steiner
23 Goethe Street
Chicago, Illinois 60610

Dear Mr. Steiner:

Thank you for inquiring about "The Seed and the Soil: A
Biodynamic Perspective," the Midwest Regional Conference of the
Biodynamic Farming and Gardening Association.  The conference
will be held from October 7-9, 1988, in the Barn Abbey at New
Harmony, Indiana.  The registration packet you requested is
enclosed.

This conference marks the first of its kind in the Midwest. If
you're new to biodynamic gardening, you'll have a rare
opportunity to learn from the experts.  If you're an experienced
biodynamic gardener, you'll be able to mingle and swap secrets
with fellow enthusiasts.


C:\WP5\BOOK\CONFER.LET                 Doc 1 Pg 1 Ln 4.33" Pos 3.4"
```

Fig. 2.6.
Part of a letter.

13. Type *Sincerely yours*, a comma (,), and press Enter five times to insert four blank lines for the signature.

14. Type *Gertrude Jekyll*.

Your letter is almost finished.

Moving Up and Down in the Document

WordPerfect has an array of shortcuts for moving the cursor around in a document. Let's try a few.

Because you just finished the letter, the cursor should be at the bottom of the screen.

The shortest distance the cursor can travel vertically is up or down one line at a time. Practice moving the cursor up a few lines by pressing the up-arrow key (↑). Return the cursor to the last line by pressing the down-arrow key (↓). Note that each press moves the cursor up or down a line unless you hold down the key so that it repeats. Try these cursor movements:

- To move to the top of the page, press PgUp.

  The cursor should be on the first line of the page. If you get the number 9 when you press PgUp, press the Backspace key to delete the number and then toggle off Num Lock by pressing the Num Lock key once.

- To move to the bottom of the page, press PgDn.

  The cursor should return to where you started, just after "Gertrude Jekyll."

You can move 24 lines up or down, to the top or the bottom of the screen:

- To move to the top of the screen, press the Screen Up key (the gray minus sign, –)

  or

  Press Home, up arrow.

- To move to the bottom of the screen, press the Screen Down key (the gray plus sign, +)

  or

  Press Home, down arrow (↓).

You can move the cursor to the beginning or end of a document:

- To move the cursor to the beginning of a file, just after any hidden codes, press Home, Home, up arrow (↑).

  If you try this with the sample letter, the cursor should be at the beginning of the inside address.

- To move the cursor to the end of the document, press Home, Home, down arrow (↓).

  The cursor should be positioned just after your name.

To position the cursor at the beginning of the document *before* any hidden codes, press Home, Home, up arrow (↑).

Moving Sideways in a Document

With WordPerfect you can move the cursor left or right on a line, from letter to letter, from word to word, or from the beginning of a line to the end of the line.

First, move the cursor to the top of the letter by pressing Home, Home, up arrow (↑). Next, press and hold down the down-arrow key (↓) until the cursor is at the beginning of the first line of the opening paragraph.

1. Press the right-arrow key (→) to move the cursor several letters into the word "Thank."

2. Press the left-arrow key (←) to move the cursor back to the "T" in "Thank."

3. Next, press and hold down the Ctrl key as you press and release the right-arrow key (→) four times.

   The cursor should be at the beginning of "about."

4. Repeat the procedure in Step 3, but this time press the left-arrow key (←).

   The cursor should be at the beginning of the first line.

5. To move to the end of the first line, press Home, right arrow (→)

   or

   Press End.

6. To return the cursor to the beginning of the line, press Home, left arrow (←).

Moving to a Different Page

With WordPerfect's GoTo command (Ctrl-Home), you can move the cursor to any page in the document. To make a two-page document of the letter, follow these steps:

1. Move the cursor to the end of the second paragraph.

2. Press Hard Page (Ctrl-Enter) to "force" a hard page break.

   Notice that a line of double dashes is inserted just after the second paragraph, in effect moving the cursor to the second page (see fig. 2.7).

```
May 13, 1988


Mr. Rudolf Steiner
23 Goethe Street
Chicago, Illinois 60610

Dear Mr. Steiner:

Thank you for inquiring about "The Seed and the Soil: A
Biodynamic Perspective," the Midwest Regional Conference of the
Biodynamic Farming and Gardening Association.  The conference
will be held from October 7-9, 1988, in the Barn Abbey at New
Harmony, Indiana.  The registration packet you requested is
enclosed.

This conference marks the first of its kind in the Midwest. If
you're new to biodynamic gardening, you'll have a rare
opportunity to learn from the experts.  If you're an experienced
biodynamic gardener, you'll be able to mingle and swap secrets
with fellow enthusiasts.
================================================================
C:\WP5\BOOK\CONFER.LET                      Doc 1 Pg 2 Ln 1" Pos 1"
```

Fig. 2.7.
Inserting a hard page break to create a two-page document.

To move the cursor to the top of the first page, now page one, follow these steps:

1. Press GoTo (Ctrl-Home).

2. At the GoTo prompt, type *1* and press Enter.

   The cursor should be at the top of page one (check the status line to be certain).

To restore the letter to its original one-page status, follow these steps:

1. Press GoTo (Ctrl-Home).

2. At the GoTo prompt, type *2* and press Enter.

   The cursor is at the top of page 2 again.

3. Press the Backspace key once to delete the hard page break. The line of double dashes should disappear from the screen.

Inserting Text

WordPerfect makes it quite easy to insert text anywhere you choose, such as in the middle of a word, sentence, or paragraph. Let's insert a sentence in the third paragraph. Use the arrow keys to move the cursor to the beginning of the last sentence in the third paragraph.

1. Type this sentence:

   You'll find a map in the registration packet to help you find your way here.

2. Press the space bar twice.

   Note how the existing text is pushed ahead. It seems to disappear off-screen to the right (see fig. 2.8) when the cursor reaches the right margin and text wraps back to the left margin.

Fig. 2.8.

Inserting text.

```
with fellow enthusiasts.

New Harmony, once the site of two utopian and agrarian
communities in the early nineteenth century, is an ideal setting
for our conference.  You'll find a map in the registration packet
to help you find your way here.  Driving time from Chicago is roughly 5 1/2 hou

Thank you for your interest in the Midwest Regional Conference of
the Biodynamic Farming and Gardening Association.  We look
forward to meeting and working with you in October.

Sincerely yours,


Gertrude Jekyll
```

3. Press the down arrow (↓) to reformat the paragraph (see fig. 2.9).

Printing the Letter

Unlike some word processors, WordPerfect doesn't require that you name and save a letter or memo before you print it.

To print an on-screen document, follow these steps:

Fig. 2.9.
*Paragraph after
reformatting.*

```
with fellow enthusiasts.

New Harmony, once the site of two utopian and agrarian
communities in the early nineteenth century, is an ideal setting
for our conference. You'll find a map in the registration packet
to help you find your way here. Driving time from Chicago is
roughly 5 1/2 hours.

Thank you for your interest in the Midwest Regional Conference of
the Biodynamic Farming and Gardening Association. We look
forward to meeting and working with you in October.

Sincerely yours,



Gertrude Jekyll
```

1. Press Print (Shift-F7).

   The Print menu appears (see fig. 2.10). Your menu may differ, depending
   on the default printer you select.

Fig. 2.10.
The Print menu.

```
Print

        1 - Full Document
        2 - Page
        3 - Document on Disk
        4 - Control Printer
        5 - Type Through
        6 - View Document
        7 - Initialize Printer

Options

        S - Select Printer          Toshiba P321/P351/P351C
        B - Binding                 0"
        N - Number of Copies        1
        G - Graphics Quality        Medium
        T - Text Quality            High




Selection: 0
```

2. Select **P**age (**2**) to print the letter.

Your printed letter should look like the one in figure 2.11.

Note that, for this example, right justification—the default setting—is turned off. For
information on how to change program defaults, see Appendix A.

Fig. 2.11.
The printed letter.

May 13, 1988

Mr. Rudolf Steiner
23 Goethe Street
Chicago, Illinois 60610

Dear Mr. Steiner:

Thank you for inquiring about "The Seed and the Soil: A
Biodynamic Perspective," the Midwest Regional Conference of the
Biodynamic Farming and Gardening Association. The conference
will be held from October 7-9, 1988, in the Barn Abbey at New
Harmony, Indiana. The registration packet you requested is
enclosed.

This conference marks the first of its kind in the Midwest. If
you're new to biodynamic gardening, you'll have a rare
opportunity to learn from the experts. If you're an experienced
biodynamic gardener, you'll be able to mingle and swap secrets
with fellow enthusiasts.

New Harmony, once the site of two utopian and agrarian
communities in the early nineteenth century, is an ideal setting
for our conference. You'll find a map in the registration packet
to help you find your way here. Driving time from Chicago is
roughly 5 1/2 hours.

Thank you for your interest in the Midwest Regional Conference of
the Biodynamic Farming and Gardening Association. We look
forward to meeting and working with you in October.

Sincerely yours,

Gertrude Jekyll

Saving the Letter

In addition to printing your letter, you may want to store a copy of it on disk. To save a document, follow these steps (these assume that the document is not yet saved):

1. Press Save (F10).

2. At the Document to be saved: prompt, type a name for the document, such as CONFER.LET. Press Enter.

WordPerfect indicates that it is saving the document under the name you indicate.

After you save your document with Save (F10), your document remains on-screen for further work. A copy with the latest additions or changes is stored on disk.

Exiting WordPerfect

When you finish creating a document, you can exit the document and stay in WordPerfect, or you can exit the document and exit WordPerfect as well.

To exit WordPerfect, follow these steps:

1. Press Exit (F7).

   WordPerfect prompts Save document? (Y/N) Yes.

2. Press *N* to clear the screen without saving what is on-screen.

   WordPerfect asks you whether you want to exit the program.

3. Press *Y* if you want to exit WordPerfect; otherwise, press *N* to stay in WordPerfect and begin another document.

WP 5 ▓▓ Summary

In Chapter 2, you learned a lot about using the word processor to help you write. You read not only about how you can type, save, and print a document in WordPerfect but also about how you can use the word processor as a composing tool, an instrument for brainstorming and freewriting. You learned how to create a template to help you plan your writing tasks and how to use an outline to develop your ideas into a more coherent package.

Now that you can brainstorm, plan, and type a document, then save it to disk and print it, you are ready to learn more sophisticated formatting techniques and more complicated word-processing strategies. On to Chapter 3!

---

[1] Ann Berthoff, *Forming, Thinking, Writing: The Composing Imagination* (Montclair, NJ: Boynton/Cook, Publishers, Inc., 1982), p. 11.

[2] Mike Rose, *When a Writer Can't Write: Studies in Writer's Block and Other Composing Process Problems*, (New York: Guilford Press, 1985), p. ix.

[3] Peter Elbow, *Writing with Power: Techniques for Mastering the Writing Process* (New York: Oxford University Press, 1981), p. 13.

[4] Elbow, p. 14.

[5] Gail Hawisher, "Research Update: Writing and Word Processing." eds. Cynthia Selfe and Kathleen Kiefer, *Computers and Composition*, 5, No. 2 (April 1988), 16.

[6] Lillian Bridwell-Bowles, Parker Johnson, and Stephen Brehe, "Composing and Computers: Case Studies of Experienced Writers," in *Writing in Real Time: Modeling Production Processes*, ed. Ann Matsuhashi (Norwood, NJ: Ablex Publishing Co., 1987), p. 90.

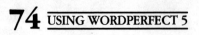

3

Editing a Document

Schuyler Lininger, Jr., is an Oregon chiropracter and vice president of sales for a major food-supplement company. Dr. Lininger is also a computer consultant and writer for the last seven years. Using WordPerfect and desktop publishing, he regularly produces a national newsletter for natural-food stores. ■

In the previous chapter, you learned how to enter text, move the cursor, make menu choices, save and print a document, and exit WordPerfect. This chapter presents the basics of editing a document. If you are switching from WordPerfect 4.2 to WordPerfect 5, you won't notice many differences in editing features between the two versions. Other chapters cover more extensive changes between the two versions.

If you are new to word processing, this chapter will be fun and exciting. You have probably wondered how using a word processor is different from using a typewriter. This chapter introduces you to some of the powerful editing tools at your disposal with WordPerfect. If you are like most people, a few minutes with WordPerfect make you wonder how you could ever again get along with only a typewriter.

This chapter includes a Quick Start. If you want, you can turn to this section first to practice the techniques described in this chapter.

In this chapter, you learn how to do the following tasks:

- Retrieve a file

- Edit basic text

- Revise text extensively

- Delete (erase) a single character, word, line, sentence, paragraph, and page

- Undelete (unerase) what you recently erased

- Overwrite text in typewriter style

- Enhance your text by using **bold** typeface or <u>underlining</u>

- Edit in Reveal Codes (Alt-F3, or F11) for greater format control

- Use the powerful search-and-replace capabilities of WordPerfect

- Use Document Comments as an aid to effective writing and control over the editing process

Retrieving a Document

In Chapter 2, you learned how to save a document. In this section, you learn how to retrieve a document into WordPerfect for editing. If you have documents created with WordPerfect 4.2, WordPerfect 5 automatically converts your 4.2 documents. (Once this conversion has taken place, the document cannot be read again by WordPerfect 4.2 without saving it in WordPerfect 4.2 format. This is done by using the Text In/Out (Ctrl-F5) key.)

Documents created with other word processors, such as WordStar or MultiMate, can be converted to WordPerfect 5 format with a utility program supplied with WordPerfect. The conversion procedure is explained in Chapter 15.

Using List Files To Retrieve a File

The simplest way to retrieve a document is to use the List Files (F5) command. The following details the procedures for retrieving a document using List Files. (A comprehensive explanation is presented in Chapter 10.)

To retrieve a document, perform the following steps:

1. Press List Files (F5).

   A prompt appears in the lower left corner of your screen, listing the current drive, subdirectory, and file specification . (The default file specification is *.*, which means *all files*.)

2. Press Enter.

   The editing screen is replaced by the List Files screen (see fig. 3.1).

Fig. 3.1.
The List Files screen.

```
05/15/88  13:38              Directory C:\WP\*.*
Document size:    61097   Free:  3389568   Used:    827081      Files:   37

.  <CURRENT>   <DIR>                    ..  <PARENT>   <DIR>
AUSTIN   .     <DIR>    12/13/87 12:31   BAHAI    .     <DIR>    04/18/87 15:15
CLASS    .     <DIR>    04/18/87 15:15   CLINIC   .     <DIR>    04/18/87 15:15
HM       .     <DIR>    06/13/87 14:25   HYPHEN   .     <DIR>    04/19/88 16:48
JANE     .     <DIR>    04/18/87 15:16   LEX      .     <DIR>    04/18/87 15:17
MACRO    .     <DIR>    04/18/87 15:28   MISC     .     <DIR>    04/18/87 15:21
MK       .     <DIR>    04/18/87 15:22   MYSTERY  .     <DIR>    04/18/87 15:36
QUE      .     <DIR>    03/13/88 00:22   RENTAL   .     <DIR>    04/18/87 15:24
REPORTS  .     <DIR>    04/18/87 15:24   STYLE    .     <DIR>    04/19/88 16:53
APLASPLU.PRS   34991    05/12/88 20:23   EPFX80   .PRS   6666    05/12/88 20:22
EPLQ2500.PRS   12485    05/14/88 22:51   GENIUS1  .WPD   4692    04/27/88 14:24
GENIUS2  .WPD   4735    04/27/88 14:24   GRABWP   .COM  14687    04/27/88 14:24
KEYS     .MRS   4800    05/04/88 23:09   STANDARD.PRS   1025    05/04/88 23:09
WP       .DRS  73356    04/27/88 14:24   WP       .EXE 244736   05/04/88 23:08
WP       .FIL 298884    05/04/88 23:09   WP       .MRS   3756    05/04/88 23:08
WPHELP   .FIL  47587    05/04/88 23:08   WPHELP2  .FIL  52121    05/04/88 23:08
WPSMALL  .DRS  13822    05/04/88 23:09   WP{WP}   .SET   4642    05/15/88 13:38
WP}WP{   .BV1      0    05/15/88 13:38   WP}WP{   .CHK      0    05/15/88 13:38
WP}WP{   .GF1      0    05/15/88 13:38 ▼ WP}WP{   .SPC   4096    05/15/88 13:38

1 Retrieve; 2 Delete; 3 Move/Rename; 4 Print; 5 Text In;
6 Look; 7 Other Directory; 8 Copy; 9 Word Search; N Name Search: 6
```

3. If you see the name of your document, use the arrow keys to position the highlight bar on the file name you want

or

If you don't see the name of your document,

   a. Press **Name** Search (**N**).

   b. Type the first few letters of the document name. The highlight bar moves to the name of your document.

   c. Press Enter to end Name Search.

If you think you've found your document but aren't positive, you can "look" before retrieving. Choose **Look** (**6**), and the text of the document is displayed. Any Document Summary is displayed first. You can scroll through the document using the arrow keys. Press Exit (F7) to return to the List Files screen.

4. Choose **Retrieve** (**1**).

WordPerfect is careful about what files are retrieved. If you try to retrieve a file other than a WordPerfect file, the following message appears:

`ERROR: Incompatible file format`

Earlier versions of WordPerfect would sometimes try to retrieve non-WordPerfect files, causing the program to freeze and making it necessary to reboot your computer. You could even damage the file you wanted to retrieve.

Changing Paths from List Files

If you cannot find your document, you may be looking on the wrong disk or in the wrong directory. To change the path, do the following steps:

1. Press List Files (F5); then press Enter.

   You see a prompt in the lower left corner of your screen that says something like, `Dir C:\WP50\*.*`.

2. If you want to change the default directory, press the equal sign (=) and then type in the new directory name, such as *C:WP50 \LETTERS*

   or

   If you want to look at a directory without changing the default path, just type in the new directory name (do not press the equal sign first).

3. Press Enter.

Changing Paths from the Document Screen

You also can change paths from the document screen. To change the directory from the document screen, perform the following steps:

1. Press List Files (F5).

2. Press Enter.

3. Choose **Other Directory** (7).

4. Type the name of the new directory.

5. Press Enter twice to access the new directory.

If you are unsure of the name of the directory you want to change to, perform the following steps:

1. Press List Files (F5).

2. Press Enter.

3. If you see a list file with the extension< DIR>, you have found a list of directories. Use the arrow keys to position the highlight bar over the name of the directory of your choice.

4. Press Enter twice.

Using Retrieve (Shift-F10) To Retrieve a Formatted File

If you know the name of the document you want to retrieve, perform the following steps to retrieve a file:

1. Press Retrieve (Shift-F10).

   A prompt Document to be retrieved: appears in the lower left corner of your screen.

2. Type the complete name of the document.

3. Press Enter.

If you see the message ERROR: File not found, verify your spelling and try again. You also may receive the error message if you have not entered the correct disk drive, directory, or subdirectory.

If the document is in a drive or subdirectory different from the one you are currently in, you must either change drives and directories or type the complete path. The following is an example of a drive, directory, subdirectory, and document name:

C:\WP50\LETTERS\SMITH.1

Combining Files by Retrieving Them

You may want to combine portions of two or more documents to create one large document. Doctors, attorneys, and other report writers often have standard paragraphs that are inserted into many documents. Journalists, authors, and thesis writers often want to use a paragraph or story fragment they have previously written. Unlike a typewriter, WordPerfect gives you a powerful editing tool by allowing you to combine two or more documents into a single document.

Whenever you retrieve a document, WordPerfect adds that document to what is on-screen. If the screen contains no text and is blank, you don't have to worry about combining. But if a document is already on-screen, the newly retrieved document is inserted at the cursor position. If the cursor is in the middle of your current document, the new document is inserted in the middle of your current document.

To combine documents, place your cursor where you want the new document inserted, and then retrieve a document with one of the methods previously described. If you use Retrieve (Shift-F10), the new document is retrieved immediately. If you then use List files (F5) and a document is already on-screen, WordPerfect warns you by asking that you confirm the retrieval process with the prompt:

`Retrieve into current document? (Y/N) No`

Press either *Y* for yes or *N* for no.

TIP: It is a good idea to save your current document before retrieving additional text. That way, if you make a mistake and retrieve the wrong text or put the text in the wrong place, you don't need to spend time correcting your error. Just erase the screen and start over again by retrieving the document you just saved.

Revising and Editing Your Text

WordPerfect serves two general groups. The first group involves writers, journalists, doctors, lawyers, and other professionals who compose original material. The second group involves typists or secretaries who must transcribe and proofread someone else's thoughts from either a recording or a manuscript.

The first group might need to extensively rewrite or substantially revise their prose. The second group might verify spelling, correct punctuation and grammar, and format the final document for an appealing presentation.

In some instances, one person may do all of the creating, revising, correcting, and formatting. In other instances, there may be a collaborative effort. Regardless of the circumstances, WordPerfect is a powerful tool for performing these tasks.

Substantive Changes (Revision)

After you create a document, you may need to revise it. Revision goes deeper than polishing the page. Polishing requires checking spelling and punctuation as well as formatting the document for attractive presentation. Revision requires polishing the thoughts behind the presentation.

Word processors in general, and WordPerfect in particular, make editing so simple that the tendency is to polish the page and not the thought. Because some of the same tools (for example, deleting and moving text) are involved in both revision and editing, sometimes it is easy to confuse one with the other. Prior to the advent of word processors, revision was a chore requiring hours of scratching out a phrase, penciling in another; cutting a paragraph, pasting in other text; and then retyping the entire document—only to have to repeat the process over and over. With WordPerfect, the drudgery is significantly reduced and rewriting easily done.

However, the same care in thinking and hard work in revision is required with WordPerfect as was required in the past with pencils, paper, scissors, glue, and typewriters. Experienced writers use WordPerfect not just for their initial thoughts but as an aid to the extensive rewriting that might involve eliminating and rewriting major sections of prose.

WordPerfect 5 offers writers an unequaled creative environment. The following suggestions show how you can use this environment to its fullest:

- Use the *transparent nature* (the large blank screen) of WordPerfect to write your thoughts quickly. (Chapter 21 shows you how you can later organize your document with WordPerfect's outlining capabilities.)

- Use the editing capabilities (described later in this chapter) to eliminate unwanted text and to add new ideas or thoughts.

- Use the powerful block moves of WordPerfect to rearrange text. (Chapter 4 examines the block feature.)

- Use WordPerfect's Thesaurus to find the "perfect" word and the Speller to find misspellings. (The Thesaurus and Speller features are explained in Chapter 7.)

- Use the editing screen or a printed copy of your document for additional revisions.

Surface Changes (Editing)

WordPerfect also has unparalleled editing capabilities. The editing process is comparable to polishing a gemstone. After the initial cut has been made, changes to the surface are what make a rock a treasure. Similarly, you can edit in two stages. In the first stage, you handle rough editing, such as correcting typographical errors by deleting or adding letters and words. At this stage of editing, WordPerfect helps you by proofreading for spelling errors and double words.

In the second stage of editing, the "polishing," you handle formatting the final document—how the document looks when printed. Most formatting can be done with the help of Format (Shift-F8) and Font (Ctrl-F8); formatting is discussed in detail in the next three chapters.

Deleting Text

Deleting text is one of the most basic editing tools. With a typewriter, deleting text is cumbersome. Even simple errors require erasing, whiting out with correction fluid or tape, and backspacing endlessly to lift off or cover the error. If substantial revision is necessary, the entire document must be retyped. What a waste of time!

With WordPerfect, deleting text is easy. You can delete single letters, entire words, whole sentences, complete paragraphs, or full pages with only a few keystrokes.

Deleting a Single Character

You can delete single characters three different ways in WordPerfect:

- Press the Backspace key to delete the character to the *left* of the cursor.

- Press the Del key to delete the character *at* the cursor.

- Press the space bar in Typeover mode (press Insert) to delete the character *at* the cursor and leave a space.

Deleting a Single Word or Portions of a Single Word

You can delete single words or portions of single words several ways in WordPerfect:

- Press Delete Word (Ctrl-Backspace) to delete a word at the cursor or to delete a word to the left of the cursor if the cursor is on a space.

- Press Home-Backspace to delete the word left of the cursor position to the beginning of the next word.

- Press Home-Del to delete everything from the cursor position to the end of the word.

- Press the space bar several times in Typeover mode (press Insert) to delete the word to the right of the cursor.

Deleting to the End of Line

To delete from the cursor position to the end of the line, press Ctrl-End. Any hard return, **[HRt]**, at the end of the line remains and is not deleted.

TIP: For those familiar with WordStar, you may miss the capability to delete a full line of text with the cursor positioned anywhere in the line (Ctrl-Y). The Macro keyboard (see Chapter 18) has a command (Alt-D) that duplicates the Ctrl-Y command in WordStar. For those of you who like this feature, use these commands in a macro:

{Home}{Home}{Home}{Left}{Delete to EOL}{Del}

Deleting to the End of Page

To delete from the cursor position to the end of the page, do the following steps:

1. Press Delete to End of Page (Ctrl-PgDn).

2. A prompt at the bottom of the screen reads, Delete Remainder of page? (Y/N) No. Press *Y* to delete or *N* to change your mind.

A hard page return **[HPg]** at the end of the page is not deleted.

Deleting Text with Esc

You can perform the following delete operations multiple times by using WordPerfect's repeat function:

- Delete
- Delete word
- Delete to end of line
- Delete to end of page

For example, to delete three words, perform the following steps:

1. Press Esc.

   A prompt appears in the lower left corner of your screen: Repeat Value = (The equal sign is followed by a number.)

2. Press the 3 key to perform the operation three times.

3. Press Delete Word (Ctrl-Backspace).

Deleting a Sentence, Paragraph, or Page

To delete discrete blocks of text, do the following steps:

1. Position your cursor at the text you want deleted.

2. Press Move (Ctrl-F4).

3. From the menu bar, choose either Sentence (**1**), **Paragraph** (**2**), or **Page** (**3**).

The sentence, paragraph, or page to delete is highlighted (see fig. 3.2).

4. From the menu bar, choose **Delete** (**3**).

The highlighted sentence, paragraph, or page is deleted.

May 15, 1988

Dear Chuck,

The idea for the book Using WordPerfect 5.0 is excellent. I like your suggestion of a multi-author collaborative effort instead of a single author approach.

Not only will we be able to get the book out more quickly, but each author will be able to concentrate effort on a specialized area. Such an approach should give us an excellent book.

Sincerely,

Schuyler W. Lininger, Jr.

1 Move; 2 Copy; 3 Delete; 4 Append: 0

Fig. 3.2.
Text block to be deleted.

Using the Undelete Command

Few things are more frustrating than accidentally deleting a large block of text. WordPerfect Corporation understands the errors that users make, so it provides a way to access your last three deletions. WordPerfect maintains a *buffer* (special files) that holds your last three deletions. To undelete text, complete the following steps:

1. Position the cursor where you want the previously deleted text placed.

2. Press Cancel (F1).

The following prompt appears in the lower left corner of your screen:

Undelete: 1 Restore; **2 P**revious Deletion: **0**

A block of highlighted text then appears on your editing screen—your most recently deleted text (see fig. 3.3).

3. Choose **Restore** (**1**) if the highlighted text is what you want undeleted

or

Choose **Previous** (**2**) (or use the ↑ and ↓ keys) if previously deleted text is what you want undeleted. When the proper text appears on-screen, choose **Restore** (**1**).

```
May 15, 1988

Dear Chuck,

The idea for the book Using WordPerfect 5.0 is excellent. I like your
suggestion of a multi-author collaborative effort instead of a single
author approach.

Not only will we be able to get the book out more quickly, but each author
will be able to concentrate effort on a specialized area. Such an
approach should give us an excellent book.

Sincerely,


Schuyler W. Lininger, Jr.




Undelete: 1 Restore; 2 Previous Deletion: 0
```

Because the deleted text is saved to a buffer file, WordPerfect could run out of memory or disk space to store the deleted text if a lot of material is deleted at once. If this happens, WordPerfect displays the warning:

Delete without saving for Undelete? (Y/N)

Press either *Y* for yes or *N* for no.

Inserting Text

As you learned in Chapter 2, the capability to insert text is a major difference between using WordPerfect and a typewriter. With a typewriter, you cannot insert a word in a previously typed sentence without retyping the sentence. With WordPerfect, you simply move the cursor to the point where you want to add the word and type away. You will see the new word inserted at the cursor point and the old text pushed to the right. Sometimes, the text pushes off the screen to the right. Just press the ↓ key, and the text will wrap correctly to the next line.

Overwriting Text

You occasionally may want to overwrite text instead of inserting text. Change by switching to *Typeover mode*. In Typeover mode, new characters you enter replace characters on the screen. This is different than the normal Insert mode which pushes existing text ahead while inserting new characters. When you press the Ins key, the word Typeover appears in the lower left corner of your screen. This message reminds you that what you type replaces what is already in the document. To return to the normal Insertion mode, press Ins again.

Understanding Hidden Codes

"Behind the scenes" of your document, WordPerfect is receiving instructions about what you want your document to look like. For instance, pressing the Underline (F8) key turns on underlining; pressing the same key a second time turns off underlining. How does WordPerfect "know" when to underline words—and when to stop? What actually happens when you press Underline (F8)?

When you press Underline (F8), a hidden code is inserted into your document. This code tells WordPerfect to begin underlining. For those of you who have used WordStar in the past, the underlining code was created by pressing Ctrl-P-S; on the screen you would see the code ^S at the beginning and end of the underlined text. Essentially the same thing happens in WordPerfect, except the code is usually not visible. By hiding the codes, WordPerfect keeps the document editing screen uncluttered.

To see the hidden codes in the text, complete the following steps:

1. Press Reveal Codes (Alt-F3, or F11).

   The screen splits in half with the same text displayed in both windows. The lower part of the screen shows the hidden codes (see fig. 3.4).

2. Press Reveal Codes (Alt-F3, or F11) again to restore the normal screen.

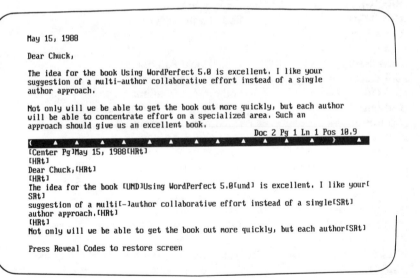

Fig. 3.4.
The Reveal Codes screen.

From figure 3.4 you can see that the hidden codes are enclosed in brackets. These brackets make codes easily distinguishable from normal text.

Besides underlining, WordPerfect has a large number of codes (see table 3.1). The codes "tell" WordPerfect about everything from tab stops to point size to where to place carriage returns and page breaks. Do not try to memorize all of the hidden codes. Some of them you may never use. If you encounter a hidden code you need to know more about, refer back to the list in table 3.1. The more important and common hidden codes will become familiar to you as you use them.

Listing Hidden Codes

Table 3.1 shows a complete listing of the hidden codes and what they represent.

Table 3.1
List of Hidden Codes

Hidden Code	Function
[ ]	Hard Space
[-]	Hyphen
-	Soft Hyphen
[/]	Cancel Hyphenation
[Adv]	Advance
[Align]	Tab Align
[Block]	Beginning of Block
[Block Pro]	Block Protection
[BOLD] [bold]	Bold ON off
[Box Num]	Caption in Graphics Box
[C/A/FlRt]	End of Tab Align or Flush Right
[Center Pg]	Center Page Top to Bottom
[Cntr]	Center Text
[Cnd EOP]	Conditional End of Page
[Col Def]	Column Definition
[Col Off]	End of Text Columns
[Col On]	Beginning of Text Columns
[Comment]	Document Comment
[Color]	Print Color
[Date]	Date/Time Function
[DBL UND] [dbl und]	Double Underlining ON off
[Decml Char]	Decimal Character/Thousands Separator
[Def Mark:Index]	Index Definition
[Def Mark:Listn]	List Definition
[Def Mark:ToC]	Table of Contents Definition
[DSRt]	Deletable soft return
[End Def]	End of Index, List, or Table of Contents
[End Opt]	Endnote Options
[Endnote]	Endnote
[Endnote Placement]	Endnote Placement
[Ext Large]	Extra Large Print
[Figure]	Figure Box
[Fig Opt]	Figure Box Options
[FINE] [fine]	Fine Font ON off
[Flsh Rt]	Flush Right Text
[Footnote]	Footnote
[Font]	Base Font

Hidden Code	Function
[Footer]	Footer
[Force]	Force Odd/Even Page
[Form]	Form (Printer Selection)
[FtnOpt]	Footnote/Endnote Options
[Full Form]	Table of Authorities, Full Form
[HLine]	Horizontal Line
[Header]	Header
[HPg]	Hard Page
[HRt]	Hard Return
[Hyph]	Hyphenation
[HZone]	Hyphenation Zone
[→Indent]	Indent
[→Indent ←]	Left/Right Indent
[Index]	Index Entry
[ISRt]	Invisible Soft Return
[ITALC] [italc]	Italic Font ON off
[Just]	Right Justification
[Just Lim]	Word/Letter Spacing/Justification Limits
[Kern]	Kerning
[L/R Mar]	Left and Right Margins
[Lang]	Language
[LARGE] [large]	Large Font ON off
[Line Height]	Line Height
[Ln Num]	Line Numbering
[←Mar Rel]	Left Margin Release
[Mark:List]	List Entry
[Mark:ToC]	Table of Contents Entry
[Math Def]	Definition of Math Columns
[Math Off]	End of Math
[Math On]	Beginning of Math
!	Formula Calculation
t	Subtotal Entry
+	Calculate Subtotal
T	Total Entry
=	Calculate Total
*	Calculate Grand Total
[Note Num]	Footnote/Endnote Number
[Outln]	Outline
[Ovrstk]	Overstrike
[Paper Sz/Typ]	Paper Size and Type
[Par Num]	Paragraph Number
[Par Num Def]	Paragraph Numbering Definition
[Pg Num]	New Page Number
[Pg Num Pos]	Page Number Position
[Ptr Cmnd]	Printer Command
[REDLN] [redln]	Redline Font ON off
[Ref]	Reference (Automatic Reference)
[Set End Num]	Set New Endnote Number

Hidden Code	Function
[Set Fig Num]	Set New Figure Number
[Set Ftn Num]	Set New Footnote Number
[Set Tab Num]	Set New Table Box Number
[Set Txt Num]	Set New Text Box Number
[Set Usr Num]	Set New User-Defined Box Number
[SHADW] [shadw]	Shadow Font ON off
[SM CAP] [sm Cap]	Small Capital Letters Font ON off
[SMALL] [small]	Small Font ON off
[SPg]	Soft New Page
[SRt]	Soft Return
[STKOUT] [stkout]	Strikeout Font ON off
[Style]	Style Definition
[Subdoc]	Subdocument for Master Document
[SUBSCPT] [subscpt]	Subscript Font ON off
[SUPRSCPT] [suprscpt]	Superscript Font ON off
[Suppress]	Suppress Page Formatting
[T/B Mar]	Top and Bottom Page Margins
[Tab]	Tab
[Tab Opt]	Table Box Options
[Tab Set]	Tab Set
[Table]	Table Box
[Target]	Target for Auto Reference
[Text Box]	Text Box
[Txt Opt]	Text Box Options
[UND] [und]	Underlining ON off
[Undrln]	Underline Spaces/Tabs ON off
[Usr Box]	User-Defined Box
[UsrOpt]	User-Defined Box Options
[VLine]	Vertical Line
[VRY LARGE] [vry large]	Very Large Font ON off
[W/O]	Widow/Orphan
[Wrd/Ltr Spacing]	Word and Letter Spacing

Some of the hidden codes have additional information about the status of the feature contained within the brackets. For example, [Just Off] means right justification is turned off; and [L/R Mar:1",1"] means the left and right margins are each set at one inch.

Editing in Reveal Codes

Editing in Reveal Codes (Alt-F3, or F11) is a little different than editing normally. As you recall, you are looking at a split screen with the upper window showing the normal edit screen and the lower window showing text plus hidden codes. The cursor in the upper window is normal, but the cursor in the lower window is a narrow highlighted bar (see fig. 3.5). When the cursor encounters a hidden code in

```
 May 15, 1988

 Dear Chuck,

 The idea for the book Using WordPerfect 5.0 is excellent. I like
 your suggestion of a multi-author collaborative effort instead of
 a single author approach.

 Not only will we be able to get the book out more quickly, but
 each author will be able to concentrate effort on a specialized
 area. Such an approach should give us an excellent book.
                                        Doc 1 Pg 1 Ln 1" Pos 1"
[   ▲    ▲    ▲    ▲    ▲    ▲    ▲    ▲    ▲    }    ▲    ▲
[Center Pg]May 15, 1988[HRt]
[HRt]
Dear Chuck,[HRt]
[HRt]
The idea for the book [UND]Using WordPerfect 5.0[und] is excellent. I like[SRt]
your suggestion of a multi[-]author collaborative effort instead of[SRt]
a single author approach.[HRt]
[HRt]
Not only will we be able to get the book out more quickly, but[SRt]
each author will be able to concentrate effort on a specialized[SRt]

Press Reveal Codes to restore screen
```

Fig. 3.5.

Cursor positioned on a hidden code in Reveal Codes.

Cursor

the lower window, the cursor expands enough to cover the entire code, while in the upper window nothing is seen except a blank space.

The Reveal Codes window can be very distracting during the initial stages of creating a document. You will use Reveal Codes most often when you are editing and formatting your document. When the codes are visible, you can get a clearer idea of what hidden codes are present and the effect those codes might have on your document. Some people like to leave the Reveal Codes window visible all the time during editing; some people find the window annoying and prefer only using Reveal Codes when they need to. Unlike WordPerfect 4.2 where editing in Reveal Codes was limited, WordPerfect 5 allows complete editing capability in Reveal Codes.

You are free to leave the screen split and do all your editing with the hidden codes revealed. Viewing the codes only when necessary is less distracting, however. You also can delete codes in Reveal Codes. The undelete feature can recall codes you accidentally delete. If a line, paragraph, or page of text is deleted and later undeleted, all the hidden codes are restored as well as the text.

If you want to add more boldface text while you are already using paired codes (codes that act as on and off switches, like **[BOLD] [bold]**) move the cursor between the **[BOLD] [bold]** codes and enter text instead of pressing the Bold (F6) key again.

Adding Simple Text Enhancements

The second part of the editing process mentioned earlier is formatting or preparing the document for printing. Some formatting is done as you enter the text; other formatting is done later. The following section focuses on simple enhancements that can be done as you enter text.

Boldfacing

To create emphasis, boldface text appears darker than regular text. Boldfacing should be used sparingly for best effect. To create boldfaced text, complete the following steps:

1. Press Bold (F6).

2. Type the text you want to boldface.

   Depending on your monitor, as you type, you see the text you enter appearing in boldface on-screen.

3. To turn off boldface type, press Bold (F6) again.

The Bold (F6) key serves as an off/on switch. Press once to turn on; press again to turn boldface off (see fig. 3.6). If you press Bold (F6) twice in a row without typing any text, the text you then enter will not be boldfaced.

Fig. 3.6.

Text in boldface in Reveal Codes screen.

```
May 15, 1988

Dear Chuck,

The idea for the book Using WordPerfect 5.0 is excellent.

Not only will we be able to get the book out more quickly, but each author
will be able to concentrate effort on a specialized area. Such an
approach should give us an excellent book.

Sincerely,
C:\WP\QUE\FIG3_6                                    Doc 2 Pg 1 Ln 9 Pos 37.13
[    ▲     ▲      ▲     ▲     ▲     ▲     ▲      ▲    }     ▲
Not only will we be able to get the book out more quickly, but each author[SRt]
will be able to concentrate effort on a specialized area. Such an[SRt]
approach should give us an [BOLD]excellent[bold] book.[HRt]
[HRt]
Sincerely,[HRt]
[HRt]
[HRt]
Schuyler W. Lininger, Jr.
```

Boldface codes

```
Press Reveal Codes to restore screen
```

Underlining

WordPerfect offers several styles of underlining. You can select either single or double underlining, and choose to have spaces between words and tab spaces underlined or not underlined. These formatting options are described in Chapter 5. For simple underlining, however, complete the following steps:

1. Press Underline (F8).

2. Enter the text you want underlined. Depending on your monitor, the text you type may appear underlined on-screen.

3. To turn off underlining, press Underline (F8) again (see fig. 3.7).

Fig. 3.7.
*Text underlined in
Reveal Codes screen.*

```
May 15, 1988

Dear Chuck,

The idea for the book Using WordPerfect 5.0 is excellent.

Not only will we be able to get the book out more quickly, but each author
will be able to concentrate effort on a specialized area. Such an
approach should give us an excellent book.

Sincerely,
C:\WP\QUE\FIG3_7                              Doc 2 Pg 1 Ln 5 Pos 32.04
[    ▲    ▲    ▲    ▲      ▲    ▲    ▲    ▲    ▲    ▲    }    ▲            ]———— Underline codes
Dear Chuck,[HRt]
[HRt]
The idea for the book [UND]Using WordPerfect 5.0[und] is excellent. [HRt]
[HRt]
Not only will we be able to get the book out more quickly, but each author[SRt]
will be able to concentrate effort on a specialized area. Such an[SRt]
approach should give us an [BOLD]excellent[bold] book.[HRt]
[HRt]
Sincerely,[HRt]
[HRt]

Press Reveal Codes to restore screen
```

Like the Bold key, the Underline (F8) key works as an off/on switch. Press once to
turn on, press again to turn off. Note the Reveal codes for underline in figure 3.7. If
you press Underline (F8) twice in a row without entering any text, the text you
then enter is not underlined.

Searching and Replacing

Two of the most powerful tools offered by WordPerfect are the Search and Replace
functions. If you have experienced the frustration of writing a long report and then
hunting for a particular phrase or name, you will appreciate the search/replace
capabilities of WordPerfect.

Searching for Text

You can search for text from any point in a document, and you can search either
direction—beginning to end or end to beginning. To search for text, perform the
following steps:

1. Press either Forward Search (F2) or Backward Search (Shift-F2)
   depending on whether you want to search to the end or to the beginning
   of the document from where your cursor is in the document. (If you
   change your mind, press ↑ or ↓ to change the direction of your search.)

   A prompt appears in the lower left corner of your screen, either → Srch:
   or ← Srch:.

2. Enter any text, up to 60 characters, for which you want to search for.

3. Press Forward Search (F2) or Esc to begin the search (regardless of the
   direction you are searching).

If one occurrence of the text matches but you'd like to look for others, repeat the previous steps; however, you need not retype the text for which you are searching—WordPerfect remembers your last search request.

You can search for parts of a word or even for words you're not sure how to spell. Look over these examples:

- If you type *and* as the text you are searching for, WordPerfect locates all words that have *and* as a part of them. For example, WordPerfect matches *and* with b*and*, R*and*y or *And*rew.

- If you want only the specific word and not a part of a word, then enter spaces before and after the search text. For example, **[space]***and***[space]** finds only occurrences of *And* or *and*.

- If you want to find text with a changing component or if you are unsure of the exact spelling, use the matching character ^X (press Ctrl-V, Ctrl-X). This character matches any single character. If you type (*^X*), the following characters match: *(1)*, *(2)*, *(3)*, and *(4)*.

- If you type in lowercase only, WordPerfect finds matches whether the text you look for is lowercase or not. For example, searching for *and* finds *And*, *AND*, or *and*. If you type in uppercase only, WordPerfect finds only uppercase matches. For example, searching for *AND* finds only *AND* but not *and* or *And*. (For more on word search, see Chapter 10.)

- If you think the text you are looking for might be in a header, footer, footnote, endnote, graphic-box caption, or text box, you must perform an extended search. Extended search is exactly the same as regular search, except before pressing the Search key, first press Home.

Searching and Replacing Text

Sometimes you may want to replace the text you find with different text. To search for and then replace text, perform the following steps:

1. Press Replace (Alt-F2).

   A prompt appears in the lower left corner of your screen saying, w/Confirm? (Y/N) No

2. If you want to be prompted for confirmation before any changes are made, press Y

   or

   If you want all changes made automatically, press N or press Enter.

3. At the →Srch: prompt at the screen's lower left, enter any text, up to 60 characters, for which you want to search.

4. If you want to change the direction of the search, press either ↑ or ↓.

5. Press Forward Search (F2) or Esc.

6. At the next prompt, `Replace with:`, type the replacement text. If you want the text simply deleted, do not enter anything and go to Step 7.

7. To begin the search and replace operation, press Forward Search (F2) or Esc.

8. If you selected *Y* for Confirm in Step 2, you see the `Confirm? (Y/N) No` prompt each time the search finds a match. Press Y to confirm a replacement or *N* to deny a replacement. If you wish to cancel the search and replace operation, press Cancel (F1) or Exit (F7).

If you want to repeat either the search or replace operation, repeat the previous steps, but you need not retype the text for which you are searching or replacing—WordPerfect remembers your last search and replace request. If you want, the previous search requests can be edited using the normal editing keys and functions. However, if you press an alphanumeric key before one of the arrow or editing keys, the new text is substituted for the old.

Both Search and Replace can be used in conjunction with Block (Alt-F4, or F12). After defining a block, begin search or replace and the operation will be confined to the block. Block functions are explained thoroughly in Chapter 4.

If a search fails to find a match, a message `* Not found *` appears in the bottom left corner of your screen. Depending on your setup, you also may hear a beep.

Using Search or Replace

You will find many uses for search or replace. Look over these ideas:

- **Check for jargon.** For example, if you are writing to a person who is unfamiliar with computers, you wouldn't want to use words that only experienced users know. You might want list your own business jargon and make sure that you replace it with more common terms.

- **Check for poor writing.** For example, you might want to search your document for the pronouns "this" or "it." These words often vaguely reference something that could confuse the reader.

- **Check for clichés.** If you have a tendency to use certain "stock" phrases that are tired or trite, you can search and replace the clichés with fresh images.

- **Check for matching punctuation.** You easily can forget to close a parenthesis or quotation mark. Double check your document for proper pairing of special punctuation.

- **Check for too many spaces.** The normal typist inserts two spaces after a period. If you are printing your document on a laser printer or are a printer that justifies the text, you should probably use only a single space after a period. You can replace all occurrences of two spaces and replace them with a single space. You can use the same technique to convert two carriage returns to one carriage return.

- **Expand abbreviations.** If you are writing a report and the name of the client is Mrs. William Danielson, III, you could type an abbreviation, say *wd*. Later, you could replace the abbreviation with the full name of the client. Each abbreviation saves you many keystrokes.

Using Hidden Codes

WordPerfect also searches or replaces hidden codes. When prompted for the search text, press the function key that normally generates the code. If the code is usually generated from a secondary or tertiary menu, those choices appear in a menu line at the bottom of the screen. When you select the options you want, the corresponding codes appear in the search or replace text area. Note that if you delete one of the paired codes (for example, **[BOLD]** or **[bold]**), both are deleted.

To search for the hidden code **[BOLD]**, do the following steps:

1. Press Reveal Codes (Alt-F3, or F11).

2. Press Forward Search (F2).

3. At the ⁻Srch: prompt, press Bold (F6).

4. Press Forward Search (F2) or Esc to begin the search.

Making Document Comments

When you are writing, you may want to insert a note, memo or comment to serve as a personal reminder of what you meant or how to follow up on what you've just written. WordPerfect provides a way to put electronic notes in a document where you can see them on-screen, but the comment won't print out. You can hide the comment on-screen so that it is only visible when you want it to be.

Inserting Document Comments

To insert a document comment in your document, use these steps:

1. Press Text In/Out (Ctrl-F5).

    You see the following menu at the bottom of the screen:

    1 DOS **T**ext; **2 P**assword; **3** Save **G**eneric; **4** Save **WP** 4.2; **5** Comment: **0**

2. Choose Comment (5) from the menu.

    You see the Comment menu at the bottom of your screen:

    Comment: 1 Create; **2 E**dit; **3** Convert to **T**ext: **0**

3. Choose **Create** (**1**) from the menu.

4. Type the text of your comment in the box that appears in the Document Comment screen (see fig. 3.8). The text cannot be longer than the length of the box—approximately seven lines of text. You may underline or boldface text in the comment box.

```
Document Comment

    ┌─────────────────────────────────────────────────────────────┐
    │ Chuck: Consider expanding this area with more examples.      │
    │                                                              │
    │                                                              │
    │                                                              │
    │                                                              │
    └─────────────────────────────────────────────────────────────┘
```

Fig. 3.8.
Document Comment screen.

5. To return to your document, press Exit (F7).

The document comment appears on-screen in the middle of your text as a box surrounded by a double line (see fig. 3.9).

```
    Normally, we would like to see several trips taken to the East
    Coast during the holiday season.

    ╔═════════════════════════════════════════════════════════════╗
    ║ Chuck: Consider expanding this area with more examples.      ║
    ╚═════════════════════════════════════════════════════════════╝
    These trips are the backbone of our December sales effort.



    C:\WP\QUE\FIG3_9                          Doc 2 Pg 1 Ln 3 Pos 18
    ▲    ▲    ▲    ▲    ▲    ▲    ▲    ▲    ▲    ▲    }    ▲    ▲
    Normally, we would like to see several trips taken to the East[SRt]
    Coast during the holiday season.[HRt]
    [Comment]These trips are the backbone of our December sales effort.
```

Fig. 3.9.
Document comment in text.

Editing Document Comments

If you like, you can change your comments. If you have more than one comment in a document, WordPerfect looks *backward* from the cursor for a comment to edit. If there are no comments preceding the cursor, WordPerfect then looks *forward* from the cursor for a comment to edit. To edit an existing document comment, perform the following steps:

1. Move the cursor past the comment you want to edit.

2. Press Text In/Out (Ctrl-F5).

3. Choose **Comment** (**5**) from the menu at the bottom of your screen.

4. Choose **Edit** (**2**) from the new menu that appears.

5. Change the text of your comments. All the normal editing keys operate.

6. Press Exit (F7) to return to your document.

If no comment is found, the error message * Not found * appears at the bottom of your screen.

Converting Comments to Text

If your document is a collaborative effort, numerous comments from various authors or editors may have been entered during the revision or editing process (see figure 3.10 for an example). Because comments are only displayed and not printed, if you decide you want any of the comments printed, they first must be converted to text.

Fig. 3.10.

Comments from various authors in a text.

```
Normally, we would like to see several trips taken to the East
Coast during the holiday season.

┌─────────────────────────────────────────────────────────────────┐
│ Chuck: Consider expanding this area with more examples.           │
└─────────────────────────────────────────────────────────────────┘

These trips are the backbone of our December sales effort.

┌─────────────────────────────────────────────────────────────────┐
│ Chuck I agree. This trip information should be more detailed. For example, │
│ last year we went to Boston but not Cambridge. Tom wants to know if we     │
│ want to repeat that or budget enough time for Cambridge this trip?         │
└─────────────────────────────────────────────────────────────────┘

┌─────────────────────────────────────────────────────────────────┐
│ Will asked me to check on whether or not the new HealthNotes product will │
│ be presented during calls made on this trip?                              │
└─────────────────────────────────────────────────────────────────┘
```

If you have a comment that you would like to insert in the document as text to be printed, perform the following steps:

1. Move the cursor past the point where you want the converted comment placed.

2. Press Text In/Out (Ctrl-F5).

3. Choose **Comment** (**5**) from the menu at the bottom of your screen.

4. Choose Convert to **Text** (**3**).

   The comment is immediately converted to text, and you are returned to the editing screen.

If no comment is found, the error message * Not found * appears at the bottom of your screen.

CAUTION: The Speller (Ctrl-F2) does not examine Document Comments for spelling errors. If you convert comments to text, check for spelling errors by running the speller.

Converting Text to Comments

Sometimes in revising a document you find some text that provides valuable information or is well written but doesn't fit with what you are writing about. Rather than delete the thought, why not save it for use at another time? One way of saving the text is to use the block command and save the text to another file. The technique for blocking and saving is described in Chapter 4. Another way to save the text but keep it separate from the document you are working on is to convert the text to a comment.

If you have some text that you want to keep but don't want printed, perhaps turning that text into a comment is an alternative to deletion. To convert text into a comment, do the following steps:

1. Press Block (Alt-F4, or F12) to mark the start of the block.

    (For more information on Block, see Chapter 4.)

2. Move the cursor to the end of the block of text (the block is highlighted).

3. Press Text In/Out (Ctrl-F5).

    The prompt Create a comment? (Y/N) No appears at the bottom of your screen.

4. Press Y for yes. The comment is immediately created and appears in a comment box on your editing screen. If you press N or any other key, the text will not be converted.

You can convert 20 lines to a comment. Because comments are treated as a single word by WordPerfect and although the comment box is large enough to hold the comment, the cursor is either before the comment box or after the comment box. Therefore, the entire comment box jumps when the cursor is moved .

Hiding Document Comments

You may find document comments distracting. To hide the comments from view as you work, do the following steps:

1. Press Setup (Shift-F1).

2. Choose **Display** (3) from the Setup menu.

3. Choose **Display** Document Comments (3) from the Setup: Display menu.

4. Press Y or N to either display or not display comments.

5. Press Exit (F7) to return to your document.

If you hide the document comments in the document you are working on, all comments are hidden in all other documents. If you want to see comments in other documents, remember to turn on the comment display.

Using Document Comments

Besides simple memos and notes, look over these additional ideas about how to use the document comment:

- **Use as a writing aid.** As you write, leave yourself little messages about what you mean, where the text could use some polish, where you have trouble completing a thought. Later, during the revision process, the comments should trigger your memory.

- **Use for collaborative writing.** If you are part of a writing team, leave messages and criticism for other team members. When the next author begins work, comments from coworkers are easily noticed.

- **Use as an editing tool.** If you are an editor, leave your author messages and comments using the document comment feature.

Quick Start

Editing a Document

This Quick Start for editing a document helps you become comfortable with the various powerful editing tools available with WordPerfect. By the time you finish this Quick Start, you will be able to delete and add text; use the undelete feature to correct accidental deletions or to move text; enhance your text with boldfacing and underlining; search for and replace text; and edit hidden codes.

To get the most out of this Quick Start, type the following paragraph (type the text exactly, including the typos):

Editing in WordPerfect is a a lot easier than using a manual typewriter. You can delete single characters, entire words, whole sentences and complete paragraphs or pages with only a few keystrokes. It is also easy to in text. Formatting is also easily done. You can. You can search for words and change them if you choose. It is also possible to see and edit hidden codes.

Is the paragraph all typed? Ready to go? Okay, let's start.

Deleting a Single Character

To delete a single character, position the cursor under the character you want to delete and then press the Del key. Try deleting a character by doing the following steps:

1. Move the cursor to the beginning of the document by pressing Home, Home, ↑.

   There are two letter "a's" in the first sentence.

2. Move the cursor to the right to the first letter "a" by pressing Word Right (Ctrl- →) four times (see fig. 3.11).

3. Press Del to delete the letter "a".

4. Press Del a second time to delete the extra space.

Fig. 3.11.

The Quick Start document screen with the cursor under the first of the doubled a's.

```
Editing in WordPerfect is a a lot easier than using a manual
typewriter. You can delete single characters, entire words,
whole sentences and complete paragraphs or pages with only a
few keystrokes. It is also easy to in text. Formatting is
also easily done. You can. You can search for words and
change them if you choose. It is also possible to see and
edit hidden codes.
```

Deleting an Entire Word

The word "manual" is not necessary to the meaning of the sentence and can be deleted. Delete a single word by doing the following:

1. Move the cursor to the word "manual" by pressing Word Right (Ctrl-→) six times.

2. Press Delete Word (Ctrl-Backspace) to delete the word "manual". Look at figure 3.12 to see what the document now looks like.

Fig. 3.12.

The Quick Start document with the word "manual" deleted.

```
Editing in WordPerfect is a lot easier than using a
typewriter. You can delete single characters, entire words,
whole sentences and complete paragraphs or pages with only a
few keystrokes. It is also easy to in text. Formatting is
also easily done. You can. You can search for words and
change them if you choose. It is also possible to see and
edit hidden codes.
```

Deleting to the End of a Line

To delete the rest of a line (not necessarily a sentence), do the following steps:

1. Move the cursor to the beginning of the document by pressing Home, Home, ↑.

2. Press Delete to End of Line (Ctrl-End).

Notice that when you use the Delete to End of Line command, the next line moves up to fill in the space left by the deleted text (see fig. 3.13). You may need to press Del to delete an extra space.

Fig. 3.13.

The Quick Start document with the first line deleted.

```
 typewriter. You can delete single characters, entire words,
whole sentences and complete paragraphs or pages with only a
few keystrokes. It is also easy to in text. Formatting is
also easily done. You can. You can search for words and
change them if you choose. It is also possible to see and
edit hidden codes.
```

Deleting to End of Page

If you want to delete the rest of a page (not necessarily the entire document), do the following steps:

1. Press Delete to End of Page (Ctrl-PgDn).

   A prompt appears on-screen, asking you to confirm the deletion (see fig. 3.14).

   Fig. 3.14.
   The Delete Remainder of page *confirmation prompt.*

   ```
   Delete Remainder of page? (Y/N) No
   ```

2. Press *Y* to confirm the deletion.

Using Undelete To Restore Deleted Text

One of the most comforting features of WordPerfect is the capability to recover from accidental deletions. Let's assume you didn't intend to delete the text you deleted in the previous example. To undelete the text, do the following steps:

1. Press Cancel (F1).

   The previously deleted text appears highlighted. At the bottom of the screen you see the **Undelete** menu (see fig. 3.15). You have three choices: **Restore (1)**, **Previous Deletion (2)**, or **0**.

2. Choose **Restore (1)** to undelete the text.

   Fig. 3.15.
   The highlighted previously deleted text and the Undelete menu.

   ```
   typewriter. You can delete single characters, entire words,
   whole sentences and complete paragraphs or pages with only a
   few keystrokes. It is also easy to in text. Formatting is
   also easily done. You can. You can search for words and
   change them if you choose. It is also possible to see and
   edit hidden codes.




   Undelete: 1 Restore; 2 Previous Deletion: 0
   ```

After undeleting, notice the cursor is positioned at the end of the undeleted block.

Deleting and Moving a Sentence

A handy capability of WordPerfect is selecting a sentence, paragraph, or page for moving, copying, or deleting. In this exercise, you first delete a sentence, then use undelete to move the sentence to another location in the paragraph. Do the following steps to move a sentence:

1. Use the arrow keys to move the cursor to any position in the sentence "Formatting is also easily done."

2. Press Move (Ctrl-F4).

3. From the Move menu, choose Sentence (**1**).

   The entire sentence (including the space after the period) is highlighted (see fig. 3.16).

Fig. 3.16.

The highlighted sentence and the Move (Ctrl-F4) submenu.

```
   typewriter. You can delete single characters, entire words,
whole sentences and complete paragraphs or pages with only a
few keystrokes. It is also easy to in text. Formatting is
also easily done. You can. You can search for words and
change them if you choose. It is also possible to see and
edit hidden codes.



1 Move; 2 Copy; 3 Delete; 4 Append: 0
```

4. From the new menu, select Delete (**3**).

   The highlighted sentence is deleted.

5. Move the cursor to the beginning of the document.

6. Press Cancel (F1).

   The sentence you just deleted is highlighted.

7. This time, do not restore the sentence; Press 0 or Cancel (F1) to leave the text deleted.

You also can move a sentence with the Move (Ctrl-F4) command without first deleting the sentence. To move a sentence, do the following steps:

1. Use the arrow keys to move the cursor to any position in the last sentence in the paragraph.

2. Press Move (Ctrl-F4).

3. From the Move menu, choose Sentence (**1**).

   The chosen sentence is highlighted.

4. From the new menu, select Move (**1**).

   The sentence disappears from the screen.

   A prompt at the bottom of the screen says, `Move cursor; press Enter to retrieve.`

5. Move the cursor to the beginning of the paragraph and press Enter. The sentence reappears in the new position. Your screen should now look like figure 3.17.

Fig. 3.17.
The last sentence moved to the beginning.

```
It is also possible to see and edit hidden codes, typewriter,
You can delete single characters, entire words, whole
sentences and complete paragraphs or pages with only a few
keystrokes, It is also easy to in text, You can, You can
search for words and change them if you choose,
```

Inserting Text

Inserting text is simple with WordPerfect. Anytime the cursor is in the middle of a word or a sentence, newly entered text is inserted; existing text is pushed to the right. To practice inserting text, do the following steps:

1. Press the space bar to move the cursor one space past the period at the end of the first sentence.

2. Type the following: *Using wordPerfect is better than using a* (see fig. 3.18). Notice that the previously existing text is pushed to the right as the new text is inserted.

Fig. 3.18.
Newly inserted text.

```
It is also possible to see and edit hidden codes, Using
wordPerfect is better than using a typewriter, You can delete
single characters, words, whole sentences and complete
paragraphs or pages with only a few keystrokes, It is also
easy to in text, You can, You can search for words and change
them if you choose,
```

Overwriting Text

Overwriting text (called *typeover* in WordPerfect) is the opposite of inserting text. With overwriting, the new text takes the place of the existing text. Sometimes it is easier to overwrite text than it is to delete existing text and then insert the new text. To practice overwriting, do the following steps:

1. Using the arrow keys, move the cursor to "w" in the word "wordPerfect."

2. Press the Ins key to turn on the typeover mode. You see the word `Typeover` appear in the lower left corner of the screen.

3. Press the W key to replace the lowercase "w" with the uppercase "W".

4. Press the Ins key again to turn off the typeover mode. The word Typeover disappears from the screen.

Making Text Bold or Underlined

Adding emphasis to text is done easily by using WordPerfect. The simplest enhancements are **boldfacing** and underlining. To practice making these enhancements, do the following steps:

1. Using the arrow keys, move the cursor to the period in the short sentence "You can."

2. Press the spacebar once to insert a space after the word "can" and before the period.

3. Press Reveal Codes (Alt-F3, or F11). This allows you to see the enhancement codes as they are inserted and lets you see what is occurring.

4. Press Bold (F6) to turn on bold.

5. Type *bold.*

6. Press Bold (F6) a second time to turn off bold.

7. Type *or.*

8. Press Underline (F8) to turn on underline.

9. Type *underline.*

10. Press Underline (F8) a second time to turn off underline.

11. Type *text.*

Look at figure 3.19 to see what the text and codes in Reveal Codes should look like.

Editing in Reveal Codes

When you view the text in Reveal Codes (Alt-F3, or F11), you easily can see the enhancement ON/off codes of **[BOLD][bold]** and **[UND][und]**. You can delete paired codes (such as these examples) just as you can delete text. To delete a hidden code, do the following steps:

1. Looking at the Reveal Codes screen, use the arrow keys to position the cursor until it highlights the **[und]** code (see fig. 3.20).

2. Press Del.

When you delete one code of a paired set of codes, the other matching code is deleted also (see fig. 3.21). If your screen is capable of showing underlining, you notice that the word "underline" is no longer underlined.

```
     It is also possible to see and edit hidden codes, Using
     WordPerfect is better than using a typewriter, You can delete
     single characters, entire words, whole sentences and complete
     paragraphs or pages with only a few keystrokes, It is also
     easy to in text, You can bold or underline text, You can
     search for words and change them if you choose,




 C:\WP\QUE\3Q,10                            Doc 2 Pg 1 Ln 5 Pos 57
 [  ▲    ▲    ▲    ▲    ▲    ▲    ▲    ▲    ▲    ▲   ] ▲
 single characters, entire words, whole sentences and complete[SRt]
 paragraphs or pages with only a few keystrokes, It is also[SRt]
 easy to in text, You can [BOLD]bold[bold] or [UND]underline[und] text▮ You can[S
 Rt]
 search for words and change them if you choose,




 Press Reveal Codes to restore screen
```

Fig. 3.19.

The Reveal Codes (Alt-F3) split screen showing the [BOLD][bold] *and* [UND][und] *hidden codes.*

```
     It is also possible to see and edit hidden codes, Using
     WordPerfect is better than using a typewriter, You can delete
     single characters, entire words, whole sentences and complete
     paragraphs or pages with only a few keystrokes, It is also
     easy to in text, You can bold or underline text, You can
     search for words and change them if you choose,




                                            Doc 2 Pg 1 Ln 5 POS 52
 [    ▲    ▲    ▲    ▲    ▲    ▲    ▲    ▲    ▲    }  ▲    ▲    ▲
 single characters, entire words, whole sentences and complete[SRt]
 paragraphs or pages with only a few keystrokes, It is also[SRt]
 easy to in text, You can [BOLD]bold[bold] or [UND]underline███ text, You can[S
 Rt]
 search for words and change them if you choose,




 Press Reveal Codes to restore screen
```

Fig. 3.20.

Screen showing the placement of the cursor on a hidden code.

Searching and Replacing Text

Looking for a word, name, or phrase in a long document can be tedious. The task can be made easy with a replace operation. To demonstrate the search and replace capabilities of WordPerfect, do the following steps:

1. Press Home, Home, ↑ to move the cursor to the beginning of the document.

Fig. 3.21.

Screen showing the paired [UND][und] have been deleted.

```
It is also possible to see and edit hidden codes. Using
WordPerfect is better than using a typewriter. You can delete
single characters, entire words, whole sentences and complete
paragraphs or pages with only a few keystrokes. It is also
easy to in text. You can bold or underline text. You can
search for words and change them if you choose.




C:\WP\QUE\3Q.12                             Doc 2 Pg 1 Ln 5 Pos 52
[ ▲  ▲  ▲  ▲  ▲  ▲  ▲  ▲  ▲  ▲  ▲  ▲  ▲  ▲ ] ▲
single characters, entire words, whole sentences and complete[SRt]
paragraphs or pages with only a few keystrokes. It is also[SRt]
easy to in text. You can [BOLD]bold[bold] or underline█text. You can[SRt]
search for words and change them if you choose.




Press Reveal Codes to restore screen
```

2. Press Replace (Alt-F2).

    w/Confirm (Y/N) No appears in the lower left corner of the screen.

3. Press Y to confirm each replacement.

    You see a → Srch: prompt.

4. Type *in text*.

5. Press Forward Search (F2).

    You see a prompt that says, Replace with:

6. Type *insert text*.

7. Press Forward Search (F2) to begin the search and replace.

8. When you see the prompt Confirm (Y/N) No, press Y to replace the text.

Examine figure 3.22 to see what the changed document looks like.

Making Document Comments

Document comments can be useful tools to remind you what you had in mind during a particular writing session. To practice entering a comment, perform the following steps:

1. Press Home, Home, ↓ to move the cursor to the bottom of the document.

2. Press Text In/Out (Ctrl-F5).

3. Choose **Comment** (5) from the menu at the bottom of the screen.

```
It is also possible to see and edit hidden codes. Using
WordPerfect is better than using a typewriter. You can delete
single characters, entire words, whole sentences and complete
paragraphs or pages with only a few keystrokes. It is also
easy to insert text. You can bold or underline text. You can
search for words and change them if you choose.
```

Fig. 3.22.
The completed text.

4. Choose **Create** (**1**) from the new menu at the bottom of the screen.

5. In the Document Comment box, type: *This is a practice Quick Start document* (see fig. 3.23).

```
Document Comment

  ┌─────────────────────────────────────────────┐
  │ This is a practice Quick Start document.     │
  │                                              │
  │                                              │
  │                                              │
  │                                              │
  └─────────────────────────────────────────────┘
```

Fig. 3.23.
The Document Comment screen.

6. Press Exit (F7).

Look at figure 3.24 to see what the comment looks like displayed in a document.

```
It is also possible to see and edit hidden codes. Using
WordPerfect is better than using a typewriter. You can delete
single characters, entire words, whole sentences and complete
paragraphs or pages with only a few keystrokes. It is also
easy to insert text. You can bold or underline text. You can
search for words and change them if you choose.
┌─────────────────────────────────────────────┐
│ This is a practice Quick Start document.     │
└─────────────────────────────────────────────┘
```

Fig. 3.24.
The completed document with a Document Comment box displayed.

WP 5 Summary

In this chapter you have learned how easily you can make simple changes to a document with WordPerfect. You can now do the following operations:

- Retrieve a previously written document

- Delete text by the character, word, line, sentence, paragraph, or page

- Recover accidental deletions using the undelete feature

- Toggle between inserting and overwriting text

You also learned how to make basic enhancements to text by making a word or phrase **boldfaced** or <u>underlined</u>. In another chapter you will learn how to add many more enhancements and how to change the size of the letters.

You learned about the powerful search and replace functions, and now you can do the following tasks:

- Find words, names, or phrases anywhere in a document

- Replace any word, name, or phrase using the Replace function

- Find basic errors in punctuation and grammar

You also learned about hidden codes and how they can be edited.

Finally, you learned about document comments and can now do the following:

- Create and edit a document comment

- Use document comments as a memo tool or as an aid to writing

- Convert comments to text and vice versa

Congratulations on mastering the basics of WordPerfect editing. Now, on to Block commands before venturing into advanced formatting.

4

Working with Blocks

Karen Rose, owner of Write on Target, uses desktop publishing to produce a variety of newsletters. ∎

With WordPerfect's Block command, you can select, or highlight, an area of text. Highlighting text is the first step in many timesaving WordPerfect functions, such as moving and copying text. The Block command, used in combination with other commands, gives you powerful editing capabilities.

The Block command is quite versatile. You use the command to apply global changes, such as underlining and boldfacing, to chunks of text of any size. You also use Block to single out areas of text for saving or printing. And you can use Block to transfer text from one WordPerfect file to another.

A block of text can be as short as a single letter or as long as several pages. Flexibility is the Block command's strength. You define the size and shape of the block, and then you specify what to do with that selected text.

In this chapter, you will learn how to do the following:

- Highlight a block of text or numbers

- Move or copy a block—both within and between documents

- Delete a block

- Append a block to a different document

- Save a block

- Print a block

- Enhance a block of characters with features such as boldface, underlining, and italics

- Enlarge or reduce the size of the characters in a block

- Make a block of text all uppercase or all lowercase

- Center a block

- Move or copy a rectangular block, such as a column

Block Operations and Revision Strategies

You can use many WordPerfect commands with or without Block. For example, you can boldface or underline text while you are typing. Often, however, completing the document before you add these enhancements is easier. Later, after your ideas are down, you can use the Block command to add enhancements or to reorganize your paragraphs into a more logical order. This approach lets your thoughts flow freely, without interruption, as you write.

Even when you are retyping a document, rather than writing from scratch, you may find that typing first and adding enhancements later is faster. When you review your typed document, you can use the Block command to rearrange or enhance your text as necessary.

How Block Works

On your computer screen, blocked text appears highlighted, as shown in figure 4.1. Blocked text is, in a sense, text that is identified as "ready." The text is ready for the second step in any of a number of operations, such as moving, copying, deleting, saving, or printing.

Fig. 4.1.

A highlighted block of text.

```
THE QUANTUM PC REPORT FOR CPAS

New Life for Your Older PCs:
Key Upgrade Products

     Change happens so quickly in the computer industry that products
seen to go obsolete before you get them paid for. But there is a
fountain of youth for over-the-hill PCs, and this month's feature
article is swimming in ideas for how to give your old PC the speed
and power of a new model.

     Within the past several months, several new products have come
along that provide attractive new alternatives for getting the kind
of speed, power and flexibility from your older PCs that would
otherwise require a new 80286- or 80386-based computer. Since many
CPAs and financial executives are in an office environment that
includes older PCs, these new alternatives can be very attractive.

The most important upgrade products include:
  - Accelerator cards
  - Larger hard disks
  - Floppy disks
  - Keyboards

Block on                              Doc 2 Pg 1 Ln 2.67" Pos 1"
```

Highlighting Text with Block

To highlight a block of text, you position the cursor at the beginning of the block of text you want to highlight, turn on the Block command, and move the cursor to the end of the block. That's it! The highlighted block of text is ready for the next step in your operation.

Here are the specific steps for highlighting a block of text:

1. Move the cursor to the beginning of the block of text you want to highlight.

2. Press Block (Alt-F4, or F12).

   Notice the Block on message blinking in the bottom left of your screen.

3. Use the cursor-arrow keys to move the cursor to the end of the block of text.

The Block on message continues to blink until you complete the operation by moving the block, underlining it, or performing any function that works with the Block command. The following functions work with the Block command:

Bold
Center
Delete
Flush Right
Font
   Appearance (All)
   Size (All)
Format
Macro
Mark Text
   Index
   List
   Table of Authorities
   Table of Contents

Move
   Block
   Tabular Column
   Rectangle
Print
Replace
Save
Search
Shell
   Append
   Save
Sort
Spell
Style
Switch
Text In/Out
Underline

You can use the cursor-arrow keys to define a block. For example, if your cursor is at the end of a line you want to block, turn on Block (by pressing Alt-F4, or F12) and press Home- ← to move the cursor to the beginning of the line. The line will then be highlighted.

TIP: You can use several shortcuts to define a block. For example, after you've turned on Block by pressing Alt-F4 or F12, you can use the Search command to find the text at the end of the block and to move the cursor to that position. Another shortcut is to turn on Block and press any character to move to the next occurrence of that character in your text. To block a sentence, for instance, turn on Block at the beginning of the sentence and type a period. The block will extend to the period at the end of the sentence. To select an entire paragraph, turn on Block and press Enter. The block will extend to the next occurrence of a hard return in your text.

Canceling a Block

To cancel a block, press either the Cancel key (F1) or the Block key (Alt-F4, or F12) while the block is highlighted. The Block on message disappears from the bottom of your screen, and the text is no longer highlighted. The cursor remains at the end of the block, where it was when you finished highlighting the block.

Rehighlighting a Block

After you highlight a block, you can perform a single editing or formatting operation. Suppose, however, that you want to make two or more changes to the same block of text. You might, for example, want to emphasize a paragraph by making it both bold and italic. After you have made one change to a block, you can use a shortcut to rehighlight the block and make the second change.

Start by highlighting the block of text and completing the first operation. Leave the cursor at the end of the block. Then complete the following steps to rehighlight the block of text:

1. Press Block (Alt-F4, or F12) to turn on the Block command.

2. Press Go To (Ctrl-Home) to activate the Go To command.

3. Press Go To (Ctrl-Home) again to return to the beginning of the block.

If you change your mind about the amount of text to highlight, return to the beginning of the block and start over. To return to the beginning of a block that is already highlighted, press Go To (Ctrl-Home) and then Block (Alt-F4, or F12). The block is no longer highlighted, but the Block command is still on. Now you can highlight the appropriate amount of text.

Moving a Block

You can use WordPerfect's capability to move blocks as a powerful editing tool. With this function, you don't have to worry about preparing your report or letter perfectly the first time. Instead, you can get the ideas down and use the Block Move command to organize them later.

When you move a block of text, you delete it from one place and insert it somewhere else. You can move a block of any size to another place in the document you currently are working on or to another document.

To move a block of text, follow these steps:

1. Use Block (Alt-F4, or F12) to highlight the text you want to move.

2. Press Move (Ctrl-F4).

    The Move menu appears in the status line at the bottom of the screen, as shown in figure 4.2.

Fig. 4.2.
The Move menu.

```
THE QUANTUM PC REPORT FOR CPAS

New Life for Your Older PCs:
Key Upgrade Products

    Change happens so quickly in the computer industry that products
seen to go obsolete before you get them paid for. But there is a
fountain of youth for over-the-hill PCs, and this month's feature
article is swimming in ideas for how to give your old PC the speed
and power of a new model.

    Within the past several months, several new products have come
along that provide attractive new alternatives for getting the kind
of speed, power and flexibility from your older PCs that would
otherwise require a new 80286- or 80386-based computer. Since many
CPAs and financial executives are in an office environment that
includes older PCs, these new alternatives can be very attractive.

The most important upgrade products include:
  - Accelerator cards
  - Larger hard disks
  - Floppy disks
  - Keyboards

Move: 1 Block; 2 Tabular Column; 3 Rectangle: 0
```

3. Select **Block** (**1**).

4. Select **Move** (**1**).

   The text disappears, and the following message appears at the bottom left of your screen:

   `Move cursor; press Enter to retrieve.`

5. Move the cursor where you want to move the block of text.

6. Press Enter.

When you press Enter, the text is retrieved and displayed at the cursor's new position.

Copying a Block

While the Move command removes a block of text from one position in your document and retrieves it to another position, the Copy command duplicates the block of text and copies it to another position. The original stays put, and the copy appears in the new position.

To copy a block of text, follow these steps:

1. Use Block (Alt-F4, or F12) to highlight the text you want to copy.

2. Press Move (Ctrl-F4).

   The Move menu appears (see fig. 4.2) just as it does when you move a block.

3. Select **Block** (**1**).

4. Select **Copy** (**2**).

The highlighting disappears, and the following message appears at the bottom left of your screen:

Move cursor; press Enter to retrieve.

5. Move the cursor to where you want to copy the block of text.

6. Press Enter.

You can retrieve the copied text as many times as you like. To duplicate the same block of text and retrieve it again, follow these steps:

1. Move the cursor to where you want to retrieve the block of text.

2. Press Move (Ctrl-F4).

3. Select **Retrieve** (**4**).

4. Select **Block** (**1**).

Deleting a Block

Deleting a block of text is as simple as highlighting the text and pressing the Del or Backspace key. The process, however, involves one final step: you must confirm your deletion.

To delete a block of text, follow these steps:

1. Use Block (Alt-F4, or F12) to highlight the text you want to delete.

2. Press the Del or Backspace key.

The following message appears at the bottom left of your screen:

Delete Block? (Y/N) No

WordPerfect assumes that you don't want to delete the text; if you don't, press Enter. The block remains highlighted. If you do want to delete the block, continue with the next step.

3. Press *Y* to answer Yes.

Deleted text is removed. You can't retrieve it like you can retrieve text that you move or copy. You can, however, change your mind about the deletion if you catch your mistake quickly. To undelete, press the Cancel key (F1). The most recently deleted text reappears in your document. Press **Restore** (**1**) to restore the deleted text.

WordPerfect lets you restore any of your last three deletions. When you press the Cancel key (F1), the following status line is displayed at the bottom left of the screen:

Undelete: 1 Restore; **2** Previous Deletion: **0**

The screen also displays in your document your most recent deletion. If you select **R**estore (**1**) now, that most recent deletion is restored. If you select **P**revious Deletion (**2**), however, the second most recent deletion is shown in your text instead. To restore that deletion, select **R**estore (**1**). If instead you want to restore your third most recent deletion, select **P**revious Deletion (**2**) again. Then select **R**estore (**1**) to restore that deletion.

Appending a Block

Sometimes you want to add information to a WordPerfect document while you are working on a different document. While you are writing a letter to a client today, for example, you might think of an idea you would like to add to a report you wrote yesterday. Rather than exiting the letter, opening the report, and adding your idea to the report, you can append the idea to the report while you still are working on the letter.

Follow these steps to append a block of text to another document:

1. Use Block (Alt-F4, or F12) to highlight the text you want to append to another document.

2. Press Move (Ctrl-F4).

3. Select **B**lock (**1**).

4. Select **A**ppend (**4**).

   The screen displays the following message at the bottom left of your screen:

   Append to:

   The cursor is positioned immediately after the message so that you can enter your response.

5. Type the file name of the document to which you want to append your block.

The appended block remains in your current document and is added to the end of the file whose name you typed in Step 5. If WordPerfect can't find a file with the name you typed, the program creates that file. The file to which you are appending a block of text can be either in the current directory or in another directory. You won't see the document to which you are appending a block unless you exit the current document and open the appended document.

Saving a Block

As you are typing a document—a legal contract is a good example—you may type a paragraph or some other block of text that you would like to use again in another document. A simple way to do that is to save the block to a separate file, independent of the document you're currently working in.

To save a block of text to a separate file, follow these steps:

1. Use Block (Alt-F4, or F12) to highlight the text you want to save to a separate file.

2. Press Save (F10).

3. Type the name of the file to which you want to save the block.

4. Press Enter.

If the name you type in Step 3 is the name of an existing file, the screen displays the following message:

```
Replace (file name)? (Y/N) No
```

To replace the file, press *Y*. If you don't want to replace the file, press *N*, type a new name, and press Enter.

The block is saved into the current default directory. That directory may be different from the directory you're currently working in. Press List Files (F5) to see what the default directory is. To save the block into a different directory, include the directory as part of the file name you type in Step 3. To save a block to a file named JUDGES in your current directory, for example, type just the name *judges* in Step 3. To save the same file into a directory called CONTRACTS, however, type the full name *contracts**judges* in Step 3.

The Block Save command works well in combination with WordPerfect's Retrieve command. You can use the two to build a document from previously created blocks of text. A legal office, for example, might use the same paragraphs repeatedly in many different contracts. Use the Block command to save each of the reusable paragraphs as individual files. Use the Retrieve command to build a contract out of the paragraphs you blocked and saved as individual files. For more about the Retrieve command, refer to Chapter 3.

Printing a Block

You do not always want to print an entire document. Sometimes you want to print only one paragraph from a letter or one page from a report. Use the Block Print command to print part of your document.

To print a block, follow these steps:

1. Use Block (Alt-F4, or F12) to highlight the text you want to print.

2. Press Print (Shift-F7).

   The following message appears at the bottom left of your screen:

   ```
   Print block? (Y/N) No
   ```

3. Press *Y* to answer Yes.

The block prints on the currently selected printer. For instructions on how to select a printer, refer to Appendix A.

Enhancing Text with the Block Command

Using the Block command, you can change the appearance of selected areas of text. You can emphasize an important paragraph by making it bold, for example, or you can call attention to a single word by underlining it. You can change the type font in a headline. You can center a title, redline edited text, or strike out text to be deleted. The Block command gives you the power to make any of these changes to a block of text that is as small as a single letter or as large as the full document.

Boldfacing and Underlining Blocked Text

You can type text that is boldfaced or underlined as you create your document. Often, however, you will find that typing the text normally and later using the Block command to add boldfacing or underlining is easier. WordPerfect offers you a choice of single or double underlines. The procedures for inserting the two types of underlines are different.

To boldface or single underline a block of text, follow these steps:

1. Use Block (Alt-F4, or F12) to highlight the text you want to boldface or single underline.

2. Press the Bold key (F6) to make the text bold

   or

   Press the Underline key (F8) to underline the text.

To double underline a block of text, follow these steps:

1. Use Block (Alt-F4, or F12) to highlight the text you want to double underline.

2. Press Font (Ctrl-F8).

3. Select Appearance (2).

4. Select Dbl Und (3).

Although enhanced text will print properly (assuming that your printer supports text enhancement features such as double underlining), the text may not appear correctly on your computer screen. Double underlining, for example, probably won't appear as double underlining and may not be legible on monochrome monitors. Figure 4.3 shows underlined and double-underlined text as it appears on a monochrome screen; figure 4.4 shows the same text when printed. The position number (to the right of Pos at the bottom right of your screen) reflects the enhancement of the text where your cursor is currently located. (Refer to this chapter's "Displaying Enhanced Text On-Screen" section for more information on this topic.)

Fig. 4.3.

Underlined text as it appears on-screen.

```
                          Karen's Nursery

                              Quantity        Price

        Bulbs
        Daffodil              24 Dz.      $144.88
        Iris                  18 Dz.       188.88
        Caladium               3 Dz.        18.88
        Subtotal:                         $278.88

        Seeds
        Zinnia                48 Pks.       24.88
        Petunia               72 Pks.       36.88
        Subtotal:                          $68.88

        Smith & Hawken Tools
        Spades                      6       38.88
        Shovels                     3       36.88
        Subtotal:                          $66.88

        Total:                            $396.88


        C:\WP5\CH4\FIG483            Doc 2 Pg 1 Ln 1.67" Pos 1"
```

Fig. 4.4.

The same underlined text as it appears when printed.

```
                              Karen's Nursery

                                  Quantity          Price

        Bulbs
        Daffodil                  24 Dz.          $144.00
        Iris                      18 Dz.           108.00
        Caladium                   3 Dz.            18.00
        Subtotal:                                 $270.00

        Seeds
        Zinnia                    48 Pks.           24.00
        Petunia                   72 Pks.           36.00
        Subtotal:                                  $60.00

        Smith & Hawken Tools
        Spades                          6           30.00
        Shovels                         3           36.00
        Subtotal:                                  $66.00

        Total:                                    $396.00
```

Changing the Type Font in a Block

WordPerfect works well with the varieties of fonts available on many printers—particularly the new laser printers, which produce high quality print in many type sizes and styles. You can use the many styles that WordPerfect offers if your printer supports them. WordPerfect offers italic, outline, shadow, and small caps. Also offered are double underlining, redlining, and strikeout, discussed in other sections of this chapter.

When you change the size or appearance of a font, your starting point is what WordPerfect calls a *base font*—your normal type font. If you increase the size of a line of Courier text, for example, the result is a line of enlarged Courier. Similarly, if you outline a line of Times Roman text, the result is outlined Times Roman.

To change the base font, refer to Chapter 5, "Formatting and Enhancing Text." You can't change to another base font using the Block command. You can change only the size or appearance of text using the Block command; the base font remains the same.

Note: Your printer may not support all the font sizes and appearances discussed in this section. Most impact printers (such as daisy-wheel and dot-matrix printers) support only a few type styles. Although laser printers can print an array of type sizes and styles, you generally need a font cartridge or downloadable fonts in order to take advantage of that capability. Check your printer manual for details.

Font Size

You can change the text in a highlighted block to any of these font sizes:

1 Suprscrpt; **2** Subscrpt; **3** Fine; **4** Small; **5** Large; **6** Vry Large; **7** Ext Large

Enlarged text, as shown in figure 4.5, is excellent for titles and headlines, while small type is ideal when you want to include "fine print" in your document. Choices 1 and 2 are useful in mathematical and scientific applications where you need superscripts and subscripts. You can use any of these font sizes in headers and footers.

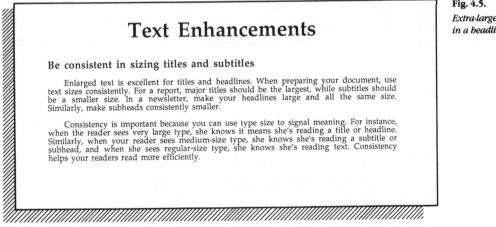

Fig. 4.5.
Extra-large text used in a headline.

To change the font size of the text in a block, follow these steps:

1. Use Block (Alt-F4, or F12) to highlight the text you want to enlarge or reduce.

2. Press Font (Ctrl-F8).

   The screen displays the following attribute line:

   Attribute: 1 Size; **2** Appearance: 0

3. Select Size (**1**).

4. Select the size you want.

Font Appearance

You can enhance the appearance—or style—of type with bold, underline, outline, and other font attributes. These are the available choices:

1 Bold **2** Undrln **3** Dbl Und **4** Italic **5** Outln **6** Shadw **7** Sm Cap **8** Redln **9** Stkout

You often use boldface text for emphasis; it works well with large type, for example, as a title or headline. You can use underlining or italics to identify a title or proper name. Use underlining if your printer won't print italics. Outline and shadow generally are regarded as special effects, to be used sparingly. In a graphic application, such as an advertisement for your company newsletter, outlined or shadowed words can be great attention-getters. Small caps give importance to a word or sentence and are not as overpowering as full-size caps. Redline and strikeout, discussed later in this chapter, are useful editing features. Figure 4.6 illustrates a number of WordPerfect's font appearance choices.

Fig. 4.6.

Text illustrating different font appearances (printed on a laser printer).

This text is emphasized by being boldfaced.

This phrase is underlined, while this is double underlined.

Titles of books and magazines should be in italics, like this.

Outline and shadow are best reserved for special effects.

SMALL CAPS GIVE EMPHASIS WITHOUT BEING AS HARD TO READ AS ALL CAPS.

Redline is useful for editing.

Strikeout is also handy for editing.

To change the appearance of a block of text, follow these steps:

1. Use Block (Alt-F4, or F12) to highlight the text you want to change.

2. Press Font (Ctrl-F8).

3. Select Appearance (**2**).

4. Select one of the font appearance attributes listed.

Uppercasing and Lowercasing Blocks

You don't have to retype in order to change a block of text to all lowercase or all uppercase. A simple command does the typing for you! Note that when you switch from uppercase to lowercase, WordPerfect leaves certain letters capitalized— including the letter I when it occurs by itself and the first letters of sentences.

To change a block of text to uppercase or lowercase, follow these steps:

1. Use Block (Alt-F4, or F12) to highlight the text you want to change to upper- or lowercase.

2. Press Switch (Shift-F3).

3. Select Uppercase (**1**)

   or

   Select Lowercase (**2**).

If you are switching from upper- to lowercase, be sure to review your text for accuracy. WordPerfect may not capitalize every word correctly. For example, the first letter following every period is capitalized. If you have a sentence that includes a decimal number, the result may have inappropriate capitalization.

Centering a Block

You can center a block of text either as you type or after you type the text. To center a block of text as you type, you center each line and end the block with a hard return. To center text after it's typed, you highlight and then center the block. WordPerfect inserts a hard return at the end of each line of centered text. Even if the block you are centering is a word-wrapped paragraph, WordPerfect inserts a hard return at the end of each line. The block appears centered both on-screen and in print. Figure 4.7 illustrates how Block Center can be used to center the text in a menu.

TIP: Keep in mind that because each line ends with a hard return, the lengths of the lines are fixed. Adding text after a block is centered, therefore, is awkward. To avoid awkward editing, don't center word-wrapped paragraphs. Instead, set off paragraphs using indents: press Indent (F4) to indent a paragraph from the left margin; press Left-Right Indent (Shift-F4) to indent from both the left and right margins. Center blocks whose lines are likely to remain fairly constant. Use the Block Center command, for example, to center a table, list, or menu.

Fig. 4.7.

A centered block.

Favorite Dishes With Robust Flavors
--John Ash & Co.--

-First Course-

Gulf prawns with a Chinese black bean
mayonnaise and spring greens
or
Latin beef tartare with jalapeno peppers,
shallots, and capers

-Second Course-

Lemon sorbet with a splash of
Russian peppered vodka

-Third Course-

Rack of lamb marinated in garlic, fresh herbs, and
red pepper roasted with Roquefort croutes
or
Salmon grilled with preserved lemon
roasted red peppers and oil cured olives

-Fourth Course-

Selection of favorite cheeses

-Fifth Course-

Choice of desserts from the menu

To center a block of text, follow these steps:

1. Use Block (Alt-F4, or F12) to highlight the text you want to center.

2. Press Center (Shift-F6).

   A screen message prompts [Cntr]? (Y/N) No

3. Press *Y*.

Using Redline and Strikeout

You can use WordPerfect's redline and strikeout features when you want to be able to compare revisions to a document. A writer, for example, submits to an editor chapters on a WordPerfect disk. The editor reads the material and marks it by redlining and striking out certain passages in the document file. Redline points to material that needs to be expanded or illustrated, while strikeout indicates text that the editor feels should be deleted. When reviewing the edited material, the writer has the advantage of seeing exactly what changes the editor wants to make rather than simply seeing the revised edited chapter.

With many printers, redline appears as a mark in the margin next to the redlined text. With other printers, such as the laser printer used to print figure 4.8, redlined text appears shaded or highlighted. If you have a color printer, redlined text prints red. Strikeout appears as characters superimposed over other characters. To define the characters you want to use for redline and strikeout, refer to Chapter 3.

Fig. 4.8.

Redlined text highlighted; strikeout text superimposed with hyphens.

```
In the old days, writers had to stop editing days before a
document was due and start combing through the main text to
prepare the document references. One of WordPerfect 5's handiest
features is that it speeds up that process. One of WordPerfect
5's handiest features is that it speeds up the process of
assembling document references. With a little foresight and
planning, you can work on a document right down to a few hours
before a deadline, confident that as your main text changes, the
document references will keep right up with it.
```

To redline or mark with strikeout a block of text, follow these steps:

1. Use Block (Alt-F4, or F12) to highlight the text you want to redline or mark with strikeout.

2. Press Font (Ctrl-F8).

3. Select **Appearance** (**2**).

4. Select **Redln** (**8**)

   or

   Select **Stkout** (**9**).

Unenhancing Text

If you use the Block command to enhance text, you generally cannot then use the Block command to return the text to its normal appearance. To unenhance text, you must delete the enhancement codes.

To delete text enhancement codes, follow these steps:

1. Move the cursor to the beginning or end of the enhanced text.

2. Press Reveal Codes (Alt-F3, or F11).

3. Delete either the beginning or ending text enhancement code.

Table 4.1 lists the text enhancement codes available in WordPerfect and explains what each code means.

Table 4.1
Text Enhancement Codes

Code	Enhancement
[Bold]	Bold
[Cntr]	Center
[Dbl Und]	Double underline
[Ext Large]	Extra-large print
[Fine]	Fine print
[Font]	Base font
[Kern]	Kerning
[Large]	Large print
[Ovrstk]	Overstrike
[RedLn]	Redline
[Shadw]	Shadow
[Sm Cap]	Small caps
[Small]	Small print
[StkOut]	Strikeout
[SubScrpt]	Subscript
[SuprScrpt]	Superscript
[Und]	Underlining
[Vry Large]	Very large print

As an alternative to deleting codes, you can cancel the effects of text enhancements by moving the cursor to the beginning of the enhanced text, pressing Font (Ctrl-F8), and selecting Normal (3). This method leaves in the codes, although they no longer bracket any text. Deleting the codes, therefore, is probably the safer of the two methods.

Displaying Enhanced Text On-Screen

Many of the text enhancements you select won't display correctly on a monochrome monitor. In fact, enhanced text may not be legible at all on-screen. Enlarged or reduced text appears in the monitor's normal text size, while italicized, underlined, and shadowed text may appear blurred. On color monitors, text enhancements appear in different colors and should be easy to read. If your screen text is illegible, press Reveal Codes (Alt-F3, or F11) to read the text.

To supplement its screen display, WordPerfect offers a command that shows how your document will look when printed: the View Document command. You can use this command by pressing the Print key (Shift-F7) and then selecting View Document (6). You can then view your document in 100%, 200%, or fit-in-the-window sizes, but you must return to the document in order to edit the text. To learn more about View Document and how to adjust the appearance of text on-screen, refer to the "Using Document Preview" section in Chapter 5 and to Appendix A.

For a true "what you see is what you get" on-screen display, you need to add a Hercules Graphics Card to your computer. With this card, enlarged text appears larger and italicized text appears in italics on-screen. Keep in mind that text, no matter how it looks on-screen, will print correctly as long as your printer supports the enhancements you've chosen.

Moving and Copying Text between Documents

WordPerfect's Block Move and Block Copy commands make moving and copying text between documents easy. In WordPerfect, you can open two documents at the same time. The first document is called Doc 1 and the second is called Doc 2. You can move between these documents by pressing the Switch key (Shift-F3). The simplest way to move or copy text between documents is to begin with both documents opened simultaneously. Then you can copy or move a block in the first document (Doc 1), press Switch (Shift-F3) to switch to the second document (Doc 2), and retrieve the text.

To open a second document, press the Switch key (Shift-F3) and retrieve the second document. Notice the message Doc 2 in the status line at the bottom right of your screen. Before you begin the moving or copying procedure, return to the first document (Doc 1) by pressing the Switch key (Shift-F3) again.

To move or copy text between documents, follow these steps:

1. Use Block (Alt-F4, or F12) to highlight the text you want to move or copy.

2. Press Move (Ctrl-F4).

3. Select **Block** (**1**).

4. Select **Move** (**1**)

   or

   Select **Copy** (**2**).

5. Press Switch (Shift-F3) to display the second document.

6. Move the cursor to the place where you want to move or copy the block.

7. Press Enter to retrieve the block.

Working with Rectangular Blocks

In WordPerfect, you can move either a grammatical block of text, such as a sentence or paragraph, or you can move any text that falls within a defined rectangular block. Being able to move or copy lines, sentences, paragraphs, and other grammatical blocks of text is a practical and useful function for editing text.

But being able to move a block of text defined not as contiguous words, but simply as a rectangle of text, opens up a whole new chapter of creative possibilities. For example, you can move or copy a single column of text or numbers from a table, as shown in figure 4.9, with WordPerfect's Move Rectangle command.

Fig. 4.9.

A blocked rectangle of text.

```
                              Assignments for the Month

        Western Region        Central Region      Eastern Region

        Karen                 Ron                 Rabbit
        Chuck                 Barb                Pegg
        Dave                  Patty               Lisa
        Leslie                Jessica Ann         Ken










    1 Move; 2 Copy; 3 Delete; 4 Append: 0
```

To move or copy a rectangular block, you first use the Block command to highlight the text. Then you use the Move Rectangle command to move or copy the block. You can retrieve the block within the current document or use Switch (Shift-F3) to retrieve the text into a different document.

When you retrieve a rectangle, be aware of how it will be integrated into the current page. If the page is empty, the rectangle simply will be placed on the page with a hard return at the end of each line. If text is currently in the position where you retrieve the rectangle, the retrieved text will be woven into the existing text, producing unexpected results. Figure 4.10 shows the same rectangle retrieved into a blank area of the screen and retrieved into an area where text existed.

When you move a column, you may move tab stops along with the text or numbers. If you do, the tab stops are included in the new location and are deleted from the previous location. Unexpected results may occur. To see whether you are including tab stops in the block, use Reveal Codes (Alt-F3, or F11) during the Block operation.

To move or copy a rectangle, follow these steps:

1. Position the cursor at the top left corner of the text you want to move as a rectangle.

2. Press Block (Alt-F4, or F12).

3. Move the cursor to the bottom right corner of the rectangle.

```
A RECTANGLE RETRIEVED INTO AN EMPTY SPACE:

Central Region

Ron
Barb
Patty
Jessica Ann

THE SAME RECTANGLE RETRIEVED AT THE BEGINNING OF AN
EXISTING PARAGRAPH:

Central Region        When you retrieve a rectangle, be aware of how it will
be integrated into the current page. If the page is empty,
Ron                            the rectangle simply will be placed on the
Barb                           page with a hard return at the end of each
Patty                  line. If text is currently in the
Jessica Ann            position where you retrieve the rectangle, the retrieved
text will be woven into the existing text, producing unexpected results.




C:\WP5\CH4\FIG410                      Doc 1 Pg 1 Ln 4.03" Pos 1"
```

Fig. 4.10.

A rectangle retrieved both into an empty area of the page and into an area where text existed.

The text is highlighted all the way across the page, as usual. In the next steps, you will define the rectangle as the area between where the cursor was when you pressed Block (Alt-F4, or F12) and where it is now. Text to the right will be excluded.

4. Press Move (Ctrl-F4).

5. Select **Rectangle** (**3**).

   Only the rectangle is highlighted, as shown in figure 4.9.

6. Select Move (**1**)

   or

   Select **Copy** (**2**).

7. Move the cursor to where you want to retrieve the rectangle.

8. Press Enter.

You also can delete a rectangle of text. You may, for example, want to delete a whole column of numbers from a table.

To delete a rectangle, follow these steps:

1. Position the cursor at the top left corner of the text you want to delete as a rectangle.

2. Press Block (Alt-F4, or F12).

3. Move the cursor to the bottom right corner of the rectangle.

4. Press Move (Ctrl-F4).

5. Select **Rectangle** (**3**).

6. Select **Delete** (**3**).

Suppose that you want to copy a selected column of data from a table and append the data to the end of another document in order to illustrate a point. Although the documentation suggests that you can append a rectangular block of text to a file on disk, this feature does not work as documented for the 5/5/88 release of WordPerfect 5. If you need to transfer a rectangle to another file, you can use this workaround:

1. Press Switch (Shift-F3) to move to the other document window (but first make certain that you do not have a file in that window).

2. Use Retrieve (Shift-F10) or List Files (F5) to retrieve the file you want to add the rectangle to.

3. Position the cursor where you want to insert the rectangle.

4. Press Switch (Shift-F3) to return to the original document window.

5. Follow the steps presented previously in this section for copying a rectangle.

   After you copy the rectangle, the following prompt is displayed on the status line:

   `Move cursor; press Enter to retrieve.`

6. Press Switch (Shift-F3) to move back to the second document window.

7. Press Enter to insert the rectangle in the second file.

8. Press Exit (F7), Enter, Enter, *Y, Y* to save the second document and return to the original document in the other window.

The file you saved to disk now contains the inserted rectangle.

Using the Block Command with Styles

When you are doing repetitive formatting in a document or series of documents (such as the chapters that make up a book), using WordPerfect's styles feature can save you time. A *style* is a set of formatting instructions that defines the appearance of the text to which it's applied. A style, for example, might define the format of a chapter title as all caps, centered, bold, and extra-large text. Other styles might define the formats of subtitles, paragraphs, and figure captions within your document. The advantage of using a style is that it applies to all the text assigned to it. By redefining a style, you change the format of all the text assigned to that style.

You can create styles in two ways. One way is to use a special Styles window. For a detailed description of this procedure, refer to Chapter 12. Perhaps an easier way to create a style, however, is by example. You format a block of text as you want it to appear, highlight it with the Block command (making sure that you include any formatting codes in the highlighted area), select the Style key (Alt-F8), and create the style.

Complete these steps to create a style using the Block command:

1. Use Block (Alt-F4, or F12) to highlight the text from which you want to copy a style.

2. Press Style (Alt-F8).

3. Select **Create** (**3**) from the menu line.

4. Select **Name** (**1**) from the Styles: Edit menu.

5. Enter the style name.

6. Press Exit (F7).

You also can choose from two ways to apply a style to text after the style is created. One way is to apply the style as you are typing (see Chapter 12 for details). Another way is to highlight the text using the Block command and then apply the style. Follow these steps to apply a style using the Block command:

1. Use Block (Alt-F4, or F12) to highlight the text to which you want to apply a style.

2. Press Style (Alt-F8).

3. Press the ↓ until you highlight the style you want to apply to your block.

4. Select **On** (**1**) to apply the highlighted style to your block.

Using this procedure, the style applies only to the block you've highlighted.

Quick Start

Working with Blocks

A WordPerfect block is an area of text that has been selected, or highlighted. In itself, the highlighted block is meaningless. What's important is that the highlighted block is poised for a second operation.

WordPerfect's Block command never works alone. Instead, it teams up with other WordPerfect commands to perform powerful editing functions. You can move the block, copy it, delete it, underline it, boldface it, center it, change its size, change its appearance, print it, save it, or add it to the end of another file. With the Block command, you can make these changes to blocks of text as small as a single letter or as large as several pages.

Highlighting a block of text is as easy as positioning your cursor and pressing a function key. Before you try it, type the following short memo so that you will have some text to experiment with:

Memo

To: All employees using WordPerfect

From: Ms. Rose

Re: Using the Block command to save time!

You can save time using the block command! With this command, you highlight the area of text you want to change, move, copy, delete, save, or print. You can use some features, like text enhancements, while you type. But often it's easiest to type your whole document, then go back through it and edit the text with the help of the Block command.

Using the Block command is easy. Position the cursor at the beginning of the block of text you want to highlight, and press Block (Alt-F4). Then move the cursor to the end of the text. That's it!

Blocked text appears highlighted on your screen. In a sense, blocked text is text that's identified as being "ready" for a second operation.

When you are finished typing, press Enter twice.

Highlighting Text with the Block Command

Highlighting a block of text is the first step in many WordPerfect operations. A highlighted block of text is singled out from the text around it. Whatever operation you next choose will perform its magic on only that block of text.

Highlight the first paragraph of the memo you typed by completing these steps:

1. Press Home-Home- ↑ to move the cursor to the beginning of the memo.

2. Press the ↓ repeatedly until the cursor is positioned at the beginning of the first paragraph.

3. Press the Block key (Alt-F4, or F12) to turn on the Block command.

   Notice the Block on message flashing in the bottom left of your screen.

4. Move the cursor to the end of the first paragraph.

The paragraph is now highlighted, as shown in figure 4.11. Leave the block highlighted for the second part of the operation.

Fig. 4.11.
A highlighted paragraph.

```
Memo

To: All employees using WordPerfect

From: Ms, Rose

Re: Using the Block command to save time!

You can save time using the block command! With this command, you
highlight the area of text you want to change, move, copy, delete,
save, or print. You can use some features, like text enhancements,
while you type. But often it's easiest to type your whole document,
then go back through it and edit the text with the help of the Block
command.

Using the Block command is easy. Position the cursor at the beginning
of the block of text you want to highlight, and press Block (Alt-F4).
Then move the cursor to the end of the text. That's it!

Blocked text appears highlighted on your screen. In a sense, blocked
text is text that's identified as being "ready" for a second
operation.

Block on                              Doc 1 Pg 1 Ln 3.12" Pos
```

Making a Block of Text Bold

The Block on message is still flashing on your screen, indicating that the highlighted block of text is ready for the second part of the operation. In this example, you want to change the first paragraph of text to boldface. To do this, you simply press a single function key:

Press the Bold key (F6) to boldface the highlighted block of text.

As soon as you press the Bold key (F6), the two-part operation of boldfacing the paragraph is complete. The Block on message disappears. The cursor remains where it was—at the end of the block. The boldface paragraph is brighter than the remaining text. (On a color monitor, the paragraph instead may appear in a different color.)

Centering a Block of Text

When you need to center more than a single line of text, the easiest approach is to type the text first. Then you can highlight the block and center it.

Try centering the heading in your sample memo. Notice that you first have to highlight the text using the Block command. This time, use the following shortcut to highlight the block:

1. Press Home, Home, ↑ to move the cursor to the beginning of the memo.

2. Press the Block key (Alt-F4, or F12) to turn on the block feature.

3. Type an exclamation point (!) to extend the block to the next exclamation point in the text—in this case, to the end of the memo heading.

   After the Block feature is turned on, any method of moving the cursor extends the block.

4. Press Center (Shift-F6) to center the block.

   The screen displays the following message asking you to confirm that you want to center the block:

   [Cntr]? (Y/N) No

5. Press *Y* to confirm the centering.

Figure 4.12 shows the result of these steps. The memo heading is centered.

Changing the Type Font with the Block Command

You can emphasize a block of text by changing the size or appearance of the type. Using very large type for a line of text creates an excellent headline. Using slightly enlarged type is a good way to display subheads within an article. Italicizing the name of a book quickly identifies the name as a title. You can modify both the size and appearance (or style) of the text in a block by using the Block command (Alt-F4, or F12) in combination with the Font command (Ctrl-F8).

To change the style of one sentence in the text you typed, complete these steps:

1. Press Home-Home- ↑ to move the cursor to the beginning of the page.

2. Press the ↓ repeatedly to move the cursor to the beginning of the second paragraph.

```
                              Memo

              To: All employees using WordPerfect

                    From: Ms. Rose

              Re: Using the Block command to save time!

    You can save time using the block command! With this command, you
    highlight the area of text you want to change, move, copy, delete, save, or
    print. You can use some features, like text enhancements, while you type.
    But often it's easiest to type your whole document, then go back through it
    and edit the text with the help of the Block command.

    Using the Block command is easy. Position the cursor at the beginning
    of the block of text you want to highlight, and press Block (Alt-F4).
    Then move the cursor to the end of the text. That's it!

    Blocked text appears highlighted on your screen. In a sense, blocked
    text is text that's identified as being "ready" for a second
    operation.


    C:\WP5\CH4\FIG414                    Doc 1 Pg 1 Ln 2.06" Pos 1"
```

3. Press Block (Alt-F4, or F12) to turn on the Block feature.

4. Type a period (.) to extend the block to the first period in your text—in this case, the end of the first sentence.

   Typing a period is a shortcut to extend the block to the first occurrence of a period in your text, as shown in figure 4.13. This is a quick way to highlight just a sentence.

```
                              Memo

              To: All employees using WordPerfect

                    From: Ms. Rose

              Re: Using the Block command to save time!

    You can save time using the block command! With this command, you
    highlight the area of text you want to change, move, copy, delete, save, or
    print. You can use some features, like text enhancements, while you type.
    But often it's easiest to type your whole document, then go back through it
    and edit the text with the help of the Block command.

    Using the Block command is easy. Position the cursor at the beginning
    of the block of text you want to highlight, and press Block (Alt-F4).
    Then move the cursor to the end of the text. That's it!

    Blocked text appears highlighted on your screen. In a sense, blocked
    text is text that's identified as being "ready" for a second
    operation.


    Block on                            Doc 1 Pg 1 Ln 3.12" Pos 3.48"
```

5. Press the Font key (Ctrl-F8).

6. Select **Size** (**1**) to change the size of the text in the highlighted sentence.

7. Select **Vry Large** (**6**).

On your screen, the sentence appears highlighted (or in a different color, if you have a color monitor). When you print the page, however, the text will be larger than the surrounding text. (The text will print larger only if your printer is capable of producing varying text sizes; check your printer manual to find the text sizes that your printer supports.)

Moving and Copying Blocks of Text

WordPerfect makes changing your mind easy. As you are composing your document, let the ideas flow freely. Get them down while they're fresh and go back later to rearrange and reorganize your text. Using the Block command along with the Move command, you can move any amount of text to another place in your document.

Move the middle paragraph in the memo to the end of the memo by completing these steps:

1. Press the ← repeatedly to move the cursor to the beginning of the middle paragraph in the memo.

2. Press Block (Alt-F4, or F12) to turn on the Block feature.

3. Press Enter as a shortcut for extending the block to the next hard return (the end of the paragraph).

   Because the paragraph ends with a hard return, pressing the Enter key is a quick way to extend the block to the end of the paragraph in order to highlight the entire paragraph.

4. Press Move (Ctrl-F4).

   The Move command displays a menu that offers you the choices listed at the bottom of figure 4.14. In this example, you are moving a block—the first choice listed.

5. Select **Block** (**1**) to indicate that you want to move a block.

   You now have four more choices, shown in figure 4.15. The Move Block subcommands are Move, to move a block; Copy, to duplicate a block; Delete, to remove a block; and Append, to add a block to the end of a separate file.

6. Select **Move** (**1**) to move the paragraph you have highlighted as a block.

   As soon as you select **Move** (**1**), the block disappears from your screen. At the bottom left of the screen, the following message is displayed:

   `Move cursor; press Enter to retrieve.`

Fig. 4.14.
The Move menu displayed in the status line.

```
                              Memo

            To: All employees using WordPerfect

                      From: Ms. Rose

            Re: Using the Block command to save time!

  You can save time using the block command! With this command, you
  highlight the area of text you want to change, move, copy, delete, save,
  or print. You can use some features, like text enhancements, while you
  type. But often it's easiest to type your whole document, then go back
  through it and edit the text with the help of the Block command.

  Using the Block command is easy. Position the cursor at the beginning of
  the block of text you want to highlight, and press Block (Alt-F4). Then
  move the cursor to the end of the text. That's it!

  Blocked text appears highlighted on your screen. In a sense, blocked text
  is text that's identified as being "ready" for a second operation.




  Move: 1 Block; 2 Tabular Column; 3 Rectangle: 0
```

Fig. 4.15.
The four Move Block subcommands.

```
                              Memo

            To: All employees using WordPerfect

                      From: Ms. Rose

            Re: Using the Block command to save time!

  You can save time using the block command! With this command, you
  highlight the area of text you want to change, move, copy, delete, save,
  or print. You can use some features, like text enhancements, while you
  type. But often it's easiest to type your whole document, then go back
  through it and edit the text with the help of the Block command.

  Using the Block command is easy. Position the cursor at the beginning of
  the block of text you want to highlight, and press Block (Alt-F4). Then
  move the cursor to the end of the text. That's it!

  Blocked text appears highlighted on your screen. In a sense, blocked text
  is text that's identified as being "ready" for a second operation.




  1 Move; 2 Copy; 3 Delete; 4 Append: 0
```

7. Use the ↓ to move the cursor two lines below the last line of text.

8. Press Enter to retrieve the text at the cursor's position.

The second paragraph has been moved from the middle of the page and retrieved at the end of the document, as shown in figure 4.16. The cursor remains where it was when you pressed Enter—at the beginning of the moved paragraph.

Copying a block of text is a procedure similar to moving a block. When you copy a block, however, you choose Copy (**2**) rather than Move (**1**) in Step 6. Also, the

```
                              Memo

              To: All employees using WordPerfect

                      From: Ms, Rose

            Re: Using the Block command to save time!

      You can save time using the block command! With this command, you
      highlight the area of text you want to change, move, copy, delete, save,
      or print, You can use some features, like text enhancements, while you
      type, But often it's easiest to type your whole document, then go back
      through it and edit the text with the help of the Block command,

      Blocked text appears highlighted on your screen, In a sense, blocked text
      is text that's identified as being "ready" for a second operation,

      Using the Block command is easy, Position the cursor at the beginning of
      the block of text you want to highlight, and press Block (Alt-F4), Then
      move the cursor to the end of the text, That's it!



      C:\CH4\FIG416                           Doc 1 Pg 1 Ln 4,11" Pos 1"
```

result is different. When you copy, the block remains in its initial position in your document and is duplicated in another place.

Deleting a Block of Text

In previous steps, you may have noticed that the Move Block submenu includes an option for deleting a block. Although you can use that option to delete a block, WordPerfect offers you an easier method—using the Del or the Backspace key.

To delete the top portion of your sample memo, complete these steps:

1. Press Home-Home- ↑ to move the cursor to the beginning of the document.

2. Press Block (Alt-F4, or F12).

3. Type an exclamation point (!) as a shortcut for extending the block to the first exclamation point—the one at the end of the memo heading.

4. Press the Del key or the Backspace key.

   WordPerfect won't delete a block until you confirm that you want to delete the highlighted text. The program displays the following message at the bottom left of the screen:

   `Delete Block? (Y/N) No`

   You can override WordPerfect's answer to its own question (No) by pressing *Y* for Yes.

5. Press *Y* to confirm the deletion.

The block is erased.

Saving a Block

Some call it "deathless prose." That's something you write that is so good, you know it will last forever. It's so good, in fact, that perhaps you will want to use it again someday. By saving the profound block of text to a file of its own, you can easily retrieve it later into another document.

Saving blocks of text in separate files is a useful technique, for example, for composing legal contracts. You can assemble the text you need from a library of previously saved paragraphs.

Follow these steps to save a short sentence into a file of its own:

1. Use the cursor-arrow keys to move the cursor to the beginning of the last sentence in your sample memo—the sentence that reads That's it!.

2. Press Block (Alt-F4, or F12) to turn on the Block feature.

3. Type an exclamation point (!) to move the cursor to the end of the sentence.

4. Press Save (F10).

5. Type the file name *thatsit*

6. Press Enter.

This short block of text is now saved to a new file named THATSIT in the current directory. Figure 4.17 shows the document containing the phrase. Note the name of the file in the bottom left corner of the screen shown in the figure.

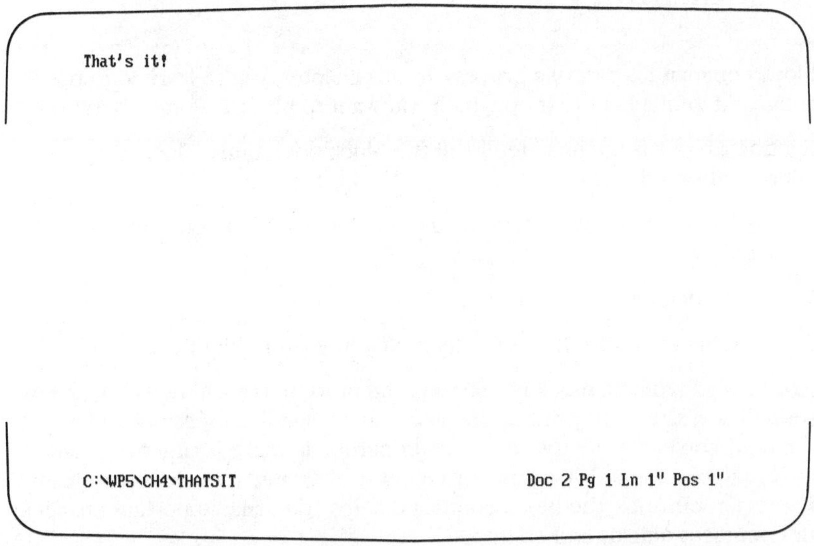

Fig. 4.17.
The sentence That's it! *saved in a file of its own.*

That's it!

C:\WP5\CH4\THATSIT   Doc 2 Pg 1 Ln 1" Pos 1"

Printing a Block

To print a block of text, you first highlight it and then issue the Print command. WordPerfect asks you to confirm that you want to print the highlighted block.

To print the first paragraph of the sample memo, follow these steps:

1. Move the cursor to the beginning of the first paragraph of the memo.

2. Press Block (Alt-F4, or F12) to turn on the Block feature.

3. Move the cursor to the end of the paragraph.

4. Press Print (Shift-F7).

   The screen displays the following message:

   Print block? (Y/N) No

5. Press *Y* for Yes to confirm that you want to print the highlighted block.

The block will print on the currently selected printer.

This Quick Start introduces you to the basics of using the Block command. Be sure to read through the chapter to learn more about the techniques illustrated here. The Block command is easy to learn. Once you've mastered it, you are on your way to using WordPerfect's powerful editing capabilities.

WP 5 Summary

The Block command is part of a process. In this chapter, you've learned to use that command to highlight text on which you want to perform some operation.

Highlighting a block is the first step in all the Block operations. The basic procedure is always the same:

1. Move the cursor to the beginning of the block of text you want to highlight.

2. Press Block (Alt-F4, or F12).

3. Move the cursor to the end of the text you want to highlight.

After you've highlighted a block of text, you can move it, copy it, delete it, append it to another file, save it, or print it. You also can change the appearance of a block of text. You can make the text bold, underline it, make it larger or smaller, change it to uppercase or lowercase, or center it. Working in tandem with many WordPerfect commands, the Block command helps you make important changes to your document quickly and easily.

5

Formatting and Enhancing Text

Schuyler Lininger, Jr., an Oregon chiropractor and owner of HealthNotes Publications, uses desktop publishing to produce fliers, brochures, and newsletters for the health food industry. ■

WordPerfect offers many useful tools that delight both novices and experienced word-processing users. If you have been using a typewriter, you will enjoy the way WordPerfect handles the mundane chores of setting margins and tabs; centering, justifying, underlining, and boldfacing text; indenting text; and hyphenating words. If you are an old hand with word processors but new to WordPerfect, you will be impressed with how simply and logically WordPerfect formats and enhances text. If you are an experienced user of WordPerfect 4.2, you will appreciate the many enhancements included in WordPerfect 5; these enhancements make your work even easier.

In this chapter, you will learn how to enhance text you have already entered. You also will learn how to format lines and paragraphs so that they appear as you want them when printed.

Text enhancements described in this chapter include the following:

- Using left and right margins (including using margin release) and indenting text from the left and from both margins

- Using various types of tabs: left, right, center, decimal, and tabs with dot leaders

- Formatting text to make it centered, flush right, or right-justified

- Changing line spacing and adjusting the height of each line (leading)

- Manually or automatically inserting hyphens into text

You also will learn how to take full advantage of your printer's capabilities, including the following:

139

- Enhancing text by changing the typeface, size, and appearance of a font

- Previewing your document before printing with the graphic View Document feature

Formatting Lines and Paragraphs

This chapter focuses on formatting the elements of the page: lines and paragraphs. The next chapter guides you through designing documents and formatting the overall page. For WordPerfect 5, WordPerfect Corporation has consolidated and completely reorganized all formatting functions; the new Format menu contains most of the functions used to format a page (see fig. 5.1). If you used WordPerfect 4.2, you will appreciate this reorganization. A beginning WordPerfect user will find that the reorganization helps make learning and recalling commands easier.

Fig. 5.1.

The Format menu.

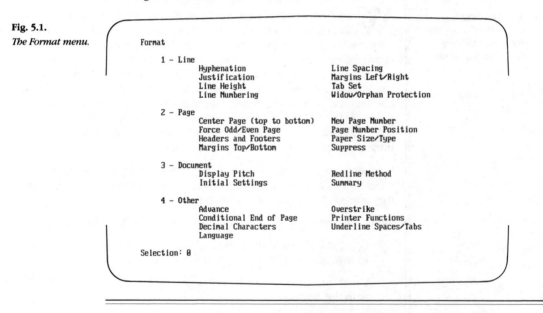

```
Format

      1 - Line
               Hyphenation              Line Spacing
               Justification           Margins Left/Right
               Line Height             Tab Set
               Line Numbering          Widow/Orphan Protection

      2 - Page
               Center Page (top to bottom)  New Page Number
               Force Odd/Even Page          Page Number Position
               Headers and Footers          Paper Size/Type
               Margins Top/Bottom           Suppress

      3 - Document
               Display Pitch           Redline Method
               Initial Settings        Summary

      4 - Other
               Advance                 Overstrike
               Conditional End of Page Printer Functions
               Decimal Characters      Underline Spaces/Tabs
               Language

      Selection: 0
```

TIP: In WordPerfect 4.2, three function keys were dedicated to formatting: Print Format (Ctrl-F8), Page Format (Alt-F8), and Line Format (Shift-F8). In WordPerfect 5, most of the functions have been moved to the new Format (Shift-F8) menu. Some of the functions on the old Print Format (Ctrl-F8) menu that were associated with Pitch/Font have been expanded and moved to the new Font key (Ctrl-F8), and the Sheet Feed Bin Number function has been moved to the Print key (Shift-F7).

Remember: If the function concerns formatting, you probably will use the Format key (Shift-F8) to do the job. You no longer have to guess, as you often did in WordPerfect 4.2, which format key to use.

WordPerfect presets all the initial or default settings for margins, tabs, and other basic features. If these settings do not fit your needs, you either can change the settings for the current document or use Setup (Shift-F1) to change many of the settings permanently.

Any changes made from the Setup menu are permanent and affect all new documents. The current document (if it contains text) and all previously created documents retain the default settings that were in place when you created those documents. Current and previously created documents do not reflect changes in the default settings. (Setup is discussed in more detail in Chapter 18 and Appendix A.)

When you are formatting and enhancing text, sometimes you will want to change only one document or a portion of one document. In this chapter, you will learn primarily how to make temporary changes that affect only your current document.

Changing Units of Measurement

The dimensions of pages and display monitors usually are defined in terms of columns (width) and rows (height). Most display monitors, for example, show 80 columns and 25 rows of text. You used to have to experiment in order to determine how many columns to include in your margins, how many columns to set in a line, and how many rows to leave for the top and bottom page margins. If you changed fonts, all calculations often were thrown off, and your printed document did not always turn out as expected. This process resulted in much wasted time.

WordPerfect 5 changes all this guesswork. Now, regardless of the font you choose, you can set absolute margins. You no longer have to calculate how many columns and rows fit on a page. In addition, you no longer need to take into account the size of the font in order to produce a printed page with perfect margins.

Examine the status line in the lower right corner of your WordPerfect screen. The screen should display something like the following (the numbers vary depending on where the cursor is positioned in your document):

Doc 1 Pg 1 Ln 1" Pos 1"

In WordPerfect 5, you can choose among the following options for units of measurement:

- " or i = inches. Inches are the best units for measuring margins and tabs. This is the default setting in WordPerfect 5.

- c = centimeters. One centimeter equals .39 inch; 1 inch equals 2.54 centimeters.

- p = points. One point equals .01384 inch or 1/72 inch; 72 points equal 1 inch. Because fonts often are measured in point sizes, use these units for measuring font height (especially with laser printers).

- u = WordPerfect 4.2 units (lines and columns). Most word processors and previous versions of WordPerfect used these units of measurement. Use this setting if your main printer is dot-matrix or letter quality, because these printers measure by lines and columns. If you have a laser printer, however, use either inches or points, because these units provide absolute control over character placement.

You easily can change the default units of measure setting from inches to one of the other available options. For example, you can use the following steps to change the units of measure for all new documents to WordPerfect 4.2 units (lines and columns):

1. Press Setup (Shift-F1).

2. From the Setup menu, choose Units of Measure (**8**).

3. From the Setup: Units of Measure menu (see fig. 5.2), choose **Display and Entry of Numbers for Margins, Tabs, etc.** (**1**), and then press *u* to select WordPerfect 4.2 Units (Lines/Columns).

Fig. 5.2.

The Setup: Units of Measure menu.

```
Setup: Units of Measure

    1 - Display and Entry of Numbers          "
            for Margins, Tabs, etc.

    2 - Status Line Display                   "


  Legend:

      " = inches
      i = inches
      c = centimeters
      p = points
      u = WordPerfect 4.2 Units (Lines/Columns)
```

4. Choose **Status Line Display** (**2**), and then press *u* to select WordPerfect 4.2 Units.

5. Press Exit (F7) to return to your document.

   The status line now should read as follows:

   Doc 1 Pg 1 Ln 1 Pos 1

The status line now gives you the cursor position in terms of WordPerfect 4.2 units (lines and columns).

The unit of measure you select for Display and Entry of Numbers for Margins, Tabs, etc. determines the units used in menu choices for hyphenation zone, margins (top, bottom, left, and right), tab settings, paper size, and display pitch. The unit of measure you select for Status Line Display determines what units are displayed in the status line at the lower right corner of the screen. If you change units of measurement, all unit displays, including those contained in hidden codes, automatically change to reflect the new choice.

Changing Left and Right Margins

WordPerfect 5 calculates margins differently than WordPerfect 4.2. Instead of the right margin being a certain number of characters from the left, the right margin is now a certain *distance* from the right edge of the paper. You now can set one-inch left and right margins, for example, without being concerned about the number of characters in the line of text. WordPerfect tracks the size of the font and automatically determines how many characters can fit on a line.

TIP: Unlike WordPerfect 4.2, the new version of WordPerfect measures margins from the edges of the paper. Simply measure your stationery or paper and decide how many inches of white space you want as margins. Because measuring in rows and columns is confusing and a matter of trial and error, set margins in inches.

After you have decided on your margins, you can change the margin settings for your current document, the document you are working on. When you enter a margin change, that change affects only text from that point forward. Text before the change retains the previous margins. If you want to change the margins for an entire document, go to the beginning of the document before setting the margins. (To move the cursor to the beginning of the document, press Home, Home, ↑.)

To change the margins in your current document, follow these steps:

1. Press Format (Shift-F8).

2. From the Format menu, select **Line** (**1**).

3. From the Format: Line menu (see fig. 5.3), select **Margins Left/Right** (**7**).

    The cursor moves to the right of the **Margins Left/Right** menu item. Notice that the left and right margins are calculated in inches.

4. Type a new value for the left margin and press Enter.

5. Type a new value for the right margin and press Enter.

6. Press Exit (F7) to return to your document.

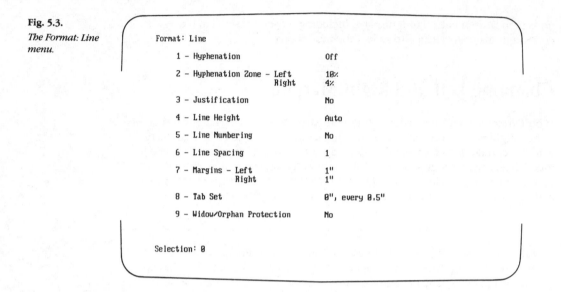

```
Format: Line

    1 - Hyphenation                    Off

    2 - Hyphenation Zone - Left        10%
                          Right        4%

    3 - Justification                  No

    4 - Line Height                    Auto

    5 - Line Numbering                 No

    6 - Line Spacing                   1

    7 - Margins - Left                 1"
                  Right                1"

    8 - Tab Set                        0", every 0.5"

    9 - Widow/Orphan Protection        No


Selection: 0
```

Changing Margins in Headers and Footers

You can set the left and right margins for footers and headers independently from the overall page margins. To change footer and header margins, complete the preceding steps while you are entering or editing a header or footer. Footers and headers are discussed in detail in Chapter 6.

Using Margin Release

Margin Release (Shift-Tab) releases the left margin and causes that margin to shift temporarily one tab stop to the left. This feature is particularly useful for creating lists. The number appears to the left of the margin, but the notation stays within the normal margins (see fig. 5.4).

To enter text to the left of the left margin, follow these steps:

1. Move the cursor to the left margin by pressing Enter or Home, ←.

2. Press Margin Release (Shift-Tab) to move the cursor one tab stop to the left. Press Margin Release (Shift-Tab) again if you want to move an additional tab stop to the left.

3. Type the text.

4. Press Tab to return to the normal left margin.

```
      Supplement List for Donna

   1.   Nature's Life Vitamin E 400 IU, 2 per day.
   2.   Liquid Calcium/Magnesium, 1 tablespoon per morning and evening
        (as needed for muscle cramping).
   3.   Vitamin B6, 100 mg, up to 3 times per day (as needed for water
        weight gain and bloating).
   4.   Add a minimum of one tablespoooat bran fiber to daily diet.



C:\WP50\QUE\FIG5.4                          Doc 2 Pg 1 Ln 2.16" Pos 4.5"
▲    (    ▲    ▲    ▲    ▲    ▲    ▲    ▲    ▲    ▲    ▲    }    ▲    ▲
[+Mar Rel]3.[Tab]Vitamin B6, 100 mg, up to 3 times per day (as needed for water[
SRt]
weight gain and bloating).[HRt]
[+Mar Rel]4.[Tab]Add a minimum of one tablespoon of [+Mar Rel]oat bran fiber to
daily diet.



Press Reveal Codes to restore screen
```

Fig. 5.4.

A list created with the Margin Release feature.

CAUTION: Don't press Margin Release (Shift-Tab) when your cursor is in the middle of a line of text. If you do, the text may not appear as you expect. Item 4 in figure 5.4 illustrates the unexpected results.

Indenting Text

An indent temporarily resets either the left or both the left and right margins. You can emphasize one or more paragraphs by offsetting them. To indent only the left margin, use Indent (F4); to indent both the left and right margins, use Left-Right Indent (Shift-F4).

CAUTION: Never use the space bar for indenting or tabbing. If your printer uses proportional typefaces, text will not align properly at the left indent or tab stop. Instead, use the Tab key or the appropriate Indent keys.

Indenting from the Left Margin

Use Indent (F4) to indent an entire paragraph one tab stop from the left margin. When you press Indent (F4), the cursor moves to the right one tab stop and temporarily resets the left margin. Everything you type until you press Enter is indented one tab stop. To indent more than one tab stop, press Indent (F4) more than once.

The Indent (F4) feature is useful when you are creating a list. You can, for example, indent and align a series of numbered blocks of text. If you use only the Tab key to indent the text next to a number, the second and consecutive lines of text are not indented. Instead, they wrap to the next line and align with the number. Figure 5.5 illustrates various types of indents.

Fig. 5.5.

A variety of indents created with the Indent (F4) and Left-Right Indent (Shift-F4) functions.

```
Schuyler W. Lininger, Jr., D.C.                    Fall Quarter

PRACTICAL NUTRITION OBJECTIVES

1.   Provide a foundation for the practice of nutritional
     therapeutics.
2.   Provide a rationale for the nutritional approach.
3.   Provide standards against which the efficacy of a therapeutic
     approach can be assessed and monitored.
4.   Offer a basis for the appreciation of the underlying relationship
     between biomechanical and biochemical functioning.

EVALUATION PROCESS

     The evaluation process will be based on the investigation of
     an assigned nutritional problem utilizing the scientific
     literature and a final examination. Grading will be on a
     straight percentage basis: 90-100 = A; 80-90 = B; etc.

     All papers must be typed on non-erasable paper.
     Papers are expected to be properly punctuated, to
     use proper grammar, and to be proofed for spelling
     errors.

C:\WP50\QUE\FIG5.5                              Doc 2 Pg 1 Ln 1" Pos 1"
```

Complete the following steps to create a list by using the Indent (F4) feature:

1. Move the cursor to the left margin.

2. Type the item number (for example: *1.*).

3. Press Indent (F4) and type the text of the item.

4. Press Enter to stop indenting and return to the normal margins.

Indenting from Both Margins

Use Left-Right Indent (Shift-F4) to indent a paragraph from both the right and left margins. When you press Left-Right Indent (Shift-F4), the cursor moves to the right one tab stop and temporarily resets both the left and right margins. Everything you type until you press Enter is indented one tab stop from the left margin and the same distance from the right margin. To indent from both margins more than one tab stop, press Left-Right Indent (Shift-F4) more than once (see fig. 5.5).

To indent a paragraph you already have typed, complete the following steps:

1. Place the cursor at the left margin and press Left-Right Indent (Shift-F4).

2. Then press ↓.

The paragraph appears indented from both margins.

Creating a Hanging Paragraph

You can create a hanging paragraph by using a combination of Margin Release (Shift-Tab) and Indent (F4). In a hanging paragraph, the first line is flush with the left margin and the rest of the paragraph is indented to the first tab stop (see fig. 5.6). Hanging paragraphs are useful in various reports, such as bibliographies.

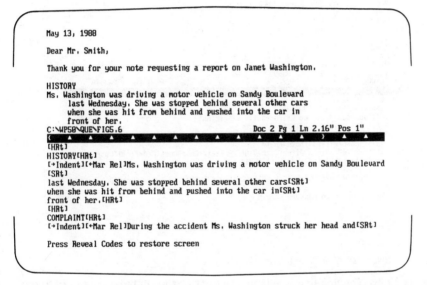

Fig. 5.6.

A hanging paragraph.

To create a hanging paragraph, you press Indent (F4) and then Margin Release (Shift-Tab) before you begin to type. Only the first line of the paragraph is outdented to the normal margins, and the rest of the paragraph is indented to the first tab stop. Pressing Enter restores the margins to their normal settings. Subsequent paragraphs are normal in appearance.

Complete the following steps to create a hanging paragraph:

1. Move the cursor to the left margin.

2. Press Indent (F4).

3. Press Margin Release (Shift-Tab).

4. Type your text.

5. Press Enter to end the hanging paragraph.

Setting Tab Stops

WordPerfect comes with tab stops predefined at intervals of one-half inch. Four basic types of tabs are available in WordPerfect: left, center, right, and decimal. In addition, each type of tab can have a *dot leader*, a series of periods before the tab. Figure 5.7 illustrates the various tab types.

Fig. 5.7.
Examples of tab types.

```
Invoice #:      12345
Date:           May 13, 1988
Ship to:        Bull Run Chiropractic Clinic

Tab Types:      Center      Center      Center      Right
Item            Qty         Cost        Total       Shipped?

Tab Types: . . Dot Leader  Decimal     Decimal     Right
Vitamin E. . . . . .4       1.19        4.76        Yes
Vitamin A. . . . . .6       1.88        6.48        Yes
Multiple . . . . . .4       3.99         .88        No
C:\WP50\QUE\FIG5.7                      Doc 2 Pg 1 Ln 1" Pos 1"
```

```
Invoice #:[Tab]12345[HRt]
Date:[Tab][Tab]May 13, 1988[HRt]
Ship to:[Tab][Tab]Bull Run Chiropractic Clinic[HRt]
[Tab Set:1",3",4",5",6.5"][HRt]
[BOLD]Tab Types:[Cntr]Center[C/A/Flrt][Cntr]Center[C/A/Flrt][Cntr]Center[C/A/Flr
t][Align]Right[C/A/Flrt][bold][HRt]
[Tab Set:1",3",4",5",6.5"]Item[Cntr]Qty[C/A/Flrt][Cntr]Cost[C/A/Flrt][Cntr]Total
[C/A/Flrt][Align]Shipped?[C/A/Flrt][HRt]
[HRt]
[Tab Set:1",3",4",4.1",5",5.1",6.5"][BOLD][bold][BOLD]Tab Types:[Cntr]Dot Leader

Press Reveal Codes to restore screen
```

Here is a description of WordPerfect's tab types:

- Left tabs. The first line is indented to the tab stop, and text continues to the right. Subsequent lines return to the normal left margin. Left tab is the most common tab type.

- Center tabs. Text is centered at the tab stop. A center tab works in a similar way as the Center (Shift-F6) feature, except a center tab can force centering anywhere in the line, not just in the center of the margins. Use center tabs to create column headings.

- Right tabs. After a right tab stop, text continues to the left. A right tab stop works in a similar same way as the Flush Right (Alt-F6) feature, except a right tab can be anywhere in the line, not just at the right margin. Use right tabs to create headings over columns of numbers or dates.

- Decimal tabs. After a decimal tab stop, text continues to the left until you type the alignment character; then text continues to the right. A decimal tab works in a similar way as the Tab Align (Ctrl-F6) feature, except you preset the alignment point as a tab stop. The default alignment character is a period; you can change this to any character you want. Use decimal tabs to line up columns of numbers.

- Tabs with dot leaders. Any of the four tab styles can be preceded by dots (periods) as a leader. Use dot leaders for long lists, such as phone lists, that require visual scanning from left to right.

Changing Tab Settings

You can use the Format menu to change the tab settings for only your current document. When you change the settings for the current document, the settings affect only the text from the point where you make the change. To change the entire document, you first must go to the beginning of the document and then reset the tab stops. (To move the cursor to the beginning of the document, press Home, Home, ↑.)

If you change the tabs after text has been entered, only left tabs reformat automatically. When you use left tabs, a **[Tab]** code that reflects the tab settings is inserted; the tab changes with any new tab settings. Center tabs insert **[Cntr][C/A/Flrt]** codes; right tabs insert **[C/A/Flrt]** codes; and decimal tabs insert **[Align][C/A/Flrt]** codes. These special codes do not replace normal **[Tab]** codes. Therefore, to change tabs to center, right, or decimal tabs, you not only must reset the tabs, but you also must delete the old **[Tab]** code and press Tab again to insert the proper codes.

A number of options are available for setting the tab stops. You can set tab stops one at a time, or you can specify the increment and set multiple tab stops. Similarly, you can delete a single tab stop, all the tab stops, or only the tabs to the right of the cursor. You can set tab stops across 8.5 inches of a page. If you want to set extended tabs (from 8.5 inches to 54.5 inches), you must set them individually. You can set a maximum of 40 tabs.

To change tab stops for the current document only, follow these steps:

1. Press Format (Shift-F8).

2. From the Format menu, select **Line (1)**.

3. From the Format: Line menu, select **Tab Set (8)**.

   The bottom of the screen displays a graphic representation of the current tab stops, called the *tab ruler* (see fig. 5.8).

```
L....L....L....L....L....L....L....L....L....L....L....L....L....L....L....L....
!    ^    !    ^    !    ^    !    ^    !    ^    !    ^    !    ^    !    ^
1"       2"       3"       4"       5"       6"       7"       8"
Delete EOL (clear tabs); Enter Number (set tab); Del (clear tab);
Left; Center; Right; Decimal; .= Dot Leader
```

Fig. 5.8.
The tab ruler.

4. *To delete a single tab stop*, use the cursor keys to move to the tab you want to delete; or type the number that represents how many units from the left margin the tab stop you want to delete is, and press Enter to position the

cursor on that tab stop. (The units can be inches, WordPerfect 4.2 units, points, or centimeters.) Press Del or Backspace to delete the tab.

or

To delete all the tab stops, move the cursor to the left margin (press Home, Home, ←), and press Delete to End of Line (Ctrl-End).

or

To delete the tab stops to the right of the cursor, type the number of units (inches, WordPerfect 4.2 units, points, or centimeters) from the point you want to delete tabs to the right and press Enter. Press Delete to End of Line (Ctrl-End).

5. *To add a single tab stop*, use the cursor keys to move the cursor to the position where you want a tab stop; or type the number that represents how many units from the left margin the tab stop you want to delete is, and press Enter to position the cursor on that tab stop. Press **Left** to add a left tab, **Center** to add a center tab, **Right** to add a right tab, or **Decimal** to add a decimal tab. To add a dot leader, type a period (.) before exiting.

or

To add multiple left tab stops, type the unit where you want the tabs to begin, a comma, and then the increment you want the tabs spaced. For example, to space tabs one-half inch apart beginning at one inch, type *1,.5* and press Enter.

or

To add multiple center, right, or decimal tab stops and dot leaders, use the cursor keys to move the cursor to the position where you want the tab stops to begin, or type the unit where you want the tabs to begin and press Enter. Then press **Center**, **Right**, or **Decimal**. If you want a dot leader, also type a period (.). Type the unit where you want the tab stops to begin, a comma, and then the increment you want the tabs spaced. For example, to space right-aligned tabs one-half inch apart beginning at one inch, position the cursor at one inch and press **Right**; then type *1,.5* and press Enter.

6. Press Exit (F7) twice to return to your document.

Comparing Tab to Indent

WordPerfect's Tab and indent features are similar in some ways, but each has specific uses. Table 5.1 lists the differences between these features.

Pressing Tab When Outline Is On

If you have turned on the Outline function, the Tab key causes changes in the hierarchy of an outline. A Roman numeral I, for example, might change to an A. If you encounter this unexpected result, be sure to turn off the Outline feature.

Table 5.1
Tab and Indent Uses

Feature	Function
Tab	Indent only the first line of a paragraph from the left margin.
Indent (F4)	Indent the entire paragraph from the left margin.
Left-Right Indent (Shift-F4)	Indent the entire paragraph equally from both margins.

Use the following steps to turn the Outline feature off or on:

1. Press Date/Outline (Shift-F5).

2. From the menu bar at the bottom of the screen, choose **Outline** (**4**) to turn the feature on or off.

   When the Outline feature is on, the word Outline appears in the lower left corner of the screen.

Chapter 21 discusses the Outline feature in more detail.

Displaying the Tab Ruler

If you want to see the current tab settings, you can use the Window feature to display a tab ruler at the bottom of the screen. Complete the following steps to display an on-screen tab ruler:

1. Press Screen (Ctrl-F3).

2. From the menu bar at the bottom of the screen, choose **Window** (**1**).

   The program displays the following prompt along with a number after the colon:

   Number of lines in this window:

   The number after the colon varies depending on the type of monitor you have or what number you entered for the /SS start-up option when you loaded WordPerfect. (For a complete discussion of start-up options, see Appendix A.)

3. Enter a number that is one less than the number in the prompt. For example, if the prompt displays 24, type *23*.

4. Press Enter.

A tab ruler appears at the bottom of the screen (see fig. 5.9). The curly braces, { and }, mark the left and right margins. The triangles mark the tab stops. Instead of braces, the program may display brackets, [and]. The brackets indicate that the tab stops have been changed from their default values.

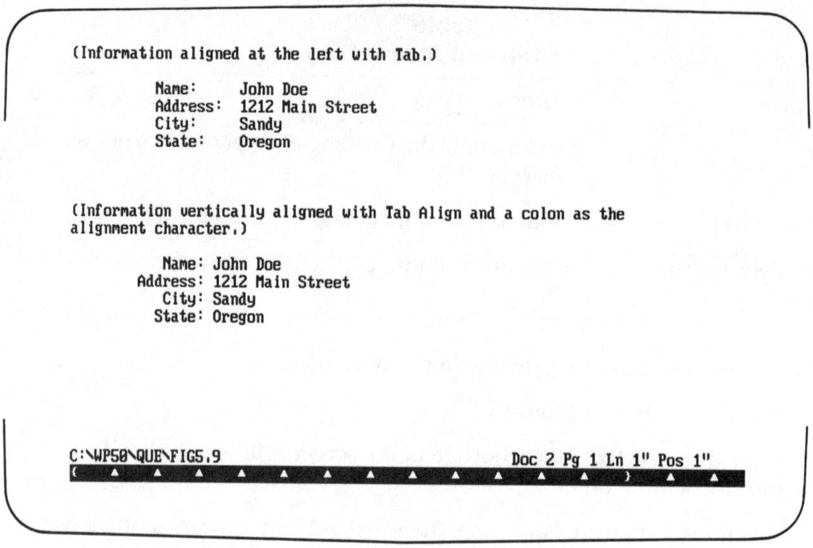

Fig. 5.9.

*The tab ruler
displayed at the
bottom of the screen;
examples of uses for
Tab and Tab Align.*

```
(Information aligned at the left with Tab.)

        Name:     John Doe
        Address:  1212 Main Street
        City:     Sandy
        State:    Oregon


(Information vertically aligned with Tab Align and a colon as the
alignment character.)

          Name: John Doe
       Address: 1212 Main Street
          City: Sandy
         State: Oregon




C:\WP50\QUE\FIG5.9                            Doc 2 Pg 1 Ln 1" Pos 1"
```

To eliminate the tab ruler, repeat the previous steps, but for Step 3, type one
more than the number the prompt displays.

Using Tab Align

Tab Align (Ctrl-F6) jumps the cursor to the right one tab stop. All text you type
moves to the left of the tab stop until you type the alignment character (the
default is a period). After you type the alignment character, the text begins
moving to the right of the tab stop. Figure 5.9 illustrates how information can be
aligned at the right with Tab Align.

Complete the following steps to create text aligned at the right on a specific
character:

1. Press Tab Align (Ctrl-F6).

   The cursor moves right one tab stop, and the following message appears in
   the lower left corner of the screen:

   Align char = .

2. Type your text.

3. Type the alignment character (in this case, a period).

   If you want to align text at the right without displaying the alignment
   character, you can press Tab Align (Ctrl-F6), type the text, and press Enter
   before pressing the alignment character. The typed text is right-justified at
   the tab stop.

TIP: You can use Tab Align (Ctrl-F6) to center text within defined text columns. To do so, position the cursor in the left margin of the column in which you want to center text, and then complete the preceding three alignment steps. (For a complete discussion of text columns, refer to Chapter 16.)

The alignment character can be any character you want. In the example in figure 5.9, the alignment character is a colon (:). To align names and addresses, use a colon. To align numbers, an equal sign (=) is best.

To change the alignment character temporarily for the current document only, follow these steps:

1. Press Format (Shift-F8).

2. From the Format menu, select **Other** (**4**).

3. From the Format: Other menu, select **Decimal/Align Character** (**3**).

   The cursor moves to the right of the **Decimal/Align Character** menu item.

4. Type a new alignment character and press Enter twice.

   (Do not change the character for the Thousands' Separator. See Chapter 17 for information about that option.)

5. Press Exit (F7) to return to your document.

Centering Text

Centering text with a typewriter can be a tedious task. With WordPerfect, you can perform this job easily. You can center a line of text either as you type it or after the text is entered.

To center a line of text that you are about to type, follow these steps:

1. Move the cursor to the left margin of a blank line.

2. Press Center (Shift-F6).

   The cursor jumps to the point midway between the two margins.

3. Type your text.

4. Press Enter.

If you type more characters than your margins can hold, the rest of the text wraps to a second line. Only the first line, however, is centered. To center several lines, use the Block function described in Chapter 4.

If you want to center text around a specific point on-screen, press the space bar until the cursor is at the point on which you want the text centered. Press Center (Shift-F6). Notice that the cursor does not move. Then begin typing.

If you want to center text within defined text columns, place the cursor in the left margin of the column in which you want the text centered. Then follow the preceding four steps for centering. Refer to figure 5.10 for examples of various types of text alignments.

Fig. 5.10.

Types of text alignments.

Centered within each of two columns

Flush right in left column

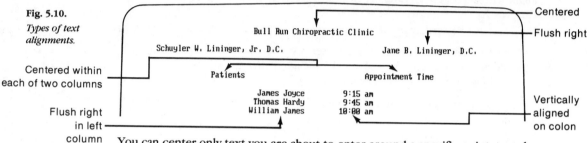

Centered

Flush right

Vertically aligned on colon

You can center only text you are about to enter around a specific point; text that is already entered cannot be centered around a specific point.

To center an existing line of text, the line must end with a Hard Return **[HRt]**. Check for the Hard Return, and then complete the following steps to center the text in a previously typed line:

1. Place the cursor at the left margin of the line of text you want to center.

2. Press Center (Shift-F6).

   The text jumps to the center of the screen.

3. Press ↓.

The text appears centered on-screen.

Making Text Flush Right

In certain documents, you might want text flush right for the far right heading of a series of columns, dates, or other business headings. Making a heading or other text flush with the right margin can be another grueling job with a typewriter. Again, WordPerfect automates this task and eliminates the difficulty. You can make text flush right either as you type it or after the text is entered.

Use the following steps to line up along the right margin the text you are about to type:

1. Move the cursor to the left margin.

2. Press Flush Right (Alt-F6).

   The cursor jumps to the right margin.

3. Type your text.

   The text you type travels from right to left.

4. Press Enter to stop typing text flush right.

CAUTION: If you type more characters than your margins can hold, the extra text travels to the left margin and beyond before wrapping to the next line (see fig. 5.11). This occurs because the Flush Right command takes precedence over any left margin command. Only the first line of text is flush right. If you want several lines of text to be right-aligned, use the Block function described in Chapter 4.

```
        This is an example of a line that begins in the left margin and
        goes to the right margin before "wrapping" to the next line.

        The next line is too long to be flush right. Notice what happens.

        n example of a line that is too long to have been flush right and
        extends beyond the left margin.



        C:\WP50\QUE\FIG5.11                    Doc 2 Pg 1 Ln 1.83" Pos 1"
        [  ▲   ▲   ▲   ▲   ▲   ▲   ▲   ▲   ▲   ▲   ▲   }   ▲   ▲ ]
        The next line is too long to be flush right. Notice what happens.[HRt]
        [HRt]
        [Flsh Rt]This is an example of a line that is too long to have been flush right
        and[C/A/Flrt][SRt]
        extends beyond the left margin.




        Press Reveal Codes to restore screen
```

Fig. 5.11.

Flush-right text that extends beyond the left margin.

To make an existing line flush right, the line must end with a Hard Return [**HRt**]. Check for the Hard Return, and then complete the following steps to make the text in a previously typed line flush right:

1. Position the cursor at the left margin.

2. Press Flush Right (Alt-F6).

    The line of text jumps to the right.

2. Press ↓.

The line appears flush right on-screen.

Using Right-Justification

Right-justification aligns the text on the printed page along the right margin. Text that is not justified in this way has a ragged right margin. Figure 5.12 is a printout that illustrates text with a ragged right margin and text that is right-justified.

Use right-justification when you have a printer capable of proportional spacing and you want a formal look. Hyphenation usually improves the appearance of justified text. If your printer is not capable of proportional spacing or if you want your document to be less formal, use ragged right printing.

Fig. 5.12.

Justified versus unjustified text, with and without hyphenation.

```
The next two paragraphs have justification turned off.

This line has so many characters that the very next
extraordinarily long word wraps to the next line, creating a gap
at the right margin.

Turn on hyphenation to improve the look of the text. The extraor-
dinarily long word is hyphenated, creating a visual appearance
that is much more attractive.


The next two lines have justification turned on.

This   line   has   so   many   characters   that   the   very   next
extraordinarily   long   word   wraps   to   the   next   line,   creating
unattractive gaps between words in the first line.

Turn on hyphenation to improve the look of the text. The extraordi-
narily long word is hyphenated, creating a visual appearance that
is much more attractive.
```

You cannot see right-justification on-screen. To see the effect of justification, you either must View the page (see this chapter's "Using Document Preview" section) or print the page. Because text is justified by adding spaces between words and letters, how attractive justified text looks depends on your printer.

TIP: Use hyphenation to reduce the white space between words. Hyphenating words makes justified text more attractive (see this chapter's "Using Hyphenation" section).

You can temporarily turn off right-justification by using the Format menu. To change the justification setting for the entire document, go to the top of the document first. (To move the cursor to the beginning of the document, press Home, Home, ↑.) If the cursor is within the body of the document, the new setting affects only the portion of the document after the cursor position.

To change the right-justification setting temporarily for the current document only, follow these steps:

1. Press Format (Shift-F8).

2. From the Format menu, select **Line** (**1**).

3. From the Format: Line menu, select **Justification** (**3**).

The cursor moves to the right of the Justification menu item.

4. Press *Y* (for yes) to justify text or *N* (for no) to leave text ragged right.

5. Press Exit (F7) to return to your document.

If you are not sure (or can't remember) whether justification is on or off, complete the preceding Steps 1 through 3 and check the setting. Then press Exit (F7) to return to your document.

Using Hyphenation

When a line of text becomes too long to fit within the margins, the last word in the line wraps to the next line. With short words, wrapping does not present a problem. With long words, however, the following problems can occur:

- If justification is off, a large gap can appear at the right margin, making the margin appear too ragged.

- If justification is on, large spaces between words become visually distracting.

Hyphenating a long word at the end of a line solves the problem and creates a visually attractive printed document. When you use WordPerfect's hyphenation feature, the program fits as much of the word as possible on one line before wrapping the balance of the word to the next line (see fig. 5.12). To control hyphenation, use one of WordPerfect's three possible settings: off, manual, or automatic.

Using Manual Hyphenation

When you select the Manual hyphenation option, WordPerfect prompts you to position the hyphen in any long word that needs to be broken. The following prompt appears at the bottom of the screen:

`Position hyphen; Press ESC`

A word that requires hyphenation follows the prompt, with the suggested hyphenation point marked by a hyphen (see fig. 5.13). You can respond to the prompt in any of three ways:

1. To accept the suggested hyphenation point, press the Esc key. The word is hyphenated at that point.

2. If the suggested hyphenation point is not acceptable, reposition the hyphenation point by moving the cursor left or right using the arrow keys. (The arrow keys move only a certain number of characters left or right.) When you have positioned the cursor to your satisfaction, press the Esc key.

3. If the word cannot be hyphenated satisfactorily, press Cancel (F1). Pressing Cancel (F1) permanently rejects hyphenation for that word. WordPerfect inserts the hidden code [/] before the word. You must manually delete this code before WordPerfect can hyphenate the word.

Fig. 5.13.

The prompt for Manual hyphenation at the bottom of the screen.

```
This paragraph has some irregular lines, and some will need hy-
phenation. If the hyphenation feature is set on manual, a prompt
will appear asking where you want to position the hyphen. Use the
arrow keys to position the hyphen, and then press Esc to place the
hyphen where you want it.

The upper paragraph already has been hyphenated. The lower para-
graph is in the process of being manually hyphenated. Notice the
prompt in the lower left portion of the screen.

This paragraph has some irregular lines, and some will need
hyphenation. If the hyphenation feature is set on manual, a prompt
will appear asking where you want to position the hyphen. Use the
arrow keys to position the hyphen, and then press Esc to place the
hyphen where you want it.




Position hyphen; Press ESC hy-phenation.
```

WordPerfect continues to prompt you for hyphenation points throughout the entire document. Manual hyphenation, therefore, can be tedious. In addition, because the hyphenation points suggested by WordPerfect are often incorrect, you can easily make mistakes in hyphenation. Keep a dictionary handy to verify syllable breaks.

Using Automatic Hyphenation

If you set hyphenation to Auto, WordPerfect uses an internal set of hyphenation rules to hyphenate words for you. Because many words are not covered by these rules, you are prompted to select hyphenation points for these words just as if you had chosen manual hyphenation. Because so many words either aren't covered or are hyphenated incorrectly by automatic hyphenation, the same advice applies for automatic hyphenation as applied to manual hyphenation. Keep a dictionary handy.

Changing the Hyphenation Setting

To change the hyphenation setting for the entire document, first go to the top of the document. (To move the cursor to the beginning of the document, press Home, Home, ↑.) If your cursor is within the body of the document, the new setting affects only the portion of the document following the cursor.

The default setting for hyphenation is off. To turn hyphenation either on or off temporarily for the current document, follow these steps:

1. Press Format (Shift-F8).

2. From the Format menu, select **Line** (**1**).

3. From the Format: Line menu, select Line **H**yphenation (**1**).

4. Make a selection from the menu that appears at the bottom of the screen:

    1 Off; **2** Manual; **3** Auto: 0

5. Press Exit (F7).

Interrupting Hyphenation

If you set hyphenation to either Manual or Auto, you are interrupted to hyphenate words while you type or edit. If you are being interrupted too much, use the steps in the preceding section to turn off hyphenation. Then wait until you complete the document before turning on hyphenation again. At that point, you can determine the proper syllable breaks for all the words in question.

If you want to interrupt the hyphenation process only briefly, press Exit (F7). Hyphenation is temporarily halted until the immediate command (such as scrolling or spell-checking) is completed. Use this feature when you turn on hyphenation and then begin spell-checking or scrolling. By pressing Exit (F7), you can complete the scroll or spell-check before resuming hyphenation.

Changing the Hyphenation Zone

WordPerfect comes with a preset hyphenation zone. When hyphenation is on, this zone determines whether a word should be hyphenated or wrapped to the next line. The hyphenation zone is preset in percentages of line length: the left hyphenation zone is preset at 10%; the right hyphenation zone is preset at 4%.

On a standard document page, 8.5 inches wide with a 1-inch left margin and a 1-inch right margin, a line of text can be 6.5 inches in length. The left hyphenation zone is .65" (10% of 6.5 inches), and the right zone is .26" (4% of 6.5 inches). If the line length becomes longer, the zones become larger but retain the same proportions.

The following examples illustrate how WordPerfect uses these zones in a standard document:

*   If the word begins at or before the left zone (.65 inches from the right margin) and continues past the right zone (.26 inches from the right margin), the word requires hyphenation. The word is too long to wrap without leaving a large gap.

- If the word begins at or after the left zone (.65 inches from the right margin) and continues past the right zone (.26 inches from the right margin), the word wraps to the next line. The word is either too short to hyphenate or short enough so that it won't leave a large gap.

You can customize the zones with the following effects:

- If you make the zone smaller, either by making the left zone a smaller percentage (for instance 9%) or the right zone a larger percentage (for instance 5%), more hyphenation is required. (The right zone should not exceed the left zone.) With justification off, a more even right margin is produced with a smaller hyphenation zone.

- If you make the zone larger, either by making the left zone a larger percentage (for instance 11%) or the right zone a smaller percentage (for instance 3%), less hyphenation is required. (The numbers should not exceed the margins.) With justification on, too large a hyphenation zone causes gaps in the line.

Refer to figure 5.14 for a better understanding of hyphenation zones.

Fig. 5.14.

Hyphenation zones

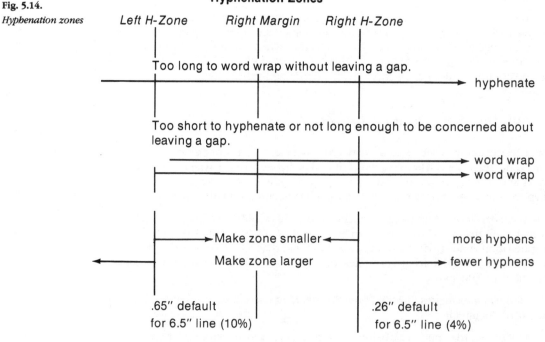

To change the hyphenation zone setting for the entire document, go to the top of the document first. (To move the cursor to the beginning of the document, press Home, Home, ↑.) If your cursor is positioned within the document, the new setting affects only the portion of the document following the cursor.

To change the hyphenation zones temporarily for the current document, follow these steps:

1. Press Format (Shift-F8).

2. From the Format menu, select **Line** (**1**).

3. From the Format: Line menu, select Hyphenation **Z**one Left/Right (**2**).

   The cursor moves to the right of the Hyphenation **Z**one Left/Right menu item.

4. Type a new value for the left zone and press Enter.

5. Type a new value for the right zone and press Enter.

6. Press Exit (F7).

Using the Optional Hyphenation Dictionary

If you plan to use WordPerfect's hyphenation feature, you should obtain the supplementary hyphenation dictionary. That dictionary solves many of the problems described in the sections on manual and automatic hyphenation. For details about ordering the dictionary, available from WordPerfect Corporation as an add-on, check the documents that came with your copy of WordPerfect 5.

The supplementary hyphenation dictionary supplied by WordPerfect Corporation includes the following files:

- WP{WP}EN.HYL contains an extensive hyphenation dictionary, available in several languages (the "EN" indicates the English version). Contact WordPerfect Corporation for details about other available language versions.

- WP{WP}EN.HYC and WP{WP}EN.HYD contain the code and exception information loaded into memory when hyphenation is turned on. If the program does not find the word in the exception dictionary, it uses either an algorithm or the extensive hyphenation dictionary.

- HYPHEN.EXE is a program file that allows you to create the exception dictionary (WP{WP}EN.HYD). You can specify words you either don't want hyphenated or words you want hyphenated in a particular way.

If you decide to use the supplemental hyphenation dictionary, you must specify where the program can find it. Complete the following steps to tell WordPerfect where to find the directory that contains the supplemental dictionary files:

1. Press Setup (Shift-F1).

2. From the Setup menu, choose **L**ocation of Auxiliary Files (**7**).

3. From the Setup: Location of Auxiliary Files menu, choose **H**yphenation Module(s) (**2**).

4. Type the drive and directory where you keep the hyphenation dictionary (such as C:\LEX) and press Enter.

5. Press Exit (F7) to return to your document.

Use experience as your guide to determine whether this supplementary dictionary is sufficiently comprehensive for your vocabulary and style of writing. If so, you may be able to turn on automatic hyphenation permanently. If not, you may need to turn on hyphenation just before printing in order to avoid being interrupted while writing.

Understanding the Types of Hyphens and Soft Returns

WordPerfect allows you to create several types of hyphens and dashes. While these hyphens and dashes may appear the same on-screen, they are interpreted by WordPerfect differently. So that you can determine which kind of hyphen or dash has been entered, you should edit text with Reveal Codes (Alt-F3, or F11) turned on. Table 5.2 shows the differences between the various types of hyphens and soft returns.

Table 5.2
Types of Hyphens and Soft Returns

Type	*Keystroke*	*Purpose*	*Hidden Code*
Hard hyphen	Hyphen key	Inserts a regular hyphen	[-]
Hyphen	Home, hyphen	Causes WordPerfect to treat a hyphenated word as a single word	-
Soft hyphen	Ctrl-hyphen	Inserts a hyphen that appears when a word breaks at the end of a line	Highlighted -
Dash	Home, hyphen, hyphen	Keeps two hyphens together	-[-]
Hard space	Home, space	Keeps two words together	[ ]
Invisible soft return	Home, Enter	Inserts a line break without hyphenating	[ISRt]
Deletable soft return	(no keystroke)	Forces a line break without hyphenating	[DSRt]

When you press the hyphen key, a *hard hyphen* is inserted into the document. That hyphen appears as [-] in Reveal Codes (Alt-F3, or F11). Hard hyphens always are visible on-screen and appear when the document is printed. If a hard hyphen appears in a word that needs to be hyphenated at the end of a line, WordPerfect uses the hard hyphen as the breaking point instead of prompting you.

When you press Home, hyphen, a *hyphen character* is inserted into the document. This character appears as an unhighlighted – in Reveal Codes (Alt-F3, or F11). Hyphen characters always are visible on-screen and appear when the document is printed. The program treats a hyphen character as part of the word, as if the hyphen were another character. If a hyphen character appears in a word being hyphenated by WordPerfect, you may be prompted for a hyphen breaking point.

Pressing Ctrl-hyphen inserts a *soft hyphen* into the document. That hyphen appears as a highlighted – in Reveal Codes (Alt-F3, or F11). Soft hyphens are inserted between syllables during hyphenation. You can insert your own soft hyphen at points you want hyphenation to occur. Soft hyphens are visible and print only when appearing as the last character in a line; otherwise, soft hyphens are hidden.

TIP: You can't produce a soft hyphen by using the numeric keypad's minus sign in combination with the Ctrl key. You must instead use the hyphen key at the top of the keyboard. Pressing the numeric keypad's minus sign by itself moves the cursor to the top of the screen. If you turn on Num Lock, you can produce a hard hyphen by pressing the numeric keypad's minus sign.

When you need to type a *dash*, use a combination of two types of hyphens. For the first hyphen, use the hyphen character (Home, hyphen). For the second hyphen, use a hard hyphen (press the hyphen key alone). This technique ensures that regardless of where the line breaks, the two hyphens stay together.

When you need to keep two or more words together, insert a *hard space* between the words. You can create a hard space by pressing Home, space. Words separated by hard spaces are not wrapped to the next line unless all the words joined by hard spaces are wrapped. Suppose, for example, that you always want the name of your business, Jones' Retail Hardware Supply, to appear on one line. You would type *Jones'*, press Home, space, type *Retail*, press Home, space, type *Hardware*, press Home, space, and type *Supply*. A hard space appears as [ ] in Reveal Codes (Alt-F3, or F11).

You can insert an *invisible soft return* manually when you want to control a line break. You may not want certain words to be broken by a hyphen or space, such as words that have a slash (and/or, either/or) or words connected with an ellipsis ("a great . . . fantastic film"). An invisible soft return breaks the line where you specify. If editing changes the line ending, the paragraph reformats; you don't have to remove the return.

If a line of text in WordPerfect 4.2 did not contain any spaces, there was no way to wrap it without hyphens. WordPerfect inserts a *deletable soft return* if hyphenation is off and a line doesn't fit between margins.

Removing Soft Hyphens

When you use manual or automatic hyphenation, WordPerfect inserts a soft hyphen at each point where a word can be hyphenated. Soft hyphens are displayed on-screen or printed by the printer if they appear at the end of a line of text; otherwise, they are hidden. If you later decide that you would like to have an unhyphenated document, you must remove these soft hyphens. Simply turning off hyphenation does not remove the hyphens already in place.

After turning off hyphenation, complete the following steps to remove the soft hyphens from a document:

1. Press Home, Home, ↑ to move the cursor to the beginning of the document.

2. Press Search and Replace (Alt-F2).

   The following prompt appears at the bottom of the screen:

   ```
   w/Confirm: (Y/N) No
   ```

3. Press Enter to select No.

   The following prompt appears at the bottom of the screen:

   ```
   Srch:
   ```

4. Press Ctrl-hyphen.

   Pressing this key combination creates a soft hyphen.

5. Press Forward Search (F2).

   The following prompt appears at the bottom of the screen:

   ```
   Replace with:
   ```

6. Press Forward Search (F2).

All the soft hyphens in the document are now removed.

Changing Line Height

The vertical distance between the base of a line of text and the base of the line of text above or below is called *line height*. Printers call line height *leading* because in the days of manual typesetting, the amount of space between lines was controlled by placing thin strips of lead between the lines. WordPerfect 5 automatically controls line height.

If you change point sizes, WordPerfect adjusts the line height. If you change the point size from 10 to 18, for example, the line height is also increased. If the line height were not adjusted, the vertical spacing would be too cramped for the 18-point type.

Automatic line height is calculated on a ratio of between 1.03 (for small point sizes) and 1.07 (for larger point sizes) of vertical height per point. Therefore, if you use a 10-point type, the line height is 10.62 points. The line height feature does not work on printers that can print only 6 lines per inch.

Because WordPerfect handles line height automatically, you usually don't need to adjust it manually. However, if you have a document that is 1 page plus 2 lines and you want all the text to fit on a single page, you could pick up the extra lines of text by reducing the line height. For instance, changing the line height to 10.18 gives you an extra 24.2 points on a 55-line page; that should be enough to fit the last 2 lines.

You do not see line height changes on-screen. To see the effect of any changes, you must either display the page with View Document (see this chapter's "Using Document Preview" section) or print the page. Figure 5.15, displayed with View Document, shows how line height changes are created automatically by WordPerfect when different fonts sizes are mixed on the same page.

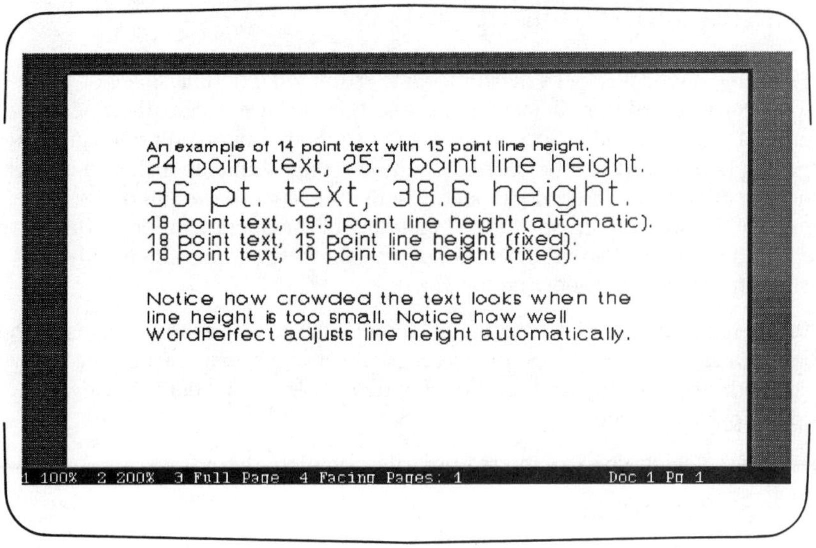

Fig. 5.15.
Line height changes displayed with View Document.

You can use the Format menu to change the line height temporarily for the current document only. Keep in mind that to change the line height for the entire document, you first must go to the top of the document. (To move the cursor to the beginning of the document, press Home, Home, ↑.) If the cursor is within the document, the new setting affects only the portion of the document following the cursor.

To change the default line height temporarily, complete these steps:

1. Press Format (Shift-F8).

2. From the Format menu, select Line (1).

3. From the Format: Line menu, select Line Height (4).

The following prompt appears at the bottom of the screen:

1 Auto; **2** Fixed: 0

4. Select Auto (**1**) to have WordPerfect calculate the line height automatically

or

Select Fixed (**2**) to enter a fixed line height. When prompted for a number, type a number with up to two decimal places, and then press Enter. Depending on what units of measurement you have selected, the number should be entered in inches, WordPerfect 4.2 units, centimeters, or points.

5. Press Exit (F7) to return to your document.

Changing Line Spacing

Single-spacing is WordPerfect's default for line spacing. To double-space or triple-space a document, you don't have to place two Hard Returns manually after each line. Instead, change the line spacing. You can use the Format menu to change the line spacing temporarily for the current document only. Remember that to change the line spacing for the entire document, you first must go to the top of the document. (To move the cursor to the beginning of the document, press Home, Home, ↑.) If the cursor is within the document, the new setting affects only the portion of the document following the cursor.

You do not see changes in line spacing on-screen except when the setting is a whole number such as 1, 2, or 3. To see the effect of any changes, you must either display the page with View Document (see this chapter's "Using Document Preview" section) or print the page.

To change the default line spacing temporarily, complete these steps:

1. Press Format (Shift-F8).

2. From the Format menu, select Line (**1**).

3. From the Format: Line menu, select Line Spacing (**6**).

   The cursor moves to the right of the Line Spacing menu item.

4. Type any number with up to two decimal places, and then press Enter.

   To double-space, type *2*. For one-and-a-half spaces between lines, type *1.5*. You can increase line spacing by small amounts by entering a number such as 1.02. Likewise, you can decrease line spacing by a small amount by entering a number that is less than 1, such as .95. Note: If the number you type reduces the line spacing too much, the lines of text may print partially one on top of another.

5. Press Exit (F7) to return to your document.

Enhancing Text

One of the exceptional features of WordPerfect 5 is the program's capability to get the most out of whatever printer you use. Although some text enhancements are evident on-screen (depending on your monitor), most are realized on the printed page. If you upgraded to WordPerfect 5 from WordPerfect 4.2, you should notice a new Font key (Ctrl-F8). This key changes the size and appearance of characters when they are printed.

Changing the Base Font

When you installed your printer, you selected an *initial font*, the default *base font*, or the *current font*. (You should consider these terms interchangeable to avoid confusion.) You choose the base font from a list of fonts available on your printer. Also, depending on the capabilities of your printer, you can change the base font's size and appearance.

To change the base font for the entire document, you first must go to the top of the document. (To move the cursor to the beginning of the document, press Home, Home, ↑.) If the cursor is within the document, the new setting affects only the portion of the document following the cursor.

To change the base font temporarily for only the current document, follow these steps:

1. Press Font (Ctrl-F8).

2. From the menu bar that appears at the bottom of the screen, choose Base Font (4).

   The Base Font menu appears, listing all the fonts that the selected printer can use (see fig. 5.16).

   Depending on the printer, the program may offer several screens of font choices. To access successive screens, scroll with the ↓. The highlighted font with an asterisk to its left is the current base font.

3. Press **Name Search (N)**, type the first letters of the font you want, and press Enter

   or

   Use the cursor keys to highlight the font you want.

4. Press Enter to change the base font and return to your document.

Fig. 5.16.

The Base Font menu.

```
Base Font

    Roman 05 Pitch
    Roman 10 Pitch
    Roman 15 Pitch
    Roman 17 Pitch
  * Roman 9 pt. PS
    Roman Italic 05 Pitch
    Roman Italic 10 Pitch
    Roman Italic 15 Pitch
    Roman Italic 17 Pitch
    Roman Italic 9 pt. PS
    Sans Serif 05 Pitch
    Sans Serif 10 Pitch
    Sans Serif 15 Pitch
    Sans Serif 17 Pitch
    Sans Serif 9 pt. PS
    Sans Serif Italic 05 Pitch
    Sans Serif Italic 10 Pitch
    Sans Serif Italic 15 Pitch
    Sans Serif Italic 17 Pitch
    Sans Serif Italic 9 pt. PS
    Script 05 Pitch

  1 Select; N Name search: 1
```

Using Proportional Spacing

Some printers allow proportional spacing—a feature that gives a printed page a more pleasing appearance by allowing for the different widths of characters. The letter *w*, for example, is wider than the letter *i*. Normally, when these letters are printed, both are given the same amount of space; the result can be gaps that are visually distracting. With proportional printing, the letter *w* is given more space than the letter *i*, creating a more aesthetic and professional looking line of text.

When you examine the list of fonts available with your printer, notice any that have proportional spacing; these are designated by the initials *PS* or the word *Proportional*. The list in figure 5.16 shows several available proportional fonts, including Roman 9 pt. PS and Sans Serif 9 pt. PS. If no fonts have the PS designation, either the printer does not allow proportional printing or WordPerfect does not support proportional printing for that particular printer.

TIP: Because proportional spacing often slows down a printer, use a nonproportional font for drafts of the document and reserve the proportionally spaced font for the final printing. Examine figure 5.17 and compare the examples of draft and proportional printing.

Choosing Font Attributes

WordPerfect divides font attributes into two categories: size and appearance. When you alter the size or appearance, the Pos indicator in the lower right portion of the

```
This line is printed in Sans Serif 10 Pitch on an Epson LQ-850 dot-
matrix printer in high text quality mode.

This line is printed in Sans Serif 9 pt. PS (proportional space) on an Epson LQ-
850 dot-matrix printer in high text quality mode.
```

Fig. 5.17.

Examples of draft and proportional printing on a dot-matrix printer.

screen takes on the characteristics of your choice. How the Pos indicator and the text look on-screen depends on what kind of monitor and display card you have. Both the Pos indicator and the text on-screen look the same.

Changing the Font Size

You can make the font size smaller or larger. Make a font smaller, for instance, for a footnote number or a mathematical formula. Make a font larger to emphasize a heading, column head, title, or letterhead.

To change the size of the base font, complete these steps:

1. Press Font (Ctrl-F8).

2. From the menu at the bottom of the screen, choose Size (**1**).

    Another menu, one with seven size attributes, appears at the bottom of the screen:

    1 Suprscpt; **2** Subscpt; **3** Fine; **4** Small; **5** Large; **6** Vry Large; **7** Ext Large

3. Choose any one of the attributes to change the size of the base font.

Keep in mind that WordPerfect automatically tracks the vertical height of the larger or smaller letters and adjusts the margins and the number of lines per page. Larger fonts use more vertical space and allow fewer letters per line; smaller fonts use less vertical space and allow more letters per line. Depending on your printer's capabilities, changing sizes has the following effects on a font:

Superscript reduces the size of the base font and places text slightly above the line of printed text. Use this option for footnote numbers and mathematical formulas.

Subscript reduces the size of the base font and places text slightly below the line of printed text. Use this option for mathematical formulas.

Fine and *Small* decrease incrementally the size of the base font.

Large, Very Large, and *Extra Large* increase incrementally the size of the base font.

Figure 5.18 illustrates some of these font size options.

Fig. 5.18.

Mixed font sizes and appearances.

> Produced on an Epson LQ-850 dot-matrix printer, the next line
> demonstrates the mixing of font sizes and appearance attributes on
> a single line.
>
> underline, **bold**, *italic*, SMALL CAPS, fine, large, double underline

Changing the Font Appearance

To emphasize certain text, you can change a font's appearance. Appearance changes such as outline, shadow, small capital letters, bold, italic, and underline are appropriate for headings, titles, letterhead, book and magazine titles, foreign words, and captions. Appearance changes such as strikeout and redline emphasize document changes and revisions.

To change the appearance of any font, follow these steps:

1. Press Font (Ctrl-F8).

2. From the menu at the bottom of the screen, choose **Appearance** (**2**).

   Another menu, one with nine appearance attributes, is displayed at the bottom of the screen:

   1 Bold; **2** Undrln; **3** Dbl Und; **4** Italc; **5** Outln; **6** Shadw; 7 Sm Cap; **8** Redln; 9 Stkout

3. Choose any one of the appearance attributes to change a font's appearance.

In general, changing appearance has the following effects on a font:

Bold darkens the font just as the Bold key (F6) does. Using the Bold key (F6) to turn the bold appearance attribute on and off takes fewer keystrokes than using the Font (Ctrl-F8) menu.

Underline turns underlining on just as the Underline key (F8) does. Using the Underline key (F8) to turn underlining on and off takes fewer keystrokes than using the Font (Ctrl-F8) menu.

Double Underline underlines text twice.

WordPerfect underlines spaces but does not underline tabs. If you want to change this feature, see this chapter's "Changing the Defaults for Underlining" section.

Text marked as *Italic* is printed in italics.

Outline and *Shadow* create special effects that depend on the printer.

When you choose *Small Capitals*, all text is printed in small capital letters.

Redline and *Strikeout* mark over text in certain ways that depend on the printer.

Placing Different Size Fonts on the Same Line

You can mix more than one appearance attribute with various font size attributes. Your printer determines whether or not these combinations work. Test your printer's capabilities by printing the file called PRINTER.TST included with the WordPerfect program. For instructions on how to print this file, see Chapter 8.

Changing the Defaults for Underlining

WordPerfect does not underline tab spaces but does underline spaces between words unless you change the default settings. You can use the Format menu to change these default settings temporarily for the current document only. Remember that to change the default underlining settings for the entire document, you first must go to the top of the document. (To move the cursor to the beginning of the document, press Home, Home, ↑.) If the cursor is within the document, the new settings affect only the portion of the document following the cursor.

To change the underlining defaults temporarily for the current document only, follow these steps:

1. Press Format (Shift-F8).

2. From the Format menu, select **Other** (**4**).

3. From the Format: Other menu, select Underline Spaces/Tabs (**7**).

   The cursor moves to the right of the Underline Spaces/Tabs menu item.

4. Press either *Y* (for yes) or *N* (for no) for each item.

5. Press Exit (F7) to return to your document.

Restoring Font Size and Appearance to Normal

You can end a change in font size and appearance in two ways. The best method for removing the attributes depends on how many you have used. After you remove the attributes, text is restored to the default font size and appearance.

When you have made a combination of attribute changes, use the first method for restoring font size and appearance to normal. From the Font (Ctrl-F8) menu, choose Normal (**3**). This selection cancels all size and appearance attributes.

When only one attribute is on, use this second method. Use Reveal Codes (Alt-F3, or F11) to display the attributes that are turned on. Note that each size or appearance attribute has a paired code. The capitalized code turns the attribute on; the lowercase one turns the attribute off. Press → to move the cursor past the attribute off code. If you have several attributes on at the same time, you need to press → enough times to move the cursor past all the codes.

Using Advanced Printer Features

You can use any of four advanced printer features to modify the way your text appears when printed. For the most part, you do not need to change WordPerfect's defaults. Once you become comfortable with these features, you can experiment with the settings on the Format: Printer Functions menu (see fig. 5.19) and observe how your document changes.

Fig. 5.19.
The Format: Printer Functions menu.

```
Format: Printer Functions

    1 - Kerning                              No

    2 - Printer Command

    3 - Word Spacing                         Optimal
        Letter Spacing                       Optimal

    4 - Word Spacing Justification Limits
          Compressed to (0% - 100%)          60%
          Expanded to (100% - unlimited)     400%
```

The first option on the Format: Printer Functions menu is **Kerning (1)**. You can turn the kerning feature on or off by specifying Yes or No. *Kerning* is the subtle altering of spaces between letters to achieve a better visual appearance. Kerned letters are unequally spaced according to a mathematical model.

Some letters take up more space than others, and normally this inequity does not present a problem. With larger point sizes, however, certain letter combinations are visually distracting when you use the default letter spacing. For instance, the letters T and *i* together can create a visual distraction. The letter T has a horizontal bar that acts as a roof. The letter *i* looks better tucked under that roof rather than spaced in the normal way. This tucking of specific letter pairs is called *kerning*. Kerning does not occur for all letter pairs—only for those defined by the font supplier. Note that monospaced typefaces (such as Courier) allow the same amount of space for each character and cannot be kerned.

The **Printer Command (2)** option, which is discussed in detail in Chapter 9, lets you send instructions directly to the printer either as a command or as a file. Any instructions you send are embedded as **[Ptr Cmnd:]** codes and remain in the document. When the program encounters a **[Ptr Cmnd:]** code, the instructions you entered are sent to the printer. The capabilities of your printer determine whether such instructions are necessary and whether advanced features are available.

When you select **Word Spacing/Letter Spacing (3)**, a Word Spacing menu appears at the bottom of the screen. That menu offers you four choices:

- **Normal (1)** sets the letter spacing at the width considered optimal by the manufacturer of the printer.

- **Optimal (2)** resets the letter spacing to the default width considered optimal by WordPerfect Corporation.

- **Percent of Optimal (3)** lets you modify spacing according to your taste or needs. At the prompt, enter a negative number to reduce the amount of space between letters and words or enter a positive number to increase the space. Zero is the same as the optimal (default) setting. Your printer may not work with the setting you choose. If you choose a setting that won't work, WordPerfect adjusts the setting.

- Pitch (4) changes the pitch (the number of characters per inch).

Selecting Word Spacing Justification Limits (4) turns on this feature and embeds in the text the following hidden code:

[Just Lim:nn,nnn]

This code affects the document from the point of insertion and on. With the Word Spacing Justification feature, you can expand or compress spacing between words and letters to justify a line of text. Once selected, enter figures for Compressed to (0%-100%) and Expanded to (100%-unlimited). For unlimited compression or expansion, type 999%. (Note: Right-justification must be on in order for this feature to have an effect.)

To make changes on the Format: Printer Functions menu, follow these steps:

1. Press Format (Shift-F8).

2. From the Format menu, select **Other** (4).

3. From the Format: Other menu, choose **Printer Functions** (6).

   The Format: Printer Functions menu appears.

4. Select any of the four options and make changes accordingly.

5. Press Exit (F7) to return to the editing screen.

Using Document Preview

WordPerfect displays text on-screen in standard-size characters. Depending on your monitor, you may see specific attributes such as bold or italic; you may not see other attributes. WordPerfect does not, for example, display 32-point text on-screen. You therefore have to guess in order to determine what the final document will look like.

To see how each attribute is displayed on your monitor and to make any desired changes, complete the following steps:

1. Press Setup (Shift-F1).

2. From the Setup menu, select **Display** (3).

3. From the Setup: Display menu, select **Colors/Fonts/Attributes** (2).

4. From the Setup: Colors menu, select **Screen Colors** (1).

   The Setup: Colors Attribute screen shows how each attribute looks on your monitor. Depending on your monitor, you can customize each attribute display.

5. Use the cursor keys to move to any attribute you want to change and press Switch (Shift-F3).

Watch how the sample changes on your monitor. You can keep pressing Switch (Shift-F3) until each attribute appears as you want it.

6. When you have finished examining or changing attributes, press Exit (F7) twice to return to the document screen.

Accurate judging of what the page will look like when printed cannot be done merely by looking at the regular WordPerfect screen. With a graphics monitor, however, you can use the View command to display on-screen a picture of the final page. You cannot edit the page, but you can view it, edit it, and then view it again.

To use the View command, follow these steps:

1. Press Print (Shift-F7).

2. Select View Document (6).

The screen displays a graphic representation of the page. Look at figure 5.20 for an example of a document displayed on an EGA monitor with the View command.

Fig. 5.20.

The View Document screen using an EGA monitor.

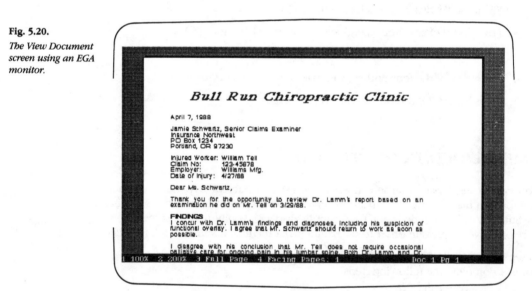

Quick Start

Formatting and Enhancing Text

This Quick Start teaches you how to enhance the visual appearance of the printed page. Use the Quick Start to try new procedures and learn them quickly. If you need more information, refer to the detailed instructions in the chapter. So that you will have some text to work with as you complete the Quick Start, type the following:

Rules of Success

1. *A positive mental attitude.*

2. *Definiteness of purpose.*

3. *Personal initiative.*

4. *Enthusiasm.*

5. *Creative vision.*

"Take your mind off the things you don't want and put it on the things you do want. Every adversity carries within it the seed of equivalent or greater opportunity."

Changing Margins

You can change the margins of your page to suit your own preferences. Change the margins for the sample document so that the printed page has a 2-inch margin on the left and a 1.5-inch margin on the right. Complete the following steps to change the margins:

1. Press Home, Home, ↑ to move the cursor to the beginning of the document.

2. Press Format (Shift-F8).

3. From the Format menu, select **Line** (**1**).

4. From the Format: Line menu, select **Margins Left/Right** (**7**).

5. Type *2* and press Enter.

6. Type *1.5* and press Enter.

7. Press Exit (F7) to return to the document.

When you print this document, the left margin will be 2 inches wide, and the right margin will be 1.5 inches wide. Position your cursor under the R in Rules and check the Pos indicator. It should read 2", as shown in figure 5.21.

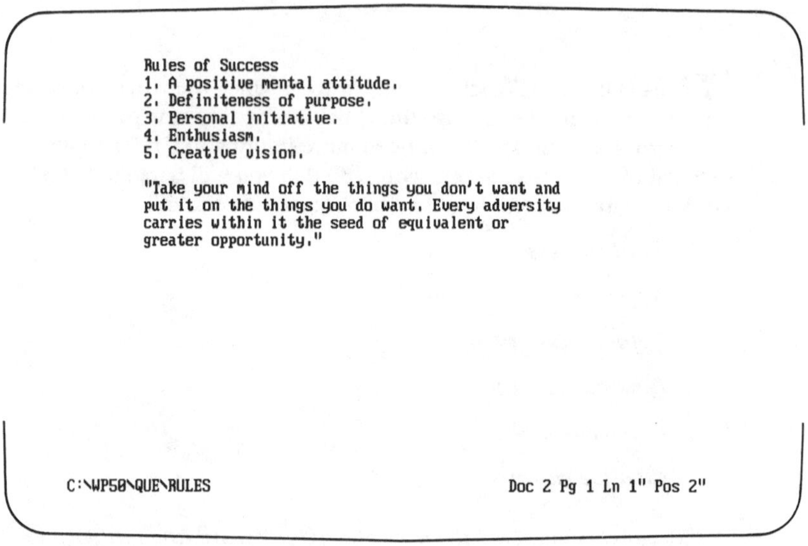

Fig. 5.21.

Inches shown as the unit of measurement in the Pos indicator.

```
Rules of Success
1. A positive mental attitude.
2. Definiteness of purpose.
3. Personal initiative.
4. Enthusiasm.
5. Creative vision.

"Take your mind off the things you don't want and
put it on the things you do want. Every adversity
carries within it the seed of equivalent or
greater opportunity."




C:\WP50\QUE\RULES                               Doc 2 Pg 1 Ln 1" Pos 2"
```

Centering Text

Next you will center the title of your sample document. Complete the following steps to center the title between the margins:

1. Position the cursor under the R in Rules.

2. Press Center (Shift-F6).

   The cursor and title jump to the center of the screen.

3. Press ↓ to center the title.

The title is now centered between the margins (see fig. 5.22).

```
                    Rules of Success
1, A positive mental attitude,
2, Definiteness of purpose,
3, Personal initiative,
4, Enthusiasm,
5, Creative vision,

"Take your mind off the things you don't want and
put it on the things you do want, Every adversity
carries within it the seed of equivalent or
greater opportunity,"
```

Fig. 5.22.
The title centered between the margins.

Using Margin Release

You can read numbered lists easier if the numbers appear in the margin. Use Margin Release (Shift-Tab) to place the numbers in the margin, one tab stop to the left:

1. Use the arrow keys to move the cursor to the first numbered item.

2. Press Home, ← to move the cursor to the left margin.

3. Press Margin Release (Shift-Tab) to move the line one tab stop to the left.

The first item of the list moves one tab stop to the left of the left margin. The Pos indicator now should read 1.5". Check your results by comparing your screen to figure 5.23.

```
                    Rules of Success
1, A positive mental attitude,
   2, Definiteness of purpose,
   3, Personal initiative,
   4, Enthusiasm,
   5, Creative vision,

   "Take your mind off the things you don't want and
   put it on the things you do want, Every adversity
   carries within it the seed of equivalent or
   greater opportunity,"




C:\WP50\QUE\RULES              Doc 2 Pg 1 Ln 1,16" Pos 1,5"
```

Fig. 5.23.
A numbered item moved left of the left margin.

Showing the Tab Ruler

The tab ruler, a useful visual aid, shows you the location of your margins and tabs. Complete the following steps to make the tab ruler visible on-screen:

1. Press Screen (Ctrl-F3).

2. From the menu at the bottom of the screen, choose **Window (1)**.

   The following prompt is displayed:

   Number of lines in this window:

3. Type a number that is one less than the number currently following the prompt. (For example, if the prompt displays 24, type *23*.)

4. Press Enter.

A tab ruler appears at the bottom of the screen, as shown in figure 5.24. The curly braces, { and }, mark the left and right margins. The triangles mark the tab stops. In the figure, notice that the tab stops are set at one-half-inch intervals.

Fig. 5.24.

The tab ruler displayed.

```
                                Rules of Success
                     1.  A positive mental attitude,
                         2, Definiteness of purpose,
                         3, Personal initiative,
                         4, Enthusiasm,
                         5, Creative vision,

                         "Take your mind off the things you don't want and
                         put it on the things you do want, Every adversity
                         carries within it the seed of equivalent or greater
                         opportunity,"




C:\WP50\RULES                                    Doc 1 Pg 1 Ln 1,16" Pos 2"
```

Using Tabs

You have shifted the first item to the left of the margin. Now complete the following steps to line up the item of text on a tab stop:

1. Using the arrow keys, place the cursor under the A in the first item.

2. Press Tab.

The Ɐ lines up at the left curly brace. The brace is the symbol for the left margin (see fig. 5.24). The Ⱥ also lines up over the left side of the other numbered items.

Using Indent

In addition to Margin Release (Shift-Tab), you can use WordPerfect's Indent functions to call attention to a list or quotation. You can indent from the left margin or both the left and right margins. Complete the following steps to indent the quotation in the sample document from both margins:

1. Using the arrow keys, move the cursor to the first quotation mark in the quotation.

2. Press Left-Right Indent (Shift-F4).

   The first line of the paragraph shifts to the first tab stop.

3. Press the ↓.

The entire paragraph indents one tab stop from both the right and left margins (see fig. 5.25).

Fig. 5.25.
The quotation indented from both the left and right margins.

```
                        Rules of Success
           1.   A positive mental attitude.
                2. Definiteness of purpose.
                3. Personal initiative.
                4. Enthusiasm.
                5. Creative vision.

                   "Take your mind off the things you don't
                   want and put it on the things you do
                   want. Every adversity carries within it
                   the seed of equivalent or greater
                   opportunity."




C:\WP50\RULES                           Doc 1 Pg 1 Ln 2.66" Pos 5.8"
```

Making Text Flush Right

Lining up text with the right margin is another way to add emphasis. Complete the following steps to line up one of the item numbers flush with the right margin:

1. Using the arrow keys, place the cursor under the 2 in the second numbered item.

2. Press Flush Right (Alt-F6).

The line jumps to the right margin.

3. Press the ↓.

The line is flush with the right margin (see fig. 5.26).

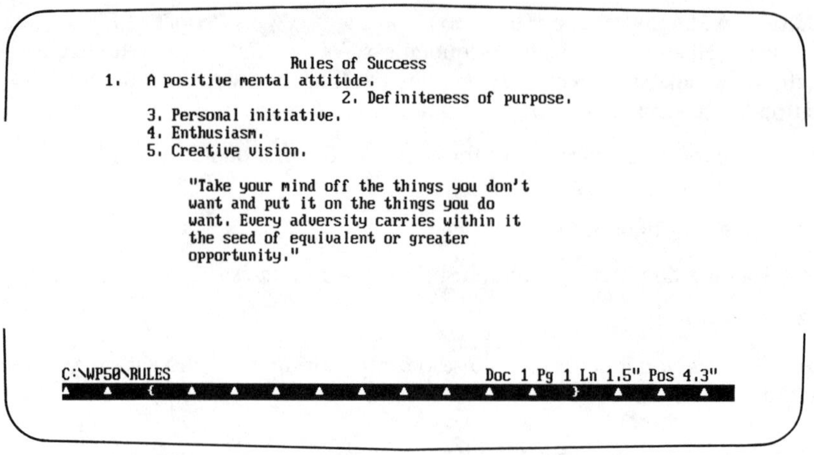

Fig. 5.26.

A line of text flush right.

```
                              Rules of Success
              1.   A positive mental attitude.
                                    2. Definiteness of purpose.
                   3. Personal initiative.
                   4. Enthusiasm.
                   5. Creative vision.

                   "Take your mind off the things you don't
                   want and put it on the things you do
                   want. Every adversity carries within it
                   the seed of equivalent or greater
                   opportunity."




C:\WP50\RULES                                    Doc 1 Pg 1 Ln 1.5" Pos 4.3"
```

Changing Line Spacing

Next you will change the line spacing of your sample document. Complete the following steps to make the entire document double-spaced:

1. Move the cursor to the beginning of the document by pressing Home, Home, ↑.

2. Press Format (Shift-F8).

3. From the Format menu, select Line (**1**).

4. From the Format: Line menu, select Line Spacing (**6**).

5. Type *2* and press Enter.

6. Press Exit (F7) to return to your document.

The entire document is now double-spaced (see fig. 5.27).

Changing Font Size

WordPerfect lets you change the font size of the text. The *font size* is the size of the characters when the document is printed. Complete the following steps to add a sentence in a larger font size to your sample document:

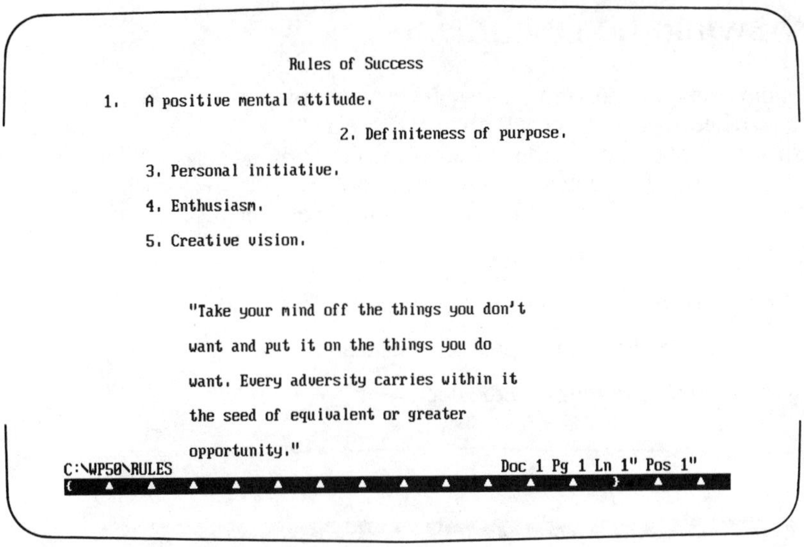

Fig. 5.27.
A double-spaced document.

```
                   Rules of Success
    1.   A positive mental attitude.

                        2. Definiteness of purpose.

        3. Personal initiative.

        4. Enthusiasm.

        5. Creative vision.


            "Take your mind off the things you don't

            want and put it on the things you do

            want. Every adversity carries within it

            the seed of equivalent or greater

            opportunity."
C:\WP50\RULES                            Doc 1 Pg 1 Ln 1" Pos 1"
```

1. Press PgDn and then Enter to move the cursor to a new line on the page.

2. Press Font (Ctrl-F8).

3. Choose Size (**1**).

4. Choose Vry Large (**6**).

5. Type the following sentence:

    "What the mind can conceive and believe, it can achieve."

Changing Font Appearance

Not only can you change the size of the font, but you also can change its appearance. To add a sentence in an italic font to your sample document, follow these steps:

1. Press PgDn and then Enter to move the cursor to a new line on the page.

2. Press Font (Ctrl-F8).

3. Choose **Appearance** (**2**).

4. Choose **Italc** (**5**).

5. Type the following sentence:

    "Success depends on the willingness to go the extra mile."

Previewing the Document

Your equipment (monitor and printer) determines how text enhancements, such as font appearance, look on-screen. With WordPerfect's View Document command, you can see an approximation on-screen of what the printed page will look like. Note that you must have a graphics monitor in order to preview a document. Complete the following steps to preview the sample document:

1. Press Print (Shift-F7).

2. Select View Document (6).

   The screen displays a graphic representation of the page (see fig. 5.28).

3. Press any key to return to the document.

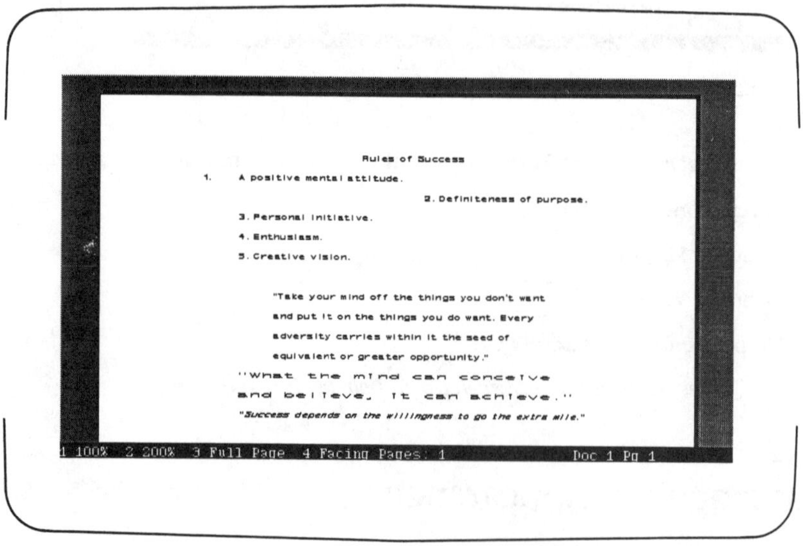

Fig. 5.28.

The View Document screen for the sample document, using an EGA monitor.

Summary

In this chapter you learned about the powerful and easily accessible features that WordPerfect 5 offers for formatting and enhancing documents. You now should be able to perform the following tasks in order to control how text appears on the printed page:

- Alter the units of measurement from inches to WordPerfect 4.2 units, points, or centimeters

- Change the left and right margins, use the margin release function, and indent text

- Change tab settings and tab types (left, right, center, decimal, and dot leader)

- Center text, make text flush right, turn justification on or off, and change line spacing and leading

- Use the hyphenation feature, change the hyphenation zone, and use the optional supplementary hyphenation dictionary

You also should be able to take advantage of your printer's capabilities by using the following procedures:

- Enhance text using font attributes such as size and appearance

- Use advanced printer functions such as letter spacing

- Verify formatting with the document preview function

6

Formatting Pages and Designing Documents

Karen Rose is the owner of Write on Target, a newsletter production and management company in Santa Rosa, CA. Write on Target produces monthly, bimonthly, and quarterly newsletters using the latest desktop-publishing technologies. ■

Whether you're a boss looking at a memo, a client looking at a report, or an employer looking at a résumé, you form a first impression of the page in your hands. And your decision whether to read the page or to put it down may depend on how that page looks.

First impressions count. Someone who just looks at text decides quickly whether to read in more detail. That choice often depends on whether a page looks friendly, inviting, and easy to read.

Ease of reading is clarity. When you look at a page, is it clear what type of information the page contains? Is it clear what page you're reading? Is it clear where you must turn for more information? Is it clear where sections begin and end?

In Chapter 6, you learn to use WordPerfect formatting features to design documents that are clear, interesting, and—above all—readable. If you need to know how to format documents quickly, see the Quick Start at the end of the chapter first, and then read the entire chapter.

Formatting Pages

Designing a document means making formatting choices at several levels. At the most global level, you make formatting choices for the entire document. At the next level, you make formatting choices for pages or groups of pages.

Page formatting includes decisions about how the pages in your document look. What are top and bottom margins? Is text centered, top to bottom, on the page? Are there headers and footers, and if so, on which pages? Are there automatic page numbers, and if so, where on the page do they appear? Is there text or a chart that must be kept together on a page? Must pages start at a certain point in the text?

185

WordPerfect conveniently includes most formatting choices in the Format menu, shown in figure 6.1. The Format Menu is displayed when you press the Format key (Shift-F8).

Fig. 6.1.

Format menu.

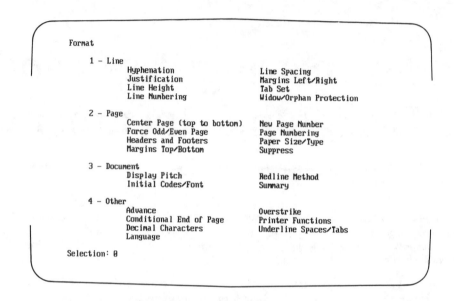

```
Format

    1 - Line
              Hyphenation                 Line Spacing
              Justification               Margins Left/Right
              Line Height                 Tab Set
              Line Numbering              Widow/Orphan Protection

    2 - Page
              Center Page (top to bottom) New Page Number
              Force Odd/Even Page         Page Numbering
              Headers and Footers         Paper Size/Type
              Margins Top/Bottom          Suppress

    3 - Document
              Display Pitch               Redline Method
              Initial Codes/Font          Summary

    4 - Other
              Advance                     Overstrike
              Conditional End of Page     Printer Functions
              Decimal Characters          Underline Spaces/Tabs
              Language

    Selection: 0
```

Notice that four categories appear on the Format menu: Line, Page, Document, and Other. These categories correspond to four levels of formatting. Line formatting commands control the appearance of individual lines; page formatting commands control the appearance of entire pages; document formatting commands control the appearance of the document as a whole; and other formatting commands control additional formatting features.

Changing Top and Bottom Margins

The top margin is the distance between the top edge of the paper and the first line of text. Bottom margins are figured the same way—by measuring the distance between the bottom edge of the paper and the bottom line of text. A margin setting applies to all text falling after it in a document until a different setting changes the margin. You set top and bottom margins in the Format Page menu, listed in the Format menu. The Format Page menu is shown in figure 6.2.

WordPerfect's default margins are measured in decimal inches. If, for example, you want a top margin of 1 1/2 inches, type *1.5* in the Format Page menu.

Follow these steps to set top and bottom margins in a document:

1. Move the cursor to where you want margin settings to begin—ordinarily at the beginning of the document.

2. Press Format (Shift-F8) to display the Format menu.

```
Format: Page

     1 - Center Page (top to bottom)      No

     2 - Force Odd/Even Page

     3 - Headers

     4 - Footers

     5 - Margins - Top                    1"
                   Bottom                 1"

     6 - New Page Number                  1
         (example: 3 or iii)

     7 - Page Numbering                   No page numbering

     8 - Paper Size                       8.5" x 11"
                Type                      Standard

     9 - Suppress (this page only)


  Selection: 0
```

Fig. 6.2.
Format Page menu.

3. Select **Page** (**2**) to display the Format Page menu.

4. Select **Margins** (**5**) to set top and bottom margins.

5. Type the new top margin, in decimal inches, and press Enter (or just press Enter to accept the current measurement).

6. Type the new bottom margin, in decimal inches, and press Enter (or just press Enter to accept the current measurement).

7. Press Exit (F7) to return to the document.

Allowing for Headers, Footers, and Page Numbers

To include headers, footers, or page numbers in a document, plan margins accordingly. WordPerfect never prints these special text features inside a margin. Headers, footers, and page numbers are printed on the margin, and additional space (about one line) is left between the text and any header, footer, or page number.

If, for example, you want text to begin printing one inch from the top of the page but you want a header to print one-half inch from the top of the page, the top margin should be one-half inch.

Hand-Feeding Pages with a Platen-Type Printer

If you hand-feed pages into a platen-type printer, WordPerfect assumes that you roll the paper in one inch. (A platen printer rolls paper through like a typewriter. Most daisy-wheel and dot-matrix printers are platen printers.) If the top margin is set for one inch or less, printing begins at the printhead. But if the top margin is set for more than one inch, the printer advances the paper by the margin amount minus one inch before printing begins. For example, if the top margin is one-half inch, the paper won't advance at all before printing begins, but if the margin is one-and-one-half inches, the paper advances one-half inch before printing begins.

If the top margin of a document is less than one inch, hand-feed paper into a platen-type printer by the amount of the margin. If the top margin is more than one inch, roll the paper in one inch.

Centering Pages Top to Bottom

At times, you may want to override the margins on a page and simply center all text on the page from top to bottom. You may, for example, want to center the title page of a report, as shown in figure 6.3.

Fig. 6.3.
A centered title page.

> # The Art of
>
> # Newsletter Design
>
> ### Chapter 1
> What's Special About Newsletters?
>
> Karen Rose

Centering top to bottom works a bit differently from setting margins. When you set margins, the settings apply to all following pages until WordPerfect encounters a new margin setting. But when you center a page top to bottom, the setting applies to just one page—the page where you make the setting.

The end of a centered page can be defined either by WordPerfect, with a soft page break (calculated from margin settings) or by you, with a hard page break (inserted by pressing Ctrl-Enter). Usually a page centered from top to bottom is a separate page, shorter than the other pages in a document. Ending the centered page with a hard page break ensures that it never merges accidentally with the next page.

When you choose the Center Page (top to bottom) (1) command, be sure that the cursor is at the very beginning of the page, before any other formatting codes. Use Reveal Codes (Alt-F3, or F11) to verify its position.

To center a page top to bottom, follow these steps:

1. Move the cursor to the beginning of the page (before other formatting codes).

2. Press Format (Shift-F8) to display the Format Page menu.

3. Select **Page** (**2**).

4. Select **C**enter Page (top to bottom) (**1**).

5. Press Exit (F7) to return to the document.

The only way to remove page centering is to delete the code. Use Reveal Codes (Alt-F3, or F11) to determine the position of the code.

Designing Headers and Footers

A header is a block of text (or numbers or graphics) appearing at the top of a page. A footer is, similarly, a block that appears at the bottom of a page. Headers and footers can appear on all pages, on even pages only, on odd pages only, or on all pages except pages on which they are suppressed.

You can include one or two headers or footers on a page. Because you can designate them to appear on even-only or odd-only pages, you can set them up so that one header or footer appears on even pages and another appears on odd pages, as shown in figure 6.4.

If two headers appear on one page, be sure they don't overlap. One header may be flush left; the other may be flush right—or they may appear on different lines.

Headers and footers can be up to a page long (but that won't leave much room for text!). Headers and footers can also employ most WordPerfect formatting functions, such as bold, underline, and centering. You can include automatic page numbering by inserting a special code, ^B (Ctrl-B), in either a header or a footer. Once created, a header or footer can easily be edited or deleted.

Headers and footers print at the top and bottom margins of pages, and WordPerfect leaves a space of about one line between the header or footer and the text of the document. (To leave more space between the text and the header or footer, include extra lines as part of the header or footer.) Headers and footers don't print inside the margins. If you have a one-inch top margin and a one-line header, for example, WordPerfect prints the header at one inch, skips a line, and begins printing text on the next line.

You can't see a header or footer on-screen. To see them, select View Document from the Print menu. Press Print (Shift-F7) and select View Document (6). Or you can read the first 50 characters of a header or footer by choosing Reveal Codes (Alt-F3, or F11).

You can remove or edit headers and footers after you create them. You also can suppress them so that they don't appear on certain pages.

Fig. 6.4.

Different headers and
footers on facing
pages.

Chapter 6

xyxy wywy nndn lsd sdjl sdfjljz mcmmdk qwewe ,s,
hhdlw sdm sdgg weremdfd ddfd ads mmvod adsf
kkadkl fkdk la dsf. zxzx ajavc zcl; dfsfgs df asdf adb
skksdfj sdff llkkdnfderr lsdf kdflpkre ifyywe iqwybd
mdna kqad qwhbasfjn ehknasd lsadnk aksjdj wejl.
ajljasd ljaejlq qaiam qekjdlaj eiuqow iqqle oqejql oie
ejlas ejlwq asn qjroasd qjd sdl oued q oua daj 2u asdj
eljfaf. xyxy wywy nndn lsd sdjl sdfjljz mcmmdk qwewe
,s, hhdlw sdm sdgg weremdfd ddfd ads mmvod adsf
kkadkl fkdk la dsf.

ajavc zcl; dfsfgs df asdf adb skksdfj sdff llkkdnfderr lsdf
kdflpkre ifyywe iqwybd mdna kqad qwhbasfjn ehknasd
lsadnk aksjdj wejl. ajljasd ljaejlq qaiam qekjdlaj eiuqow
iqqle oqejql oie ejlas ejlwq asn qjroasd qjd sdl oued q
oua daj 2u asdj eljfaf. xyxy wywy nndn lsd sdjl sdfjljz
mcmmdk qwewe ,s, hhdlw sdm sdgg weremdfd ddfd
ads mmvod adsf kkadkl fkdk la dsf.

ajavc zcl; dfsfgs df asdf adb skksdfj sdff llkkdnfderr lsdf
kdflpkre ifyywe iqwybd mdna kqad qwhbasfjn ehknasd
lsadnk aksjdj wejl. ajljasd ljaejlq qaiam qekjdlaj eiuqow
iqqle oqejql oie ejlas ejlwq asn qjroasd qjd sdl oued q
oua daj 2u asdj eljfaf.

June, 1988

Formatting Pages

xyxy wywy nndn lsd sdjl sdfjljz mcmmdk qwewe ,s,
hhdlw sdm sdgg weremdfd ddfd ads mmvod adsf
kkadkl fkdk la dsf. zxzx ajavc zcl; dfsfgs df asdf adb
skksdfj sdff llkkdnfderr lsdf kdflpkre ifyywe iqwybd
mdna kqad qwhbasfjn ehknasd lsadnk aksjdj wejl.
ajljasd ljaejlq qaiam qekjdlaj eiuqow iqqle oqejql oie
ejlas ejlwq asn qjroasd qjd sdl oued q oua daj 2u asdj
eljfaf. xyxy wywy nndn lsd sdjl sdfjljz mcmmdk qwewe
,s, hhdlw sdm sdgg weremdfd ddfd ads mmvod adsf
kkadkl fkdk la dsf.

ajavc zcl; dfsfgs df asdf adb skksdfj sdff llkkdnfderr lsdf
kdflpkre ifyywe iqwybd mdna kqad qwhbasfjn ehknasd
lsadnk aksjdj wejl. ajljasd ljaejlq qaiam qekjdlaj eiuqow
iqqle oqejql oie ejlas ejlwq asn qjroasd qjd sdl oued q
oua daj 2u asdj eljfaf. xyxy wywy nndn lsd sdjl sdfjljz
mcmmdk qwewe ,s, hhdlw sdm sdgg weremdfd ddfd
ads mmvod adsf kkadkl fkdk la dsf.

ajavc zcl; dfsfgs df asdf adb skksdfj sdff llkkdnfderr lsdf
kdflpkre ifyywe iqwybd mdna kqad qwhbasfjn ehknasd
lsadnk aksjdj wejl. ajljasd ljaejlq qaiam qekjdlaj eiuqow
iqqle oqejql oie ejlas ejlwq asn qjroasd qjd sdl oued q
oua daj 2u asdj eljfaf.

Page 3

Creating New Headers and Footers

Create headers and footers at the beginning of a document. If you create them
elsewhere, they may move when you insert or delete text.

To create a new header or footer, follow these steps:

1. Press Format (Shift-F8) to display the Format menu.

2. Select **Page** (**2**) to display the Format Page menu.

3. Select **Headers** (**3**) to create a header

   or

   Select **Footers** (**4**) to create a footer.

   You can create two headers (A and B) and two footers (A and B).

4. Select Header **A** (**1**) or Header **B** (**2**)

   or

   Select Footer **A** (**1**) or Footer **B** (**2**).

5. Select Every **Page** (**2**) if you want the header or footer to appear on every page in the document

   or

   Select **Odd** pages (**3**) if you want the header or footer to appear on odd pages only

   or

   Select **Even** pages (**4**) if you want the header or footer to appear on even pages only.

6. Type the text of the header or footer.

   Use any WordPerfect formatting command as you type the text of a header or footer. You can, for example, create a bold header or an underlined footer.

7. Press Exit (F7) to save the header or footer and return to the Page Format menu.

8. Press Exit (F7) again to return to the document.

Including Automatic Page Numbering in a Header or Footer

To include automatic page numbering in a header or footer, simply type the special code ^B (Ctrl-B) as part of the header or footer text. If, for example, you want the header to read "Page 1" on the first page and continue numbering pages consecutively, type *Page*, press the space bar once, then press the Ctrl key while you type *B*.

To include automatic page numbering in a header or footer, follow these steps:

1. Start a new header or footer, or edit an existing one.

2. Type any text you want to precede the page number.

3. Type ^*B* (Ctrl-B).

4. Press Exit (F7) twice.

Editing Headers and Footers

After you create a header or footer, you can change it. You can edit its text so that it reads differently, or you can change its formatting so that it looks different.

To edit a header or footer, follow these steps:

1. Press Format (Shift-F8).

2. Select **Page** (**2**) to display the Format Page menu.

3. Select **Headers** (**3**) to edit a header

   or

   Select Footers (**4**) to edit a footer.

4. Select Header **A** (**1**) or Header **B** (**2**)

   or

   Select Footer **A** (**1**) or Footer **B** (**2**).

5. Select Edit (**5**).

6. Edit the header or footer.

7. Press Exit (F7) to return to the Format Page menu, and press Exit again to return to the document.

To remove a header or footer, follow these steps:

1. Press Format (Shift-F8).

2. Select **Page** (**2**) to display the Format Page menu.

3. Select **Headers** (**3**) to remove a header

   or

   Select Footers (**4**) to remove a footer.

4. Select Header **A** (**1**) or Header **B** (**2**)

   or

   Select Footer **A** (**1**) or Footer **B** (**2**).

5. Select **Discontinue** (**1**).

Suppressing Headers and Footers

You can suppress any or all headers and footers so that they don't appear on a specified page. You don't, for example, want a header with the title of a report on the title page. Start by moving the cursor to the beginning of the page on which you want the header or footer suppressed.

To suppress a header or footer, follow these steps:

1. Move the cursor to the beginning of the page where you want to suppress the header or footer.

2. Press Format (Shift F-8).

3. Select **Page** (**2**).

4. Select Suppress (this page only) (**9**).

5. Select the header or footer to suppress:

   Suppress **All** Page Numbering, Headers, and Footers (**1**)

   Suppress Headers and Footers (**2**)

   Suppress **Header** A (**5**)

   Suppress Header B (**6**)

   Suppress Footer A (**7**)

   Suppress Footer B (**8**).

6. Type *Y* to suppress the header or footer.

7. Press Exit (F7) to return to the Format Page menu. Press Exit again to return to the document.

Searching and Replacing in Headers and Footers

Searching and replacing text in a header is only one step different from searching and replacing text in a document. Simply press the Home key before you press the Forward Search (F2) or Replace (Alt-F2) key, and continue the search or replace as usual. Search and replace is a quick way to change the title or date in all headers and footers in a report.

To search for text in a header or footer, follow these steps:

1. Press the Home key.

2. Press Forward Search (F2).

3. Type the text to search for.

4. Press Forward Search (F2) again.

   WordPerfect searches through headers, footers, endnotes, and footnotes to find the text. When the text is found, you can edit it as usual.

5. Press Exit (F7) to return to the document.

To replace text in a header or footer, follow these steps:

1. Press the Home key.

2. Press Replace (Alt-F2).

3. Type *Y* to confirm each replacement or *N* to replace without confirming.

4. Press ↑ to search backward through headers and footers. Press ↓ to search forward.

5. Type the text to replace.

6. Press Forward Search (F2).

7. Type the new text.

8. Press Forward Search (F2) to start the search.

    Headers and footers are usually embedded in a document before text begins. To find the text, you may have to press ↑ (as in Step 4) to search backward. When the text to be replaced is found, confirm or deny the replacement.

9. Type *Y* to make the replacement or type *N* to leave the text as it is.

10. Press Exit (F7) to return to the document.

Including Graphics in Headers and Footers

You can include graphics as part of a header or footer in two ways: by drawing boxes or by retrieving a graphic created in a graphics program. Use a box around a footer, for example, to call attention to a page number. Or include a previously drawn logo in a header to create stationery for your business. Follow the general steps below to add a graphic—such as a horizontal line appearing across the tops and bottoms of all pages—to your document.

1. Press Format (Shift-F8) to display the Format menu.

2. Select **Page** (**2**) to display the Format Page menu.

3. Select **Headers** (**3**) to create a header

    or

    Select Footers (**4**) to create a footer.

4. Select Header **A** (**1**) or Header **B** (**2**)

    or

    Select Footer **A** (**1**) or Footer **B** (**2**).

This series of commands puts you in the header/footer creation screen, where you can type and format text or create graphics. Or you can create a combination of text and graphics. To continue creating a graphic, follow these steps:

5. Press Graphics (Alt-F9).

6. Create the box or line.

    Feel free to use the Reveal Codes feature when you create a graphic. For example, to delete an incorrect line, it's easiest to press Reveal Codes

(Alt-F3, or F11), find the line code, delete the line code, and re-create the line.

7. Press Exit (F7) to return to the Page menu.

8. Press Exit (F7) again to return to the document.

See Chapter 24 for more information about creating and editing graphics.

Numbering Pages

Automatically numbering pages in a document is as easy as telling WordPerfect how and where you want the numbers to appear on the page. Page numbering begins with whatever number you specify. If you write a book, you will probably print Chapter 1 beginning with page number 1. But you may print Chapter 6 beginning with page number 147.

Page numbers print on the margin. You won't see them on the page until you print a document, but you can preview them if you press Print (F7) and select View Document (6).

Page numbering options include printing page numbers on facing pages for double-sided documents like newsletters and multipage reports and suppressing page numbers for individual pages.

Positioning the Page Number

The page number can appear in any of six positions on the page or in either of two positions on alternating pages. You choose which position from a visual Page Number Position menu, shown in figure 6.5.

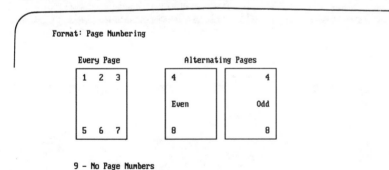

Fig. 6.5.

Choosing a position for page numbers.

Page numbers can appear at the top of the page—on the left, center, or right. They can also appear at the bottom of the page—on the left, center, or right. For facing pages, such as in a book or newsletter, page numbers can appear on the left side of even pages (left-facing pages) and on the right side of odd pages (right-facing pages), as shown in figure 6.6.

The currently selected page number position is listed on the Format Page menu.

Fig. 6.6.

Page numbers on facing pages.

2

xyxy wywy nndn lsd sdjl sdfjljz mcmmdk qwewe ,s, hhdlw sdm sdgg weremdfd ddfd ads mmvod adsf kkadkl fkdk la dsf. zxzx ajavc zcl; dfsfgs df asdf adb skksdfj sdff llkkdnfderr lsdf kdflpkre ifyywe iqwybd mdna kqad qwhbasfjn ehknasd lsadnk aksjdj wejl. ajljasd ljaejlq qaiam qekjdlaj eiuqow iqqle oqejql oie ejlas ejlwq asn qjroasd qjd sdl oued q oua daj 2u asdj eljfaf. xyxy wywy nndn lsd sdjl sdfjljz mcmmdk qwewe ,s, hhdlw sdm sdgg weremdfd ddfd ads mmvod adsf kkadkl fkdk la dsf.

ajavc zcl; dfsfgs df asdf adb skksdfj sdff llkkdnfderr lsdf kdflpkre ifyywe iqwybd mdna kqad qwhbasfjn ehknasd lsadnk aksjdj wejl. ajljasd ljaejlq qaiam qekjdlaj eiuqow iqqle oqejql oie ejlas ejlwq asn qjroasd qjd sdl oued q oua daj 2u asdj eljfaf. xyxy wywy nndn lsd sdjl sdfjljz mcmmdk qwewe ,s, hhdlw sdm sdgg weremdfd ddfd ads mmvod adsf kkadkl fkdk la dsf.

ajavc zcl; dfsfgs df asdf adb skksdfj sdff llkkdnfderr lsdf kdflpkre ifyywe iqwybd mdna kqad qwhbasfjn ehknasd lsadnk aksjdj wejl. ajljasd ljaejlq qaiam qekjdlaj eiuqow iqqle oqejql oie ejlas ejlwq asn qjroasd qjd sdl oued q oua daj 2u asdj eljfaf.

3

xyxy wywy nndn lsd sdjl sdfjljz mcmmdk qwewe ,s, hhdlw sdm sdgg weremdfd ddfd ads mmvod adsf kkadkl fkdk la dsf. zxzx ajavc zcl; dfsfgs df asdf adb skksdfj sdff llkkdnfderr lsdf kdflpkre ifyywe iqwybd mdna kqad qwhbasfjn ehknasd lsadnk aksjdj wejl. ajljasd ljaejlq qaiam qekjdlaj eiuqow iqqle oqejql oie ejlas ejlwq asn qjroasd qjd sdl oued q oua daj 2u asdj eljfaf. xyxy wywy nndn lsd sdjl sdfjljz mcmmdk qwewe ,s, hhdlw sdm sdgg weremdfd ddfd ads mmvod adsf kkadkl fkdk la dsf.

ajavc zcl; dfsfgs df asdf adb skksdfj sdff llkkdnfderr lsdf kdflpkre ifyywe iqwybd mdna kqad qwhbasfjn ehknasd lsadnk aksjdj wejl. ajljasd ljaejlq qaiam qekjdlaj eiuqow iqqle oqejql oie ejlas ejlwq asn qjroasd qjd sdl oued q oua daj 2u asdj eljfaf. xyxy wywy nndn lsd sdjl sdfjljz mcmmdk qwewe ,s, hhdlw sdm sdgg weremdfd ddfd ads mmvod adsf kkadkl fkdk la dsf.

ajavc zcl; dfsfgs df asdf adb skksdfj sdff llkkdnfderr lsdf kdflpkre ifyywe iqwybd mdna kqad qwhbasfjn ehknasd lsadnk aksjdj wejl. ajljasd ljaejlq qaiam qekjdlaj eiuqow iqqle oqejql oie ejlas ejlwq asn qjroasd qjd sdl oued q oua daj 2u asdj eljfaf.

To position page numbers, follow these steps:

1. Press Format (Shift-F8).

2. Select **P**age (**2**).

3. Select **P**age Numbering (**7**).

4. Type the number corresponding to the position where you want page numbers to appear on the page:

   1 top left

   2 top center

   3 top right

   5 bottom left

   6 bottom center

   7 bottom right

   4 top outside, facing pages

   8 bottom outside, facing pages

   9 No page numbers.

5. Press Exit (F7) to return to the document.

Page numbering begins where you select page numbering. Be sure you're at the beginning of the document if you want page numbering to begin on page 1.

Starting a New Page Number

Page numbering, which can begin with any number, can be numeric (1, 2, 3) or lowercase Roman (i, ii, iii). You can change page numbering at any point in your document, and the change takes effect from that point forward.

To change the starting page number, follow these steps:

1. Move the cursor where you want new page numbering to begin.

2. Press Format (Shift-F8) to display the Format menu.

3. Select **P**age (**2**) to display the Format Page menu.

4. Select **N**ew Page Number (**6**).

5. Type the starting page number.

6. Press Exit (F7) to return to the document.

To number with Roman numerals, use this procedure to change the starting page number, even if you plan to start at Roman numeral i.

Suppressing Page Numbering

You can suppress page numbering for a single page so that no page numbers appear on that page. Numbering continues on the following pages.

To suppress page numbering for one page, follow these steps:

1. Move the cursor to the beginning of the page where you want to suppress page numbering.

2. Press Format (Shift-F8) to display the Format menu.

3. Select **Page** (**2**) to see the Format Page menu.

4. Select **Suppress** (this page only) (**9**).

5. Select Suppress **Page** Numbering (**4**).

6. Press Y.

In long documents you may occasionally want to force a page to be even-numbered or odd-numbered. For example, the first page of a chapter in a book or a subsection in a report usually begins on an odd-numbered page. On a double-sided document, the odd-numbered page is the page on the right.

Look at the status line at the bottom right of the screen to see the page number of the page you're currently on.

To force a page to be even- or odd-numbered, follow these steps:

1. Move the cursor to the top of the page you want to force to be even- or odd-numbered.

2. Press Format (Shift F8) to display the Format menu.

3. Select **Page** Format (**2**) to display the Format Page menu.

4. Select Force Odd/Even Page (**2**).

5. Select **Odd** (**1**) if you want the current page to be odd-numbered, or select **Even** (**2**) if you want the current page to be even-numbered.

6. Press Exit (F7) once to return to the document.

If you force an even page number for a page that's already even-numbered, no change is made. Page 4 remains page 4. But if you force an even page number on an odd-numbered page, then the page number changes to the next higher number. Page 3 becomes page 4. The same principle applies when you force an odd page number on a currently even-numbered page.

Keeping Text Together

WordPerfect calculates the length of each page in a document, depending on the set margins. When one page is full, a new page begins. In many cases, though, you want to prevent a block of text from breaking between two pages. A chart, for example, should be kept on a single page.

With WordPerfect you have three ways to prevent unwanted page breaks (discussed in detail in the following sections). The Conditional End of Page command groups a given number of lines so that they won't break across two pages. The Block Protect command protects a given block of text from breaking. And you can avoid widows and orphans with the Widow/Orphan Protection command so that the first or last line isn't separated from a paragraph.

When WordPerfect encounters a protected block of text, it calculates whether enough room exists to print the whole block on the page. If not, the page ends, and the block shifts to the top of the following page. The page before the protected block may be shorter than other pages.

WordPerfect's automatic page breaks are called soft page breaks. Another way to prevent unwanted page breaks is to insert hard page breaks by pressing Ctrl-Enter. A hard page break forces the page to break. But a hard page break may be the least desirable way to prevent unwanted page breaks because it must be removed manually (just as it is inserted manually). A soft page break, on the other hand, is automatically recalculated when you make adjustments affecting page length. (See "Understanding Soft and Hard Page Breaks," later in this chapter.)

A soft page break appears as a single dashed line across the page. A hard page break appears as a double dashed line.

Using the Conditional End of Page Command

Use the Conditional End of Page command to keep a specified number of lines together on a page. You may, for example, want to make sure that all titles or subheads in a document are followed by at least three lines of text. Figure 6.7 shows how the Conditional End of Page command keeps a title, its subhead, and three lines of text together.

To ensure that a particular type of title or subhead is always followed by the correct number of lines, you can include a Conditional End of Page command in style sheets.

To apply the Conditional End of Page command, follow these steps:

1. Move the cursor to the line above the lines you want to keep together.

2. Press Format (Shift-F8) to display the Format menu.

3. Select **Other** (**4**) to display the Format Other menu.

4. Select Conditional End of Page (**2**).

5. In response to the prompt, type the number of lines you want to keep together and press Enter.

6. Press Exit (F7) to return to the document.

7. Press ↓ enough times to see the new page break.

Fig. 6.7.

Using Conditional End of Page command to insert a page break in front of a title.

```
the page will print with different fonts, character styles, columns, and
graphics. You now have the power to create simple newsletters, brochures,
or high-level reports. Your typed reports can now include spreadsheets with
enhanced text and graphics from Lotus 1-2-3 or drawing programs. When
printed on a laser printer, they look typeset.

    We have two primary goals for the people we teach. First, people
should learn PC skills they can directly apply to specific tasks at their job.
Second, we teach people how to find answers to their own PC related
questions and how to learn more about applications by themselves.

----------------------------------------------------------------
TWO GOALS: PRACTICALITY AND LEARNING TO LEARN

Our Instructors Are Experienced

    Our instructors are experienced as both teachers, consultants, and as
business people using the applications we teach. Karen Rose, our desktop
publishing instructor, was the marketing communications manager for Texas
Instruments and owns Write On Target, a desktop publishing company that
produces newsletters and an international quarterly. My experience includes
a technical MS, an MBA, and seven years as an industry analyst for Texas

C:\CH6\FIG607B.DOC                          Doc 1 Pg 2 Ln 8.95" Pos 1"
```

Using the Block Protect Command

With Block Protect you can protect any block of text from being broken by a soft page break. Use Block Protect, for example, to prevent a chart from breaking across two pages, as shown in figure 6.8.

Fig. 6.8.

A page break in a chart.

```
When WordPerfect encounters a protected block of text, it calculates
whether there is enough room to print the whole block on the page. If not,
the page ends, and the block shifts to the top of the following page. The
page before the protected block may be shorter than other pages. The
following chart of meeting times is an example.

                          STAFF MEETING TIMES
                             July, 1988

                  Dept. A          Dept. B          Dept. C

Week 1             9:00            10:00             1:30
--------------------------------------------------------------------
Week 2            10:00             1:30             3:00
Week 3             9:00            10:00             1:30
Week 4            10:00             1:30            10:00


WordPerfect's automatic page breaks are called "soft page breaks." Another
way to prevent unwanted page breaks is to insert "hard page breaks" by
pressing the Ctrl-Enter keys. A hard page break forces the page to break.
But a hard page break may be the least desirable way to prevent unwanted
page breaks, because it must be removed manually (just as it is inserted
manually). A soft page break, on the other hand, is automatically
C:\CH6\FIG608A.DOC                          Doc 1 Pg 2 Ln 3.55" Pos 1"
```

```
When WordPerfect encounters a protected block of text, it calculates
whether there is enough room to print the whole block on the page. If not,
the page ends, and the block shifts to the top of the following page. The
page before the protected block may be shorter than other pages. The
following chart of meeting times is an example.

---------------------------------------------------------------------------
                        STAFF MEETING TIMES
                           July, 1988

                   Dept. A          Dept. B          Dept. C

        Week 1       9:00            10:00             1:30
        Week 2      10:00             1:30             3:00
        Week 3       9:00            10:00             1:30
        Week 4      10:00             1:30            10:00

WordPerfect's automatic page breaks are called "soft page breaks." Another
way to prevent unwanted page breaks is to insert "hard page breaks" by
pressing the Ctrl-Enter keys. A hard page break forces the page to break.
But a hard page break may be the least desirable way to prevent unwanted
page breaks, because it must be removed manually (just as it is inserted
manually). A soft page break, on the other hand, is automatically
C:\CH6\FIG600B.DOC                              Doc 1 Pg 2 Ln 3.55" Pos 1"
```

Fig. 6.9.

*An application of
Block Protect to
prevent a page break
in a chart.*

To protect a block of text, follow these steps:

1. Move the cursor to the beginning of the block you want to protect.

2. Press Block (Alt-F4, or F12).

3. With the arrow keys, move the cursor to the end of the block (but don't include the final return at the end of a paragraph).

4. Press Format (Shift-F8).

5. Type *Y* to protect the block.

Choose the Block Protect command to protect blocks that may vary in size. If you protect a chart (see fig. 6.9), for example, you can add lines of data later, and the protection remains in effect.

Preventing Widows and Orphans

An *orphan* is the first line of a paragraph that appears by itself at the end of a page. A *widow* is the last line of a paragraph that appears by itself at the top of a page. Most page designers prefer to avoid widows and orphans.

Activating the Widow/Orphan Protection command at the beginning of a document prevents their occurrence throughout an entire document.

Figure 6.10 shows how a page may look before Widow/Orphan Protection is activated. Before Widow/Orphan Protection is activated, only the last line of a paragraph appears after a soft page break (a widow); after Widow/Orphan Protection, two lines appear after the page break (see fig. 6.11).

Fig. 6. 10.

A "widow," separated from the rest of the paragraph by a page break.

> WordPerfect 4.2 is the most widely sold word-processing software in the United States. Its speed, clutter-free screen, and large number of professional-level features have made it the word processor of choice for most businesses. But a competitor is out now that will take the place of WordPerfect 4.2.
>
> It's WordPerfect 5! In WordPerfect 5 the menus are easier to follow. Complex features such as printer and font selection have been simplified, and the power to incorporate graphics has been added.
>
> One of the most striking features of WordPerfect 5 is the ability to create documents involving multiple character fonts, columns of text, and graphics. With the Preview command you can see on-screen exactly how the page will print with different fonts, character styles, columns, and graphics. You now have the power to create simple newsletters, brochures, or high-level reports. Your typed reports can now include spreadsheets with enhanced text and graphics from Lotus 1-2-3 or drawing programs. When
> --
> printed on a laser printer, they look typeset.
>
> We have two primary goals for the people we teach. First, people should learn PC skills they can directly apply to specific tasks at their job. Second, we teach people how to find answers to their own PC-related questions and how to learn more about applications by themselves.
> C:\CH6\FIG609A   Doc 1 Pg 3 Ln 2.1" Pos 1"

Fig. 6.11.

Widow/orphan protection on.

> WordPerfect 4.2 is the most widely sold word-processing software in the United States. Its speed, clutter-free screen, and large number of professional-level features have made it the word processor of choice for most businesses. But a competitor is out now that will take the place of WordPerfect 4.2.
>
> It's WordPerfect 5! In WordPerfect 5 the menus are easier to follow. Complex features such as printer and font selection have been simplified, and the power to incorporate graphics has been added.
>
> One of the most striking features of WordPerfect 5 is the ability to create documents involving multiple character fonts, columns of text, and graphics. With the Preview command you can see on-screen exactly how the page will print with different fonts, character styles, columns, and graphics. You now have the power to create simple newsletters, brochures, or high-level reports. Your typed reports can now include spreadsheets with
> --
> enhanced text and graphics from Lotus 1-2-3 or drawing programs. When printed on a laser printer, they look typeset.
>
> We have two primary goals for the people we teach. First, people should learn PC skills they can directly apply to specific tasks at their job. Second, we teach people how to find answers to their own PC-related questions and how to learn more about applications by themselves.
> C:\CH6\FIG609B   Doc 1 Pg 3 Ln 2.25" Pos 1"

To prevent widows and orphans, follow these steps:

1. Move the cursor to the beginning of the document (or to wherever you want protection to begin).

2. Press Format (Shift-F8) to display the Format menu.

3. Select **Line** (**1**) to display the Format Line menu.

4. Select **Widow/Orphan Protection** (**9**).

5. Type *Y* for Yes to turn on protection.

6. Press Exit (F7) to return to the document.

Widow and orphan protection takes effect where you activate it and remains in effect until you turn it off. To turn it off, repeat the process, responding *No* in Step 5. Or press Reveal Codes (Alt-F3, or F11) and delete the code.

Understanding Soft and Hard Page Breaks

WordPerfect uses two types of page breaks. Soft page breaks, calculated automatically, depend on margin settings. Hard page breaks are inserted manually.

Using Soft Page Breaks

WordPerfect inserts a soft page break when it gets to the end of a page of text (or when it encounters a protected block of text that won't fit on the current page). Text then continues on the following page.

When text is added to a document or deleted from it, soft page breaks are automatically recalculated so that pages always break correctly.

On-screen, a soft page break appears as a single dashed line. When you press Reveal Codes (Alt-F3, or F11), a soft page break code appears as **[SPg]**.

Using Hard Page Breaks

To force a page to break at a certain spot—for example, at the beginning of a new section in a report—enter a hard page break. The page always breaks there, no matter what.

On-screen, a hard page break appears as a double dashed line. When you press Reveal Codes (Alt-F3, or F11), a hard page break code appears as **[HPg]**.

To insert a hard page break, follow these steps:

1. Move the cursor to the beginning of the text that should appear on a new page.

2. Press Ctrl-Enter.

The only way to override a hard page break is to delete it.

To delete a hard page break, follow these steps:

1. Move the cursor to the beginning of the line just below the double dashed line on-screen.

2. Press the Backspace key.

   or

1. Move the cursor to the last space before the double dashed line.

2. Press the Delete key.

You can also delete a hard page break by pressing Reveal Codes (Alt-F3, or F11) and deleting the code.

Choosing Paper and Form Sizes

In WordPerfect, you must specify the size, type, orientation, and location (in the printer) of the paper to print a document on. Your paper may be letterhead—a vertical sheet of standard-size paper on which you print in normal "portrait" orientation. Or your paper may be a business envelope—a horizontal piece of paper measuring only 4 by 9-1/2 inches—that you print on lengthwise.

Specifying paper size is a two-part process. In a document, you identify paper size and type through the Format Page menu. But you must also define form size and type for the printer (or printers, if you use more than one). Define printer forms through the Printer menu. Paper and form really mean the same thing. *Paper*, however, refers to how you specify paper size within a document, and *form* refers to how you define paper size for a printer.

Paper and form must match. If you specify in the document that the paper is an envelope, a corresponding envelope form must be listed in the print menu.

Access the two steps in defining paper and forms through two different function keys—the Format (Shift-F8) key, used for specifying paper size and type in a document, and the Print (Shift-F7) key, used for identifying available forms for the printer.

Specifying Paper Size and Type in a Document

To print on the paper size and type WordPerfect chooses for you, do nothing. Your document prints on standard 8-1/2 by 11 inch vertical paper.

To print on a different paper size, however, change the setting within the document. You can change paper size and type for the entire document by choosing a different setting at the beginning or—for individual pages—by changing the setting at the top of the page. The paper size and type you choose remain in effect until you choose a different setting. Each time you change the paper size and type, WordPerfect inserts a code in the document.

You can choose any of nine predefined paper sizes, or you can define your own size. Paper sizes and their dimensions are listed in the Paper Size menu, shown in figure 6.12.

To choose a predefined paper size and type, follow these steps:

1. Press the Format (Shift-F8) key.

2. Select **Page** (**2**).

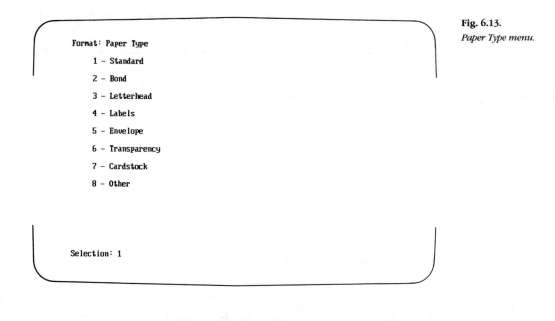

Fig. 6.12.
Paper Size menu.

```
Format: Paper Size
        1 - Standard              (8.5" x 11")
        2 - Standard Landscape    (11" x 8.5")
        3 - Legal                 (8.5" x 14")
        4 - Legal Landscape       (14" x 8.5")
        5 - Envelope              (9.5" x 4")
        6 - Half Sheet            (5.5" x 8.5")
        7 - US Government         (8" x 11")
        8 - A4                    (210mm x 297mm)
        9 - A4 Landscape          (297mm x 210mm)
        0 - Other

Selection: 1
```

3. Select Paper Size (**8**).

4. Select any predefined paper size listed.

After you choose a paper size, you advance to the next menu, Paper Type, shown in figure 6.13.

Fig. 6.13.
Paper Type menu.

```
Format: Paper Type
        1 - Standard
        2 - Bond
        3 - Letterhead
        4 - Labels
        5 - Envelope
        6 - Transparency
        7 - Cardstock
        8 - Other




Selection: 1
```

Continue the selection process:

5. Select any of the seven predefined paper types listed.

6. Press Exit (F7) to return to your document.

To define your own paper size and type, follow these steps:

1. Press the Format (Shift-F8) key to display the Format menu.

2. Select **Page** (**2**).

3. Select **Paper Size** (**8**).

4. Select **Other** (**0**).

5. Type, in inches, the width of the paper and press Enter.

6. Type, in inches, the height of the paper and press Enter.

After you type the dimensions of the new paper size, you advance to the Paper Type menu, where you must define the paper type. You can choose one of eight standard types so that you simply redefine the dimensions of an existing type. Or you can give the paper type a new name. Be sure to use the same name later, in the Print menu.

7. Select **Other** (**8**).

8. Then select **Other** (**2**).

9. Type in a name for the new paper type and press Enter.

10. Press Exit (F7) to return to your document.

Figure 6.14 shows the Format Page menu set up with a unique form: a 5 by 9 inch notepad.

Fig. 6.14.

Format Page menu with a 5 by 9 inch notepad.

```
Format: Page

    1 - Center Page (top to bottom)    No

    2 - Force Odd/Even Page

    3 - Headers

    4 - Footers

    5 - Margins - Top                  1"
                  Bottom               1"

    6 - New Page Number                1
          (example: 3 or iii)

    7 - Page Numbering                 No page numbering

    8 - Paper Size                     5" x 9"
                  Type                 notepad

    9 - Suppress (this page only)

    Selection: 0
```

Identifying Available Forms for the Printer

For each paper size and type you specify in your document, a corresponding form size and type must be defined through the print menu. Forms are specific to each printer. If you use more than one printer, you may have to set forms for each of them.

To define forms, you must work through several menus. Begin with the Print command (the Shift-F7 function key), select the printer for which you're identifying forms, and—finally—identify paper type and form.

Just as you did from within the document, you can choose a predefined form, or you can define a form of your own. Nine paper types are listed in the Form Type menu shown in figure 6.15.

```
Select Printer: Form Type

        1 - Standard

        2 - Bond

        3 - Letterhead

        4 - Labels

        5 - Envelope

        6 - Transparency

        7 - Cardstock

        8 - [ALL OTHERS]

        9 - Other



    Selection: 1
```

Fig. 6.15.
Form Type menu.

Seven paper types are predefined. An eighth type, All Others, is a generic category that WordPerfect looks to when it encounters an unrecognizable paper size code in the document. The ninth form type, Other, is for you to define. If, for example, you define a 5-by-9-inch notepad in a document, choose Other in this step and type *Notepad*. Use the Forms menu, shown in figure 6.14, to define the size and orientation of your special paper, Notepad.

To define a standard form for your printer, follow these steps:

1. Press the Print (Shift-F7) key.

2. Select **S**elect Printer (**S**).

3. Use the arrow keys to highlight the printer for which you want to define a form.

Fig. 6.16.

Forms menu.

```
Select Printer: Forms

          Filename              HPLASEII.PRS

          Form Type             Standard

     1 - Form Size              8.5" x 11"

     2 - Orientation            Portrait

     3 - Initially Present      Yes

     4 - Location               Continuous

     5 - Page Offsets - Top     0"
                        Side    0"




     Selection: 0
```

    4. Select Edit (**3**).

    5. Select Forms (**4**).

At this point, you see a list of existing forms. You can add a new form, or you can edit a listed one. To add a new form, continue following the instructions. To edit a form on the list, highlight it and select Edit (**3**). Then continue the instructions at Step 7.

To add a form, follow these steps:

    6. Select Add (**1**).

        Now you see the Form Type menu shown in figure 6.15.

    7. Select a paper type.

        After you select a paper type, advance to the Forms menu, shown in figure 6.16. Here you must make a series of choices. The choices are described later under "Understanding Printer Forms."

    8. Enter the form information (see "Understanding Printer Forms").

    9. Press Exit (F7) twice to return to the Select Print menu.

    10. Press Exit (F7) three more times to return to your document.

Understanding Printer Forms

In the Forms menu, shown in figure 6.16, you see five choices. At the top of the menu, two items are listed: the Filename, which tells you for which printer you're defining forms, and the Form Type, which tells you which paper type you selected (or defined) in the previous menu. You can't change either of these.

Make any of the selections described below and press Exit (F7) enough times to return to the document.

Form Size (1): When you select this option from the Forms menu, you're presented with a list of nine standard paper sizes and one Other category.

Select one item on the list. If you select Other to define your own form size, first type the width of the form in inches and press Enter; then type the length of the form in inches and press Enter.

Orientation (2): Orientation refers to the direction you want to print on the page. To print a standard vertical page, select **Portrait (1)**. To print lengthwise on the page, select **Landscape (2)**. If you'll print both ways, select **Both (3)**.

Initially Present (3): In this step, you tell the printer where to look for the form. But there are only three possible locations. To compensate, you can set up several forms for each location. The form marked Initially Present is the form in the specified location when the job starts.

During printing, if WordPerfect encounters a form definition that isn't marked Initially Present, printing stops, and you are prompted to insert the form into the proper location.

To identify a form as initially present, select **Initially Present (3)**.

Location (4): WordPerfect can look for only three form locations on your printer; **Continuous (1)**, for sheet or roll-fed paper; **Bin (2)**, for bin-fed paper; or **Manual (3)**, for manually fed paper.

Select the location where the printer can find the form. If you select **Bin (2)**, follow the selection by typing the bin number.

Page Offsets (5): If you want printing to begin at a specified distance from the top and side edges of a form, select **Page Offsets (5)**. Then type a distance, in inches, for the printing to be offset from the top and the sides.

Keep in mind that Page Offset doesn't override margin settings. If your document already has top and side margins of one inch and you include top and side page offsets of one inch, printing begins two inches from the top and sides of the form.

Notice that although paper size and type (defined through the Format Page menu) are specific to the document, form size and type (defined through the Print menu) are specific to your printer (or printers) and apply to all documents.

Designing Documents

Line formatting commands concern the appearance of lines of text in a document. Page formatting commands affect the appearance of pages. And document formatting commands affect the overall design of a document. To see the options available for document formatting, press Format (Shift-F8) and then **Document (3)**.

The Format Document menu lists five document formatting functions (see fig. 6.17). With the first option, **Display Pitch (1)**, you can set the space between letters for the document. Initial Codes /(2)Settings lets you modify WordPerfect's default settings for the document. With **Redline** Method (4), you define how redlining appears on printed pages. And with Summary (5), you can fully describe a document for future reference. For a discussion of Initial Font (3), see Chapters 8 and 9.

Fig. 6.17.

The document formatting section of the Format menu.

```
Format: Document

    1 - Display Pitch - Automatic        Yes
                        Width            0.07"

    2 - Initial Codes

    3 - Initial Font                     Times Roman 10 pt

    4 - Redline Method                   Printer Dependent

    5 - Summary
```

Many line formatting commands are explained in Chapter 5. Page formatting commands are explained earlier in this chapter.

Changing Initial Document Settings

WordPerfect comes equipped with a set of default format settings—margins, tab settings, paper size, and others. If you make no format changes, these settings govern the appearance of the document. Or you can override these default settings individually by using Format commands.

As an alternative to using the individual Format commands, you can use the Initial Codes menu to change format settings for an entire document before you begin working.

The changes you make apply to the current document and are saved with the document. They override WordPerfect's default settings, and they override Initial Settings made through the Setup (Shift- F1) command.

To make formatting choices for all WordPerfect documents, use the Setup command (Shift-F1). Select Initial Settings (5); then select Initial Codes (4). WordPerfect displays a ruler. At this point, press Format (Shift-F8), and make formatting choices. These choices apply to the current document and all WordPerfect documents, but they have lowest priority in your document. Formatting choices made directly through the Format command have first priority in a document, and formatting choices made through the Initial Settings menu within the Format menu have second priority. Format settings made with the Setup command have third priority.

To change initial settings for a document, follow these steps:

1. Press Format (Shift-F8) to display the Format menu.

2. Select **Document** (3) to display the Format Document menu.

3. Select Initial Codes (2).

4. Press Format (Shift-F8) again to redisplay the Format menu.

5. Make any format changes you want.

6. Press Exit (F7) three times to return to the document.

You also can use Initial Codes to create *templates*—formatted, but text-empty model documents. Templates are extremely useful when you do the same type of project over and over. A template is like a blank document. You open it, and it contains the settings and the basic information you need to start. Before you make any changes to the template, save it with a unique name so that it is preserved for next time.

Adjusting Display Pitch

Pitch—the number of characters per inch—is familiar to typists as pica or elite. And just as on a typewriter, WordPerfect's display pitch refers to the fractional value of an inch occupied by each character in a document.

With the Display Pitch feature, you can control the amount of space between characters. But this capability to tighten or loosen text is used by WordPerfect only when it's needed. If, for example, you create a chart including centered columns of numbers and overlapping columns, WordPerfect adjusts the display pitch to prevent overlapping characters, as shown in figure 6.18.

Fig. 6.18.
Condensed overlapping columns.

```
When WordPerfect encounters a protected block of text, it calculates whether
there is enough room to print the whole block on the page. If not, the page
ends, and the block shifts to the top of the following page. The page before
the protected block may be shorter than other pages. The following chart of
meeting times is an example.

                        STAFF MEETING TIMES
                            July, 1988

                        Dept. ADept. B Dept. C

        Week 1            9:00 10:00 1:30
        Week 2           10:00  1:30 3:00
        Week 3            9:00 10:00 1:30
        Week 4           10:00  1:3010:00
```
Adjusted display pitch
```
WordPerfect's automatic page breaks are called "soft page breaks." Another way
to prevent unwanted page breaks is to insert "hard page breaks" by pressing the
Ctrl-Enter keys. A hard page break forces the page to break. But a hard page
break may be the least desirable way to prevent unwanted page breaks, because
it must be removed manually (just as it is inserted manually). A soft page
break, on the other hand, is automatically recalculated when adjustments
-------------------------------------------------------------------------
                        Doc 1 Pg 1 Ln 9.72" Pos 1"
```

You either can let WordPerfect adjust the display pitch automatically, or you can set the display pitch yourself.

To set the display pitch, follow these steps:

1. Press Format (Shift-F8) to display the Format menu.

2. Select **Document** (**3**) to display the Format Document menu.

3. Select **Display Pitch** (**1**).

4. Type *N* to set your own display pitch.

5. Type a display pitch width (in inches, from .03 to .5), and press Enter.

6. Press Exit (F7) to return to the document.

To let WordPerfect adjust display pitch automatically, follow the same procedure as for setting display pitch, but type *Y* rather than *N* in Step 4.

The display pitch setting is saved with the document. It regulates the entire document.

Using Redlining To Mark Text

Redlining is a method of marking text that has been edited, added to, or deleted from a document. When several people have an input in the final appearance of a document, redlining is a useful way to let everyone know what changes are proposed or made.

The term "redlining" originated when people used red pens to edit draft copies of documents before passing them on to the next editor. Today, people share disks instead, and redlining is a word-processing function. In WordPerfect, you can choose how redlining appears on a printed page.

To set WordPerfect's redlining method, follow these steps:

1. Press Format (Shift-F8) to display the Format menu.

2. Select **Documents** (**3**) to display Format Document menu.

3. Select **Redline Method** (**4**).

4. Select one of three redlining methods:

   Printer Dependent (**1**)—marks redlined text according to your printer's definition of redlining.

   Left (**2**)—prints a redline character in the margin to the left of the redlined text.

   Alternating (**3**)—prints a redline character in the outside margins of alternating pages.

5. If you choose Left or Alternating in the preceding step, you can now type a redline character—if not, go on to the next step.

6. Press Exit (F7) to return to the document.

To learn how to use (and remove) redlining in a document, refer to Chapter 3.

Using Document Summaries

Sometimes it helps to keep track of information about your documents. With the Document Summary command, you can keep a record of a file's name, the date it was originally created, its subject, its author, and its typist. You can also write a several-line comment about the document.

Document summary information is stored in a special window. Every file has a document summary, and it automatically includes some information, including file name, date the file was created, and the first several lines of the document. (You can replace the text in the comment box with your comments.) Under some conditions (discussed later in this section), the summary includes a subject or account.

Besides the information automatically included in the document summary, you can add or change a descriptive file name (a handy feature when the eight-character file name isn't long enough to describe your file very well), the author's name, the typist's name, and comments.

Follow these steps to create a document summary:

1. Press Format (Shift-F8).

2. Select **Document** (**3**).

3. Select **Summary** (**5**).

4. Select any of the changeable items listed in the Document Summary window:

   Descriptive Filename (**1**)

   Subject/Account (**2**)

   Author (**3**)

   Typist (**4**)

   Comments (**5**)

5. Type the new information and press Enter.

6. Press Exit (F7) to return to the document.

You cannot change the system file name nor the date of creation. But you can enter up to 40 characters of information in selections **1**, **2**, **3**, and **4**, and you can type up to 780 characters in the comments box. In the comments box, you can also format text with bold and underline.

You may not always remember to create a document summary, so WordPerfect has a way to remind you. Using the Setup menu, you activate a reminder; then when you save or quit, the Document Summary window pops up on-screen.

Follow these steps to activate the reminder:

1. Choose Setup (Shift-F1) to display the Setup menu.

2. Select **Initial Settings** (**5**).

3. Select Document **S**ummary (**3**).

4. Select **C**reate on Save/Exit (**1**).

5. Type *Y.*

6. Press Exit (F7) to return to your document.

In the Document Summary window, the second selection is Subject Search Test (**2**). If your document contains the word "RE" in its first 400 or so characters, as many memos do, then the 40 characters following the "RE" are included to the right of the Subject Search Text selection. It's a good way to keep track of the subjects of memos. But if you prefer, you can change the word "RE" to some other word. Perhaps your custom is to use the heading "Subject" in memos.

You can change the word WordPerfect searches for in the Document Summary window by doing the following:

1. Choose Setup (Shift-F1) to display the Setup menu.

2. Select **I**nitial Settings (**5**).

3. Select Document **S**ummary (**3**).

4. Select **S**ubject Search Text (**2**).

5. Type the new word to search for and press Enter.

6. Press Exit (F7) to return to your document.

When you use the Setup menu to turn on the document summary reminder or to change the search word, these features remain in effect for all WordPerfect documents until you change them again.

Using Other Format Options

Among the four categories of commands listed in the Format menu, the Other category, shown in figure 6.19, is the miscellaneous category. It includes commands that don't specifically apply to lines, pages, or a document as a whole.

Three commands that let you modify WordPerfect's conventions are listed under Other: Decimal Character, Language, and Overstrike.

Changing the Decimal Character and the Thousands' Separator

With the Decimal Character command, you can change the appearance of numbers in two ways. First, you can redefine the decimal character, usually a period. Second, you can redefine the thousands' separator, usually a comma. Decimal characters and thousands' separators are changed in a single operation.

```
Format: Other

     1 - Advance

     2 - Conditional End of Page

     3 - Decimal/Align Character          .
         Thousands' Separator             ,

     4 - Language                         EN

     5 - Overstrike

     6 - Printer Functions

     7 - Underline - Spaces               Yes
                     Tabs                 No




     Selection: 0
```

Fig. 6.19.

Other submenu of the Format menu.

WordPerfect's tabbing options include decimal tabs. When you use a decimal tab, numbers line up under a decimal character embedded in the number, rather than from the right or left edge of the number. This feature is quite useful when you create tables including columns of dollar amounts or fractional numbers.

With the Decimal Character command, you can change the decimal character used for tab alignment. Usually the decimal is a period. If you change the decimal character to a colon (:), for example, the column of numbers lines up by the colon in each number. Figure 6.20 shows a list of meeting times neatly arranged in a column using the colon as the decimal character.

```
                        STAFF MEETING TIMES
                            July, 1988

              Dept. A         Dept. B         Dept. C

Week 1         9:00           10:00            1:30
Week 2        10:00            1:30            3:00
Week 3         9:00           10:00            1:30
Week 4        10:00            1:30           10:00




A:\CH6FIGB2                              Doc 1 Pg 2 Ln 1" Pos 1"
```

Fig. 6.20.

Columns of meeting times using the colon (:) as the decimal character.

As a default, WordPerfect includes left-aligned tabs set at every half inch. When you want different tabs for a project such as a table that lists prices, you can set decimal tabs at the spacing you need. Refer to Chapter 5 for more information about setting tabs.

WordPerfect also can perform math calculations for you (see Chapter 17). When it does, results may include a number in the thousands, with the thousands separated by a comma. If you want the thousands separated by a character other than a comma, use the Thousands' Separator command to change it.

In Swedish, for example, thousands are separated by a period, and decimals are indicated by a comma—just the opposite of how they appear in English.

To change the decimal character and the thousands' separator, follow these steps:

1. Press Format (Shift-F8) to display the Format menu.

2. Select **Other** (**4**) to display the Format Other menu.

3. Select **Decimal/Align Character Thousands' Separator** (**3**).

4. Type the new decimal character.

5. Type the new thousands' separator.

6. Press Exit (F7) to return to the document.

Changing the Language Code

If you write in a language other than English, or if your documents include sections written in another language, you can check your work with spelling, hyphenation, and thesaurus files specific to the language.

WordPerfect's default language is English. When you check spelling in a document, WordPerfect refers to its English dictionary. But if a document includes a section in Spanish, you can instruct WordPerfect to refer to a Spanish dictionary instead. To cause WordPerfect to refer to a spelling, hyphenation, or thesaurus dictionary in another language, insert a language code at the beginning of the section written in the other language.

The language code remains in effect until WordPerfect encounters a different language code. So if only a section of a document is in another language, be sure to insert EN, the code for English, where English resumes.

Here are the available language codes:

CA	Canadian French
DA	Danish
DE	German
EN	English
ES	Spanish
FR	French
IC	Icelandic

IT	Italian
NE	Dutch
NO	Norwegian
PO	Portugese
SU	Finnish
SV	Swedish
UK	British English

To change the language code, follow these steps:

1. Press Format (Shift-F8) to display the Format menu.

2. Select **Other** (4) to display the Format Other menu.

3. Select **Language** (4).

4. Type the language code.

   Be careful to type the correct code. WordPerfect does not prompt you if the code is incorrect.

5. Press Exit (F7) twice to accept the change and return to the document.

WordPerfect comes equipped with only English dictionaries. Order other dictionaries (for a price) from the WordPerfect Corporation.

Using Overstrike

Usually only one character per space appears in a WordPerfect document. Sometimes, though, you want two (or more) characters to appear in the same space. For example, you may want to create foreign characters, such as û, é, or ñ.

Use Overstrike to create foreign and scientific characters that your printer doesn't support. If your printer does support these characters, use the printer's characters instead. To use the printer's characters, insert a printer escape code where you want the character to appear.

To create an overstrike, follow these steps:

1. Type to the point in your document where you want two (or more) characters to print in the same space.

2. Press Format (F8) to display the Format menu.

3. Press **Other** (4) to display the Format Other menu.

4. Press **Overstrike** (5).

5. Press **Create** (1).

6. Type each character you want to appear in the same space.

7. Press Enter.

8. Press Exit (F7) to return to the document.

Overstrike characters do not appear on-screen, but they appear on the document when you print or in the View Document mode. On-screen, only the last character of the overstrike appears. Use the Reveal Codes command (Alt-F3, or F11) to check the accuracy of overstrikes before you print.

Note that you can't create an overstrike character and use it again and again in a document. You must create it anew each time it is to appear.

You also can edit an overstrike character once it's been created by following these steps:

1. Move the cursor to just after the overstrike.

2. Press Format (Shift-F8) to display the Format menu.

3. Press **Other** (**4**) to display the Format Other menu.

4. Press **Overstrike** (**5**).

5. Press **Edit** (**2**).

6. Type the new overstrike characters.

7. Press Enter.

8. Press Exit (F7) to return to the document.

When you select **Edit** (**2**), WordPerfect searches backward through text and displays the first overstrike character the program finds. If none is found, WordPerfect then searches forward through the text.

Checking Document Format with View Document

One of WordPerfect's handiest features is the View Document command. View Document shows you as closely as possible what a document will look like when you print it.

Use View Document to preview page breaks, headers and footers, page numbers, columns, lines, illustrations, and graphics. Use it frequently to check your progress when you create a complex document—it can often save you time by identifying mistakes before you print them, and it can alert you early to problem areas. Figure 6.21 shows a Full Page View Document look at a document.

If you don't have a graphics card in your computer, View Document functions in the same way as it does in version 4.2. You do not have a Full Page option, and you see only such items as margins, headers and footers, page numbers, and foot- and endnotes.

The following four View Document display sizes are available:

- Full Page—shows you the entire page, reduced to fit on-screen

- 100%—displays the page in actual size

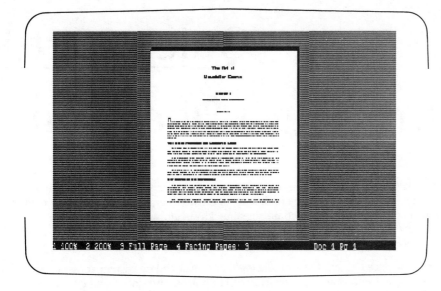

Fig. 6.21.
A Full Page view of a document.

- 200%—displays the page in twice actual size
- Facing Pages—displays a full page view of two pages, with even-numbered pages on the left and odd-numbered pages on the right. (Page 1 has no facing page, so it's always by itself.)

To view a document, follow these steps:

1. Press Print (Shift-F7).

2. Select View Document (**6**).

3. Select a display size:

   100% (**1**)

   200% (**2**)

   Full Page (**3**)

   Facing Pages (**4**)

4. Press any direction arrow to scroll through the page, or press Home and a direction arrow to scroll one screen at a time. Press PgUp or PgDn to scroll to a different page.

5. Press Exit (F7) to return to the document.

If you scroll to a different page, that's the page where you are when you press the Exit key to return to your document.

When you are in the View Document display, you can press **1**, **2**, **3**, or **4** to change the view to another size.

Quick Start

Formatting a Document

Quick Start 6 introduces you to some of WordPerfect's most powerful formatting commands. You can use these commands to create clear, interesting, easy-to-read pages. If you need to use formatting commands quickly, begin with this Quick Start section. Then reread the entire chapter later for more complete information about formatting strategies.

Setting margins creates top and bottom spacing that is neat and consistent across each page in a document. Centering one page from top to bottom presents a single page—usually the document's title page—that stands out from the rest.

With headers and footers, you quickly advise your reader of the document's topic or title. And with automatic page numbering, you let your reader know which page is which.

You also can issue format commands to keep blocks of text intact. Keeping text together prevents awkward page breaks.

And when you use WordPerfect's View Document command, you can see how the document looks before you print.

Setting Top and Bottom Margins

Margin settings apply to all text that follows them. You usually set margins before you begin typing.

To set top and bottom margins in a new WordPerfect document, follow these steps:

1. Press Format (Shift-F8).

   Pressing Format displays the Format menu, shown in figure 6.22. Notice that the Format menu lists three levels of formatting choices: line, page, and document. A fourth category includes other formatting choices.

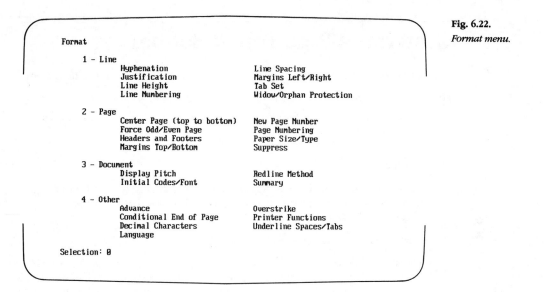

Fig. 6.22.
Format menu.

```
Format
    1 - Line
            Hyphenation                    Line Spacing
            Justification                  Margins Left/Right
            Line Height                    Tab Set
            Line Numbering                 Widow/Orphan Protection

    2 - Page
            Center Page (top to bottom)    New Page Number
            Force Odd/Even Page            Page Numbering
            Headers and Footers            Paper Size/Type
            Margins Top/Bottom             Suppress

    3 - Document
            Display Pitch                  Redline Method
            Initial Codes/Font             Summary

    4 - Other
            Advance                        Overstrike
            Conditional End of Page        Printer Functions
            Decimal Characters             Underline Spaces/Tabs
            Language

    Selection: 0
```

2. Select **Page** (**2**).

   Now the Format Page menu is displayed. It lists formatting choices affecting the appearance of pages.

3. Select **Margins** (**5**).

   WordPerfect's default margin choices—one inch (1″) on the top and one inch (1″) on the bottom—are already listed.

4. Type *.75* for the top margin and press Enter.

5. Type *.5* for the bottom margin and press Enter.

   You changed the margins to .75 (3/4-inch) for the top and .5 (1/5-inch) for the bottom. The changes apply to this document only.

6. Press Exit (F7) to return to your document.

Now type the text within the rules to use in the following Quick Start sections. Press Enter when you finish typing.

AN OZONE HOLE OVER CAPITOL HILL

The heat is on Congress to safeguard the atmosphere.

Few scientists doubt that something ominous is happening to the sky. And they know what the culprit is: it's a group of chemicals known as CFCs (chlorofluorocarbons). CFCs are used to cool refrigerators and to put the bubbles in plastic food containers used to keep fast foods warm.

Centering a Page Top to Bottom

You can override margin settings if you want to center a page from top to bottom.

To center the text you just typed from top to bottom, follow these steps:

1. Press Home, Home, ↑ to move the cursor to the beginning of the page.

2. Press Format (Shift-F8).

3. Select Page (2).

   Take a look at the first command listed on this menu. It's the Center Page command, and No appears to the right. That means that this page is currently NOT centered top to bottom.

4. Select Center Page (top to bottom) (1).

   The word No changes to Yes. The page is now centered on the page from top to bottom. You won't see a difference on-screen, but you can use the View Document command (next in the Quick Start) to see how the page looks.

5. Press Exit (F7) to return to the document.

Keep in mind that although margin settings apply to all text that follows them in a document, top to bottom page centering applies only to the current page.

Viewing a Document

You can't see many page and document formatting changes on-screen. They appear only when you print a document. Using the View Document command, however, you can see what the page looks like before you print—complete with headers and footers, page numbers, and top-to-bottom centering. Without a doubt, this is one of WordPerfect's handiest features!

To view a document, follow these steps:

1. Press Print (Shift-F7) to display the Print menu.

2. Select View Document (6).

   You see a small picture of the page, in Full Page mode, as shown in figure 6.23. You can't read the text in this view, but you can get an idea of how the page looks.

3. Press 100% (1).

   You can choose four possible page views. The initial view, Full Page (3), shows you the whole page. Pressing 1 gives you 100% or a full-size picture of the page. Other views include 200% (2) for a double-size view and Facing Pages (4), which shows you left- and right-facing pages (but only

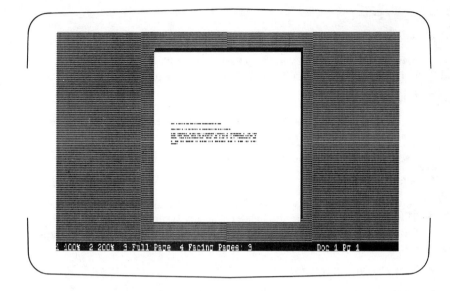

Fig. 6.23.

A Full Page view of a document.

when you have more than one page or when you are not on page 1, which usually has no facing page).

4. Press the ↓ several times.

    You can scroll through a view of the page using any of the arrow keys. (If a document has more than one page, you can press the PgUp or PgDn keys to scroll through the pages.)

5. Press Exit (F7) to return to the document.

If you scroll to another page or even another part of the page, that's where you'll be when you press Exit to return to the document.

You can only look at a page with the View Document command. You can't edit it until you return to the document.

Creating Headers and Footers

Headers and footers are lines of text that appear at the tops and bottoms of every page in a document. In a book, headers often tell you the book's title and the name of the chapter you're reading. In a newsletter, footers often specify the month and date of the issue.

To create a header, follow these steps:

1. Press Home, Home, ↑ to move the cursor to the beginning of the document.

2. Press Format (Shift-F8).

3. Select **Page** (**2**).

4. Select **Headers** (**3**).

You can have up to two headers and two footers. WordPerfect calls them Header A and Header B, and Footer A and Footer B. You create them one at a time.

5. Select Header **A** (**1**).

   To create Header A, you have to decide where the header will appear. Your choices are on every page, on odd pages, or on even pages.

   Use this menu to discontinue or edit the header later.

6. Select **Odd Pages** (**3**).

   Now you advance to a screen that looks like the usual WordPerfect screen. This is where you create the header. Use any WordPerfect command to format the header. Because you chose **Odd Pages** (**3**), Header A appears only on odd-numbered pages in the document.

7. Type *Business Week article*.

8. Press Exit (F7) to return to the Format Page menu.

   A header reading "Business Week article" appears on all odd-numbered pages in the document. Notice that in the Format Page menu, the message HA Odd pages now appears to the right of **Headers** (**3**). The message tells you that you created Header A to appear on odd pages.

Create a second header by following these steps:

1. Select **Headers** (**3**).

2. Select Header **B** (**2**).

3. Select **Even Pages** (**4**).

4. Press Flush Right (Alt-F6) to move to the right of the screen.

5. Type *April 4, page 35*.

6. Press Exit (F7).

7. Press Exit (F7) again to return to the document.

This header appears only on even pages. Thus you have Header A, which appears on the left edge of odd pages, and Header B, which appears on the right edge of even pages.

Creating footers is just the same as creating headers—just choose Footers (**4**) from the Format Page menu instead of Headers (**3**).

Like many formatting choices, headers and footers can't be seen on your document screen. But you can see them in the View Document mode.

Use View Document to see the header by following these steps:

1. Press Print (Shift-F7).

2. Select View (**6**).

   Notice Header A at the top left of the page.

3. Press Exit (F7) to return to the document.

Numbering Pages Automatically

Numbering pages in a document can't be any easier than in this version of WordPerfect. WordPerfect does it for you automatically! All you have to do is indicate where page numbers should appear on the page.

To number pages automatically, follow these steps:

1. Press Home, Home, ↑ to move the cursor to the beginning of the document.

2. Press Format (Shift-F8).

3. Select **Page** (**2**).

4. Select **Page** Numbering (**7**).

What you see now is a screen (see fig. 6.24) that represents the nine possible page positions for page numbers.

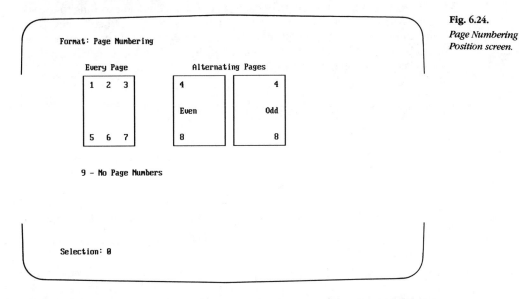

Fig. 6.24.
Page Numbering Position screen.

Page numbers can appear in one of six positions on every page or in either of two positions on alternating pages. To remove page numbering, choose the last selection on-screen, **No** Page Numbers (**9**).

5. Select **6**.

This command puts automatic page numbering at the bottom center of every page and returns you to the Format Page menu (where you can make additional formatting choices if you like).

6. Press Exit (F7) to return to the document.

Again, you can't see page numbering on-screen. Use View Document to see the page number at the bottom of the page.

To view the document, follow these steps:

1. Press Print (Shift-F7).

2. Select View Document (**6**).

3. If necessary, select 100% (**1**) to see the page in 100% size.

4. Press Home, ↓ to scroll to the bottom of the page.

You can see the number 1 at the bottom center of the page.

5. Press Exit (F7) to return to the document.

Keeping Text Together

WordPerfect calculates the length of each page in a document according to the set margins. When it reaches the end of a page, a new page begins. What if a new page begins automatically in the middle of a chart or just after the title of a new section? You probably don't want the page to break just there. WordPerfect offers you three ways to keep text together on a page.

Setting a Conditional End of Page

With the Conditional End of Page command, you specify that a certain number of lines be kept together on the page. In effect, you're setting a condition for how the page will end.

To set a conditional end of page, follow these steps:

1. Move the cursor to the empty line between the two paragraphs of text.

Always move the cursor to the line above the group of lines you want to keep together.

2. Press Format (Shift-F8).

3. Select Other (**4**).

4. Select Conditional End of Page (**2**).

Now you see the following prompt at the bottom of the screen: Number of lines to Keep Together:. At the end of the prompt, the cursor is flashing.

5. Type *5*.

6. Press Exit (F7).

7. Press Exit (F7) again to return to the document.

   You want to keep five lines together. Rather than break that group of five lines across two pages if the lines fall at the end of a page, WordPerfect inserts a page break before the lines so that they start on the next page instead.

Protecting a Block

Another way to protect text from breaking is the Block Protect command.

To protect a block of text, follow these steps:

1. Move the cursor to the beginning of the document.

2. Press Block (Alt-F4, or F12).

3. Press the ↓ enough times to highlight the entire three paragraphs.

   You just selected a block of text, and now you'll protect it so that it does not break across two pages.

4. Press Format (Shift-F8).

5. Press *Y* to protect the block.

Preventing Widows and Orphans

An orphan is the first line of a paragraph that appears by itself at the bottom of a page. A widow is the last line of a paragraph that appears by itself at the top of a page. Usually, it's best to prevent widows and orphans.

To prevent widows and orphans, follow these steps:

1. Move the cursor to the beginning of the document.

2. Press Format (Shift-F8).

3. Select **Line (1)**.

4. Select **Widow/Orphan protection (9)**.

5. Press *Y* for Yes.

6. Press Exit (F7) to return to the document.

   Widow/Orphan protection takes effect from this point forward in the document.

Now that you've quickly rehearsed the basic formatting commands, you can apply what you just learned to a document you are creating. Or you can go back and read Chapter 6 in its entirety for a fuller explanation of formatting strategies.

WP 5 Summary

If you hold a WordPerfect document at arm's length and look at it, you notice its overall appearance. You notice how the text fits on the pages, where headers and footers and page numbers fall, whether new sections begin on new pages.

Most formatting is done through the Format menu, accessed through the Format key (Shift-F8). In this chapter you learned that the Format Menu contains four options—Line, Page, Document, and Other. Selecting any of these four options advances you to a menu containing commands specific to the option. In the Line menu, you see commands such as hyphenation, justification, and left and right margins—all of which control line formatting in a document. Similarly, in the Page menu, you see commands such as headers and footers, top and bottom margins, and page numbering—all of which regulate the appearance of pages in a document. In the Document menu, you find commands with which to establish initial settings for a document. And in the Other menu, you find commands for protecting areas of text from breaking across two pages and for creating special decimal and overstrike characters.

In a sense, each of the sections on the Format menu controls a different level of document formatting—from the very local level, line formatting; to the intermediate level, page formatting; to a much more global level, document formatting.

In a related menu, the Print menu, you learned to view a document as it looks when you print it, including headers, footers, and automatic page numbers.

These formatting choices are part of document design. And when your document's design is consistent and clear, your document looks attractive. But more importantly, it is clear and readable.

Although conveying a message through words is your most important task, don't underestimate the importance of good document design. Good design makes your document readable. And no matter how meaningful your message is, it will never get across if someone doesn't pick it up and read it.

7

Using the Speller
and the Thesaurus

*Susan Hafer has been
using, supporting, and
teaching WordPerfect at
Wellesley College since
1986 and brings her
knowledge of version 5
to this chapter.* ■

WordPerfect's Speller and Thesaurus provide you with two
valuable tools for increasing your efficiency and accuracy as a
writer. The Speller contains a dictionary with more than 100,000
words and helps you proofread your work by searching for spelling
mistakes and common typing errors such as transposed, missing, extra,
or wrong letters, and double words like "the the." You can use the
Speller also when you know what a word sounds like but aren't sure of
its spelling.

You can look up words in the Speller, add words to the built-in
dictionary, or create your own dictionaries of terms specific to your
profession. The Speller contains only the correct spelling of words; it
does not contain definitions. If you need to look up a word's meaning,
use a conventional dictionary.

If you write in a language other than English, spell-checking a
document is a tedious chore; the Speller stops at almost every word.
Fortunately, WordPerfect dictionaries in other languages are available.
If you need a foreign language dictionary, contact WordPerfect
Corporation to see if it can provide the dictionary you need.

The on-line Thesaurus, with more than 10,000 *headwords* (words that
serve as primary references), saves you time. You can quickly find
synonyms (words with similar meanings) and *antonyms* (words with
opposite meanings) as you type or edit your document. You no longer
have to thumb through a printed Thesaurus.

When you can't find quite the right word, or when you can think only
of the opposite of the word you want, use the Thesaurus to suggest
other possible words. If you repeat one word over and over again in
your text, add freshness and variety to your writing by using the
Thesaurus to find other words.

229

The Speller and the Thesaurus work essentially the same way in version 5 as they did in version 4.2. To convert a dictionary from 4.2, see "Using the Speller Utility." Because letters are used as a reference menu to select individual words within the Speller or Thesaurus, you select options by numbers, not mnemonics.

This chapter shows you how to use the Speller and the Thesaurus as part of the cycle of drafting, revising, editing, and proofreading. You learn how to do the following tasks:

- Access the Speller or Thesaurus on a floppy or a hard disk system

- Spell-check a word, page, document, or block of text

- Create and use your own customized dictionaries

- Add or delete words in the built-in dictionary

- Use the Thesaurus as an aid to composition: replacing words, viewing words in context, and looking up additional words

Using the Speller

WordPerfect's Speller compares each word in your document against the words in its dictionary. This dictionary is made up of a list of *common* words (words most frequently used) and a list of *main* words (words generally found in dictionaries). WordPerfect checks every word against its list of common words, and if the program does not find the word there, WordPerfect looks in its list of main words. If you have your own supplemental dictionary, WordPerfect looks there as well. Words found in any of the dictionaries are considered correct by the program.

For words that the program does not find, you can use the Speller to replace the misspelled words with an alternate spelling that the program suggests, or you can edit words by typing the correct spelling. You also can add words to a supplemental dictionary. You can create several supplemental dictionaries of specialized terms— for instance, terms used for law, engineering, medicine, literary criticism, or entomology—and use these special dictionaries during a spell-check.

The Speller does not find all typos, so although using this feature does help, the Speller doesn't completely replace a human proofreader. If you type "them" when you meant to type "then," for example, or "their" instead of "there," your mistake is not noted by the Speller. Because these words are actual words in the dictionary, the Speller considers them correct, even though they are incorrect in the context of the sentence. You still should proofread your document after using the Speller.

The Speller's built-in dictionary contains some variant spellings. For example, the Speller includes "fetish" and "fetich," "doughnut" and "donut," "etiology" and "aetiology," "flutist" and "flautist," "numbskull" and "numskull," "soubriquet" and "sobriquet," and "yogurt" and "yoghurt."

Setting Up the Speller

If you have an IBM PS/2 machine, the Speller and Thesaurus files are found on one 3 1/2-inch Speller/Thesaurus disk. If you have an IBM PC XT, PC AT, or compatible, the Speller and Thesaurus files are on two separate 5 1/4-inch floppy disks.

The main dictionary file, WP{WP}EN.LEX, contains both the main and common word lists. When you run the Speller for the first time and add words to the dictionary, a supplemental dictionary file, WP{WP}EN.SUP, is created. Use the Speller Utility, SPELLER.EXE, to make changes to the main dictionary and to create or make changes to a supplemental dictionary (see "Using the Speller Utility").

To install WordPerfect and copy the Speller and Thesaurus files, see Appendix A of this book.

If you have a floppy disk system, be sure that you specify the locations of your supplemental dictionaries from Setup. If you omit this step, the program cannot find the dictionaries.

If you have a hard disk drive, you may have created a separate subdirectory for the Speller and Thesaurus files during installation. You need to tell WordPerfect where to locate these files when you run the Speller or the Thesaurus. (You don't have to store these files in a separate subdirectory, but doing so keeps your main program directory from becoming cluttered with too many files.)

If you have a hard drive and created a separate subdirectory for the Speller and Thesaurus files, do the following to specify the file locations:

1. Press Setup (Shift-F1).

2. Press Location of Auxiliary Files (**7**).

3. Select the file location you want to change.

    For instance, select **T**hesaurus (**8**).

4. Type the directory of this file and press Enter.

    For instance, you may have stored this file in a directory called C:\WP5\LEX.

Figure 7.1 shows file locations chosen for the main dictionary, supplemental dictionaries, and the Thesaurus. If you have a special supplemental dictionary that you want to store elsewhere—such as a special file of medical, legal, or discipline-specific terms—you also can specify a directory for this dictionary.

TIP: If your computer does not have a hard disk but does have expanded or extended memory, you can put the Speller and Thesaurus files in a RAM or virtual disk to make these WordPerfect features easier and faster to use.

Fig. 7.1.

Auxiliary file location for the Speller and Thesaurus files.

```
Setup: Location of Auxiliary Files

    1 - Backup Directory

    2 - Hyphenation Module(s)

    3 - Keyboard/Macro Files

    4 - Main Dictionary(s)           C:\WP5\LEX

    5 - Printer Files                C:\WP5

    6 - Style Library Filename

    7 - Supplementary Dictionary(s)  C:\WPDOCS

    8 - Thesaurus                    C:\WP5\LEX




    Selection: 8
```

Starting the Speller

You can use the Speller on dual floppy disk systems as well as on hard disk systems. A disadvantage to using the Speller on a dual floppy system is that you must first retrieve your document from your data disk in drive B:; then you must remove your data disk and insert the Speller disk in drive B: before you can spell-check a document. When you want to save the spell-checked document, you must remember to remove the Speller from drive B: and reinsert the document disk. Moreover, floppy disk storage space puts some constraints on the size of the dictionaries you can use. With a hard disk system, you don't need to swap disks or worry about dictionary size for the most part.

To practice spell-checking a document, type the text in italics, including the spelling errors. Use this text to complete the steps for using the Speller. When you finish typing, your file should look like the one in figure 7.2.

In Pide and Prejudice *by Jane Austen, for example, there are both men and women characters with selfcentered personalities: Bingley's sisters and brother-in-law, the cousin Mr. Collins. We see this as Elizabeth goes to see her sister Jane, who became ill while visiting the neighbors:*

> *[Elizabeth] was shown into the breakfast-parlour, where all but Jane were assembled, and where her appearance created a great deal of surprise. . . . Mr. Darcy said very little, and Mr. Hurst nothing at all. The former was divided between admiration of the brilliancy which exercise had given to her complexion, and doubt as to the occasion's justifying her her coming so far alone. The latter was thinking only of his breakfast.*

. . . . Jane was by no means better. [Mrs. Hurst and Miss Bingley], on hearing this, repeated three or four times how much they were grieved, how shocking it was to have a bad cold, and how excessively they diskliked being ill themslves; and then thought n more of the matter. . . .

Fig. 7.2.
Sample text.

To start the Speller, follow these steps:

1. If you want to check just a word or just a page, place the cursor anywhere within the word or page

    or

    If you want to check the entire document, you do not need to place the cursor.

2. If you have a floppy disk system, remove the data disk from drive B: and insert the Speller disk

    or

    If you have installed the Speller on the hard disk, you do not need to change disks.

CAUTION: Before you remove the disk, make sure that WordPerfect isn't doing a backup of your work. * Please wait * appears at the bottom of the screen during backup. You can lose your document if the computer is writing to the disk when you take it out.

---

3. Press Spell (Ctrl-F2).

The following Spell menu appears at the bottom of the screen:

Check: 1 Word; **2** Page; **3** Document; **4** New Sup. Dictionary; **5** Look Up; **6** Count: **0**

4. Select the menu choice you want.

Because you want to spell-check the entire document for this example, select **Document (3)**.

If you forgot to insert the Speller disk and do not have the Speller files on a hard disk or if you forgot to specify the location of the speller files in the Setup menu, you see the following message:

WP{WP}EN.LEX not found: **1** Enter Path; **2** Skip Language; **3** Exit Spell; *3*

If you forgot to insert the speller disk, insert the disk and select Enter **Path (1)**. Then type *B:* and press Enter.

If you forgot to specify the location, select Enter **Path (1)**. Then type the path *C:\wp5\lex* and press Enter.

To look up the word where your cursor is located, select **Word (1)**. If WordPerfect finds the word in its dictionary, the cursor moves to the next word in your document, and the Spell menu remains at the bottom of the screen. You can continue checking words or choose some other option from the Spell menu. If the word isn't found, you are offered alternative spellings. You can also press Exit (F7) to exit the Speller.

If you select **Page (2)**, WordPerfect looks up every word on the page where your cursor is located. After checking the page, the Spell menu remains. Again, continue checking words or choose another option.

You can use a new supplemental dictionary to spell-check the document (see "Using a Supplemental Dictionary") if you select New Sup. Dictionary **(4)**.

To enter a new word to spell-check, select Look Up **(5)** (see "Looking Up a Word"). To count the words, select Count **(6)** (see "Ending the Speller").

As soon as the Speller finds a word not in its dictionary, the Speller stops, highlights the word, and provides a list of alternative spellings (see fig. 7.3).

You have several options: you can select a correct spelling from the replacements, skip the word (for instance, if it is spelled correctly), add the word to the supplemental dictionary, or edit the word (type the correct spelling).

Selecting a Correct Spelling

The Speller highlights a word not found and displays a list of alternative spellings and the following Not Found menu:

Not Found: 1 Skip Once; **2** Skip; **3** Add Word; **4** Edit; **5** Look Up: **0**

Fig. 7.3.

A misspelled word.

```
   In Pide and Prejudice by Jane Austen, for example, there are both
men and women characters with selfcentered personalities: Bingley's
sisters and brother-in-law, the cousin Mr. Collins. We see this as
Elizabeth goes to see her sister Jane, who became ill while
visiting the neighbors:

          [Elizabeth] was shown into the breakfast-parlour,
          where all but Jane were assembled, and where her
          appearance created a great deal of surprise...., Mr. Darcy
          said very little, and Mr. Hurst nothing at all. The
          former was divided between admiration of the brilliancy

================================================================================

   A. pede             B. pie              C. pied
   D. pike             E. pile             F. pine
   G. pipe             H. pride            I. pad
   J. paddy            K. paid             L. pat
   M. pate             N. patio            O. pawed
   P. payday           Q. payout           R. peat
   S. peaty            T. pet              U. pete
   V. peyote           W. piety            X. pit
Press Enter for more words

Not Found: 1 Skip Once; 2 Skip; 3 Add Word; 4 Edit; 5 Look Up:  0
```

To select a word from the replacement list, complete the following steps:

1. Find the correct spelling among the list of alternative spellings.

   If you do not see the correct spelling and WordPerfect tells you to Press Enter for More Words (as it does in fig. 7.3), press Enter to display more alternatives. Otherwise, refer to the subsequent sections of this chapter.

   For this example, you see many alternative spellings for the typo "Pide" (see fig. 7.3). The correct spelling is, of course, "Pride."

2. Press the letter next to the replacement spelling you want to select.

   For instance, press *h* for "pride."

   The new word automatically replaces the misspelled word in the text; notice that the Speller was smart enough to leave the word capitalized!

TIP: You do not need to wait for all the alternatives to be displayed on-screen. As soon as you see the correct spelling, press its letter and the Speller immediately replaces the word.

Once you correct the word, the Speller continues checking the rest of the text.

Skipping Words Spelled Correctly

Many correctly spelled words are not included in the WordPerfect dictionary. Remember that the dictionary contains only a limited number of words. In the sample text, for example, the next word not found is "Austen," the author's name. "Austen" is spelled correctly but is not found in the dictionary. However, note that the author's first name, "Jane," passes with no problem. The dictionary contains many common American proper names, like "Catherine"; other less common names, like "Kathryn," are not included.

When the Speller notes a word as incorrect, the Not Found menu appears at the bottom of the screen. When a word on which the Speller stops is spelled correctly, you can skip the word or add it to your supplemental dictionary.

How do you decide which method to use for a correctly spelled word? If a word appears only once or twice in your document, skip the word by selecting Skip (**2**) and continue with the rest of the spell-check. Choosing this option ignores the word now and throughout the rest of the document. If you want to skip the word the first time only, select Skip Once (**1**) instead. Then if the Speller encounters the word in the document again, the Speller stops and prompts you once more. Skip Once (**1**) is the better choice if the word is spelled correctly but may be a misspelling of another word elsewhere in your document. (For example, you might abbreviate "thesaurus" in your text as "thes"; however, you might later have mistyped "these" as "thes." You would want the Speller to catch that typo for you.)

Adding Words Spelled Correctly

If you use the word frequently, select Add Word (**3**). The Speller then stores the word in memory and skips any future occurrences of the word in the document. At the end of the spell-check, all words you added to the dictionary are saved to the current supplemental dictionary. (The supplemental dictionary is named WP{WP}EN.SUP unless you specify otherwise from the Spell menu.)

Words in the supplemental dictionary are not offered as alternative spellings; therefore, if you misspell one of these words ("Aussten" instead of "Austen"), the correct spelling is not one of your alternatives. Instead you have to correct the word yourself. However, you can add the word to the main dictionary by using the Speller Utility, and then the word is offered as an alternative.

For your example, select Add Word (**3**) so that you can see what the supplemental dictionary looks like later. WordPerfect stores "Austen" in memory and creates a supplemental dictionary at the end of this spell-check session.

You also want to add "Bingley," "Darcy," and "Hurst" (names of characters from *Pride and Prejudice*) to the supplemental dictionary when the Speller stops at those words in a few moments.

Editing a Word

When the correct alternative is not offered and when the word is incorrect, you have to enter the correct spelling yourself. For instance, the hyphen is missing in the word "selfcentered" in the example (see fig. 7.4).

Fig. 7.4.

Editing a misspelled word.

```
In Pride and Prejudice by Jane Austen, for example, there are both
men and women characters with selfcentered personalities: Bingley's
sisters and brother-in-law, the cousin Mr. Collins. We see this as
Elizabeth goes to see her sister Jane, who became ill while
visiting the neighbors:

        [Elizabeth] was shown into the breakfast-parlour,
        where all but Jane were assembled, and where her
        appearance created a great deal of surprise.... Mr. Darcy
        said very little, and Mr. Hurst nothing at all. The
        former was divided between admiration of the brilliancy

================================================================================




    Not Found: 1 Skip Once; 2 Skip; 3 Add Word; 4 Edit; 5 Look Up:  0
```

To enter a correct spelling, complete the following steps:

1. Select Edit (**4**).

   The cursor moves to the word in your text.

2. Press → or ← to move right or left, respectively, and make the corrections.

   For instance, move the cursor between "self" and "centered" and type a hyphen.

3. Press Exit (F7) when you have finished the correction.

   The Speller rechecks the word you just corrected and stops at the same place again if the corrected version is not in its dictionary.

Eliminating Double Words

In addition to finding misspelled words, the Speller notes double words. In the example, the next problem the Speller finds is a double word, "her her" (see fig. 7.5).

When WordPerfect encounters a double word, the program does not show alternative spellings; however, the program does display the following Double Word menu, which differs slightly from the normal Not Found menu:

Double Word: 1 2 Skip; **3** Delete 2nd; **4** Edit; **5** Disable Double Word Checking

If you accidentally typed two words instead of one, select Delete 2nd (**3**). The program deletes one word and leaves the other.

Select Skip (**1** or **2**) if the double word is legitimate. Both options **1** and **2** from the Double Word menu do the equivalent of Skip Once (**1**) from the normal Not Found menu. There is no "skip this word now *and* throughout the rest of this document"

Fig. 7.5.

A double word.

```
where all but Jane were assembled, and where her
appearance created a great deal of surprise.... Mr. Darcy
said very little, and Mr. Hurst nothing at all. The
former was divided between admiration of the brilliancy
which exercise had given to her complexion, and doubt as
to the occasion's justifying her her coming so far alone.
The latter was thinking only of his breakfast.

....Jane was by no means better. [Mrs. Hurst and Miss
Bingley], on hearing this, repeated three or four times
how much they were grieved, how shocking it was to have
```

```
Double Word: 1 2 Skip; 3 Delete 2nd; 4 Edit; 5 Disable Double Word Checking
```

for double words. For example, the double word in the following sentence is correct:

She had explained that that job would be difficult for him.

If one of the words is a typo, select Edit (4) and enter the correct spelling (for instance, "that that" when you meant "than that").

If a document contains many legitimate double words, select Disable Double Word Checking (5). If you use this option, carefully proofread the text yourself for double words you do not want in the document.

To take care of a double word, complete the following steps:

1. Read the text and determine whether the double word is a mistake.

2. Select the action you want to perform.

   For instance, select Delete 2nd (3).

   The Speller then continues to check the rest of your text.

For your example, two more words are not found in the Speller's main dictionary: "diskliked," which you should replace with "disliked," and "themslves," which you should replace with "themselves."

Notice also that the "n," which should have been "no" in the text, was not caught by the Speller; all single letter words are accepted as valid. You really do need to proofread your work even after running the Speller.

Ending the Speller

When the Speller finishes, it automatically stops and tells you the number of words checked on-screen. Because you spell-checked the entire document for your example, the word count shows the number of words in the entire document (see fig. 7.6). All words are counted, even the articles and conjunctions. (If you need a word count of your document, you could spell-check the entire document or simply select **Count** (6) from the Spell menu.)

```
        said very little, and Mr. Hurst nothing at all. The
        former was divided between admiration of the brilliancy
        which exercise had given to her complexion, and doubt as
        to the occasion's justifying her coming so far alone.
        The latter was thinking only of his breakfast.

        ....Jane was by no means better. [Mrs. Hurst and Miss
        Bingley], on hearing this, repeated three or four times
        how much they were grieved, how shocking it was to have
        a bad cold, and how excessively they disliked being ill
        themselves; and then thought n more of the matter....




    Word count: 167      Press any key to continue
```

Fig. 7.6.

The word count at the end of a spell-check.

If you need to interrupt the spell-check to do something else with your computer, just press Cancel (F1) instead of selecting a menu option. You will be given a count of the words checked and will be told to Press any key to continue to return to your document. Later you can check the rest of the document, skipping over the section that was already checked (see "Spell-Checking a Block").

To continue, press any key and then save your document by pressing Save (F10). Floppy disk users should keep in mind that spelling corrections are made to your document in the computer's temporary memory. To save the changes to a floppy disk, you must exit the Speller, remove the Speller disk from drive B:, and reinsert the appropriate data disk before saving your spell-checked document.

Looking Up a Word

As you type, you can look up words you don't know how to spell. The word "geiger," for example, is one of those pesky "ie vs. ei" words you probably use very rarely and might forget how to spell.

To look up a word by using the Speller, complete the following steps:

1. If you use floppy disks, put the Speller disk in drive B:.

2. Press Spell (Ctrl-F2).

3. Select Look Up (5).

   You are prompted with Word or word pattern:

4. Type the word or word pattern and press Enter.

   A *word pattern* is a rough guess at a word's spelling. You type an asterisk (*) to replace an unknown number of letters or a question mark (?) to replace one unknown letter. After you press Enter, WordPerfect shows you all the words that match the word pattern.

   For the example, type *g*ger* and press Enter. The Speller displays all words that begin with the letter "g" followed by some number of letters and ending with "ger" in its dictionary (see fig. 7.7).

Fig. 7.7.
Looking up "g*ger."

```
================================================================================
A. gager           B. gauger          C. geiger
D. ginger          E. gouger          F. gunslinger



Word or word pattern:
```

5. Press Exit (F7) twice to return to your document

   or

   Enter another word or word pattern.

   For your exercise, type *g??ger* and press Enter.

Fig. 7.8.
Looking up "g??ger."

```
================================================================================
A. gauger          B. geiger          C. ginger
D. gouger



Word or word pattern:
```

You can see the difference between using asterisks and question marks (see fig. 7.8). Fewer words appear when you use question marks because each question mark represents a single letter, whereas an asterisk can represent any number of letters.

When you use Look Up, you cannot select a word and automatically insert it in your document, so be sure to write down the correct spelling!

You do not have to enter question marks and asterisks in every case, however; you simply can enter a phonetic spelling (spelling a word the way it sounds or the way it is pronounced). For instance, you can type *sikotic* and press Enter.

```
=================================================================================

       A. psychotic              B. saccadic




    Word or word pattern:
```

Fig. 7.9.

Phonetic Look Up of "psychotic."

You can see that in addition to checking for similar spellings, the Speller selects words that are *phonetically* close (those with similar pronunciations) to the spelling (see fig. 7.9); therefore, for any word you know how to pronounce but not spell, you should be able to find that word's spelling.

You can look up a word from the Not Found menu in exactly the same way. For example, if the Speller stops at a word and you want to look up some possibilities that don't appear in the list of alternatives, you can select Look Up (5), type a word pattern, and then select Edit (4) to replace the word in your text with a word you looked up.

Spell-Checking a Block

In addition to being able to spell-check a word, a page, or an entire document, you can pick out a particular block of text to spell-check.

To spell-check a block, complete the following steps:

1. Press Block (Alt-F4, or F12) at one end of the block of text you want to spell-check.

2. Use the cursor-movement keys to move to the other end of the text you want to check.

3. If you are using floppy disks, replace your data disk with the Speller disk in drive B:.

4. Press Spell (Ctrl-F2).

You skip the Spell menu because you already have told WordPerfect how much of the text to check with Block (Alt-F4, or F12). Otherwise the Speller runs no differently.

Use the Block option if you have to Cancel (F1) in the middle of a spell-check, leaving the first part of a document corrected but the last half untouched. You could go back later and block off the part of the document that you did not check and then press Spell (Ctrl-F2).

Handling Words with Numbers

Unlike earlier versions of WordPerfect, the Speller now treats words containing numbers as if they were regular words. The advantage is that you can add words that contain numbers (for instance, x1234 or F1-F10) to dictionaries; the disadvantage is that you no longer can request that all words that contain numbers be ignored. If your text includes many legitimate words containing numbers, speed up the spell-check by adding the list of words to a supplemental dictionary or by blocking the words in a temporary comment.

Document comments are blocked-off sections of text that can be displayed on-screen but are not printed (see Chapter 3). These comments are not included in a spell-check, so if your document contains one or more sections of abnormal text (tables containing abbreviations or many words containing numbers), you can block off each section and turn it into a comment. You may have to break up the abnormal text into smaller groups of text if it is too long to fit into a comment. Then, after the spell-check, convert the comments back into normal text.

Creating a Supplemental Dictionary

You can create a supplemental dictionary by adding words during the spell-check, or you can create a supplemental dictionary from scratch. You also can have more than one supplemental dictionary. If you create the supplemental dictionary before you begin typing your document, the spell-check process runs faster because you have pre-empted the Speller from asking you about those words.

To create a dictionary specific to one document or project, you can keep a list of words in Doc 2 while typing a document in Doc 1. Then save the list and select that dictionary from the Spell menu when you spell-check that document or any other document on a related topic.

To create a supplemental dictionary, complete the following steps:

1. If you use floppy disks, insert a blank formatted disk in drive B:.

2. Begin a new document.

   If you just started WordPerfect, you have begun a new document. If you have a document on-screen, press Exit (F7), save your text, and press *N* for No when asked Exit WP?

3. Type your list of words, pressing Enter after each word.

4. Press Save (F10) to save the list.

CAUTION: Be sure to do a Fast Save, unformatted (Fast Save is determined by the main Setup menu). If you save a supplemental dictionary with printer information (formatted), the Speller can use those words. Your computer, however, may lock up if you use the Add Word option from the Not Found menu.

5. When prompted for a file name, type the name of the directory and the name of the file.

   For instance, hard disk users who want to name the file MEDICAL.SUP and store the file with their Speller files in the directory C:\WP5\LEX should type the following:

   C: \ WP5 \ LEX \ MEDICAL.SUP

   Floppy disk users: type *B:* and then the file name before using this supplemental dictionary. However, you must copy it to either the Speller disk or the second WP disk because these disks will be in your computer when you run the Speller.

Figure 17.10 shows MEDICAL.SUP, a supplemental dictionary of medical terms.

```
 Filename C:\WP5\LEX\MEDICAL.SUP                    File size:      536
    akathisia
    amytal
    BSP
    CBC
    CNS
    CPK
    CSF
    DAP
    EOM
    eos
    FBS
    FTA
    FTI
    Gardnerella
    glabellar
    GYN
    Hct
    HEENT
    hematest
    hemoccult
    Hgb

    Press Exit when done                  (Use Cursor Keys for more text)
```

Fig. 7.10.
MEDICAL.SUP dictionary.

TIP: WordPerfect's main dictionary already contains many medical terms (for instance, "folate," "lymphadenopathy," and "Rorschach"). To avoid duplications and save space in memory and on your disk, check your list of words through the Speller before saving the list as a supplemental dictionary. Delete any entries that WordPerfect passes (finds in its dictionary).

You can set up several supplemental dictionaries for different projects. You are limited to one supplemental dictionary per spell-check, but you can merge two or more together by retrieving them together and saving them (unformatted) under a new name. (To retrieve the two files together, first retrieve one from List Files, leave the cursor at the end of the list, and retrieve the second one from List Files. Answer *Y* when asked Retrieve into current document?.) Then select the merged file as the New Supplemental Dictionary from the Speller's Check menu.

Viewing the Contents of a Supplemental Dictionary

If you added any words to a dictionary during a spell-check or if you created another supplemental dictionary, you can review the words that the supplemental dictionary contains. (If you haven't done either of these options, a supplemental dictionary has not been created yet and cannot be reviewed.)

To review the supplemental dictionary, complete the following steps:

1. Press List Files (F5).

2. Type the directory name for the location of your supplemental dictionaries and press Enter.

   For instance, if you store the supplemental dictionary in a directory called C:\WP5\LEX, type *C:\WP5\LEX* and press Enter.

   Floppy disk users should type *B:* or *A:* and press Enter.

3. Move the cursor to the file WP{WP}EN.SUP. (This name is automatically given to a supplemental dictionary.)

   If you don't see this file, check the location of your auxiliary files to be sure that you specified the correct directory (see "Setting Up the Speller").

4. Select Look (6).

   Figure 7.11 displays the supplemental dictionary created in a previous exercise in this chapter. Notice that only one word appears per line. The words are in alphabetical order and are all lowercase.

5. Press Exit (F7) twice to return to your document.

From the List Files menu, you can select Retrieve (1) to edit this dictionary file like a regular document. Be sure to save it with Fast Save (unformatted) if you make any changes to it.

Using a Supplemental Dictionary

WordPerfect automatically uses the supplemental dictionary during spell-check if the supplemental dictionary you want to use is called WP{WP}EN.SUP (see "Setting Up the Speller") and is stored in the location you specified for Location of Auxiliary Files (7). You can select different supplemental dictionaries, however.

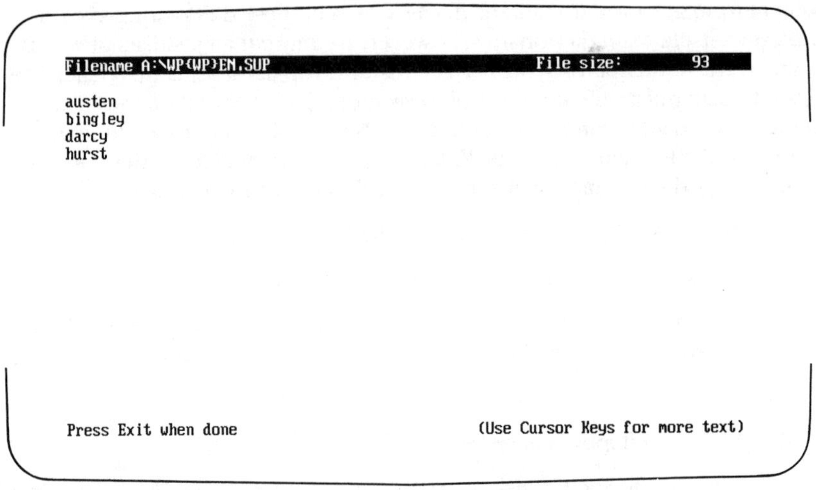

Fig. 7.11.
*A supplemental
dictionary.*

To use another supplemental dictionary, do the following:

1. Insert the Speller disk in drive B: if you have a floppy disk system.

2. Press Spell (Ctrl-F2).

3. From the Spell menu, select **New** Sup. Dictionary (4).

4. When prompted with `Supplemental dictionary name:`, type the name of the supplemental dictionary and press Enter.

   Be sure to include the drive and directory if they do not match the location of files you specified with Setup.

   For example, you would type *C:\WP5\LEX\MEDICAL.SUP* and press Enter if you had created the supplemental dictionary MEDICAL.SUP in the directory \WP5\LEX on your hard disk (C:).

5. Continue the spell-check as you would normally, requesting a check of a word, page, or entire document.

If the dictionary does not exist, the Speller does not tell you because it assumes that you will be adding words to the new supplemental dictionary while spell-checking the document. If you find that the Speller stops at words contained in your supplemental dictionary, go back and verify the name and location of your supplemental dictionary and try again.

Using the Speller Utility

In addition to using the Speller from within a document in WordPerfect, you can use the Speller Utility (the spell program) to manipulate the contents of a dictionary. Supplemental dictionaries are just alphabetical lists of words in normal WordPerfect document format, so you can add or delete words in these dictionaries within WordPerfect itself. Main dictionaries, however, are more than just lists of words, so you can't retrieve them into WordPerfect. Instead, you use a separate Speller Utility program to manipulate the contents of these more complex dictionaries. For example, you can add words to or delete words from dictionaries, including the common word and main word lists. You can optimize new dictionaries you have created, display the common word list, or check the location of a word.

To use the Speller Utility options, complete the following steps:

1. Press Exit (F7) to exit WordPerfect and begin at DOS level.

2. If you have a hard disk, change to the directory containing the Speller files (for instance, C:\WP5\LEX)

   or

   If you have a floppy disk system,

   a. Insert the Speller disk in drive A: and the document disk containing your supplemental dictionary in drive B:.

   b. If you are not at the B> prompt, type *B:* and press Enter.

3. If you use a hard disk, type *spell* and press Enter

   or

   If you use floppy disks, type *A:spell* and press Enter.

   The Speller Utility menu appears on-screen; the name of the dictionary that you can modify appears in the upper right corner (see fig. 7.12).

Fig. 7.12.
The Speller Utility menu.

```
Spell -- WordPerfect Speller Utility                    wp{wp}en.lex

0 - Exit
1 - Change/Create dictionary
2 - Add words to dictionary
3 - Delete words from dictionary
4 - Optimize dictionary
5 - Display common word list
6 - Check location of a word
7 - Look up
8 - Phonetic look up
9 - Convert 4.2 Dictionary to 5.0

Selection:
```

Within the Speller Utility menu, you have several options. If you want to change the dictionary being edited, select Change/Create Dictionary (1), enter a dictionary name, and perform any of the available options for this dictionary.

Select Add words to dictionary (2) to add words to either the common word list or the main word list. With Delete words from dictionary (3) you can delete words from the main or common word list. The following sections cover these two options in detail.

After you create a new dictionary, select Optimize dictionary (**4**), which helps WordPerfect access the words in your list more quickly and efficiently.

To review the words contained in the common word list, select Display common word list (**5**). After reviewing the list, press Exit (F7) to return to the Speller Utility menu.

You can determine in which word list (main or common) a word is located by choosing Check location of word (**6**). Type the word and press Enter. The location appears on-screen. Press Exit (F7) to return to the Speller Utility menu.

Look up words just as you do during a spell-check with options Look up (**7**) and Phonetic look up (**8**).

And finally, WordPerfect 4.2 users can convert their dictionaries to WordPerfect 5 by choosing Convert 4.2 Dictionary to 5.0 (**9**). (However, this option may not work if you have the 5/5/88 release of WordPerfect 5.)

Adding Words to the Main Dictionary

If you often use certain words in many documents, you can add these words to the main dictionary rather than include them in a supplemental dictionary. For example, you can add words that you use in your work to the main dictionary. (If you have a floppy disk system, the lack of free disk space may limit the number of words you can add, however.) One advantage of adding words to the main dictionary is to improve the effectiveness of spell-checking. Remember that words in the main dictionary are offered as alternative spellings for similar words in a document; words in a supplemental dictionary are not.

You can create a supplemental dictionary—a list of words with one word per line— and then add all its words to the main dictionary, or you can type individual words to be added. Be aware that updating the dictionary takes some time, however. For your example, add the list of words in the supplemental dictionary created earlier in this chapter.

To add words to the main dictionary, do the following:

1. Start the Speller Utility.

2. Select Add words to dictionary (**2**).

   The Add Words menu appears (see fig. 7.13).

CAUTION: If you are using the 5/5/88 release of WordPerfect 5 on a dual floppy system, the Spell program causes your computer to lock up and invalidates your dictionary file if you try to add words to the dictionary. If you are not sure whether your Spell program will work, be sure that you make a copy of the Speller disk before trying to use the Speller Utility.

Fig. 7.13.

The Add Words menu.

```
Spell -- Add Words                                           up{up}en.lex

0 - Cancel - do not add words
1 - Add to common word list (from keyboard)
2 - Add to common word list (from a file)
3 - Add to main word list (from keyboard)
4 - Add to main word list (from a file)
5 - Exit

Selection:
```

You can add words to the main or common word list either from the keyboard (typing one word at a time) or from a list in a file on disk.

3. Select the type of action you want to perform.

   For your example, you want to add the words from WP{WP}EN.SUP (the supplemental dictionary) to the main word list; therefore, select Add to main word list (from a file) (**4**).

4. When prompted with Enter file name:, type the file name and press Enter.

   For instance, type *up{WP}en.sup* and press Enter.

5. The words are not added immediately, so you either can pick more words to add (menu options **1-4**) or cancel the additions (menu option **0**)

   or

   Select Exit (**5**) to add the words and exit the menu.

   When you select Exit (**5**), you see the following message:

   Updating dictionary
   * Please Wait *

   WordPerfect then begins to write the words in the dictionary, starting with "A" and proceeding through the entire alphabet; the message Writing a's appears. Gradually the entire alphabet is done, but the process takes a while to complete.

CAUTION: Do not continue with the process—press Cancel (F1) instead—if you see the following message rather than the preceding one:

Insufficient room on drive A: for temporary files.

Do not remove diskette in drive A:

Enter drive letter for temporary files:

---

7. When the additions are complete and you return to the Speller Utility menu, select Exit (**0**) to exit back to DOS level.

Be sure that you delete the supplemental dictionary after it has been added to the main dictionary.

During a spell-check, the Speller no longer stops at the words you have added; the words may even appear as alternative spellings for other words.

Deleting Words from the Main Dictionary

Besides adding words, you also can delete words from the main dictionary to make room for other words or just to clean up the dictionary. For example, you might want to get rid of single-letter words like "n" or obscure terms you never use.

For this exercise, delete the words you added in the previous example.

To delete words from the main dictionary, complete the following steps:

1. Start the Speller Utility.

2. Select Delete words from dictionary (**3**).

   The Delete Words menu appears (see fig. 7.14). This menu is similar to the Add Words menu in figure 7.13.

CAUTION: If you are using the 5/5/88 release of WordPerfect 5 on a dual floppy system, the Spell program causes your computer to lock up and invalidates your dictionary file if you try to delete words from the dictionary. If you are not sure whether your Spell program will work, be sure that you make a copy of the Speller disk before trying to use the Speller Utility.

```
  Spell -- Delete Words                              wp{wp}en.lex

  0 - Cancel - do not delete words
  1 - Delete from common word list (from keyboard)
  2 - Delete from common word list (from a file)
  3 - Delete from main word list (from keyboard)
  4 - Delete from main word list (from a file)
  5 - Exit

  Selection:
```

Fig. 7.14.
The Delete Words menu.

Note that you can delete words from the keyboard (by typing each word) or from a file and that you can delete words from both the main and common word list.

4. Select the action you want to perform.

   For instance, select Delete from main word list (from a file) (**4**).

5. When prompted with Enter file name:, type the file name and press Enter.

For instance, type *up{WP}en.sup* and press Enter.

6. The words are not deleted immediately, so you either can delete other words (menu options **1-4**) or cancel the deletions (menu option **0**)

or

Select Exit (**5**) to delete the words.

When you select Exit (**5**), the dictionary is updated and you see the following message:

```
Updating dictionary
* Please Wait *
```

CAUTION: Do not continue with the process—press Cancel (F1) instead—if you see the following message rather than the previous one:

```
Insufficient room on drive A: for temporary files.

Do not remove diskette in drive A:

Enter drive letter for temporary files:
```

WordPerfect then begins to write the words in the dictionary, starting with "A" and proceeding through the entire alphabet; the message `Writing a's` appears. Gradually the entire alphabet is done. Updating the dictionary will take some time.

7. When the deletions are complete and you return to the Speller Utility menu, select Exit (**0**) to exit back to DOS level.

Using the Thesaurus

The Thesaurus can add freshness and variety to your writing by suggesting alternate words for your use. The Thesaurus also helps you to be more precise in your writing—when you can't find quite the word you need, use the Thesaurus.

For instance, you might be writing an evaluation, and you want to say that the person is "not lazy." Because this phrasing has a negative emphasis and you want your statement to be complimentary, use the Thesaurus to look up "lazy." From the list of antonyms, you can find the word with the positive meaning you want—for instance, "hard working."

The Thesaurus offers antonyms and synonyms. Synonyms have meanings *similar* to but not exactly the same as the word looked up. One word might be more or less formal or have positive or negative connotations. The Thesaurus only lists these words; you must decide which one most closely fits your meaning. Avoid abusing the Thesaurus by using inappropriate words.

If you want to use the Thesaurus, you must know how to spell the word in order to look it up. If you are not sure of the spelling of a word, you first can look up the spelling by using * and ? with the Speller and then use the Thesaurus.

Starting the Thesaurus

To practice using the Thesaurus, type the following paragraph:

Jonathan has been working for me in this office for the past year. He had just finished his graduate work in Policy Studies when he joined our staff, and while we hesitated to hire him because of his lack of professional experience, he has proved to be bright, reliable, resourceful and not lazy.

To start the Thesaurus, complete the following steps:

1. If you have a floppy disk system, remove the data disk from drive B: and insert the Thesaurus disk.

CAUTION: Make sure that WordPerfect is not doing a backup of your work, echoing * Please wait * at the bottom of the screen, before removing the disk! You can damage your disk if the computer is writing to the disk when you take it out.

---

2. Place the cursor anywhere between the first character and the space following the word you want to look up.

   For instance, place your cursor under the "l" in "lazy."

3. Press Thesaurus (Alt-F1).

The screen splits; your normal text (if any) appears in the top half, and the Thesaurus menu and word list appear in columns in the bottom half (see fig. 7.15).

If your menu is empty and Word: appears at the bottom of the screen, then either your cursor was not within a word boundary when you pressed Thesaurus (Alt-F1) or the Thesaurus could not find the word you requested. In either case, type the word you want to look up at the Word: prompt and press Enter.

Understanding the Parts of the Thesaurus Menu

Several items that help you use the Thesaurus appear in the Thesaurus menu. The word you look up, called a *headword* because it has a body of similar words attached to it, appears at the top of the column. Some of the synonyms and antonyms for your headword are headwords themselves and are noted with a small bullet.

Fig. 7.15.

The Thesaurus menu.

Part of speech (adjective)

Headword

Numbered subgroups

Antonym

Reference menu

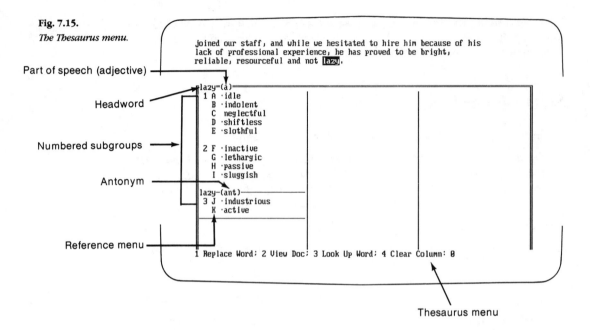

Thesaurus menu

The words are divided into parts of speech—such as nouns, verbs, adjectives, and so on (see table 7.1)—and numbered subgroups. The column of letters to the left of the words is called the Reference menu; you refer to the words by these letters.

Table 7.1
Parts of Speech from Thesaurus menu

Part of speech	Abbreviation
Adjective	(a)
Noun	(n)
Verb	(v)
Antonym	(ant)

Replacing a Word

If you see a word with which you would like to replace the one in your text, select the replacement. For your example, you can select "industrious" from the list to replace "not lazy."

To replace a word with one from the Thesaurus menu, do the following:

1. Select Replace Word (**1**) from the Thesaurus menu.

    You are prompted with Press letter for word.

2. From the Reference menu, press the letter that corresponds to the replacement word.

For example, press *j* for the word "industrious."

The Thesaurus menu disappears, and the program inserts in the text the word you selected (see fig. 7.16).

(Remember to delete the word "not" from the sentence!)

```
Jonathan has been working for me in this office for the past year.
He had just finished his graduate work in Policy Studies when he
joined our staff, and while we hesitated to hire him because of his
lack of professional experience, he has proved to be bright,
reliable, resourceful and industrious.




                                   Doc 1 Pg 1 Ln 1.66" Pos 4.8"
```

Fig. 7.16.

The words "not lazy" replaced with "industrious."

3. If you use floppy disks, remember to remove the Thesaurus disk, replace it with your data disk, and save your document.

Selecting More Words

If you don't see a word that is exactly right or you want to try other words, you can expand the word list.

For example, suppose you think the meaning of "industrious" is close to the word you're looking for but not exactly right. You could replace "not lazy" with "industrious" and then call up the Thesaurus for "industrious"; but that would be tedious. Instead, request more words from within the Thesaurus menu before making the decision about the replacement.

For this example, start over again. To view other words, delete the word "industrious," type *not lazy* again (to get back to your original document), and press Thesaurus (Alt-F1). Remember to replace disks if you're using floppies.

Take another look at the Thesaurus menu. Remember that words marked with a bullet also are headwords, such as "idle" and "indolent" in figure 7.15. You can look up any of these words for more ideas.

Words without bullets, such as "neglectful" in figure 7.15, are not headwords. If you look up a word without a bullet, either the message Word not found appears, or WordPerfect looks up a similar word in its place. For instance, rather than looking up "neglectful," WordPerfect looks up "neglect."

To see additional words from the Thesaurus menu, complete the following steps:

1. From the words listed by the Thesaurus, choose one that is close to the meaning you want.

2. Press the letter beside the word.

   For your example, press *j* for the word "industrious" so that you can see some synonyms for that word.

   Words associated with the new headword appear in the next column to the right of the previous headword (see fig. 7.17).

Fig. 7.17.

A second headword selected.

```
 joined our staff, and while we hesitated to hire him because of his
 lack of professional experience, he has proved to be bright,
 reliable, resourceful and not  lazy .

 ┌lazy-(a)──────────┐┌industrious-(a)────┐┌─────────────────┐
 │1    ·idle        ││1 A ·enterprising  ││                 │
 │     ·indolent    ││                   ││                 │
 │      neglectful  ││2 B ·assiduous     ││                 │
 │     ·shiftless   ││  C ·diligent      ││                 │
 │     ·slothful    ││  D  hard working  ││                 │
 │                  ││  E ·tireless      ││                 │
 │2    ·inactive    ││                   ││                 │
 │     ·lethargic   │industrious-(ant)───│                 │
 │     ·passive     ││3 F ·indolent      ││                 │
 │     ·sluggish    ││                   ││                 │
 │                  ││                   ││                 │
 │lazy-(ant)────────│                   ││                 │
 │3    ·industrious ││                   ││                 │
 │     ·active      ││                   ││                 │
 └──────────────────┘└───────────────────┘└─────────────────┘
 1 Replace Word: 2 View Doc: 3 Look Up Word: 4 Clear Column: 0
```

3. Select a replacement word or select another headword to see additional words.

   For your example, press *c* to select "diligent" as the next headword (see fig. 7.18).

Maneuvering inside the Thesaurus

When you select a new headword, the Reference menu (the column of letters) automatically moves to the new column of words. Each column contains one headword and its associated words. Use ← and → to move the Reference menu between columns.

You can select three headwords to view at one time (see fig. 7.18). When you select a fourth headword, the third is replaced with your new selection. Or you can select Clear Column (4) to clear the column and select another word.

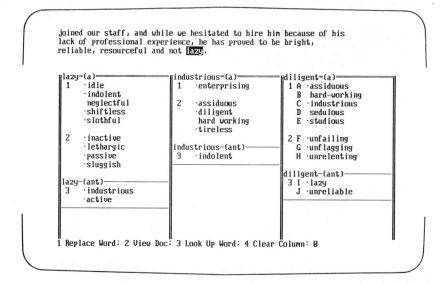

Fig. 7.18.
*A third headword
selected.*

If the words continue past the bottom of the screen, use ↑ and ↓ to move from one numbered group to the next within the columns. The unbroken lines below the groups of words in a column indicate the end of a headword's groupings of alternative words. For instance, note the line below "active" in the first column, "indolent" in the second column, and "unreliable" in the third column (see fig. 7.18).

To move the Reference menu and select a replacement, follow these steps:

1. Use the ← or → keys until the Reference menu is in the correct column.

   For this example, press ← so you can get to the word "diligent" in the second column.

2. Replace the word in your text with the desired alternative.

   For this example, you decide that "diligent" is the best replacement for "not lazy," so select Replace Word (**1**) and press the letter *c*. (Remember to delete the word "not.") Your final memo should look like the one in figure 7.19.

Viewing a Word in Context

If you are unsure of a word's exact meaning in the context of your writing, you can see more of the text surrounding the word in the document. You can Exit (F7) the Thesaurus, scroll through the text, and then reselect Thesaurus (Alt-F1); or you can select View Document from within the Thesaurus menu.

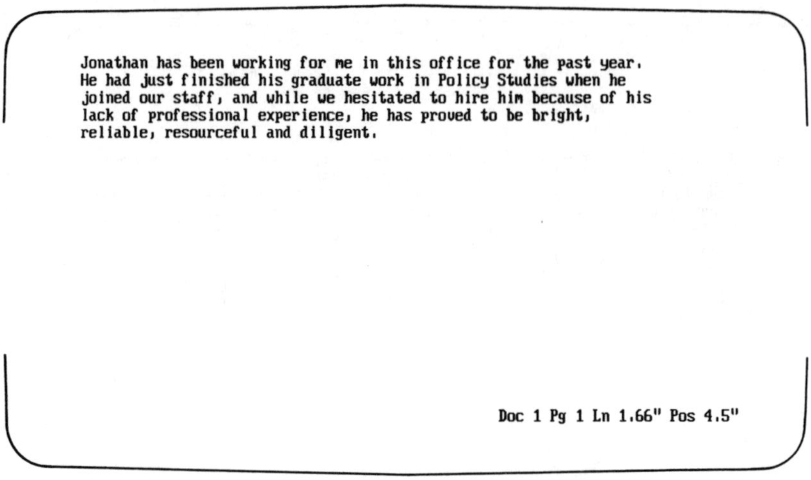

Fig. 7.19.

The words "not lazy" replaced with "diligent."

Jonathan has been working for me in this office for the past year.
He had just finished his graduate work in Policy Studies when he
joined our staff, and while we hesitated to hire him because of his
lack of professional experience, he has proved to be bright,
reliable, resourceful and diligent.

Doc 1 Pg 1 Ln 1.66" Pos 4.5"

To see more of your document without exiting the Thesaurus, complete the following steps:

1. From the Thesaurus menu, select View Doc (**2**).

   The cursor moves within the text to the word you are looking up.

2. Use the cursor keys to see the rest of your document.

3. Press Exit (F7) to return to the Thesaurus

   or

   Place your cursor on another word and press Thesaurus (Alt-F1) to look up a new word.

Looking Up Words

While in Thesaurus, you can look up other words that come to mind by doing the following:

1. Select Look Up Word (**3**).

2. When prompted with Word:, type the new word you want to look up and press Enter.

If the word is a headword, the Thesaurus displays the word with all its subgroups of synonyms and antonyms. If the word is not a headword, either WordPerfect looks up another similar word or the message Word Not Found appears. You can choose to look up another word, or you can press Cancel (F1).

WP 5 Summary

Although you may still need a conventional dictionary to look up the meanings of words, WordPerfect's Speller and Thesaurus are handy tools that can help you improve your writing. In this chapter, you have learned how to use the Speller with either a floppy disk system or a hard disk system to complete the following tasks:

- Replace typos and misspelled words by selecting the correct alternative spelling offered by the Speller

- Correct a word yourself by using the Edit option from the Spell menu

- Leave out parts of a document from a spell-check by using Block or document comments

- Create and use your own supplemental dictionaries for various projects

- Count the number of words in your document

- Add and delete words from the main or common word list by using the Speller Utility

You have learned also how to use the Thesaurus for the following purposes:

- To look up synonyms and antonyms

- To review additional words for your selection

- To replace a word with another that is more fitting

8

Printing and Print Options

Joel Shore is president of Documentation Systems, a Southborough, MA, private consulting firm providing microcomputer services, including printer training as a phase of software development. He teaches a range of personal-computing courses at Massachusetts Bay Community College and conducts private corporate in-house seminars. ■

With all of WordPerfect's sophisticated tools to aid in the composition and formatting of a document, you can lose sight of the program's primary function: committing your words to paper. Because printing is what word processing is all about, WordPerfect has paid special attention to this function. In fact, much of WordPerfect 5 has been redesigned and rewritten to take advantage of the latest advances in printer technology.

In this chapter, you examine all aspects of printing. First, you tell WordPerfect what kind of printer you have, a process called *defining and selecting*. You indicate the styles of type that you have available and which one you expect to use most of the time. Next, you list the sizes and kinds of material on which you plan to print, from regular continuous forms to letterheads, envelopes, transparencies, or labels. You learn how to print an entire document or just a portion. Perhaps most important, you learn techniques to help you efficiently manage your printing activities. No matter what kind of printer you have, this chapter is for you. For more information on laser printers, see the next chapter.

The designers of WordPerfect have gone to great lengths to make printing as easy and flexible as possible. Not only can you edit a document at the same time it is being printed, you can even edit two documents simultaneously with the split screen feature while printing a third document directly from a disk file!

WordPerfect's Protection As You Print

WordPerfect is smart enough to place a protective barrier between you and your printer. It's virtually impossible for printing problems to result in your document being lost or scrambled.

259

How does WordPerfect protect you? When you print, WordPerfect creates a temporary file on your disk and stores in it a copy of the document to be printed (up to the last page you want to print). The actual printing is done from this file. While WordPerfect prints the document from the newly created file, you can continue to edit the text being displayed on-screen. Any changes that you make are *not* reflected in the file being printed. When the print job has finished, WordPerfect automatically erases the temporary print file from your disk.

By using this complex procedure, WordPerfect can store many of these temporary print files and use them to build a *job list*. Fortunately, all of this activity takes place behind the scenes.

The Print Key (Shift-F7)

Most of WordPerfect's printing features are found on the Print key (Shift-F7). Pressing this key displays the Print screen shown in figure 8.1. This menu, completely redesigned for version 5 now uses the entire screen and replaces the single-line menu in version 4.2.

Fig. 8.1.

The Print screen.

```
Print

        1 - Full Document
        2 - Page
        3 - Document on Disk
        4 - Control Printer
        5 - Type Through
        6 - View Document
        7 - Initialize Printer

    Options

        S - Select Printer            Standard Printer
        B - Binding                   0"
        N - Number of Copies          1
        G - Graphics Quality          Medium
        T - Text Quality              High




    Selection: 0
```

If you are in the process of installing WordPerfect, you need to do some work before you can print. This process, called selecting printers, tailors WordPerfect to your specific printer make and model.

Selecting Printers

Printers are like people from around the world; they don't speak the same language. Printer manufacturers, in an effort to differentiate themselves and provide unique features, have developed proprietary printer command languages. Even different models by the same manufacturer may use incompatible commands. Sending the same command from your computer to two different printers may, for example, produce a margin change in one and turn on underlining in the other. If WordPerfect had a huge chart listing every printer make and model across the top and every possible printing feature along the left margin, all the resulting boxes could be filled in with the appropriate printer command. Fortunately, WordPerfect Corporation has done this exhaustive research by working with printers on loan from the manufacturers. The results have been saved in the files that are found on the Printer disks shipped with WordPerfect.

Literally hundreds of printers are supported by WordPerfect. To make sure you achieve the results you expect, you must tell WordPerfect which printer make and model you are using. You use the Select Printer feature to do this.

When To Use the Select Printer Feature

The Select Printer feature is actually a combination of two other features—*defining* a printer or printers in which you tell WordPerfect the kind of equipment you have, and *selecting* one of those defined printers for your current needs. You use Select Printer to define printers when you initially install WordPerfect and then only when you change or add printers or change the port to which your printer is connected. You can select a printer from the list of those you have defined, as often as needed. For a quick draft of a long document, you may use your dot-matrix printer and then switch to another printer for the final, letter-quality copy.

Using Select Printer To Define a New Printer

WordPerfect must know many things about your printer before the program can take full advantage of the printer's features. What is the make and model? What printing styles (fonts) are built in? Which one do you intend to use for "normal" printing? What computer port is the printer connected to? Is the printer a parallel or serial type? Are you using a sheet feeder? If so, how many bins does it have? Does your printer generate both draft and letter-quality output? If so, which will you normally use? And on, and on.

In the following example, you tell WordPerfect that you plan to use a Hewlett-Packard LaserJet Series II printer and that it will be connected to the computer's standard parallel printer port called LPT1. If you're using a different printer, you may not need to make some of the choices shown here. Follow the steps that are appropriate for your printer. The example assumes that you are in the process of installing WordPerfect and that no printers have been selected.

To select a printer, complete the following steps:

1. Press Print (Shift-F7) to display the main Print screen.

2. Choose Select Printer (**S**).

Because selecting printers is done only occasionally, this choice is in the less frequently chosen Options section. Note that WordPerfect is shipped with one predefined printer labeled Standard Printer. The standard printer has few features defined and cannot take advantage of many of WordPerfect's capabilities.

WordPerfect displays the Select Printer screen (see fig. 8.2). At the top of the screen, you can see a list of all currently identified printers. If you have previously defined any printers, they are listed here. Because WordPerfect can speak only one printer language at a time, an asterisk (*) indicates the currently chosen printer.

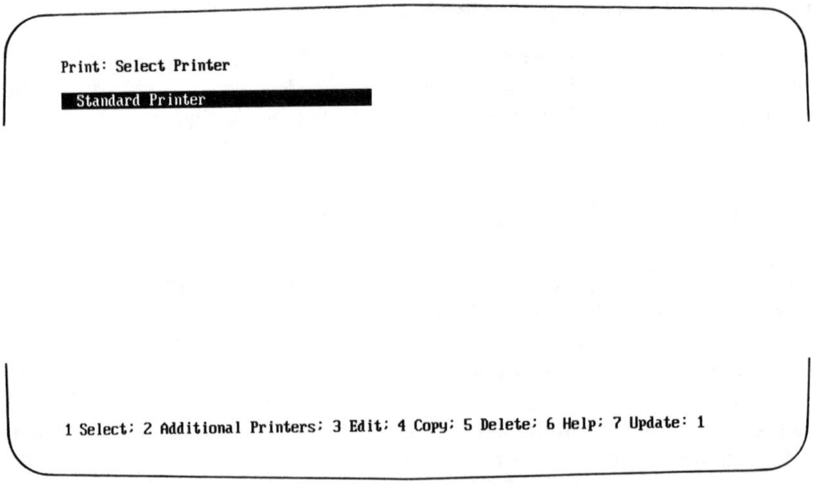

Fig. 8.2.
The Select Printer screen.

```
Print: Select Printer

   Standard Printer




                1 Select; 2 Additional Printers; 3 Edit; 4 Copy; 5 Delete; 6 Help; 7 Update: 1
```

3. Select Additional Printers (**2**).

   If you didn't copy the printer disks to your hard disk, or if you are using a floppy disk system, WordPerfect displays the Printer files not found error message.

4. Insert the Printer 1 disk in a disk drive and select Other Disk (**2**) to tell WordPerfect that the printer files are on a different disk.

5. Next, type the appropriate drive letter (always followed by a colon), and then press Enter.

TIP: Copying the printer files (with a file extension of .ALL) to your hard disk needlessly wastes a substantial amount of valuable space. Because you use these files only when selecting printers, it's more efficient, in terms of disk space, to use floppy disks.

---

6. Move the highlight bar to the desired printer brand and model (see fig. 8.3).

Use the up (↑) and down (↓) arrows and the gray screen up (–) and screen down (+) keys to move through this list.

```
Select Printer: Additional Printers

    Alphacom Alphapro 101
    Alps ALQ200/300/P2400C
    Alps P2000/P2100
    AMT Office Printer (Diablo)
    AMT Office Printer (IBM Color)
    Apple ImageWriter / DMP
    Apple ImageWriter II
    Apple Laserwriter Plus
    AST TurboLaser
    AST TurboLaser/PS
    Blaser
    Brother HR-15XL/35
    Brother HR-20
    C.ITOH 8510 Prowriter
    C.ITOH C-310 CP
    C.ITOH C-310 EP/CXP
    C.ITOH C-715F
    C.ITOH C-815
    C.Itoh D10-40
    C.Itoh ProWriter jr. Plus
    C.Itoh Starwriter/Printmaster

1 Select; 2 Other Disk; 3 Help; 4 List Printer Files; N Name Search: 1
```

Fig. 8.3.

The Select Printer: Additional Printers screen.

If the desired printer is not listed, press **Other Disk (2)** again and replace the Printer 1 disk with the Printer 2 disk. Repeat with Printer disks 3 and 4 if necessary. If you still cannot find your printer listed, call the WordPerfect customer support line to see if a driver for your printer is available.

TIP: In a pinch you may be able to substitute printer definitions. If your dot-matrix printer is not listed, try using the Epson-FX definition. It's as close to a universal dot-matrix printer as there is. If you have a print-wheel or thimble-type letter-quality printer which is not listed, try using the Diablo 630 printer definition.

---

7. To select the highlighted printer, press **Select (1)**.

The file name displayed on-screen is WordPerfect's suggested name for the printer definition file it is about to create. If you like, you can edit this name, but it is best, and easier, to accept the suggested name. Printer definition files should always have a file extension of .PRS.

CAUTION: Version 4.2 stores the printer definitions for all defined printers in a file called WPRINTER.FIL and stores all font definitions for the defined printers in the file WPFONT.FIL. You cannot use these files in version 5.

Printer and font definitions are now stored in separate .PRS files for every printer you select.

8. Press Enter to name the printer-definition file.

A progress report at the bottom of the screen shows the number of fonts remaining to be created. While the ".PRS" file is being created, WordPerfect displays some helpful information and hints about the selected printer (see fig. 8.4). Reading this information carefully now may save you time later.

Fig. 8.4.

The Select Printer:
Help screen.

```
Printer Helps and Hints:  HP LaserJet Series II

The HP LaserJet family of printers allows only 16 different fonts per
printed page.  Also, the printer can only store 32 soft fonts at one time.

If you choose the option to initialize your printer, all soft fonts in its
memory will be erased.

The printer can be either serial or parallel.  You need to select the
setting through the front panel.  If the printer is set as serial, be sure
to use the following parameters:
     Baud Rate:  9600
     Parity:     None
     Stop Bits:  1
     Character Length (or Data Bits):  8

Unless you have upgraded the printer's memory from the standard 512 Kbytes,
do not change the quantity for memory.  If you have added 1 Meg memory,
change the quantity to 1000, 2 Meg, 2000, 4 Meg, 4000.  Not all of the
printer's memory is user accessable, and some memory is required for
buffering.



Press Exit to quit, Cursor Keys for More Text, Switch for Sheet Feeder Help
```

9. Press Exit (F7).

The Select Printer: Edit screen (shown in fig. 8.5) displays the current settings for this printer.

10. Press Enter to accept the current settings or press a menu number (or highlighted letter) to change that item. (See the following section, "Editing Printer Settings.")

WordPerfect returns to the Select Printer screen, which has been fully updated and now lists the printer you have just defined. You have completed defining your printer. Next, you need to *select* it to tell WordPerfect that you intend to print on the printer.

11. Move the highlight bar to your printer and press Enter, or choose Select Printer (**1**) to make this the active printer.

You are returned to the main Print menu, which has been updated and now shows that the printer you have just defined is the active printer. Any print operation from now on will use this printer until you select a different one.

12. Press Enter to return to your document.

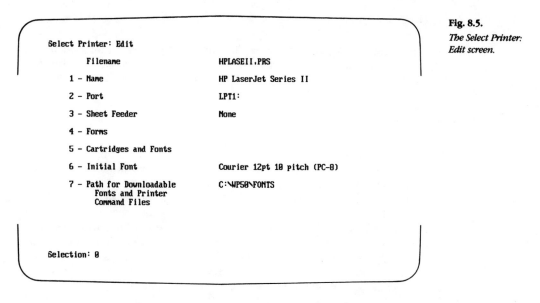

```
Select Printer: Edit

        Filename                 HPLASEII.PRS

    1 - Name                     HP LaserJet Series II

    2 - Port                     LPT1:

    3 - Sheet Feeder             None

    4 - Forms

    5 - Cartridges and Fonts

    6 - Initial Font             Courier 12pt 10 pitch (PC-8)

    7 - Path for Downloadable    C:\WP50\FONTS
        Fonts and Printer
        Command Files




    Selection: 0
```

Fig. 8.5.

The Select Printer: Edit screen.

Remember, you can define as many printers as you like, but only one can be active at a time.

TIP: To save disk space, don't create more printer definitions than you need, and delete definitions you no longer use.

Editing Printer Settings

Now that WordPerfect knows what kind of printer you are using, you need to indicate your specific configuration. The printer settings initially displayed are WordPerfect's best guess.

You can change these settings at any time: when you first create a printer definition or later.

To change a printer setting, complete the following:

1. Press Print (Shift-F7).

2. Choose Select Printer (**S**).

3. Move the highlight bar to the printer setting you want to edit, using up (↑) and down (↓) arrow keys.

4. Select Edit (**3**).

You can now select any of the features described in the following sections.

Name

This full name (up to 36 characters) is the one that WordPerfect uses when referring to this printer. You can see this full name displayed when you press the Print (Shift-F7) key. Chances are you will never need to change this description.

Port

The *port* is the socket on the back of your computer to which your printer is connected. Ports are of two types: *parallel* and *serial*. If your printer is of the parallel variety (as most are), it is connected to a port named *LPT*. The first parallel port is LPT1, and the second, if you have one, is LPT2. Serial printers are connected to ports named *COM1* and *COM2*. If you select a COM port, WordPerfect automatically asks you to enter additional information including the speed at which the computer sends data to the printer (baud rate) and information about the how the data is organized (parity, stop bits, and start bits). This is not the place to make an educated guess. Refer to your printer's technical reference manual (or, in some cases, the WordPerfect Printer Help screen) for the appropriate values.

Sheet Feeder

The Sheet Feeder setting lets you indicate whether your printer is equipped with a cut-sheet feeder. The procedure for selecting a sheet feeder is the same as that for selecting a printer. WordPerfect displays a list of compatible sheet feeders; simply move the highlight bar to the correct choice and choose **S**elect (**1**) or press Enter.

Forms

Forms, a new feature in version 5, lets you define the different kinds and sizes of paper you use and whether the printer must pause so that you can load the specified form type (see Chapter 9).

Cartridges and Fonts

This option lets you tell WordPerfect which optional typefaces (fonts) you have available for use by your printer. Depending on your printer's capabilities, these optional fonts may be plug-in cartridges, special font files stored on your hard disk and downloaded from your computer to your printer as needed, or both. If your printer is not able to use optional fonts, WordPerfect displays the message `This printer has no other cartridges or fonts` on the status line at the bottom of the screen.

Depending on your printer, when you select this option, WordPerfect first displays the number of slots available for plug-in font cartridges, the amount of memory in the printer for storing downloaded font files, or both (see fig. 8.6).

```
Select Printer: Cartridges and Fonts

Font Category              Resource                 Quantity

Cartridge Fonts            Font Cartridge Slot          2
Soft Fonts                 Memory available for fonts  350 K




1 Select Fonts; 2 Change Quantity; N Name search: 1
```

Fig. 8.6.

*The Select Printer:
Cartridges and Fonts
screen.*

To choose where you want to specify fonts, do the following:

1. Move the highlight bar to the location for which you want to specify fonts, and choose Select Fonts from the menu.

WordPerfect displays a list of optional predefined fonts. Fonts built into the printer by the manufacturer are not listed here. (You will see them listed in the next section, "Initial Font.")

2. Move the highlight bar to the fonts you are selecting and (depending on your printer) indicate whether they must be loaded prior to the print job or whether they can be loaded during the print job.

If you are choosing downloadable fonts, WordPerfect subtracts the memory required for that font from the total memory available. Both figures are displayed at the top right of the screen.

Initial Font

Initial font is the typeface (Times, for example), style (Roman), and size (10 points in height, where 1 point is 1/72″) in which WordPerfect prints standard text and around which other fonts (large, small, etc.) are defined. For example, if you specify 10-point Times Roman to be the initial font, then (using the Font key [Ctrl-F8] and selecting Size) large might be 12 point; but if you choose 12 point to be the initial font, then large might be 14-point type.

All defined fonts, both those built in by the manufacturer and optional fonts chosen in the Cartridges and Fonts option, are listed on the Select Printer: Initial Font screen (see fig. 8.7). If you defined additional fonts with the Cartridges and Fonts option, you'll probably want to use one of them for the initial font.

Fig. 8.7.

*The Select Printer:
Initial Fonts screen.*

```
Select Printer: Initial Font

* Courier 10 pitch (PC-8)
  Courier 10 pitch (Roman-8/ECMA)
  Courier Bold 10 pitch (PC-8)
  Courier Bold 10 pitch (Roman-8/ECMA)
  Line Draw 10 pitch
  Line Printer 16.66 pitch (PC-8)
  Line Printer 16.66 pitch (Roman-8/ECMA)
  Prestige Elite 10pt 12 pitch (D/J/M)
  Prestige Elite 10pt Bold 12 pitch (D/J/M)
  Prestige Elite 10pt Italic 12 pitch (D/J/M)
  Solid Line Draw 10 pitch
  Tms Rmn 06pt (AC)
  Tms Rmn 08pt (AC)
  Tms Rmn 08pt Bold (AC)
  Tms Rmn 08pt Italic (AC)
  Tms Rmn 10pt (AC)
  Tms Rmn 10pt Bold (AC)
  Tms Rmn 10pt Italic (AC)
  Tms Rmn 12pt (AC)
  Tms Rmn 12pt Bold (AC)
  Tms Rmn 12pt Italic (AC)

1 Select; N Name search: 1
```

TIP: When working with your document, you can temporarily change the initial font by using the Base Font (**4**) option on the Font key (Ctrl-F8).

Path for Downloadable Fonts and Printer Command Files

If you store font files on your hard disk drive, enter the full path and directory in which the fonts are stored. Note that you are limited to one directory.

TIP: Store your font files in a directory all their own; housekeeping is easier if they are not intermixed with your WordPerfect files.

Printing the Test Document

Before you begin printing your documents, it makes sense to test the printer definition you have just created and selected. To do this, WordPerfect includes a file named PRINTER.TST.

To print the test document, complete the following steps:

1. Retrieve the file PRINTER.TST to the screen.

   You can use Retrieve (Shift-F10) and type the file name, or you can press List Files (F5), move the highlight bar to the file name, and select Retrieve (**1**).

2. Press Print (Shift-F7) to display the main Print screen.

3. Select Full Document (**1**).

   Features that do not print are probably not supported by your particular printer.

Now that WordPerfect knows about your printer, you can begin printing your documents.

An Overview of WordPerfect Printing Methods

One of WordPerfect's great flexibilities is its numerous ways of printing documents. The most common method, printing the document you are currently editing, is called *printing from the screen*. When printing in this way, you have the option of printing the entire document, a specific page, or a block of any size. When you print from the screen, WordPerfect allows you to continue editing while your job is printing.

The second method of printing is called *printing from disk*. When choosing this option, you can print a file directly from your disk without the need to retrieve the document to the screen, and you can specify which pages to print.

With WordPerfect, there's never a need to wait until one print job is finished before submitting the next. You can submit as many print jobs as you want as often as you like. WordPerfect keeps track of all these jobs by creating a *job list*.

To manage the job list, WordPerfect provides one of its most important and powerful features: *Control Printer*. With Control Printer, you can display a progress report on the current print job, cancel or suspend print jobs, move any print job to the top of the job list, and display the entire list of jobs waiting to be printed. Control Printer is examined in detail later in this chapter.

Printing from the Screen

You can print all or any part of the document you are currently editing. Printing the entire document or just the current page requires only three keystrokes. If you'd like to print just part of a page, a sentence, or a paragraph, for instance, WordPerfect can do that almost as easily by using the block Function.

Printing the Entire Document from the Screen

To print the entire document from the screen, do the following steps:

1. Press Print (Shift-F7).

   WordPerfect displays the main Print menu.

2. Press **Full** Document (**1**) to print the entire document.

WordPerfect automatically creates and formats a print job for the active printer. The active printer name is displayed on the lower portion of the print screen.

Or to see a progress report about this or other pending print jobs, select Control Printer (**4**) to display the Printer Control screen. Otherwise, press Enter to return to your document and continue editing.

When the document has finished printing, WordPerfect automatically begins printing the next print job if there is one.

Printing a Page from the Screen

Before WordPerfect can print a single page from the screen, the program needs to know which page you want to print. Simply move the cursor to any location on the desired page. It is not necessary to enter a page number.

To print one page of the document on the screen, perform these steps:

1. Position the cursor anywhere on the page you want to print.

2. Press Print (Shift-F7).

3. Select **Page** (**2**) to print the current page.

If the selected page is not near the beginning of the document, you may notice a pause before printing actually begins. The reason is that WordPerfect begins scanning your document from the beginning to find your last format settings (tabs, margins, fonts, etc.) before printing the page.

To see a progress report about this print job, select Control Printer (**4**) to display the Control Printer screen; otherwise, press Enter to return to your document and continue editing.

When the document has finished printing, WordPerfect automatically begins printing the next print job if there is one.

Printing a Block from the Screen

Sometimes printing the entire document or an entire page just won't do. If you need to a print a single sentence, a paragraph, a page and a half, or five pages from a larger document, then you need to use WordPerfect's Block feature.

As we have seen, printing the entire document or a full page from the screen is easy because WordPerfect knows where your document begins and ends and where page breaks occur. This isn't the case with the kinds of structures listed in the preceding paragraph. You need to tell WordPerfect where the beginning and end of the block lie.

To print a block, complete these steps:

1. Move the cursor to the beginning of the block you want to print.

2. Press Block (Alt-F4, or F12).

   The phrase Block on flashes at the lower left corner of the screen.

3. Move the cursor to the end of the block you want to print.

TIP: Use good cursor-movement technique to save time. Remember that the block automatically advances to the next occurrence of any character you type. You can advance the block to the end of the current paragraph simply by pressing Hard Return (Enter). Press PgDn to advance the block to the next page. Press the period key to advance to the end of the current sentence.

---

4. Press Print (Shift-F7).

Something different happens when you press the print key while Block is on. Instead of displaying the full screen Print menu, WordPerfect displays a prompt message on the status line at the bottom of the screen: Print Block? (Y/N) No

5. To be on the safe side, WordPerfect has already suggested No as its choice. If you choose not to print the block, press Enter or *N* to confirm the choice.

   or

   Press *Y* to print the block.

   You must press *Y* to print the block. Pressing any other key confirms the *No* choice and cancels the print operation.

The block turns off once you have chosen to print it. If you choose not to print, the block stays highlighted because WordPerfect assumes that you intend to perform a Block operation other than printing.

Printing a Document from Disk

With WordPerfect, you can print a document directly from disk without the need to display the document on-screen. You can do this either from the main Print menu or from the List Files screen.

Documents saved with the Fast Save option must be retrieved to the screen before being printed. If you intend to print documents directly from disk, you must use the Setup key (Shift-F1) to change the Fast Save setting to No.

CAUTION: If the file you are printing is on a disk, never remove the disk from the drive until the print job is complete.

Using the Main Print Menu

When you know the name of the file you want to print, use this method to type the file name and specify the pages you want printed.

You must know the complete file name before starting this operation. No provision is made for looking at the List Files screen once you have pressed the Print key.

To print from disk, using the Print menu, perform these steps:

1. Press Print (Shift-F7).

   WordPerfect displays the main Print menu.

2. Select **Document on Disk (3)**.

3. Enter the file name for the document.

   Pages: (All) displays on the status line.

4. Press Enter to print the entire document, or enter the pages you want printed (see the section "Selecting Pages").

WordPerfect reads the file from disk and creates a print job that is added to the job list.

Using List Files

If you are not sure what the name of the file is, you can use the List Files feature to display the files. Then you can highlight the desired file and instruct WordPerfect to print it.

To print from disk, using the List Files screen, complete the following steps:

1. Press List Files (F5) and then Enter to display the file list.

2. If the file is not on the disk drive (or directory) shown, enter the appropriate information before pressing Enter.

3. Move the highlight bar to the file you want to print.

4. Select **Print (4)**.

   Pages: (All) displays on the status line.

5. Press Enter to print the entire document, or enter the pages you want printed (see the section "Selecting Pages").

WordPerfect reads the file from disk and creates a print job that is added to the job list.

Selecting Pages

When printing from a disk file, you can specify which pages to print. Pages specified need not be consecutive; if you need to, for example, you can specify pages 3 through 6, 11, 21 and 22, and 30 to the end of the document.

Imagine that you are working with a document in which you have used the New Page Number feature (Shift-F8, 2, 6) several times to mix Roman and Arabic numerals or restart the page numbering for a new chapter. The document looks like this:

Front Matter	pages i - vii
Chapter 1	pages 1 - 10
Chapter 2	pages 1 - 17
Chapter 3	pages 1 - 28

The front matter includes a title and acknowledgment page as well as a table of contents page and a list of diagrams.

Table 8.1 lists several scenarios for printing selected pages from the example and shows what you must enter. WordPerfect defines a new section as any point at which a New Page Number code is inserted. (When referring to a section, you must enter the section followed by a colon.)

Table 8.1
Specifying Pages To Print from Disk

What You Want To Print	*What You Must Enter*
The entire document	i-
All front matter	i-vii
All front matter and all of Chapter 1	i-10
All of Chapter 1	1-10 or 2:1-10
Chapter 1, page 1 only	1 or 1:1
Chapter 1, pages 4 and 5	4,5 or 1:4,5
All of Chapter 2 only	2:1-17
Chapter 2, pages 5-7	2:5-7
Chapter 3, pages 1, 4, 7-9, and 13	3:1,4,7-9,13

Controlling the Printer

WordPerfect's Control Printer feature is a powerful tool for managing your printing activities. You can cancel individual print jobs or all jobs. You can display a list of all jobs waiting to be printed. You can move any print job to the top of the list. You can even temporarily suspend and then resume printing if your printer has jammed or needs a new ribbon.

All of these control activities are located on the Control Printer screen.

To display the Control Printer screen, perform the following two steps:

1. Press Print (Shift-F7) to display the main Print menu.

2. Select Control Printer (4).

WordPerfect displays the Control Printer screen (see fig. 8.8), which conveys a great deal of information. For purposes of illustration, the example shows several print jobs.

Fig. 8.8.

The Print: Control Printer screen.

```
Print: Control Printer

Current Job

Job Number: 1                          Page Number:  1
Status:      Printing                  Current Copy: 1 of 1
Message:     None
Paper:       Standard 8.5" x 11"
Location:    Continuous feed
Action:      None


Job List

Job  Document           Destination       Print Options
 1   (Screen)           LPT 1


Additional Jobs Not Shown: 0



 1 Cancel Job(s); 2 Rush Job; 3 Display Jobs; 4 Go (start printer); 5 Stop: 0
```

The screen is divided into three sections: Current Job, Job List, and a printer control menu. Let's examine each section in detail.

Information about the Current Print Job

The most important print job is the one currently printing. WordPerfect maintains constant watch over the status of the print job and continually updates the Control Printer screen.

Job Number

Every time you attempt to print, WordPerfect creates a *print job*. A print job can be the entire document, a page, or a block of any size. WordPerfect keeps track of each print job by assigning a job number. Each time you start WordPerfect, the first job you print is assigned job number one. The job number is incremented by one for every print job.

Job Status

The *job status* tells you what WordPerfect is trying to do. If your job is printing normally, the message displayed is Printing. If you forgot to turn your printer on and WordPerfect cannot communicate with it, then the message would say Trying to Print.

Paper

This element lists the type of paper that you specify for the currently selected form. If you are using regular continuous form 8 1/2 by 11-inch paper, this setting displays Standard 8.5 by 11.

Location

This setting is the location from where the paper is being fed into the printer. For standard continuous-form paper, this is Continuous Feed; but for printers with sheet feeders, this setting may say Bin 1, Bin 2, and so on.

Message

If everything is printing normally, WordPerfect displays None. If WordPerfect is unable to communicate with your printer, it displays Printer not accepting characters. As intuitive as WordPerfect is, it now needs your help to solve the problem.

Page Number

Look at this element to see the page number currently being sent to your printer. The displayed number may not be the page being physically printed; it depends on the amount of your printer's built-in memory. If your printer can store five pages, then WordPerfect sends that much and indicates that the current page number is five even though the printer may still be printing page one.

Current Copy

This element tells you two things: the number of copies requested and which copy is currently printing.

Other Jobs Waiting To Be Printed

The center of the Control Printer screen, labeled Job List, displays information about the next three print jobs. If more than three print jobs are pending, WordPerfect tells you how many there are in the message Additional Jobs Not Shown.

Job

This setting is the job number assigned by WordPerfect when you submitted the print job.

Document

This is the name of your document. When you print from the screen, the name (screen) displays. If you are printing directly from a disk file, the full path and file name are shown.

Destination

The printer port for the currently selected printer displays here. For standard parallel printers, this setting is LPT1.

Print Options

Special options selected for a print job such as Rush are displayed here.

Using the Control Printer Menu

The bottom line of the screen presents five printer control options: Cancel Job(s), Rush Job, Display Jobs, Go (start printer), and Stop.

Cancel Job(s)

Select Cancel Job(s) (1) to cancel any print job. WordPerfect asks if you want to cancel all jobs or just the current one. To cancel the current print job, simply press

Enter. To cancel all print jobs, type an asterisk (`*`) and then press Enter. If your printer doesn't respond immediately, you may also see the message `Press Enter if Printer Doesn't respond`.

Rush Job

The **Rush** Job (**2**) option lets you print any job immediately no matter how far down it is in the list of jobs waiting to be printed. You have the option to interrupt the current print job or wait until the current job is done.

If you choose to interrupt the current job, it will automatically resume printing when the rush job is done. If necessary, WordPerfect prompts you first to change forms in the printer for the rush job and again to reinsert the original forms for the resumed job.

Display Jobs

Select **Display** Jobs (**3**) to display any additional print jobs not displayed on the Control Printer screen. The Control Printer screen can display information for a maximum of three print jobs. The information displayed is the same as that for the Control Printer job list. Press any key to continue.

Go (Start Printer)

Select **Go** (start printer) (**4**) to resume printing after a form change or after suspending printing with the Stop option. You may also need to send a Go command after canceling a print job.

Printing resumes on page 1 if your document consists of a single page, or if your print job stopped on the first page of a multipage document. Otherwise, WordPerfect asks for the page number on which you want printing to resume.

Stop

Select **Stop** (**5**) to stop or suspend printing without canceling the print job. Use this option if your printer runs out of paper or jams, or if you need to replace the ribbon or otherwise intervene in the printing operation. If you don't want to resume this print job, you should press Cancel instead of stopping.

Using the Print Menu

You have already seen the main Print menu (Shift-F7) several times. You have used it to select printers; print the entire document or just a page from the screen; print a document from disk; and most important, control the printer. Some additional choices, located on the Print menu, are also important tools in your overall management of printing activities. These choices include: Type Through, View Document, **Initialize Printer**, **Binding**, **Number of Copies**, **Graphics Quality**, and **Text Quality**. Though not used as often, these choices help you manage your printing efficiently.

Type Through

Type Through (**5**) makes WordPerfect act like a typewriter. This is useful for filling in preprinted forms or addressing an envelope.

To access Type Through, complete the following steps:

1. Press Print (Shift-F7) to display the main Print menu.

2. Select Type Through (**5**).

If WordPerfect does not support Type Through for the currently selected printer, the error message Feature not available on this printer displays on the status line at the bottom of the screen.

3. Choose **Line Type Through** (**1**), or **Character Type Through** (**2**).

TIP: Use Line Type Through so that you can edit the line before sending it to the printer. Character Type Through sends each character as you type; if you make a typing mistake, it's too late to correct it.

---

4. Type the text.

5. If you are using Line Type Through (**1**) press Enter to end a line and send it to the printer.

With Line Type Through, you can use the cursor keys and the Backspace and Delete keys to edit the line of text before pressing Enter.

WordPerfect prints the text beginning at the current print-head location on the paper. Margin settings are ignored. You must have the paper properly positioned before you send the text to the printer.

If you are filling out a preprinted form, you will probably need to reposition the form for each line to be filled out.

TIP: Make a copy of the preprinted form and practice with it before printing on the real thing.

View Document

View Document (**6**) lets you preview the appearance of a page before you print it. Everything that can appear on a page, including headers, footers, graphics, page numbers, and footnotes, is displayed in addition to the text. The page is shown exactly as it will be printed within any limitations imposed by your display hardware.

If your computer cannot display graphics, the Preview feature displays text only; this does not accurately portray the actual printed page.

To view a document, perform the following steps:

1. Position the cursor anywhere on the page you want to view.

2. Press Print (Shift-F7) to display the main Print menu.

3. Select View Document (**6**).

WordPerfect shifts your computer into graphics mode and displays the current page and the page number on the status line. To see the "bigger picture," several options are provided to help you move in for a close-up or take a step back.

100% Page

Choose the 100% (**1**) option to view the page at full size (see fig. 8.9). Because most display monitors cannot show an entire page at full size, you will probably see only a portion of the page. Use the cursor keys to shift the image up, down, right, or left until the desired portion of the page comes into view. You should be able to read text at this size.

Fig. 8.9.
View Document at 100%.

An Overview of Printing

One of WordPerfect's great flexibilities is its numero most common method, printing the document you ar from the screen. When printing in this way, you have document, a specific page, or a block of any size. W WordPerfect allows you to continue editing while yo printing is called printing from disk. When choosing from your disk without the need to retrieve the docu which pages to print.

With WordPerfect there's never a need to wait until submitting the next. You can submit as many print j

1 100% 2 200% 3 Full Page 4 Facing Pages: 2   Doc 1 Pg 6

200% Page

The 200% (**2**) option displays the page at twice the normal height and width (see fig. 8.10). At this magnification, you can see only a small portion of the page, but text is clearly legible. If you are using a proportional font, WordPerfect reproduces it as faithfully as possible within the limitations of your particular hardware configuration. Use the cursor keys to shift the image up, down, right, or left until the desired portion of the page comes into view.

Fig. 8.10.
View Document at 200%.

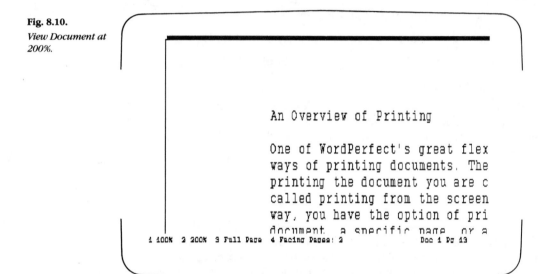

```
An Overview of Printing

One of WordPerfect's great flex
ways of printing documents. The
printing the document you are c
called printing from the screen
way, you have the option of pri
document. a specific page. or a
1 100% 2 200% 3 Full Page 4 Facing Pages: 2          Doc 1 Pg 13
```

Full Page

Choose the Full Page (**3**) option to view the entire current page (see fig. 8.11). Text is not readable at this size, but the layout of the page is clearly visible. Use PgUp and PgDn to view the preceding or succeeding page, or use GoTo (Ctrl-Home) with a specific page number to view that page.

Facing Pages

Select Facing Pages (**4**) to display the full-page images of two consecutive pages as they would appear in a book (see fig. 8.12). There are a few guidelines to remember when using this option. First, in a book, page one is always a right-hand page and, therefore, has no facing page. If you choose this option with the cursor on page one, WordPerfect does not display a facing page. Second, an even-numbered page always displays on the left; its facing page is the next page number. For example, facing pages would be 20 and 21; they could never be 19 and 20.

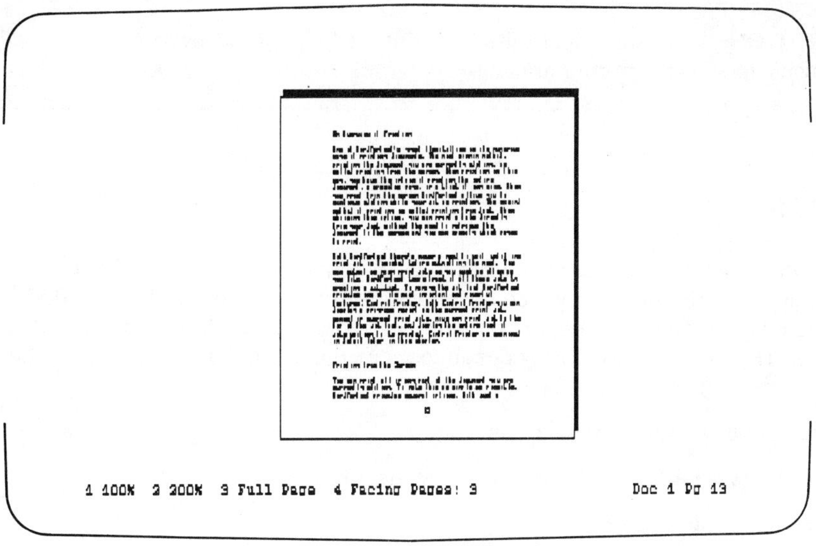

Fig. 8.11.
View Document with the Full Page option.

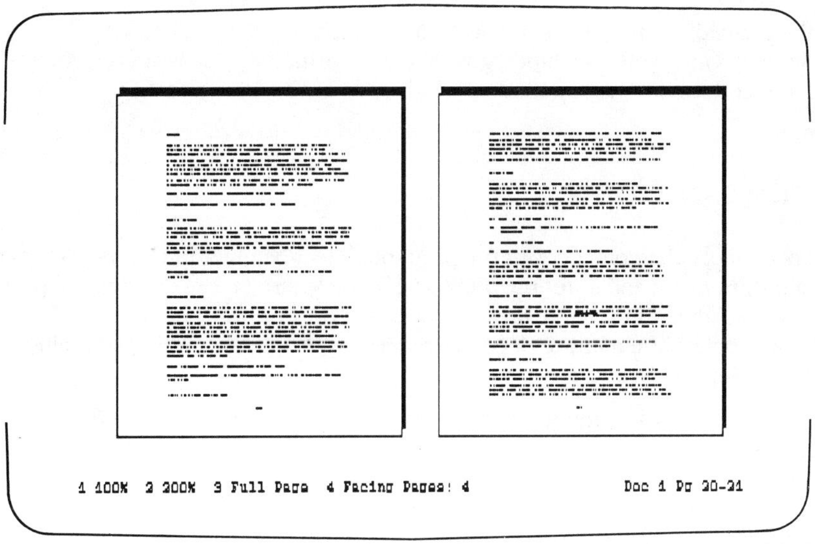

Fig. 8.12.
View Document with the Facing Pages option.

Initialize Printer

Initialize Printer (7) on the main Print menu *downloads* (sends) to your printer any font files you designate `present at beginning of job` with the Cartridges and Fonts option on the Select Printer: Edit screen. WordPerfect looks for these files in the disk directory you specified in the Path for Downloadable Fonts and Printer Command Files option.

CAUTION: When you select Initialize Printer (**7**), any fonts previously downloaded to the printer are erased.

Binding

Select **Binding** (**B**) from the main Print menu if you plan to make two-sided xerographic copies of your printed document. Setting a binding width shifts odd-numbered pages to the right and even-numbered pages to the left by the indicated amount. The Binding option provides an extra margin along the inside edge of the paper for binding your final copy.

To set a binding width, complete these steps:

1. Press Print (Shift-F7) to display the main Print screen.

2. Select **Binding** (**B**).

3. Type the amount of binding width desired and press Enter.

The binding-width setting stays in effect until you change it again or Exit WordPerfect. Once you set a binding width, every print job you create is shifted. WordPerfect does not insert a binding-width code in your document.

Number of Copies

If you need more than one copy of the print job, select **Number of Copies** (**N**) from the main Print menu and enter the number of copies here *before* creating the print job. WordPerfect uses the same print job over and over to print the requested number of copies. The number of copies requested remains set at the new value until you change it back to 1.

Note for 4.2 users: The temporary print option for number of copies has been eliminated.

Graphics Quality

Use the **Graphics Quality** (**G**) option on the Print menu to control the degree of resolution (sharpness) your printer uses to print graphics images. Higher-resolution images take longer to print than lower-resolution images. If your printer has trouble printing text and graphics simultaneously, select the Do Not Print (**1**) option to print your text first. You can then reload the paper and choose the degree of graphics quality you need to print the graphics image.

Text Quality

Text Quality (**T**) is identical to Graphics Quality except that it controls text only. If you must print text and graphics as two separate print jobs, remember to set **Text Quality** (**T**) to Do Not Print (**1**) when you want to print the graphics images.

Printing in Color

If your printer supports color printing, use this feature to specify the color in which you want your text to print. You can change colors as often as you like.

You can also use this option to create a color mix of your own design by adjusting the mix of component colors (red, green, and blue) that make up the color you select.

Entering Text in Color

You can specify a color for text as you type.

To specify a color, complete these steps:

1. Press Font (Ctrl-F8).

2. Select Print Color (**5**).

WordPerfect displays the Print Color screen (see fig. 8.13).

```
Print Color


                              Primary Color Mixture
                            Red      Green     Blue

          1 - Black         0%        0%        0%
          2 - White         100%      100%      100%
          3 - Red           67%       0%        0%
          4 - Green         0%        67%       0%
          5 - Blue          0%        0%        67%
          6 - Yellow        67%       67%       0%
          7 - Magenta       67%       0%        67%
          8 - Cyan          0%        67%       67%
          9 - Orange        67%       25%       0%
          A - Gray          50%       50%       50%
          N - Brown         67%       33%       0%
          0 - Other

          Current Color     0%        0%        0%



        Selection: 0
```

Fig. 8.13.

The Print Color screen.

3. Press the highlighted number or letter to select the color for your text.

4. Press Enter to return to your text.

WordPerfect inserts a code into your document, specifying the color name. All text that you enter from that point on is printed in that color. To return to normal black text, choose Print Color (5) again and select Black (1).

You cannot use the Block feature to assign a color to a block of existing text. You must, instead, move the cursor to where you want the color change to take place, insert a color code, then move the cursor to where you want to change the color again and insert another color code.

Creating a Custom Color

If none of the predefined colors suits your needs, you can create a custom color.

To create a custom color, complete these steps:

1. Press Font (Ctrl-F8).

2. Select Print Color (5).

3. Select Other (O).

4. Enter a percentage for the red, green, and blue components.

The percentages you enter can (and probably will, in many cases) add up to more than 100%. Cyan, for example, is a mixture of 0% red, 67% green, and 67% blue. The percentages total more than 100% because green is contributing 67% of the total green available, and blue is doing the same.

5. Press Enter to return to your text.

WordPerfect inserts a code into your document specifying the red, green, and blue percentages entered. All text that you enter from that point on is printed in the custom color. To return to normal black text, choose Print Color (5) again and select Black (1).

Printing Files Created with Previous Versions of WordPerfect

Moving from version 4.2 (or any other previous version) to version 5 is bound to create problems for even the most experienced user. Some common problems follow.

Printing from Disk

You cannot print files created with previous versions of WordPerfect directly from disk. If you try this, WordPerfect displays the message ERROR: Incompatible file format. You must retrieve the file into WordPerfect 5 with Retrieve (Shift-F10) before trying to print. WordPerfect automatically converts the file to version 5 format when it is retrieved.

Converting Pitches and Fonts

In previous versions, you always select a particular typeface and size by specifying the font number and the pitch—for example, Font 1 at 10 Pitch. This selection no longer works in version 5.

When a file is retrieved into version 5 for the first time, WordPerfect automatically creates a comment box on the screen with a message telling you that your font and pitch setting must be manually converted (see figs. 8.14 and 8.15). Because fonts are no longer chosen by number and because you are no longer limited to eight fonts, WordPerfect unfortunately has no way to correlate your old font numbers with the new method of choosing them by name. (But see Appendix B for the use of a *conversion resource file* to convert some codes.)

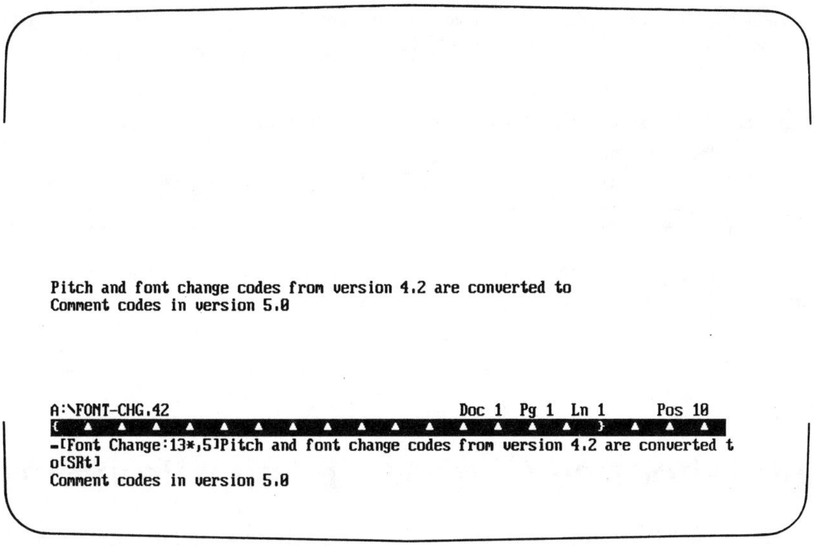

Fig. 8.14.
A version 4.2 document with pitch and font codes.

```
Pitch and font change codes from version 4.2 are converted to
Comment codes in version 5.0




A:\FONT-CHG.42                          Doc 1  Pg 1  Ln 1     Pos 10
[  ▲  ▲  ▲  ▲  ▲  ▲  ▲  ▲  ▲  ▲  ▲  ▲  ▲  ▲  ▲  }  ▲  ▲  ▲
-[Font Change:13*,5]Pitch and font change codes from version 4.2 are converted t
o[SRt]
Comment codes in version 5.0
```

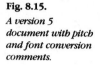

Fig. 8.15.

*A version 5
document with pitch
and font conversion
comments.*

Note: The change to pitch`(13*) and font (5) must be converted manually.

Pitch and font change codes from version 4.2 are converted to
Comment codes in version 5.0

A:\FONT-CHG.42   Doc 1 Pg 1 Ln 1.16" Pos 3.8"

[Comment]Pitch and font change codes from version 4.2 are converted to[SRt]
Comment codes in version 5.0

Press Reveal Codes to restore screen

Printing Version 5 Documents with Version 4.2

Never use an earlier version of WordPerfect to perform any operation on a file
created with version 5. You will cause your computer to freeze up, and you may
damage your file beyond repair. Files saved in version 5 contain hundreds of internal
codes that previous versions could never hope to recognize (new features, for
example).

If you must print a version 5 file with a version 4.2 environment (usually when you
give a file to someone who has not yet upgraded), you *must* save your document in 4.2
format by pressing Text In/Text Out (Ctrl-F5) and then choosing Save **WP** 4.2 (**4**).

CAUTION: If you save your file in 4.2 format, all new version 5 features are
stripped out permanently. It's wise to save this 4.2 file under a different file
name so that you don't accidentally erase the corresponding version 5 file.

Troubleshooting Common Printer Problems

There are so many links in the chain from creating to printing a document that it's a
marvel things don't go wrong more often. WordPerfect Corporation has striven to
anticipate most of the difficulties that can occur and to provide you with immediate
feedback by the Control Printer screen (Shift-F7, 4). Unfortunately, sometimes
things just seem to go wrong for no reason at all. Here is a list of some common
printing problems and solutions.

Display the Control Printer screen (Shift-F7, 4) and act on any displayed messages before attempting any of these suggestions.

Printer Does Not Print

- Make sure the printer is plugged in and turned on.

- Make sure the printer is on-line.

- Make sure WordPerfect is not waiting for a Go command on the Control Printer screen.

- Make sure the current print job (if any) has not been stopped with the Stop (5) option. Check the Control Printer screen.

- Check the printer. Is it out of paper? Has the paper jammed? Is the ribbon out?

- Check all plugs and connections including the keyboard and both ends of the printer cable.

- Make sure you have selected the correct printer definition.

- Make sure the printer has been defined correctly. If the printer is of the serial variety, make sure the baud rate, parity, and start/stop bits have been entered accurately.

- Shut off your printer, wait several seconds, and then turn it back on. This clears any commands (and downloaded fonts) previously sent to the printer.

- As a last resort, save your documents, exit WordPerfect, and shut your printer off. Start everything again and try printing.

Printer Is Printing Nonsense

- Check all plugs and connections including the keyboard and both ends of the printer cable.

- Make sure the printer has been defined correctly. If the printer is of the serial variety, make sure the baud rate, parity, and start/stop bits have been entered accurately.

- If the nonsense occurs on every other character, chances are you have a serial printer and may have entered incorrect values for the baud rate, parity, or start/stop bits. Check your printer's technical reference manual.

- Big chunks of good text followed by big chunks of nonsense also usually indicate problems defining a serial printer.

WP 5 Summary

You've seen that WordPerfect is equipped with a broad range of powerful tools designed to let you get the most out of your printer. To use these tools, you first must properly define and select your printer. Although not difficult, many steps along the way deserve your careful consideration.

Next, you learned how to print entire documents, single pages, or blocks from the screen. You also used similar techniques to print a document from disk. You worked with the Control Printer screen—WordPerfect's nerve center for managing all of your printing activities—and with the main Print screen from which other printing options are accessed.

This chapter covered a great deal. As you work and grow with WordPerfect, you may find some features that you virtually never use—that's perfectly natural. But every WordPerfect user prints and prints often. Mastering WordPerfect's numerous printing options and management tools will make you more efficient; increase your productivity; and, most important, allow you to concentrate on your writing. After all, isn't that what word processing is for?

9

Printing with Laser Printers

Joel Shore's private consulting firm, Documentation Systems, produces computer-training materials and documentation, using the most recent developments in laser printing.

Schuyler Lininger, a computer consultant and writer, uses a PostScript-based system to produce a monthly national newsletter for natural-foods stores. ∎

In the preceding chapter, you learned how to use WordPerfect to manage printing activities. This basic knowledge is important, whether you use a dot-matrix, daisywheel, or laser printer.

Because laser printing differs from other printing technologies, however, this chapter examines additional techniques essential to using a laser printer. You learn the basic vocabulary of laser printing, examine WordPerfect's use of fonts, discover how to define various types of forms, and investigate some problems that commonly occur when you use a laser printer. Regardless of the laser printer you own, this chapter helps you produce better documents more efficiently.

To help you find the information for your particular printer in this chapter, first read the introductory sections through the section "Defining Forms." If you have a LaserJet, the next section features information specific to the LaserJet family of printers, followed by a section for PostScript users. Finally, read the section entitled "Other Considerations" to conclude the chapter.

Learning Laser Printing Vocabulary

Because laser printers have more features than other printers, new words are needed to describe these features. It's important to understand the vocabulary. You'll find new terms introduced throughout this chapter.

At the very heart of laser printing are fonts. Printing text with lasers means working with fonts. A font is a complete set of all characters of a single typeface in the samesize, style, and weight. Let's look at these terms in more detail, referring to the three typefaces in figure 9.1.

289

Fig. 9.1.

Three categories of typeface.

This is Helvetica, a sans-serif typeface. Note the straight strokes. Helvetica looks good at larger point sizes.

This is Times, a serif typeface. Note the tails on each letter. Good for body text and long stretches of smaller point sizes since it is easy to read.

This is Cloister Black. A decorative typeface and not easy to read. It should be used only for impact.

- *Typeface* refers to the overall artistic design of the character set or to a style of type. In the example, the typefaces are Helvetica, Times, and Cloister Black. The three basic typeface categories are *serif*, which has fine lines that finish off the main strokes (Times); *sans-serif*, which has only straight strokes (Helvetica); and *decorative* type, which has a special look (Cloister Black).

- *Font* refers to a set of characters with specific typeface, point size, and weight. For example, *10-point Times* constitutes a font. Using Font (Ctrl-F8), you can change the Size (**1**) and Appearance (**2**) of a font. In WordPerfect documentation, "font" is used inexactly—sometimes when "typeface" is more accurate. WordPerfect relies heavily on the use and management of fonts to vary the appearance of text on a laser printer. After you learn to work with fonts, you will find that printing with a laser is no more difficult than printing with your dot-matrix or daisywheel printer.

- *Style* tells you whether the font is upright (Roman) or slanted (italic).

- *Size*, measured in points, determines the nominal character height. There are 72 points to an inch; therefore, 10 points equal approximately 0.14 inches.

Most text in books is set in 10-point type. In WordPerfect, seven different point sizes are predefined in the Size (**1**) submenu of Font (Ctrl-F8). These sizes are superscript, subscript, fine, small, large, very large, and extra large. How these sizes correlate to specific point sizes is discussed later. You can see examples of different point size in figure 9.2.

Fig. 9.2.
*Helvetica typeface at
different point sizes.*

This is 8 point type. It is hard to read.

This is 10 point type. Good for body text.

This is 12 point type. Good for body text.

This is 14 point type. Good for subheads.

This is 18 point type. Good for subheads and some heads.

This is 24 point type. Good for headlines.

This is 36 point type. Good for mastheads.

This is 72 pts.

- *Weight* refers to thickness of characters, such as light, normal, or bold. In WordPerfect, weights are chosen by pressing Font (Ctrl-F8) and selecting Appearance (**2**). (Don't forget that you can still press Bold [F6] for boldface type.) In addition to bold and italic, you can select underline, double underline, outline, shadow, small capitals, redline, and strikeout. You will read more about these features later.

- *Spacing*, either fixed or proportional, describes whether all characters in the font are of equal width. Typewriter-like fonts such as Courier or Prestige use *fixed-spacing*, where every character is exactly the same width. *Proportional* fonts, on the other hand, vary the width of every character; an "i" or "l" requires much less space than a "W" or "M". See examples of fixed and proportional spacing in figure 9.3.

- *Pitch* specifies the number of characters that can fit in one horizontal inch. Courier is normally printed at 10 pitch, and Prestige Elite is normally printed at 12 pitch. Pitch is never specified with proportional fonts.

- *Portrait* and *Landscape* describe the orientation of the paper. Normal text is printed in portrait mode, where an 8 1/2 by 11 inch paper prints

Fig. 9.3.
Examples of
character spacing.

```
This is a fixed-space typeface (Courier).
```
This is a proportionally-spaced typeface (Times).

vertically. In landscape orientation, the paper prints horizontally, like an artist's rendering of a landscape. Portrait mode is the most common orientation, but landscape mode is often used for printing lengthy, multiple-column charts and spreadsheets.

- *Symbol Set* describes the collection of characters in a font. The Roman-8 symbol set includes many characters used in foreign languages, such as

  ç, u, é, â, and ñ

  The *IBM-US* symbol set includes all characters that can be displayed on an IBM Personal Computer. Note: not all characters in the symbol set are available to your printer. Print the CHARACT.DOC file on the Learning disk to see which symbols your printer can produce.

Comparing LaserJet and PostScript Printers

Two general kinds of laser printers are available: the Hewlett-Packard LaserJet family and its compatibles, and PostScript printers. These printers differ chiefly in the way they regard a page. The LaserJet printers handle a page as an assortment of characters, whether the page contains text, graphics, or a combination of the two. On the other hand, the PostScript printers operate with a page description language (PDL) that treats a page as a picture or a graphic rather than a collection of characters.

What are the implications of these differences? With a character-based printer, like the LaserJet, all fonts must be available at the time of printing. In addition to the LaserJet's built-in type fonts, you can add additional typefaces with either a *cartridge* (which fits into a slot on the printer) or in *soft fonts* that are downloaded by WordPerfect to the printer at the time of printing. A PostScript printer can use a mathematical model or outline of a typeface to create type in any point size. Rather than store each point size in a cartridge or on a disk, PostScript printers require only a single outline for each typeface.

You will find information about each kind of laser printer in this chapter. But before examining each specific kind of printer, you see how to use WordPerfect with laser printers in general.

Note: To demonstrate WordPerfect's laser printing capabilities in the procedures throughout this chapter, we chose the Hewlett-Packard LaserJet Series II as a standard non-PostScript laser printer. These references to the LaserJet are neither a recommendation nor an endorsement; they merely reflect the popularity of the LaserJet family of printers.

Surveying Improvements in WordPerfect 5 for Laser Printers

In WordPerfect 4.2, the choice of PostScript fonts is limited unless you send special (and complicated) commands to the printer. You can choose between only two fonts, Helvetica and Times, and between two orientations, landscape and portrait. Changing point sizes is laborious and produces unpredictable results on margins, tab settings, and vertical spacing.

WordPerfect 5 is, however, capable of driving both LaserJet and PostScript printers. The program has been redesigned to take advantage of the vast capabilities of laser printers. If you're an old hand at WordPerfect, you should be aware of these improvements. Some improvements may force you to rethink your work habits. WordPerfect 5 now has the following capabilities:

- Virtually no limit to the number of fonts (PostScript is currently limited to 10 downloaded per job)

  Version 4.2 limits you to eight fonts per printer definition. No such limitation exists in version 5.

- Automatic font management

  In version 4.2, fonts have to be downloaded manually to the printer before printing. Version 5 downloads fonts automatically as needed.

- Minute control over vertical line-spacing

  Version 4.2 prints text at either six or eight lines per vertical inch. In version 5, the distance between lines (called *leading* by typographers) is calculated automatically for each font. You can also adjust line height manually.

- Advanced printer control

  You can now send commands to the printer and use new tools to control the relationship of letters within a single word.

WordPerfect 5 has several new keys that affect laser printing. These keys are Print (Shift-F7), Font (Ctrl-F8), and Format (Shift-F8).

With Print (Shift-F7), you can permanently alter the initial font (the default base font or normal text font) to any font built into the printer or to any available downloadable font.

Using Font (Ctrl-F8), you can temporarily alter the base font from that point forward in any given document.

Also, WordPerfect now uses an intelligent formatter. If the document you want printed was originally designed with the base font choice as Epson Roman 10 CPI and you change the base font to PostScript Palatino 10 point, the document *automatically* reformats and prints correctly on either printer. This automatic reformatting adjusts line height, number of characters in a line, number of lines on a page, and number of pages in a document.

Additionally, WordPerfect now has absolute margins. For example, instead of a margin or tab set at five spaces, the margin or tab can be set in inches. This method keeps margins and tabs correct even if multiple font changes occur in a document.

With Font (Ctrl-F8), you can also select various font attributes, including bold, underline, double underline, italic, outline, shadow, small capital, redline, and strikeout. You can also easily choose from seven sizes of type: superscript, subscript, fine, small, large, very large and extra large.

TIP: Because PostScript printers allow unlimited font-size selection, better control is maintained by setting the point size through the base-font feature than through the fine, small, large, very large, and extra large size attributes.

With WordPerfect 5, advanced printer functions are available through Format (Shift-F8). These functions include kerning, sending commands to the printer (either from a command line or from a file), word and letter spacing, and underlining spaces and tabs.

Configuring WordPerfect To Work with Your Laser Printer

The WordPerfect configuration procedure is identical for both types of laser printers. You must first define your printer, which is explained in the preceding chapter. Then you must select the fonts you wish to use in normal printing. After this initial setup is completed, there are numerous options you can invoke in normal editing. Font selection is covered next.

Note: If you have a Hewlett-Packard LaserJet printer, you must also select either a font cartridge or specific soft fonts before you can select printer fonts. (This is not necessary for PostScript printers.) Refer to the special section on LaserJet printers at the end of this chapter f r instructions on how to install hard and soft fonts on your LaserJet.

TIP: Each typeface has its own personality. The personalities of typefaces can interact on the page—with certain consequences for the reader. An error that beginners often make is to use too many fonts on one page. Experienced typesetters agree that many different fonts, point sizes, and weights on a single page obscure rather than facilitate communication.

Setting the Initial Font

Once your printer has been installed, and—on the LaserJet—you've selected the proper soft or hard fonts, you must now assign the initial fonts for your printer. This process is identical for both LaserJet and PostScript printers.

The initial font (also called *base font* on the Font key) is the font in which ordinary text is printed and around which font sizes and attributes are defined. If, for example, you specify Times Roman 10-point as the initial font, choosing Large from the Font key automatically prints in the next largest Times font available. Choosing Very Large prints in the second largest size, and so on.

Any font from either the Initial Font or Base Font list can serve as the base font (the default font). Remember, if you change the base font in the middle of a document, you see font changes displayed in the text only after the point of change. If you intend to change the base font for an entire document, first press Home, Home, ↑ (in sequence) to move the cursor to the beginning of the document.

TIP: After you move the cursor to the top of the document, if you want to return the cursor to where you were, press GoTo (Ctrl-Home) twice in sequence.

To change the initial font permanently, follow these steps:

1. First, press Print (Shift-F7).

2. Choose **Select Printer** (**S**).

3. From the Print: Select Printer menu, choose **Edit** (**3**).

4. Choose **Initial Font** (**6**).

5. Using the arrow keys, move the highlighted bar until your choice of initial font is covered.

6. Choose **Select** (**1**) to choose an initial font. (If you have a PostScript printer, you will be prompted for Point size:. Type a number and press Enter.)

7. Press Exit (F7) three times to return to your document.

A base font of either 10 or 12 points is easiest on the eyes. Fonts smaller than 10 points are hard to read; ones larger than 12 points are useful for headings but not ordinary business text.

Choosing a serif typeface (like Times) or a sans-serif typeface (like Helvetica) is a matter of personal taste. Serif fonts are easier to read for long stretches, so serif is usually a good choice for the body of a text. Notice that most newspapers and magazines use serif type. (Times type was developed for the London *Times* itself.) Sans-serif looks best in larger point sizes (notice street and traffic signs).

It is possible to change the initial font for a document without making a permanent change. To make an initial font change for the document you are currently editing, follow these steps:

1. Press Format (Shift-F8).

2. From the Format menu, choose **Document** (**3**).

3. Choose Initial Font (**3**).

4. Using the arrow keys, move the highlighted bar until your choice of initial font is covered.

5. Chose **Select** (**1**) to select the initial font. (If you have a PostScript printer, you will be prompted for ^D Point size: ^D. Type a number and press Enter.)

6. Press Exit (F7) to return to your document.

Selecting Typeface Size

WordPerfect 5 has greatly improved the procedure for mixing fonts within a document. With 4.2, you adjust margins every time you changed font and pitch. If you switch to a large type size, you also adjust vertical line-spacing so that characters from one line do not print on top of characters from the next.

Fortunately, version 5 makes that constant adjusting unnecessary. Because version 5 can set margins and tabs in absolute distances such as inches, you never need to adjust margins and tabs when you change fonts. Vertical line-height is also adjusted automatically. When you change to a large font from a smaller one, or vice versa, WordPerfect maintains proper leading.

WordPerfect provides two ways to change fonts: by size and by name. Both are located on the Font key (Ctrl-F8).

Selecting Fonts by Size

This method of changing fonts uses WordPerfect's new printer intelligence so that someone else can print your document even without the same fonts or printer. Because fonts are specified by size ("large") or appearance ("italic"), WordPerfect can formulate a best guess, no matter what kind of printer you use.

Font attributes like large and italic may or may not appear on your screen. Depending on your monitor type, different attributes are visible in either edit or View Document mode. See Chapter 5 for more information.

Select typeface size by following these steps:

1. Press Font (Ctrl-F8).

2. From the menu at the bottom of the screen, select **Size** (**1**). Another menu bar appears along the bottom of the screen, presenting the following choices:

1 Suprscpt; **2** Subscpt; **3** Fine; **4** Small; **5** Large; **6** Vry Large; **7** Ext Large

3. Choose the size you want.

When you alter the size, the Pos (Position) indicator in the lower right portion of the screen shows your choice. (What the Pos indicator and text size look like on-screen depends on what kind of monitor and display card you have. Both the Pos indicator and the text look the same.) WordPerfect automatically tracks the vertical height of the larger or smaller letters and adjusts margins and number of lines per page.

With PostScript printers, the base font is scaled larger or smaller by a certain percentage (see fig. 9.4). For example, you must experiment to determine just how much bigger "extra large" makes a 14-point base font. You can maintain more control by changing the base font and entering an exact point size instead of relying on relative scaling from the size menu.

fine-6 pts small-8 pts no change-12 pts large-14 pts

very large-22 pts extra large-30 pts

Fig. 9.4.
Changing point size.

Selecting Fonts by Name

Changing fonts by name gives you more control over fonts. To change fonts by name, follow these steps:

1. Press Font (Ctrl-F8).

2. Select Base Font (4).

WordPerfect displays the Base Font screen (see fig. 9.5), listing all fonts defined for the printer.

3. Move the highlight to the desired font; press Enter to select the font and return to your document.

Note: With Postscript printers, you see a prompt Point size:. You must then enter any point size from .1 to as large as the page can hold. Point sizes can be entered with up to two decimal places.

4. If you press Reveal Codes (Alt-F3, or F11), you can see that WordPerfect inserts a font change code that identifies the new font by name (see fig. 9.6).

Fig. 9.5.

Base Font screen.

```
Base Font

    Condensed
*   Courier
    Courier Double Wide
    Courier Double Wide Italic
    Courier Italic
    Courier PS
    Prestige Elite
    Prestige Elite Double Wide
    Prestige Elite Double Wide Italic
    Prestige Elite Italic




    1 Select; N Name search: 1
```

Fig. 9.6.

Reveal Codes showing font changes by name.

```
Suite 100, Tower Plaza¶
Portland, OR 97200¶
 ¶
Re:  Bill Williams¶
DOI: 1/9/88¶
¶
Dear Mr. Smith,¶
¶
In response to your letter of 2/10/88, I submit the following:¶
¶
1. HISTORY AND EXAMINATION¶
C:\WP50\QUE\FIG9.6                          Doc 2 Pg 1 Ln 5.33i Pos 1.07i
[   ▲    ▲    ▲    ▲     ▲     ▲    ▲     ▲     ▲     ▲     ▲
In response to your letter of 2/10/88, I submit the following:[HRt]
[HRt]
[Font:Times Roman Bold 13 pt]1. HISTORY AND EXAMINATION[HRt]
On June 19, 1987 at approximately 3 pm, Mr. Williams was involved[SRt]
in a vehicular accident at Highway 26 and 362nd in Sandy, Oregon.[SRt]
As reported by Mr. Williams:[HRt]
[HRt]
[→Indent←][ITALC]Stopping to let vehicle #3 turn left, I was immediately struck
by[SRt]
a 2 ton truck, vehicle #2. The impact pushed my vehicle #1 into[SRt]

Press Reveal Codes to restore screen
```

All text following this code prints in the new font. To return to the original font, perform this process again. You cannot choose the Normal option on the Font key to return to the original font, because you have explicitly changed the base font. This method works well as long as the specified font exists and is available when the document is printed. If, however, another printer is used or some fonts are unavailable, WordPerfect will substitute available fonts. These substitutions may make your final document printout look different from the one you planned.

Changing Typeface Appearance

Change the appearance of a typeface by following these steps:

1. Press Font (Ctrl-F8).

2. From the menu bar that appears at the bottom of the screen, select Appearance (**2**), and another menu appears along the bottom of the screen, presenting the following choices:

   1 Bold **2** Undrln **3** Dbl Und **4** Italc **5** Outln **6** Shadw **7** Sm Cap **8** Redln **9** Stkout

To see how each appearance affects output, print out the PRINTER.TST file on your Learning disk. Figure 9.7 shows various appearances.

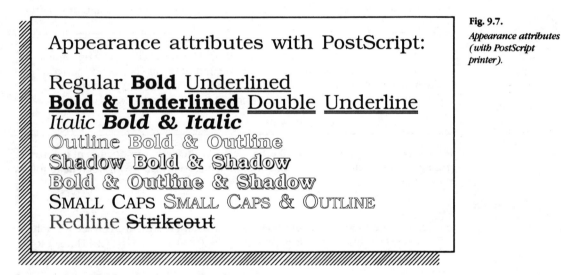

Fig. 9.7.
Appearance attributes (with PostScript printer).

3. Choose the typeface modification that you want.

When you select an attribute, depending on your monitor, the text and the Pos (Position) indicator in the lower right portion of the screen show your choice.

Facilitating Printer Configuration

To help you use different base fonts for different documents or change the printer port easily, you may want to have the same printer configured several different ways. Rather than change the configurations each time, you can copy the definition, make changes, and save them under a new name. To reconfigure your printer, follow these steps:

1. Press Print (Shift-F7).

2. Choose Select Printer (**S**).

3. Highlight the printer for which you want an alternative configuration, and select Copy (**4**).

The Printer Helps and Hints screen appears.

4. Press Exit (F7).

5. Select **Name** (**1**) and type a new name for the printer that describes the new default font or printer port (for example, type *Palatino 10-pt* or *LaserWriter COM 2*).

Now you can select one or the other printer with a simple command. You no longer need to reconfigure your printer for different uses.

If you configure your printer for more than one use, you can easily, for example, print the two letters in figures 9.8 and 9.9—each of which has a different typeface.

TIP: PostScript files are *device independent*. This means that your document can be printed to disk and that file can be output on any PostScript device including a Linotronic™, which will print the document in typeset quality. Many service bureaus around the country offer this service for a nominal per-page charge.

If your monitor is capable, WordPerfect lets you preview your document before printing by using the View Document command. To preview your document, follow these steps:

1. Press Print (Shift-F7).

2. Choose **View Document** (**6**) from the main Print menu. You see a graphics representation of your page. Use PgUp, PgDn, and GoTo (Ctrl-Home) to view different pages.

3. Press the space bar to return to the editing screen.

Defining Forms

The concept of *forms* is new with version 5. With the Forms feature, you can predefine and name different media on which you print, specify their size, and indicate the place where forms are stored. Indicating location is especially useful for multiple-bin sheet feeders. You can feed forms either manually or automatically from the paper tray.

You can create as many form definitions as you like. You may, for example, create one definition for a letterhead, another for subsequent pages, a third for envelopes, and another for labels. Because margins are set in inches, WordPerfect needs to know the size of the paper to figure the right and bottom margins. When you insert a Paper Size/Type code in a document, WordPerfect goes to the requested location and uses the appropriate media—if you load it.

1. HISTORY AND EXAMINATION

On June 19, 1987 at approximately 3 pm, Mr. Williams was involved in a vehicular accident at Highway 26 and 362nd in Sandy, Oregon. As reported by Mr. Williams:

Stopping to let vehicle #3 turn left, I was immediately struck by a 2 ton truck, vehicle #2. The impact pushed my vehicle #1 into vehicle #3 causing extensive damage to latter vehicle. My head lurched forward, then whipped back. The glass in the cab of vehicle #1 shattered.

Mr. Williams reported neck and sore throat pain immediately after the accident. This pain made work difficult. He denies any pain prior to the accident and has not been in previous accidents of this sort since he had a resolved whiplash injury in 1978.

Mr. Williams is a pleasant and cooperative 39 year old man weighing 190 pounds and standing 6'1". He was examined in my office on January 10, 1988. Cervical range of motion was reduced to 60 from 70 degrees in both left and right rotation. Left lateral flexion was reduced from 40 to 30 degrees and right lateral flexion was only 25 degrees. Flexion and extension were normal. All restricted ranges were painful.

Fig. 9.8.

Letter in Helvetica typeface printed by PostScript printer.

1. HISTORY AND EXAMINATION

On June 19, 1987 at approximately 3 pm, Mr. Williams was involved in a vehicular accident at Highway 26 and 362nd in Sandy, Oregon. As reported by Mr. Williams:

Stopping to let vehicle #3 turn left, I was immediately struck by a 2 ton truck, vehicle #2. The impact pushed my vehicle #1 into vehicle #3 causing extensive damage to latter vehicle. My head lurched forward, then whipped back. The glass in the cab of vehicle #1 shattered.

Mr. Williams reported neck and sore throat pain immediately after the accident. This pain made work difficult. He denies any pain prior to the accident and has not been in previous accidents of this sort since he had a resolved whiplash injury in 1978.

Mr. Williams is a pleasant and cooperative 39 year old man weighing 190 pounds and standing 6'1". He was examined in my office on January 10, 1988. Cervical range of motion was reduced to 60 from 70 degrees in both left and right rotation. Left lateral flexion was reduced from 40 to 30 degrees and right lateral flexion was only 25 degrees. Flexion and extension were normal. All restricted ranges were painful.

Fig. 9.9.

Letter in Times typeface printed by PostScript printer.

To define forms, follow these steps:

1. Press Print (Shift-F7) to display the main Print menu.

2. Choose **S**elect Printer (**S**) to display the Print: Select Printer screen.

3. Move the highlight bar to the appropriate printer, then press Edit (**3**) to display the Select Printer: Edit screen.

4. Select Forms (**4**).

WordPerfect displays the Select Printer: Forms screen (see fig. 9.10).

One form, Standard, is predefined. Across the top of the screen you can see the items you need to specify when you define a form: Form type, Size, Orientation, Initially Present, Location, and Offset.

5. Select Add (**1**).

WordPerfect displays the Select Printer: Form Type screen (see fig. 9.11). This is the first of several screens that WordPerfect displays during the Forms Definition process.

Fig. 9.10.

The Select Printer:
Forms screen.

```
Select Printer: Forms
                                      Orient Init          Offset
Form type            Size             P L   Pres Location  Top    Side

Envelope             4" x 9.5"        N Y    Y   Manual     0"     0"
Standard             8.5" x 11"       Y Y    Y   Contin     0"     0"
[ALL OTHERS]         Width ≤ 8.5"            N   Manual     0"     0"




If the requested form is not available, then printing stops and WordPerfect
waits for a form to be inserted in the ALL OTHERS location.  If the requested
form is larger than the ALL OTHERS form, the width is set to the maximum width.

1 Add; 2 Delete; 3 Edit: 3
```

Fig. 9.11.

The Select Printer:
Form Type screen.

```
Select Printer: Form Type
         1 - Standard

         2 - Bond

         3 - Letterhead

         4 - Labels

         5 - Envelope

         6 - Transparency

         7 - Cardstock

         8 - [ALL OTHERS]

         9 - Other



Selection: 1
```

6. Press the appropriate number or letter to select a name for the form from the list. (These names don't mean anything specific to WordPerfect; they help you keep track of different forms.)

After you make a choice, WordPerfect displays the Select Printer: Forms screens (see fig. 9.12). You will return to this screen several times during the forms definition process.

7. Select Form Size (**1**).

WordPerfect displays the Select Printer: Form Size screen. The `Inserted Edge` heading refers to the edge of the form that is fed into the printer first. Usually you feed the shorter edge first, *even when you print in landscape mode.*

```
Select Printer: Forms

         Filename              HPLASERJ.PRS

         Form Type             Bond

     1 - Form Size             8.5" x 11"

     2 - Orientation           Portrait

     3 - Initially Present     Yes

     4 - Location              Continuous

     5 - Page Offsets - Top    0"
                        Side   0"
```

Fig. 9.12.

The Select Printer: Forms screen.

8. Press the appropriate number or letter to choose a form size. Note that some of the forms are common sizes that you use everyday; others are less common forms for more specialized uses.

   You return to the Select Printer: Forms screen (see fig. 9.12).

9. Select Orientation (**2**).

   WordPerfect displays three choices at the bottom of the screen:

   Orientation: 1 Portrait; **2** Landscape; **3** Both:

10. Select the appropriate Orientation choice.

Choose **Portrait** (**1**) if you plan to print only in portrait mode, **Landscape** (**2**) if you plan to print on this form only in landscape, or **Both** (**3**) to print in either portrait or landscape mode.

TIP: Choose **Both** (**3**). Although you may never need to print in landscape mode, WordPerfect is then ready for that "once in a blue moon" special job.

---

11. Select Location (**4**).

    WordPerfect displays three choices at the bottom of the screen:

    Location: 1 Continuous; **2** Bin Number; **3** Manual:

12. Choose **Continuous** (**1**) if you are feeding from the paper tray (even though it uses cut sheets instead of continuous paper). If you purchase an optional multibin sheet feeder, choose **Bin Number** (**2**) and enter the appropriate value. To feed individual sheets manually (useful when you print on heavyweight stock), choose **Manual** (**3**).

13. Select **P**age Offsets (**5**).

Offsets tell WordPerfect to begin printing at a specific location on the form. For example, if the top and left margins are both one inch, offsets of zero cause printing to begin one inch down and one inch in. By changing the offsets, you can make allowances for such different forms as letterhead paper and envelopes.

14. Enter the vertical and horizontal offsets; then press Enter twice.

You return to the Select Printer: Forms screen, which now displays the newly defined form. If everything is correct, press Exit (F7) until you return to the document. Choose the **E**dit (**3**) option if you want to make corrections.

To specify a form in a document, press Format (Shift-F8), and select **P**age (**2**), and then Paper **S**ize/Type (**8**); then enter the appropriate information for sizes you select (see Chapter 6 for detailed information on this feature).

Using WordPerfect with LaserJet Printers

Hewlett-Packard LaserJet printers differ from some other laser printers in that the fonts used in printing can come from up to three sources: internal fonts, cartridge fonts, and soft fonts. Naturally, the internal fonts are already in your printer when you remove it from the shipping carton, and WordPerfect realizes this on the various setup menus. But WordPerfect must be made aware of any cartridge or soft fonts you may be using. This section discusses the three types of LaserJet fonts and shows you how to set up WordPerfect for proper LaserJet use.

Considering Internal Fonts

Internal fonts are easiest to work with. Built into the printer by the manufacturer, they are always available. You find internal fonts in the LaserJet Series II listed in table 9.1.

Considering Cartridge Fonts

Cartridge fonts (sometimes called *hard fonts*), available from Hewlett-Packard and a few third-party manufacturers, contain from three to eight fonts in a cartridge roughly the size of an old eight-track audio tape. (These cartridges contain just computer chips, no tape.)

The 27 cartridges currently available from Hewlett-Packard include special fonts to print Internal Revenue Service tax forms, supermarket style UPC (Universal Product Code) bar codes, and machine readable OCR (optical character recognition) text.

Table 9.1
LaserJet Series II Internal Fonts

Typeface	Weight	Spacing	Pitch	Point Size	Style	Symbol Set	Orientation
Courier	Medium	Fixed	10	12	Upright	Roman-8	Portrait
Courier	Medium	Fixed	10	12	Upright	Roman-8	Landscape
Courier	Medium	Fixed	10	12	Upright	IBM-US	Portrait
Courier	Medium	Fixed	10	12	Upright	IBM-US	Landscape
Courier	Bold	Fixed	10	12	Upright	Roman-8	Portrait
Courier	Bold	Fixed	10	12	Upright	Roman-8	Landscape
Courier	Bold	Fixed	10	12	Upright	IBM-US	Portrait
Courier	Bold	Fixed	10	12	Upright	IBM-US	Landscape
LPC*	Medium	Fixed	16.66	8.5	Upright	Roman-8	Portrait
LPC	Medium	Fixed	16.66	8.5	Upright	Roman-8	Landscape
LPC	Medium	Fixed	16.66	8.5	Upright	IBM-US	Portrait
LPC	Medium	Fixed	16.66	8.5	Upright	IBM-US	Landscape

* Line Printer Compressed

Cartridge fonts don't use any LaserJet internal memory—an important advantage. Unfortunately, because of the engineering and manufacturing complexities and costs inherent in cartridge fonts, few manufacturers have entered this market. The selection is limited.

Considering Soft Fonts for LaserJets

Soft fonts are files stored on disk and *downloaded* from your computer to the laser printer's internal memory as needed. Because these fonts are stored in the printer's internal memory, they reduce the memory available for storing pages to print.

Thousands of soft fonts—virtually any typeface in any size—are available from hundreds of manufacturers. Because soft fonts are inexpensive to manufacture, their price is relatively low. If you can't find a font to fit your needs, you can buy software to design your own. If the graphic artist in you is yearning for expression, creating your own soft font is the answer.

Choosing between Cartridges and Soft Fonts

Choosing between cartridges and soft fonts for your LaserJet is not an easy task. Fortunately, with many laser printers, you can use both types simultaneously; the LaserJet Series II, for example, is equipped with two slots for cartridge fonts and internal memory for storing soft fonts. Still, you should understand the differences between the two LaserJet printing strategies.

Cartridge fonts offer these advantages:

- Available as soon as you plug them in—without downloading.

- Completely self-contained and do not use internal memory.

- Easily and quickly installed; however, selection is limited and prices are higher than soft font prices.

Soft fonts offer these advantages:

- Less expensive than hardware-based cartridges.

- Widely available. You can find a huge selection of typefaces from hundreds of manufacturers.

- Versatile. You can mix and match them, downloading only those fonts you need and designing your own fonts with available software. (However, soft fonts use valuable internal memory and must be stored on a hard disk for maximum efficiency.)

Developing a Font Strategy

Many people combine cartridge and soft fonts. This technique balances the cost of fonts against memory usage, and ease of use against the need to download. Table 9.2 summarizes a mix of fonts commonly used in a business environment. Hewlett-Packard font cartridges are identified by a single letter ("G" and "Z" in the table). Soft fonts, sold as a family containing several point sizes and weights in both Roman and italic style, are identified by two letters ("AD" in the table).

Table 9.2
Sample Font Strategy

Typefaces	Type	Remarks
Courier	Internal	Always available, good for typewriter-like output
Line Printer	Internal	Always available, good for spreadsheets.
Prestige Elite	Cartridge G	Saves memory, good for executive correspondence, includes line-drawing characters
Times and Helvetica	Cartridge Z1A	Saves memory; normal point sizes and styles are adequate for most standard office work.
Times and Helvetica	Soft *AD* Set	Excellent supplement to Z cartridge; includes a broad range of larger and smaller sizes; download only what you need for a given job.

You need not limit your library of soft fonts to the AD set. Hewlett-Packard distributes several handsome text font families—including ITC Garamond, Century

Schoolbook, and Zapf Humanist 601; and headline typefaces—including Broadway, Coronet Bold, Cooper Black, University Roman, and Bauer Bodini Black Condensed. In addition, over a hundred independent manufacturers market thousands of different fonts licensed from type foundries worldwide. Whatever your needs are, you should be able to find a font to satisfy them.

Installing Fonts

To install fonts on the LaserJet II, you use different techniques, depending on the font installed. These same procedures can be used for the older Hewlett-Packard LaserJet and LaserJet +, except that soft fonts cannot be used with the original LaserJet. (They can be used with the LaserJet +, however.)

Installing Cartridge Fonts

Few things in life are easier than installing a cartridge font. To install a cartridge font, follow these steps:

1. Take the printer off-line by pressing the On-Line key on the printer's control panel. Make sure the On-Line light goes off after you press the key.

2. Insert the cartridge all the way.

   Make sure that the label is facing up and double-check that the cartridge is inserted all the way.

3. Press the On-Line key to return the printer to on-line status.

   The On-Line light should be lit.

TIP: You must take the printer off-line before removing or installing a font cartridge. Failure to do so will require turning the printer off, then back on.

You learn how to tell WordPerfect to use the font cartridge later in this chapter.

Installing Soft Fonts

You don't install soft fonts in the LaserJet. Instead, you copy them to your computer's hard disk and instruct WordPerfect to download them to the printer when you deem it necessary.

TIP: Although you can use soft fonts without a hard disk, you may not like the disk-swapping that floppy disks require.

To install a set of soft fonts on your hard disk, first create a subdirectory to hold font files. You can create this subdirectory from DOS, but this example shows how to accomplish subdirectory creation from within WordPerfect.

1. Press List Files (F5) to display the List Files screen.

```
03/28/88  12:24              Directory C:\WP50\*.*
Document size:        0   Free: 11130880   Used:  3358943        Files:  99

.  <CURRENT>    <DIR>                    ..  <PARENT>    <DIR>
ALTA     .WPM       88  03/08/88 10:03   ALTB     .WPM       97  03/09/88 11:05
ALTH     .WPM       91  03/23/88 13:55   ALTL     .WPM       83  03/23/88 13:34
ALTQ     .WPM       69  03/11/88 14:56   ALTW     .WPM       81  03/09/88 10:56
AMD      .WPG     1466  02/06/88 07:17   APPLAUSE.WPG     1774  02/06/88 07:17
ARROW1   .WPG      342  02/06/88 07:17   ARROW2   .WPG      352  02/06/88 07:17
ARROW3   .WPG      340  02/06/88 07:17   ARROW4   .WPG      404  02/06/88 07:17
ARROW5   .WPG      698  02/06/88 07:17   AWARD    .WPG     1746  02/06/88 07:17
B        .         1085  06/04/80 05:24   BADNEWS  .WPG     4167  02/06/88 07:17
BOMB     .WPG      950  02/06/88 07:17   BOOK     .WPG     1904  02/06/88 07:17
BOOK002  .QUE    34425  03/09/88 14:30   BORDER   .WPG    13662  02/06/88 07:17
CHARACTR.DOC     52559  02/05/88 17:36   CHECK    .WPG     1070  02/06/88 07:17
CLOCK    .WPG     6030  02/06/88 07:17   COMPASS  .WPG     2126  02/06/88 07:17
CONFID   .WPG     2242  02/06/88 07:17   EGA512   .FNT     7160  02/06/88 07:16
EGAITAL  .FNT     3504  02/06/88 07:16   EGASMC   .FNT     3504  02/06/88 07:16
EGAUND   .FNT     3504  02/06/88 07:16   EPSONFX-.PRS     5370  03/09/88 13:45
FACTORY  .WPG      972  02/06/88 07:17   FATARROW.WPG      342  02/06/88 07:17
FC       .DOC     1906  02/06/88 07:17   FC       .EXE    23552  02/06/88 07:17
FEET     .WPG     1304  02/06/88 07:17 ▼ FLAG     .WPG      554  02/06/88 07:17


New directory = C:\WP50\FONTS
```

If your WordPerfect directory is C:\WP50 and that appears on the status line, press Enter. If not, type *C:\WP50* and press Enter.

2. Choose **Other Directory** (7) and edit the status line to C:\WP50\FONTS.

   To edit the status line, press End to move the cursor to the end of the current directory; then type the new information.

3. Press Enter.

   WordPerfect displays Create C:\WP50\FONTS? (Y/N) No.

4. Press *Y* to confirm the creation of the new subdirectory.

   WordPerfect updates and redisplays the List Files screen with the new subdirectory (see fig. 9.13).

5. With the highlight bar still on the<CURRENT> directory, select Look (6).

   With this command, you can see the files in a different directory without making it the default.

6. Type the letter of the disk drive (A: or B:) in which you have inserted the font disk; then press Enter.

   WordPerfect lists the files on the specified drive.

7. Mark the font files you want to copy to the hard disk.

8. To copy all files, press Home, either asterisk (*) key, and then select Copy (**8**).

   WordPerfect displays Copy marked files? (Y/N) No.

9. Press *Y* to confirm your decision.

10. Enter the full drive and path to indicate the destination when you see the prompt Copy marked filed to:.

    In this exercise, type *C:\WP50\FONTS*, and press Enter.

Installing Bitstream

The WordPerfect package contains information about ordering a Bitstream Installation Kit for WordPerfect. Included with the kit are Swiss (Bitstream's version of Helvetica) in four weights, Dutch (Bitstream's version of Times Roman) in four weights, and the regular weight of Bitstream Charter (other weights of Bitstream Charter are for sale). The kit is sent at no charge by WordPerfect on request. Bitstream Fontware works with either PostScript or with Hewlett-Packard compatible LaserJet printers.

Note: Bitstream Fontware does not work with dot-matrix or other non-LaserJet or non-PostScript-compatible printers.

Setting Up Fonts

WordPerfect needs to be told what fonts you will be using. This will vary depending on whether you use cartridge fonts or soft fonts. An explanation of how to relay this information for each kind of font is provided next.

Setting Up Cartridge Fonts

The next section explains how to tell your LaserJet which cartridges you will be using.

1. Press Print (Shift-F7) to display the main Print menu (see fig. 9.14).

2. Choose Select Printer (**S**) to display the Print: Select Printer screen (see fig. 9.15).

3. Move the highlight bar to the appropriate printer; then select Edit (**3**) to display the Select Printer: Edit screen (see fig. 9.16).

4. Select Cartridges and Fonts (**5**) to display the Select Printer: Cartridges and Fonts screen (see fig. 9.17).

   For the LaserJet Series II, WordPerfect lets you specify two cartridges simultaneously because the printer is equipped with two cartridge slots.

Fig. 9.14.
Print menu.

```
Print

      1 - Full Document
      2 - Page
      3 - Document on Disk
      4 - Control Printer
      5 - Type Through
      6 - View Document
      7 - Initialize Printer

Options

      S - Select Printer          HP LaserJet Series II
      B - Binding                 0"
      N - Number of Copies        1
      G - Graphics Quality        Medium
      T - Text Quality            High




      Selection: 0
```

Fig. 9.15.
The Print: Select Printer screen.

```
Print: Select Printer

   * HP LaserJet Series II
     Standard Printer








   1 Select; 2 Additional Printers; 3 Edit; 4 Copy; 5 Delete; 6 Help; 7 Update: 1
```

```
Select Printer: Edit

        Filename                HPLASEII.PRS

   1 - Name                     HP LaserJet Series II

   2 - Port                     LPT1:

   3 - Sheet Feeder             None

   4 - Forms

   5 - Cartridges and Fonts

   6 - Initial Font             Courier 10 pitch (PC-8)

   7 - Path for Downloadable
       Fonts and Printer
       Command Files




Selection: 0
```

Fig. 9.16.
The Select Printer:
Edit screen.

```
Select Printer: Cartridges and Fonts

Font Category               Resource                    Quantity

Cartridge Fonts             Font Cartridge Slot             2
Soft Fonts                  Memory available for fonts    350 K




1 Select Fonts; 2 Change Quantity; N Name search: 1
```

Fig. 9.17.
The Select Printer:
Cartridges and Fonts
screen.

5. With the highlight bar on the Cartridge Fonts line, choose **Select Fonts (1)**.

    WordPerfect displays a list of the font cartridges currently available from Hewlett-Packard (see fig. 9.18).

6. Move the highlight bar to the cartridge or cartridges you want; then press the asterisk key (`*`) to select the cartridge.

    Because you cannot change cartridges during a print job, your only choice is **Present** when Print Job Begins.

Fig. 9. 18.

The Select Printer: Cartridges and Fonts screen for cartridges.

```
Select Printer: Cartridges and Fonts

                                          Total Quantity:    2
                                      Available Quantity:    2

    Cartridge Fonts                                    Quantity Used

        A Cartridge                                         1
        B Cartridge                                         1
        C Cartridge                                         1
        D Cartridge                                         1
        E Cartridge                                         1
        F Cartridge                                         1
        G Cartridge                                         1
        H Cartridge                                         1
        J Cartridge                                         1
        K Cartridge                                         1
        L Cartridge                                         1
        M Cartridge                                         1
        N Cartridge                                         1
        P Cartridge                                         1
        Q Cartridge                                         1

    Mark Fonts: * Present when print job begins        Press Exit to save
                                                       Press Cancel to cancel
```

The top right corner of the screen tells you how many slots the printer has and how many you used.

7. Press Exit (F7) to complete the selection process.

Setting Up Soft Fonts

Just as with cartridge fonts, you must inform WordPerfect about the various soft fonts you intend to use with your LaserJet. To select soft fonts, follow these steps:

1. Press Print (Shift-F7) to display the main Print menu.

2. Select **Select Printer** (**S**) to display the Print: Select Printer screen.

3. Move the highlight bar to the appropriate printer. Then select **Edit** (**3**) to display the Select Printer: Edit screen.

4. Select **Cartridges and Fonts** (**5**) to display the Select Printer: Cartridges and Fonts Screen.

5. WordPerfect says that for the LaserJet Series II, 350K of printer memory is available for storing soft fonts. If you added memory to your LaserJet, you can change this figure by pressing Change **Quantity** (**2**) and entering the new figure.

6. With the highlight bar on the Soft Fonts line, chose **Select Fonts** (**1**).

   WordPerfect displays a list (see fig. 9.19) of soft fonts currently available from Hewlett-Packard.

7. Move the highlight bar to the cartridge or cartridges you want, and press either * or + to select.

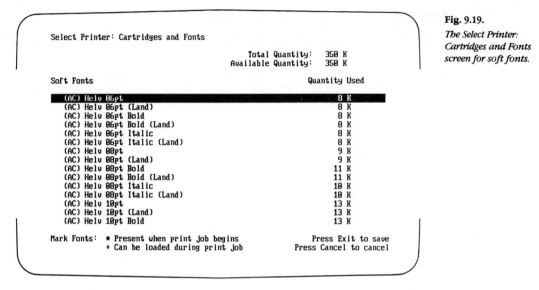

Fig. 9.19.
*The Select Printer:
Cartridges and Fonts
screen for soft fonts.*

You can download soft fonts to the LaserJet during a print job. Select ˙ for
fonts that *must* be present in the printer at the beginning of a print job.
Select + for fonts that can be downloaded at any point in the print job.

The top right corner of the screen tells you how much total memory is
available and how much you have used.

TIP: Fonts you use only occasionally should be marked +.

8. Press Exit (F7) to complete the selection process.

When you are done installing the soft fonts on your printer, you must configure
WordPerfect to work with these fonts, as explained earlier in this chapter. One
additional configuration must be made for soft fonts, however; you must tell
WordPerfect where the soft fonts are located.

Downloading Bitstream

Once you install Bitstream fonts, you can select them the same way you select any
other font. WordPerfect automatically downloads them to the printer.

Setting the Path for Soft Fonts and Printer Command Files

WordPerfect needs to know where the soft fonts (and command files, if you have any) are located, so you must indicate the location—or set the path to find them.

To set the path, follow these steps:

1. Press Print (Shift-F7) (**S**) to display the main Print menu.

2. Choose Select Printer (**S**) to display the Print: Select Printer screen.

3. Move the highlight bar to the appropriate printer; then select Edit (**3**) to display the Select Printer: Edit screen.

4. Select Path for Downloadable Fonts and Printer Command Files (**7**).

5. Type the full path name and press Enter.

6. Press Exit (F7) three times to return to your document.

Using Forms

The LaserJet Series II can handle several different sizes of media. It is useful to know this information when you are defining new forms with WordPerfect (discussed earlier this chapter). Each media size requires its own paper tray. Table 9.3 lists the names, sizes, and the various Hewlett-Packard paper trays available. Keep in mind that for portrait- or landscape-mode printing, you change fonts rather than paper tray.

Table 9.3
Hewlett-Packard Series II Paper Sizes and Trays

Form Type	Paper Tray Size	Hewlett-Packard Part Number
Letter Size	8 1/2 x 11 inches	92295B
Legal Size	8 1/2 x 14 inches	92295C
A4	210mm x 297mm	92295D
Executive Size	182mm x 257mm	92295E
Envelope Tray	—	92295F

The envelope tray is special; it can handle four different envelope sizes, listed in table 9.4.

Table 9.4
Envelope Sizes Supported by the Envelope Tray

Envelope Type	Size
Com-10	4 1/8 x 9 1/2 inches
Monarch	3 7/8 x 7 1/2 inches
C5	229mm x 162mm (9 x 6.4 inches)
DL	110mm x 220mm (4.3 x 8.6 inches)

Troubleshooting Problems for Your LaserJet Printer

All troubleshooting items listed in the preceding chapter on printing also apply generally to laser printers. The items listed in this section, however, apply specifically to LaserJet printers.

Troubleshooting Cartridge Font Problems

If you have trouble with cartridge fonts, any of the following items may be the cause:

- Installed cartridges may not be identified to WordPerfect. You must use the Cartridges and Fonts option on the Select Printer: Edit screen to tell WordPerfect which cartridges are installed.

- You may be using the wrong font for regular printing. Use the Initial Font option on the Select Printer: Edit screen to tell WordPerfect which font to use for normal printing.

- The cartridge may no longer work. Hewlett-Packard specifies font cartridge life expectancy in *number of insertions*. If you frequently swap font cartridges, you may need to replace them.

- If you receive an FE Cartridge error message on the control panel, you removed the font cartridge without first taking the printer off-line. You must shut the printer off, then turn it back on. You must also re-download the soft fonts with the Initialize Printer option on the main Print screen.

Troubleshooting Soft Font Problems

If you have problems with soft fonts, here are some possible causes and solutions:

- The soft fonts may not be downloaded. Make sure that WordPerfect knows where the fonts are. Do this with the Path for Downloadable Fonts and Printer Command Files option on the Select Printer: Edit screen.

- The desired fonts may not be selected. Use the Cartridges and Fonts option on the Select Printer: Edit screen to tell WordPerfect which fonts you have. Don't select fonts you don't have.

- The fonts may be erased from the LaserJet's memory. If you turn the printer off, its memory is cleared. Use the Initialize Printer option on the main Print menu to reload the fonts you marked as *Must be present at beginning of job*.

- You may have an old set of soft fonts. If you use the AA, AB, or AC font sets, you may need to change to the .PRS file for your printer. Use the PTR.EXE program to do this.

- The computer may be unable to download soft fonts. You probably have the original LaserJet. To use soft fonts, you must have a LaserJet +, LaserJet 500 +, or a LaserJet Series II.

- You may be using the wrong font for normal printing. Use the Initial Font option on the Select Printer: Edit screen to tell WordPerfect which font should be used for normal printing.

- If you have trouble printing soft fonts, or have trouble printing complete graphics images, chances are you need to install more memory in your LaserJet. Both soft fonts and graphics images consume large amounts of memory. Fortunately, Hewlett-Packard and other manufacturers offer several add-on memory boards for the LaserJet. Consult your dealer for more details.

If a page is incomplete, the printer may be out of memory. Everything printed on a single page must fit into the printer's memory simultaneously. The LaserJet should display 2Ø ERROR on its control panel when it has insufficient memory.

For a quick remedy, redo the page so that it contains fewer graphics, downloads fewer soft fonts, or both. For a permanent remedy, add a memory expansion board (see table 9.5).

Table 9.5
Hewlett-Packard LaserJet Series II Memory Boards

Amount of Memory	Part Number	Remarks
1 megabyte	33443A	Recommended for the single-user environment.
2 megabytes	33444A	Recommended for multiuser (network) environments or single-user environments in which many soft fonts are downloaded simultaneously.
4 megabytes	33445A	Recommended for special memory-intensive applications like CAD (computer-assisted drafting); certainly not needed for word processing.

Getting the Most from Your PostScript Laser Printer

If you have a PostScript laser printer, you'll learn how to use your printer to best advantage with WordPerfect in this part of the chapter. If something doesn't happen in the sequence described, double-check your work and begin again.

Considering Downloadable Fonts for PostScript Printers

Downloadable fonts are stored on-disk and *downloaded* from your computer to the laser printer's internal memory as needed. Only a few vendors now supply WordPerfect/PostScript compatible downloadable fonts. Among them are Adobe and Bitstream. Many more font choices are becoming available, and selection is rapidly expanding.

Installing and Setting Up Fonts on the PostScript Printer

If you use a PostScript printer, you will want access to as many fonts as you can for flexibility in designing all your documents. This next section shows you how to get the most from downloadable fonts.

Installing Downloadable Fonts from Adobe

Copy the downloadable fonts to your computer's hard disk and instruct WordPerfect to download them to the printer when you deem it necessary.

To copy a set of downloadable fonts on your hard disk, first create a subdirectory to hold font files. You can create this subdirectory from DOS, but this example shows how to accomplish subdirectory creation from within WordPerfect.

1. Press List Files (F5) to display the List Files screen. (see fig. 9.13).

   If your WordPerfect directory is C:\WP50 and that appears on the status line, press Enter. If not, type *C:\WP50* and press Enter.

2. Choose Other Directory (7) and edit the status line to C:\WP50\FONTS.

   To edit the status line, press End to move the cursor to the end of the current directory; then type the new information.

3. Press Enter.

   WordPerfect displays Create C:\WP50\FONTS? (Y/N) No.

4. Press *Y* to confirm creation of the new subdirectory.

   WordPerfect updates and redisplays the List Files screen with the new subdirectory.

5. With the highlight bar still on the <CURRENT> directory, press Look (**6**).

   With this command, you can see the files in a different directory without making it the default.

6. Type the letter of the disk drive (A: or B:) in which you have inserted the font disk; then press Enter.

   WordPerfect lists the files on the specified drive.

7. Mark the font files you want to copy to the hard disk.

8. To copy all files, press Home, either asterisk (*) key, and then select Copy (**8**).

   WordPerfect displays Copy marked files? (Y/N) No.

9. Press *Y* to confirm your decision.

10. Enter the full drive and path to indicate the destination when you see the prompt Copy marked filed to:.

    In this exercise, type *C:\WP50\FONTS* and press Enter.

Setting Up WordPerfect for PostScript Downloadable Fonts

You must inform WordPerfect about the various downloadable fonts you intend to use with your PostScript printer. To select downloadable fonts complete these steps:

1. Press Print (Shift-F7) to display the main Print menu (see fig. 9.20).

2. Choose Select Printer (**S**) to display the Print: Select Printer screen (see fig. 9.21).

3. Move the highlight bar to the appropriate printer. Then select Edit (**3**) to display the Select Printer: Edit screen (see fig. 9.22).

4. Select Cartridges and Fonts (**5**) to display the Select Printer: Cartridges and Fonts Screen.

Note: If the printer files were not copied to your hard drive or are not on your current disk, WordPerfect will ask for the directory for the printer files. Either specify a directory or insert the correct Printer disk in the drive, press the appropriate drive letter, and press Enter.

```
   Print

        1 - Full Document
        2 - Page
        3 - Document on Disk
        4 - Control Printer
        5 - Type Through
        6 - View Document
        7 - Initialize Printer

   Options

        S - Select Printer        Apple Laserwriter Plus
        B - Binding               0
        N - Number of Copies      1
        G - Graphics Quality      Medium
        T - Text Quality          High




   Selection: 0
```

Fig. 9.20.
The Printer Options menu.

```
   Print: Select Printer

   * Apple Laserwriter Plus
     Epson FX-80/100
     Epson LQ-2500




   1 Select; 2 Additional Printers; 3 Edit; 4 Copy; 5 Delete; 6 Help: 1
```

Fig. 9.21.
The Print: Select Printer menu.

Fig. 9.22.

The Select Printer:
Edit menu.

```
Select Printer: Edit

          Filename              APLASPLU.PRS

      1 - Name                  Apple Laserwriter Plus

      2 - Port                  COM1:9600,N,8,1

      3 - Sheet Feeder          None

      4 - Forms

      5 - Cartridges and Fonts

      6 - Initial Font          Helvetica 10 pt

      7 - Path for Downloadable C:\WP50\FONTS
          Fonts and Printer
          Command Files



    Selection: 0
```

5. WordPerfect says that for the Apple LaserWriter Plus, 120K printer memory is available for storing downloadable fonts. If you have more memory, you can change this figure by pressing Change **Quantity** (**2**) and entering the new figure.

6. Choose Select Fonts (**1**).

   WordPerfect displays a list (see fig. 9.23) of downloadable fonts currently available.

Fig. 9.23.

The Select Printer:
Cartridges and Fonts
screen for
downloadable fonts.

```
Select Printer: Cartridges and Fonts

Font Category              Resource              Quantity

Downloadable fonts         Memory                120 k








1 Select Fonts; 2 Change Quantity; N Name search: 1
```

7. Move the highlight bar to the cartridge or cartridges you want, and press either * or + to select.

You can download fonts to the printer during a print job. Select * for fonts that *must* be present in the printer at the beginning of a print job. Select + for fonts that can be downloaded at any point in the print job.

The top right corner of the screen tells you how much total memory is available and how much you have used.

8. Press Exit (F7) to complete the selection process.

When you are through installing the downloadable fonts on your printer, you must tell WordPerfect where the fonts are located.

Setting the Path for Downloadable Fonts and Printer Command Files

WordPerfect needs to know where the downloadable fonts (and command files, if you have any) are located, so you must indicate the location—or set the path to find them.

To set the path, follow these steps:

1. Press Print (Shift-F7) to display the main Print menu.

2. Choose Select Printer (**S**) to display the Print: Select Printer screen.

3. Move the highlight bar to the appropriate printer, then select Edit (**3**) to display the Select Printer: Edit screen.

4. Select Path for Downloadable Fonts and Printer Command Files (**7**).

5. Type the full path name and press Enter.

6. Press Exit (F7) three times to return to your document.

Using Forms with PostScript Printers

PostScript printers can handle several different sizes of media. It is useful to know this information when you are defining new forms with WordPerfect (discussed earlier this chapter).

Using Downloadable Fonts

As wonderful as is the selection of fonts that come with a PostScript printer, an even more incredible selection is available. New font choices become available every day. Several companies offer software fonts (fonts that are not built-in) for use with PostScript printers. Two of these companies are Bitstream and Adobe.

CAUTION: These disk-based fonts require a lot of disk space, so using them requires a hard disk with enough available space.

Adobe has a magnificent library of PostScript fonts. Many of these fonts are available for use with WordPerfect. To see which fonts are supported by WordPerfect, follow these steps:

1. Press Print (Shift-F7).

2. Choose Select Printer (**S**).

3. Use the arrow keys to position the highlight bar over the PostScript printer you are using.

4. Press Help (F3). You see a Printer Helps and Hints screen that gives you the latest information about which Adobe fonts are supported by WordPerfect.

Installing Bitstream

The WordPerfect package contains information about ordering a Bitstream Installation Kit for WordPerfect. Included with the kit are Swiss (Bitstream's version of Helvetica) in four weights, Dutch (Bitstream's version of Times Roman) in four weights, and the regular weight of Bitstream Charter (other weights of Bitstream Charter are for sale). The kit is sent at no charge by WordPerfect on request. Bitstream Fontware works with either PostScript or with Hewlett-Packard compatible LaserJet printers.

The documentation accompanying the Bitstream Installation Kit for WordPerfect is clear, and installing the fonts is a straightforward process. Here is an overview and some suggestions for quick installation:

1. From the Fontware Control Panel, you are asked for three directory names. Remember the directory name for Printer Fonts because you will need it later for WordPerfect.

2. You have several choices for Printer Model and Character Set. Select PostScript Printer for the model and PostScript Outline for the character set. Because WordPerfect does not display different typefaces with screen fonts (it uses a text display that does not show graphic displays of fonts), no screen fonts are available with WordPerfect.

3. On the Fontware Typefaces menu, you are prompted to Add/Delete Fontware Typefaces.

TIP: Most PostScript printers come with Helvetica and Times already built-in. If you already have these two typefaces, don't add the Swiss and Dutch Fontware typefaces because they duplicate fonts you already have under a different name. Bitstream Charter is not a typeface you will have in your printer. Bitstream offers a large variety of different fonts for different purposes. With the installation kit, you can take advantage of them all.

If you use any of these fonts or later add new ones, put the directory information into WordPerfect by following these steps:

1. Press Print (Shift-F7).

2. From the Print menu, choose **S**elect Printer (**S**).

3. Then, from the Print: Select Printer menu, select **E**dit (**3**).

4. From the Select Printer: Edit menu, select **P**ath for Downloadable Fonts and Printer Command Files (**7**).

5. Then, type the drive and path name where the Fontware fonts reside—for example, *C:\WP50\FONTS*. Press Enter. If you see an ERROR: invalid path/ drive specification message, double-check the path name and try again.

6. Press Enter four times to return to the document.

Downloading Bitstream

Once you install the Bitstream fonts, select them the same way you select any other font. WordPerfect automatically downloads them to the printer.

Using Specialty Typefaces with PostScript Printers

Most typefaces built into PostScript or other laser printers are useful for business correspondence and reports. The typeface you choose can add or detract from the communication. Enjoy experimenting; find out what appeals to you and what your correspondents find pleasing.

Considering Typeface Suggestions

A variety of available typefaces can be more confusing than limited choices. Here are some suggestions to help you decide which font to use for what occasion:

- For legibility and ease of reading long stretches of text, try a serif typeface like Times, ITC Bookman, Palatino, and New Century Schoolbook.

- For a modern look, try Avant Garde.

- For lists or tabular material, try Courier (monospaced type, like a typewriter—not proportional), Helvetica, or Helvetica Narrow.

- For headlines or text with a larger point size, try a sans-serif typeface like Helvetica or Avant Garde.

- For a calligraphic look or for invitations, try Zapf Chancery.

- For mathematical or Greek letters, use Symbol.

- For emphasis and for fun, try Zapf Dingbats (a collection of nonalphabet characters such as check marks, pointing hands, stars, boxes, playing card symbols, circled numbers, and arrows). These fonts are not available for the HP LaserJet.

  Because Symbol and Zapf Dingbats typefaces have nonalphabetic characters and no counterparts in the IBM character set, they do not show up on-screen except as letters or numbers. They do, however, print correctly as the Dingbat or Symbol you choose. Used sparingly, these special characters can greatly enhance a document's appeal.

Using Display Fonts

Certain fonts are not appropriate for everyday usage but, carefully used, can create great impact in flyers or in brochures. Bitstream has several sets of Headline typefaces. One set includes Cooper Black, Broadway, Cloister Black, and University Roman. Another set includes Brush Script, Blippo Black, Hobo, and Windsor. See figure 9.24 for an example of these eight typefaces.

Using Other Features with PostScript Printers

Most PostScript laser printers are serial printers, and serial printers are notoriously slow. In reality, this slowness is due to the speed at which your computer transmits data through the serial printer port. If the slowness of your computer becomes a problem, you can purchase a "speed up" program, such as Blitz, to make your laser printer run faster.

Troubleshooting Problems with Your PostScript Printer

If your printer won't print, start with this list to see whether you can isolate and correct the problem:

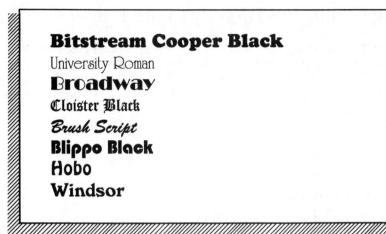

Fig. 9.24.
*Bitstream headline
series display fonts.*

- Check power. Are both printer and computer plugged in?

- Check printer status lights. Is the printer on-line? Is paper in the paper tray? Is the toner cartridge installed properly?

- Check the cable. Do you have the correct cable? If there is more than one place to plug the cable into the computer, have you plugged it into the correct one?

- Check the printer emulation switch. Some PostScript printers have switches or dials that offer choices between PostScript and Diablo or Epson emulation. If there is a switch or dial, is it set correctly?

- Check your selection in the main Print menu. Have you selected the correct printer? Is it installed? Is the correct port selected? If it is a serial port (COM), have you chosen the correct baud, parity, etc.?

- If none of the previous suggestions corrects the problem, try reinstalling WordPerfect and reselecting the printer. This sometimes works.

- Contact WordPerfect customer support, where a whole group of support people can help you with your problem. If you buy a printer and can't find it on the printer choices and can't find an emulation listed in the manual, call WordPerfect. You can get help selecting correct printer definition, or you may even have a new printer definition sent to you.

Other Considerations

Two additional issues that apply to both LaserJet and PostScript printers are important for getting the most from your printer. One is sending commands to the printer; the other is troubleshooting printing problems in general.

Sending Commands Directly to the Printer

In WordPerfect 4.2, accessing some features of a PostScript printer (such as fonts other than Times or Helvetica) requires sending commands directly to the printer. WordPerfect 5, on the other hand, handles most commands automatically. Advanced users may still send commands (instructions) to the printer; if you prefer not to, you may skip this section.

You can send instructions directly to the printer in one of two ways. The first is to use Print (Shift-F7) and select Initialize Printer (7) from the main Print menu. (PostScript printers do not require initializing.) The second is to send a command directly to the printer with the following steps:

1. Press Format (Shift-F8).

2. From the Format menu select **Other** (4).

3. From the Format: Other menu, select **Printer Functions** (6).

4. From the Format: Printer Functions menu, select **Printer Command** (2).

5. Then, from the prompt at the bottom of the screen select either **Command** (1) or Filename (2).

   a. If you press Command (1), you are prompted for a command. Enter the command and press Enter four times to return to the document.

   Any characters you type are embedded as a **[Ptr Cmnd:]** code and remain in the document. During printing, when the **[Ptr Cmnd:]** code is encountered, the character string you previously entered is sent to the printer. You may never need this advanced technique, but if you do, your printer manual has information on the effect of different commands on your printer.

   b. If you press Filename (2), you are prompted for a file name. You must then enter the path and file name of a command file. After you enter the file name, press Exit (F7) two times to return to the document.

   If you use printer commands often, you may store some of the more common ones in a file. Create and save a file with the commands you want sent to the printer. When WordPerfect encounters the **[Ptr Cmnd:]** code, it transmits the instructions contained in the command file to the printer.

CAUTION: If you incorrectly enter a command file name or path, you are not warned. If your printer does not seem to respond to the command file, double-check the instructions in the file as well as the path and file name you entered.

If your document file is used by someone else on a different computer, the command file must be available on that computer in a directory of the correct name.

If you use command files frequently, you may want to enter permanently the name of the subdirectory where the files are stored. Follow these steps to enter a permanent subdirectory:

1. Press Print (Shift-F7).

2. From the main Print menu, choose Select Printer (**S**).

3. From the Print: Select Printer menu, choose Edit (**3**).

4. From the Select Printer: Edit menu, select Path for **D**ownloadable Fonts and Printer Command Files (**7**).

5. Finally, type the drive and path name where the command files are. For example, *C:\CMNDFILE*. Press Enter. (If you see an ERROR: Invalid drive/ path specification message, double-check spelling and try again.)

Troubleshooting Printing Problems

If your print quality is inferior, consider the following solutions:

- The toner cartridge may need replacing. Replace the toner cartridge when print output is too light or uneven. Lines running the length of the paper indicate a scratched photoconductor drum inside the toner cartridge.

- The paper path or corona wires may need cleaning. Turn the printer off and use a cotton swab moistened with isopropyl alcohol to clean the interior as the owner's manual instructs.

- The fuser roller pad may need cleaning or replacing. A new pad is included with every replacement toner cartridge.

- You may be using an improper paper type. For general work, use photocopy paper. For cotton bond letterheads, use paper that does not create paper dust. Textured or woven papers may not work well.

If the printer seems to take a long time to print pages, perhaps the text contains graphics. Pages containing graphics always take longer to print than text-only pages. Waiting time varies with the number of graphics on the page and the amount of memory your printer has.

Printing Your Laser Documents on Another Printer

An unusual feature in WordPerfect 5 is its "intelligent printing capability." In order to achieve the best possible output from a particular printer, WordPerfect takes the capabilities of that printer into account from the very beginning. When you create a document, WordPerfect assumes that it will be printed on the printer that is currently selected. When you change fonts in the document, WordPerfect lets you choose among only those fonts that are actually available for that printer, in the orientation you are using. With a LaserJet, you cannot choose a landscape font if you are using a portrait orientation, and vice versa; fonts of the wrong orientation do not even appear on the list of available fonts. With PostScript printers, orientation is not a concern.

Each version 5 document, therefore, is printer-specific. The name of the printer for which the document is formatted is stored in the document header, along with information about the fonts available for that printer. If you instruct WordPerfect to print the document on a different printer, WordPerfect reformats the document for the new printer. Reformatting involves substituting fonts and forms that are available to the new printer for the ones that were available to the original printer.

If you always use the same printer, you may not ever be aware of this reformatting. If you switch back and forth between two printers, however, you should get into the habit of selecting the printer you plan to use before you begin a new document, especially if you change fonts and/or paper sizes frequently. You can write a simple macro to select each printer.

WP 5 Summary

In this chapter, you learned how to coexist peacefully with your Hewlett-Packard or other non-PostScript laser printer. You learned how to work with internal, cartridge, and soft fonts, and why each can be a powerful tool in your everyday work. You have also seen that it takes patience and work to get the most out of your laser printer.

The chapter has also shown you much about PostScript printers. You now know what a PostScript printer is, how it differs from other laser printers, and what special features it offers. You have seen how the new features in WordPerfect 5 can help you get the most out of your PostScript printer.

Now that your printer is operational, you can quickly print letters, reports, and other documents that look the way *you* want them to look.

10

Using List Files

Doug Hazen, Jr., is a computer programmer and ex-machinist who lives in the Boston area. He is a member of the Boston Computer Society WordPerfect Special Interest Group and has used WordPerfect for almost three years. He works for Intellution, Inc., in Norwood, Mass. ■

In this chapter, you learn how WordPerfect can help you deal with DOS and manage your computer system. You read about one of WordPerfect's major features, List Files, with which you can manipulate files and directories to a much greater degree than most word-processing programs allow.

You learn the following skills:

- Review the various parts of the List Files screen: the heading, the file listing, and the menu

- Use List Files to help you with common DOS and WordPerfect operations, such as deleting, moving, copying, and renaming files; making, changing, and deleting directories; and retrieving and printing documents

- Perform List Files operations on multiple files with a feature called *file marking*

- Search several files at once for a word or phrase with the Word Search option

To get the most from this chapter, you need some elementary understanding of DOS features such as files, directories, wild cards, and basic DOS commands. If you aren't familiar with this information, you may want to read Que's best-selling books on DOS: Chris DeVoney's *Using PC DOS*, 2nd Edition, or *MS-DOS User's Guide*, 3rd Edition, depending on the DOS your system uses. For an easy-to-use rapid reference, see also *DOS QueCards*™ by Glenn Larsen and Denise Slingsby.

Discovering List Files

List Files (F5) is one of WordPerfect's nicer features. With List Files, you can—from within WordPerfect—accomplish much of the file and directory management you ordinarily do in DOS. To get to the List Files screen, press List Files (F5). WordPerfect displays a message in the lower left corner: Dir, followed by a file specification for all files in the current directory, such as Dir C:\WP5\BOOK*.*.

This message says that WordPerfect is ready to give you a *file listing* of all files in the current directory. If this is the file listing you want, simply press Enter. If it is not the listing you want, you can change the specification. If you type a new file specification, the original one disappears and is replaced by the new one you type. You can also edit the file specification, just as you edit regular text, by using many ordinary WordPerfect command keys:

Key	Key Movement
End	Moves cursor to end of file specification
Home -	Moves cursor to beginning of file specification
Del	Deletes character at cursor
Backspace	Deletes character to left of cursor
Ctrl-End	Deletes to end of file specification

If you use these editing commands, the old file specification stays on-screen for you to edit. Change the file specification to what you want; then press Enter.

For now, use the default file specification (list all files in the current directory). Press List Files (F5), then Enter. You now see the List Files screen (see fig. 10.1). The three areas on this screen are the *heading*, the *file listing*, and the *menu*.

Fig. 10.1.

List Files screen.

```
04/02/88  08:33              Directory C:\WP\D\BUSLTR\*.*
Document size:       0  Free:  1593344  Used:      18564        Files:  21

  . <CURRENT>  <DIR>                    .. <PARENT>  <DIR>
DEDUCT   .       314  10/20/87 16:53  DRAFT    .       974  03/14/88 14:03
DS       .      6498  06/02/87 19:35  DS2      .       410  01/14/88 23:46
ENV42X   .MAC    352  12/16/87 22:58  INMAC    .       715  11/19/87 13:45
IRA86    .       332  01/07/87 16:02  LTR      .FMT     89  07/12/86 15:07
LTR      .MAC     79  03/14/88 23:13  LTRFMT   .        85  01/14/88 23:56
MACDOC   .       323  11/30/86 21:11  NEIL     .      2298  01/08/87 21:35
QUE      .       464  02/26/88 17:58  TRNSCRPT.2       357  03/03/88 09:06
TURBO    .       565  10/04/87 11:52  VISA2    .       684  05/28/87 20:43
VISA21   .       442  06/10/87 23:05  WP5      .       404  01/23/88 13:53
WPIMPRV .1       545  05/24/87 13:03  WPIMPRV .2       721  11/05/87 12:16
WPLET    .      1913  01/20/88 10:35

1 Retrieve; 2 Delete; 3 Move/Rename; 4 Print; 5 Text In;
6 Look; 7 Other Directory; 8 Copy; 9 Word Search; N Name Search: 6
```

Understanding the Heading

At the top of the List Files screen, you see the two-line heading, which contains useful information. Listed at the top left and going across to the right are the date, the time (given as 24-hour time), and the directory being listed. On the second line, starting again at the left, are the size of the document currently being edited, the amount of free space left on the disk, the amount of disk space taken by files in the current file listing, and the number of files shown in the listing.

Understanding the File Listing

The second section is a two-column file listing in alphabetical order across the screen (files whose names start with numbers are listed first). This listing shows the complete file name, file size, and date and time the file was created or last modified. You can print this listing, along with most of the information in the heading, on your currently selected printer by pressing Print (Shift-F7) (see fig. 10.2).

```
04/02/88  08:33              Directory C:\WP\D\BUSLTR\*.*
Free:  1593344

.  <CURRENT>    <DIR>              :  ..  <PARENT>     <DIR>
DEDUCT   .           314   10/20/87  16:53  :  DRAFT    .          974   03/14/88  14:03
DS       .          6498   06/02/87  19:35  :  DS2      .          410   01/14/88  23:46
ENV42X   .MAC        352   12/16/87  22:50  :  INMAC    .          715   11/19/87  13:45
IRA86    .           332   01/07/87  16:02  :  LTR      .FMT        89   07/12/86  15:07
LTR      .MAC         79   03/14/88  23:13  :  LTRFMT   .           85   01/14/88  23:56
MACDOC   .           323   11/30/86  21:11  :  NEIL     .         2298   01/08/87  21:35
QUE      .           464   02/26/88  17:50  :  TRNSCRPT .2         357   03/03/88  09:06
TURBO    .           565   10/04/87  11:52  :  VISA2    .          684   05/28/87  20:43
VISA21   .           442   06/10/87  23:05  :  WP5      .          404   01/23/88  13:53
WPIMPRV  .1          545   05/24/87  13:03  :  WPIMPRV  .2         721   11/05/87  12:16
WPLET    .          1913   01/20/88  10:35
```

Fig. 10.2.
List files screen printed with Print (Shift-F7).

Notice the top name in each column of the List Files file listing contains the following:

. <CURRENT>   <DIR>   .. < PARENT>   <DIR>

< DIR > indicates that items are directories. Other directories in the listing are similarly labeled. The entry labeled < CURRENT > refers to the currently listed directory. The other entry, labeled < PARENT >, refers to the parent directory of the listed directory.

A highlight bar also appears on the top left name. You can move this bar with the cursor keys to highlight any name in the listing. You can move it also with the usual WordPerfect cursor movement command keys, as in table 10.1.

Using the List Files Menu

The List Files menu appears at the bottom of the screen. You can select from ten command choices on the menu. You can select each with either a number, as in WordPerfect 4.2, or with the highlighted letter. Each choice acts on the highlighted file or directory.

Table 10.1
WordPerfect Cursor Movement Command Keys

Keys	Move to Location
Home ↓	Last file on-screen
keypad -	First file on-screen
Home ↑	First file on-screen
keypad +	Last file on-screen
Home, Home, ↓	Last file in listing
Home, Home, ↑	First file in listing

WordPerfect often asks for confirmation when you pick one of the menu commands. Trying to be as safe as possible, WordPerfect initially presents a No choice when asking for confirmation. For example, if you press **Delete (2)** to delete the file EXAMPLE.WP, WordPerfect asks

`Delete C:\BOOK\EXAMPLE.WP? (Y/N) No`

You can, of course, answer either *Y* (to delete the file) or *N* (to cancel the command).

Using Retrieve

Retrieve (1) works like Retrieve (Shift-F10) from the editing screen: it brings a file into WordPerfect for editing. Like Retrieve (Shift-F10), this command inserts the newly retrieved file into the old file at the cursor position—if you already have a file on-screen. Because many people accidentally combined files this way in previous WordPerfect versions, WordPerfect 5 asks, `Retrieve into current document? (Y/N)` if you pick this List Files menu choice with a file already on-screen. Answer *Y* if you want to combine the new file with the file you already have on the screen. Answer *N* if you don't want to combine the files.

WordPerfect tries to protect you from retrieving improper files. It does not retrieve *program* files, nor does it retrieve any temporary or permanent WordPerfect system files (see the "WordPerfect Files" section in the Appendix of the WordPerfect 5 manual for information on these types of files) or macro files (see Chapter 11).

Using Delete

Delete (2) deletes either files or directories. If the highlight bar is on a file, that file is deleted. If the bar is on a directory, the directory is deleted *as long as there are no files in it*. If the directory has some files in it, WordPerfect gives you an error message. Whether you're deleting files or directories, WordPerfect asks Delete name? (Y/N) No. Press *Y* to confirm deletion, or press *N* to cancel deletion.

Using Move/Rename

To rename a file, put the highlight bar on the file name you want to change, and press Move/Rename (3). WordPerfect displays the message New name: followed by the current name of the file. Type the new name for the file (the displayed name disappears), and press Enter. You can't rename a file with the name of an existing file.

Moving a file means transferring it to a different directory or disk drive. To move one or more files, complete the following steps:

1. Press List Files (F5), change the file specification if you want, and press Enter.

2. Move the highlight bar to the first file you want to move and *mark* it (see the section on marking files) by pressing the asterisk key.

3. Similarly mark all the files you want to move.

4. Press Move/Rename (3) and answer *Y* in response to the Move marked files? (Y/N) No question.

   If you answer *N* to the Move marked files? question, WordPerfect displays the New name message to see if you want to rename the file where the highlight bar is, as described at the beginning of this section.

5. When prompted Move marked files to: type the directory or drive where you want to move the files, and press Enter.

Using Print

Print (4) prints the highlighted file on the currently selected printer. Unlike many programs, WordPerfect can print *while you continue to edit another document*. You can even tell WordPerfect to print more than one file. WordPerfect tracks and prints all the files in the order in which you specify them. If you have more than one printer, you can even send each file to a different printer—and WordPerfect can keep track of everything.

If you are using the Fast Save option (see Appendix A), you can't print files saved with this option. If you try, you see the message ERROR: Document was Fast Saved-Must be retrieved to print.

For more information on printing with WordPerfect 5, see Chapters 8 and 9.

Using Text In

Text In (5) retrieves a *text* (sometimes called an ASCII) file, not a WordPerfect format file. This command is the same as retrieving a DOS Text file in the editing screen with Text In/Out (Ctrl-F5, 1). See Chapter 15 for more information on retrieving text files.

Using Look

Look (6) displays the highlighted file *without* retrieving it into WordPerfect (see fig. 10.3). You *cannot* edit the file.

Fig. 10.3.

Look screen.

```
Filename C:\WP5\BOOK\APPENA.LJ                    File size:    54569

(b)Using DOS

What is DOS? DOS is an "operating system" (the letters stand for
Disk Operating System). All modern computers, big and small, have
some kind of operating system. An operating system is a sort of
"manager" or master program that helps all other programs do many
of the things that all programs need to do. In effect, other
programs that you run ask the operating system for certain kinds
of services.

When you press Save (F10), for instance, WordPerfect asks DOS
(without you being aware of it) to save the file onto the disk
and DOS does it. When you press Retrieve (Shift-F10) to retrieve
a new file, WordPerfect asks DOS to start passing it the data in
that file. DOS manages all disk activity and the video display,
loads programs into memory and starts them running, and many
other things that you don't see or know about.

One of the most important things DOS does is provide the
framework for saving programs and data on a disk. Virtually all
programs you'll ever use make use of this important DOS service.

Press Exit when done                    (Use Cursor Keys for more text)
```

The file name and size are displayed at the top of the screen. You can move the cursor through the file with the usual WordPerfect cursor-movement commands. The Look option also continuously displays or scrolls each succeeding line of the document if you press S. Pressing S again stops the scroll. Press Exit (F7) or Enter to leave Look.

You can search for text with Forward Search (F2) and Backward Search (Shift-F2). You can't, however, search for text in headers, footers, or footnotes with the Look option.

If you look at a file containing a Document Summary (see Chapter 2), you find that, in Look, the Summary is displayed first, as in figure 10.4.

You can thus examine quickly a number of files with Document Summaries to find the one you want. To see the rest of the document, press either PgDn or ↓.

Fig. 10.4.
Looking at a file containing a document summary.

```
Filename C:\WP5\BOOK\APPENA.50              File size:      55047

  April 2, 1988
  Appendix A for 5.0

  Doug Hazen, Jr.
  Doug Hazen, Jr.
  This is Appendix A - DOS Guide in WP 5.0 form. It has 7176 words, with
  footers and page numbers. All figures are in place, though not all are yet
  numbered.




  Document Summary                    (Use Cursor Keys for more text)
```

Note current directory and highlighted directory

Fig. 10.5.
Preparing to Look at a new directory.

```
04/02/88  08:25              Directory C:\*.*
Document size:         0  Free:  1546240  Used:   122413      Files:  20

  . <CURRENT>   <DIR>                    .. <PARENT>    <DIR>
  BAT      .    <DIR>    11/27/86 23:39   COMM     .    <DIR>    02/19/88 11:14
  DOS      .    <DIR>    11/27/86 23:39   INSET    .    <DIR>    04/02/88 07:39
  KW       .    <DIR>    11/27/86 23:39   MISC     .    <DIR>    11/27/86 23:40
  MS       .    <DIR>    02/26/88 20:18   PRGM     .    <DIR>    11/27/86 23:45
  SCHOOLD  .    <DIR>    11/27/86 23:55   SCHOOLM  .    <DIR>    11/27/86 23:55
  SQRNOTE  .    <DIR>    10/17/87 10:41   TYPTUTR  .    <DIR>    11/27/86 23:56
  UTILS    .    <DIR>    11/27/86 23:56   WP       .    <DIR>    11/28/86 00:06
  WP5      .    <DIR>    03/08/88 13:05   WPLBRY   .    <DIR>    11/28/86 00:08
  AUTOEXEC.BAT    456    02/16/88 15:45   BACKUP   .M_U    60928 04/02/88 07:18
  CONFIG  .SYS    101    05/11/87 21:35   OLDBACK  .M_U    60928 04/02/88 07:18




  Dir C:\WP5\*.*
```

Use Look to examine files quickly. You may, for example, forget which file you need to edit. Note that 6 is the default menu choice. You don't have to press 6 to Look at a file (though you can if you want); you can just press Enter.

You can also Look at other directories. With the highlight bar at the top left, press Enter once, edit the displayed file specification or type a new one, and press Enter again. You have NOT changed directories. You are simply seeing a file listing of the other directory.

You can use the Look command to inspect directories another way. Place the highlight bar on a directory entry (other than < CURRENT >) in the file listing, as in figure 10.5. Press Enter, and WordPerfect displays a `Dir` message followed by the file specification (see the previous section on changing directories). Press Enter again, and WordPerfect displays the file listing of this highlighted directory. You can look at any directories in this new listing the same way, as in figure 10.6.

Fig. 10.6.

Looking at a directory further down the tree.

Note current directory now

```
04/02/88  08:27              Directory C:\WP5\*.*
Document size:      0   Free:  1546240   Used:  1039265      Files:  21

. <CURRENT>    <DIR>                  .. <PARENT>    <DIR>
BOOK     .    <DIR>    03/08/88 14:35  MACROS   .    <DIR>    03/09/88 09:15
THDIC    .    <DIR>    03/12/88 16:37  TMP      .    <DIR>    03/12/88 10:41
DI630ECS.PRS    2170   04/01/88 14:04  EPFX80  .PRS    8311   04/01/88 13:47
IBPCGRPR.PRS    2311   04/01/88 13:48  PAKXP109.PRS    3946   04/01/88 13:49
PTR     .EXE  202240   03/28/88 15:42  PTR     .HLP  126446   03/28/88 15:42
WP      .DRS   73360   03/28/88 15:03  WP      .EXE  239104   03/28/88 15:01
WP      .FIL  296771   03/30/88 15:09  WPHELP  .FIL   57139   03/28/88 15:01
WPHELP2 .FIL   19535   03/28/88 15:01  WPTEXT  .PRS     997   03/30/88 19:19
WP)WP(  .SET    2839   04/01/88 19:35  WP)WP(  .BV1       0   04/02/88 08:13
WP)WP(  .CHK       0   04/02/88 08:13  WP)WP(  .SPC    4096   04/02/88 08:13
WP)WP(  .TV1       0   04/02/88 08:13




Dir C:\WP5\BOOK\*.*
```

In this way, you can travel up or down the directory tree, examining each directory in turn. Remember, though, you have not changed your current directory. You are simply listing files in other directories.

TIP: When you delete a file, WordPerfect leaves an empty space on-screen where the file name was. If you delete a number of files at once, reading the listing becomes hard. Simply move the highlight bar to the top left (Home, Home, ↑) and press Enter twice. This lets you perform a Look at the current directory, so WordPerfect re-creates the file listing without all the holes.

TIP: You can use the Look option to discover the purpose of macros you may have forgotten about. If you look at a macro file, you can see the description you entered when you created the macro (you *do* put in macro descriptions, don't you?). This Look feature is the main reason for entering a description for *every* macro you create.

Using Other Directory

Press **Other Directory** (**7**) to change the current directory. The result of making this choice depends where the highlight bar is.

If the highlight bar is on any directory name other than <CURRENT> when you press **Other Directory** (**7**), WordPerfect displays in the lower left corner of the screen the message New directory = followed by the name of the highlighted directory, as in figure 10.7.

```
05/16/88  00:03              Directory C:\WP5\*.*
Document size:       0    Free: 1744896   Used:  1012112        Files:  19

. <CURRENT>   <DIR>                     .. <PARENT>   <DIR>
BOOK     .   <DIR>    03/08/88 14:35    MACROS   .    <DIR>    03/09/88 09:15
THDIC    .   <DIR>    03/12/88 16:37    TMP      .    <DIR>    03/12/88 10:41
TMP2     .   <DIR>    04/11/88 12:04    GRAB     .COM    14687 04/27/88 14:24
PAKXP109.PRS    3992  05/15/88 14:52    PTR      .EXE   204288 04/27/88 11:32
PTR      .HLP 139898  04/27/88 11:32    WP       .EXE   244736 05/05/88 12:47
WP       .FIL 298884  05/05/88 12:47    WPHELP   .FIL    47587 05/05/88 12:47
WPHELP2  .FIL  52121  05/05/88 12:47    WP}WP>   .SET     1823 05/15/88 22:56
WP}WP(   .BV1      0  05/15/88 20:32    WP}WP(   .CHK        0 05/15/88 20:32
WP}WP(   .GF1      0  05/15/88 22:02    WP}WP(   .SPC     4096 05/15/88 20:32
WP}WP(   .TV1      0  05/15/88 20:32



New directory = C:\WP5\BOOK
```

Fig. 10.7.
Preparing to change directories in List Files.

Press Enter and WordPerfect displays the message Dir followed by the file specification for all the files in the highlighted directory. Press Enter again and WordPerfect changes to the new directory and displays its listing. If you decide you don't want to change directories after all, just press Cancel (F1) before pressing Enter the second time.

If the bar is on the upper left directory name (<CURRENT>) or a file name when you give the Other Directory command, WordPerfect does nothing except redisplay the same directory listing.

You can edit both the New directory = and Dir messages (see fig. 10.8), just as you could edit the original message you got when you first pressed List Files (F5) from the editing screen. You can thus directly change to any directory on your hard disk.

Regardless of where the highlight bar is, you can create a new directory by entering a nonexistent name. If you enter *frog*, WordPerfect asks Create frog? (Y/N) No. If you answer *Y*, WordPerfect creates a new subdirectory called FROG. If this isn't what you want, answer *N*.

You can also use the List Files key (F5) to change or create directories right from the WordPerfect editing screen. Press F5, then =. WordPerfect responds the same way as in the List Files screen.

Fig. 10.8.

Editing the New Directory name.

```
04/02/88  12:01              Directory C:\WP5\BOOK\*.*
Document size:    25891   Free:  1515520   Used:    347445        Files:  44

.  <CURRENT>   <DIR>              ..  <PARENT>    <DIR>
ALTF   .MAC       4  03/27/88 16:28    ALTI   .MAC       8  03/27/88 14:50
ALTM   .MAC       2  03/27/88 16:27    ALTP   .MAC      11  03/27/88 15:16
APPENA .42    45193  03/30/88 12:05    APPENA .50    55047  04/02/88 08:22
APPENB .      34584  03/14/88 09:22    APPNAOTL.      3840  03/28/88 19:23
APPNAOTL.42    2484  03/30/88 12:21    APPNBOTL.      9111  03/14/88 08:51
BADAPPNB.     34584  03/14/88 08:51    BANK   .       532  04/02/88 10:17
BANKABLE.        27  04/01/88 21:57    BANKCOM .      319  04/02/88 11:00
BANKER .         28  04/01/88 21:57    BANKP  .        13  04/01/88 21:56
BANKROLL.         8  04/01/88 21:48    BAT    .      4674  03/14/88 12:41
BIO    .        726  03/09/88 12:04    BIZNESS .LTR   778  04/02/88 09:54
CH1042 .      16923  03/30/88 11:25    CH1050 .     25933  04/02/88 10:12
CH1050 .BK!   25866  04/02/88 09:53    CH10COPY.BAD 47064  03/26/88 14:52
CH10OTL.42     2226  03/30/88 22:02    CHK    .      1018  03/26/88 10:44
DON    .       3373  03/12/88 12:34    DON2   .      1196  03/12/88 14:19
DON3   .       2385  03/14/88 19:57    DONREP .      2165  03/27/88 23:41
FB     .MAC       4  03/27/88 16:28    FTR    .        76  03/27/88 14:35
GO     .BAT      50  03/14/88 09:40    GO1    .BAT     7  03/14/88 09:54
LTR    .FMT     523  03/12/88 11:41  ▼ LTRFMT .        85  01/14/88 23:56


New directory = \wp5\t
```

Using Copy

The Copy (**8**) option copies the highlighted file, just like the DOS COPY command. If you press Copy (**8**), WordPerfect displays the message Copy this file to: . You can copy the file to another disk or directory, or you can make a copy of the file in the current directory by entering a new file name instead of a drive or directory.

Using Name Search

With the Name Search (**N**) choice, you can move the highlight bar to a file name in the listing as you type the name. To start, press **N**, then type the first letter of the file name (BIZNESS.LTR) for which you want to search. For example, if you type *b*, the highlight bar jumps to the first file name starting with that letter (see fig. 10.9).

Now if you type *i* as the second letter of the name, the highlight jumps to the first file name that starts with these *two* letters (see fig. 10.10) or as close to them as it can get.

If you still don't find the file, type the third letter—for example, type *z*—and the highlight jumps to the first file name starting with these *three* letters (see fig. 10.11).

If you make a mistake or change your mind, press Backspace, and the highlight bar jumps to the previous position. Once the file name you want is highlighted, turn off Name Search by pressing either Cancel (F1), Enter, or one of the arrow keys. Then you can do any of the operations described in this chapter—for example, Retrieve, Delete, Print, and so forth.

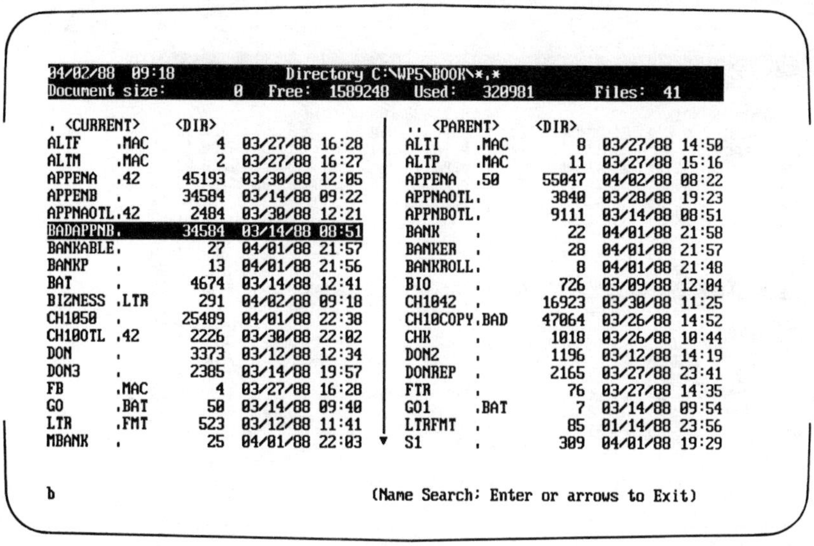

Fig. 10.9.
Starting with a name search.

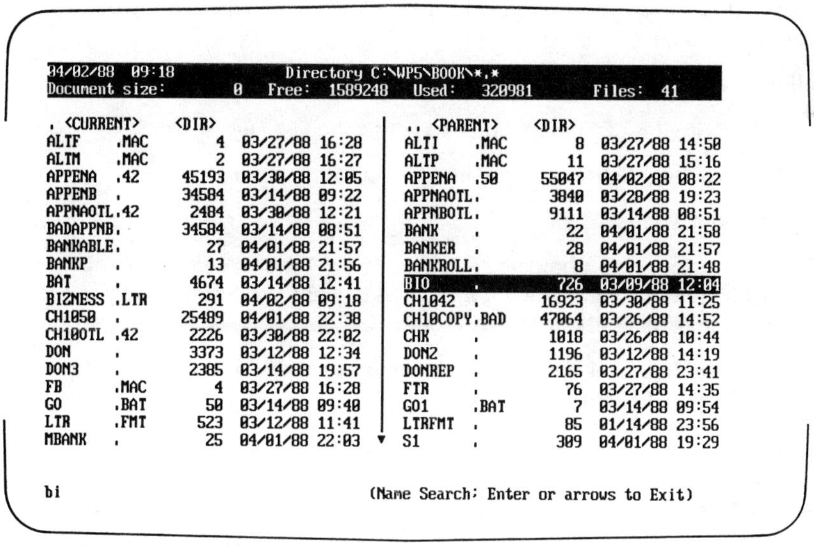

Fig. 10.10.
Continuing a name search.

Marking Files

Is there a way to perform one of the List Files operations (such as deleting or copying) on a number of files simultaneously? If you can specify this subgroup with a wild-card file specification such as *.DOC or CH10.*, you can type this pattern after pressing List Files (F5). Only those files fitting the pattern appear on the List Files screen for you to work on.

Fig. 10.11.

A successful Name Search.

```
04/02/88  09:18              Directory C:\WP5\BOOK\*.*
Document size:       0   Free: 1589248   Used:   320981      Files:  41

  . <CURRENT>    <DIR>                 .. <PARENT>     <DIR>
ALTF    .MAC         4  03/27/88 16:28   ALTI    .MAC       8  03/27/88 14:50
ALTM    .MAC         2  03/27/88 16:27   ALTP    .MAC      11  03/27/88 15:16
APPENA  .42      45193  03/30/88 12:05   APPENA  .50    55047  04/02/88 08:22
APPENB  .        34584  03/14/88 09:22   APPNAOTL.       3840  03/28/88 19:23
APPNAOTL.42       2484  03/30/88 12:21   APPNBOTL.       9111  03/14/88 08:51
BADAPPNB.        34584  03/14/88 08:51   BANK    .         22  04/01/88 21:58
BANKABLE.           27  04/01/88 21:57   BANKER  .         28  04/01/88 21:57
BANKP   .           13  04/01/88 21:56   BANKROLL.          8  04/01/88 21:48
BAT     .         4674  03/14/88 12:41   BIO     .        726  03/09/88 12:04
BIZNESS .LTR       291  04/02/88 09:18   CH1042  .      16923  03/30/88 11:25
CH1050  .        25489  04/01/88 22:38   CH10COPY.BAD   47064  03/26/88 14:52
CH10OTL .42       2226  03/30/88 22:02   CHK     .       1018  03/26/88 10:44
DON     .         3373  03/12/88 12:34   DON2    .       1196  03/12/88 14:19
DON3    .         2385  03/14/88 19:57   DONREP  .       2165  03/27/88 23:41
FB      .MAC         4  03/27/88 16:28   FTR     .         76  03/27/88 14:35
GO      .BAT        50  03/14/88 09:40   GO1     .BAT       7  03/14/88 09:54
LTR     .FMT       523  03/12/88 11:41   LTRFMT  .         85  01/14/88 23:56
MBANK   .           25  04/01/88 22:03 ▼ S1      .        309  04/01/88 19:29

biz                          (Name Search: Enter or arrows to Exit)
```

But what if you want to delete some files that don't fit any pattern? With a List Files feature called *marking*, you can individually indicate which files you want to concentrate on.

Just follow these steps:

1. Press List Files (F5), then Enter to get to the List Files screen.

2. Move the highlight bar to the first file you want to mark.

3. Press the asterisk key.

   WordPerfect puts a bold asterisk next to the file-size column of the highlighted file name, then moves the highlight bar automatically to the next file name in the listing.

4. Move the highlight bar to each file you want to include, and mark them. See figure 10.12 for an example.

If you want to mark *all* the files in the listing, press Home and then the asterisk key. Note that all files are now marked with a bold asterisk. To unmark all marked files, press the same keys again.

Whenever you have files marked on a List Files screen, you can move the highlight bar directly to each marked file by pressing either Tab (to go down through the list) or Shift-Tab (to go back up through the list). If you have five files marked as a result of a Word Search, for example, you can press Tab to move to the first marked file, press Enter to Look at the contents of the file, then repeat this sequence for the rest of the marked files.

With marked files, the last two fields of the screen heading change. The Used: field shows the combined size of the marked files. The Files: field changes to Marked: and shows the number of marked files.

Fig. 10.12.
*List Files screen with
marked files.*

```
04/02/88  08:31                Directory C:\WP5\BOOK\*.*
Document size:        0   Free:  1597440   Used:    185383        Marked: 10

  . <CURRENT>   <DIR>               .. <PARENT>    <DIR>
ALTF   .MAC      4  03/27/88 16:28  ALTI   .MAC       8  03/27/88 14:50
ALTM   .MAC      2* 03/27/88 16:27  ALTP   .MAC      11* 03/27/88 15:16
APPENA .42   45193* 03/30/88 12:05  APPENA .50    55047* 04/02/88 08:22
APPENB .       34584* 03/14/88 09:22  APPNAOTL.      3040  03/28/88 19:23
APPNAOTL.42     2484  03/30/88 12:21  APPNBOTL.      9111  03/14/88 08:51
BADAPPNB.      34584  03/14/88 08:51  BANK   .         22  04/01/88 21:58
BANKABLE.         27  04/01/88 21:57  BANKER .         28  04/01/88 21:57
BANKP  .          13  04/01/88 21:56  BANKROLL.         8  04/01/88 21:48
BAT    .        4674  03/14/88 12:41  BIO    .        726* 03/09/88 12:04
CH1042 .       16923  03/30/88 11:25  CH1050 .       25489  04/01/88 22:38
CH10COPY.BAD   47064* 03/26/88 14:52  CH100TL.42      2226* 03/30/88 22:02
CHK    .        1010  03/26/88 10:44  DON    .        3373  03/12/88 12:34
DON2   .        1196  03/12/88 14:19  DON3   .        2385  03/14/88 19:57
DOMREP .        2165  03/27/88 23:41  FB     .MAC        4  03/27/88 16:28
FTR    .          76  03/27/88 14:35  GO     .BAT       50  03/14/88 09:40
GO1    .BAT        7* 03/14/88 09:54  LTR    .FMT      523* 03/12/88 11:41
LTRFMT .          85  01/14/88 23:56  MBANK  .         25  04/01/88 22:03
S1     .         309  04/01/88 19:29  SEA    .        335  04/01/88 19:25

  1 Retrieve; 2 Delete; 3 Move/Rename; 4 Print; 5 Text In;
  6 Look; 7 Other Directory; 8 Copy; 9 Word Search; N Name Search: 6
```

Printing a directory listing containing marked files with Shift-F7 prints the marks as well. Printing the marks is useful, for example, for saving a record of what files were printed or deleted.

Not all the usual menu operations work on marked files. You cannot, for instance, retrieve all marked files at once. You can, though, use the following options with marked files:

- **Delete (2)**

- **Move (3)**—but not rename

- **Copy (8)**—to a different drive or directory

In all these cases, WordPerfect asks you to confirm the requested operation on the marked files. If you answer *Y*, it goes ahead. If you answer *N*, WordPerfect then asks whether you want to perform the operation on the file the highlight bar is on (Move/Rename asks if you want to Rename). With marked files, you also can use these options:

- **Print (4)**—on the currently selected printer

- **Word Search (9)**. This feature works as usual, except that the Word Search Conditions screen shows the number of *marked* files rather than the total number of files in the listing.

If you return to the editing screen after marking some files in WordPerfect 4.2, you lose the marks. WordPerfect 5 has a new means of redisplaying the marked files from the editing screen. Press List Files (F5) twice, and you see the previous List Files screen with files marked.

Using Word Search

Using Word Search (**9**), you can search one or more files in the file listing for a word or phrase without Retrieving the files into WordPerfect. You can, for example, determine which documents are about a certain subject by searching for a word or phrase related to that subject.

The Word Search feature has been enhanced considerably since WordPerfect 4.2. You can now specify a search of only parts of files, a speedy operation. To start a search, press Word Search (**9**) (see fig. 10.13).

Fig. 10.13.

Starting a Word Search in List Files.

```
04/02/88  14:50                Directory C:\WP5\BOOK\*.*
Document size:         0   Free:  1531904   Used:   350526      Files:  43

.  <CURRENT>    <DIR>                      ..  <PARENT>    <DIR>
ALTF    .MAC          4  03/27/88 16:28    ALTI    .MAC          8  03/27/88 14:50
ALTM    .MAC          2  03/27/88 16:27    ALTP    .MAC         11  03/27/88 15:16
APPENA  .42       45193  03/30/88 12:05    APPENA  .50       55047  04/02/88 08:22
APPENB  .         34584  03/14/88 09:22    APPNAOTL.          3840  03/28/88 19:23
APPNAOTL.42        2404  03/30/88 12:21    APPMBOTL.          9111  03/14/88 08:51
BADAPPNB.         34584  03/14/88 08:51    BANK    .           532  04/02/88 10:17
BANKABLE.            27  04/01/88 21:57    BANKCOM .           319  04/02/88 11:00
BANKER  .            28  04/01/88 21:57    BANKP   .            13  04/01/88 21:56
BANKROLL.             8  04/01/88 21:48    BAT     .          4674  03/14/88 12:41
BIO     .           726  03/09/88 12:04    BIZNESS .LTR        778  04/02/88 09:54
CH1042  .         31316  04/02/88 14:43    CH1050  .         39644  04/02/88 14:11
CH10COPY.BAD      47064  03/26/88 14:52    CH10OTL .42        2226  03/30/88 22:02
CHK     .          1018  03/26/88 10:44    DON     .          3373  03/12/88 12:34
DON2    .          1196  03/12/88 14:19    DON3    .          2385  03/14/88 19:57
DONREP  .          2165  03/27/88 23:41    FB      .MAC          4  03/27/88 16:28
FTR     .            76  03/27/88 14:35    GO      .BAT         50  03/14/88 09:40
GO1     .BAT          7  03/14/88 09:54    LTR     .FMT        523  03/12/88 11:41
LTRFMT  .            85  01/14/88 23:56 ▼  MBANK   .           314  04/02/88 10:12


Search: 1 Doc Summary: 2 First Page: 3 Entire Doc: 4 Conditions: 0
```

You can search only the Document Summaries (see Chapter 6) in the files, you can search only the first page of each file, or you can search (as in WordPerfect 4.2) the entire file. To perform a word search, complete the following steps:

1. Press Word Search (**9**).

2. Select Doc Summary (**1**) to search only the Document Summary in each file

   or

   Select First Page (**2**) to search only the first page of each document

   or

   Select Entire Doc (**3**) to search an entire file.

3. When WordPerfect displays the Word pattern: message, type the word or pattern you're looking for and press Enter.

WordPerfect displays the total number of files to be searched and a running tally of the number of files it has searched.

When the search is finished, WordPerfect marks with the usual bold asterisk all files in which it finds the word and places the highlight bar on the first of these matching files (see fig. 10.14).

Fig. 10.14.

Results of a Word Search on all files.

```
04/02/88  14:51              Directory C:\WP5\BOOK\*.*
Document size:        0  Free:  1531904  Used:      96219        Marked: 10

. <CURRENT>      <DIR>              .. <PARENT>      <DIR>
ALTF    .MAC       4  03/27/88 16:28   ALTI    .MAC       8  03/27/88 14:50
ALTM    .MAC       2  03/27/88 16:27   ALTP    .MAC      11  03/27/88 15:16
APPENA  .42    45193  03/30/88 12:05   APPENA  .50    55047  04/02/88 08:22
APPENB  .      34584  03/14/88 09:22   APPNAOTL.       3840  03/28/88 19:23
APPNAOTL.42     2404  03/30/88 12:21   APPNBOTL.       9111  03/14/88 08:51
BADAPPNB.      34584  03/14/88 08:51   BANK    .        532* 04/02/88 10:17
BANKABLE.         27* 04/01/88 21:57   BANKCOM .        319* 04/02/88 11:00
BANKER  .         28* 04/01/88 21:57   BANKP   .         13* 04/01/88 21:56
BANKROLL.          8* 04/01/88 21:48   BAT     .       4674  03/14/88 12:41
BIO     .        726  03/09/88 12:04   BIZNESS .LTR     778  04/02/88 09:54
CH1042  .      31316* 04/02/88 14:43   CH1050  .      39644* 04/02/88 14:11
CH10COPY.BAD   47064  03/26/88 14:52   CH100TL .42     2226  03/30/88 22:02
CHK     .       1018  03/26/88 10:44   DON     .       3373  03/12/88 12:34
DON2    .       1196  03/12/88 14:19   DON3    .       2385  03/14/88 19:57
DONREP  .       2165  03/27/88 23:41   FB      .MAC       4  03/27/88 16:28
FTR     .         76  03/27/88 14:35   GO      .BAT      50  03/14/88 09:40
G01     .BAT       7  03/14/88 09:54   LTR     .FMT     523  03/12/88 11:41
LTRFMT  .         85  01/14/88 23:56 ▼ MBANK   .        314  04/02/88 10:12

1 Retrieve; 2 Delete; 3 Move/Rename; 4 Print; 5 Text In;
6 Look; 7 Other Directory; 8 Copy; 9 Word Search; N Name Search: 6
```

You can then Look at each file in turn by pressing Enter (or **Look 6**). Or, you can Retrieve each file individually into WordPerfect by pressing **Retrieve** (**1**). If you use Look, the files are still marked when you Exit (F7) the Look screen. If you Retrieve a file, however, remember that to retain the marks in the file listing, you have to go back to the List Files screen by pressing List Files (F5) *twice* (rather than F5 followed by Enter).

Reducing the Number of Files To Search

Obviously, the fewer files you have to search, the faster the search goes. You can reduce the number of files for a Word Search in a couple of ways. The first is by calling up the List Files screen with a file specification other than the default '.'. Remember that this file specification means *all* the files in the current directory. If possible, it is more efficient to reduce the number of files in the listing by specifying some subgroup of files. For example, in your PERSLTR directory, you may have five letters to Don:

DON1

DON2

DONBOOK1

DONBOOK2

DONVACAT

If one of these documents has a bit of information you need (something about Jack, for instance), but you can't remember which one, you can have List Files list *only* these five documents. Then you have only five files to Word Search rather than all the files in a directory. Follow these steps:

1. Press List Files (F5).

2. After the file specification appears, type *DON**; then press Enter. The List Files screen appears with only these five files listed. Press Word Search (9) to get the search menu.

3. Press Entire (3).

4. Type the word that you want to search: *Jack*.

5. Press Enter to start the search.

The other method of restricting the number of files you need to search is to *mark* only the files you want to search (see the preceding section on Marking Files). Use this method if you cannot specify the files you want to search with a wild-card file specification. Suppose that, because you haven't learned the advantages of consistent file naming, you have this group of files to search:

DON1

2.DON

BOOK1.DON

2BOOK

VACATDON

To search these files is less convenient than searching files that are consistently named (thus you learn a lesson in efficient file naming), but the search is still not difficult:

1. Press List Files (F5), then Enter.

2. Move the highlight bar to each of the five files and press the asterisk key.

3. Press Word Search (9) to display the Word Search menu.

4. Press Entire (3).

5. Type the word you're searching for: *Jack* (see fig 10.15). Press Enter to start the search.

When WordPerfect finishes the search, it leaves marked *only those files that match the search criterion (see fig. 10.16)*.

Fig. 10.15.

Ready to Word Search marked files.

```
04/02/88  14:57              Directory C:\PERSLTR\*.*
Document size:        0   Free:  1435648   Used:     10093        Marked: 5

. <CURRENT>   <DIR>                    .. <PARENT>   <DIR>
2       ,DON    1196* 03/12/88 14:19   2BOOK     .     2165* 03/27/88 23:41
BOOK1   ,DON    2385* 03/14/88 19:57   CH100TL .42     2226  03/30/88 22:02
DEDUCT  .        314  10/20/87 16:53   DOM1      .     3373* 03/12/88 12:34
DS      .       6498  06/02/87 19:35   DS2       .      410  01/14/88 23:46
GNCURLT2.        718  03/04/88 10:40   INMAC     .      715  11/19/87 13:45
INTELLUT.CUR     815  02/08/88 10:11   INTRMET2.CUR     892  03/27/88 12:25
INTRMET3.CUR     893  03/27/88 12:27   IRA86     .      332  01/07/87 16:02
JOBADDR .        414  01/12/88 10:19   KURZWEIL.CUR     889  02/29/88 12:00
LOTUS2  ,CUR     898  03/07/88 20:15   LTR     ,FMT      89  07/12/86 15:07
LTRFMT  .         85  01/14/88 23:56   MACDOC    .      323  11/30/86 21:11
MEDSCI  ,CUR     892  02/21/88 18:39   META    ,CUR     946  03/04/88 10:16
NEIL    .       2298  01/08/87 21:35   QUE       .      464  02/26/88 17:50
REFERS  .       1416  03/04/88 11:40   RES1      .     2003  01/29/88 23:06
RES2    .       2145  03/12/88 09:51   RES21     .     2436  03/12/88 10:07
SCHLUM  ,CUR     924  02/29/88 12:52   STRATUS ,CUR     824  01/29/88 14:28
TRNSCRPT,2       357  03/03/88 09:06   VACATDON.        974* 03/14/88 14:03



Word pattern: Jack
```

Fig. 10.16.

Results of a Word Search on marked files.

```
04/02/88  15:04              Directory C:\PERSLTR\*.*
Document size:        0   Free:  1431552   Used:      3092        Marked: 2

. <CURRENT>   <DIR>                    .. <PARENT>   <DIR>
2       ,DON    1196  03/12/88 14:19   2BOOK     .     2191* 04/02/88 15:00
BOOK1   ,DON    2385  03/14/88 19:57   CH100TL .42     2226  03/30/88 22:02
DEDUCT  .        314  10/20/87 16:53   DOM1      .     3373  03/12/88 12:34
DS      .       6498  06/02/87 19:35   DS2       .      410  01/14/88 23:46
GNCURLT2.        718  03/04/88 10:40   INMAC     .      715  11/19/87 13:45
INTELLUT.CUR     815  02/08/88 10:11   INTRMET2.CUR     892  03/27/88 12:25
INTRMET3.CUR     893  03/27/88 12:27   IRA86     .      332  01/07/87 16:02
JOBADDR .        414  01/12/88 10:19   KURZWEIL.CUR     889  02/29/88 12:00
LOTUS2  ,CUR     898  03/07/88 20:15   LTR     ,FMT      89  07/12/86 15:07
LTRFMT  .         85  01/14/88 23:56   MACDOC    .      323  11/30/86 21:11
MEDSCI  ,CUR     892  02/21/88 18:39   META    ,CUR     946  03/04/88 10:16
NEIL    .       2298  01/08/87 21:35   QUE       .      464  02/26/88 17:50
REFERS  .       1416  03/04/88 11:40   RES1      .     2003  01/29/88 23:06
RES2    .       2145  03/12/88 09:51   RES21     .     2436  03/12/88 10:07
SCHLUM  ,CUR     924  02/29/88 12:52   STRATUS ,CUR     824  01/29/88 14:28
TRNSCRPT,2       357  03/03/88 09:06   VACATDON.       1701* 04/02/88 15:03


1 Retrieve; 2 Delete; 3 Move/Rename; 4 Print; 5 Text In;
6 Look; 7 Other Directory; 8 Copy; 9 Word Search; N Name Search: 6
```

Using the Word Search Conditions Menu

The fourth menu choice in Word Search provides even more flexible search options than the basic Word Search menu options. To use the Word Search Conditions option, follow these steps:

1. Press Word Search (9) in List Files to display the Word Search menu.

2. Press Conditions (4) to display the Word Search Conditions menu (see fig. 10.17).

```
Word Search

   1 - Perform Search on              All 32 File(s)

   2 - Undo Last Search

   3 - Reset Search Conditions

   4 - File Date                       No
         From (MM/DD/YY):              (All)
         To   (MM/DD/YY):              (All)

                  Word Pattern(s)

   5 - First Page
   6 - Entire Doc                      Jack
   7 - Document Summary
         Creation Date (e.g. Nov)
         Descriptive Name
         Subject/Account
         Author
         Typist
         Comments

   Selection: 1
```

Each item on this screen has a search specification or search control option on the left side of the screen. On the right side, you find an area where information for each option is displayed or entered.

The first choice on the menu, **Perform Search On (1)**, starts a search. In the right column, this option displays the number of files to be searched. The display says either All x File(s) (where x is the number of files) if you're searching all files in the directory or x Marked File(s) if you've marked files to search. When the search is finished, WordPerfect displays the List Files screen with all files matching the search criteria marked with the bold asterisk.

The second choice, Undo Last Search (**2**), undoes or reverses the results of the last search. For example, a Word Search of all files in the directory ends with eight files marked. A second Word Search of those eight files ends with two files marked. If you decide that the second search was a mistake, press Undo Last Search (**2**), and all eight previously marked files are marked again. Now you can search them with different criteria. You can undo up to three levels this way.

To eliminate any search criteria you've previously entered and return all Word Search Conditions options to their pristine state, choose **Reset Search Conditions (3)**.

Using the File **Date (4)** choice, you can restrict the search to files that fall within the range of specified dates. Press File **Date (4)** to turn on the File Date feature. Press this key again to turn File Date off when you no longer need it. To enter dates after you turn on the File Date selection, follow these steps:

1. Press Enter to move the cursor to the From date field.

2. Type a date in *mm/dd/yy* format.

3. Press Enter again to move the cursor to the To date field.

4. Type the date.

5. Press Enter once more.

The remaining choices, **5-7**, control what part of a document to search, the same as the basic Word Search menu in List Files. Indeed, choices **First Page (5)** and **Entire Doc (6)** are the same as choices in the List Files Word Search menu. For either option, press the number or highlighted letter of the option, then type the word for which you want to search.

The **Doc Summary (7)** option is more flexible than its List Files/Word Search counterpart. You can search either the whole Summary or any one of its individual fields: date, name, subject, author, typist, or comments. Follow these steps:

1. From the Word Search Conditions screen, select Document Summary (**7**).

2. If you want to search the whole Summary (which is just like the Doc Summary option on the List Files Word Search menu), type a word for which to search

   or

   To search just one field of the Summary, press ↓ or ↑ to move to the field you want. Type a word for which to search.

3. Press Enter.

4. Press **Perform Search On (1)** to start the search.

Searching for Phrases

You can search for phrases as well as for single words. You must, however, enclose the phrase to be searched for in quotation marks:

"my car"

"she's my friend, the electrical engineer"

"she said that"

Using Wild Cards in Searches

You can use wild-card characters in the word for which you're searching. The wild-card characters are the same as the DOS wild cards, * and ?. They are also used the same way. For example, the word pattern *b*k* is matched by

book

buck

bonk

block

black

The pattern *art?* is matched by

art1

art9

arty

Phrases can contain wild cards, too. For example, the pattern *she·shore* matches

she's ashore

she sells sea shells by the sea shore

she's at the shore

Using Caution with Word Search

Word Search actually searches for a *pattern of letters* rather than for words. It finds your pattern not only by itself but also at the beginning of words. Thus, if you tell WordPerfect to search for *bank*, it will find, among other possibilities,

bank

banker

bankroll

bankable

You cannot overcome this limitation completely. If you add a space to the end of your pattern, then enclose the whole pattern in quotation marks, *"bank "*, you eliminate all patterns at the beginning of words, but you then won't be able to find the word if it's followed by punctuation, such as:

bank.

bank,

There is another complicating factor to remember about Word Search searches. Word Search finds words anywhere in a document, including in headers, footers, and footnotes. A search in Look (6) does *not*, however, find words in these places. So, if Word Search finds some files with the word you're searching for, you won't be able to find the word in those files if you use the Look (6) option with them (even if you use the Look search feature) *if* the word is in a header, footer, or footnote. In WordPerfect's editing screen, a Forward Search (F2) also does not find words in headers, footers, or footnotes. You must use Extended Search (Home, F2).

Locking Your Files

You can assign a password to files so that no one but you can retrieve them, examine them with the Look option (6) in List Files, or print them. If you decide that you want to guard your files with password protection, keep one important caution in mind: if you forget the password, the file will be inaccessible to you. *Don't forget your password!*

Let's assume that you have a file on-screen and want to save and "lock" it with a password. Press Text In/Out (Ctrl-F5) and select **P**assword (**2**). You see the following menu:

   Password: 1 Add/Change; **2** Remove: **0**

Choose **A**dd (**1**). At the Enter Password: prompt, type up to 23 characters to identify your password, then press Enter. WordPerfect prompts you to reenter your password. Type the password again and press Enter. If you make a typing error or don't enter the correct password, you get an error message and are prompted to go through the process again for identifying a password for your file. To complete the process of password protection, you must Save (F10) or Exit (F7) the file, thereby "locking" it.

Before you retrieve a locked file, make certain that you have a clear editing screen. When you attempt to retrieve a file with either Retrieve (Shift-F10) or List Files (F5), WordPerfect prompts you to enter the password. Unless you enter the correct password, WordPerfect will not retrieve the document to the screen.

When you want to "unprotect" a file, you begin by retrieving the file as you would retrieve any password-protected file. With the document on-screen, press Text In/Out and select **P**assword (**2**). Next, choose **R**emove (**2**). To verify that your document is now unlocked, save the file and then retrieve it again. WordPerfect no longer prompts you to enter a password.

WP 5 Summary

In this chapter, you learned about WordPerfect's List Files feature. Remember that with List Files, you can perform many file and directory operations that you ordinarily have to do from DOS.

You can do the following tasks:

- Delete files and directories (with **Delete 2**)

- Rename and move files (with **Move/Rename 3**)

- Look at a file's contents (with **Look 6**)

- Change the current directory (with **Other Directory 7**)

- Create new directories (with **Other Directory 7**)

- Copy files (with **Copy 8**)

In addition, with List Files you can perform many WordPerfect functions more conveniently:

- Retrieve WordPerfect files (with **Retrieve 1**)

- Retrieve ASCII files (with **Text In 5**)

- Print WordPerfect files (with **Print 4**)

- Search for words or phrases in files on the disk (with **Word Search 9**)

List Files can make your WordPerfect sessions more convenient, efficient, and effective. Using List Files is also easier to learn and use than the corresponding DOS commands. The time and effort you spend learning List Files will certainly be rewarded.

Part
II

Using WordPerfect's
Advanced Features

Includes

11

Creating Macros

Elias Baumgarten,
associate professor of
philosophy at the
University of Michigan at
Dearborn, was a beta
tester for WordPerfect 5.
He has developed hundreds
of macros for himself and
others. ■

Macros are one of the most useful and exciting features of WordPerfect 5. A *macro* is a file you create to represent a whole series of keystrokes.

After you create a macro, you can just type the name of the macro instead of typing all the keystrokes.

If you perform any task repeatedly, even one as simple as deleting a line, you can do it more quickly with a macro. Macros can automate simple tasks, such as typing *Sincerely yours* and your name. Macros also can perform complex operations that include both text and WordPerfect commands. After you set up a macro, you can use it to do almost instantly what would otherwise require many keystrokes.

Using even a few macros can help to "complete" WordPerfect for you by tailoring it to your personal needs. In WordPerfect, for example, you can delete a word in one step (Ctrl-back space), but you need more keystrokes to delete a sentence or a paragraph. If you are someone who often deletes whole sentences or paragraphs, you can create macros that make those tasks—or any others—just as easy as deleting a word.

You can create a macro to perform nearly any task that you could accomplish with a series of keystrokes. Suppose, for example, that you occasionally need to do something intricate, such as set up a format for columns. If you don't do this often, you might have trouble remembering how you last did it. You can create a macro that collects and saves all the required keystrokes under one name. Then, whenever you want to set up columns, you won't need to search your desk drawer for your notes. You simply can invoke your macro, which tells WordPerfect: "do all that again."

Macros are like tiny programs within the larger WordPerfect program. Just as you invoke WordPerfect (WP.EXE) by pressing the keys *wp*, you run each of your macros by pressing the keys for its name. You have more control, however, over the macros you create than you have over commercial programs like WordPerfect. You decide what to name your macros. Also, you decide what your macros will do when they run.

353

A typical macro works like this. Suppose that you want to change the format in your document from single-spacing to double-spacing. Without a macro, you would need to complete a sequence of six keystrokes: press Format (Shift-F8); press L for **L**ine (**1**); press S for Line **S**pacing (**6**); type *2* to change to double-spacing; press Enter; and press Exit (F7). A macro lets you assign all those keystrokes to an easy-to-remember name, such as DS for double-spacing. Then, whenever you want to change to double-spacing, you invoke your DS macro. WordPerfect "remembers" that DS means all six commands and executes them automatically—and a lot faster than you could enter them one at a time.

Aside from their obvious advantages, macros also are fun to create and use. In this chapter, you first will learn the following basic macro concepts and skills:

- Types of macros
- Creating macros
- Running macros
- Stopping macros
- Replacing macros
- Controlling how your macros run

You then will learn how to create a library of useful macros and how to manage your macro files. Finally, you will learn how to use the macro editor, which allows you to alter a macro without having to create it from scratch.

Throughout the chapter, you will find the following features to help you quickly become familiar with WordPerfect macros:

- Samples of useful macros
- Techniques to apply when you create your own macros
- Tips on using macros

You will best learn macro techniques if you practice creating the sample macros in this chapter. Because macros draw on other procedures of WordPerfect, you may learn some new tricks for using WordPerfect as you work through this chapter. Be sure, in particular, to create the AD macro. That macro is used in many of the examples throughout this chapter.

You should know some bad news and some good news about WordPerfect 5. The bad news is that WordPerfect 5 will run only WordPerfect 5 macros; you cannot use macros created in any earlier version of WordPerfect. The Conversion disk that comes with WordPerfect 5 does include a macro conversion utility (MACROCNV.EXE). This utility will convert some of your 4.x macros to WordPerfect 5 macros, but it will not do the whole job for all your macros. For specific instructions on converting macros, see this chapter's "Converting WordPerfect 4 Macros to WordPerfect 5" section.

The good news is that WordPerfect 5 includes a macro editor that is built into the program. The macro editor not only allows you to modify macros after you create them, but also lets you create more powerful and flexible macros than in previous versions of WordPerfect. In addition, the macro editor includes a command language. Although you can create powerful macros even without learning this language, you may find the programming commands useful if you have some programming experience. The command language is discussed separately in Appendix C.

Understanding Types of Macros

Macros can be either permanent or temporary. A *permanent macro* is a file that you name and that is stored on disk. You can use a permanent macro in any session of WordPerfect by issuing a special command that refers to the macro's name. A *temporary macro* is a file that WordPerfect names WP{WP}.WPM and that works as you have defined it until you create another temporary macro. Each temporary macro you create replaces the previous one.

Permanent Macros

You can create two kinds of permanent macros: Alt-*letter* macros and descriptive macros. Alt-*letter* macros have names that consist of the Alt key plus a letter from A to Z—for example, Alt-K or Alt-X. Descriptive macros have names of one to eight characters—for examples, TABS or MARGIN5.

The macros that are simplest to create and use are the Alt-*letter* macros. Therefore, choose Alt-*letter* names for the macros you will use most often. Be sure to use macro names that will remind you of what your macros do; for example, you might use the name Alt-C for a macro that centers text.

All permanent macros have file names that include the three-letter extension .WPM. The full file name of a descriptive macro called TABS, for example, would be TABS.WPM. You do not need to be concerned about the .WPM extension except when you manipulate macros as files, either in DOS or in List Files. You will learn more about handling macros as files later in this chapter.

Temporary Macros

A temporary macro works only until you create another one. You can have only one temporary macro at a time because each temporary macro you create replaces the previous one. In WordPerfect 5, a temporary macro is preserved from one session to another. If you create a temporary macro that types your name, for example, and then you exit WordPerfect before creating another temporary macro, you still will be able to use that temporary macro the next time you use WordPerfect. You will learn how to create and use temporary macros later in this chapter.

Creating Permanent Macros

Before you can use a permanent macro, you need to create it. In this section you will learn the five steps required to create a permanent macro. You then will create your first macro, something short but useful.

Before practicing with macros, use Save (F10) to store your current document. That way you won't need to worry about affecting any of your permanent files. You can safely practice macros with the document that remains on your screen right after you save it. (Just be sure not to save it again using the same name!) Or you can start with a blank screen and type a few lines of text whenever you need something for a macro to act on.

You create a permanent macro in five steps:

1. Press Macro Define (Ctrl-F10).

   The bottom of the screen displays the prompt

   `Define macro:`

   In plainer English, this prompt is asking: "What is the *name* of your macro?"

2. Type the name of the macro. For an Alt-*letter* macro, press the Alt key and a letter from A to Z. For a descriptive macro, type one to eight characters (letters or numbers) and press Enter.

   You don't have to provide the .WPM extension for either type of macro.

   The screen displays the prompt `Description:`.

3. Type a short description of what the macro does. Use any description, up to 39 characters, that will help remind you of the macro's commands. Then press Enter.

   `Macro Def` blinks at the bottom of your screen. Think of this blinking message as a reminder that the program is recording and remembering all your keystrokes.

4. Type the keystrokes that you want recorded for this macro. Type them in the exact order that you will want them played back when you run the macro.

5. Press Macro Define (Ctrl-F10) again to end macro recording.

Note: All the keystrokes that you use to define your macro also will affect your current document. When you create a macro to change your tab settings, for example, you also change your tab settings at the cursor position in your document. You can use Reveal Codes (Alt-F3, or F11) to verify the tab setting changes in your current document.

You now can practice these five steps by creating a useful macro, one that inserts your return address. The macro you will create assumes that you want to make each line of your address flush with the right margin. Later in this chapter, you will create an address macro that uses a different format. Follow these steps to create the return address macro:

1. Press Macro Define (Ctrl-F10).

   The screen displays the prompt Define macro:, which is asking for the name of the macro.

2. Type *ad* and press Enter.

   The prompt Description: appears.

3. Type *Return address, flush right* and press Enter.

   The blinking Macro Def message appears.

4. Press Flush Right (Alt-F6).

5. Type *1010 Rose Avenue* (or the first line of your actual address) and press Enter.

6. Press Flush Right (Alt-F6).

7. Type *Gabe, CA   90505* (or your actual city, state, and ZIP code).

8. Press Enter to position the cursor one line below the return address.

   Figure 11.1 shows how your screen looks at this point.

```
                                      1010 Rose Avenue
                                      Gabe, CA   90505




 Macro Def                            Doc 1 Pg 1 Ln 1.33" Pos 1"
```

Fig. 11.1.
The AD macro being created.

9. Press Macro Define (Ctrl-F10) to end macro recording.

TIP: If a formatting code (such as Enter in Step 8) or certain punctuation will almost always be desired together with the text in a macro, include the formatting or punctuation as part of the macro.

Running Permanent Macros

When you run a permanent macro, the steps vary depending on whether you are running an Alt-*letter* macro or a descriptive macro. Before you run either type of permanent macro, of course, you first must have created it.

To run an Alt-*letter* macro, simply press the Alt-*letter* combination. If you have created an Alt-C macro to center a line of text, for example, you invoke the macro by holding down the Alt key while pressing the letter C. WordPerfect knows that Alt and a letter mean "run a macro."

To run a descriptive macro, you first press Macro (Alt-F10), then type the name of the macro (one to eight characters), and then press Enter. The Macro (Alt-F10) command informs WordPerfect that what you type next is the name of the macro you want to run.

Notice that the command to *run* a descriptive macro (Alt-F10) is different from the one you used to *define* a macro (Ctrl-F10). If you press Macro Define (Ctrl-F10) by mistake, simply press Cancel (F1).

Go ahead and try using your return address macro. Because the macro you created is a descriptive one, the procedure is as follows:

1. Save any needed files and then clear your screen by pressing Exit (F7), *N*, and *N*.

2. Press Macro (Alt-F10).

3. Type *ad*

4. Press Enter.

Your return address will appear on the screen, flush right.

Creating Temporary Macros

You can create a temporary macro to use only until you create a different one. A temporary macro can be especially useful when you have a long or complicated name or title that you must type repeatedly in a particular document. Temporary macros are created just like descriptive macros except that instead of entering one to eight characters and pressing Enter, you just press Enter.

To create a temporary macro, follow these steps:

1. Press Macro Define (Ctrl-F10).

   The screen displays the prompt Define macro:.

2. Press Enter.

   Notice that you are not prompted for a description when you create a temporary macro.

   The screen displays the blinking message Macro Def.

3. Type the keystrokes that you want to record in the temporary macro.

4. Press Macro Define (Ctrl-F10) again to stop recording keystrokes for the temporary macro.

Next you will practice creating a temporary macro. Imagine that you have a document that includes repeated references to an article with the title *Selma Stanislavsky and Modern Russian Theater*. Use the following steps to create a temporary macro that will save you the trouble of repeatedly typing that title:

1. Press Macro Define (Ctrl-F10).

   The screen displays the prompt Define macro:.

2. Press Enter.

   The blinking prompt Macro Def appears.

3. Type *"Selma Stanislavsky and Modern Russian Theater*

   Be sure to type the opening quotation mark.

4. Press Macro Define (Ctrl-F10) to end macro recording.

TIP: When you create macros, you should keep in mind the following guidelines for punctuation and formatting:

- Include any punctuation or formatting that will almost always go with the text of the macro.

- Don't include punctuation or formatting that will often need to be modified after the macro runs.

In the temporary macro you just created, if "Selma Stanislavsky and Modern Russian Theater" were a book title instead of an article, you would want to include underlining as part of the macro itself (because book titles are underlined). In the preceding macro (and for most article titles), closing quotation marks are not included because a comma or a period will often precede the closing quotation mark, as in the following sentence:

Three interesting articles to read are "Selma Stanislavsky and Modern Russian Theater," "Elizabeth Deter's Theory of Creative Writing," and "Mary Anne Ericson's Approach to Spiritual Counseling."

Running Temporary Macros

To run your most recent temporary macro, press Macro (Alt-F10) and then press Enter. You can try this with the temporary macro you just created. Imagine that you are in the midst of typing an article on modern theater as you complete the following steps:

1. Type the following:

   The best article on this subject is

2. Press the space bar once so that your cursor is immediately after the space following *is*.

3. Press Macro (Alt-F10).

4. Press Enter.

"Selma Stanislavsky and Modern Russian Theater will appear at the current cursor position. You would then type the rest of the sentence.

Stopping Macros

You use the Cancel key (F1) in many situations to "back out" of a process that you started. You can use this key also to back out of a definition you are creating for a macro or to stop a macro in progress.

Stopping Macro Definition

You can stop a macro definition either before or after you name the macro. If you start to create a macro using Macro Define (Ctrl-F10) and have not yet named it, pressing Cancel (F1) will cancel the macro definition and return you to your document. If you already have named a permanent macro, you cannot cancel it, but you can end macro definition by pressing Macro Define (Ctrl-F10) again. Although the macro still is created with the name you assigned it, you then can delete, rename, replace, or edit it. These procedures are normal parts of working with macros, and you will learn about them in this chapter.

Stopping a Macro in Progress

You can stop a macro while it is running by pressing Cancel (F1). For example, if the macro is not doing what you expected, just press Cancel (F1).

CAUTION: Even an incomplete macro can create codes in your document that you don't want. After you cancel a macro, press Reveal Codes (Alt-F3, or F11) and delete any unwanted codes.

Replacing Macros

Fortunately, imperfect macros are easily replaced. You may want to replace a macro you created for any of several reasons:

- You get an error message when you run the macro, and you press Cancel (F1).

- The macro finishes but does not do what you want.

- You change your mind about exactly what you want the macro to do.

You might decide, for example, that your return address macro doesn't do everything that you want. Because you will be using your return address in letters, you decide that you usually will want to include a third line with the current date. You must decide which way you want your macro to run:

- If you want to add the date manually when you need it, keep your macro the way it is.

- If you sometimes will want your macro to insert only the return address and other times to insert both your return address and the date, create a second macro that includes both the return address and the date.

- If you need only one macro that inserts both the return address and the date, then keep the AD macro name and change what it does.

You can change what your AD macro does in either of two ways:

- Replace the AD macro.

- Edit the AD macro.

Often, the simpler procedure is to replace a macro than to edit it. To replace a macro with another one of the same name, you use the following steps:

1. Press Macro Define (Ctrl-F10).

2. Enter the same name as the old macro.

   The program asks whether you want to **Replace** (**1**) or **Edit** (**2**) the named macro.

3. Choose **Replace** (**1**).

4. Enter a description of the macro.

5. Type the keystrokes you want the macro to record.

6. Press Macro Define (Ctrl-F10) to end macro recording.

The procedure is exactly like creating a macro for the first time except that you are prompted to replace or edit the macro.

Before you replace your AD macro, be sure to save any file you need. Then follow these steps to replace your AD macro with a macro that inserts both your return address and the current date:

1. Press Macro Define (Ctrl-F10).

   The prompt Define macro: appears on-screen.

2. Type *ad* and press Enter.

WordPerfect does not let you change an existing macro without warning. The program displays the prompt

AD.WPM is Already Defined. 1 Replace; 2 Edit: 0

3. Choose **Replace** (**1**).

The same Description: prompt appears as when you created the macro the first time.

4. Type *Return address and date, flush right* and press Enter.

The blinking Macro Def message appears.

5. Press Flush Right (Alt-F6).

6. Type *1010 Rose Avenue* (or the first line of your actual address) and press Enter.

7. Press Flush Right (Alt-F6).

8. Type *Gabe, CA 90505* (or your actual city, state, and ZIP code) and press Enter.

9. Press Flush Right (Alt-F6).

10. Press Date/Outline (Shift-F5).

11. Select Date Format (**3**).

12. Regardless of the date format already shown, type *3 1, 4* and press Enter. (Be sure to press the space bar after the 3 and the comma.)

TIP: When creating a macro, you should supply information for items such as date format (or search) even if the desired response already is displayed. This technique is the only way to ensure that the correct information will be used whenever you run the macro.

---

13. Select Date **Text** (**1**).

The current date appears on-screen below the return address. The date will be correct if your computer has a built-in clock that remembers the date or if you answered a prompt for the date when you started your computer. Even if the date is wrong, your macro still will work properly; you can go back and reset your computer's clock in order to correct the date.

Because you almost always will want two blank lines after your return address, include them as part of your macro.

14. Press Enter twice.

15. Press Macro Define (Ctrl-F10) to end macro recording.

Now you can test your new AD macro. Press Macro (Alt-F10), type *ad*, and then press Enter. Your return address and date appear on-screen, flush right.

You probably will replace macros often while you are learning to create them. Later in this chapter you will learn how to change what a macro does without creating it again from scratch. You will learn to "get inside" a macro and edit it; that procedure is especially useful for modifying complex macros.

Controlling How Your Macros Run

WordPerfect macros offer you a great deal of flexibility. When you create a macro, you can control not only *what* you want each macro to do but *how* you want it to do it. You can run a macro visibly or invisibly, one time or repetitively, silently or with bells and whistles. (Well, at least bells.)

You use the Macro Commands key (Ctrl-PgUp) to access many of these "how to run" options. When you press Macro Commands (Ctrl-PgUp) while recording a macro, the blinking Macro Def message temporarily is replaced with a menu of options:

   1 Pause; **2** Display; **3** Assign; **4** Comment: **0**

Your next keystroke chooses among these options and is not included as something for the macro to record and play back. You will learn about Macro Commands (Ctrl-PgUp) and some of the other "how to run" options in this section.

Making a Macro Visible

Among the options for controlling the way a macro runs, you can choose whether you want the macro to run invisibly or whether you want to see each command in the macro carried out, just as if it were being typed very quickly. If you don't instruct WordPerfect otherwise, it runs macros invisibly. This is the way you have run the macros you have created so far in this chapter.

You may want to run macros with the display feature turned on so that you can watch each step of execution. This feature may be especially useful when you are learning to create your own macros. Because you easily can turn the display feature off and on (using the macro editor) even after you have created a macro, don't hesitate to experiment.

To see how WordPerfect's macro display feature works, you can create a macro to delete a sentence. WordPerfect requires three steps to erase a sentence or block. You can create a macro that executes those three steps instantly. Because this procedure is something you will do often, you probably should assign the macro an Alt-*letter* name.

To create an Alt-E macro that erases a sentence or block while WordPerfect's display feature is turned on, follow these steps:

1. Press Macro Define (Ctrl-F10).

2. Respond to the `Macro Def` prompt by pressing Alt-E.

3. To answer the `Description:` prompt, type *Erase a sentence or block* and press Enter.

   `Macro Def` flashes at the bottom of the screen.

   This time you don't want the macro to start recording keystrokes right away. You first want to tell WordPerfect how to run the macro.

4. Press Macro Commands (Ctrl-PgUp).

   WordPerfect obliges by displaying the following menu at the bottom of the screen:

   1 Pause; **2** Display; **3** Assign; **4** Comment: **0**

5. Select **Display** (**2**).

   The screen displays the following prompt:

   `Display execution? (Y/N) No`

6. Press *Y*.

   The blinking `Macro Def` reappears and you proceed to enter the keystrokes that define the macro.

7. Press Move (Ctrl-F4).

   The following menu appears at the bottom of the screen:

   Move: 1 Sentence; **2** Paragraph; **3** Page; **4** Retrieve: **0**

8. Select **Sentence** (**1**).

   Type *1*, not *S*, so that this same macro can also erase a block.

   Another menu appears at the bottom of the screen:

   1 Move; **2** Copy; **3** Delete; **4** Append: **0**

9. Select **Delete** (**3**).

10. Press Macro Define (Ctrl-F10) to end macro recording.

Now try your "erase a sentence" macro by placing your cursor anywhere in a sentence and pressing Alt-E. Although the macro performs very quickly, the "display on" feature allows you to verify that the sentence you want to delete is indeed the one that is blocked and erased.

You may want to create another macro that deletes a paragraph rather than a sentence. To create that macro, you select **Paragraph** (**2**) in Step 8 instead of **Sentence** (**1**).

Making a Macro Repeat

You occasionally may want to make a macro run more than one time. Perhaps you want to delete three consecutive sentences with your Alt-E macro. Although you could, of course, press Alt-E three times, there is an easier way.

Pressing the Esc key repeats any WordPerfect command. If you press Esc and then the letter *e*, the screen displays eight *e*'s. You also can change the default of eight to some other number. For example, if you press Esc, type *4*, and then press ↑, the cursor moves up four lines.

You can repeat a macro the same way. You press Esc, indicate the number of times you want the macro to run, and then invoke the macro. You can invoke the macro either by pressing Alt and a letter or by pressing Macro (Alt-F10), typing the name of the descriptive macro, and pressing Enter. Be sure that you invoke the macro *immediately* after indicating the number of repetitions.

You can practice making a macro repeat by using your Alt-E macro that erases a sentence. First type four short sentences and position your cursor anywhere in the first sentence. Then follow these steps to erase the first three sentences:

1. Press Esc.

2. Type *3*.

3. Press Alt-E.

The first three sentences are deleted.

Making a Macro Pause

One of the most useful options for controlling how a macro runs is the pause feature. You can make a macro pause while it is running so that you can enter a command or some text. Then the macro can continue running.

You access the pause option in the same way you accessed the option for making your Alt-E macro visible. When you are creating a macro, you press Macro Commands (Ctrl-PgUp) to display the options for controlling the way your macro runs.

To practice using the pause feature, you will create two macros: one to create headings and another to format letters.

A Macro To Create Headings

A useful macro that includes a pause is one that sets up the format for a heading. Suppose that you want most of your headings to be centered, in boldface type, and in all uppercase letters. Instead of giving each of those formatting commands, you can have a macro perform them for you.

Place your cursor at the beginning of the line where you want your heading. A blank screen is fine. Then follow these steps to create a macro that displays a heading:

1. Press Macro Define (Ctrl-F10).

2. Respond to the Macro Def prompt by pressing Alt-H (for heading).

3. In response to the `Description:` prompt, type *Centered, bolded, uppercase heading* and press Enter.

   `Macro Def` flashes at the bottom of the screen.

4. Press Center (Shift-F6).

5. Press Bold (F6).

   Now that the format is set up, you can have the macro pause so that you can enter a particular heading.

6. Press Macro Commands (Ctrl-PgUp).

   The screen displays the following menu:

   1 Pause; 2 Display; 3 Assign; 4 Comment: 0

7. Select **Pause (1)**.

   Nothing noticeable happens at this point. `Macro Def` keeps blinking, but the macro does not record actual keystrokes until you press Enter. Before pressing Enter, you should type some kind of "stand in" heading so that the rest of the macro is easier to create. This heading, however, does not become part of your macro.

8. Type *the jacqueline lawson teaching award* and press Enter.

   Notice that you don't need to capitalize anything in your heading. The next steps of the macro take care of that.

9. Press Block (Alt-F4, or F12).

10. Press Home, Home, ←.

11. Press Switch (Shift-F3).

    The screen displays the following menu:

    1 Uppercase; 2 Lowercase: 0

12. Select **Uppercase (1)**.

    The heading you typed changes to all uppercase.

    The macro could stop right here. But because you almost always will want at least two blank lines after your heading, include the next two steps.

13. Press End to position the cursor at the end of the heading.

14. Press Enter twice to insert two blank lines after the heading.

15. Press Macro Define (Ctrl-F10) again to turn off macro recording.

Now clear your screen and test your new macro by completing these steps:

1. Press Alt-H.

   The cursor moves to the center of the line, the bold feature is turned on, and the macro pauses for your input.

You need to type some kind of heading in order to see the macro work. Because the macro will change the heading to uppercase, you can type the entire heading in lowercase letters.

2. Type *delap's endearing dandelions*

3. Press Enter.

The heading changes to uppercase, and the cursor positions itself two lines beneath the heading.

TIP: If you want the program to display a prompt when the macro pauses, you can use the special {PROMPT} command, which is accessed through the macro editor. The special macro commands are discussed briefly toward the end of this chapter and in Appendix C.

A Macro To Format Letters

Earlier in this chapter, you created a macro that inserts your return address and the date. Using the additional features you have learned, you now can create a more powerful macro that combines text with formatting commands. The next macro you will create will format a letter in the following way:

- Format the page for a two-inch top margin

- Include your return address, using tab settings (instead of flush right)

- Pause three times to allow you to enter three lines of a recipient's address

- Enter the salutation

To create the letter-formatting macro, first save any needed files and clear your screen. Then follow these steps:

1. Press Macro Define (Ctrl-F10).

2. In response to the Macro Def prompt for naming your macro, type *let* (for letter) and press Enter.

3. In response to the Description: prompt, type *Format for letter* and press Enter.

   The blinking message Macro Def appears on-screen.

4. Press Format (Shift-F8).

5. Press **Page** (**2**).

6. Press **Margin** (**5**).

7. Type *2"* and press Enter twice.

If you have used the Setup menu to display units in something other than inches, WordPerfect automatically converts inches to the other unit of measure.

8. Press Enter again to leave the Format: Page menu and return to the general Format menu.

9. Press Line (**1**).

10. Press **T**ab Set (**8**).

11. Press Home, Home, ← to move to the beginning of the line.

12. Press Ctrl-End to clear the current tab settings.

13. Type *5.7"* and press Enter.

   Note: If this tab setting is not the best one for your address, you can change it later.

14. Press Exit (F7) twice to return to the editing screen.

15. Press Tab.

16. Type *1317 Ohio Street* (or your own street address) and press Enter.

17. Press Tab.

18. Type *Norway, MI   48104* (or your own city, state, and ZIP code) and press Enter.

19. Press Tab.

20. Press Date/Outline (Shift-F5).

21. Select Date Format (**3**).

22. Regardless of the date format already shown, type *3 1,   4* and press Enter. (Be certain to press the space bar after the 3 and the comma.)

   Reminder: You should supply this information even if the correct response already is displayed, because that is the only way to be sure that the date format will be correct at the time you run the macro.

23. Select Date Text (**1**).

   The current date appears on-screen below the return address. The date will be correct if your computer has a built-in clock that remembers the date or if you answered a prompt for the date when you started your computer. Even if the date is wrong, your macro still will work properly; you can go back and reset your computer's clock to correct the date.

24. Press Enter four times.

25. Press Macro Commands (Ctrl-PgUp).

   The program displays the following menu:

   1 Pause; **2** Display; **3** Assign; **4** Comment: **0**

26. Select **Pause** (**1**).

    Keep in mind that what you type during a pause (up until you next press Enter) does not become part of the macro.

27. Type any name, for example *Dr. Sanford Kessler*, and press Enter twice.

    The first Enter ends the pause; the second Enter is recorded in the macro.

28. Press Macro Commands (Ctrl-PgUp) again.

    Figure 11.2 shows how your screen looks at this point.

Fig. 11.2.
The Macro Commands menu while the LET macro is created.

```
                                        1317 Ohio Street
                                        Norway, MI  48104
                                        May 24, 1988



       Dr. Sanford Kessler










   1 Pause; 2 Display; 3 Assign; 4 Comment: 0
```

29. Select **Pause** (**1**) again.

30. Type any street address, for example *286 Biltmore Avenue*, and press Enter twice.

31. Press Macro Commands (Ctrl-PgUp) again.

32. Select **Pause** (**1**) again.

33. Type any city, state, and ZIP code, for example *Lapland, NC   27605*, and press Enter to end the pause.

34. Press Enter twice to insert a blank line below the address.

35. Type *Dear* and then press the space bar once.

36. Press Macro Define (Ctrl-F10) to end macro recording.

Now clear your screen and try your new macro by completing these steps:

1. Press Macro (Alt-F10).

2. In response to the Macro: prompt, type *let* and press Enter.

   The macro pauses four lines below the return address and waits for you to enter the recipient's name and address.

3. Type the recipient's name, for example *Susan M. Day, President*, and press Enter.

The macro pauses again for your input.

4. Type the first line of the recipient's address, for example *Singer Famine Relief Fund*, and press Enter.

The macro pauses for the last line of the address.

5. Type the recipient's city, state, and ZIP code, for example *Ann Arbor, MI   48104*, and press Enter.

Dear appears with the cursor in the appropriate place, ready for you to type a name and begin the letter.

Figure 11.3 shows your screen after you run the macro.

Fig. 11.3.

The result of the LET macro.

```
                                                    1317 Ohio Street
                                                    Norway, MI  48104
                                                    May 24, 1988




              Susan M. Day, President
              Singer Famine Relief Fund
              Ann Arbor, MI  48104

              Dear
```

You now have created a fairly complicated macro that combines formatting commands, text, and pauses. Although intricate macros like this one can save you a lot of time, you also may want to have several smaller macros that can be pieced together in different ways to make up a longer macro, as described in the next section.

Making a Macro Call Another Macro

You can connect macros to one another in two ways. One method is to *chain* one macro to another. If macro B is chained to macro A, for example, then macro B will run when macro A is completed. The second technique is *nesting*. If macro B is nested within macro A, for example, then macro A will start running, it will then call macro B, macro B will run to completion, and then the rest of macro A will run to completion (or until another nested macro is called).

The basic technique in both cases is the same. You create one macro with Macro Define (Ctrl-F10). While you are creating the first macro, you call the second macro, which you must create separately. The difference between chaining and nesting is in the way you call the second macro.

If the second macro will be chained to the first, you use Macro Define (Ctrl-F10) and define the first macro completely. Then, before pressing Macro Define (Ctrl-F10) again to end macro recording, you press Macro (Alt-F10) and provide the name of the second macro. If you are calling an Alt-*letter* macro, you can press Alt and the letter instead of typing the macro's name, but you still must press Macro (Alt-F10) first. You then end macro recording for the first macro by pressing Macro Define (Ctrl-F10).

If you want to nest a second macro within the first macro, you also will call that second macro while creating the first, but in a different way. The second macro *must* be an Alt-*letter* macro, not a descriptive macro (unless you use the macro editor as explained later in this chapter). You call the second macro by pressing the Alt key and the letter; you don't use Macro (Alt-F10) as you do when you chain a second macro to the first. Pressing Alt-*letter* tells WordPerfect to run the second macro immediately and then return to running the first one. The second macro does not come at the end of the first macro. You call it at the point where you want it to be invoked when the first macro runs. You then continue defining the first macro.

TIP: When you call a macro, WordPerfect looks for it in your current drive and directory, in the drive or directory where WordPerfect's program files are stored, and in the place specified in the Setup menu. If the macro is not in any of those places, you must call it by its full path name (but you don't have to include the .WPM extension). For more about path names, see this chapter's "Managing Your Macro Files" section.

Creating a Simple Chained Macro

Chaining macros is an easy way to simplify the task of creating a complex macro. If the macro you want to create ends with a series of commands that you already have stored in a different macro, you can make that other macro the last command of your new macro.

Suppose, for example, that you are a teacher and you want to create a macro for the different handouts you distribute to students. You want all the handouts to include the name of the university, the semester, and your name. You also want the macro to pause so that you can insert the name of the course. Then you want the macro to do what your Alt-H macro does: specify the format for a boldfaced, centered, uppercase heading and pause for you to insert its contents.

You don't need to re-create all the commands that are already in the Alt-H macro. You can create the beginning of the macro, which will consist of new commands, and then end with a command to run your Alt-H macro. The Alt-H macro then will be chained to your new macro.

Because the new macro will "set up" your handouts, you can name it SU. Notice that the last command in the macro definition links the Alt-H macro with the new SU macro. Follow these steps to chain the two macros that will set up your handouts:

1. Press Macro Define (Ctrl-F10).

2. In response to the `Define macro:` prompt, type *su* and press Enter.

3. In response to the `Description:` prompt, type *Setup for course handouts* and press Enter.

   `Macro Def` blinks on-screen.

4. Type *Socrates University*.

5. Press Flush Right (Alt-F6).

6. Press Macro Commands (Ctrl-PgUp).

   The program displays the following menu:

   1 Pause; 2 Display; 3 Assign; 4 Comment: 0

7. Select **Pause** (**1**).

8. As stand-in text, type *Ethical Theory* and press Enter to end the pause.

9. Press Enter again.

10. Type *Fall 1988*

    Later in this chapter, you will learn how to modify a small part of a macro, such as this date.

11. Press Flush Right (Alt-F6).

12. Type *Professor Rochelle Gatlin* (or a name of your choice).

13. Press Enter twice.

    Because the cursor now is positioned where you want to include your heading, you are ready to chain this macro to your Alt-H macro.

14. Press Macro (Alt-F10).

15. Press Alt-H.

    The command to run the Alt-H macro is now chained to your SU macro.

16. Press Macro Define (Ctrl-F10) to end recording of the SU macro.

Because you already have created the Alt-H macro, your SU macro should work right away. Follow these steps to run the SU macro:

1. Press Macro (Alt-F10).

2. Type *su* and press Enter.

   `Socrates University` appears on-screen, and the cursor is positioned at the right, ready for your input.

3. Type a course name, for example *American Women Since 1945*, and press Enter.

   The rest of the SU macro runs, and then your Alt-H macro begins. The cursor is in a centered position, waiting for you to enter a heading.

4. Type a heading, such as *women's art and spirituality*.

    You don't need to capitalize any of the letters.

5. Press Enter to indicate that your input is completed.

The macro does the rest of its work. Figure 11.4 shows the result.

```
Socrates University          American Women Since 1945
Fall 1988                    Professor Rochelle Gatlin
              WOMEN'S ART AND SPIRITUALITY
```

Fig. 11.4.
The result of the SU macro.

You can use this method of chaining to establish other formats that also end with your Alt-H macro. You may, for example, use certain margins and tab settings for particular documents. You can create a macro to format the margins and tabs in a particular way and then to run your Alt-H macro.

Your chain of macros is not limited to two. You can have a second macro call a third, and a third call a fourth. Obviously, the more intricate the chain you want to create, the more advance planning you will need to do.

Chaining a Macro to Itself

Another way to repeat a macro, aside from using the Esc key, is to chain the macro to itself. The problem with this method, however, is that you create an endless loop. Your first macro calls itself, which calls itself again, which calls itself yet again—theoretically, for eternity. The problem is not as awesome as it seems because in practice you can stop the macro by pressing Cancel (F1).

This odd repetition has a practical use. Because WordPerfect macros stop automatically when a search fails, you can include a search within a macro and then chain the macro to itself. The macro will perform the search, do whatever you created the macro to do, and then search again. The macro will perform the specified action on each item it finds and then stop when the search fails. You will discover more uses for this looping technique after you have learned some of WordPerfect's advanced features.

Creating a Nested Macro

With WordPerfect 5, you can nest macros as well as chain them. When you nest macros, you can include one or more macros in the middle of another macro. The host macro (the one with macros nested inside it) runs the nested macros at the points where it finds them in its list of commands. Then the host macro takes back control and completes the rest of its own commands. Notice how nesting differs from chaining: a nested macro need not come at the end of the original macro, whereas a chained macro must be the last command of the macro it is chained to.

You create a nested macro in a similar way as you create a chained macro. With a nested macro, however, you *first* must create all the inside macros that will be nested. Then you can create the host macro that will refer to, and instantly execute, the nested macros. When you chain macros, on the other hand, you can create the macros in any order. Another requirement for creating a nested macro is that the inside macros, the ones referred to by the host macro, must be Alt-*letter* macros if you are creating the host macro in the normal way, using Macro Define (Ctrl-F10). Later in this chapter, you will learn how to use the macro editor to nest descriptive macros as well as Alt-*letter* macros.

For practice in creating a nested macro, first create a simple Alt-Z macro that includes text. Then create a host macro and nest the Alt-Z macro within it. Start by completing the following steps to create the Alt-Z macro:

1. Press Macro Define (Ctrl-F10).

2. Respond to the Define macro: prompt by pressing Alt-Z.

3. Press Enter to bypass the Description: prompt.

4. Type some text, for example *This is a nested macro.*

5. Press Macro Define (Ctrl-F10) to end macro recording.

Next create the host macro with the Alt-Z macro nested within it:

1. Press Macro Define (Ctrl-F10).

2. In response to the Define macro: prompt, type *host* and press Enter.

3. Press Enter to bypass the Description: prompt.

4. Type *This is a host macro that will call Alt-Z* and press Enter.

5. Press Alt-Z.

   Notice that you do not press Macro (Alt-F10) first when you call a nested macro.

   Your nested Alt-Z macro (unlike a chained macro) is executed immediately.

6. Press Enter.

7. Type some text, such as *This text follows the execution of a nested macro.*

8. Press Macro Define (Ctrl-F10).

Now, press Macro (Alt-F10), type *host*, and press Enter to run your host macro. Notice that the Alt-Z macro runs as part of the host macro, and then control returns to the host macro itself.

You may later want to delete the practice macros ALTZ.WPM and HOST.WPM. You will learn how to delete macros from within WordPerfect later in this chapter. Note that you also can delete macro files from DOS.

Creating Some Useful Permanent Macros

You don't have to be a macro expert to create macros that will help you with your everyday work. In this section, you will learn to create some useful permanent macros. As you create these macros, think about how you can use the following techniques you have learned to create other macros on your own:

- Use Macro Commands (Ctrl-PgUp) to insert a pause or turn the display feature on or off at any point in your macro.

- Repeat a descriptive or Alt-*letter* macro by using Esc, indicating the number of times you want the macro to repeat, and then giving the command to execute the macro.

- Connect macros to each other by chaining or nesting them.

A Macro To Underline Your Previous Word

WordPerfect makes underlining a word easy: you press Underline (F8) to turn on underlining, type the word, and then press Underline (F8) again to turn off underlining. When you need to underline just one word, however, you can use an even easier method. You can type the word first, then use a macro to underline the last word you typed.

Suppose that you were asked to type the following sentence:

Corporations should focus *only* on profits.

(Of course *you* would never create such a sentence yourself.) Complete the following steps to create an Alt-U macro that underlines the word *only* after you type it:

1. Type *Corporations should focus only*

   The cursor is positioned immediately after the last character you want to underline.

2. Press Macro Define (Ctrl-F10).

   The program displays the prompt Define macro:.

3. Press Alt-U.

   The prompt Description: appears.

4. Type *Underline previous word* and press Enter.

   The program displays the blinking message Macro Def.

5. Press Block (Alt-F4, or F12).

6. Press Word Left (Ctrl- ←).

7. Press Underline (F8).

   The word only is underlined.

8. Press GoTo (Ctrl-Home) twice.

9. Press the → twice.

The cursor returns to its original position.

10. Press Macro Define (Ctrl-F10) to end macro recording.

You can use this macro either to underline the last word you typed or to underline a word you typed previously. In both cases, you position the cursor immediately after the word you want to underline and then press Alt-U. This method is simpler than blocking a word and pressing Underline (F8).

After the word is underlined, you can press the space bar and continue typing. Note that you could have included the space as part of the macro, but you would then need to use Backspace whenever you wanted the word to be followed instead by punctuation.

A Macro To Change Directories

If you have a hard disk, you often need to change from one directory to another. You can create a macro for each directory you want to change to, and you can use an abbreviated form of each directory's name for the names of the macros. You can make your macro end so that you remain at the editing screen, or you can have your macro take you to the List Files screen for your new directory. Of course, you can use macros that change directories only if you first have created the directories you are changing to.

Suppose that you have a directory called \BUSINESS\ACCOUNTS. The following macro changes your current directory to C:\BUSINESS\ACCOUNTS while keeping you at the editing screen. The macro assumes that you already are in drive C:. Complete these steps to create the macro:

1. Press Macro Define (Ctrl-F10).

The prompt Define macro: appears.

2. Type *acc* to name the macro, and then press Enter.

The prompt Description: appears.

3. Type *Change to "\business\accounts" directory* and press Enter.

Macro Def blinks at the bottom of the screen.

4. Press List Files (F5).

5. Type =

Typing = informs WordPerfect that you want to change directories, not just look at the files in a directory.

6. Type *\business\accounts* and press Enter.

The current directory is now C:\BUSINESS\ACCOUNTS.

7. Press Cancel (F1) to return to the editing screen.

8. Press Macro Define (Ctrl-F10) to end macro recording.

If you want a macro to take you to the List Files screen instead of ending at the editing screen, the process is only slightly different. The next macro changes directories to C:\BUSINESS\ACCOUNTS\OVERDUE and ends at the List Files screen for that new directory. The macro assumes that you already are in drive C:. Complete these steps to create the macro:

1. Press Macro Define (Ctrl-F10).

   The prompt Define macro: appears.

2. Type *odf* to name the macro, and then press Enter.

   The *od* stands for drive overdue; the *f* stands for files.

   The prompt Description: appears.

3. Type *Change to "overdue" and List Files* and press Enter.

   Notice that the full path name of \BUSINESS\ACCOUNTS\OVERDUE is too long to include in the macro description.

   Macro Def blinks at the bottom of the screen.

4. Press List Files (F5).

5. Type =

   Typing = informs WordPerfect that you want to change to another drive or directory, not just look at the files in that drive or directory while remaining in your current drive.

6. Type *business\accounts\overdue* and press Enter.

   The current directory is now \BUSINESS\ACCOUNTS\OVERDUE.

7. Press Enter (or the space bar).

   The screen displays your list of files for the directory \BUSINESS\ACCOUNTS\OVERDUE.

8. Press Macro Define (Ctrl-F10) to end macro recording.

A Macro To Change Margins

You can create a macro to make any formatting command easier. Suppose, for example, that your default right and left margins are each 1 inch. Because you often need to change each margin to 1.5 inches, however, you want to create a macro to make the changes in one step. Complete the following steps to create that macro:

1. Press Macro Define (Ctrl-F10).

   The prompt Define macro: appears.

2. Type *mar15* to name the macro, and then press Enter.

   You can't use a period as part of a macro name, but you can use a hyphen to name the macro MAR1-5 if you prefer that name.

   The prompt Description: appears.

3. Type *Change right and left margins to 1.5"* and press Enter.

   Macro Def blinks at the bottom of the screen.

4. Press Format (Shift-F8).

5. Select Line (**1**).

6. Select Margins (**7**).

7. Type *1.5"* and press Enter.

8. Type *1.5"* and press Enter again.

   Figure 11.5 shows how your screen might look at this point. The added arrow calls your attention to the margin change.

Fig. 11.5.

The Format: Line menu with new margin settings.

```
Format: Line

    1 - Hyphenation                        Off

    2 - Hyphenation Zone - Left            10%
                          Right            4%

    3 - Justification                      Yes

    4 - Line Height                        Auto

    5 - Line Numbering                     No

    6 - Line Spacing                       1

    7 - Margins - Left                     1.5"    <-----------
                  Right                    1.5"

    8 - Tab Set                            0",0.5"

    9 - Widow/Orphan Protection            No


Selection: 0
```

9. Press Exit (F7) to return to your editing screen.

10. Press Macro Define (Ctrl-F10) to end macro recording.

After you run this macro, you can verify the margin change by checking Reveal Codes (Alt-F3, or F11).

A Macro To Set Tabs for Numbered Lists

You can use macros to shorten any WordPerfect commands that you use often. Suppose, for example, that you often change your tab settings when you create numbered lists. The setting you find most useful for numbered lists is 1.4". (This tab setting assumes that you are using 1″ margins and a 10-pitch font.) To create a macro that changes your tab settings, follow these steps:

1. Press Macro Define (Ctrl-F10).

2. In response to the Define macro: prompt, type *tablist* and press Enter.

3. In response to the Description: prompt, type *Format tabs for lists* and press Enter.

   The screen displays the blinking Macro Def message.

4. Press Format (Shift-F8).

5. Select **Line (1)**.

6. Select **Tab** Set (**8**).

7. Press Home, Home, ←.

8. Press Del to EOL (Ctrl-End).

9. Type *1.4″* and press Enter.

   If you have set up WordPerfect to use another unit of measure, WordPerfect converts inches to the unit of measure you selected.

10. Press Exit (F7) twice.

11. Press Macro Define (Ctrl-F10) to stop macro recording.

Your tab settings now have been changed. Retain these tab settings as you work through the next few macros. You next will use these tab settings in a macro that simplifies numbered lists.

A Macro To Simplify Numbered Lists

With your tabs set for numbered lists, you next can create another macro to help you enter the numbered items. This macro indents each item in the list and saves you the trouble of continually pressing the Indent key (F4). Follow these steps to create the macro:

1. Press Macro Define (Ctrl-F10).

2. Respond to the Define macro: prompt by pressing Alt-N (for number).

3. In response to the Description: prompt, type *Numbered lists* and press Enter.

   The screen displays the blinking Macro Def message.

4. Press End to move the cursor to the end of any line it might be on.

5. Press Enter twice to move the cursor to the left margin and insert a blank line.

6. Press Macro Commands (Ctrl-PgUp) to give a "how-to-run" command.

The program displays the following menu:

1 Pause; 2 Display; 3 Assign; 4 Comment; 0

7. Select **Pause (1)**.

   Note: In this case, you can create the macro easily without typing a "stand in" for the item number.

8. Press Enter to end the pause.

9. Type a period (.).

10. Press Indent (F4).

11. Press Macro Define (Ctrl-F10) to end macro recording.

    Only a period (.) is now visible on-screen.

Now you can try your new Alt-N macro. Because you want to keep the tabs that were set by your TABLIST macro, don't clear the screen. Complete these steps to test the macro:

1. Press Alt-N.

   The cursor moves down two lines, and the macro pauses for your input.

2. Type the number *1* and press Enter.

   A period is inserted, and the cursor moves one tab stop to the right. Turn on Reveal Codes (Alt-F3, or F11) and notice that an [→**Indent**] code has been inserted. Keep Reveal Codes on.

3. Type *This is the first item in a numbered list, and I want each item to be indented two spaces after each number.*

   The text is indented and forms an even left margin two spaces after the number and the period.

4. Press Word Left (Ctrl- ←).

   You now will see that the macro works even if the cursor is not at the end of the line when you press Alt-N. (The End command in Step 4 of the preceding steps takes care of cursor positioning.)

5. Press Alt-N again.

   Each time you press Alt-N, the macro inserts a blank line and pauses for you to type a number.

6. Type the number *2* and press Enter.

Figure 11.6 shows what your screen looks like at this point if you are in Document 1 and have Reveal Codes turned on.

You may want to experiment in order to vary or enhance this macro. You can add a tab align feature, for example, so that the periods after each number line up evenly. Later, when you learn about WordPerfect's automatic numbering feature, you may want to create a macro that inserts automatic paragraph numbers instead of pausing and having you type the numbers manually (see Chapter 21).

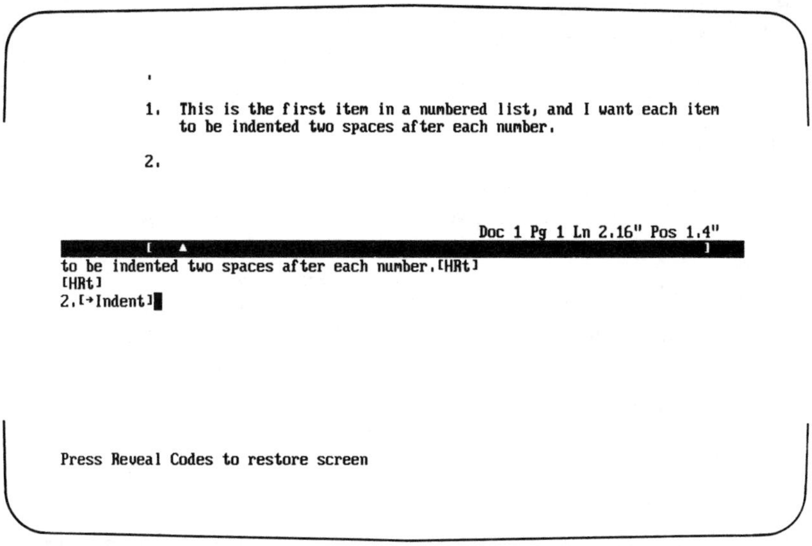

Fig. 11.6.
A numbered list being created with the Alt-N macro.

A Macro To Reinstate Old Tab Settings

Using a little imagination, you can develop a macro that reinstates the tab settings you had before the last time you changed your tabs. This macro would allow you to change tabs for something like numbered lists or a return address and then easily restore the tabs you had just before you made the change.

Because you have used the TABLIST macro to change your tab settings for the previous examples, this is a good time to create a macro to restore your original tab settings. Turn on Reveal Codes (Alt-F3, or F11) and watch what this macro does as you create it. You may learn some tricks that you can apply elsewhere as well.

This macro works only if you have typed something since your most recent change in tab settings. (Changing tabs twice in succession would be pointless anyway.) Complete these steps to create the macro that reinstates your original tab settings:

1. Press Macro Define (Ctrl-F10).

2. In response to the Define macro: prompt, type the name *oldtabs* and press Enter.

3. In response to the Description: prompt, type *Restore previous tab settings* and press Enter.

   Macro Def begins blinking.

4. Press Backward Search (Shift-F2).

   Reminder: When creating a macro, you should supply information for items such as a search string (or date format) even if the correct response already is displayed. You cannot be sure that the correct response will exist when you run the macro.

5. Press Format (Shift-F8).

6. Select **L**ine (**1**).

7. Select **T**ab Set (**7**).

8. Press Search (F2).

   The block cursor in Reveal Codes (Alt-F3, or F11) is positioned immediately after the code for your most recent tab setting.

9. Press ⊸.

   The block cursor in Reveal Codes (Alt-F3, or F11) now appears to be on the tab setting code. This position actually is *before* the tab change takes effect.

10. Press Format (Shift-F8).

11. Select **L**ine (**1**).

12. Select **T**ab Set (**8**).

    You see the tab settings that are currently in effect. The old settings appear because the cursor is positioned before the tab code.

13. Press Exit (F7) twice to insert temporarily in the document the code for the old tab settings.

14. Press Backspace.

    The old tab setting code is deleted. Like all deletions in WordPerfect, that code is held in memory in case you later decide to undelete it.

15. Press GoTo (Ctrl-Home) twice.

16. Press Cancel (F1).

    The last deletion, your previous tab setting, appears. Figure 11.7 shows your screen at this point.

17. Select **R**estore (**1**) from the Undelete menu.

    Your old tab settings are restored.

18. Press Macro Define (Ctrl-F10) to end macro recording.

Be sure that you keep your cursor *after* the Tab Set code if you want to use the tab settings you have just restored.

You probably will want to turn off Reveal Codes after you define the macro. To do so, press Reveal Codes (Alt-F3, or F11) again.

Managing Your Macro Files

Before learning how to use the macro editor, you will benefit by knowing about macros as files. In Chapter 10 you learned how to manipulate your document files

Fig. 11.7.

The previous tab setting ready to be restored.

```
          '

      1,  This is the first item in a numbered list, and I want each item
          to be indented two spaces after each number,

      2,




Undelete: 1 Restore; 2 Previous Deletion: 0
▲     ▲   {   ▲    ▲    ▲    ▲   ▲    ▲    ▲    ▲    ▲    ▲    }
to be indented two spaces after each number,[HRt]
[HRt]
2,[→Indent][Block][Tab Set:0", every 0,5"]█
```

```
    Press Reveal Codes to restore screen
```

using WordPerfect's List Files feature. You can apply some of those same techniques to macro files.

All permanent macros are stored as files on disk, just as your document and program files are stored. Macro files are similar to document files in that you create them, but they are also like program files (such as WP.EXE or SPELL.EXE) because they can instruct your computer to perform a series of operations.

Just as program files have a unique file name extension, typically .EXE, permanent macros have the three-letter extension .WPM that identifies them as WordPerfect macros. Descriptive macros have exactly the full file name that you would expect: the name of the macro, a period, and the .WPM extension. Your AD macro, for example, is saved in a file called AD.WPM. Alt-*letter* macros also are files with regular file names. An Alt-*letter* macro has a full file name consisting of ALT and one additional letter—with no hyphen between ALT and the letter. The .WPM extension is added just as it is in descriptive macros. An Alt-L macro, for instance, is saved in a file called ALTL.WPM, and both WordPerfect and DOS treat it as a file with a regular file name.

In any macro command where you press the Alt key and a letter, you can instead type each letter of the file name—for example, *a, l, t, l*. In a few situations, discussed later in this chapter, you *must* type the full file names of macros in this way.

Keep in mind that a macro file, like all other files, has a full path name that identifies the drive and directory where the macro file is stored. The file name of your AD macro is AD.WPM, but its full path name might be something like C:\MACROS\AD.WPM or B:AD.WPM. The full path name of an Alt-K macro that is in your COURSES directory on drive C: would be C:\COURSES\ALTK.WPM. On a few occasions, you will need to refer to macros by their full path names.

Creating Global Macros

If you do not tell WordPerfect where to store your macros, the program will store them in whatever drive and directory you are in when you create a macro. And if you do not instruct WordPerfect otherwise, the program will look for macros you want to run in your current directory, the one you are working in. WordPerfect also will look in the drive or directory where your WordPerfect program files are stored. Therefore, if you are working in the LETTERS directory of drive C: and you press Alt-L to run a macro stored in your ACCOUNTS directory, WordPerfect will not find it. The screen will display the following message:

```
ERROR: File Not Found - ALTL.WPM
```

One way to run a macro that is in a different drive or directory is to use the macro's full path name. If your Alt-L macro is in C:\ACCOUNTS and you are not, you press Macro (Alt-F10); and instead of pressing only Alt-L, you type *c:\letters\altl*. (If you already are in drive C:, then *letters\altl* is sufficient.) Now WordPerfect knows where to look. Because you are using a macro command, the .WPM extension is assumed even if you don't provide it. When you manipulate macro files from List Files (F5), however, you must type the .WPM extension.

An easier way to run macros from other drives or directories is to make all your macros *global*. You do this by pressing Setup (Shift-F1) and telling WordPerfect where you want your macros stored. Then, when you create a macro, it is stored in the location specified in Setup rather than in your current drive or directory. Even more important, when you call a macro, WordPerfect always will look for that macro in the place where your macros have been stored, regardless of where you are when you call the macro.

With Setup, you easily can make all your future macros global. You already may have done this, or someone may have done it for you. To check the location of your macro files, follow these steps:

1. Press Setup (Shift-F1).

2. Select Location of Auxiliary Files (7).

3. Check Keyboard/Macro Files (3) to see whether a drive or directory is indicated on the right side of the screen.

Figure 11.8 shows what your screen might look like if C:\MACROS (for WordPerfect macros) has been designated as the drive and directory for storing your macros.

Make a note of where your macro files are being stored; you will use this information later. If no drive or directory is indicated, then each macro is being stored in whatever drive and directory you are working in when you create the macro. Press Exit (F7) to leave the Setup menu.

After you have used Setup to specify a place to store your macro files, all macros you create from that point on are global macros. Those macros work any time you use the WordPerfect program (as long as the macros are on a disk in your computer).

```
Setup: Location of Auxiliary Files

     1 - Backup Directory             C:\BACKUP

     2 - Hyphenation Module(s)        C:\LEX

     3 - Keyboard/Macro Files         C:\MACROS

     4 - Main Dictionary(s)           C:\LEX

     5 - Printer Files                C:\PRINTER

     6 - Style Library Filename

     7 - Supplementary Dictionary(s)  C:\LEX

     8 - Thesaurus                    C:\LEX
```

Fig. 11.8.
The Setup menu for specifying the location of auxiliary files.

Creating Local Macros

Although you usually will want your macros to work from any drive or directory, you sometimes may find that having *local* macros in certain drives or directories is useful. Suppose, for example, that you have a number of different macros to format a letter, each called LET.WPM. Assume that each LET macro is on the working disk or the directory of your hard disk that goes with the kind of documents for which the macro is appropriate. Perhaps you have a LET macro in your directory for business letters, and a LET macro in your directory for personal letters.

Although you can set up local macros of this kind, they probably are more trouble than they are worth, given the way WordPerfect handles macros. A better approach is to create separate macros. If you want one macro for personal letters and one for business letters, call one something like PLET and the other BLET, and you will save yourself a lot of trouble.

Suppose, however, that you have a compelling reason to have local macros. Perhaps your officemate works in one directory (or with one floppy disk) and you work in another directory or with another disk, and you each have your own macros. You can take two precautions to make sure that WordPerfect keeps the different macros straight. First, go to the Setup menu (Shift-F1), select Location of Auxiliary Files (7), and delete any entry beside Keyboard/Macro Files (3). Now, in any new session, WordPerfect will look for macros in your current directory first.

Changing the Setup alone is not enough if different local macros with the same name will be run during a single session of WordPerfect. In that case, you also must press Shell (Ctrl-F1), select Go to DOS (1), and then return to WordPerfect by typing *exit* at the DOS prompt.

WordPerfect ordinarily remembers the last time you used a particular macro. If you use a LET macro (from any drive or directory) during the current session, WordPerfect keeps that macro in its memory and uses it whenever a LET macro is invoked again—even if you specify a different path name! This feature allows macros to be executed more quickly, but it makes the use of local macros awkward. By exiting WordPerfect and then returning to the program, you can induce WordPerfect to "forget" any previous use of a macro. This procedure clears WordPerfect's memory of any macro that you or anyone else used earlier in the session. The fastest way to exit and return to WordPerfect is by selecting Shell (Ctrl-F1) and going to DOS, as just described.

Viewing a List of Your Macro Files

You can use List Files (F5) to display the names of your macro files. At this point, you should have at least one macro—the AD macro that you just created. Before you can see that macro on the List Files screen, you must determine where the macro is stored. If no drive or directory was indicated when you went to Setup (Shift-F1) and checked Location of Auxiliary Files (7), then your AD macro is in your current directory. If a particular drive or directory was listed, then your AD macro is stored in that location.

Note: The drive or directory you indicate on the Setup screen affects only the macros you create after you change the location of your auxiliary files. If your AD macro is not in the directory indicated on the Setup screen, you can move it there. You will learn how to move macros later in this chapter.

Use List Files (F5) to display the names of any macros you have stored:

1. Press List Files (F5).

2. If your macros are in your current drive or directory, type *.wpm* and press Enter (or the space bar). This command displays a list of all files with a .WPM extension.

   If your macros are in a different drive or directory, type its name followed by \ *.wpm*, and then press Enter (or the space bar). For example, if your macros are stored in C:\MACROS, type *c:\macros\ *.wpm*. If your macros are stored on a floppy disk in drive B:, type *b:\ *.wpm* (or simply *b:*.wpm*).

   Reminder: If the directory you want to look at is on your current drive, you don't need to include the letter of the drive. For example, if you are working in C:\LETTERS and want to see files in C:\MACROS, you can just press List Files (F5), type *\macros*, and press Enter.

3. To find AD.WPM among the files, select Name Search (N), type *ad*, and press Enter.

   AD.WPM is highlighted.

The program lists the files with a .WPM extension in the drive or directory you selected. Figure 11.9 shows a List Files screen from drive B: with the AD.WPM file highlighted. On your screen this file may be the only one you see; or, if you have other macros, AD.WPM will be one of several files, as it is in the figure.

Storing Macros on a Hard Disk

If you are using a hard disk and expect to have more than a few global macros, you will find them easier to work with if you store them in their own special directory. You can give the directory any name you want, such as \MACROS, \MAC, or \WPM (for WordPerfect macros). If you prefer, you can store your macros together with your WordPerfect program files. Or you can store global macros in any other

Fig. 11.9.
The List Files screen.

```
05/08/88  14:23              Directory B:\*.WPM
Document size:    1339  Free:    212992  Used:    1328      Files:  12

  . <CURRENT>   <DIR>                  .. <PARENT>   <DIR>
A        .WPM       171  03/10/88 12:19    AD      .WPM      165  05/07/88 23:34
ALTC     .WPM        57  05/08/88 00:39    ALTD    .WPM      108  05/06/88 11:17
ALTE     .WPM        98  04/30/88 21:20    ALTF    .WPM      109  04/30/88 21:49
ALTG     .WPM        88  04/10/88 21:30    ALTH    .WPM       96  05/05/88 22:41
ALTI     .WPM       132  04/15/88 12:48    ALTK    .WPM      117  03/15/88 17:51
BOLD     .WPM        90  02/10/88 20:50    COPY    .WPM       97  05/06/88 21:03




1 Retrieve; 2 Delete; 3 Move/Rename; 4 Print; 5 Text In;
6 Look; 7 Other Directory; 8 Copy; 9 Word Search; N Name Search: 6
```

directory you choose, as long as you indicate the name of the directory with Setup
(Shift-F1), Location of Auxiliary Files (7).

Suppose that you want to store your WordPerfect macros in a special directory
called \MACROS. First you need to create the directory by completing these steps:

1. Press Shell (Ctrl-F1) and choose **Go** to DOS (1) to go to DOS without
   exiting WordPerfect.

   The DOS prompt is displayed.

2. Type *md \macros* and press Enter.

   MD is the DOS command to make (create) a new directory.

3. Type *exit* and press Enter.

   You exit DOS and return to the WordPerfect editing screen.

4. Press Setup (Shift-F1).

5. Select **L**ocation of Auxiliary Files (7).

6. Select **K**eyboard/Macro Files (3).

7. Type *c:\macros* and press Enter.

8. Press Exit (F7).

From now on, all the macros you create will be stored in C:\MACROS.

Storing Macros on Floppy Disks

If you are using a floppy disk system, you can have global macros by storing them on
the WordPerfect working program disk #2. This is the program disk that must
remain in drive A: while you are running WordPerfect. You can instruct WordPerfect
to store your macros and run them automatically from drive A: by completing these
steps:

1. Press Setup (Shift-F1).

2. Select **L**ocation of Auxiliary Files (**7**).

3. Select **K**eyboard/Macro Files (**3**).

4. Type *a:* and press Enter.

5. Press Exit (F7).

Your macros will be stored on whatever disk is in your A: drive. If you later use a different working program disk #2, you will need to copy your macro files to the new disk in order to access them.

You can store only as many macros in drive A: as you have free space for on your floppy disk. If you look again at figure 11.9, you can see that the amount of free space is indicated on the second line of the List Files screen. Each macro (except an extremely long one) requires about a thousand bytes on a floppy disk. The more printer or other files you keep in drive A:, the less free disk space you will have for macros. If you run out of space for macros in drive A:, you can store macros in drive B: along with your documents. If you do that, however, you will have access to the macros in drive B: only when you are using the disk where the macros are stored.

Manipulating and Viewing Macro Files

You already know how to use List Files (F5) to manipulate your regular documents. Although macro files (like program files) cannot be retrieved or printed, they can be deleted, moved or renamed, and copied. Descriptions of your macros also can be viewed from List Files (F5) with the Look command. When you first start creating macros, you may rarely need to manipulate your macro files; you might simply let them remain stored away on your disk, like your program files. As you develop more and more of your own macros, however, you probably will find that performing a few simple file management tasks can be useful.

Keep in mind that List Files (F5) performs actions on an *entire* file by deleting the file, moving or renaming it, or creating a copy of the whole file in another directory or drive. If you want to manipulate the contents of a file, such as a part of one of your documents, you must go inside the file itself and make changes rather than use List Files (F5). You use List Files (F5) when you want to delete, move or rename, or copy a whole macro as a file rather than to change the contents of a macro.

TIP: When you manipulate macros in List Files, you always must include the .WPM extension as part of the file name. Otherwise, WordPerfect does not recognize the file as a macro.

The List Files (F5) options work the same way for macro files as they do for regular document files. For a fuller explanation of these options, see Chapter 10. You can use any of the following List Files (F5) options to manipulate your macro files:

1. **Delete** (**2**) a macro file (or group of files). You delete a macro file when you don't want to have any macro with that name.

2. **Move/Rename** (**3**) a macro file when you want to move a macro to another directory or disk, or when you want to rename a macro. Be sure to include the .WPM extension in the new name.

3. **Copy** (**8**) a macro file to another directory or disk while leaving the original file in place.

4. **Look** (**6**) at a macro to check the macro description.

In Chapter 10, you learned how to manipulate a group of files by marking them first. You can use the same technique to delete, move, or copy macro files. You mark the files with asterisks and respond to the prompts just as you would if you were acting on any other group of files. For example, you can use the Copy command to back up all your macros to a floppy disk. Particularly if you have just a few macros, you may want to use the Copy command in List Files (F5) instead of the DOS BACKUP command. You mark the files you want to back up and then use the Copy command.

Just as you can use the Look (6) command to see one of your document files from List Files (F5) without actually retrieving it, you can also look at your macro files. The only part of the display that will mean anything to you will be the macro description. If you wrote a clear description when you created the macro, you now will reap your reward.

Imagine that a year from now, after having created hundreds of useful macros for yourself and your friends, you chance upon an odd-looking file in your \MACROS directory called AD.WPM. You wonder what in the world this macro does. With the cursor on this macro name in List Files, you press Look (6) or just press Enter, and you see the description you wrote when you first created the macro. Below the description you see some other things that don't make any sense. Computer people call these symbols "garbage" because they are not readily intelligible as ordinary language. Figure 11.10 shows how AD.WPM appears using Look from List Files (F5).

Using the Macro Editor

You now have learned to create a variety of macros. You also know how to replace a macro with an entirely new one. Sometimes, however, you will want to make just a small change in a macro. If the macro is an intricate one, you won't want to create it from scratch. Fortunately, you don't have to: WordPerfect 5 includes a macro editor.

The macro editor allows you to modify a macro by using some of the same editing commands that you use in the normal editing screen. The macro editor also makes available to you powerful programming commands that you can include in your macros only by using the editor. In this section you will learn how to modify a macro, and you will become acquainted with a few of the additional commands. A complete survey of the programming commands is provided in Appendix C.

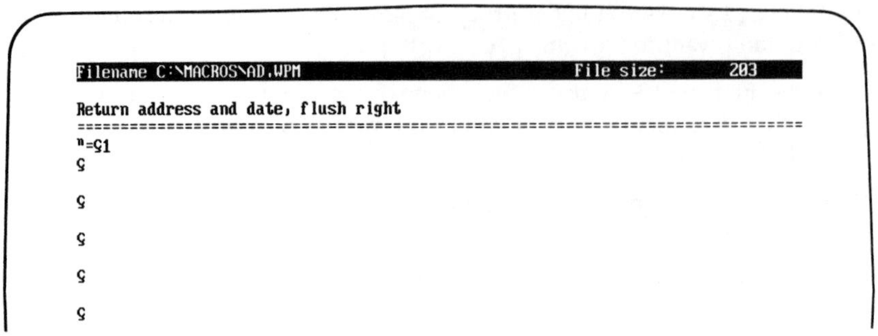

Fig. 11.10.

A look at a macro from List Files.

```
Filename C:\MACROS\AD.WPM                          File size:      203

Return address and date, flush right
================================================================================
"=§1
§

§

§

§

§
```

Making a Simple Text Change

Suppose that you have a macro which includes your return address and the date, such as the AD macro you created earlier in this chapter. What do you do if you want to change some part of the address but keep everything else in the macro the same? This task is a prime candidate for the macro editor.

To edit a macro, you begin as if you were going to create the macro from scratch, using the same name. Complete these steps to modify the address in the AD macro:

1. Press Macro Define (Ctrl-F10).

2. In response to the Macro Def prompt, type *ad* and press Enter.

   Keep in mind that WordPerfect will not let you change an existing macro without warning. The program displays the following prompt:

   AD.WPM is Already Defined. 1 Replace; **2** Edit: **0**

3. Select Edit (**2**).

   A macro editing screen appears, as shown in figure 11.11.

   You now can edit either the description of the macro or the action performed by the macro.

4. Select Action (**2**).

   The cursor moves inside the box containing the commands and text that make up AD.WPM. Each WordPerfect command is enclosed in braces, text is shown as regular text, and spaces are shown as small dots. Text is the easiest of these elements to edit.

5. Press End.

6. Backspace nine times to erase CA   90505.

7. Type *MA*, press the space bar twice, and type *02154*.

   Figure 11.12 shows how the macro editing screen should appear at this point.

8. Press Exit (F7) twice to exit the macro editor and save the changes.

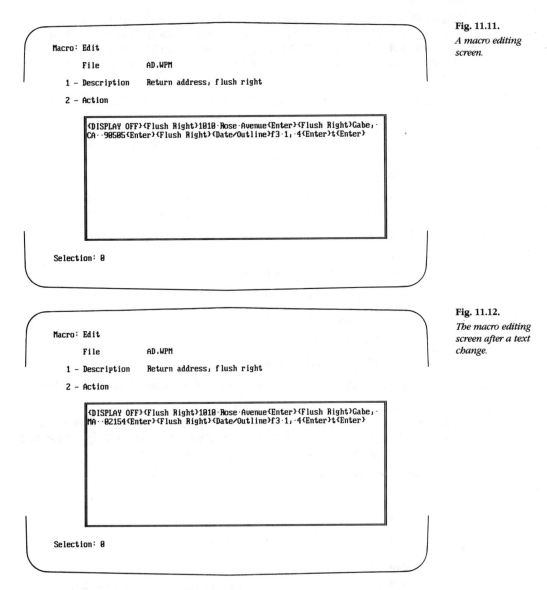

Fig. 11.11.
A macro editing screen.

```
Macro: Edit

     File          AD.WPM

  1 - Description   Return address, flush right

  2 - Action

    ┌───────────────────────────────────────────────────────────────┐
    │ {DISPLAY OFF}{Flush Right}1010·Rose·Avenue{Enter}{Flush Right}Gabe,· │
    │ CA··90505{Enter}{Flush Right}{Date/Outline}f3·1,·4{Enter}t{Enter}   │
    │                                                               │
    │                                                               │
    │                                                               │
    │                                                               │
    │                                                               │
    └───────────────────────────────────────────────────────────────┘

  Selection: 0
```

Fig. 11.12.
The macro editing screen after a text change.

```
Macro: Edit

     File          AD.WPM

  1 - Description   Return address, flush right

  2 - Action

    ┌───────────────────────────────────────────────────────────────┐
    │ {DISPLAY OFF}{Flush Right}1010·Rose·Avenue{Enter}{Flush Right}Gabe,· │
    │ MA··02154{Enter}{Flush Right}{Date/Outline}f3·1,·4{Enter}t{Enter}   │
    │                                                               │
    │                                                               │
    │                                                               │
    │                                                               │
    │                                                               │
    └───────────────────────────────────────────────────────────────┘

  Selection: 0
```

Deleting WordPerfect Commands

You can change more than just text with the macro editor. You might decide, for
example, that you want a return address macro that does not include the Flush Right
commands. Although you could edit the macro to delete those commands, you
might instead want to have two macros: one with the Flush Right commands and
one without them.

You can't use WordPerfect's built-in macro editor to save a second copy of the macro under a different name, but that doesn't mean that you have to create the second macro from scratch. You first can use List Files (F5) to make a copy of your AD.WPM macro and call it AD2.WPM. Then you can use the macro editor to edit the AD2 macro.

Complete these steps to make a copy of your AD.WPM macro called AD2.WPM:

1. Press List Files (F5).

   The name of your current directory appears. You want to work with the files in your macro directory without changing the directory you are working in.

2. Type the name of the directory where your macros are located and press Enter. For example, type *macros* and then press Enter (or the space bar).

3. To find your AD macro, select Name Search (N), type *ad.wpm*, and press Enter.

   Your AD.WPM macro is highlighted.

4. Select Copy (8) from the List Files menu.

   The screen displays the following prompt:

   Copy this file to:

5. Type *ad2.wpm* and press Enter.

6. Press Exit (F7) or the space bar to exit List Files and return to the editing screen.

You now have an AD2 macro identical to your AD macro. You can modify the AD2 macro, knowing that you will not affect the original AD macro. Complete these steps to eliminate the Flush Right commands from your AD2 macro:

1. Press Macro Define (Ctrl-F10).

2. In response to the Macro Def prompt, type *ad2* and press Enter.

   The screen displays the following prompt:

   AD2.WPM is Already Defined. 1 Replace; 2 Edit: 0

3. Select Edit (2).

4. Select Action to edit the macro's action rather than its description.

   You now can use the Del key to erase all three {Flush Right} codes.

5. Use the → to position the cursor on the opening brace of the first {Flush Right} code.

6. Press Del.

   The {Flush Right} code is deleted.

7. Press the ↓ or → until the cursor is on the opening brace of the second {Flush Right} code.

8. Press Del again to delete the second {Flush Right} code.

9. Use the ↓ or ← key to position the cursor on the opening brace of the third {Flush Right} code.

10. Press Del again to delete the third {Flush Right} code.

11. Press Exit (F7) to exit the Action section of the macro editor.

    You now need to edit the Description.

12. Select **Description**.

    You can use many of the same editing commands you are used to.

13. Press End.

14. Use the Backspace key to delete the comma (,) and flush right from the description.

    Note: You cannot use Block to edit the description.

15. Press Exit (F7) to leave the Description portion of the editing screen.

Inserting and Editing WordPerfect Commands

You can do much more with the macro editor than simply edit text or delete commands. You also can add new commands or edit old ones. To add most commands, you select Action, position your cursor within the box of macro commands, and press the same keys you would press if you were in the regular WordPerfect editing screen. To add commands to a macro, you need to remember or write down in advance *exactly* what commands you want to include.

Suppose, for example, that you want to change the date format in your AD2 macro so that the day of the week is included before the date. To find out what commands are required, you probably will need to exit the macro editor and write down exactly the commands you will need. If you do this, you will see that you need the following formatting commands to enter the day of the week plus the date:

    Date/Outline (Shift-F5)
    Date Format (3)
    6, 3 1, 4

Now, using the macro editor, you need to determine where the old codes for the date are located. Notice the section in figure 11.12 that reads as follows:

    {Date/Outline}f3 1, 4

(Remember that the macro editor inserts dots to indicate spaces.)

To change the command to include the day of the week, you need to change the original commands to the following:

    {Date/Outline}f6, 3 1, 4

Position the cursor on the 3 and type a 6, a comma, and a space.

You can reformat the codes in the macro editor by using the Enter key. Used within the macro editor, the Enter key (when used in the usual way) only rearranges the appearance of the commands; it does not insert an {Enter} command in the macro.

The Enter key is one of several exceptions to the general rule that any text or commands you enter in the macro editor become inserted as part of the macro itself. If you press Underline (F8), for example, you insert an {Underline} code into the macro editing screen, and that Underline command becomes part of the macro. To edit the commands in the macro editor, however, you can use keys such as Del, Backspace, and Enter without adding codes to the macro itself. You also can use Exit (F7) to leave the macro editor without adding an {Exit} code, and you can use Cancel (F1) or Esc to back out of changes you have made.

Sometimes you *will* want to add to a macro itself codes such as {Backspace}, {Del}, {Enter}, {Exit}, and {Cancel}. You can add those commands in either of two ways: you can add one code at a time, or you can add a string of codes. To add only one code, press Ctrl-V and then press the key for the code you want to add. Ctrl-V tells the macro editor that the next command is a code to insert in the macro itself. For example, if you press Ctrl-V and then press Enter, an {Enter} code is inserted in the macro.

To add a string of codes, press Macro Define (Ctrl-F10), add the codes you need, and then press Macro Define (Ctrl-F10) again. Any commands you enter after first pressing Macro Define (Ctrl-F10) become part of the macro itself. Figure 11.13 shows how your macro editing screen looks after you press Macro Define (Ctrl-F10) the first time. The program displays the following message at the bottom of the screen:

`Press Macro Define to enable editing`

This message is computerese for "Press Macro Define (Ctrl-F10) again when you want to stop inserting codes in the macro." Pressing Macro Define (Ctrl-F10) will put you back in regular editing, where pressing keys such as Enter and Exit (F7) do not insert codes in the macro.

If you don't make the mistake of inserting a few unwanted codes after pressing Macro Define (Ctrl-F10) in the macro editor, you may be the first WordPerfect user not to do so. You may, for example, press Exit (F7) to stop editing and then find that you mistakenly inserted an {Exit} code in the macro. Or you may try to erase a code you just entered by mistake and then make the further mistake of pressing Backspace, only to insert the {Backspace} code. These errors are easily corrected. You first press Macro Define (Ctrl-F10) to "enable editing," and then you can use the Backspace key to delete any unwanted codes. You then also can use Exit (F7) to leave the macro editor, saving any changes you have made.

You have another option for correcting your mistakes in the macro editor. You can back out of changes you have made to a macro by pressing Cancel (F1) or Esc. If you are editing the Action commands, the program displays the following prompt:

`Cancel changes? (Y/N) No`

Press *Y* and then press Cancel (F1) again to exit the macro editor without saving any changes.

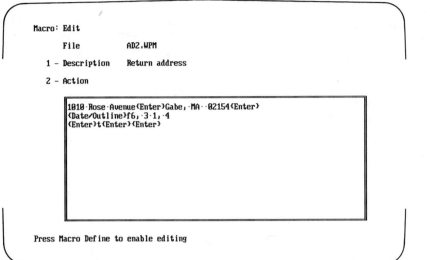

Fig. 11.13.
The macro editing screen while codes are being inserted.

```
Macro: Edit

        File        AD2.WPM

  1 - Description    Return address

  2 - Action

    ┌────────────────────────────────────────────────────┐
    │1010·Rose·Avenue{Enter}Gabe,··MA···02154{Enter}      │
    │{Date/Outline}f6,·3·1,·4                              │
    │{Enter}t{Enter}{Enter}                               │
    │                                                     │
    │                                                     │
    │                                                     │
    │                                                     │
    │                                                     │
    │                                                     │
    └────────────────────────────────────────────────────┘

  Press Macro Define to enable editing
```

Inserting Special Macro Commands

While editing the Action section in the macro editor, you can not only add or modify regular WordPerfect commands, but also insert special macro commands at any point in the macro. You are familiar with some of these special macro commands— for example, "display on" and "prompt." These and other commands allow you to create intricate programs. To gain access to these special commands, you press Macro Commands (Ctrl-PgUp) while inside the macro editor.

Complete these steps to access the macro editor and to add the {DISPLAY ON} command to your AD2 macro:

1. Press Macro Define (Ctrl-F10).

2. In response to the prompt, type *ad2* and press Enter.

3. In response to the prompt, select Edit (**2**).

4. Select Action.

   The cursor is positioned at the beginning of the macro.

5. Press Del to delete the {DISPLAY OFF} command.

6. Press Macro Commands (Ctrl-PgUp).

   A window that lists the special commands opens in the upper right corner of the screen. A block cursor is on the first command, {;}comment ~. To move the block cursor to other commands, you either use the cursor keys or type the first letters of the command.

7. To move the block cursor to the {DISPLAY OFF} command, type *d*.

8. Press the ↓ once to position the block cursor on {DISPLAY ON}, as shown in figure 11.14.

Fig. 11.14.

Macro commands in the macro editor.

```
Macro: Edit                                    ┌──────────────────────────────┐
                                               │{CHAR}variable~message~       │
              File        AD2.WPM              │{DISPLAY OFF}                 │
                                               │{DISPLAY ON}                  │
         1 - Description   Return address      │{ELSE}                        │
                                               │{END IF}                      │
         2 - Action                            │{GO}label~                    │
                                               │{IF}value~                    │
                                               └──────────────────────────────┘
         ┌──────────────────────────────────────────────────────────────┐
         │1010·Rose·Avenue{Enter}Gabe,·MA··02154{Enter}                  │
         │{Date/Outline}f6,·3·1,·4                                       │
         │{Enter}t{Enter}{Enter}                                         │
         │                                                               │
         │                                                               │
         │                                                               │
         └──────────────────────────────────────────────────────────────┘

                                  (Name Search: Enter or arrows to Exit)
```

9. To insert the command on which the block cursor is positioned, press Enter.

   That command is inserted at the point in your macro where you were when you invoked Macro Commands (Ctrl-PgUp).

A {DISPLAY ON} code is inserted in your macro. You can delete it by pressing Backspace. As you experiment further in the macro editor, remember that you always can delete changes or back out of changes you have made by pressing Cancel (F1).

Experimenting Further with the Macro Editor

As you experiment further with the macro editor, keep these guidelines in mind:

- Press Macro Commands (Ctrl-PgUp) to display the list of special macro commands. With your cursor on one of the special commands, press Enter or Exit (F7) to insert that command in your macro.

- Press Cancel (F1) or Esc to return to the regular macro editor without inserting the command.

- From the regular macro editing screen, press Macro Commands (Ctrl-PgUp) to place the cursor in the list of special macro commands.

- Press the space bar to go to the top of the list of special macro commands.

You may find several of the special macro commands useful in your own macros. Here are some ideas:

- You may want to add a {BELL} to a macro such as your Alt-H macro so that you would be reminded that the macro is pausing for your input.

- You could have the macro ask you a question or remind you of something while it is running, by using the {PROMPT} command.

- The {;}comment ~ command allows you to add comments to your macro without affecting the way it runs. This feature can be helpful when you want to go back and edit a complicated macro.

- Use the {DISPLAY ON} and {DISPLAY OFF} commands if you change your mind about how you want your macro to run.

- Use the {NEST} command to nest either a descriptive or an Alt-*letter* macro. You will recall that outside the macro editor, your nested macros had to be Alt-*letter* macros.

Each of the special macro commands has a particular required *syntax*—an exact way that you must insert it in the macro editor. These commands make possible the creation of complicated routines. Like all programming, programming with WordPerfect macros requires careful planning and organization. Although these advanced techniques are beyond the scope of this book, Appendix C gives you a glimpse of the possibilities.

Converting WordPerfect 4 Macros to WordPerfect 5

WordPerfect 5's macro conversion utility (MACROCNV.EXE), which is on the program's Conversion disk, will convert some of your WordPerfect 4.x macros to WordPerfect 5 macros. The macro conversion program first converts whatever parts of your old macro it is able to. Then the program informs you whether you need to do further editing to make the macro work. To make those editing changes, you can either use the WordPerfect 5 macro editor or create the macro from scratch.

You run the conversion program from DOS, not from within WordPerfect. At the DOS prompt, you change to the drive or directory where your conversion files are stored. (Of course, you also could insert the original Conversion disk supplied by WordPerfect into a floppy drive.) To convert a 4.x macro, you type *macrocnv* and then the name of the 4.x macro. Be sure to provide the complete path name. For help with the conversion program, type *macrocnv/h* at the DOS prompt.

Suppose that MACROCNV.EXE is stored in C:\WP5 and your WordPerfect 4.x macros are in C:\WP4. Follow these steps to convert an Alt-L WordPerfect 4.x macro to WordPerfect 5:

1. Press Shell (Ctrl-F1) and choose **G**o to DOS (**1**) to go to DOS without exiting WordPerfect.

   The DOS prompt is displayed.

2. Type *cd\wp5* to make your current directory the one where MACROCNV.EXE is stored.

3. Type *macrocnv \wp4\altl* and press Enter.

Your WordPerfect Alt-L macro, \WP4\ALTL.MAC, is converted into a WordPerfect 5 macro with the name ALTL.WPM and is stored in your current directory, \WP5. If you have a special directory for your macros, you will want to move ALTL.WPM from \WP5 to that special macros directory.

WP 5 ≡≡≡ # Summary

In this chapter you have learned how macros can save you time by storing a group of keystrokes. When you want to insert those keystrokes in a document, you just run the macro.

You have learned to perform the following macro techniques:

- Create both permanent and temporary macros

- Manage your macros as files with the List Files feature

- Change the Setup screen so that you can run any macro regardless of what drive or directory you are working in

- Control the way your macros run. Specifically, you learned how to set up a macro so that you can see each step it performs, how to make a macro pause so that you can insert a command or some text, and how to include in a macro a command to run a different macro.

- Create some macros for everyday use

- Use the macro editor to modify macros after you have created them

Don't expect to create perfect macros every time you try. You can improve your odds of success by working through the steps of a macro before you begin creating it. If the steps work when you perform them one-by-one, they almost always will work in a macro. Before you create a complicated macro, you may want to write down each of the steps. Even experienced macro users, however, often create their macros through trial and error. Don't be afraid to experiment.

If you're interested in learning how to assign macros to various keyboard layouts, see Chapter 18.

12

Using Styles

As a beta tester for WordPerfect Corporation, **Marilyn Horn Claff** *offers expert advice and suggestions for the development of WordPerfect. She is also Director of the Boston Computer Society's WordPerfect Special Interest Group and a WordPerfect Certified Instructor.* ■

S tyle (Alt-F8) is a powerful tool for controlling the format of an individual document or a group of documents. Each style consists of regular WordPerfect codes that you can turn on or off in your document. Styles can include almost any formatting code that you can use manually. Using Style (Alt-F8) is simple: you define and name a style, and then when you want to use that style, you select it from a list.

Style definitions are saved in the current document. You also can save your style definitions in a master style library file so that you can use the styles in other documents.

This chapter teaches the following skills:

- Create different types of styles, opened and paired

- Use a style in a document; apply a style to a block

- Edit, save, and delete style definitions

- Save style definitions to a style library to use with other documents

- Retrieve styles from your library, update your documents with styles from the library, and maintain your style library

- Review sample style libraries

- Use macros with styles

Deciding To Use Styles

If you are a novice, you may be tempted to skip this chapter and return to it later. Don't! If you understand how to use individual WordPerfect formatting codes in your document, you can define and use styles.

399

Unless you examine a document in Reveal Codes, a document formatted with styles does not look different from a document formatted manually. If the results look the same whether you use styles or individual codes, why do you need styles?

Suppose that you write a forty-page proposal with three sets of margins and four levels of section headers. Your boss approves the proposal, but she doesn't like the margin settings for the tables. She also wants you to use a different font for your third-level headings.

If you inserted the formatting codes manually, you must find each wrong code, delete it, and insert a new code. Changing the format codes this way is no easy task because you cannot search for specific code settings. You can search for generic formatting codes, such as margin change or font change codes, but you cannot use Replace (Alt-F2) to replace a code that sets the left margin to 1.25 inches with a code for a 1.5-inch margin, nor can you replace an 11-point Helvetica font code with a code for 12-point Chancellor font.

Styles provide a simple solution to this problem. If you use styles to format your proposal, you can make the changes effortlessly, just by changing two of the style definitions in your style list! Even better, you can save the new styles in your master style list so that the next time you write a proposal, you can use exactly the same format.

Realizing the Advantages of Using Styles

Using the Style feature offers many advantages over manual formatting:

- Styles save formatting time and keystrokes.

- Styles facilitate revisions.

- Styles encourage formatting consistency within a single document.

- Styles enable you to share formatting specifications with other users easily.

- Styles reduce "code clutter" in Reveal Codes and let you choose formatting by name and description.

- Styles treat a group of codes as a single object so that codes that belong together stay together.

- Styles free you to think about your writing.

Comparing Styles to Macros

If you are an intermediate or advanced user, your first question may be, Why use styles instead of macros? In previous versions of WordPerfect, macros accomplished many of the tasks that the Style feature performs in WordPerfect 5. You still can use macros for formatting in WordPerfect 5, but you miss one of WordPerfect's most powerful features.

Styles have one clear advantage over macros. When you use a macro to insert formatting codes in your document, you save keystrokes, but the file is identical to a file that is formatted manually. Once you have entered the codes in your document, you still cannot change them easily. If you need to change the font used for all the embedded quotations, you must change each font code individually; you also can miss a code easily.

Instead, you can create a style called Quotations and assign the style to each quotation. Then, if necessary, you can change the format of all the quotations by redefining the Quotations style.

Defining Open and Paired Styles

WordPerfect styles fall into two categories: *open* and *paired*.

Open styles remain in effect until you override the style codes, either by using another style or by inserting other formatting codes manually. You do not turn off open styles.

Use open styles for formatting that affects an entire document. For instance, you can use an open style to set your document margins, tabs, line spacing, base font; choose the hyphenation type and zone; turn on or off justification; turn on widow/orphan protect; and select a form type.

Remember that if you want an open style to affect an entire document, move the cursor to the beginning of the document before turning on the style.

Paired styles are turned on and off. For example, you can create a paired style called Heading that makes a section heading bold and italic. When you use this style, WordPerfect inserts a **[Style On: Heading]** in your document before the cursor position and a **[Style Off: Heading]** after the cursor position. After you type your heading text, turn off the style. If you need to change the text of the heading, just position the cursor between the **[Style On: Heading]** and the **[Style Off: Heading]** codes and make your changes.

Use paired styles for titles, section headings, tables, embedded quotations, or even entire chapters. Paired styles are appropriate for any element of your document that has a beginning and an end.

Paired styles can be divided into three subgroups, according to the method you choose to turn off the style.

Enter = HRt You can choose to keep the style on until you explicitly turn off the style by returning to the Styles menu and choosing Off (**2**). Use this method for styles that extend over multiple paragraphs or that must contain hard returns. Pressing Enter simply inserts a new line.

Enter = Off If you choose this option, WordPerfect turns off the style when you press Enter. Use this method for styles that affect only a single paragraph, such as a section heading.

Enter = Off/On If you choose this option, WordPerfect turns off and immediately turns on a style when you press Enter. Off/On styles are ideal for formatting a series of similar paragraphs. For example, you can use an Off/On style to create consecutive hanging paragraphs or numbered lists.

Creating an Open Style

A letterhead is a typical application for an open style. You need to leave enough white space at the top of the first page of the document for your preprinted name and address. On all other pages, you use regular paper so that the text starts higher on the page.

To create an open style, complete the following steps:

1. Press Style (Alt-F8).

   The Styles List appears with the following menu at the bottom:

   1 On; 2 Off; 3 Create; 4 Edit; 5 Delete; 6 Save; 7 Retrieve; 8 Update: 1

2. Press Create (**3**).

   The Styles: Edit menu appears (see fig. 12.1).

Fig. 12.1.
The Styles: Edit menu.

```
Styles: Edit

    1 - Name

    2 - Type          Paired

    3 - Description

    4 - Codes

    5 - Enter         HRt
```

Notice that two of the five items on this list are already filled in with WordPerfect's default values.

3. Select Name (**1**).

4. Type the name of your style and press Enter.

   For your example, type *Letterhead* and press Enter.

   Choose a name whose meaning will be clear to you when you see the style name in a document six months from now. (Remember that although you can read the style description in the Styles menu, you see the name, not the description, when you look at your document in Reveal Codes.)

   The style name is not a file name, so you can use any characters you want; you can enter up to 11 characters including spaces. Style names are not case-sensitive; WordPerfect considers header, HEADER, and Header as the same style name.

5. Select **Type** (**2**).

   The following menu appears:

   Type: 1 Paired; 2 Open: 0

6. Select **Open** (**2**).

7. Select **Description** (**3**).

8. Type a short description of what the style does and press Enter.

   For your example, type *formats business letters* and press Enter.

   The file description can contain up to 54 characters. Make the description as precise as you can. (You can edit the description later if you change the definition of the style.)

TIP: To keep track of revised styles, include the date in the style description whenever you create or revise a style definition.

---

9. Select **Codes** (**4**).

   A screen which resembles a document editing screen with Reveal Codes active appears. You can see the codes you are inserting as you create the style in the lower half of the screen. If you include text in your style definition, the text is visible in both halves of the screen.

10. Insert the formatting codes and text that you want to be included in the style, just as though you are editing a WordPerfect document.

11. Press Exit (F7) three times to return to your document.

The Advance feature used in this style moves the cursor down one inch. Instead of changing the top margin, use the Advance feature to make a two-inch top margin for this page only. Then, you do not have to set the margin back so that subsequent pages print correctly.

Note that the Reveal Codes show the codes you have entered (see fig. 12.2).

```
Press Exit when done                          Doc 1 Pg 1 Ln 2i Pos 1.5i
▲    ▲    ▲   {    ▲    ▲    ▲    ▲    ▲    ▲    ▲    ▲  ]
[T/B Mar:1i,1i][Just Off][L/R Mar:1.5i,1.25i][Tab Set:0i, every 0.5i][W/O On][Pg
Numbering:No page numbering][Paper Sz/Typ:8.5i x 11i,Letterhead][AdvDn:1i]█
```

Fig. 12.2.

The Reveal Codes for Letterbead style.

TIP: You may be tempted to include the date as part of your Letterhead style. Unfortunately, neither Date Text nor Date Code is very useful in a style definition. If you use the Date Text code, every letter is date stamped with the date on which you created the Letterhead style. If you use the Date Code, whenever you retrieve a file created with the style, the date changes to the current date. If you need to print a copy of a letter a week later, the date is no longer valid.

Use a macro to turn on the style and insert the Date Text. The macro can insert the date of the day you invoke the macro, not the date that the macro was written.

Creating a Paired Style

The process of creating a paired style is a bit more involved than creating an open style. A paired style gives you two added capabilities. First, you can specify the position of the formatting codes relative to your own text. Second, you can choose a method for turning off the style.

Many of WordPerfect's formatting codes actually consist of two codes: one code to turn on a feature, and another to turn off the feature. For example, when you underline a word, you press Underline (F8), type the word, and press Underline (F8) again. In Reveal Codes, you see these formatting options: **[UND]**word**[und]**. As with several other pairs of WordPerfect codes, capital letters indicate the beginning of a formatting feature, and lowercase letters indicate the end.

Instead of manually inserting formatting codes, like Underline and Bold, you can use a style to format the text. For instance, if you want a heading in your document to be both bold and underlined, you can create a paired style to turn on and off Bold and Underline.

To create a paired style, complete the following steps:

1. Press Style (Alt-F8).

   The following menu appears:

   1 On; 2 Off; 3 Create; 4 Edit; 5 Delete; 6 Save; 7 Retrieve; 8 Update: 1

2. Select Create (**3**).

   The Styles: Edit menu appears (see fig. 12.1).

3. Select Name (**1**).

4. Type the name of the style and press Enter.

   For your example, type *Emphasized* and press Enter.

   Because Paired style is the default, you don't need to change the Type of the style.

5. Select **Description** (**3**).

6. Type a description of the style and press Enter.

 For your example, type *bold and underlined* and press Enter.

7. Select **Codes** (**4**).

 The Paired Codes screen appears (see fig. 12.3). Notice that your cursor is before the comment box. The comment box represents the text that you will type when you use this paired style. You can insert formatting codes and text before the comment, after the comment, or both before and after.

```
┌──────────────────────────────────────────────────────────────────┐
│ Place Style On Codes above, and Style Off Codes below.            │
└──────────────────────────────────────────────────────────────────┘



Press Exit when done                    Doc 1 Pg 1 Ln 1i Pos 1i
{          ▲   ▲   ▲    ▲   ▲   ▲      ▲  ▲ ▲   }  ▲   ▲
[Comment]
```

Fig. 12.3.
The Paired Codes screen.

8. Enter the formatting codes that should appear before the text.

 For your example, press Bold (F6) and Underline (F8).

9. Press ↓ to move beyond the comment.

10. Enter the ending format codes.

 For your example, press Bold (F6) and Underline (F8).

 Note that your codes appear in the Reveal Codes half of the screen.

11. Press Exit (F7) to return to the Styles: Edit menu.

12. Select **Enter** (**5**).

 The following menu appears:

 Enter: 1 Hrt; 2 Off; 3 Off/On: 0

13. Select the effect pressing Enter has with this style.

 This selection controls how you turn off the style.

 For your example, select Off (**2**). When you press Enter, you turn off the style.

14. Press Exit (F7) twice to return to your document.

Turning Off a Paired Style

Steps 12 and 13 in the preceding procedure specify the effect pressing Enter has on your style and how you turn off a paired style. Because you will mainly use Emphasized style on text that does not contain any hard returns, you can use Enter to turn off the style. Use this style for chapter titles and section headings. Note that a hard return is not inserted; pressing Enter simply turns off the style, and your cursor stays where it is. If you want a blank line following the heading, insert a hard return in the style itself, after the comment box.

For other types of formatting, you can make other selections. For instance, if you plan to format longer sections of text, you do not want to turn off the style when you press Enter. Instead, you can select **Hrt** (**1**) for this option. Pressing Enter simply inserts new lines, and the style remains in effect until you turn it off. To turn off the style, press Style (Alt-F8) and select Off (**2**). Use this method for parallel columns and tables.

If you want to format a series of paragraphs, use Off/On (**3**). With this selection, pressing Enter turns off and then immediately turns on the style. Use this option when you need to format a series of similar paragraphs or single lines, such as bulleted items or hanging paragraphs.

Inserting Paired Codes with Block

Not all WordPerfect's paired codes can be entered directly into a style definition. Several codes, such as Block Protect, Table of Contents, and Lists, require that Block be on. In the Styles Codes screen, you must press Block (Alt-F4, or F12), move the cursor to the other side of the Comment, and press the key that corresponds to the code you need.

If you want to mark your heading for the first level of the table of contents, you must use Block. To insert paired codes with Block, complete the following steps:

1. Within the Styles Codes screen, press Home, Home, ↑ to move cursor to beginning of style.

2. Press Block (Alt-F4, or F12).

3. Press Home, Home, ↓ to block the entire style.

4. Press Mark Text (Alt-F5).

5. Select ToC (**1**).

6. When prompted for the **ToC Level**, type the level and press Enter.

7. Press Exit (F7) three times to return to your document.

Note that because WordPerfect lets you define a Block in either direction, you could block text with the cursor on either side of the Comment.

Selecting a Style

Once you define a style, you simply select it to use in your document. For instance, when you want to format a heading, use the Emphasized style.

To select a style, complete the following steps:

1. Press Style (Alt-F8).

   The styles you have defined are listed alphabetically by name (see fig. 12.4).

```
Styles

  Name        Type  Description

  Emphasized  Paired bold and underline
  Letterhead  Open    Formats business letters




  1 On; 2 Off; 3 Create; 4 Edit; 5 Delete; 6 Save; 7 Retrieve; 8 Update: 1
```

Fig. 12.4.
The Styles list.

2. Use the cursor keys to highlight the style you want.

   For your example, highlight Emphasized.

   You can use PgUp (or the gray minus key) to move the cursor to the first style in the list, or PgDn (or the gray plus key) to move the cursor to the end of the list. Press Home, Home, ↑ to move to the beginning of the list; press Home, Home, ↓ to move to the end of the list.

   If your list contains many styles, you can use Name Search (F2 or N) to move quickly to the style you want. Press Forward Search (F2) and type the name of the style. When the cursor is positioned on the name, press Enter.

3. Select **On** (**1**).

   You return to your document. Remember that the style you select affects only the text after the cursor.

4. Type your heading and press Enter.

   For instance, type *Chapter 1* and press Enter. Note your text is both bold and underlined.

This style turns off automatically when you press Enter. If the style does not turn off automatically, press Style (Alt-F8) and select Off (**2**) to turn off the style.

Viewing a Style with Reveal Codes

To confirm that you inserted the style code, press Reveal Codes (Alt-F3, or F11).
You should see a **[Style On:]** code with the style name after the colon. Move your
cursor to the **[Style On:]** code; it expands to display all the formatting codes that
the style contains. If you ever forget what a style does, you can use Reveal Codes
(Alt-F3, or F11) to view the style, instead of returning to the style menu to read the
style description.

Applying Styles to Existing Text

Frequently, you do not make the final decisions about how a document should be
formatted until you have already typed a draft. You therefore need to be able to
apply styles to text you have already typed. Use Block (Alt-F4, or F12) to apply styles
to existing text.

To use a paired style with block, complete the following steps:

1. Place the cursor at one end of the block you want to define.

2. Press Block (Alt-F4, or F12).

3. Highlight the block.

4. Press Style (Alt-F8).

5. Use the cursor keys to highlight the style you want.

6. Select **On (1)**.

You return to your document, and the block is formatted with the style you selected.

Creating a Style by Example

WordPerfect does not have a true style-by-example feature, but you can use Block to
create a new style from existing codes in your document:

1. Press Reveal Codes (Alt-F3, or F11).

2. Move your cursor to the formatting codes in the document you wish to
    copy.

3. Press Block (Alt-F4, or F12).

4. Highlight the codes you want to copy.

5. Press Style (Alt-F8).

6. Select **Create (3)**.

The codes become part of a style. Then simply, name the style, enter a style
definition, and decide how the style should be turned off.

Editing a Style

One of the best features of Style is the capability to change easily the formatting codes in a document. Remember that you cannot search for specific styles, so you cannot search for one style and replace it with another style. Instead, redefine the current document style. For example, if you decide headings should be only bold, not bold and underlined, you can change the style.

To edit a style definition, complete the following steps:

1. Press Style (Alt-F8).

   The Styles list appears.

2. Use the cursor keys to highlight the style you want to change.

   For instance, highlight Emphasized.

3. Select **Edit** (4).

   The Styles: Edit screen appears.

4. Select the item you want to change and make any changes.

   For instance, select Codes (4) and delete the Underline codes.

5. Press Exit (F7) twice (or three times if you edited Codes) to return to your document.

CAUTION: You can edit a style definition name and description any time. While you should update the description whenever you modify the style, do not change the style's name after you use it. WordPerfect does not maintain a dynamic link between the name in the style list and style codes in the document. If you change the name of a style you used, you cannot reformat sections to which the style had been assigned.

Changing Styles

Sometimes it is necessary to employ a different style in place of the one you originally chose. Although you cannot search for exact style codes, you can search for three generic style codes: **[Style On]**, **[Style Off]**, and **[Open Style]**. You can search for these codes to find the styles you want to change.

Suppose you use three style definitions for section headers called First, Second, Third. You decide to simplify the appearance of your paper by eliminating the second-level headers. Some will become first-level headers; the rest will become third-level headers. You can search for the generic style code and delete it. Then you can block the text and reassign it to another style.

To change a style code, complete the following steps:

1. Press Forward Search (F2).

2. Press Style (Alt-F8).

   The following menu appears:

   1 Style **On**; **2** Style **Off**; **3** Open Style: **0**

3. Press the style code you want.

   For instance, select Style **On** (**1**).

4. Press Forward Search (F2).

5. When you locate the text you want to change, delete the style code.

   For instance, delete the **[Style On:Second]** code.

6. Press Block (Alt-F4, or F12).

7. Highlight the text you want to reassign.

8. Press Style (Alt-F8).

9. Use the cursor keys to highlight the new style.

10. Select **On** (**1**).

Deleting Styles from a Document

In addition to changing the style for a section of text, you may want to delete the style code. To delete an open style, simply delete the **[Open Style]** code. To delete a paired style, delete either the **[Style On]** or the **[Style Off]** code. A quick way to delete style codes is to use Replace (Alt-F2) to replace the style code with nothing.

To delete a style code from a document using Replace, complete the following:

1. Press Reveal Codes (Alt-F3, or F11).

2. Press Replace (Alt-F2).

3. When prompted w/Confirm (Y/N) No, press Y.

4. Press Style (Alt-F8) and select one of the generic codes for which you want to search.

5. Press Forward Search (F2).

6. When prompted Replace with, press Forward Search (F2) to replace the code with nothing.

7. When you stop on a code, press Y to delete the code.

If you used several different styles in a long document, searching for all the instances of a particular style may be very time-consuming. In this case, leave the style codes in the document and redefine the style so that it does nothing. While this method is not a "clean" solution, you can use this method to reformat a complex document quickly.

Saving Styles with a Document

When you create a style, the style definition becomes part of the document you are currently editing. If you exit the document without saving, or if your power goes off and you lose the document, your style definition is lost also. If you are working in Doc 1, switch to Doc 2, and call up your style list, you may not necessarily see the same style list that you saw in Doc 1.

When you save a document, the styles that you defined on the Styles list are saved as part of the document header, whether or not you used any of the styles to format your text.

Each time you use a style in your document, the information in the style definition is repeated. (Styles were not invented to save disk space.) While this design may seem wasteful, it has two advantages: WordPerfect can format the document on-screen quickly, without having to look up the information in a table, and if you inadvertently delete a style definition that is active in your document, your text still formats correctly.

Deleting a Style from the Style List

Because all the styles are saved with a document regardless of whether you used the styles in the document, you should delete any unused style definitions from the list. Your original formatting intentions are clearer to someone else (or to you six months later) if extraneous style definitions are not present to confuse things.

To delete a style definition from the list, complete the following steps:

1. Press Style (Alt-F8).

    The Styles list appears.

2. Use the cursor keys to highlight the style you want to delete.

3. Select **Delete** (**5**).

CAUTION: Do not delete style definitions you used in the document.

Even though your document's format is retained if you delete a style you have used in your document, you should not delete active style definitions. The style definition is your key to controlling and changing the format of your document. If you delete the definition, you may forget that you used a style by that name. Several things can go wrong if you delete an active style.

First, if you change the format of the document (either with styles or manually inserted codes), you may find that the document does not reformat as expected because portions of the document are controlled by the style definition you forgot.

If you forget you used a style, you may assign a different style to the same text inadvertently. If the two styles contain contradictory codes, the results are unpredictable.

Also, you may reformat the document unwittingly, by retrieving a style library with a style of the same name. Normally, if a style is already defined, WordPerfect warns you if you try to retrieve a style library with a style definition by the same name, and you can retrieve only the styles that are not defined in the current document.

Creating a Style Library

WordPerfect's Style feature is designed so that you can use styles not only in the document in which you create them but also in other WordPerfect documents.

To use styles in more than one document, you must save the style to a style library. A style library file is a WordPerfect document that consists solely of style definitions. You can make as many style libraries as you want, and each style library can contain as many styles as you want. Each style must have a unique name within the style library, but you can name styles the same name if they are located in different libraries.

Beginners may find it easier to keep all their style definitions in one library file; you can specify a default style library that WordPerfect uses when you press Style (Alt-F8).

More advanced users can create several style libraries; with several libraries, you simply retrieve the appropriate library and select the style.

CAUTION: If you have multiple style libraries, designating a default style library may be more a hindrance than a help because you cannot clear the default style definitions from your screen. When you retrieve a style library, style definitions with different names and definitions in the default library are added to the list. (Style definitions with the same name can override current styles if you choose.) All of these style definitions are saved with the document whether you use them or not.

Using Multiple Style Libraries

Multiple style libraries are an extraordinarily powerful tool for writers who need to format the same material differently for different purposes. If each style library contains a set of style definitions whose name and function correspond to the style definitions of your other style libraries, you can reformat your work instantaneously by retrieving a different style library.

For example, an aspiring writer has three different style libraries for three different magazine formats. Each library uses identical names for each of the style definitions the library contains. The writer formats the first version of an article according to his default style library file. When the article is rejected by his first-choice magazine, the writer retrieves the document, uses the Styles menu to retrieve the style library for his second-choice magazine, and prints the second version. When that version is returned to him, he formats it with the style library for his third-choice magazine.

Setting the Default Style Library File

To manage your styles, you can designate one of your style library files as your default style list. You do not need to choose a default list, but you can manage your styles more easily if you do. Unless you plan to use multiple style library files, you should designate a default style library file.

You specify the default style using Setup (Shift-F1), selecting Location of Auxiliary Files (7), and entering a file name for Style Library File (6). (See Chapter 18 for additional information on specifying the Location of Auxiliary Files.) Figure 12.5 shows a default style library file.

Fig. 12.5.
Selecting the default style library file.

```
Setup: Location of Auxiliary Files

     1 - Backup Directory              C:\BACKUP

     2 - Hyphenation Module(s)         C:\LEX

     3 - Keyboard/Macro Files          C:\MACROS

     4 - Main Dictionary(s)            C:\LEX

     5 - Printer Files                 C:\PRINTER

     6 - Style Library Filename        C:\STYLES\LIBRARY.STY

     7 - Supplementary Dictionary(s)   C:\LEX

     8 - Thesaurus                     C:\LEX
```

LIBRARY.STY is the library supplied by Wordperfect (see "Using LIBRARY.STY"). You can use this library or create your own.

Choose a name that you won't confuse with other documents and file names. Also, be sure that you enter a file name, not a subdirectory (note that all other entries in this menu are subdirectories). If you specify a subdirectory, you encounter the following error messages when you attempt to use the Style feature: ERROR: File is locked--C:\STYLES. Although you can enter a file name that does not exist, you encounter the following error messages later when you press Style (Alt-F8): ERROR: File not found--C:\STYLES\MASTER.LST.

Be sure to specify the path also. If you do not specify the path, WordPerfect adds the current directory as the path. For example, if you are working in the C:\LETTERS directory and enter MASTER.STY for the name of your style library file, WordPerfect adds the current path, making the file name C:\LETTERS\MASTER.STY.

TIP: To manage your style library files, keep them in a separate directory.

Saving Style Definitions in a Style Library

If you create styles that you plan to use in other documents, you need to save the styles to the style library. Then you can use the styles to format other documents.

To save a style definition to a style library, complete the following steps:

1. Create the style.

2. Select Save (6).

    You are prompted for Filename:

3. Type the path name and the file name and press Enter.

4. Press Exit (F7) to return to your document.

You can use any valid file name you like. If you want to save the styles definitions to your default style library, you must type its name and path; WordPerfect does not automatically save your definitions to the default file. If you do not include the path, WordPerfect saves the style library file in your current working directory.

CAUTION: Always specify the path name. If you save your style to the current directory, you may forget or lose the style library file, create multiple versions of the style library by mistake, and even confuse the library file with a regular WordPerfect document.

Suppose you set the default style library file as C:\STYLES\MASTER.STY. As you work on a report in the C:\REPORTS directory, you retrieve and modify a style from the MASTER.STY style library. Because you made changes, you want to save your changes back to your original file (C:\STYLES\MASTER.STY). If you type MASTER.STY and do not include the path (C:\STYLES\), WordPerfect saves your style as a file called MASTER.STY in your C:\REPORTS directory.

When you use the style again, WordPerfect loads the default style library; this library contains the old, unmodified file. You now have two MASTER.STY files. If you work and save the style file in other directories, you can end up with even more copies of the same file. Then, determining which style library files to keep and which to discard can be quite a task.

To avoid duplicate copies of the same style file, consider the following options:

- Use a macro to save your style definition changes. The macro can remember to use the full path name even if you won't.

- Include the date in the style description. You then can tell from looking at your file list if something is wrong.

Note that you save all the style definitions on the style list to the file you specify, whether they are active in your current document or not.

TIP: You can also save your style definitions by pressing Save (F10) at the Styles menu and entering the name of the file.

CAUTION: Remember that WordPerfect treats library files like document files. Don't name styles with the name of a document, or you easily can lose that document when you save the style file. Saving your style definitions to a separate file has nothing to do with saving the current document.

Retrieving a Style Library

Once you create and save a style library file, you can use the styles from the file in your documents. If you have a default style library, it appears when you press style (Alt-F8); if you don't have a default style library, the style list is blank (unless your current document already contains styles). You can select a style from this list or retrieve another style library file. For instance, although your default library style file is C:\STYLES\LIBRARY.STY, you may want to use another library style file called C:\STYLES\REPORT.STY.

To retrieve another style library file, complete the following steps:

1. Press Style (Alt-F8).

   The style list from the default library style appears.

2. Select **Retrieve** (7).

3. Type the path name and file name of the style library file and press Enter.

   If you have defined styles in your current document, you are prompted:

   Styles already exist, Replace? (Y/N) No

4. Press *Y* to read in all the style definitions, overwriting the ones already in your document

   or

Press *N* to read in only the style definitions with different names from the ones in your document.

5. Press Exit (F7) to return to your document.

Remember that only the style definitions on-screen (and in the current document, if you are in one) are affected by your choice. If you have not yet used any styles in a document, you can safely overwrite the default styles.

Also, note that you retrieve only a *copy* of the style library file. If you modify any of the styles and want to save the new version, you must save the style definitions to the style library again.

Updating Styles in Your Document

You can use the style library to update styles in your documents. For instance, say you create a report with REPORT.STY. While working on another report, you change the headings and save the style. Use Update to format your first document with the new style from the file library.

Update copies the styles from the default library to the document on-screen. Update works in one direction only, from the default style library to the document on-screen. Use Update to reformat easily the current document if you changed your default style master library.

Update is like using Retrieve, but when you use Retrieve, you must designate the name of the style library file you wish to use. Update always uses the default library file. Also, Retrieve warns you if the retrieved file will overwrite style definitions in the current file; if you want, you can retrieve only the styles with different names. Update assumes that you want to overwrite your current styles with the ones in your default style library , so you are not warned about duplicate style names. And finally, Update is much faster and easier to use than Retrieve and requires considerably fewer keystrokes.

To update your document with the current style in the library file, complete the following steps:

1. Retrieve the document.

2. Press Style (Alt-F8).

3. Select Update (**8**).

4. Press Exit (F7) to return to your document.

5. Save your document.

TIP: If you are unsure of what styles your default style library file contains, switch to Doc 2, clear your screen (if you have a document loaded), and press Style (Alt-F8). You see a list of the style definitions in your default style list.

TIP: Save your document before using either the Retrieve or Update command. Then look your document over; you may want to print a few pages. If your document is not formatted the way you expect, exit the document without saving it and Retrieve the document again.

Deleting a Style from the Style Library

To delete a style definition from the current document, press Style (Alt-F8), highlight the name of the style, and select **Delete** (**5**); the style is deleted only from the list saved with the document. Your style library file is not affected.

When you delete a style, you do not delete the style from the master style list unless you use **Save** (**6**) and specify the same master style file name.

Maintaining Style Libraries

To manage your library file, consider the following tips:

- Choose a file name extension such as .STY or .WPS for your style library files, and use the extension consistently. Do not use that extension with any other files. With a unique extension, you are unlikely to lose your library files or to overwrite them with regular WordPerfect documents.

- Keep all your style library files in the same directory and make a backup of that directory whenever you update one of your style libraries.

- Keep track of the styles in each library file. One easy way to keep your style lists current is to do a print screen of the style list in each library whenever you edit the style; keep the printouts together in a notebook.

- Make the style descriptions as detailed as possible so that you (or your colleagues) do not have to study the codes to figure out what the style does.

- Include the date in the style definition so you can tell at a glance when the style was last revised.

- Get rid of outdated style definitions from your library files, especially from your primary library file. Your master library file does not need to contain a copy of every style you have ever used in a document. Remember that style definitions are stored in the document in which they were defined. The master library files should include only the styles you might use for future documents.

- Delete any unused style definitions from your document, but do not delete any active styles from your document.

Reviewing Sample Style Libraries

WordPerfect supplies LIBRARY.STY, which you may use; or you can use the sample libraries contained in this chapter; or you can create your own personalized style library.

Using LIBRARY.STY

WordPerfect's sample style library, LIBRARY.STY, is found on the Conversion disk. To use this style library, copy the file to your style directory. LIBRARY.STY includes the following predefined styles:

Bibliogrphy	Paired	Bibliography
Heading	Paired	Chapter Heading
Right Par	Paired	Right-Aligned Paragraph Numbers
Subheading	Paired	Subheading

Bibliography style creates hanging paragraphs often used in bibliographies. You don't have to press Indent (F4) and Margin Release (Shift-Tab) for each entry. The hard returns included in the definition create double spacing. This style is an Off/On paired style.

Heading style marks the text you enter for level one in the table of contents; the text is centered, bold, and large. The Hard Page code forces a new page.

Right Par style creates paragraph numbers right-aligned. The two hard returns separate the paragraph wiith a blank line. This style is defined as an Off/On Style.

Subheading style makes the text bold, marks the text for level two in the table of contents, and numbers the paragraph. This style is defined so that pressing Enter turns off the style.

Investigating Another Style Library

This chapter includes some style libraries that you can use as models when designing your own style library. Keep in mind that you can change any of the attributes to match your needs.

Dissertation Chapter Style

If you must write a dissertation, check with your academic department for precise requirements, then use or alter this dissertation style to use on your dissertation.

Many formatting requirements are needed to make your dissertation easier to read in this medium. For this reason, footnotes (printed at the bottom of each page) are preferable to endnotes (printed at the end of the chapter or at the end of the dissertation). Margins must be generous and uniform to ensure that nothing is lost when the dissertation is copied.

This style turns off Right Justification, turns on Widow/Orphan Protection, and selects Courier 10 pitch (PC-8) as the base font.

The paragraph numbering style definition code customizes the paragraph numbering to eliminate trailing periods. The new footnote number code ensures that the footnote numbers begin at 1 even if chapters are combined in a Master Document. The author has included an underline definition code to keep spaces from being underlined in book titles.

The [**Ln Spacing:2**] code sets double spacing. Top, bottom, and right margins are set at 1″ inch; the left margin is 1.5″ to allow for binding. Page numbers print in the upper right corner, except for the first page of each chapter. The [**Suppress:PG BC**] code causes the page number to print at the bottom center on the first page of every chapter.

An Advance Down code causes the printer to advance down 2.5 inches on the first page of the chapter. The word *CHAPTER* is followed by a first-level paragraph number code, all within the Center codes. When you combine your files, the paragraph number will indicate the number of the chapter.

On the next line, your chapter title is centered, underlined, and marked for the first level of the table of contents. (Note that the underline codes are outside the table of contents codes so that the chapter titles will not be underlined in the table of contents.) The final Advance Down code causes the printer to advance 3/4 inches before the text begins.

Figure 12.6 shows the Reveal Codes for Dissertation Chapter style.

Fig. 12.6.
Dissertation Chapter style.

```
                                CHAPTER I



  ┌────────────────────────────────────────────────────────────┐
  │ Place Style On Codes above, and Style Off Codes below.      │
  └────────────────────────────────────────────────────────────┘




Press Exit when done                    Doc 2 Pg 1 Ln 3.58" Pos 4.5"
▲    {   ▲   ▲   ▲   ▲   ▲   ▲   ▲   ▲   ▲   ▲   }   ▲   ▲
[Force:Odd][Font:Courier 10 pitch (PC-8)][Just Off][W/O On][L/R Mar:1.5",1"][Ln
Spacing:2][T/B Mar:1",5"][Pg Numbering:Top Right][Suppress:Pg BC][Undrln:][Par N
um Def][Ftn Opt][New Ftn Num:1][AdvToLn:2.5"][Cntr]CHAPTER [Par Num:1][C/A/Flrt]
[HRt]
[UND][Mark:ToC,1][Comment][End Mark:ToC,1][und][Cntr][C/A/Flrt][AdvDn:0.75"]█
```

While working with drafts, do not worry about setting the initial page or footnote number for each chapter. If you want the numbering to be consecutive, simply combine the chapters into one large file or use the Master Document feature (see Chapter 23).

TIP: If you plan to use a different printer for the final copy of your dissertation, include all the formatting codes that could affect your document, even if they duplicate your own default settings. Although you could include these codes as Document Initial Codes instead, you should include these codes in your style definition so that you can change the format of all your chapters at once if necessary.

Secondary Chapter Heading Style

This style automatically numbers and marks the heading for the second level of the table of contents. (Because the paragraph number code is included between the table of contents codes, the number carries over to the table of contents.) To allow two blank lines between the heading and text, Line Spacing is set for single-spacing at the beginning and back to double-spacing at the end.

A Conditional End of Page Code is set to keep the next five lines together on a page. Because the secondary header style includes two blank lines after the header, the **[Cndl EOP:5]** code guarantees that at least two lines of text remain on the same page as the secondary header.

Figure 12.7 shows the Reveal Codes used to create Secondary Chapter Heading style.

Fig. 12.7.

*Secondary Chapter
Heading style.*

```
                                            A.
        ┌─────────────────────────────────────────────────────────────┐
        │ Place Style On Codes above, and Style Off Codes below.        │
        └─────────────────────────────────────────────────────────────┘



    Press Exit when done                   Doc 2 Pg 1 Ln 1.16" Pos 1"
    [  ▲    ▲    ▲    ▲    ▲    ▲    ▲    ▲    ▲    ▲    }    ▲    ▲ ]
    [Ln Spacing:1][Cndl EOP:5][HRt]
    [Mark:ToC,2][Cntr][Par Num:2] [Comment][End Mark:ToC,2][C/A/Flrt][HRt]
    [HRt]
    [HRt]
    [Ln Spacing:2]
```

Quotation Style

Use the quotation style to set off quotations. This style is very simple: single-spacing, italics, and Left-Right Indent. Figure 12.8 shows the Reveal Codes for this style.

```
┌─────────────────────────────────────────────────────────────┐
│ Place Style On Codes above, and Style Off Codes below.       │
│                                                              │
│                                                              │
│                                                              │
│                                                              │
│ Press Exit when done              Doc 1 Pg 1 Ln 1.16i Pos 1i │
│ ▲     ▲     ▲    ▲    ▲    ▲    ▲    ▲   ▲ ▲   }   ▲  ▲  ▲   │
│ [Ln Spacing:1][ITALC][→Indent][Comment][italc][HRt]          │
│ [Ln Spacing:2]▌                                              │
└─────────────────────────────────────────────────────────────┘
```

Fig. 12.8.
Quotation style.

The style is defined as an Off/On style because Left-Right Indent codes only affect single paragraphs.

TIP: If you often quote passages of several paragraphs, or poetry (in which each verse ends with a Hard Return), use an extended paired style (Enter = HRt) instead. Substitute a margin change for the Indent code.

Footnotes use the same margins as the text to which they are attached. If you use a margin change in embedded quotations, you also need a margin change in each footnote attached to a quotation.

French Style

If your writing requires you to mix languages in the same document, use a language code that tells WordPerfect which dictionary, thesaurus, and hyphenation modules to use (see Chapter 7). By including the language codes in a paired style, WordPerfect automatically switches to the new language when you turn on the style, and back to English (or another language) when you turn off the style. Review figure 12.9 for the Reveal Codes in this style.

In this example, when you press Enter, the style is turned off. You also could define the style as an extended pair style. If you write entire documents in different languages, you could define an open style containing the appropriate language code for each.

TIP: If you tend to use foreign languages primarily in quotations, combine the language styles with your quotation style.

Fig. 12.9.
French style.

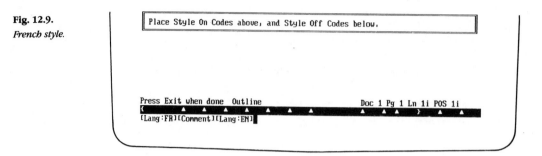

Fig. 12.9.
French style.

Parallel Columns Style

Use column formats for both open and paired styles. If you typically use columns for an entire document, use an open style to turn on columns. If you use columns for only sections of your documents, use a paired style. With a paired style, you can turn on and off the style as needed.

A **[Columns On]** code affects only the text after the cursor position until a **[Column Off]** code is encountered. If you try to write two pages of columns beginning on page 10 of a 50-page document, you must insert both the **[Columns On]** code and the **[Columns Off]** before you begin to type. If not, the previously typed text reformats into columns (whether you wanted columns or not), and editing becomes excruciatingly slow. Using a paired style to set up your columns eliminates this problem.

Figure 12.10 shows the Reveal Codes used to create Parallel Columns style.

Fig. 12.10.
Parallel Columns style.

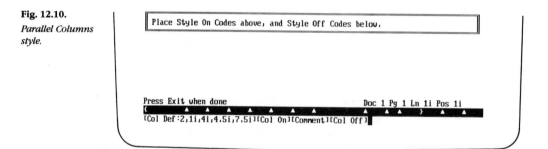

Bullet Style

If you use bullets to set off text in your writing, you can create a bullet style. An Off/On style works well for paragraphs with bullets. You can include the paragraph number in the style or use a specific character. For instance, this example uses a block (ASCII character 254) for the bullet. (You might want to review a list of available ASCII characters.)

Figure 12.11 shows the Reveal Codes for Bullet style.

```
■
┌─────────────────────────────────────────────────────────────────┐
│ Place Style On Codes above, and Style Off Codes below.          │
└─────────────────────────────────────────────────────────────────┘




Press Exit when done                        Doc 1 Pg 1 Ln 1i Pos 1.1i
{      ▲    ▲    ▲    ▲    ▲    ▲           ▲   ▲ ▲   }    ▲    ▲
■[→Indent][Comment][HRt]
```

Fig. 12.11.
Bullet style.

TIP: If you use automatic paragraph numbering, use a macro to switch to the bullet style of paragraph numbering, to adjust the amount of indentation if desired, and to turn on the style. (If you change the amount of indentation, be sure to change it back after you turn off the Bullet style.)

Table Style

Table style illustrates how you can combine text and formatting codes to create a template for math tables. Note that the math definition and **[Math On]** and **[Math Off]** codes are incorporated into the style definition.

Regular Tabs have been set two inches apart. You do not need to define the tabs as decimal tabs because all tabs are treated as decimal tabs when Math is on. Enter any text (for instance, table headings) before the **[Math Def]** code because WordPerfect treats some letters as math symbols when Math is on. You can set up the Math Definition with a calculation column. Figure 12.12 shows the Reveal Codes for Table style.

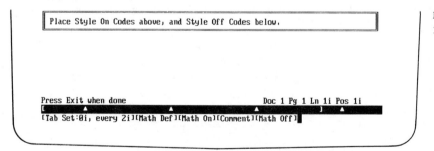

```
┌─────────────────────────────────────────────────────────────────┐
│ Place Style On Codes above, and Style Off Codes below.          │
└─────────────────────────────────────────────────────────────────┘




Press Exit when done                        Doc 1 Pg 1 Ln 1i Pos 1i
[          ▲              ▲              ▲              ]    ▲
[Tab Set:0i, every 2i][Math Def][Math On][Comment][Math Off]
```

Fig. 12.12.
Table style.

To use the style, use tabs to move to columns and enter data. Press Enter to start a new line. When you finish entering data, you can use a simple macro to calculate the results.

Using Macros with Styles

Although using the Style feature may replace many of your formatting macros, you still can use macros with styles. For instance, you can use macros to turn on or off a style with a minimum of keystrokes.

To create a macro to turn on a style, complete the following:

1. Press Macro Define (Ctrl-F10).

2. Press the keys that you want to use to invoke macro.

   For instance, press Alt-O.

3. Type a description of the macro and press Enter.

   For instance, type *turn on style* and press Enter.

4. Press Style (Alt-F8).

5. Press Forward Search (F2).

6. Type the name of the style.

7. Press Enter.

8. Select **On (1)** to turn on the style.

9. Press Macro Define (Ctrl-F10).

To invoke the style, just press Alt-O.

Note that you must use Name Search for the macro to move directly to the style name you want. If you use the cursor keys to move the cursor bar to a particular style name, the macro calls up a different style if you add or delete style definitions from your list.

You can use this technique to create macros to turn on each of the styles you use frequently, especially the paired styles that you use repeatedly in the same document. (You probably don't need macros for open styles because you use open styles only once in each document.)

If a style should take effect at the beginning of the document, you can press Home, Home, ↑ as part of the macro. Adding these keystrokes to the macro lets you call up the style from anywhere in the document, without worrying about the cursor position.

In addition to using a macro to turn on a style, you can create a macro that turns off any paired style:

1. Press Macro Define (Ctrl-F10).

2. Press the key combination that you will use to invoke this macro.

   For instance, press Alt-F.

3. Type a description of the macro and press Enter.

   For instance, type *turn off style* and press Enter.

4. Press Style (Alt-F8).

5. Select Off (**2**).

6. Press Macro Define (Ctrl-F10).

Assessing Style Limitations

While you will find that using styles can simplify formatting, you should note that there are limitations:

- Not all WordPerfect features (such as graphics) can be used in a style, and you cannot set document specifications for all WordPerfect features.

- You cannot copy a style definition to use as a model for another style.

- You can search for only generic style codes; you cannot search and replace specific style definitions. You cannot search for an individual code or text that is part of the style definition.

- If you edit a document and then retrieve another document into the first, you lose the styles in the second document. (In most cases, you would want the styles of the first document to control the formatting.)

- You cannot convert the style definitions to regular WordPerfect codes, and you cannot purge documents of unused style definitions. You can delete style codes only one by one.

WP
5 Summary

WordPerfect's styles are well worth the effort to learn to use. With styles you can accomplish many tasks that were impossible to do in previous versions of WordPerfect:

- Create an open style to format an entire document

- Create a paired style to format sections of the text of a document

- Make formatting revisions by simply changing the style

- Create a library of styles to use on documents

- Use style libraries to simplify formatting and revision, to maintain consistent formatting on a set of documents, and to share styles with other users

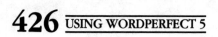

13

Assembling Documents with Merge

*An author of two books on WordPerfect, **Forest Lin** uses his knowledge of the program to write about the Merge function in version 5.* ∎

T he Merge feature, frequently referred to as mail merge, is probably WordPerfect's most versatile tool to increase office productivity. The Merge feature has many functions that allow you to set up a system in which WordPerfect does most of the routine steps normally requiring human intervention.

Taking advantage of the Merge features can make the cumbersome job of assembling a complex document relatively easy. For example, names and addresses can be inserted in the proper places in a letter for personalized mass mailing. Different boilerplates can be put together to form a completed document. Math codes can be placed in a document and WordPerfect can be instructed to calculate the merged numbers. A menu system can be created, and an inexperienced user prompted to use it.

Merge is a complicated topic, its complexity rivaled only by the new and much expanded Macro feature. To master Merge, you need time and dedication. You can use more than a dozen codes to maneuver different situations. Together, these codes constitute an elementary programming language. If you can master this feature, however, you will be amply rewarded because Merge does much of the work for you.

This chapter first introduces the basic concepts and terms of Merge and demonstrates the three kinds of merge: merging to the keyboard, merging two files, and merging to the printer. Then you learn about the different merge codes and how to apply them to various concrete situations.

Understanding the Basics of Merging

A merging operation requires a primary file, often in combination with a secondary file. A secondary file contains records, which in turn are comprised of fields. You need to understand these terms before you can explore the mechanism of merging.

A *primary file* is the main document in a merging operation. The primary file contains two items: the fixed text and the merge codes implanted where variable items are to enter the fixed text. When a merge is completed, the codes are replaced with entries from the keyboard or a secondary merge file. The document is thus completed with a minimum of human effort.

The most typical and timesaving merge requires a *secondary merge file* that contains related variable data, such as an address list. The address list includes names, streets, states, and ZIP codes. These items then enter the primary file in the manner determined by the matching codes in both the primary and secondary files.

A secondary merge file is divided into records, and each record is divided into fields. Using the address list as an example, all the information related to one person is a *record*; the separate items, such as name, street, and ZIP code, are *fields*.

Fields, records, and other items are controlled by merge codes. These codes have to be placed in the right places in the right order for a merge to be successful.

Merging from the Keyboard

The simplest form of merge is the keyboard merge. It can serve as our first example of an actual merge. With a minimum of investment, however, you should not expect a great deal of return: the time saved in the keyboard merge is minimal.

To do a keyboard merge, you need only a primary file with text and a few merge codes. Create a primary file for the memo in figure 13.1 so that you can practice the keyboard merge. Save the file as MEMO.PF, and you are ready to merge.

Fig. 13.1.

A sample primary file with merge codes.

```
                           Office Memo

           To : ^C
         From : ^C
      Subject : ^C
         Date : ^D

      Our regular monthly office meeting will be held ^C. Our
      main topic for this month is ^C. Please spend some time
      studying the issue and come with suggestions.
```

Two kinds of merge codes are in this primary file: ^C indicates where an entry from the console or keyboard is placed, and ^D indicates where the current date is displayed. To implant these codes, hold down Ctrl and type an appropriate letter. Do not use the caret; WordPerfect does not recognize the caret as a merge code when placed at the beginning of a letter. If you do not remember whether you entered a code in your primary file as Ctrl-C or caret-C, try to erase the code. If it is the former (Ctrl-C), it is erased as one unit.

Follow these steps to begin a keyboard merge:

1. Press Merge/Sort (Ctrl-F9).

2. Select **Merge (1)**.

3. Type *MEMO.PF* as the primary file and press Enter.

4. Press Enter again to indicate no secondary file.

The primary file appears on-screen, and the cursor rests at the location of the first ^C code, which has disappeared. You now can enter the first line (see fig. 13.2). Press Merge R (F9) to continue; do not press Enter unless you mean to enter a hard return. The cursor goes to the second ^C code in order for you to type another line.

```
                    Office Memo

     To : All Professional Personnel
   From : The President
Subject : Monthly Office meeting
   Date : March 25, 1988

Our regular monthly office meeting will be held 3:00 PM,
Thursday, March 31. Our main topic for this month is the
company's sagging profit. Please spend some time studying
the issue and come with suggestions.
```

Fig. 13.2.
A sample primary file with merge codes replaced with text.

When the merging process reaches the ^D code, it is replaced automatically with the default text of the current date. If you have a battery-backed clock/calendar or have entered the correct date at the beginning of each session, the display shows the correct date; otherwise, an incorrect date may appear.

When a merge is in progress, WordPerfect displays the message * Merging * on the status line. When you enter the last item and press Merge R another time, the message disappears. The merge is now complete (see fig. 13.2). The document then can be saved and/or printed.

Merging Text Files

A file merge combines two existing files—a primary and a secondary file. Before you can execute such a merge, these files must exist. You can create either file first, but the next example begins with the creation of a secondary file.

Creating a Secondary Merge File

A secondary file consists of records (ending with ^E), which have a number of fields (ending with ^R). The structure must be uniform, or a merge will go awry. Examine carefully the secondary merge file in figure 13.3 and create this file for a practice merge.

Fig. 13.3.

A sample secondary merge file.

```
         John^R
         Wane^R
         1234 Big Bull Street
         Big Sky, MT 94333^R
         718 543-4433^R
         ^E
=================================================================================
         Mumbo Jumbo^R
         Rambo^R
         Soldier of Fortune Corp.
         999 Venture Rd.
         Bravado, MS 22111^R
         ^R
         ^E
=================================================================================
         James^R
         Bondo^R
         Studio 007
         Paramour Production Co.
         1010 Sunrise Boulevard
         Holywart, CA 99999^R
         888 777-0707^R
         ^E
=================================================================================
                                            Doc 2 Pg 1 Ln 1 Pos 10
```

Figure 13.3 has three records, each ending with a ^E code in a separate line and a hard page (indicated by a double line). Each record also has four fields ending with a ^R code and a hard return. First names are in the first fields; last names are in the second fields; and so on. Where no entry exists in a record, such as the fourth field in the second record, just enter ^R. Thus, a field can have no lines or multiple lines, as long as the field ends with ^R and a hard return.

To enter ^R, just press Merge R (F9), or press Ctrl-R followed by Enter. To enter ^E, press Merge Codes (Shift-F9) and press *E*, or press Ctrl-E followed by hard page (Ctrl-Enter). The hard page is new with version 5. Previous versions required a hard return after ^E rather than a hard page. The hard return after the ^E works also with version 5, however.

Merge R and Merge Codes, F9 and Shift-F9 respectively, are used for different purposes when a merge is in progress. You use Merge R to resume a merge after it is halted by a ^C code. Use Merge Codes, sometimes combined with pressing *E*, to terminate a merge in progress.

You can sort a secondary merge file and select certain records from the file. To sort and then select files requires your familiarity with the Sort feature, explained in the next chapter.

Save the secondary file as ADDRESS.SF, or any other name; the SF merely serves as a reminder that the file is a secondary file. Clear the screen so that you are ready to create a primary file.

Creating a Primary File

A *primary file* contains fixed text and certain merge codes. The codes guide WordPerfect to bring in certain items from the secondary merge file and place the items where the codes are implanted. The most commonly used code is the field number code, ^F*n*^. The *n* indicates a field number (or name, as explained later) of each record in the secondary file. For example, if you implant ^F3^ at a certain location in the primary file, you instruct WordPerfect to enter at that particular location the information found in field number 3 (the address in our example) of the secondary file (see fig. 13.4). To create a sample primary file, type the letter in figure 13.4.

```
                          Save America Federation

                                    ^D

   ^F1^ ^F2^
   ^F3^


   Dear Mr. ^F2^:

   The Save America Federation earnestly invites you to a massive
   rally in Washington, D.C., on July 4.

   This rally is intended to rouse America's spirit from the current
   slumber, laxity, and flabbiness, and restore it to its former
   bristle and bluster. We truly believe that the involvement of true
   blue he-men heroes like you will make America number one again.


   Sincerely,


   Ronald George Head,
   Founder
                                           Doc 2 Pg 1 Ln 12 Pos 47
```

Fig. 13.4.
A sample primary file with merge codes.

You can enter ^F*n*^, a field number code, in two ways. The first way is to press Merge Codes (Shift-F9), press *F*, enter a field number at the prompt displayed on the status line, and press Enter. The second way is to press Ctrl-F and press a number and the ending caret (Shift-6 key). Make sure that you enter the field numbers correctly. Each field number must match the appropriate field in the secondary file; otherwise, an incorrect item will be merged. In the example in figure 13.4, if you want the last name to appear at a certain location of the document, you have to enter ^F2^ at that location.

Save this file as INVITE.PF, or any other name; the PF serves as a useful reminder that this is a primary file.

Merging a Primary and a Secondary File

Now that the two necessary files exist, we are ready to merge. Follow these steps:

1. Press Merge/Sort (Ctrl-F9).

2. Select **Merge (1)**.

3. Type *INVITE.PF* as the primary file and press Enter.

4. Type *ADDRESS.SF* as the secondary file and press Enter.

The merge is now complete and three letters have been created because three records are in the secondary file. The screen shows the last completed letter. If you move the cursor to the beginning of the document, you will find the first completed letter (see fig. 13.5).

Fig. 13.5.

The first letter, after the merge.

```
                        Save America Federation

                           March 25, 1988


     John Wane
     1234 Big Bull Street
     Big Sky, MT 94333

     Dear Mr. Wane:

     The Save America Federation earnestly invites you to a massive
     rally in Washington, D.C., on July 4.

     This rally is intended to rouse America's spirit from the current
     slumber, laxity, and flabbiness, and restore it to its former
     bristle and bluster. We truly believe that the involvement of true
     blue he-men heroes like you will make America number one again.

     Sincerely,


     Ronald George Head,
     Founder
                                       Doc 2 Pg 1 Ln 23 Pos 25
```

All the necessary items are filled in, and each letter is separated from the others with a hard page. The letters are ready to print. If you now print the whole document, each letter prints on a separate page.

Naming Fields in a Secondary File

Rather than using field number codes such as ^F2^ in a primary file to reference the fields in a secondary merge file, you may find it easier to remember the fields if you assign names to them. By using names, the likelihood of entering incorrect field numbers into the primary file is reduced.

To use names to designate fields in a secondary file, you must observe certain rules about the special first record you create. The first record must provide a model for WordPerfect to handle the "real" records (see fig. 13.6). The first record also must start with ^N (for Name), followed by the names for each field and ending with a hard page.

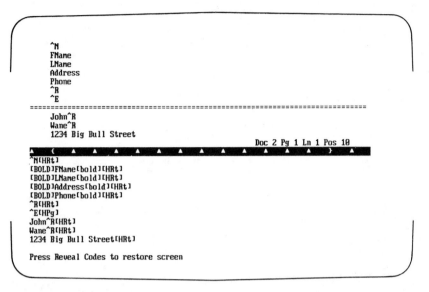

Fig. 13.6.
A sample first record, in Reveal Codes, that provides names for fields.

The last and most important point to remember about the first record is to make sure that each line of the names is surrounded by a set of bold codes, starting with **[Bold]** and ending with **[bold]**, as seen on the Reveal Codes screen. If these names (FName, LName, Address, and Phone) are not in bold or are inadvertently put in bold codes together, WordPerfect recognizes only the first item and enters it in all the fields, regardless of their names, in the primary file.

To bold each field name, do the following:

1. Press Bold (F6).

2. Type a name (FName, for example).

3. Press Bold (F6) again.

You also can type a name and then bold it afterwards. Just move the cursor to one end of the name, press Block (Alt-F4, or F12), move the cursor to the other end of the name, and press Bold.

Once a secondary file's fields are assigned names, these names can be used in a primary file, as shown in figure 13.7. To enter a field name code, such as ^Flname^, in a primary file, you can use either one of the two methods of entering a field number code explained in the "Creating a Primary File" section. The only difference is typing a name instead of a number.

Designing a Secondary Merge File

Before creating a secondary file, you should design it carefully. If you break each record into several fields, the file is more laborious to create, but the benefit is worth the extra trouble because more fields give you more flexibility.

Fig. 13.7.

Field names used in a primary file.

```
                         Save America Federation

                                  ^D

   ^Ffname^ ^Flname^
   ^Faddress^

   Dear Mr. ^Flname^:

   The Save America Federation earnestly invites you to a massive
   rally in Washington, D.C., on July 4.

   This rally is intended to rouse America's spirit from the current
   slumber, laxity, and flabbiness, and restore it to its former
   bristle and bluster. We truly believe that the involvement of true
   blue he-men heroes like you will make America number one again.


   Sincerely,


   Ronald George Head,
   Founder
                                           Doc 2 Pg 1 Ln 1 Pos 10
```

Let's look at an example. In the following record, three separate fields make up the record. Notice that both Jane and John are considered as one entity in the following example:

    Jane and John Wane^R
    1234 Big Bull Street
    Big Sky, MT 94333^R
    718-543-4433^R
    ^E

What if you want to address separately a letter to Jane or John? You could not do so with the previous example. However, by adding more fields to the record, you give yourself more flexibility. The next example has five fields that make up the same record; each name has its own field. Now you can address Jane, John, or both Jane and John, as follows:

    Jane^R
    John^R
    Wane^R
    1234 Big Bull Street
    Big Sky, MT 94333^R
    718 543-4433^R
    ^E

The second example gives you more items that you selectively can put in a primary file. Now you can put the following names (upper or lower case, or a mixture of both) in the letter: "ffname" for female first name, "lname" for last name, "mfname" for male first name. Figure 13.8 illustrates a letter using female names only. If you want to have male names alone, you can enter ^Fmfname^. If you want to put both female and male names together, you can enter ^Fffname^ and ^Fmfname^ ^Flname^.

```
^Fffname^ ^Flname^
^Faddress^


Dear ^Fffname^:
```

Fig. 13.8.
Field names in a letter using female names.

Merging to the Printer

If you have a large job to do, it is easier to merge the primary and the secondary file and send each completed document directly to the printer instead of the screen. To send the document directly to the printer, you need to plant the merge codes ^T^N^P^P at the end of the primary file (see fig. 13.9).

```
                        Save America Federation

                                ^D

^Ffname^ ^Flname^
^Faddress^


Dear Mr. ^Flname^:

The Save America Federation earnestly invites you to a massive
rally in Washington, D.C., on July 4.

This rally is intended to rouse America's spirit from the current
slumber, laxity, and flabbiness, and restore it to its former
bristle and bluster. We truly believe that the involvement of true
blue he-men heroes like you will make America number one again.

Sincerely,


Ronald George Head,
Founder
^T^N^P^P
                                    Doc 2 Pg 1 Ln 24 Pos 18
```

Fig. 13.9.
Merge codes that send a completed document directly to the printer.

These codes give WordPerfect different directives. ^T instructs WordPerfect to send to the printer any text merged up to this point. ^N fetches the next record in the secondary file. ^P is for primary file. If you want to use another primary file, enter it between the two ^P codes, as in ^Pfile2.pf^P. If the same primary file is to be used again and again, enter nothing between the two codes.

If you merge the new primary file to the secondary file, your computer may freeze while the screen displays the * Merging * message. If your computer freezes, don't panic—you probably forgot to turn on your printer. If you turn on the printer, it will start to print and the screen will return to normal. If you go to the Printer Control screen—Shift-F7, Control Printer (4)—you may see the notation (Merge) in the Job List.

You also can take out the ^T and leave the other merge codes (^N^P^P) in the same place. When you remove the ^T, the merged text is sent to the screen and your computer does not freeze when the printer is off.

The difference between merging files with and without the ^N^P^P codes is that the completed letters in the first merge (without the codes) are separated with hard pages (double lines), but the letters with the codes are not.

Merging to the printer could be the ultimate office automation you can achieve. If you have a fast printer, thousands of personalized mass-mailing letters can be printed without any human intervention. On the other hand, you could save printing costs by printing a master copy without the personal information, making copies, and finally having your printer fill in the missing information. This technique is explained in the section "Using Merge To Fill In Forms."

Using Other Merge Codes

Altogether, you can choose from fourteen merge codes. One of the merge codes, ^R, is accessed by pressing Merge R (F9) when no merge is in progress. You can enter the other codes by pressing Merge Codes (Shift-F9) and the proper letter. The following codes appear on the status line when you press Merge Codes:

  ^C; ^D; ^E; ^F; ^G; ^N; ^O; ^P; ^Q; ^S; ^T; ^U; ^V:

Most of these codes can be entered also by pressing a letter while holding down Ctrl. The only exception is ^V, which requires pressing *V* twice while holding down Ctrl.

So far you have used eight of these codes (^C, ^D, ^E, ^F, ^N, ^P, ^R, and ^T) in the examples. You used ^E and ^R in the secondary file and the rest in different primary files. The other codes are explained and illustrated in the following paragraphs and are used in various simulations in later sections.

^G activates a macro. For example, ^Gxyz^G (or ^Gxyz.wpm^G) runs the macro named XYZ.WPM—the WPM (for WordPerfect macro) is not necessary. The macro does not start immediately when the merging process reaches the location where you have entered the macro; instead, it is activated only after the other merge codes are executed. Of course, the macro must exist for the merge to activate it. If the macro does not exist, an error message (ERROR: File not found-XYZ.WPM) appears for a while, but the merge continues with the other instructions. If you have named a macro by pressing the Alt key during the macro's definition, include the letters in the macro name, such as ^Galtz^G. Later sections provide more details about using macros in primary files.

^O displays a message, which could be one line or a screenful. When a merge reaches the point where the code is located, the message between the ^O codes is displayed at the bottom of the screen. For example, a message might appear like the following:

  ^OEnter your social security number^O

You can put this message in the part of the primary file where you want a user to make an entry. When a merge reaches this point, the message appears on the status line. At this point, the merge can be halted with a ^C code for a response from the keyboard. Without the ^C code to halt temporarily the merge, the message simply flashes and quickly disappears from the screen.

In actual application, ^O usually is combined with ^C. When a merge is halted by ^C, the cursor position varies, depending on where ^C is planted. In the following example, ^C is located after the message following "Name":

   Name: ^OEnter last name first^O^C

The status line displays Enter last name first, and the cursor appears after "Name," which appears at the top of the screen. A user now can read the displayed message and enter the necessary information at the cursor.

On the other hand, the following example shows the placement of ^C within a message:

   ^OEnter a secondary file: ^Slist^C.sf^S^O

The status line displays the message Enter a secondary file: list, and the cursor stays after the message, waiting for you to enter something. If you have secondary files with names like LIST1.SF, LIST2.SF, and LIST3.SF, all you need to do is type a number and press Enter.

The previous example also shows how you can nest certain codes. The nesting must be arranged correctly; if not, WordPerfect refuses to execute the line and displays the error message.

Multiple lines can be entered between ^O codes. You can use multiple lines to create a menu system for your convenience or for that of an inexperienced user. See the following sections for more details.

^Q quits a merge. You can plant ^Q at the location where the merge is to terminate. Some features—Math, for example—cannot operate when a merge is on. By terminating the merge at the right point, you can direct WordPerfect to calculate Math formulas and enter the result in a document. See "Integrating Math, Macro, and Merge Functions" in this chapter for more details.

^U lets you view a merge in progress. (Think of the equivalent French word *vUe* to remind you of the purpose of ^U.) Normally, a file merge operation is not displayed on-screen until it is over. If you place ^U in a primary file, however, you can see what is happening. When the primary file is merged, the screen displays the items brought in from a secondary file, and the text continues to scroll until the merge is completed.

^V lets you transfer merge codes to a document being created by a merge. The new document, with merge codes transferred to it during the merge, then can be used as a primary or secondary file. Figure 13.10 shows an example of a primary file marked with ^V codes.

Notice that a pair of ^V codes flank the ^R and ^E codes in figure 13.10. When this file is merged without a secondary file, the screen displays the whole file, and

Fig. 13.10.

A sample primary file marked with ^V codes.

```
^OName:^O^C^U^R^U
^OAddress:^O^C^U^R^U
^OPhone:^O^C^U^R^U
^U^E
===========================================================================
^U
```

the status line displays the Name: message, prompting you to enter a name. Pressing Merge R (F9) leads to the display of the message inside the next pair of ^O codes. When the process is completed, the file appears as you see it in figure 13.11.

Fig. 13.11.

A sample secondary merge file with merge codes.

```
Sirhan Wilson Damien^R
1666 Pennsylvania Avenue
Pandemonia, Transylvania^R
666 100-1010^R
^E
===========================================================================
```

The transfer mechanism works in the following manner: As the merge progresses, an entry from the keyboard, such as a name, becomes part of the merged file, and all the merge codes disappear except those between a pair of ^V codes. These codes, such as ^E and ^R, are combined with keyboard entries. The merged file now contains necessary codes for other purposes. In our example, the merged file has become a secondary merge file, which in turn can be used to merge with other files.

You can use the ^V method to create efficiently a large secondary file. All you need to do is to define a macro and enter it into the primary file. This macro appends the completed document to an existing file, clears the screen, and starts another merge.

Table 13.1 lists all the merge codes and briefly explains the purpose for each. While the table can serve as a quick reference, the text and examples in this and other sections provide more details for the actual application of the codes.

Applying Merge to Various Situations

The codes explained in the previous section can be combined in many ways to apply to different situations. The following sections demonstrate how you can combine the codes to solve different problems.

Assembling a Document from Boilerplates

A primary file does not have to be combined with a secondary file. You can combine a primary file with entries from the keyboard or with another primary

Table 13.1
Merge Codes

Code	Function
^C	To temporarily halt a merge in order to display a message or to allow an entry from the keyboard
^D	To insert the current date into the merged document
^E	To mark the end of a secondary file record
^Fn^	To indicate a field name or number in a primary file
^G	To activate a macro
^N	To look for the next record to continue the merge in progress (for a primary file)
	To reference a field by name (for a secondary file)
^O	To display menu, prompt, message, or instruction
^P	To activate a primary file
^Q	To quit (terminate) a merge
^R	To mark the end of a field in a secondary file
^S	To activate a secondary file
^T	To send to the printer the merged text
^U	To update (rewrite or view) the screen displaying the merge in progress
^V	To transfer merge codes to a document created by a merge

file, with or without merge codes in it. Without merge codes, a primary file is just a regular file.

By merging a primary file to other primary files, you quickly can assemble a document. As the merge progresses, it pauses at the prearranged places for you to select certain *boilerplates*—existing text files—to enter into the main primary file. The document is assembled when the merge is completed. The whole process is like putting a number of prefab panels together to build a house.

Figure 13.12 shows an example of document assembly made easy. Suppose you write lots of letters and you like to use varied complimentary closings to give your monotonous message a little variety. Type the document in figure 13.12 and save it as LETTER.PF.

This primary file has most fixed items for a letter already in place. Before you can merge the file, however, you need to create another primary file. Type the primary file in figure 13.13 and name it CLOSE (not CLOSE.PF).

Fig. 13.12.
A sample primary file.

```
M^C

^D

Dear M^C:

^U^Pclose^P,


Major Sargent Minor, Jr,
U.S, Army Recruiter
```

Fig. 13.13.
A second sample primary file.

```
^OClosing Options:

        1, Truly yours        4, Best wishes
        2, Sincerely          5, Sincerely yours
        3, Best regards       6, Best of luck

^Pclose^C^P^O
```

Certain codes, such as Tab, are not allowed within a pair of ^O codes because these special codes may interfere with or even abort a merge. One solution is to avoid using such codes to shape a menu display—use the space bar instead. Another solution is to save your merge file in the generic format—press Text In/Out (Ctrl-F5) and select Save Generic (**3**). This extra measure saves a file without the embedded codes.

You still need to create six more primary files. The first is named CLOSE1 and contains only one line of text, "Truly yours"; CLOSE2 stores "Sincerely"; and so on. After you make the additional primary files, you are ready to merge.

When you merge LETTER.PF as the primary file with no secondary file, the skeleton letter appears on-screen. The cursor rests at the first location for you to enter proper information. Press Merge R to continue. When the merging process reaches close, the primary file CLOSE is activated. The bottom of the screen displays the six options, and the cursor rests at the very bottom, at the location of the ^C code. You now can type one of the six numbers and press Enter or Merge R to retrieve a complimentary close.

If you regularly create documents by combining different existing passages, you can save time by exploiting the boilerplate technique. This technique is like a worker, putting a piece of meat, a few pieces of green, and a shot of catsup on a hamburger in a McDonald's restaurant. The technique is fast and efficient—and that's what productivity is about.

Using Merge and Macro To Create Menus

A menu presents to a user a list of options and enables him to select an option to perform a function. A menu is created with ^O. The ^O code is often used to display prompts, messages, and instructions. It can instruct a user to enter text on-screen, select an option to bring up a primary file, or start a macro to perform other chores.

If you are in business, you probably wish you had some efficient ways to keep track of your dealings with your clients. Suppose you maintain a separate file for each client. You could use the system represented in figure 13.14 to tie those files (accounts) together.

Figure 13.14 is a menu that displays all the available accounts and lets you enter a single number or letter to bring an account to the screen for modification. You no longer will be confused about what accounts you have and how you get them.

```
^O
0 - Abrams    1 - Bakker    2 - Block    3 - Brown
4 - Carter    5 - Dicky     6 - Dinen    7 - Foxx
8 - Hubart    9 - Jones, D. A - Jones, L. B - Linan
C - Norman    D - Smith, R. E - Smith, Z. F - White

^Pclient^C^P^O
```

Fig. 13.14.
A sample menu of available accounts.

If you create a file like the one in figure 13.14 and save the file as ACCOUNTS.PF, you can merge it without a secondary file. If you have used the Tab key, remember to save in generic format: press Text In/Out (Ctrl-F5) and select Save Generic (3). The screen displays your clients' names and their corresponding option numbers. The status line also displays the Client message. You then can enter a corresponding option number to activate a particular client's file.

Before you can activate a client's file, you must create it first. Such a file—with a name like CLIENT0, CLIENTA, and so on—can include transactions related to this particular client. You can add Math functions in that file to keep track of numbers, and you can use Sort (see next chapter) to sort and select records. You also can put a macro at the end of such a file. The macro would save the updated file and take you back to the main menu when you are through with this account.

Another example of using Merge to create and manage a menu system is shown in figure 13.15. This menu lets you select a number to activate a corresponding macro. The macro then does a specific task, such as printing the completed letter and returning to the main menu for another selection. Create a file like the one in figure 13.15 and name it END.PF.

```
^O   Menu for Ending the Letter:

     1 - Append to LETTERS file
     2 - Print this letter
     3 - Print envelope
     4 - Clear screen

     Enter a # to select an option.

     Press Shift-F9 and type E to terminate the merge
     (break out of the above loop). ^O

^Gend^C^G^Q
```

Fig. 13.15.
A menu with four options to activate macros.

You could put such a system at the end of the LETTER.PF file in the preceding section. When the merging process reaches this area, a menu is displayed, and the status lines shows the end message. A user can type a number (1 through 4) and activate one of the four macros named END1, END2, END3, and END4.

Because a macro does not start until the end of a merge, place the ^Q code at the end of the file. The ^Q code terminates the merge and starts the macro. In the example, this macro leads to one of the four macros, which also can include macros to start another merge and return you to the main menu, thus forming a continuous loop until you break it by pressing Merge Codes.

You must define the four macros before you merge the file. END1 blocks the completed letter, appends (saves) it to an existing file named LETTERS, and merges END.PF without a secondary file. When you save the letter, the main menu reappears for you to choose other options. END2 simply prints the full text and returns to the main menu. END3 fetches pertinent items, arranges them in the format of an envelope, and prints the envelope. END4 simply clears the screen without doing anything else. If you need a challenge, creating a merge file with macros may be a project for you. You could spend considerable time setting up the project; when it is in place, however, it simplifies the laborious steps of producing a letter.

Using Merge To Fill In Forms

Sometimes you may have a form like the one in figure 13.16, and you want to use your printer to fill in the blanks. You can use Merge to speed up the process. Again, this Merge process requires a little preparation, but once a system is properly set up, it is easy to use.

Fig. 13.16.

A sample preprinted form.

```
Name: _____  Phone: _____  Date: _____
Address: _____
Profession: _____  Title: _____
Company: _____  Phone:_____
Address: _____
Remarks: _____
         _____
```

You need to pinpoint the locations where merge codes are to enter so that an entry from the keyboard prints in the intended place on the form. The most convenient way to determine where to place merge codes is to print out a grid like the one in figure 13.17.

Type the characters as shown in figure 13.17. Select a nonproportional font and print the grid. If a proportional font is used, the grid may be skewed and cannot provide a guide for your form.

```
A123456789B123456789C123456789D123456789E123456789F123456789G12
A123456789B123456789C123456789D123456789E123456789F123456789G12
A123456789B123456789C123456789D123456789E123456789F123456789G12
A123456789B123456789C123456789D123456789E123456789F123456789G12
A123456789B123456789C123456789D123456789E123456789F123456789G12
A123456789B123456789C123456789D123456789E123456789F123456789G12
A123456789B123456789C123456789D123456789E123456789F123456789G12
```

Put your form over the grid and carefully align them. Use a sharp object (a pin will do) to pierce a hole in each location where a code is to enter. The holes on the grid then can guide you to where you enter the merge codes (see fig. 13.18). For example, if a phone number is to enter at line 1, position D7, move the cursor to line 1, position 47 (check the status line) and implant a ^C code.

Fig. 13.18.
A primary file with merge codes only.

```
^C               ^C        ^D
  ^C
   ^C           ^C
 ^C             ^C
 ^C
 ^C
 ^T^N^P^P
```

When such a primary file is merged, it is hard to handle. The cursor stops at each location of a merge code so that you can enter pertinent information. However, because the screen is mostly blank, you may have a hard time entering correct items in correct places. One remedy is to add a message for each entry, as shown in figure 13.19.

Fig. 13.19.
A primary file with merge codes and prompts.

```
^OName^O^C          ^OPhone^O^C      ^D
  ^OAddress^O^C
     ^OProfession^O^C    ^OTitle^O^C
  ^OCompany^O^C         ^OPhone^O^C
  ^OCo. Address^O^C
  ^ORemark^O^C
  ^T^P^P
```

If you now merge this primary file without a secondary file, the file is retrieved to the screen and the cursor rests at the first location. In the meantime, the status line displays the Name: message. Enter a name and press Merge R to continue. If there is no entry for a particular merge stop, just press Merge R. Continue this procedure until Merge R is pressed for the last time. The merge is now complete and is sent to the printer. Make sure that you set up your printer properly and that you put the form in the right place. You may want to use a blank sheet of paper to test the outcome first.

Another merge begins, and a new form appears. You can begin to fill in another form; or if you are ready to stop, press Merge Codes (Shift-F9) and press *E*. Clear the screen, and you can begin to do something else.

Using Merge To Print Mailing Labels

The previous techniques can be used also to print mailing labels. All you need to do, in addition to having a secondary file, is to create a primary file with proper merge codes and then merge this primary file to the existing secondary file.

Let's use ADDRESS.SF (created in the "Merging Text Files" section) as an example. Because that file already exists as a secondary file, you need to create the following primary file to use with ADDRESS.SF:

```
^Ffname^ ^Flname^
^Faddress^
```

Save the primary file as LABELS.PF and merge it to ADDRESS.SF. The result is shown in figure 13.20.

Fig. 13.20.

A file merge for mailing labels.

```
        John Wane
        1234 Big Bull Street
        Big Sky, MT 94333
        ==========================================================================
        Mumbo Jumbo Rambo
        Soldier of Fortune Corp.
        999 Venture Rd.
        Bravado, MS 22111
        ==========================================================================
        James Bondo
        Studio 007
        Paramour Production Co.
        1010 Sunrise Boulevard
        Holywart, CA 99999
        ==========================================================================
```

A hard page separates each address so that each address is one page. If your label sheet has one column, you can print the completed file. Before you can print correctly, however, you need to adjust page size and top and bottom margins to fit the size of each label. Make sure that you embed the necessary codes at the beginning of the document.

If your label sheet has multiple columns, you need to create text columns before or after the merge. The labels appear from left to right—the first label in the first column, the second label in the second column, and so on. If necessary, adjust the line and column widths so that address lines are not broken up.

To arrange the labels to appear in two columns, move the cursor to the beginning of the document and follow these steps:

1. Press Math/Columns (Alt-F7).

2. Select Column Def (4).

3. Press Exit (F7) to accept the default settings.

4. Select Column On/Off (3) to turn on Columns.

Printing multicolumn labels requires considerable finesse and patience. Line width, page length, and top and bottom margins all need to be adjusted in order for the addresses to be printed correctly. First print the labels on a regular sheet of paper until you are sure you have everything properly arranged.

When you find the right combinations, you may want to store the keystrokes in a macro. Then the next time you complete a merge, you simply can go to the beginning of the document and activate the macro to embed the necessary codes (concerning specs for line, page, and text columns) and start printing the labels. If you print mailing labels often, this macro can save you plenty of time.

Handling Blank Lines in Mailing Labels

Sometimes a field in a secondary file record is empty. If you print such a record, you may find empty lines occurring in the middle of a record, as shown in figure 13.21.

Fig. 13.21.
A record with an empty line.

```
John Wane
718 543-4433
1234 Big Bull Street
Big Sky, MT 94333
===============================================================================
Mumbo Jumbo Rambo

Soldier of Fortune Corp.
999 Venture Rd.
Bravado, MS
22111
===============================================================================
James Bondo
888 777-0707
Studio 007
Paramour Production Co.
1010 Sunrise Boulevard
Holywart, CA 99999
===============================================================================
```

When a blank line occurs, you can remedy the problem with a question mark added to a field name or number, as in the following example:

> ^Ffname^ ^Flname^
> ^Fphone?^
> ^Faddress^

Then when the primary file is merged to the secondary file, blank lines no longer are present. Whenever WordPerfect encounters a blank line in the Phone field, the entry from the next field is brought in to fill the gap, because a question mark (?) at the end of a field causes WordPerfect to skip this field if it is empty.

Using Merge To Retrieve Data

You can use Merge to create a system to store certain information and retrieve it selectively at a moment's notice. Creating such a system requires careful planning and repeated testing. When the system is completely debugged, however, it is a joy to use—quick and efficient.

Suppose you run a hamburger restaurant and need to find out quickly the workers you have for a certain day. The first thing you do is create a secondary file like the one in figure 13.22 and save it as WORKERS.SF. The example has 12 fields, each ending with ^R. The first six fields also have field numbers to reference other fields.

Fig. 13.22.

A secondary file for retrieving stored data.

```
          Workers for Monday:
          ^F7^^R
          Workers for Tuesday:
          ^F8^^R
          Workers for Wednesday:
          ^F9^^R
          Workers for Thursday:
          ^F10^^R
          Workers for Friday:
          ^F11^^R
          Workers for Saturday:
          ^F12^^R
              Tim, Jim, Kim
          ^R
              Tamy, Camy, Hammy
          ^R
              Bob, Tub, Cob
          ^R
              Tim, Bob, Kim
          ^R
              Jim, Tamy, Tub
          ^R
              Hammy, Camy, Bob
          ^R
                                    Doc 2 Pg 1 Ln 1 Pos 10
```

The ending caret in each field number, such as ^F7^, is important. If the ending caret is missing, a merge still works, but an incorrect list (usually the one prior to the desired list) is retrieved.

The next step is to type a primary file like the one in figure 13.23 and save the file as SCHEDULE.PF. This file contains two headlines and five merge codes (explained in the following paragraphs).

Fig. 13.23.

A primary file for retrieving data.

```
          Harbor Burger Workers
          Enter 1-6 to show workers for that day.

          ^U^F^C^^P^P
```

Now merge SCHEDULE.PF to WORKERS.SF. The screen displays the primary file at the top, and the status line shows the Field: prompt. Type a number (1 through 6) and press Enter or Merge R to retrieve the names of a particular day's workers. If you enter 1 (for Monday), the information in figure 13.24 appears.

```
Harbor Burger Workers
Enter 1-6 to show workers for that day.

Workers for Monday:
     Tim, Jim, Kim

^U^F^C^^P^P
```

Fig. 13.24.
*The list of workers
for Monday.*

The Field: prompt reappears after each operation. You can enter another number to retrieve another list.

Each of the merge codes plays a role. ^U displays on-screen the merge in progress; without ^U, the screen does not display a selected list. ^F lets you select a field (list) to display. ^C halts the merge to allow keyboard entry. Make sure that you put an ending caret (just press the caret key or Shift-6) after ^C; without the ending caret, the merge ends after only one record is selected. ^P^P recycles the same primary file to allow you more selections.

The mechanism of this merge works in the following manner: When you enter field 1, WordPerfect displays the text in the first field before the first ^R, thus showing "Workers for Monday." Because ^F7^ is located before the first ^R, the program also displays the text in field 7, thus showing "Tim, Jim, Kim."

If you enter a number other than 1 through 6, you can get two different results. If the number you enter is between 7 and 12, WordPerfect displays only the list (such as Tim, Jim, Kim), but not the headline (such as Workers for Monday). If a number is higher than 12, the program terminates the merge.

Therefore, as you operate this system for the example, you can enter any number between 1 and 6 again and again. When you are ready to quit, either enter a number higher than 12 or press the Merge Codes key (Shift-F9).

Integrating Math, Macro, and Merge Functions

In this section, you see the final demonstration of how to integrate merge codes to do a complex task. The example involves several of the functions covered previously in the chapter.

Let's assume that you teach WordPerfect classes and that every few weeks you need to process a large number of student reports. The system demonstrated here could save you a great deal of time.

This system requires several items (see fig. 13.25). The main primary file is REPORT.PF, and the only secondary file is GRADES.SF. You also have four other primary files ASSESS1.PF through ASSESS4.PF and a macro named AVERAGE.WPM.

The Main Primary File

The main primary file, REPORT.PF, appears in figure 13.25. The file clearly shows the visible text and merge codes.

Fig. 13.25.
REPORT.PF, the main primary file.

```
^F1^ ^F2^                                                              ^D
^F3^

Dear ^F1^,

Here is the report for your semester grade in the WordPerfect
class. The grade is calculated as follows:

     Test 1    Test 2    Test 3    Average

      ^F4^      ^F5^      ^F6^         !

^Gaverage^G

^U^0^PAssess^C.pf^P^0


Sincerely yours,


Forest Lin

==============================================================================
^T^N^Preport.pf^P^Q
                                          Doc 2 Pg 1 Ln 1 Pos 10
```

Fig. 13.26 shows the crucial codes displayed in the Reveal Codes screen. The file includes two Tab Set codes, with the first code shown in figure 13.26 and the second, not shown, placed at the end of the document.

To enter the first Tab Set code, follow these steps:

1. Press Format (Shift-F8).

2. Select **Line** (**1**).

3. Select **Tab Set** (**8**).

4. Press Home, Home, ← to move to the left end of the menu.

5. Press Ctrl-End to delete the existing tab stops.

6. Type *10,10* and press Enter.

7. Press Exit (F7) twice.

Place a second Tab Set code that appears as **[Tab Set:5, every 5]** in the Reveal Codes screen at the end of this primary file to make the display appear neat and orderly. To embed the code, just follow the above steps and type "5,5" instead of "10,10."

You also need to enter the Math codes shown in figure 13.26. To define Math, follow these steps:

Fig. 13.26.
*REPORT.PF, as shown
in Reveal Codes.*

```
   Dear ^F1^,

   Here is the report for your semester grade in the WordPerfect
   class. The grade is calculated as follows:

        Test 1    Test 2    Test 3    Average

         ^F4^      ^F5^      ^F6^        !

      ^Gaverage^G
Math                                      Doc 2 Pg 1 Ln 13 Pos 10
     {        ▲        ▲        ▲        ▲        ▲        ▲       ]
[Tab Set:10, every 10][Math Def][Math On][Align]^F4^[C/A/Flrt][Align]^F5^[C/A/Fl
rt][Align]^F6^[C/A/Flrt][Align][!][C/A/Flrt][HRt]
[HRt]
^Gaverage^G[HRt]
[HRt]
^U^O^PAssess^C.pf^P^O[HRt]
[HRt]
[HRt]
Sincerely yours,[HRt]
[HRt]

Press Reveal Codes to restore screen
```

1. Press Math/Columns (Alt-F7).

2. Select Math Def (**2**).

3. Move the cursor to column D and type *0*.

4. Type *+/* and press Enter.

   The Math Definition screen appears, as shown in figure 13.27.

5. Press Exit (F7).

6. Select Math On (**1**).

   The [**Math Def**] and [**Math On**] codes are embedded, and the status line
   displays the Math message.

The line where the grades are to enter in the merging process requires special
treatment. Tab once, press Ctrl-F, enter the field number, and type the ending
caret. Tab the second time and enter the second field. Do the same with the third
field. Press Tab a fourth time to display ! as a calculation field.

The Four Other Primary Files

To assemble the document with some prepared passages, you need four more
primary files. Create the following files and save them with the names shown. You
use these files later to assemble a document:

ASSESS1.PF
You are an excellent student and did impressive work in this class. I enjoyed
having you in the class.

ASSESS2.PF

You did a reasonably good job in this class. You gave quite a few positive contributions to the class. It was fun to have you.

ASSESS3.PF

You did an average job in this class. You are a bright student and I think you can do better than what you have demonstrated in this class.

ASSESS4.PF

I am sorry to give you a failing grade. You have the potential to do better, and I hope you will try a little harder in the future.

Fig. 13.27.

The Math definition for REPORT.PF.

```
Math Definition            Use arrow keys to position cursor

Columns                    A B C D E F G H I J K L M N O P Q R S T U V W X

Type                       2 2 2 0 2 2 2 2 2 2 2 2 2 2 2 2 2 2 2 2 2 2 2 2

Negative Numbers           ( ( ( ( ( ( ( ( ( ( ( ( ( ( ( ( ( ( ( ( ( ( ( (

Number of Digits to        2 2 2 2 2 2 2 2 2 2 2 2 2 2 2 2 2 2 2 2 2 2 2 2
  the Right (0-4)

Calculation   1     D    +/
   Formulas   2
              3
              4

Type of Column:
      0 = Calculation    1 = Text     2 = Numeric    3 = Total

Negative Numbers
      ( = Parentheses (50.00)        - = Minus Sign  -50.00


Press Exit when done
```

The Secondary File

Create a secondary file like the one in figure 13.28 and label it GRADES.SF. Make sure that the test scores are arranged properly—the first in field 4, the second in field 5, and the third in field 6.

The Macro File

The only macro in this report automatically calculates the average score of each report.

To define the macro, follow these steps:

1. Press Math/Columns (Alt-F7) and then Math On (**1**) to turn on Math.

2. Press Macro Define (Ctrl-F10).

```
           Jim^R
           Jones^R
           1010 West Easton St.
           Tulsa, OK 74119^R
           87^R
           97^R
           92^R
           ^E
===================================================================
           Tim^R
           Tomms^R
           2121 East Westin St.
           Bugsy, OK 73004^R
           87^R
           78^R
           77^R
           ^E
===================================================================
           Kim^R
           James^R
           Apt. 201
           9044 North Southern Rd.
           Wagaloo, OK 74333^R
           55^R
                                 Doc 2 Pg 1 Ln 1 Pos 10
```

Fig. 13.28.
GRADES.SF, the secondary file.

3. Type *AVERAGE* for the macro name and press Enter.

4. Press Enter for no description.

5. Press Math/Columns (Alt-F7).

6. Select Calculate (**2**).

7. Press Macro Define (Ctrl-F10).

The Merge

After you have created all the files, you finally are ready to merge. Merge REPORT.PF to GRADES.SF. The first name, last name, address, and grades enter the designated locations. The merge encounters the macro, but it is not activated until the end of the merge. The merge then stops at the ^C location, and the status line displays the Assess message. You are to enter 1 through 4 to bring in one of the four primary files (see fig. 13.29).

^N fetches the next secondary file record, and ^P^P brings in the same primary file for another merge until the end of the secondary file. The merge is then terminated when it encounters ^Q. The ^Q code is necessary because Math does not function when a merge is in progress. At this point the macro is activated. It calculates the average and inserts the number in the fourth field of every letter.

The hard page inserted in the main primary file breaks each letter into a separate page. If the whole document is now printed, each letter prints on a separate page.

Fig. 13.29.

The final version of a merged letter.

```
Jim Jones
1818 West Easton St.
Tulsa, OK 74119                          May 3, 1988

Dear Jim,

Here is the report for your semester grade in the WordPerfect
class. The grade is calculated as follows:

     Test 1   Test 2   Test 3    Average

       87       97       92      92.88!

You are an excellent student and did impressive work in this class.
I enjoyed having you in the class.

Sincerely yours,

Forest Lin
                                    Doc 2 Pg 1 Ln 1 Pos 19
```

Creating Complete Automation

In this chapter, you have attempted different devices of automation and have used timesaving merge codes after starting a merge. If you now can automate the beginning part, you will have a completely automated cycle.

You can use your previous examples for this total automation. Start with the MEMO.PF file you created at the beginning of this chapter.

To define a macro to automate the beginning of a merge, follow these steps:

1. Press Macro Define (Ctrl-F10).

2. Enter Alt-M (hold down Alt and press *M*) as the macro name.

3. Type *To write a memo* as the macro description and press Enter.

4. Press Merge/Sort (Ctrl-F9).

5. Select **Merge** (**1**).

6. Type *MEMO.PF* as the primary file and press Enter.

7. Press Enter for no secondary file.

8. Press Merge Codes (Shift-F9) and type *E.*

You do not need to press Macro Define at the end. After Step 8, the definition is complete and the merge is terminated. The MEMO.PF file remains on-screen. Clear the screen and you are ready to use the macro.

The next time you are ready to write a memo, simply use this macro by holding down Alt and pressing *M.* The primary file appears on-screen. Then you type any necessary items and press Merge R to continue till the end. If you put the ^T code at the end of the primary file, the completed document is sent automatically to the printer.

If you manage a number of workers with irregular shifts, as described in the "Using Merge To Retrieve Data" section, you can create a system that lets you press a few keys to find out quickly the names of the employees for each shift. The initial steps can be stored in a macro that merges the specified primary and secondary files.

To create the macro for this function, do the following:

1. Press Macro Define (Ctrl-F10).

2. Enter Alt-W as the macro name.

3. Type *To retrieve workers' names* as the macro description and press Enter.

4. Press Exit (F7) and press *N* twice to clear the screen.

5. Press Merge/Sort (Ctrl-F9).

6. Select **Merge (1)**.

7. Type *SCHEDULE.PF* as the primary file and press Enter.

8. Type *WORKERS.SF* as the secondary file and press Enter.

9. Press Merge Codes (Shift-F9).

Step 9 terminates the merge and completes the macro definition.

Clear the screen, and the macro is ready for use. When you want to find out who is working on a certain day, just press Alt-W and enter a field number.

Beware that this macro will wipe out anything on-screen. If you are working with a file, it will be cleared before a merge begins. If you don't want to lose the document, switch to the Doc 2 screen (Shift-F3) and activate the macro as many times as you wish. When you are finished, return to Doc 1 to continue your work. If it is not convenient to use the Doc 2 screen, take out Step 4 so that you will not wipe out your data.

If you are the person managing the system, you need to keep it current. When a change is needed, just edit WORKERS.SF and save it over the original. When the macro is activated next time, the updated list will be used.

WP 5 Summary

Merge is a highly sophisticated and relatively complex feature used for office automation. Merge contains 14 merge codes with which you can direct WordPerfect to do many chores automatically. You need to be familiar with the merge codes in order to do complex merges. Among the codes, the most commonly used include the following:

^C—to halt a merge for keyboard entry
^G—to activate a macro
^O—to display prompts, messages, and instructions
^P—to enter a primary file
^T—to send a merged file to the printer

A typical merge requires a primary file and a secondary file, each of which contains necessary codes for a proper merge. When you have those files, follow these steps to do a merge:

1. Press Merge/Sort (Ctrl-F9) and select **Merge (1)**.

2. Enter the primary and secondary files.

In the middle of a merging operation, observe these rules:

- When the merge is halted by ^C, enter the necessary information and press Merge R (F9) to continue.

- When a merge is to be terminated before its natural completion, press Merge Codes (Shift-F9) and, if necessary (when the list of codes appears), press *E*.

Designing complex primary and secondary files requires considerable finesse. Merge codes need to be placed in proper locations and nested in the correct order. You should review the numerous applications in this chapter if you intend to use Merge extensively.

14

Sorting and Selecting Data

Forest Lin, Ph.D., an expert on WordPerfect products, is writing a book on PlanPerfect®, a spreadsheet program from WordPerfect Corporation. He brings his spreadsheet expertise to this chapter as he writes about the Sort function in WordPerfect 5. ■

The Sort feature provides some important functions to manage a database. Sort can maneuver the items in a database in several ways. For example, the Sort feature can sort the items by line or by paragraph. Sort also can *select* (extract) items that meet specified criteria.

Database management programs, such as dBASE III® and dBASE IV™, have become popular with businesspeople because they use the programs to keep business records of all kinds. Running a business today without such a database management program to keep track of payroll, inventory, and other items is hard to imagine.

While WordPerfect's Sort feature cannot match specialized database management programs in certain areas, it has enough power and versatility to handle most situations where you need to keep track of records. When Sort is combined with other WordPerfect features—such as Search, Replace, Merge, Math, and Macro—it becomes a useful management tool.

In this chapter, you learn how to build a variety of databases and how to use Sort to rearrange them and select records from them. You learn also how to use macros to save time in different sorting operations.

The Basics of Sort

Before you can perform a sorting operation, you need to have an adequate background. This section introduces you to the basic terms you encounter in this chapter, the options you use in the Sort menu, and the techniques you need to create a simple database, which you use in the next section.

455

Database Terms

A *database*, also known as a data bank, is a collection of data. In its organization, a database consists of records, which in turn comprise of fields, which in turn contain words, the smallest units. A *record* is a collection of related pieces of information; each piece of information in a record is stored in a *field*; and a *word* is a combination of letters and/or numbers.

To use a concrete example, an address list is a simple database. All the pieces of information relating to one person constitute a record. Each piece of information—such as name, street number, city, state, and ZIP code—is placed in a separate location called a field. The pieces of information must enter the correct fields: names in the first field, streets in the second, and so on. If the information is not arranged properly, WordPerfect cannot maneuver it properly.

A database is saved as a file with a unique name to distinguish the database file from other files. Like any WordPerfect file, a database can be as large as your disk space permits.

WordPerfect can maneuver three types of records: a line, a paragraph, or a secondary merge file record. A *line record* ends with a hard or soft return, and a *paragraph record* ends with two hard returns. You must distinguish between line sort and paragraph sort because using an improper sort can distort a database. As explained in Chapter 13, a *secondary merge file* contains records, each of which has fields. A field ends with a ^R merge code, and a record ends with ^E. Other than the difference in merge codes, a secondary merge file is treated like any database.

When you create a database, remember that fields are separated by tab codes. Suppose you want to create a database containing the names, home phone numbers, and office phone numbers of your sales contacts. In each line, you enter a name and press Tab; enter the home phone number and press Tab; and finally enter the office phone number and press Enter to end the line (record). Arranged in this manner, WordPerfect understands that names are in the first field, home phone numbers in the second field, and office phone numbers in the third field.

A field can have one or more words. A word can contain any printable character or number and is separated from other words with a space. In the previous example, the first field can have a name with two or more words, each separated with a space. When you want to sort the names, you need to tell WordPerfect by which word in that field to sort.

When you do a sorting operation, WordPerfect asks you for an input and an output file. An *input file* is the database, saved on disk, that you intend to sort; an *output file* is the sorted (or selected) file, which you can send to the screen or save on disk.

WordPerfect can sort numeric or alphanumeric records in ascending (from low to high) or descending (from high to low) order. *Numerics* are sorted according to their arithmetic values, and *alphanumerics* are sorted according to ASCII values, except that upper- and lowercase letters are placed next to each other. (In the ASCII order, the lowercase alphabet as a group appears after the uppercase alphabet.) For example, the items in the first line of the following example appear as they do in the second line after an ascending alphanumeric sort:

A B C D a b c d 1 2 3 4 ! @ # - + ( )

- ! ( ) + # @ 1 2 3 4 A a B b C c D d

The Sort Menu

At the beginning of each sorting operation, after the entering of input and output files, WordPerfect displays the Sort menu (see fig. 14.1). You need to understand the menu thoroughly before you can use Sort effectively, particularly if you intend to do complex maneuvers.

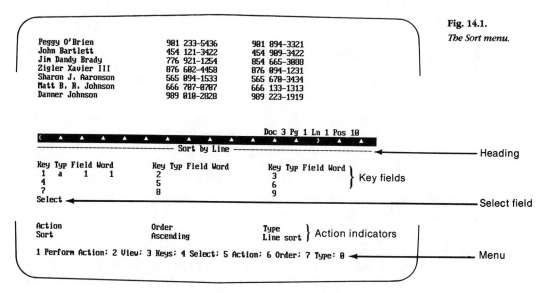

Fig. 14.1.

The Sort menu.

The Sort menu is divided into five parts. The first part, the heading, shows the preset default Sort by Line. The second part shows nine keys, each of which has three fields where you can enter the criteria to sort your data. The third part is the Select field where you enter the formulas to select (extract) certain records from a database. The fourth part indicates the Action, Order, and Type (which coincides with the heading) of the Sort. The fifth part, at the very bottom, shows the menu with seven options. The menu options are explained in the next few paragraphs.

The first menu option, **P**erform Action (**1**), instructs WordPerfect to begin sorting. Before you select this option, however, make sure that everything is in order. By examining the different parts of the display, you can tell whether the type and order of the Sort are correct. If not, you have to change them before starting action.

When you select the View (**2**) option, the cursor jumps to the data to be sorted. You can move the cursor around to view the data, but you are not allowed to edit. Press Exit (F7) to return to the Sort menu.

The **Keys** (**3**) option enables you to define and change the keys (criteria) for sorting. Because nine keys are represented on the menu, you can establish nine sets of criteria by which to sort your file. When you select this option, the bottom of the screen displays the following instructions:

Type: **a** = Alphanumeric; **n** = Numeric; Use arrows; Press **Exit** when done

The cursor jumps to the first item in the first key and awaits your action. You now can move the cursor to make necessary changes—to add or delete, for example. Pressing Ctrl-End deletes all the entries in all the fields of any key except Key1.

The default values in Key1 are preset at "a 1 1". These values mean that the Sort type is alphanumeric and that the first word in the first field is to be used as the basis for sorting.

Negative values can be entered in each key. For example, if you want to use the third word from the end, enter –3 under the Word category. When a **[Mar Rel]** code is embedded, a negative number may be necessary under the Field category (see the "Managing a Bibliography" section).

If sorting by Key1 results in ties (equal values, such as same names or numbers), you can use Key2, Key3, and so on, to break the ties. If your database contains many people with Smith as the last name, for example, you may want to sort their last names as Key1 (with a Field value of –1), first names as Key2 (with a Field value of 1), and middle names as Key3 (with a Field value of 2).

Select (**4**) lets you enter a formula so that you can direct WordPerfect to select certain records. This option is explained in greater detail in "The Select Function" section.

Action (**5**) is activated only when you choose **Select** (**4**). Action (**5**) gives you two options: Select and Sort (**1**) and Select Only (**2**). Choosing the first option allows you to sort selected records; choosing the second option allows you only to select the records.

By selecting the **Order** (**6**) option, you choose an Ascending (**1**) or Descending (**2**) order for your Sort.

Selecting the **Type** (**7**) option produces the following choices:

> **Type:** **1** Merge; **2** Line; **3** Paragraph: **0**

All three types are explained in "The Three Kinds of Sort" section.

A Simple Database

To illustrate how to use the Sort function, let's build a simple database as shown in figure 14.2.

If you intend to experiment with this database, ignore the heading lines for now. If you do add the heading lines, you need to block the database (excluding the

```
                    SALES CONTACTS 1

   Name                    Home Phone        Office Phone

   Peggy O'Brien           901 233-5436      901 894-3321
   John Bartlett           454 121-3422      454 909-3422
   Jim Dandy Brady         776 921-1254      854 665-3088
   Zigler Xavier III       876 602-4458      876 894-1231
   Sharon J. Aaronson      565 894-1533      565 670-3434
   Matt B. R. Johnson      666 707-0707      666 133-1313
   Danner Johnson          989 010-2828      989 223-1919




                    Doc 1 Pg 1 Ln 1 Pos 6
```

Fig. 14.2.
A simple database.

headlines) before doing a sorting or selecting operation (see the "Sorting a Block" section for details). You also need to keep in mind that the examples in this chapter are based on WordPerfect units of measure, not inches.

Before entering the records (lines), you must change the tab stops. First go to the Tab Set screen by pressing Format (Shift-F8), selecting Line (**1**), and selecting Tab Set (**8**). Erase the existing tab stops by pressing Home, Home, ←, and Ctrl-End. Enter tabs at the 40th and 60th positions by moving the cursor to 40 and pressing **L** for Left-justified tab and then moving to 60 and pressing **L**. Finally, exit from the Tab Set screen by pressing F7 twice, and begin entering the lines.

Make sure to press Tab after entering each field. The three fields must be separated by two **[Tab]** codes. If you just press the space bar to move the cursor to the next field, WordPerfect cannot sort these records correctly. Press Enter at the end of each record (line). This arrangement satisfies the requirement that each record is separated by a **[HRt]** (hard return) code and each field by a **[Tab]** code.

If you intend to keep a database you have created, you should always save it before attempting to sort it or select records from it. After a sorting operation, the database on-screen may be distorted, so having a backup file is convenient.

To save a database, follow these steps to save it to disk:

1. Press Save (F10).

2. Type a file name (SALES, for example) and press Enter.

The Three Kinds of Sort

Sort can maneuver three kinds of databases—line, paragraph, and a secondary merge file. You need to use a different type of sort for each kind of database. Use line sort when records are lines, paragraph sort when records are paragraphs, and merge sort when sorting a secondary merge file.

Sorting by Line

Now that you have a database sample with lines as records, you will learn the simple technique of sorting by line.

To sort by line, follow these steps:

1. Press Merge/Sort (Ctrl-F9).

2. Select Sort (**2**).

3. Type the input file name and press Enter.

4. Type the output file name and press Enter.

   The Sort menu appears.

5. Select **Type** (**7**), if it is necessary to change to another type.

6. Select **Keys** (**3**), if it is necessary to change existing values.

7. Select **Perform Action** (**1**).

When you press Merge/Sort (Ctrl-F9), WordPerfect displays the following menu:

1 Merge; **2** Sort; **3** Sort Order: **0**

Selecting **Sort** (**2**) produces the following question on-screen:

Input file to sort: (Screen)

If you want to sort the file already in memory, just press Enter. If you want to sort another file instead, you need to indicate the directory (if the file is in a directory or drive other than the current one) and the file name. Then pressing Enter leads to the following question:

Output file for sort: (Screen)

You can press Enter to sort to the screen. Later, you can save the output file as a regular file. If you want the sorted file to be saved to disk right away, however, enter a file name. If you use the original name, the new (sorted) file overrides the original. If you give a different name, the file is saved as a separate file.

If you are not familiar with Sort, direct the output (sorted) file to the screen. If a sorting operation is not satisfactory, try again. When the Sort works correctly, you then can save the file over the original or as a new file, whichever suits your purpose.

After you have taken care of these items, the screen is divided into two halves. The top half displays the beginning lines of the file you intend to sort, and the bottom half shows the Sort menu (refer to fig. 14.1).

If you select **Perform Action** (**1**), the outcome appears as in figure 14.3. Something is not right. If you look closely, you see that WordPerfect has sorted the lines by first names—namely, the first word in the first field.

```
                    SALES CONTACTS 1

    Name                   Home Phone        Office Phone

    Danner Johnson         989 010-2828      989 223-1919
    Jim Dandy Brady        776 921-1254      854 665-3088
    John Bartlett          454 121-3422      454 909-3422
    Matt B. R. Johnson     666 707-0707      666 133-1313
    Peggy O'Brien          901 233-5436      901 894-3321
    Sharon J. Aaronson     565 094-1533      565 670-3434
    Zigler Xavier III      876 602-4458      876 894-1231




                        Doc 1 Pg 1 Ln 1 Pos 6
```

Fig. 14.3.
Records sorted by first names.

If you re-examine the Sort menu, you see that WordPerfect indicated it would sort by these criteria. If you want to sort by the last names, you need to change some items in the menu.

Repeat the steps in the previous procedure in order to display the Sort menu. When the menu appears, select **Keys** (**3**). The cursor jumps to Key1, resting at the "a" position under the Type category. The "a" character is intended to sort alphanumeric items, anything containing characters and numbers. You do not have to change this setting. Press → to move the cursor to the 1 under the Field category. Because we intend to sort the first field, this category needs no change. Press → again to move the cursor to the area under the Word category. Because we do not want to sort by the first word (first name), we need to change the number. Type –1 to replace 1. Typing –1 directs WordPerfect to sort by the last word or the first word from the end.

Because the names in the database contain two that have the same last name, we need to tell WordPerfect to sort by the first names when it encounters such a tie. Press → three more times to move the cursor to Key2 and to the Word category; Key2 now shows the values of "a 1 1". Press Exit (F7), and the cursor returns to the bottom of the screen. Select **Perform Action** (**1**), and the result changes to that in figure 14.4.

The sort in figure 14.4 looks much better. However, if you look closely, you see that "Mr. Xavier" is misplaced. His name is out of order because WordPerfect identifies him as "Mr. III." To remedy this odd situation, replace the space between "Xavier" and "III" with a hard space by deleting the space, pressing Home, and then pressing the space bar. If you now go to the Reveal Codes screen, you see the [   ] code

Fig. 14.4.

Records sorted by last names.

```
                          SALES CONTACTS 1

        Name                      Home Phone       Office Phone

        Sharon J. Aaronson        565 894-1533     565 678-3434
        John Bartlett             454 121-3422     454 989-3422
        Jim Dandy Brady           776 921-1254     854 665-3888
        Zigler Xavier III         876 682-4458     876 894-1231
        Danner Johnson            989 818-2828     989 223-1919
        Matt B. R. Johnson        666 787-8787     666 133-1313
        Peggy O'Brien             981 233-5436     981 894-3321




                                               Doc 1 Pg 1 Ln 4 Pos 16
```

connecting the two words. From now on, the two words are treated as one by WordPerfect and are sorted correctly (see fig. 14.5).

Fig. 14.5.

The final sort of the records by last name.

```
                          SALES CONTACTS 1

        Name                      Home Phone       Office Phone

        Sharon J. Aaronson        565 894-1533     565 678-3434
        John Bartlett             454 121-3422     454 989-3422
        Jim Dandy Brady           776 921-1254     854 665-3888
        Danner Johnson            989 818-2828     989 223-1919
        Matt B. R. Johnson        666 787-8787     666 133-1313
        Peggy O'Brien             981 233-5436     981 894-3321
        Zigler Xavier III         876 682-4458     876 894-1231




                                               Doc 1 Pg 1 Ln 6 Pos 12
```

Sorting by Paragraph

A database can contain paragraphs, each separated with two consecutive hard returns. Such a database gives you considerable freedom to organize your data. The records no longer have to adhere to the rigid structure of lines and fields. A record can be one line or a full page, as long as one record is separated from the next record with two hard returns. A database made up of paragraphs is often referred to as a free-form database, or simply a text base.

As your freedom to organize data increases, the room to maneuver data decreases—the price you pay for not adhering to rigid structure. If you enter your data without any order, you limit your ability to maneuver the data. In a paragraph database, you no longer can sort by line, field, or word. Even if you could find a way to sort under certain circumstances, the sorting would be relatively meaningless.

To make a paragraph database more manageable, however, you can add some structure. For example, you can designate the first one or two lines of each record for certain uniform items, each entered into a fixed field. After you designate the fixed fields, the entry can be completely free-form. Figure 14.6 is an example of this compromise arrangement.

Fig. 14.6.
A paragraph database with fixed fields in the first line.

```
                    SALES CONTACTS 2

    Name                    Home Phone         Office Phone

    Sharon J. Aaronson      565 094-1533       565 670-3434
    Met in Chicago computer show, a charming lady, about 30. Info
    manager for IMB Co, a large retail chain of soft goods. Her
    company is in the market for a large number of new PC's within a
    year. Good prospect of selling our products.

    John Bartlett           454 121-3422       454 909-3422
    VP for finance of ABC Finance Co. The company has a large fund to
    finance startup high-tech ventures. Could be tapped if future
    clients need financing to purchase our products.

    Jim Dandy Brady         776 921-1254       854 665-3088
    A slick salesman, dynamic, has an impressive record. Met him a
    few times in different computer shows. Could hire him if we need
    more sales people.

    Zigler Xavier III       876 602-4458       876 094-1231
    Dynamic positive-thinking, fast-talking, sometimes mouth-foaming
    professional speaker. Heard him speak to enthusiastic audiences.
    Could invite him to talk to our sales people to pep them up. Fee
    is $5,000 plus expenses.

    Danner Johnson          989 010-2828       989 223-1919
    Sales manager for Chip Tech. Company makes high-quality add-on
    boards for PC. A potential supplier for us.

    Matt B. R. Johnson      666 707-0707       666 133-1313
    Met in IBM seminar in New York. Runs a chain of retail stores
    selling IBM products. While he competes with us for similar
    clientele, there could be some way we could cooperate someday.

    Peggy O'Brien           901 233-5436       901 894-3321
    Personnel director for IBM. Could approach her to employ our
    laid-off workers.
```

Figure 14.6 keeps the original first line of each record while you add the variable lines after the fixed fields. The first line of each record (paragraph) is rigidly structured. But the lines below the fixed fields can be anything, as long as each record is together. Remember to separate each record from the other records by inserting two consecutive hard returns.

The database in figure 14.6 now can be maneuvered like the original database in figure 14.2. However, you must be careful when you sort the paragraph database. Make sure that the heading in the Sort menu shows Sort by Paragraph.

To select Paragraph sort, first select **Type (7)** from the Sort menu and then choose **Paragraph (3)**. The Type column in the menu now indicates Paragraph sort, and the heading shows Sort by Paragraph. Now you can choose other options, including **Perform** Action (**1**).

If line sort is used to sort paragraphs, the outcome is predictable. Each line is treated as a separate unit. After sorting, the data are completely jumbled and the neatly arranged paragraphs are gone forever—unless you have a copy on disk.

When paragraph sort is selected, the menu display is different. Each key displays four items instead of three, as in line sort. The reason for the added Line item is that a paragraph can contain multiple lines, and you need to tell WordPerfect by which line to sort. The paragraph sort key display looks like the following:

```
Key Typ Field Line Word
1   a   1     1    1
```

To sort the modified paragraph database on-screen, follow these steps:

1. Press Merge/Sort (Ctrl-F9).

2. Select **Sort (2)**.

3. When the message Input file to sort: (Screen) appears, type a file name and press Enter.

4. When the Output file message appears, press Enter to output to the screen.

5. Select **Type (7)**.

6. Select **Paragraph (3)**.

7. Select **Keys (3)**.

8. Move the cursor to the Word category in Key1 and type −1.

9. Press → twice to display "a 1 1 1" in Key2.

10. Press Exit (F7).

11. Select **Perform Action (1)**.

Some of the steps may not be necessary. For example, Steps 5 and 6 are not needed if you have previously selected paragraph sort.

The database is now sorted according to the last name located in the first line of each record, as shown in figure 14.7.

Adding records to a paragraph database (or any database) is relatively simple, as long as you adhere to certain rules. You have to separate the items in the structured lines

```
                        SALES CONTACTS 2

     Name                        Home Phone        Office Phone

     Sharon J. Aaronson          565 094-1533       565 670-3434
     Met in Chicago computer show, a charming lady, about 30. Info
     manager for IMB Co, a large retail chain of soft goods. Her
     company is in the market for a large number of new PC's within a
     year. Good prospect of selling our products.

     John Bartlett               454 121-3422       454 909-3422
     VP for finance of ABC Finance Co. The company has a large fund to
     finance startup high-tech ventures. Could be tapped if future
     clients need financing to purchase our products.

     Jim Dandy Brady             776 921-1254       854 665-3088
     A slick salesman, dynamic, has an impressive record. Met him a
     few times in different computer shows. Could hire him if we need
     more sales people.

     Danner Johnson              989 010-2828       989 223-1919
     Sales manager for Chip Tech. Company makes high-quality add-on
     boards for PC. A potential supplier for us.

     Matt B. R. Johnson          666 707-0707       666 133-1313
     Met in IBM seminar in New York. Runs a chain of retail stores
     selling IBM products. While he competes with us for similar
     clientele, there could be some way we could cooperate someday.

     Peggy O'Brien               901 233-5436       901 894-3321
     Personnel director for IBM. Could approach her to employ our
     laid-off workers.

     Zigler Xavier III           876 602-4458       876 094-1231
     Dynamic positive-thinking, fast-talking, sometimes mouth-foaming
     professional speaker. Heard him speak to enthusiastic audiences.
     Could invite him to talk to our sales people to pep them up. Fee
     is $5,000 plus expenses.
```

Fig. 14.7.

A paragraph database after a sort on the last name field.

with **[Tab]** codes, and you must place two hard returns at the end of each record. After you type new records on-screen, block and append them (including the last two hard returns) to the existing file.

If you are not familiar with the Block and Append functions, follow these steps to append (add) records to an existing file on disk:

1. Move the cursor to the beginning of the first record.

2. Press Block (Alt-F4, or F12).

3. Move the cursor to the end of the last block.

4. Press Move (Ctrl-F4).

5. Select **Block** (**1**).

6. Select Append (**4**).

7. Type a file name (such as SALES) and press Enter.

Sorting a Secondary Merge File

A secondary merge file is nothing more than a database with implanted merge codes, which WordPerfect uses to do a merge. Once a database exists, you can convert it to a secondary merge file by using the Replace feature to convert some codes. In this section, you build a database, convert it to a secondary merge file, and learn how to sort the merge file.

Suppose you are the current president of Okie Bird Watchers Society. You could use a database like the one in figure 14.8 to keep track of your flock. Building such a database is simple. Just set proper tab stops and enter each line (just as you did to create figure 14.2).

Fig. 14.8.

A sample database.

```
                    Okie Bird Watchers Society

    LName     FName    Address          City         Phone     $$$

    Wing      Red      1234 5th St.     Oakdale      299-4533  100
    Foxxe     Fanny    999 Broad St.    Cedar City   990-5544  250
    Jay       Blu      222 Main St.     Ridge City   858-3322  300
    Byrd      Ina      290 Center Rd.   Jinx         922-2166  50
    Byrd      Ura      290 Center Rd.   Jinx         922-2166  220
    Fish      Ham      3030 Circle Dr.  Spring       404-4949  120
    Fish      Golda    3030 Circle Dr.  Spring       404-4949  110
    Salmon    Whitey   844 Gill St.     Crease City  888-4040  60
    Salmon    Smokey   844 Gill St.     Crease City  888-4040  70




                                         Doc 1 Pg 1 Ln 1 Pos 12
```

When you want to notify the members of certain upcoming events, you can convert the database to a secondary merge file, which you can use to merge to your letter.

To convert a database to a secondary merge file, do the following:

1. Move the cursor to the beginning of the file (or block the needed portion) and press Replace (Alt-F2).

2. Press *N* for No Confirm.

3. Press Enter and Esc to enter **[HRt]** (hard return code) as the search string.

4. Press Ctrl-E and Enter to enter ^E**[HRt]** as the replace string.

5. Press Esc to begin the operation.

   All the lines now end with ^E.

6. Go back to the beginning of the file (or reblock the necessary portion) and replace each **[Tab]** code (by pressing Tab) with ^R**[HRt]** (by pressing F9 and Enter).

At the end of the operation, the database is converted to a secondary merge file like the one that follows:

Wing^R
Red^R

1234 5th St.^R
Oakdale^R
299-4533^R
100^E
Foxxe^R
Fanny^R2
999 Broad St.^R
Cedar City^R
990-5544^R
250^E
Jay^R
Blu^R
222 Main St.^R
Ridge City^R
858-3322^R
300^E
Byrd^R
Ima^R
290 Center Rd.^R
Jinx^R
922-2166^R
50^E
Byrd^R
Ura^R
290 Center Rd.^R
Jinx^R
922-2166^R
220^E
Fish^R
Ham^R
3030 Circle Dr.^R
Spring^R
484-4949^R
120^E
Fish^R
Golda^R
3030 Circle Dr.^R
Spring^R
484-4949^R
110^E
Salmon^R
Whitey^R
844 Gill St.^R
Crease City^R
888-4040^R
60^E
Salmon^R
Smokey^R
844 Gill St.^R

Crease City^R
888-4040^R
70^E

If you already have a secondary merge file, it can be converted to a tabular-form database. All you need to do is replace the search strings in the previous example with replace strings, thus reversing the operation. First, replace the ^R and hard return codes with tab codes. Then replace the ^E codes with nothing, thus deleting them. You may then need to adjust tab stops to make the columns appear in a neat order.

This secondary merge file now can be sorted. From the Sort menu (refer to fig. 14.1), make sure to select **Type** (**7**) and then **Merge** (**1**). The heading should show `Sort Secondary Merge File`. Set the values of Key1 as "a 1 1 1" (to sort by last names) and Key2 as "a 2 1 1" (to sort by first names). If you now select **Perform Action** (**1**), the result is the following:

Byrd^R
Ima^R
290 Center Rd.^R
Jinx^R
922-2166^R
50^E
Byrd^R
Ura^R
290 Center Rd.^R
Jinx^R
922-2166^R
220^E
Fish^R
Golda^R
3030 Circle Dr.^R
Spring^R
484-4949^R
110^E
Fish^R
Ham^R
3030 Circle Dr.^R
Spring^R
484-4949^R
120^E
Foxxe^R
Fanny^R
999 Broad St.^R
Cedar City^R
990-5544^R
250^E
Jay^R
Blu^R
222 Main St.^R

Ridge City^R
858-3322^R
300^E
Salmon^R
Smokey^R
844 Gill St.^R
Crease City^R
888-4040^R
70^E
Salmon^R
Whitey^R
844 Gill St.^R
Crease City^R
888-4040^R
60^E
Wing^R
Red^R
1234 5th St.^R
Oakdale^R
299-4533^R
100^E

If you want to have a hard page separating each record to conform to the version 5 format, you need to change the replace string of ^E**[HRt]** to ^E**[HPg]**. Press Ctrl-Enter to get the hard page code. However, the absence of a hard page after each record does not interfere with a merge.

This file now can be used to merge with a primary file as explained in the previous chapter. If you want to select only certain records to merge, "The Select Function" section explains the techniques. This file also can be saved as a separate file for future use.

Other Sort Features

You can use the Sort feature to maneuver all kinds of records. This section demonstrates how you can apply Sort to three practical situations: managing a bibliography, sorting a block, and sorting numbers.

Managing a Bibliography

For your first application, let's assume that you write profound treatises and need to manage a bibliography (see fig. 14.9). In the old days, scholars kept such information on individual index cards, which became unwieldy in large numbers. Now you can use Sort to manage the "index cards" for you.

A bibliography requires that you rigidly adhere to a format of hanging indents for the first lines; therefore, you need to press Indent (F4) and then Margin Release (Shift-Tab) before entering each first line. Do not press Enter until the end of an entry. A long line automatically wraps to the next line starting at the left margin. Press Enter twice at the end of each entry to make it a paragraph.

Fig. 14.9.

*A sample
bibliography before
sorting.*

```
Hayek, Friedrich A. The Road to Serfdom. Chicago: University of
     Chicago Press, Phoenix Books, 1960.

Cole, Margaret. The Story of Fabian Socialism. Stanford: Stanford
     University Paperbacks, 1969.

Fried, Albert (ed.). Socialism in America: From the Shakers to
     the Third International--A Documentary History. Garden City,
     N.Y.: Doubleday Anchor Books, 1970.

Schumpeter, Joseph A. Capitalism, Socialism, and Democracy. New
     York: Harper Torchbooks, 1962.

Myrdal, Gunmar. The Challenge of World Poverty: A World Anti-
     Poverty Program in Outline. New York: Pantheon Books, 1970.




                              Doc 1 Pg 1 Ln 2 Pos 10
```

Once you have the bibliography, you can sort it or select records from it. Because the last name is entered as the first word of the first line in each entry, we can use the last name to sort the database. Make sure to save the bibliography to disk if you intend to keep it.

With the bibliography on-screen, follow these steps to sort the bibliography:

1. Press Merge/Sort (Ctrl-F9).

2. Select **Sort** (**2**).

3. Press Enter twice.

4. Select **Type** (**7**).

5. Select **Paragraph** (**3**).

6. Select **Keys** (**3**).

7. Move the cursor to the Field position in Key1 and type *–1*.

8. Press Exit (F7).

9. Select **Perform Action** (**1**).

Step 7 changes the values of Key1 to "a 1 –1 1", with the Field number as –1. If you sort with the values of Key1 as "a 1 1 1", the outcome will not be correct. Because a [←**Mar Rel**] code is embedded at the beginning of each first line, WordPerfect considers that line to be located in the field before the first. If you now select **Perform Action** (**1**), the result should look like the bibliography in figure 14.10.

Sorting a Block

Occasionally, you may not want to sort the whole database. To sort only a portion of a database, you need to use the Block function to block the necessary portion and go

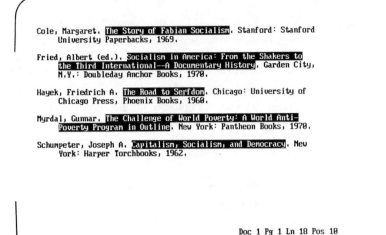

Fig. 14.10.
*The sample
bibliography after
sorting.*

through the routine of sorting. The first database example in this chapter has two heading lines. If you sort the whole database, these lines are included among the items to be sorted. In order to sort correctly, however, you need to block the database, minus the heading lines.

Let's use the first database (refer to fig. 14.2) to demonstrate how to sort a block. First, type in the two heading lines, if you have not already done so, so that you can see how to sort a block.

To sort a block, do the following:

1. Move the cursor to the beginning of the first record or the empty line just above it.

2. Press Block (Alt-F4, or F12).

3. Move the cursor to the line just below the last record.

4. Press Merge/Sort (Ctrl-F9).

   The Sort menu appears.

When Block is on, pressing Merge/Sort (Ctrl-F9) automatically takes you to the Sort menu. Because a defined block is already in memory, WordPerfect does not prompt you to enter input and output files. Once in the Sort menu, you can select any option and set any values as usual.

While the bottom of the screen displays the Sort menu, the top portion shows the beginning of the block. If you want to view the file being sorted, you can scroll only in the blocked area; other parts of the file are off-limits.

When the sorting operation is complete, only the blocked part is affected; the rest remains intact.

Sorting Numerics

Numbers can be sorted as alphanumerics or numerics. Numbers of equal lengths, such as phone numbers or social security numbers, can be sorted correctly as numerics or alphanumerics. If you have numbers of unequal lengths, you must do a numeric sort to arrange the numbers correctly according to their arithmetic values.

Let's use the Okie Bird Watchers Society database as an example of doing a numeric sort. To sort this database according to the $$$ column, you need to go to the Sort menu and change several values. Make sure that you are in line sort before you do anything else. Then change the values of Key1 to "n 6 1" and the order to descending. If you now select **Perform Action** (**1**), the result is shown in figure 14.11.

Fig. 14.11.

The database after a numeric sort.

LName	FName	Address	City	Phone	$$$
Jay	Blu	222 Main St.	Ridge City	858-3322	300
Foxxe	Fanny	999 Broad St.	Cedar City	990-5544	250
Byrd	Ura	290 Center Rd.	Jinx	922-2166	220
Fish	Ham	3030 Circle Dr.	Spring	484-4949	120
Fish	Golda	3030 Circle Dr.	Spring	484-4949	110
Wing	Red	1234 5th St.	Oakdale	299-4533	100
Salmon	Smokey	844 Gill St.	Crease City	888-4040	70
Salmon	Whitey	844 Gill St.	Crease City	888-4040	60
Byrd	Ima	290 Center Rd.	Jinx	922-2166	50

Okie Bird Watchers Society

Doc 1 Pg 1 Ln 1 Pos 12

The numerics column also can be totaled, averaged, and maneuvered in other ways as explained in Chapter 17. You also can add the dollar sign ($) in front of each number without interfering with the sorting or selection of records (true only in a numeric, not alphanumeric, sort).

The Select Function

If you have a large database, you can make good use of the Select function to manage your database. Select enables you to extract the records that meet the criteria you specify. Only the selected records, a smaller and more manageable number, appear on-screen, and you can do whatever you want with them.

When you choose **Select** (**4**) from the Sort menu, the cursor moves to the middle of the menu, just under the Select heading. At the same time, the bottom of the menu displays the following message:

+(OR), *(AND), =, <>, >, <, =, < =; Press **Exit** when done

Use the displayed operators to enter a selection formula. You need to combine an accurate formula with the correct values in pertinent keys to do a successful selection, or you could do a *Global Select* (to select the records satisfying the selection formula, regardless of the values in key fields), as explained in the following paragraphs.

Using the first database in this chapter as an example, let's select the two "Johnsons." With the database on-screen, go through the routine of using Sort.

When the Sort menu appears, follow these steps:

1. Select **Keys** (**3**).

   The cursor moves to Key1.

2. Press → twice, type *–1*, and press Exit (F7).

   The values of Key1 change to "a 1 –1".

3. Choose **Select** (**4**).

   The cursor moves to the Select field.

4. Type *key1=johnson* and press Enter.

5. Select **Perform Action** (**1**).

   All the records disappear except the two "Johnson" lines.

If you do a Global Select, however, you do not need to key the values of any key; the Global Select works regardless of values. All you need to do is enter a formula like the following:

keyg=johnson

The "g" after the "key" directs the sorter to select any record that has the value of "johnson" anywhere in that record.

To continue demonstrating this versatile Global Select function, let's use the paragraph database in figure 14.6 to select the records that contain references to IBM. With the database on-screen, go to the Sort menu (Ctrl-F9). Select **Type** (**7**) and then **Paragraph** (**3**). (If you select line sort for this example, WordPerfect will select lines and not paragraphs.) Choose **Select** (**4**) and enter the following formula:

keyg=IBM

Press Enter and select **Perform Action** (**1**). Theoretically two records (paragraphs) should be selected—the Matt Johnson and the Peggy O'Brien records—but only Matt Johnson's record remains on-screen. Peggy O'Brien's record contains a reference to IBM, but the reference ends with a period, and the period interferes with the selection. One remedy for this discrepancy is to change the formula to the following:

keyg=IBM + keyg=IBM.

With the added selection criterion, the two records are now selected from the database. The new formula instructs the sorter to select any record containing "IBM." or "IBM".

A similar complex formula also can be applied to the bibliography database (refer to fig. 14.9) to select specific books. For example, you can use the following formula to select all records (paragraphs) containing the words capitalism OR socialism OR communism:

keyg=capitalism + keyg=socialism + keyg=communism + keyg=socialism.

Using this formula, the program selects three bibliography entries: Cole, Fried, and Schumpeter.

You can enter a long formula in the Select field. The screen continues to move the entered text leftward to make room for more typed text. You also can use the cursor keys to move left or right and do limited editing. Pressing Enter or Exit takes you back to the menu bar at the bottom.

Let's use the Okie Bird Watchers Society database (refer to fig.14.8) to create another example of a complex formula used to select records. In this case, let's assume that you want to select the records of people who live in a particular town and contribute a particular sum of money.

With the database on-screen, go to the Sort menu. Select line sort, if necessary. Select **Keys** (**3**) and change the values of Key1 to "a 4 1" and Key2 to "n 6 1". With these values, you select the records according to fields 4 (City) and 6 ($$$). Press Exit, choose **Select** (**4**), and enter the following formula:

key1=spring ' key2>100

Press Enter or Exit. The formula tells the sorter to select anyone that lives in Spring (field 4) AND contributes more than 100 dollars (field 6). If you now choose **Perform Action** (**1**), WordPerfect selects two records meeting the criteria: Ham Fish and Golda Fish.

If you enter a complex formula, you have to observe some rigid rules. You must insert a space before and after the Select operators + (or) and ' (and). In addition, you must use parentheses to separate some variables. As in the Math function, parentheses can alter the meaning of a formula, and you need to put them in the right place.

For example, the following complex formula has the first two formulas inside a pair of parentheses (refer to fig. 14.8):

(key1=jinx + key1=spring) ' key2>=100

This complex formula tells the sorter to select any record that has the city of Jinx OR Spring, AND the dollar amount (of both Jinx and Spring) greater than or equal to 100. WordPerfect would select the following three records: Ura Byrd, Ham Fish, and Golda Fish.

If you alter the placement of parentheses in the complex formula, you get different results. Look at the following formula, for example:

key1=jinx + (key1=spring ' key2>=100)

Now you are telling the sorter to select any record from the city of Jinx OR any record that has a dollar amount greater than or equal to 100 from Spring. This formula results in four selected records: Ima Byrd, Ura Byrd, Ham Fish, and Golda Fish.

When a formula is in the Select field, you no longer can do an ordinary sort. To do a sort again, you must first erase the formula.

To erase a formula, do the following:

1. Choose Select (4) from the Sort menu.

2. When the cursor goes to the Select field, press Ctrl-End to erase the formula.

3. Press Enter and proceed to the other Sort steps.

If you have a large number of records selected, you may want to sort them. You can select Action (5) from the Sort menu and then Select and Sort (1). If you choose Sort Only (2), the selected records are not sorted. This last option takes a shorter time to implement.

Macros in Sort

The Macro feature can be put to good use if you use Sort often. The repetitive keystrokes can be stored in a macro and quickly replayed, thus saving you the time and trouble of pressing them one by one on each occasion.

If you often do a screen sort, for example, you can create a macro to store the beginning keystrokes.

To create a macro to store the beginning keystrokes for a screen sort, do the following:

1. Press Macro Define (Ctrl-F10).

2. Press Alt-S to indicate the name of the macro.

3. Type the description *To sort from screen to screen* and press Enter.

4. Press Merge/Sort (Ctrl-F9).

5. Select Sort (2).

6. Press Enter twice.

7. Press Macro Define (Ctrl-F10).

8. Press Cancel (F1).

The macro definition is complete after Step 7. However, the Macro Def message continues to blink on the status line, and the Sort menu is still on-screen. Pressing Cancel returns the screen to the regular document.

When you want to sort a database, just retrieve the file and activate the macro by pressing Alt-S. In a short time, the bottom half of the screen displays the Sort menu. You now can examine the messages and select options. When you have made your choices, select **Perform Action (1)**. If you want to sort with the same criteria a second time in the same session, just activate the macro and type *1*; everything is done for you.

If your needs are specific and fixed, you can enter all the keystrokes into a macro. Let's use the paragraph database in figure 14.6 as an example. Suppose you have built a large file and often need to select the records that contain the word "sales."

The following macro can help you select the records that contain the word "sales":

1. Press Macro Define (Ctrl-F10).

2. Type *sales* and press Enter.

3. Type the description *To select sales-related records* and press Enter.

4. Press Merge/Sort (Ctrl-F9).

5. Select **Sort (2)**.

6. Type a file name (such as SALES) and press Enter twice.

7. Select **Type (7)** and then **Paragraph (3)**.

8. Choose **Select (4)**, press Ctrl-End, type the formula *keyg =sales*, and press Exit (F7).

   The Ctrl-End keystroke is an extra precaution intended to erase any formula that may remain there.

9. Select **Perform Action (1)**.

10. Press Macro Define (Ctrl-F10).

To use this macro, press Macro (Alt-F10) and then enter the name *sales*. The macro retrieves the named file and automatically selects only the records containing the word "sales"; all the others files do not appear on-screen.

If you want to select the records containing the word "personnel" rather than "sales," you could define another macro, or you could edit the previous one.

To edit a macro, do the following steps:

1. Press Macro Define (Ctrl-F10).

2. Type *sales* and press Enter.

3. Select **Edit (2)**.

   The edit screen appears.

4. Select **Action (2)**.

   The cursor moves inside the edit box.

5. Change "sales" to "personnel" and press Exit twice.

If you use this macro now (after clearing the screen), it selects only those records that contain the word "personnel."

WP 5 Summary

After studying this chapter, you have learned how to build databases, how to sort and select records from the databases, and how to apply macros to save time in sorting operations. You are probably thinking of applying these techniques to your specific needs.

When you build a database, keep the following points in mind:

- Each line record is separated from another line record by a hard return.
- Two hard returns must separate paragraph records.
- A field inside a record is separated from another field by a tab code.

When you are ready to sort a database, follow these essential steps:

1. Press Merge/Sort (Ctrl-F9) and select Sort (2).

2. Enter the name(s) of input and output files. If the database is already in the computer memory, press Enter twice.

3. Examine the Sort menu and the displayed values. Change the values if necessary.

   To change a type of sort, select Type (7) from the Sort menu and choose Merge (1), Line (2), or Paragraph (3).

   To set the values of different Sort keys, select Keys (3) from the Sort menu, move the cursor left or right, and enter new values.

   To select records, choose Select (4) from the Sort menu and enter a formula.

4. If you want to sort only a portion of your document, block the portion and repeat the previous steps.

5. The final step is to select Perform Action (1).

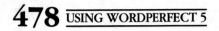

15

Converting Files

Judy Housman is a microcomputer software consultant and trainer in such programs as WordPerfect, 1-2-3, dBASE, Reflex, and Quattro. She is a WordPerfect Certified Training Instuctor based in Cambridge. Her training sessions afford the user hands-on WordPerfect experience. Housman currently leads the Boston Computer Society's Training and Documentation Group. ■

A s you've learned from earlier chapters, WordPerfect is a superb word processor. In most offices, however, tasks are so varied that even the most sophisticated word processor must be supplemented with other programs. For this reason, an office is likely to choose several programs that meet special needs—perhaps a spreadsheet to handle budgets and a database to track customers and their orders, in addition to a word-processing program.

Specialized software packages make transferring information necessary. WordPerfect is designed to read the information created within different programs and convert that information to a workable WordPerfect file. This chapter explains how to make file conversions between WordPerfect and spreadsheets, databases, and other word processors, including how to use the following:

- DOS text files (ASCII files)
- WordPerfect's Text In/Out feature
- WordPerfect's Convert and conversion facilities in other programs

This chapter concentrates on the most common translation problems, but it also offers techniques for solving more specialized problems. Many users won't perform every conversion discussed here, so you may prefer to concentrate on techniques that apply to your own situation. If you skim, though, do pay attention to the tips; many suggest strategies that can apply to various situations. If you use WordPerfect exclusively, you can skip this chapter. You may, though, learn ways to perform more efficiently using WordPerfect with another program.

Perhaps you haven't yet realized how using another program with WordPerfect can be useful. Let's look at some common situations that require file conversion.

Let's assume that you create a spreadsheet with one software package and now need to include that information in a long budget report—a cumbersome or impossible task with most spreadsheets. The ideal way to perform this task is to create the spreadsheets with 1-2-3 or PlanPerfect and incorporate the budget within a WordPerfect document. You then can take advantage of both the spreadsheet's calculation capabilities and WordPerfect 5's superb print formatting.

Because WordPerfect offers limited database capabilities, you probably keep customer and order information in a dedicated database (a software package, such as dBASE or Rbase®, designed to handle information organized in tables). To send personalized letters to clients without retyping information already in the computer, you can use WordPerfect's merge capabilities. Simply transfer information from your database to a WordPerfect secondary-merge file.

Finally, if you switch from another word processor to WordPerfect or if you work with a document created in a different word processor, you must convert documents to WordPerfect format. WordPerfect offers several methods for conversion; the one you choose determines how much additional work is required to reestablish the format of the original documents.

Here's some advice before you begin the tasks of conversion. An important consideration in choosing software is the ease with which you can move data between programs—*portability*. Choose software carefully, and you will minimize data-transfer problems. Avoid software that recognizes only products made by its manufacturer. One software expert explains, "There are three criteria for choosing software: portability, portability, and portability."

And once more, before you attempt any translation, be sure to backup your original data! It is easy to accidentally overwrite a WordPerfect file or another important file with a translated version. Finding the original may not be so easy.

Using DOS Text Files for Transfer

One common means of transferring information between software programs is with an ASCII or DOS text file. As you recall from Chapter 10, ASCII (American Standard Code for Information Interchange) is a standardized code for translating ones and zeros to numbers, punctuation marks, symbols, and special computer characters. A DOS text file, also called an ASCII file, consists of letters, numbers, punctuation marks, math symbols, and a few special codes, such as tabs and carriage returns, that share the same meaning across programs. You can type a DOS text of characters without translation.

Many programs create files with characters peculiar to the program. If you type a file at the DOS prompt (by typing the DOS command *TYPE* followed by the file name), and you hear bells, or see hearts, musical notes, or little happy faces, the file is not a DOS text file.

Many programs, including WordPerfect, can create and accept DOS text files. DOS text files, therefore, provide a way of transferring information between programs. One caveat: when you use DOS text files to transfer information, you can lose some special program characteristics (in WordPerfect, for example, bold or underlined characters).

Transferring 1-2-3 Spreadsheets into WordPerfect

You may need to create a report that combines budgets and text. Fortunately, incorporating 1-2-3 spreadsheets within a WordPerfect document with the help of a DOS text file is fairly easy. 1-2-3 can print to disk a DOS text file that looks just like the original spreadsheet. After converting the text file to WordPerfect, you can spruce up a budget with bolding, double underlining, and other special print characteristics.

To create a print file in 1-2-3, perform the following steps:

1. In 1-2-3, bring up the menu with a slash (/). Type *P* to indicate that you want to print, then type *F* to print to a file.

2. Type the name for the print file (see fig. 15.1) and press enter. If you do not provide an extension, 1-2-3 supplies the default extension .prn.

Fig. 15.1.
A 1-2-3 print file.

```
A1: [W4] 'The Secret Guide to Computers, Disbursement of Purchases      EDIT
Enter print file name: c:\work\text50\disburse.prn

        A         B              C           D         E
1    The Secret Guide to Computers, Disbursement of Purchases
2    For the month of May, 1984
3
4                                                   Master Chg.
5    DatePaid to:                 For:          Check #:  SG Check
6    =============================================================
7      1 Cab & Subway             CPA & Photos
8      2 Express Mail             Infoworld
9      3 Trevor Atkinson          Refund         952
10     3 Salem Postmaster         Postage        953
11     3 Romonow Box Co.          boxes          954
12     6 Ruggles                  lunch with Irene
13     6 Brighams                 lunch with Irene
14     7 Essex Office Assoc.      Refund         955
15     2 Irene Vassos             office supplies 956
16     2 Bank of Boston           Master Card
17       Computerland            Disk cleaner    957     $31.45
18       Electronic Supermart    R:Base          957     $310.88
19       Pan AM                  Refund-Pris travel 957  ($177.88)
20       Milbrook Off Furn.      Office chairs   957     $198.47
21-Mar-88  12:15 PM
```

If you want to store the file in the default directory, you simply type the file name and press Enter. The extension .prn is added automatically.

If, you want the file in a different directory, press the Esc key twice to clear the file name and path. Then type the full file name, including the directory where the file should appear.

    a. If a print file of the same name exists, 1-2-3 responds with the question Cancel Replace. Cancel is highlighted as the default. If you want to overwrite the file with the same name, choose **R**eplace (the older file then disappears). Otherwise choose **C**ancel, and begin the process again.

3. Choose **R**ange, then indicate the range you want to transfer to WordPerfect, either by using the point mode or by typing a previously defined range name and pressing Enter.

4. Choose **O**ptions **O**ther **U**nformatted.

The file now appears without headers, footers, and page breaks. Otherwise, the differences in formatting between 1-2-3 and WordPerfect would be confusing.

5. Choose **M**argins, then **L**eft. Enter the numeral **0**.

This step ensures that when you retrieve the file into WordPerfect, the first column is flush with the left margin.

6. Then choose **M**argins and **R**ight. Decide what number you want for the right margin. You cannot specify a right margin greater than 240.

The number you choose determines how many characters print in a line of the file. If you choose 80, the first 80 characters of all rows print before the next 80 characters in each row. Think about how many characters of each row will fit into a line of your WordPerfect document. Determine this number by the size of your paper, by whether you are printing in landscape or portrait mode, and by the type size. You may want to experiment.

7. **Q**uit the Options menu and return to the Print menu. Type **G**o (start printing). Then **Q**uit the Print menu.

Note: If you print a small file to disk, you may not notice the red light on your disk drive going on. Printing the file to disk is completed when you type *Q* for Quit. Do not press **G**o again, or more than one copy of the range will appear in the print file.

8. Bring up the menu with a slash (/) and quit 1-2-3 with **Q**uit **Y**es.

If you are in a hurry, you can print a file to disk by rote. Just follow these steps:

1. Type */PF followed by the name of the print file.*

2. Type *R* to highlight the range to print.

3. Press Enter.

4. Type *OOUML0* (This last *0* is a numerical zero, not the letter O.).

5. Type *MR* and a number of your choice no greater than 240.

6. Type *QGQ*

Now that you have turned your 1-2-3 data into a print file, you can bring the print file into WordPerfect.

1. Enter WordPerfect and retrieve the document where you want to place the spreadsheet.

2. Place the cursor where you want the spreadsheet to appear.

3. Press List Files (5), and retrieve the file you created in 1-2-3 with the command **Text**/In (**5**). The file should have the name you gave it, with an extension .prn.

Alternately, press Text In/Out (Ctrl-F5), and choose DOS **Text** File (**1**). With a spreadsheet, choose **Retrieve** (**2**) (CR/LF to [HRt]). This command changes carriage returns/line feeds (CR/LF) to the reveal code for hard returns ([**HRt**]). This marks the edges of the spreadsheet range with hard returns. Although some single rows may wrap, this command prevents rows from merging into one another.

When you initially import the print file, some lines of the file may have more characters than can fit in a line of the WordPerfect document. If this happens, the longer lines wrap around so that column headers appear in the second row (see fig. 15.2).

```
The Secret Guide to Computers, Disbursement of Purchases
For the month of May, 1984

                                         Master
Chg,    SG Check        Cash
DatePaid to:              For:          Check #:   SG
Check      Amount:    Amount:
==========================================================
============================
   1 Cab & Subway        CPA & Photos
                 $7,20
   2 Express Mail        Infoworld
                 $9,35
   3 Trevor Atkinson     Refund          952
         $1,60
   3 Salem Postmaster    Postage         953
      $105,75
   3 Romonow Box Co.     boxes           954
      $301,00
   6 Ruggles             lunch with Irene
                 $6,00
   6 Brighams            lunch with Irene
                 $3,00
   7 Essex Office Assoc, Refund          955
C:\WORK\TEXT50\DISBURSE,PRN              Doc 1 Pg 1 Ln 1 Pos 10
```

Fig. 15.2.
Wrapping that occurs with margin disparity.

One remedy for misshapen margins is to set the left and right margins to zero in WordPerfect. Another is to reduce the size of the characters (see fig. 15.3).

You may want to print the spreadsheet in landscape mode after you "pretty" it with bold and double underlining and other WordPerfect features. You may find, however, that the spreadsheet is still wider than the margins of your document and that wrapping still occurs. In this case, you must make some design choices: You can print different spreadsheet ranges to different print files. Or you can temporarily set the paper size to a width larger than you will actually print and use the Move Rectangle feature to create an attractive document.

```
The Secret Guide to Computers, Disbursement of Purchases
For the month of May, 1984

                                                    Master Chg.   SG Chec
   DatePaid to:                For:          Check #:  SG Check    Amount
   ==================================================================
     1 Cab & Subway            CPA & Photos
     2 Express Mail            Infoworld
     3 Trevor Atkinson         Refund           952                   $1.6
     3 Salem Postmaster        Postage          953                 $105.7
     3 Romonow Box Co.         boxes            954                 $301.0
     6 Ruggles                 lunch with Irene
     6 Brighams                lunch with Irene
     7 Essex Office Assoc.     Refund           955                   $2.3
     2 Irene Vassos            office supplies  956                 $140.0
     2 Bank of Boston          Master Card
       Computerland            Disk cleaner     957    $31.45
       Electronic Supermart    R:Base           957   $310.00
       Pan AM                  Refund-Pris travel 957 ($177.00)
       Milbrook Off Furn.      Office chairs    957   $198.47
       Radio Shack             Phone cords      957    $10.40
       Charette Corp.          Office Supplies  957    $11.97
     2 Russ Walter             Draw
       $10,000.00                               958
   C:\WORK\TEXT50\DISBURSE.PRN          Doc 1 Pg 1 Ln 1 Pos 17.14
```

Incorporating dBASE Reports within WordPerfect

With dBASE, you can print reports to disk. You can then retrieve the reports into WordPerfect with Text In/Out (Ctrl-F5).

Suppose that you define a report called SUBSCRIBE in dBASE that you want to incorporate in a WordPerfect document. You can accomplish this by having dBASE print the report SUBSCRIBE to a disk file. Let's call the disk file LIST.DOC.

Follow these steps within dBASE to print SUBSCRIBE to the disk file LIST.DOC:

1. At the dot prompt in dBASE, *Use* the file to which the report refers.

2. Type *REPORT FORM* followed by the name of the report, *TO FILE*, then type the name of the new file.

   For the example type the following the command:

   REPORT FORM Subscribe TO FILE List.doc

You can use any extension for the file; but if you do not provide an extension, dBASE supplies the extension .txt. If you would like to shorten your command, you can leave out the word "FILE" in this command.

The steps within WordPerfect to incorporate a dBASE report printed to disk in a WordPerfect document are identical to those used with 1-2-3 print files:

1. Enter WordPerfect, and retrieve the document where you want to place the spreadsheet.

2. Place the cursor where you want the spreadsheet to appear.

3. Press List Files (F5).

4. Select **Text In** (**5**) to retrieve the file created in dBASE.

As an alternative, you can press Text In/Out (Ctrl-F5) and choose DOS Text File (1). With a database report, choose Retrieve (2) (CR/LF to [HRt]). This step marks the end of the last column of the report with hard returns. Although a single row may wrap, this command prevents rows from merging into one another.

The remedies suggested for coping with wrapping rows in a spreadsheet also apply to database reports. You can widen margins, choose smaller typeface, or print in landscape mode. If none of these techniques corrects wrapping, you must make design choices.

Creating and Retrieving DOS Text Files

In this section, you use WordPerfect's capability to incorporate DOS text files produced in 1-2-3 or dBASE, using the Text In/Out key (Ctrl-F5).

WordPerfect also can create DOS text files. To use this feature, follow these steps:

1. Press Text In/Out (Ctrl-F5).

    The following menu appears:

    1 DOS **T**ext; **2 P**assword; **3** Save **G**eneric; **4** Save **WP** 4.2; **5 C**omment:0

2. Choose DOS **T**ext (1), then **S**ave (1).

Many word processors can import DOS text files. The file produced by this feature produces tabbed, indented, and centered text with spaces. Any date code or paragraph number changes into text. The end of each line appears marked with a hard return (a carriage return followed by a line feed). Hard page breaks are marked with the code for a form feed ASCII, code 12.

Using Text In/Out (Ctrl-F5) does not reproduce WordPerfect headers and footers, footnotes, or other special features. You can preserve these features when you print a file to disk using the DOS text printer, described in a later section.

You can, however, encounter major problems with such spacing formats as indentation and centering if you use DOS text files as a medium of transfer. When you try to edit an imported DOS text file, your troubles begin. For example, if you add text, indented paragraphs wrap at the margin rather than remain indented. The WordPerfect Convert program or a third-party conversion utility is a better method of translating between WordPerfect and other word processors.

Nevertheless, if your main goal is to transfer text with little or no special formatting between word processors, DOS text files provide a convenient universal language.

As you have seen, WordPerfect also can import DOS text files created by other programs. Press List Files (F5), move the cursor to the DOS text file, and choose Text In (5). This option retains forced returns at the ends of lines.

You also can bring a DOS text file into WordPerfect by pressing Text In/Out (Ctrl-F5), then choosing DOS Text (1). You then have the option of retaining hard returns or converting hard returns within the hyphenation zone to soft returns.

Using DOS Text Files To Transfer Tabular Reports

If you retrieve a DOS text file from a spreadsheet or a database report, you should retain hard returns to maintain columnar format.

The simplest way to retrieve a DOS text file from a spreadsheet is to use the Text In (5) option under List Files. As an alternative, follow these steps:

1. Press Text In/Out (Ctrl F5).

2. Select DOS **Text** (1).

3. Choose **Retrieve** (CR/LF to [HRt]) (2).

Using DOS Text Files To Transfer Text from a Word Processor

If you retrieve a DOS text file created by a word processor, you should convert carriage return/line feeds that occur near the end of the line to soft returns. Otherwise, you will have additional spacing in undesirable places when you edit. To convert hard returns within the hyphenation zone to soft returns, follow these steps:

1. Press Text In/Out (Ctrl-F5).

2. Select DOS **Text** (1).

3. Select **Retrieve** (3) (CR/LF to [SRt] in HZone).

With this set of commands, a single carriage return followed by a line feed near the end of a line becomes a soft return. A CR/LF occurring in the middle of a line is converted into a hard return. If two CR/LFs occur in succession, both become hard returns.

The substitutions this option makes for a carriage return followed by a line feed should largely match the type of line ending in the original text. A CR / LF occurring near the end of a line is usually the result of word wrap—the feature that pushes text to the next line when more text is typed than can fit within the margins. These CR /LFs become soft returns—returns whose position is monitored by WordPerfect. When more text is added, the appropriate place to wrap text changes. So WordPerfect repositions the soft return. As a consequence, text is always adjusted to stay neatly within margins.

Two CR/LFs in succession, no matter what their location within a line, are usually part of paragraph spacing. The author wants to retain the paragraph spacing of the original document.

Creative use of WordPerfect macros and of the search-and-replace feature can help to fine-tune conversions in this and other instances.

Installing the DOS Text Printer

You can print to a disk and create a DOS text file. To do this, you must first install the **DOS** Text Printer definition. You can find the DOS Text Printer on Printer Disk 3 in early editions of WordPerfect 5.

To install the DOS Text Printer, complete the following steps:

1. Press Print (Shift-F7).

2. Choose **S**elect Printer (**S**).

3. Place the disk with the DOS text file definition in drive A:

4. Choose **A**dditional Printers (**2**).

5. Choose **O**ther Disk (**2**).

6. Type *A:* and press Enter.

7. Use the cursor to highlight DOS Text Printer.

8. Choose **S**elect (**1**).

9. Press Enter to accept DOTEXPRI.PRS.

At the Printer Helps and Hint Screen, press Exit (F7) to go to the Select Printer: Edit menu. At the Select Printer: Edit menu, perform these steps.

1. Choose **P**ort (**2**).

2. Choose **O**ther (**8**).

3. Type in a file name such as *textfile* and press Enter.

4. Press Exit (F7) three times to return to the document screen.

Creating a DOS Text File to Using the DOS Text Printer

Now you can use the DOS text printer.

1. Press Print (Shift-F7).

2. Choose **S**elect Printer (**S**).

3. Use the cursor to highlight DOS Text Printer.

4. Choose **S**elect (**1**).

5. Press Exit (F7) to go back to the document screen.

You now can print a WordPerfect file to a DOS Text file simply by printing as you normally would. (The DOS Text file will contain the text of WordPerfect headers, footers, footnotes, endnotes, and other text not in the body of the document.)

To print a WordPerfect file to a **DOS Text** file, complete these steps:

1. Press Print (Shift-F7).

2. Choose **F**ull Document (**1**).

Remember to reselect your normal printer.

1. Press Print (Shift-F7).

2. Choose **S**elect Printer (**S**).

3. Use the cursor to highlight your usual printer.

4. Choose Select (**1**).

5. Press Exit (F7) to go back to the document screen.

CAUTION: If you print another document to disk, that document will have the same name as the first document and will overwrite the first document. The simplest solution is to rename the first document you printed to disk.

Saving a File in Generic Word-Processing Format

Saving a file in generic word-processing format is similar to saving the file as a DOS Text file. The DOS Text option replaces soft returns with CR/LFs, but the generic word-processing format replaces soft returns with spaces. This format, known as *streaming ASCII*, facilitates data transfer and controls word wrap.

To save a WordPerfect file in generic word-processing format, follow these steps:

1. Press Text In/Out (Ctrl-F5).

2. Choose Save **G**eneric (**3**).

Converting between WordPerfect 5 and 4.2

When you first use WordPerfect 5, you will doubtless find several occasions to convert documents between WordPerfect 5 and 4.2. Many older documents were created, for example, in WordPerfect 4.2 format. But you may want to reedit the documents with WordPerfect 5. Occasionally, you may need to share files with people still using WordPerfect 4.2.

Fortunately, converting 4.2 documents into version 5 occurs automatically on retrieving a 4.2 document into version 5, then saving the document. WordPerfect 5, however, is a dramatically enhanced program that handles print formatting in a very different manner. Certain codes such as 4.2 pitch and font changes cannot be converted automatically. Instead, a comment is inserted into the document that tells you to convert the code manually.

As you become more familiar with WordPerfect 5, you may wish to use a Conversion Resource File to automate the process of converting your font, bin, and page-length changes. See Appendix B for more information about upgrading to version 5. This appendix also contains valuable information about converting 4.2 macros to version 5 format and converting a 4.2 dictionary that you have customized to the 5 format.

Incidentally, before you attempt a mail merge within version 5, make sure that both the primary- and secondary-merge files are saved in WordPerfect 5 format.

Almost all software packages provide a way to convert files from an earlier format into the current format. WordPerfect is no exception. But many packages provide no means of converting from the current version to an earlier version. You are fortunate because WordPerfect also helps you convert WordPerfect 5 to WordPerfect 4.2 format.

Translating WordPerfect files to version 4.2 is easy. Follow these steps:

1. Retrieve the document to be converted to 4.2. format.

2. Press Text In/Out (Ctrl-F5).

3. Choose Save **WP** 4.2 (**4**).

WordPerfect translates the document into 4.2 format. Of course, WordPerfect 5 features not available in 4.2 are lost.

The capability for translating files between WordPerfect 4.2 and version 5 is particularly important for documentation conversion. Many word-processing conversion packages and other translation aids currently work only with WordPerfect 4.2, but these packages will soon be upgraded to work with WordPerfect 5. At present, however, using many of these conversion aids to translate from WordPerfect requires that you first translate a file from WordPerfect 5 to WordPerfect 4.2. Conversely, these translation aids produce WordPerfect 4.2 files, which must then be brought into WordPerfect 5.

CAUTION: Remember to give the new 4.2 document a new name. Otherwise, the 4.2 version will overwrite your version 5 document.

Using the WordPerfect Convert Program

WordPerfect Corporation provides a separate program, Convert, to aid file translation. The program is an important tool for data transfer.

Fig. 15.4.

Convert menu.

```
Name of Input File? letter.doc
Name of Output File? letter.wp5

1 WordPerfect to another format
2 Revisable-Form-Text (IBM DCA Format) to WordPerfect
3 Navy DIF Standard to WordPerfect
4 WordStar 3.3 to WordPerfect
5 MultiMate 3.22 to WordPerfect
6 Seven-Bit Transfer Format to WordPerfect
7 WordPerfect 4.2 to WordPerfect 5.0
8 Mail Merge to WordPerfect Secondary Merge
9 WordPerfect Secondary Merge to Spreadsheet DIF
A Spreadsheet DIF to WordPerfect Secondary Merge

Enter number of Conversion desired
```

If you are familiar with WordPerfect 4.2, you will find that the Convert program has not changed significantly with version 5. To run Convert, you must exit or shell from WordPerfect to the DOS prompt. Convert is not available from within WordPerfect.

Change to the directory where the file you want to convert is located, type *CONVERT* and press Enter. When promted for the name of the Input file, type the file name and press Enter. Next, type the name of the Output file and Press Enter. The menu in figure 15.4 appears.

From this menu, you can convert WordPerfect files to and from various formats. The following sections explain your options.

Using Convert To Translate between WordPerfect and Other Word Processors

The WordPerfect special Convert program preserves most formatting and special characteristics of the MultiMate®, WordStar, or WordStar 2000 file.

To translate files, access the Convert program. When the program asks Name of output file?, type the name for the output file. Include a path if you want the new file placed in a directory other than the current default directory.

The Convert program warns you if a file by the name you have chosen already exists and asks Confirm Overwrite of <*filename*> (Y/[N]). If you want to replace the old file, type *Y*. Otherwise, type *N*, and enter a new name.

The menu shown in figure 15.4 appears.

Options 1, 2, 4, and 5 are especially useful in translating between WordPerfect and other word processors.

Translating from WordStar

To translate from WordStar to WordPerfect, choose WordStar 3.3 to WordPerfect (4). The Convert program completes translation of the original WordStar document into WordPerfect format.

WordStar 2000 provides for translation into WordStar. First, translate WordStar 2000 into WordStar Professional Format. Then choose WordStar 3.3 to WordPerfect (4) to translate the resulting WordStar file into WordPerfect.

Translating from MultiMate ®

To translate from MultiMate to WordPerfect, choose MultiMate 3.22 to WordPerfect (5).

If a file is in MultiMate Advantage™, you'll have one additional step. First, within MultiMate Advantage, translate the MultiMate Advantage file into regular MultiMate format. Then choose this option to translate the resulting MultiMate file into WordPerfect.

If you get the message `Error--Invalid Input File Name` or `File does not exist`, try specifying the directory in which the file is kept, or check the spelling of the file name.

Using WordStar as an Intermediary Format

Because many word processors can translate files to and from WordStar, WordStar can be used as an intermediary format for translating between certain word processors such as Palantir. You can, for example, translate Palantir files into WordStar, using Palantir's conversion capabilities, then translate the resulting WordStar file into WordPerfect using Convert. Using WordStar as an intermediary preserves more formatting than converting the original program to a DOS text file and using WordPerfect's Text In feature.

If you have access to Document Content Architecture (DCA), however, you may find it even better as an intermediary. DCA is designed to preserve features when translating between different word processors.

Using Document Content Architecture

Document Content Architecture (DCA) is a standard established by IBM for the transfer of word-processing programs across IBM systems—from microcomputers to mainframe computers. Some word processors can translate files to and from DCA.

If Convert does not provide direct translation to and from a particular word processor, you may be able to translate the word processor's files to DCA and then use Convert to translate the resulting DCA file to WordPerfect. This method preserves much of the original formatting.

You also can use DCA format as an intermediary between WordPerfect and Microsoft Word.

Using Convert To Translate WordPerfect into Other Word Processors

Using Convert to translate *from* WordPerfect into other word processors is also straightforward. After you specify the name of the input file and the name for the output file, Convert presents a list of possible types for input file types and asks Enter Number of Conversion desired. Select WordPerfect to another format (1). WordPerfect then asks Enter number of output file format desired (see fig. 15.5).

Fig. 15.5.

Options for output file format.

```
Name of Input File? kahn.wp
Name of Output File? kahn.doc


1 Revisable-Form-Text (IBM DCA Format)
2 Final-Form-Text (IBM DCA Format)
3 Navy DIF Standard
4 WordStar 3.3
5 MultiMate 3.22
6 Seven-Bit Transfer Format
7 ASCII text file

Enter number of output file format desired
```

If you are translating WordPerfect into WordStar or MultiMate, choose the appropriate option. If you are translating into WordStar 2000, translate the WordPerfect file into WordStar. WordStar 2000 can accept Wordstar files. If you are translating into MultiMate Advantage, MultiMate can be used as an intermediary. (When you translate into MultiMate, remember that the output file must have the extension .doc.)

In general, if a word processor can accept DCA format, use DCA format (Revisable-Form-Text) as the intermediary. If a word processor cannot accept DCA format, you may be able to use Wordstar or MultiMate in this role. If the word processor does not accept files in any of these formats, you may want to purchase a specialized conversion program or use DOS text files as the medium of transfer.

The Navy DIF format was developed by the U.S. Navy to assist in the translation of word-processing files. This format is rarely used outside its special-purpose area.

Transferring dBASE into a WordPerfect Secondary Merge File

You are likely to keep information about clients or prospects in dBASE or another database. If, however, you want to send customized letters to names in your database, you can use WordPerfect's merge capability. In this case, you must translate dBASE files into a WordPerfect secondary-merge format.

If you look at the options for input file type, you see that dBASE does not appear (see fig. 15.4). Do not despair. Although dBASE files do not appear on the menu of the Convert program, dBASE is, fortunately, capable of producing mail-merge files. And the Convert program can translate mail-merge files into WordPerfect secondary-merge form.

This translation process has two phases. The first phase takes place within dBASE; a dBASE file is translated into mail-merge format. The second phase takes place within WordPerfect's Convert program; the mail-merge file is translated into WordPerfect's secondary-merge file.

Translating to WordPerfect Mail Merge from within dBASE

If you want to translate a file to a WordPerfect mail merge from within dBASE, follow these steps:

1. Start dBASE by typing *dbase* at the DOS Prompt.

2. To translate a dBASE file called CUSTOMER into mail-merge form (also called comma-delimited files), type *USE customer* at the dot prompt.

3. Then type *COPY TO customer DELIMITED* to create a mail-merge file, CUSTOMER.TXT.

If you want only certain fields from the original file to appear, list their field names after the word copy. For example, you can type the following command:

.COPY FIELDS first, last, company, street, city, state, zip TO customer DELIMITED

Only those fields which are part of the address to customer.txt are transferred.

4. Leave dBASE by typing . *quit*

TIP: You can give the resulting mail-merge file an extension. For example, the file can be called CUSTOMER.MRG. If, however, you don't supply an extension, dBASE adds the extension .txt to the file name you use. dBASE calls the same mail-merge file CUSTOMER.TXT.

Understanding Mail-Merge File Structure

You could easily learn to answer the questions asked by the convert program by rote and convert data without any problems. Let's take a moment, however, to examine the structure of a mail-merge file. Then you will understand what the questions mean and why certain answers are appropriate.

A mail-merge file (also called a *comma delimited file*) looks like the following:

```
"Eugene Povirk/Marlene Znoy","South Paw Books","Elmer
Road","Conway","MA","",12500.00
"Braverman, Ed","Ed Braverman Studio","337 Summer
Street","Boston","MA","",23750.50
"Demeter, John","Xerox Artists","One Sommers
Street","Somerville","MA","02141",55770.00
"Walsh, Sheila","Paragraphics","321 Harvard
Street","Cambridge","MA","02139",67450.00
"Bird, Larry","The Celtics","","French Lick","IN","",99999.00
```

Each field or different piece of information is separated from the next field by a comma. Each record or complete set of information about one item is separated by a hard return. (Every new record starts at a new line.) In the language of ASCII characters, a hard return has two components. The first of these is a carriage return (represented by the number 13), which moves the output device to the beginning of the same line. The second is a line feed (represented by the number 10), which moves the output device to the next line.

In a mail-merge file, quotation marks are placed around the contents of character fields (fields where alphabetic characters can occur). This ensures that fields containing commas are not divided. For example, a field might contain the name "Bird, Larry" with quotation marks around it. Because of the quotation marks, the name is not divided into two fields. Numeric fields, however, are not surrounded by quotation marks.

Translating Mail Merge to Secondary Merge from Within Convert

When you translate a mail-merge file to a secondary-merge file, follow these steps:

1. When the Convert program first asks `Name of input file?` type the name of the mail-merge file. In this example, type *customer.txt*. Remember that you may need to include the directory path as part of the file name.

2. The Convert program then asks `Name of output file?` Type the name for the output file. Include a path if you want the file to be placed in a directory other than the current default directory.

3. The Convert program warns you if a file by the name you have chosen already exists and asks `Confirm Overwrite of` <*filename*> `(Y/[N])`. If you want to replace the old file, type *Y*. Otherwise, type *N*, and enter a new name.

In this example, CUSTOMER.SF is a good name to give the output file. Naming secondary-merge files with the extension .sf (for secondary file) helps with file organization.

4. Then choose Mail Merge to WordPerfect Secondary Merge (**8**).

   Convert then tells you to `Enter Field Delimiter Characters or Decimal ASCII values Enclosed in { }`.

5. Fields in mail-merge files are separated by a comma. Type a comma (**,**) and press Enter.

   Convert then says `Enter Record delimiter characters or decimal ASCII values enclosed in {}` (see fig. 15.6).

```
Name of Input File? client.txt
Name of Output File? client.sf
Confirm Overwrite of client.sf (Y/[N])

1 WordPerfect to another format
2 Revisable-Form-Text (IBM DCA Format) to WordPerfect
3 Navy DIF Standard to WordPerfect
4 WordStar 3.3 to WordPerfect
5 MultiMate 3.22 to WordPerfect
6 Seven-Bit Transfer Format to WordPerfect
7 WordPerfect 4.2 to WordPerfect 5.0
8 Mail Merge to WordPerfect Secondary Merge
9 WordPerfect Secondary Merge to Spreadsheet DIF
A Spreadsheet DIF to WordPerfect Secondary Merge

Enter number of Conversion desired 8

Enter Record delimiter characters or decimal ASCII values enclosed in {}
{13}{10}
```

Fig. 15.6.

Prompts for mail merge to secondary merge.

Records in mail-merge files are separated by a hard return; this hard return is represented by a carriage return (ASCII code 13) followed by a line feed (ASCII code 10).

6. Type {*13*}{*10*} and press Enter. Remember that ASCII codes for nontext characters must be surrounded by curly brackets.

   Convert then instructs you to Enter character to be stripped from file or press Enter if none

7. A mail-merge file may include extra quotation marks designed to keep a field including commas from being split up. In response to this question, type *"* and press Enter.

In short, the responses to the questions asked by the Convert utility translating a mail-merge file into WordPerfect secondary mail merge include the following:
  < name of input file><name of output file>8,{13}{10}"

TIP: This section concentrates on translating comma-delimited format with fields separated by commas and records, separated by a line feed followed by a carriage return. You can, however, use the Convert utility to translate formats using other symbols to mark fields or records. When the Convert utility requests that you enter the field delimiter, simply enter the symbol or symbols (or an ASCII code encased in curly brackets). Similarly, you can enter another appropriate symbol or symbols for record delimiter or character to be stripped.

Converting dBASE Dates

Dates present special problems. When dBASE converts a dbf file to mail-merge format, the date "12/31/87" is changed to the number "19871231"—not a pretty, or even intelligible, sight in a letter. You may want to copy the original dBASE file to another temporary file and change date fields to character fields. Then "12/31/87" appears as the character string "12/31/87".

Better yet, you can add a few new fields to the temporary file and separate the date into three dBASE fields that give the month, date, and year. Thus, instead of a date field with the contents "12/31/87", your database will contain fields with the contents "December", "31", and "1987". The following process lets you create mail-merge letters with dates in the more usual form of December 31, 1987.

Suppose one of the fields is a date field called BIRTHDAY. You can modify the structure to include new fields named BIRMONTH, BIRDAY, and BIRYEAR.

Follow these steps to create mail-merge files with the year, day, and month in separate fields. At the dot prompt in dBASE, type the following commands, pressing Enter after each command:

1. Type *copy <filename> to temp* and press Enter.

   (Substitute the name of your file for *<filename>*.)

2. Type *use temp* and press Enter.

3. Type *modify structure* and press Enter.

4. After you have typed *modify structure*, add the following fields:

   birmonth A character field with a width of nine

   birday   A numerical field with a width of two and no decimal places

   biryear   A numerical field with a width of four and no decimal places

At the dot prompt:

1. Type *replace all birmonth with cmonth (birthday)* and press Enter.

2. Type *replace all birday with day (birthday)* and press Enter.

3. Type *replace all biryear with year (birthday)* and press Enter.

4. Type *copy to newfile delimited* and press Enter.

Thus if a certain record has the birthday 12/15/60, birmonth is December, birday is 15, and biryear is 1960.

The WordPerfect merge file you create includes fields with the contents December, 15, and 1960. These contents clearly have more potential in merged letters than 19601215.

An important principle is illustrated here. Think about whether it is easier to perform a necessary manipulation in the program where data is originally entered or in the program to which data is transferred. Sometimes WordPerfect macros are the ideal way to clean up data transfer. And sometimes cleaning up the file before you transfer it into WordPerfect is easier.

TIP: Although two programs may not directly transfer to one another, they may both have a third program in common. You can then use the third program as a conduit to transfer data.

You may want to translate a particular program such as dBASE into WordPerfect. Unfortunately, the program's translation program cannot create or import WordPerfect files, and the WordPerfect Convert program does not list the program in question as an option. Determine whether the program you want to translate into WordPerfect can create a file that the Convert program does recognize. In this case, dBASE can create a mail-merge file; and Convert can translate a mail-merge file into a WordPerfect secondary merge. Although, for example, Convert does not list 1-2-3 as an option, both 1-2-3 and Convert can accept and create the DIF format.

Using Spreadsheet DIF To Convert WordPerfect Secondary-Merge Files

Spreadsheet DIF (Data Interchange Format) is a format created and documented by Software Arts, creators of the original spreadsheet VisiCalc ®, to facilitate data transfer. Both 1-2-3 and dBASE can create and accept data in DIF.

To transfer a WordPerfect secondary merge into DIF format, complete the following steps:

1. Type *CONVERT* at the DOS prompt in the subdirectory where the Convert program is located.

2. Type the name of the file to be converted as the input file and press Enter.

3. Type the name of the output file and press Enter. You must give the output file the file extension *.dif*.

4. Then choose WordPerfect Secondary Merge to Spreadsheet DIF (**9**). The secondary- merge file is transformed into DIF form.

Then, to translate DIF into 1-2-3, complete these steps:

1. Enter the Lotus translate facility, either through the Lotus Access Menu or by typing *trans*.

2. The translate menu walks you through translating a file in DIF format into a 1-2-3 or Symphony worksheet. Make selections by moving the cursor to the appropriate choice and pressing Enter.

3. Translate a DIF file column by column.

CAUTION: If the DIF file you want to translate is in a directory other than the current one, it does not appear in the list of available files.

When the translate utility lists available files, press the Esc key twice. The cursor is then positioned at a blank space entitled Source. Type the drive and directory where the file you want to translate is located. Follow that with the file template: *.dif(i.e. c:\data\ *.dif*.

The translate utility produces a file with the same file name as the translated DIF file—and an appropriate extension such as wk1 or wks. You can retrieve this file into 1-2-3. You will, however, probably have to change column width settings.

Generally, use the print-file option to incorporate spreadsheets into WordPerfect. To translate a 1-2-3 spreadsheet into a WordPerfect secondary-merge file, first use the Lotus translate utility to change the worksheet to DIF format. Then run the Convert program, using option Spreadsheet DIF to WordPerfect Secondary Merge (**A**).

Translating a WordPerfect secondary-merge file into dBASE using just Convert and dBASE can be cumbersome. The dBASE file to hold the data is not created automatically—you have to define each field.

TIP: The 1-2-3 translate facility can simplify the process of converting a secondary-merge file into a dBASE file. Translate the WordPerfect merge file to DIF format with WordPerfect Secondary Merge to Spreadsheet DIF (9). Then use 1-2-3's translate facility to transform the DIF file into a spreadsheet. Finally, use 1-2-3's translate facility once again to turn the resulting spreadsheet into a dBASE file. You may need to adjust column widths or manipulate other format before you change the worksheet into a dBASE file. (You will find this task even easier if PlanPerfect is available.)

Using Seven-Bit Transfer Format

The Convert program also offers an option for conversion to Seven-Bit Transfer Format to WordPerfect (6). This option is used to send WordPerfect files through a modem. But most communication programs have protocols such as XMODEM which can transfer WordPerfect files without using this conversion, so this option is rarely used.

Using Convert without Menus

If you perform a particular conversion often, WordPerfect's prompts and your responses become second nature. The Convert program menus become unnecessary, and indeed you may regard them as a nuisance. Fortunately, you can bypass Convert menus. At the DOS prompt in the subdirectory where the convert program is located, simply type *convert*, then type each response in turn, separated by spaces, to conveniently bypass the Convert menus. If you remember only the first few steps, just type *convert* and those responses you do remember, separated by spaces at the DOS prompt. The program bypasses the steps you remember.

At the DOS Command line, use the following format to convert without menus:

convert (input file name) (output filename) (number for input file type) (number for output file type—only needed if **1** WordPerfect is selected for input type) (field delimiter) (record delimiter) (characters to be stripped)

You have to supply field delimiter, record delimiter, and characters to be stripped only if Mail Merge to WordPerfect Secondary Merge (**8**) is the input file type. If you need to use the following responses, enter them as they appear at Convert menu prompts:

Typing *CONVERT letter.doc letter.wp 5* converts a MultiMate file to a WordPerfect document. Remember that the MultiMate file must be in the current directory, or the Convert program responds with Error-Invalid

Input File Name or File does not exist. The letter.wp file is placed in the current subdirectory.

Typing *CONVERT c:\work\contract.doc c:\data\contract.wp 5* converts a MultiMate file in the C:\WORK directory to the WordPerfect document contract.wp. CONTRACT.WP is found in the subdirectory C:\DATA.

Typing *CONVERT c:\data\clients.txt clients.sf 7 , {13}{10} "* converts a mail-merge file named CLIENTS.TXT located in the C:\DATA directory to a WordPerfect secondary-merge file CLIENTS.SF, located in the current directory.

Performing Mass Conversion

With WordPerfect, you can use the DOS wild card *. Thus, the command *CONVERT *.doc *.wp 5* converts all MultiMate files in the current directory to WordPerfect files with the extension .wp. Be careful, however, that all files in the directory with the .doc extension are, in fact, MultiMate files.

Translating WordPerfect 4.2 into WordPerfect 5.0

WordPerfect's Convert utility now includes the capability to translate WordPerfect 4.2 files into WordPerfect 5.0 as option 7. Usually, you only want this option when you are converting a group of 4.2 documents into 5.0. An easier way to convert a single 4.2 document to 5.0 format is simply to retrieve the document through List Files.

If all the files in the current directory are 4.2 files, the following command converts all the files in the current directory to 5.0 format files with the extension .old:

*CONVERT *.* *.new 7*

Translating WordPerfect 5 to ASCII Text Files

WordPerfect's Convert utility now includes the capability to translate Wordperfect 5 into ASCII text files by choosing WordPerfect to another format (1), followed by ASCII Text Files (7). Usually, you use this option only when you are converting a group of version 5 documents into ASCII text. An easier way to convert a single version 5 document to ASCII is simply to use the options under the Text In/Out key (Ctrl-F5) for saving a file as a DOS text file (described earlier).

If all the files in the current directory are 5 files, the following command converts all the files in the current directory to ASCII text files with the extension .dos:

*CONVERT *.* *.dos 1 7*

Using PlanPerfect for Data Translation

Sometimes it is easier to translate a file in one software package to a file in another software package, using a third package as an intermediary. WordPerfect Corporation's PlanPerfect is versatile at translating WordPerfect and WordPerfect merge files to and from various popular software. Translating a WordPerfect merge file into dBASE becomes, for example, much less tedious with the help of PlanPerfect. You may find that PlanPerfect's data-conversion capabilities alone justify the cost of the package.

PlanPerfect now converts to and from 4.2 format. Fortunately, WordPerfect 5 automatically converts 4.2 files as they are retrieved, so you do not have to take special steps for files imported into WordPerfect.

When you translate from WordPerfect into other formats, the file must first be converted into 4.2 format. Just retrieve the file and press Text In/Out (Ctrl-F5). Then choose Save **WP** 4.2 (**4**). You can then import the resulting file into PlanPerfect.

No more than three major steps are involved in software to and from WordPerfect formats when you use PlanPerfect. For WordPerfect files, simply complete the following steps:

1. Translate the original file into 4.2 format.

2. Translate the 4.2 file into PlanPerfect.

3. Translate the PlanPerfect file into the new format.

For other software, simply translate the file into PlanPerfect format, then translate the PlanPerfect worksheet into WordPerfect.

To illustrate this process, the following steps show how to use PlanPerfect to translate a WordPerfect merge file into a dBASE file. You change a WordPerfect secondary-merge file, CLIENT.SF, into a dBASE file, CLIENT.DBF.

Translating the 5 File into 4.2 Format

Within WordPerfect, follow these steps:

1. Press Retrieve (F10), and retrieve the file, CLIENT.SF.

2. Press Text In/Out (Ctrl-F5).

3. Choose Save **WP** 4.2 (**4**).

To make sure the new file does not overwrite the original, give the file a new name—CLIENT.42

Translating the 4.2 File into PlanPerfect Format

First, translate the WordPerfect merge file into PlanPerfect. Follow these steps:

1. Within PlanPerfect, press Convert (Ctrl-F5). The menu shown in figure 15.7 appears.

Fig. 15.7.

PlanPerfect Convert menu.

```
Convert Menu

    1 - Import a file into worksheet

    2 - Export worksheet to a file

    3 - Select import/export format      [WP Doc]

    4 - Add password

    5 - Delete password

    6 - Save worksheet in MP 2.1 format




    Selection: 0
```

2. Type **3** to Select import/export format. The menu shown in figure 15.8 appears.

Fig. 15.8.

PlanPerfect Text In/ Out menu.

```
Import/Export Format              [WP Merge]

    1 - WordPerfect Document

    2 - WordPerfect Merge File

    3 - DOS Text File (space-filled)

    4 - DOS Text File (with tabs)

    5 - Lotus 1-2-3 Worksheet

    6 - Dbase II/III File

    7 - DIF File

    8 - Other
            Row Delimiter
            Column Delimiter
            Spaced-Filled (Y/N)    N


    Selection: 0
```

3. Choose **2** for WordPerfect Merge File and press Enter.

4. List files and choose **5** Import to retrieve CLIENT.42 into PlanPerfect

   or

   Press Convert (Ctrl-F5), and choose **1** Import a File into Worksheet. Type CLIENT.42 as the name of the file.

5. Press Save (F10), and call the file CLIENT. PlanPerfect saves the file as CLIENT.MPW.

Translating the PlanPerfect File into the New Format

Complete the second set of commands to translate the PlanPerfect file into a dBASE file. Follow these steps:

1. Press Text In/Out (Ctrl-F5).

2. Type **3** to Select import/export format.

3. Choose **6** for Dbase II/III File.

4. Choose Export a Worksheet to a File (**2**). Type the name *CLIENT.TXT.*

You will then have a mail-merge file. Enter dBASE and create a database file with the appropriate number of fields, data types, and lengths. You can then complete the creation of a dBASE file by entering the command *append from new delimited* at the dot prompt.

You easily can adapt the steps for translating WordPerfect merge into a dBASE format to other programs listed on the MathPlan convert. Simply substitute the original software in Step 3 of the first set of commands and the software you want to convert to in Step 3 of the second part of the sequence.

Translating 1-2-3 spreadsheets into WordPerfect files through PlanPerfect offers certain advantages. The resulting file is a WordPerfect file that can be incorporated into a document using Retrieve (Shift-F10). Therefore, even if you change numerical entries, the decimal place remains aligned. Furthermore, decimals line up if the document is printed with proportional spacing. This alignment does not happen with a 1-2-3 print file, which uses spaces rather than tabs to separate columns. Columns and decimals do not line up if you print the document with proportional spacing.

WP 5 Summary

In this chapter, you've learned that WordPerfect can exchange information with other software. This exchange feature allows you to accomplish any task with the best tool.

For example, you can now do the following tasks:

- Incorporate budgets from 1-2-3 by printing the spreadsheet to disk, then bringing the file into WordPerfect with the Text In option of List Files (F5).

- Translate other word processors to and from WordPerfect using the Convert program.

- Merge information from a dBASE file into a WordPerfect letter with the help of Convert.

- Use DCA, DIF, and Mail Merge formats as useful intermediaries for data transfer.

- Decide between performing a necessary manipulation in the original program or in the program to which data is transferred.

Transferring data in and out of WordPerfect sometimes takes many steps, but with a little practice it becomes routine. Because most business presentations involve both numbers and texts, which must be combined to create a useful report, data transfer has assumed increasing importance. Data transfer is an important method of combining powerful numerical and data analysis with WordPerfect's superior text-handling capabilities.

Part
III

Using WordPerfect's Specialized Features

Includes

16

Working with Text Columns

Hans Lustig, a copy chief for an industrial advertising agency, uses WordPerfect to write copy for industrial brochures and manuals. Through his work, he has developed an expertise in working with text columns in WordPerfect. ■

WordPerfect offers you a powerful feature that lets you put your text in one of two types of columns: newspaper style, also called *snaking* columns, and parallel columns. *Newspaper columns* provide flowing text that wraps from the bottom of one column to the top of the next column and then wraps back to the first column on the left on the next page. *Parallel columns* are read from left to right across the page, unlike newspaper columns, which are read from top to bottom.

In this chapter, you explore WordPerfect's Column feature. The basic procedure for invoking the Column feature is the same for both newspaper-style columns and parallel columns. You learn how to set up both kinds of columns, how to work with them, and how to edit them. You learn how to mix columns with regular text and how to preview your masterpiece. You learn also how to use macros, the keyboard mapping capability of WordPerfect, to speed up the process. You start with newspaper columns and walk through the various procedures step by step; then you do the same with parallel columns.

Newspaper Columns

If you're a newspaper reporter, a copywriter for an advertising agency, or simply have been roped into doing the newsletter for your club, you probably want your text in column format. Even simple newsletter copy, such as you see in figure 16.1, looks better and is easier to read if the copy is in newspaper-column format. Text in columns is easier for the eye to follow, particularly if the text is spaced correctly (neither too close together nor too far apart), than text in page-wide printing.

Fig. 16.1.

*An example of
newspaper columns.*

New Drivers School Location

There's been a change in the location for this year's drivers school for the Windy City Chapter, and I know you'll love this one! Instead of going to Blackhawk Farms, we'll be going up to Road America in beautiful Elkhart Lake, Wisconsin.

This way, all you hotshoes will have about 4.5 miles instead of 2.5 miles to thrash your Bimmers around the track. It'll also be easier on your brakes than Blackhawk, due to the longer straights that'll give them a chance to cool off between turns.

The dates will remain the same, May 21 and 22. Lodging, as always, will be available at Siebkens and Barefoot Bay in Elkhart Lake, or at Motels in Sheboygan or Fond du Lac. Remember, you must make your own reservations. Remember also that Siebkens is basically a summertime resort, which means NO HEAT in the rooms. Also no phones and no credit cards. But LOTS of ATMOSPHERE. The rates at both Siebkens and Barefoot Bay are quite reasonable, $24 and $48 (single/double) at Siebkens and $59.95 at Barefoot Bay for either single or double. Driving directions to Elkhart Lake will be included with your registration package, along with a map of the area.

SATURDAY DINNER

There'll be dinner at Siebkens Saturday night, with a choice of fish, duck or prime rib. The cost will be $15 plus tip. We'll have a cash bar also, but remember you'll want a clear head the next morning or your Bimmer will start playing tricks on you. So go easy on the liquid stuff.

If you want to join us for dinner, let Registration know Saturday morning what your choice of entree is, otherwise there'll be no food waiting for you.

PRETECH AT LEO'S

Pretech will as always be at Leo Franchi's Midwest Motor Sports. The date is April 23. This will give you a chance to get anything fixed before the drivers school. A tech sheet is enclosed with the registration package. Be sure to fill it out and bring it along. There is no charge for the tech inspection. We're planning to start at 9 a.m. and go until everybody is done.

If you miss the tech at Leo's, you'll have to go to your favorite mechanic and bring proof of the inspection and any repairs that were made. Remember, NO TECH - NO TRACK.

We look forward to seeing you all at Elkhart Lake.

Enjoy!

Defining Newspaper Columns

WordPerfect allows you to have as many as 24 columns on a page and gives you many choices for setting them up. The program displays the first set of options for text and math columns in the following menu when you press Math/Columns (Alt-F7):

1 Math On; **2** Math Def; **3** Column On/Off; **4** Column Def: 0

Options **1** and **2** deal with creating math columns (see Chapter 17). The last two menu choices concentrate on text columns.

When you choose Column **Def** (**4**) from the menu, the Column Definition screen appears (see fig. 16.2) and displays the default settings. If you want the default settings for your document, simply press Exit (F7). Then select Column On/Off (**3**) at the place where you want to start typing your text. For a different format, follow the steps as outlined below.

```
Text Column Definition

   1 - Type                        Newspaper

   2 - Number of Columns           2

   3 - Distance Between Columns

   4 - Margins

   Column   Left    Right   Column   Left    Right
     1:     1"      4"        13:
     2:     4.5"    7.5"      14:
     3:                       15:
     4:                       16:
     5:                       17:
     6:                       18:
     7:                       19:
     8:                       20:
     9:                       21:
    10:                       22:
    11:                       23:
    12:                       24:

   Selection: 0
```

Fig. 16.2.

The Column Definition screen.

To define newspaper-style columns, do the following:

1. Move the cursor to the position where you want to start the columns.

2. Press Math/Columns (Alt-F7) to access the Math/Column Definition menu.

3. Select Column **Def** (**4**) to display the Column Definition menu (see fig. 16.2).

4. Select Number of Columns (**2**) if you want to have more than two columns of text and type in the number of columns you want; press Enter.

(To define newspaper columns, you do not need to select **Type** (**1**) because Newspaper is the default setting in WordPerfect.)

5. Select **Distance Between Columns** (**3**) if you want a different amount of space between your columns than the default 0.5″ (one-half inch) allows. Type in the amount and press Enter.

6. Now select **Margins** (**4**).

In most cases, you can accept the default margins offered by WordPerfect, which automatically calculates the margins of the columns, based on the margins you set for your document.

The columns that the default margins give you are of equal width and are spaced evenly across the page. If you want columns of different width, you must type in the margins for the columns you want and press Enter after each number.

7. Press Exit (F7) when you're finished defining the columns.

8. Select Column On/Off (3) to turn on Columns.

You're ready to start typing your newsletter or document.

WordPerfect inserts a column definition code, **[Col Def: {column margins}]**, into your document, which you can check in Reveal Codes (Alt-F3, or F11). As figure 16.3 shows, all your formatting codes are included, from hyphenation to justification to column definition. For columns, you may want to reset the hyphenation zone to reduce the raggedness of the right side of the column. (The defaults are 10% left and 4% right.)

Fig. 16.3.

Hidden codes for a newspaper column definition.

```
                        New Drivers School Location

There's been a           summertime resort,          what your choice of
change in the loca-      which means NO HEAT          entree is, otherwise
tion for this year's     in the rooms.  Also          there'll be no food
drivers school for       no phones and no             waiting for you.
the Windy City Chap-     credit cards.  But
ter, and I know          LOTS of ATMOSPHERE.
you'll love this         The rates at both                Pretech at Leo's
one! Instead of go-      Siebkens and Bare-
ing to Blackhawk         foot Bay are quite          Pretech will as al-
C:\WP50\QUENEW\NEWSCOL2.EVN                          ways be at Leo
                                           Doc 1 Pg 1 Ln 0.5" Pos 1"
{   ▲      ▲      ▲      ▲      ▲      ▲      ▲      ▲      ▲      ▲      }
[Hyph On][HZone:10%,4%][Just Off][T/B Mar:0.5",1"][BOLD][Cntr][Font:*Courier 18
PT  5 CPI]New Drivers School Location[Font:*Courier  9 PT 10 CPI][bold][Col Def:
3,1",3",3.25",5.25",5.5",7.5"][C/A/Flrt][HRt]
[HRt]
[Col On]There's been a[SRt]
[/]change in the loca-
tion for this year's[SRt]
drivers school for[SRt]
the Windy City Chap-
ter, and I know[SRt]

Press Reveal Codes to restore screen
```

You need to experiment to see which hyphenation zone fits your particular column setup best. To change the hyphenation zone, press Format (Shift-F8), select Line (1), choose Hyphenation Zone (2), and enter your new settings. Be sure that you do not have Hyphenation turned off.

If your text will be printed in a newsletter or brochure, keep the following rule of thumb in mind when defining column width for readability: for 9-point type, the text should not be wider than 18 picas (3 inches); for 10-point type, the text should not be wider than 20 picas (about 3.3 inches); and so on in the same relationship (based on 6 picas per inch).

You can change both the left and the right outside margins if you want your columns to be wider or narrower than the basic document. Set the remaining margins according to the spacing you want between columns. WordPerfect's default for spacing between columns is 0.5" (one-half inch), which is generous. When you print your newsletter with the default spacing, you get lots of white space between columns, so you might want to change the spacing to 0.25″ or 0.35″, which gives you a more attractive printed page.

Typing Columnar Text

Typing in Column mode is the same as typing in a regular document—you simply type as you normally would anything else. The text wraps automatically within the column and wraps to the top of the next column when you reach the bottom of the page. WordPerfect inserts a soft page code **[SPg]** at the bottom of each column because each is considered a separate page by the program.

Moving the Cursor

Cursor movement in columns is the same as in a regular document—with some exceptions. The GoTo keys (Ctrl-Home) work in combination with the arrow keys in the following way:

- GoTo (Ctrl-Home), → moves the cursor to the next column.

- GoTo (Ctrl-Home), ← moves the cursor back to the previous column.

- Home, ↓ moves the cursor to the bottom of the column on the current screen.

- Home, ↑ moves the cursor to the top of the column on the current screen.

- The ↑ and ↓ keys by themselves work as in any document and scroll all columns consecutively.

- The → and ← keys work within the column and move the cursor from the bottom of one column to the top of the next one.

- The gray plus (+) and minus (–) keys move the cursor to the bottom or the top of your on-screen column, respectively.

Centering Column Headings

To center a column heading over the text in a column, move the cursor to the left-hand margin of the column, press Center (Shift-F6), type the heading, and press Enter. If the heading already exists, move the cursor to the beginning of the heading, block the heading by pressing Block (Alt-F4, or F12), move the cursor to the end of the heading, press Center (Shift-F6), and answer *Y* (for Yes) to the prompt.

Combining Columns with Regular Text

You can switch back and forth between columns and regular text as many times as you like (see fig. 16.4). The original column definitions stay in effect for your document until you insert new definitions.

Fig. 16.4.

Combining newspaper columns with regular text.

```
Bay in Elkhart Lake,     playing tricks on      NO TECH - NO TRACK.
or at Motels in She-     you. So go easy on
boygan or Fond du        the liquid stuff.      We look forward to
Lac. Remember, you                              seeing you all at
must make your own       If you want to join    Elkhart Lake.
reservations. Remem-     us for dinner, let
ber also that Sieb-      Registration know      Enjoy!
kens is basically a      Saturday morning

        Note:        For those of you who have never been to Road
                     America, here's a little tip: At this time of
                     year, the weather up there in dairy country is
                     rather unpredictable.  Be prepared for either to
                     fry or freeze.

That's all there is      pads! They may come
for now.                 in handy.
Oh - bring brake
_____
        One more thing, watch out for the Wisconsin constabulary.
        They always find a great chance to help balance their
        budgets when we come up there.  So take it easy on highway
        57. That's their favorite money maker.

C:\WP50\QUENEW\NEWSCOL2.EUM              Doc 1 Pg 2 Ln 1.16" Pos 1"
```

At the point in your columnar document where you want to change to regular text, do the following:

1. Press Math/Columns (Alt-F7).

2. Press Column On/Off (**3**) to turn off Columns.

3. Type the regular text.

4. Press Math/Columns (Alt-F7).

5. Press Column On/Off (**3**) to turn on Columns.

If you mix text with this technique and want to keep your columns an even length, figure out in advance how many lines deep the columns will be before the start of the regular text. Then type your columnar text that many lines and press Ctrl-Enter, which inserts a **[HPg]** code into your document and takes you to the top of the next column. If you don't go through this procedure, you will probably end up with lots of white space in your printed text. If your last column is shorter than the ones on the left, the cursor jumps to the bottom of your columns when you press Enter after turning off Columns.

Creating Newspaper Columns from Existing Text

If you have an existing document that you want to convert to columns, you easily can change the text to a newspaper column format.

To change existing text to a newspaper column format, do the following:

1. Position the cursor at the beginning of the document.

If your document has a centered heading, position the cursor on the line below the heading, unless you want to include the heading in the first column.

2. Press Math/Columns (Alt-F7), define your columns, and turn on Columns by pressing **Column On/Off (3)**.

3. Press ↓.

WordPerfect automatically reformats your text into columns.

If you have Hyphenation turned on, WordPerfect either hyphenates the text automatically or continually asks you to confirm hyphenation. Depending on the length of your text, this can be a fairly lengthy operation.

Editing Newspaper Columns

Editing newspaper columns is not much different from editing standard text. You can delete text, insert text, and change attributes (Bold, Underline, and so on) just as you do in regular text; and cursor movement in columns is similar to cursor movement in regular text. Because the basic editing is the same as the procedures you learned in Chapter 3, this section concentrates on the procedures for manipulating columns.

In Column mode, the editing keys work within the column as illustrated in table 16.1.

Table 16.1
Editing Keys in Columns

Editing Keys	Function
Ctrl-End	Erases to the end of the line in the column you are editing
Ctrl-PgDn	Erases to the end of the column starting at the cursor position
→	Moves the cursor to the right within the column
←	Moves the cursor to the left within the column
↑	Scrolls up all columns together
↓	Scrolls down all columns together

You can use Move (Ctrl-F4) to cut or copy a sentence or paragraph within the column, but if you want to manipulate a whole column, you must block the column first.

To cut or move within the column, do the following:

1. Press Move (Ctrl-F4).

2. Select either **Sentence** (**1**), **Paragraph** (**2**), or **Page** (**3**).

Even though WordPerfect considers each column a page, the program moves, copies, or deletes the full page of text, not just one column, when you select **Page** (**3**).

3. Select either **Move** (**1**), **Copy** (**2**), **Delete** (**3**) or **Append** (**4**).

If you want to move or copy information within a column, WordPerfect asks you to put the cursor at the new location and press Enter. To move or copy the whole page, you should have a hard page break just before the place to which you want to move or copy. If you don't, WordPerfect inserts a soft page code for you.

To manipulate (move, copy, delete, or append) a complete column, do the following:

1. Go to the top of the column.

2. Press Block (Alt-F4, or F12).

3. Press PgDn.

4. Press Move (Ctrl-F4).

5. Press **Block** (**1**).

6. Press **Move** (**1**), **Copy** (**2**), **Delete** (**3**), or **Append** (**4**).

If you want to copy or move, move the cursor to the new location.

7. Press Enter.

Displaying One Column at a Time

If you feel the on-screen display of your columns looks too crowded, you can eliminate the multiple-column display and have WordPerfect show one column at a time on-screen.

To display one column at a time on-screen, do the following:

1. Press Setup (Shift-F1).

2. Select **Display** (**3**).

3. Select Side-by-side Columns Display (**8**).

4. Press *N* if you don't want side-by-side display, or press *Y* if you want to have all columns displayed on-screen.

5. Press Exit (F7).

In a single-column display, scrolling through the columns displays them as separate pages, but in their respective positions. In other words, the first column is on the left side on page 1 (see fig. 16.5); the second column is in its proper margins on page 2, and so forth. (This technique does not work the same way with parallel columns;

each parallel column segment is separated by hard page rules, but the columns all show on-screen at the same time.)

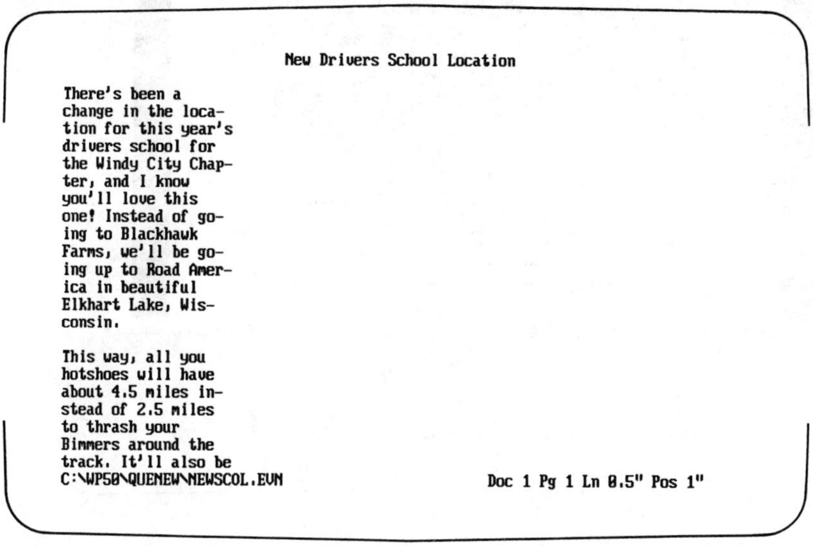

```
                    New Drivers School Location
There's been a
change in the loca-
tion for this year's
drivers school for
the Windy City Chap-
ter, and I know
you'll love this
one! Instead of go-
ing to Blackhawk
Farms, we'll be go-
ing up to Road Amer-
ica in beautiful
Elkhart Lake, Wis-
consin.

This way, all you
hotshoes will have
about 4.5 miles in-
stead of 2.5 miles
to thrash your
Bimmers around the
track. It'll also be
C:\WP50\QUENEW\NEWSCOL.EVN            Doc 1 Pg 1 Ln 0.5" Pos 1"
```

Fig. 16.5.
A single column display.

If you are in List Files (F5) and press Enter with the cursor on a columnar document, the display appears as a single column, just as if you had specified it.

Previewing Newspaper Columns

You can preview your columns with the View Document (**6**) feature of the Print menu (Shift-F7). Choose 100% (**1**) to see the document at approximately the size it will be on the printout (see fig. 16.6). If you want to see what the full page looks like (see fig. 16.7), press Full Page (**3**).

To preview your document, do the following:

1. Press Print (Shift-F7) to bring up the Print menu.
2. Press View Document (**6**) to see what your document will look like on the printed page.
3. Press Exit (F7) to return to your document.

If the number of lines in each column is unequal and you don't like the way your columns look on the page, you can even things out with a little mathematics. Simply add the number of lines and divide the total by the number of columns.

If you're working with 3 columns, for example, you may end up with 2 columns of 54 lines and 1 column of 20 lines (see figure 16.7). Adding the lines (54 + 54 + 20 = 128) and dividing by 3 columns produces 42.666, close enough to 43 lines. Next, go to the first column and insert a hard page (Ctrl-Enter) at the end of line 43.

Fig. 16.6.
View Document at 100%.

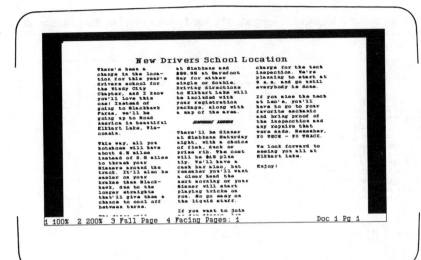

Fig. 16.7.
View Document at Full Page.

Insert another hard page at line 43 in the second column. You then have 2 columns of 43 lines each and 1 column of 42 lines (see fig. 16.8).

Printing Mailing Labels

Using the Column feature of WordPerfect can reduce the drudgery of printing mailing labels in multiple columns, particularly if you frequently produce many labels. The enhanced printing capabilities of WordPerfect 5 make printing mailing labels easy.

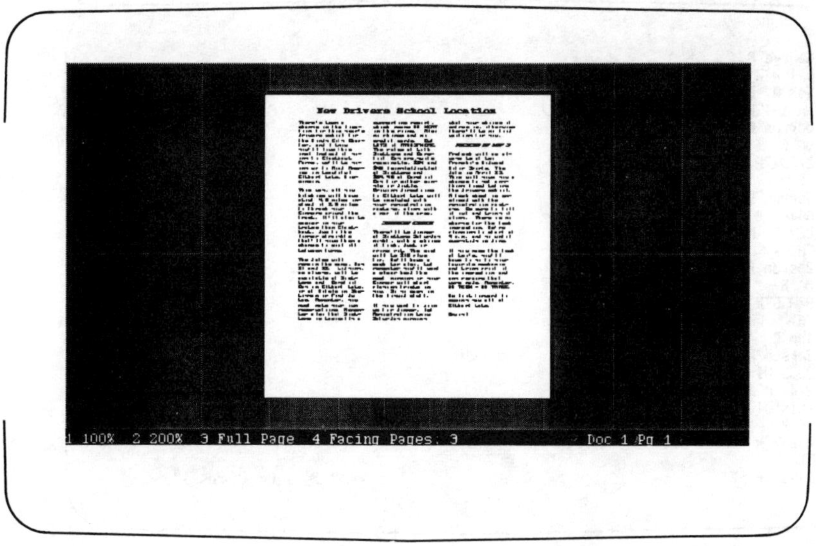
1 100% 2 200% 3 Full Page 4 Facing Pages: 3
Doc 1 Pg 1

Fig. 16.8.
Newspaper columns with even column length.

The first part of the procedure for creating mailing labels is to create two merge files and run a merge. (For more information about the Merge process, see Chapter 13.)

To begin the mailing label process, do the following:

1. Create a secondary merge file with your mailing-list data (see fig. 16.9).
2. Create a primary merge file with the field numbers coded the way you want them to print on your labels (see fig. 16.10).
3. Merge the secondary and primary files to create a single-column mailing list (see fig. 16.11).

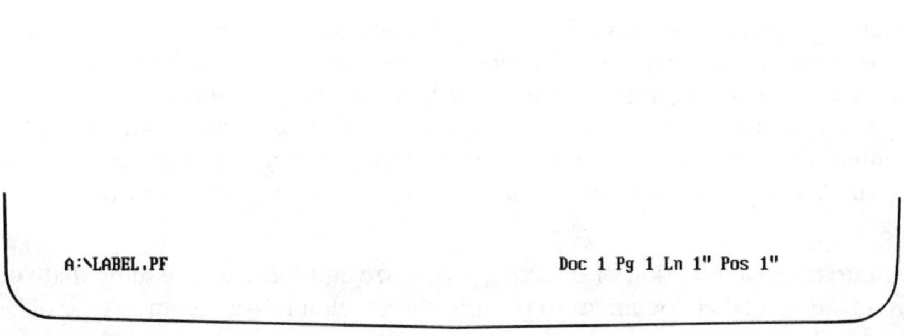
^F1^ ^F2^
^F3^
^F4?^
^F5^, ^F6^ ^F7^
A:\LABEL.PF
Doc 1 Pg 1 Ln 1" Pos 1"

Fig. 16.9.
A secondary merge file with mailing list data.

Fig. 16.10.

A primary merge file with codes for mailing labels.

```
George^R
Walsh^R
543 W. Broad^R
Rm 101^R
Vernon^R
VA^R
22234^R
^E
Johnny^R
Adams^R
222 E. Main^R
^R
Boston^R
MA^R
02355^R
^E
Tom^R
Jefson^R
3333 Virgin^R
Bldg A^R
Bristol^R
VA^R
23252^R
^E
A:\TEMP.SF                                    Doc 1 Pg 1 Ln 1" Pos 1"
```

Fig. 16.11.

The result of a merge, displayed in one column.

```
George Walsh
543 W. Broad
Rm 101
Vernon, VA 22234

===============================================================
Johnny Adams
222 E. Main
Boston, MA 02355

===============================================================
Tom Jefson
3333 Virgin
Bldg A
Bristol, VA 23252

===============================================================
Jim Madson
4040 E. 1st
2nd Flr
Conway, VA 20203

===============================================================
Andy Jack
                                              Doc 2 Pg 1 Ln 1" Pos 1"
```

After merging a primary file containing field-number (or field-name) codes and a secondary file containing names and addresses, the screen displays the merged document in one column, as shown in figure 16.11. Each name and its accompanying address are separated from the others by a hard-page code ([**HPg**]), represented on-screen by a double line. If you print the merged document as is, the mailing labels will print in the one-column format, and each label will print on one page.

To illustrate the vital function of selecting paper size and form, let's assume that you want your merged label document to print in three columns—a common type of label sheet—with a 1-inch height for each label and an 11-inch width for the whole sheet. To accommodate a wide sheet with vertically short labels, you need to tell WordPerfect to use a special paper size.

Unlike the simple steps in version 4.2 for setting left/right margins and page length, version 5 requires a more detailed process. The first step is to tell your printer to accept a form with 11-x-1-inch measurements.

With your merged label document on-screen, press Home, Home, ↑ to move the cursor to the top of the file.

Next, to indicate a new page form for your printer, do the following:

1. Press Print (Shift-F7).

2. Select **Select Printer** (**S**).

3. Select **Edit** (**3**) to edit your selected printer.

4. Choose **Forms** (**4**).

5. Choose **Add** (**1**).

6. Select **Labels** (**4**).

7. Select **Form Size** (**1**).

8. Select **Other** (**O**).

9. Type *11* (inches) for width and press Enter.

10. Type *1* (inch) for length and press Enter.

11. Press the space bar five times to save the selected information.

Now that your printer knows the form size, ask WordPerfect to use it by following these steps:

1. Press Format (Shift-F8).

2. Select **Page** (**2**).

3. Select **Margins** (**5**); type *0* for the top margin and press Enter; type *0* for the bottom margin and press Enter.

   The top/bottom margins are set to 0.

4. Choose **Page Numbering** (**7**).

5. Choose **No Page Numbers** (**9**).

6. Choose **Page Size** (**8**).

7. Select **Other** (**O**).

8. Type *11* (inches) as the width and press Enter; type *1* (inch) as the height and press Enter.

9. Select **Labels** (**4**) and press Enter twice.

The last step in the mailing label process is to create a three-column format by embedding necessary column codes in the label file:

1. Press Math/Columns (Alt-F7).

2. Select Column **Def** (**4**).

3. Select **Type** (**1**) and choose **Newspaper** (**1**).

4. Select **Number of Columns** (**2**).

5. Type *3* and press Enter twice to accept the preset values.

6. Select **Column On/Off** (**3**).

This procedure now has embedded the **[Col Def]** and **[Col On]** codes. When you press Home, Home, ↓, the label document is displayed in three columns.

The Reveal Codes screen in figure 16.12 shows the three critical codes—top/bottom margins, page numbering, and page size—embedded at the location of execution (the beginning of the document). You must embed these codes in front of all other codes, such as the codes for column definition, or WordPerfect may not recognize the codes or accept the specifications.

For example, if you put column definition codes *before* the page size/form codes, WordPerfect ignores the latter and uses the standard paper size of 8.5 x 11. Notice in figure 16.12 that the column definition codes reflect the paper size/type settings.

The third row of labels does not appear on-screen because when you defined the columns, the margins were expanded to accommodate the 11-x-1-inch paper size.

Fig. 16.12.

Three-column mailing labels shown in Reveal Codes.

```
   George Walsh              Johnny Adams                    T
   543 W. Broad              222 E. Main                     3
   Rm 101                    Boston, MA 02355                B
   Vernon, VA 22234                                          B

===================================================================================
   Jim Madson                Andy Jack                       A
   4040 E. 1st               456 Hickory                     1
   2nd Flr                   Memphis, TN 37703               P
   Conway, VA 20203


                                      Col 1 Doc 1 Pg 1 Ln 0" Pos 1"
   ▲    ▲    ▲    ▲    ▲    ▲ ] ▲ [ ▲    ▲    ▲    ▲    ▲ ] ▲ [
[T/B Mar:0",0"][Pg Numbering:No page numbering][Paper Sz/Typ:11" x 1",Labels][Co
l Def:3,1",3.66",4.16",6.83",7.33",10"][Col On]George Walsh[HRt]
543 W. Broad[HRt]
Rm 101[HRt]
Vernon, VA 22234[HRt]
[HPg]
Johnny Adams[HRt]
222 E. Main[HRt]
Boston, MA 02355[HRt]
[HPg]

Press Reveal Codes to restore screen
```

If you print your labels now, they will print as they appear on-screen. If the printing does not fit well on your actual labels, you may need to adjust the left and right margins or fine-tune the preceding specifications.

A Macro To Define Newspaper Columns

If you expect to use the same column definition frequently, save yourself time by writing a macro that lets you call up your predefined columns with just a few keystrokes. (For a more detailed explanation of WordPerfect macros, see Chapter 11.)

If you have macros from previous versions of WordPerfect, they do not work with version 5. You can use the Macro Editor to edit them for the new version, or you can rewrite them. Be aware, however, that the Macro Editor in version 1.0 and 1.1 of WordPerfect Library also does not work with your new macros.

To help ease the change to WordPerfect 5, a utility on the Conversion disk, MACROCNV.EXE, lets you convert those macros or parts of macros that contain text, cursor movements, and functions that have not changed. Functions that do not convert directly generate comments.

To define a macro that speeds up creating newspaper or parallel columns, do the following:

1. Press Macro Define (Ctrl-F10) and name your macro Alt-C for "columns."

    (You can use any Alt-key combination and call the macro whatever helps you to remember its function.)

2. Type a short macro description, such as *Newsletter Columns*, and press Enter.

    The words Macro Def start flashing in the lower left corner of your screen.

3. Press Math/Columns (Alt-F7) and select Column **Def** (**4**).

4. Select **Number** of Columns (**2**), type *3*, and press Enter.

5. Select **Distance** Between Columns (**3**), type *0.25*, and press Enter.

6. Press Enter to accept the margins calculated by WordPerfect.

    The Math/Columns menu reappears at the bottom of your screen.

7. Select **Column** On/Off (**3**) to turn on Columns.

8. Press Macro Define (Ctrl-F10) again to finish the macro.

    It appears in your list of files with the name ALTC.WPM.

The next time you want to use columns, simply position the cursor at the point where you want them to begin, press Alt-C, and start typing the text in your columns.

If you later decide to edit the macro, perhaps to change the margins of your columns, the Column Definition screen does NOT come up when you press Math/Columns (Alt-F7). Only the column code appears in the edit box. Therefore, you have to know the keystrokes to enter in advance. You may find it easier to rewrite the macro and erase the old one.

Parallel Columns

Listings, schedules, and so on, are ideal for parallel columns. Parallel columns are handy if you're setting up a tour itinerary, for instance. The first column might contain the date, the next the location, the third the hotel or dinner location, the next any special attractions to visit, and another any comments you might want to include regarding that particular point in the tour. Once the columns are set up, you easily can go from one column to the next. And if you save your column setup as a macro or a style, the setup is always available with only a few keystrokes.

Putting your information into parallel columns is much easier than using Tab and Indent to produce columns. Once you begin with Tab and Indent, you must continue to use them for every paragraph because a hard return takes you back to the left margin. In addition, depending upon how wide you want each column, you must reset your margins before you start and reset them back to the original when you finish.

Defining Parallel Columns

Unlike newspaper columns, parallel columns are designed to be read across the page from left to right. Setting up parallel columns follows the same basic steps as setting up newspaper columns; however, parallel columns require some preplanning because most columns are not the same width. First figure out how many columns you need and then decide how wide each column should be. Finally, consider the hyphenation zone for the columns.

If you normally work with Hyphenation on, be aware that the hyphenation zone in columns, particularly narrow ones such as you might use with parallel columns, is small. WordPerfect figures the hyphenation in percentages, the default being 10% left and 4% right. For a 2-inch column, for instance, the default settings mean that your left hyphenation zone is 0.2 inches and your right hyphenation zone 0.08 inches. With a 10-character-per-inch font, the zone allows you only 2 characters on the left and less than 1 character on the right. Because of this narrow zone, you may have to insert hyphens manually to straighten out your column lines. The same, of course, applies to newspaper columns, but the hyphenation problems are less noticeable there because the columns are wider.

The examples in this chapter have been created with Hyphenation on and by manually inserting hyphens in several places to improve the final appearance of the columns. You will have to experiment with different hyphenation zones to get the look you want for your text.

Let's use a tour itinerary example to set up parallel columns (see fig. 16.13).

To define parallel columns, do the following:

1. Press Center (Shift-F6) and type the overall heading for your document.

   For this example, type *Windy City Tour Schedule*.

```
                    Windy City Tour Schedule

     Date      Location      Hotel      Sightseeing      Remarks

    Oct 24    Luxembourg    Hotel       Tour of the      The Kasematten
                           Aerogolf-    Kasematten       are an ancient
                           excellent    and if time      fortification;
                           restaurant   permits, a       the Luxembourg
                           serving      short visit      Swiss area is one
                           French and   to the Lux-      of the most pic-
                           Luxembourg   embourg          turesque areas of
                           cuisine -    Swiss area.      the country.
                           the frog
                           legs and
                           Chateau-
                           briand are
                           highly re-
                           commended.


    Oct 25    Trier         Dorint      Porta Nigra;     Supposedly found-
                           Hotel        Cathedral        ed in 2000 B.C.,
                                        and Imperial     this small city
                                        Baths            became the capi-
    C:\WP50\QUENEW\PARALLEL              Col 3 Doc 1 Pg 1 Ln 4.33" Pos 3.4"
```

Fig. 16.13.

An example of parallel columns.

2. Press Enter twice to space down.

3. Press Math/Columns (Alt-F7).

4. Select Column **Def** (**4**).

5. Select **Type** (**1**).

6. Select either **Parallel** (**2**) or Parallel with **Block** Protect (**3**).

   If you choose Parallel with **Block** Protect (**3**) to set up a tour itinerary, for instance, each item in the listing begins with a **[BlockPro: On]** code, ends with a **[BlockPro:Off]** code, and automatically is kept together by WordPerfect.

7. Next, select **Number** of Columns (**2**).

8. Type in the number *5* and press Enter.

9. Select **Distance** Between Columns (**3**), and either accept the default of 0.5″ or enter a distance of your choosing.

   For your example, set the distance to 0.25″.

10. Type *0.25* and press Enter.

11. Finally, select **Margins** (**4**).

    For your example, type the margins that appear in figure 16.14 and press Enter after each one. Remember, you can set the margins wider or narrower than your regular document to suit your specific requirements.

12. Press Enter when you are completely finished.

13. Select **Column** On/Off (**3**) to turn on Columns.

Fig. 16.14.

*The Parallel Column
Definition screen.*

```
Text Column Definition

    1 - Type                          Parallel

    2 - Number of Columns             5

    3 - Distance Between Columns      0.25"

    4 - Margins

    Column   Left     Right     Column   Left     Right
       1:    0.5"     1.5"         13:
       2:    1.75"    2.75"        14:
       3:    3"       4"           15:
       4:    4.25"    5.5"         16:
       5:    5.75"    7.5"         17:
       6:                          18:
       7:                          19:
       8:                          20:
       9:                          21:
      10:                          22:
      11:                          23:
      12:                          24:

    Selection: 0
```

If you have upgraded from WordPerfect 4.2, you will be happy to know that the
program no longer rearranges your parallel columns when you get to the end of a
page. Version 5 takes page breaks in stride without losing a beat. Figure 16.15 shows
how column 3 breaks across the page. Notice that the soft page line extends only
through column 3 because no text appears in either columns 4 or 5.

Fig. 16.15.

*A page break in
parallel columns.*

```
                                                    times still
                                                    exist.

Oct 26   Bus tour     Overnight    Nürburgring–    A MUST stop for
         down along   at Heidel-   the mecca of    any car crazy.
         the Mosel    berg, At-     German, if     For a small fee,
         River        las Hotel    not European    you can drive
                                   auto racing,    your car around
                                   recently re-    the track.
                                   built

Oct 27   Bus to Mu-   Holiday
         nich         Inn, one
                      of best
         ----------------------------------
                      anywhere,
                      excellent
                      restaurant
                      (Omas
                      Küche)

Oct 28   Munich                                    Free day for
                                                   shopping. Munich
                                                   has some excel-
C:\WP50\QUENEW\PARALLEL                   Col 5 Doc 1 Pg 2 Ln 2.33" Pos 5.75"
```

Typing Text in Parallel Columns

Typing text in parallel columns is different from typing text in newspaper columns
because you need to move from column to column to set up your list. In the tour

itinerary, for instance, after you type the text for the first column (Date), press Hard Page (Ctrl-Enter) to position the cursor at the next column, where you type in the location. Again press Hard Page to get to the third column, and so on across the page. When you press Hard Page at the end of your text in the right-hand column, the program returns the cursor to the left-hand column, and you can start a new entry.

WordPerfect inserts hidden codes for each column, depending upon the type of column. Regular parallel columns start with **[Col On]**, have a hard page code **[HPg]** between columns, and end with **[Col Off]** at the end of your text in the right-hand column. Unlike earlier versions of WordPerfect, page breaks do not interrupt the columns, so you can keep typing as far as necessary. You remain in your column until you press Hard Page (Ctrl-Enter).

Parallel columns with Block Protect start with **[Block Pro:On][Col On]**, have a **[HPg]** code between columns, and end with **[Block Pro:Off][Col Off]**. The Block Protect column is useful when you do not want to split a column across a page break but want to keep all your text together on one page. If the right-hand column, for instance, is too long to fit on the same page, WordPerfect inserts a soft page code **[SPg]** at the beginning of the left-hand column and moves the columns as a block to the next page.

Let's see how typing in parallel columns works. You have established the format for your columns, and you're ready to start your text. First, put in the individual column headings, center them, and put them in bold (refer to fig. 16.13).

To enter the columns headings, do the following:

1. Press Center (Shift-F6).

2. Press Bold (F6), type *Date*, and press Bold (F6).

3. Press Ctrl-Enter to go to the next column and press Center (Shift-F6).

4. Press Bold (F6), type *Location*, and press Bold (F6).

5. Press Ctrl-Enter to go to column 3 and press Center (Shift-F6).

6. Press Bold (F6), type *Hotel*, and press Bold (F6).

7. Press Ctrl-Enter to go to column 4 and press Center (Shift-F6).

8. Press Bold (F6), type *Sightseeing*, and press Bold (F6).

9. Press Ctrl-Enter to go to the last column and press Center (Shift-F6).

10. Press Bold (F6), type *Remarks*, and press Bold (F6).

Now that you have set up your headings, you are ready to start typing the body of the document. Be sure that Hyphenation is on. Insert hyphens manually if you must so that your tour schedule looks like the one in figure 16.13.

To type text in your columns, do the following:

1. Press Ctrl-Enter to go back to the left-hand column and type *Oct 24*.

2. Press Ctrl-Enter to go to the next column and type *Luxembourg*.

3. Press Ctrl-Enter to go to column 3 and type the following text:

Hotel Aerogolf—excellent restaurant serving French and Luxembourg cuisine—the frog legs and Chateaubriand are highly recommended.

4. Press Ctrl-Enter to go to column 4 and type the following text:

Tour of the Kasematten and if time permits, a short visit to the Luxembourg Swiss area.

5. Press Ctrl-Enter to go to the last column and type the following text:

The Kasematten are an ancient fortification; the Luxembourg Swiss area is one of the most picturesque areas of the country.

Combining Parallel Columns with Regular Text

As with newspaper columns, you can mix parallel columns with regular text (see fig. 16.16). You must, however, be at the end of your text in the right-hand column in order to combine the two properly. If you turn off Columns while the cursor is in a middle column, your columns will get out of alignment.

Fig. 16.16.

Combining parallel columns with regular text.

```
   Oct 24      Luxembourg   Hotel        Tour of the    The Kasematten
                            Aerogolf-    Kasematten     are an ancient
                            excellent    and if time    fortification;
                            restaurant   permits, a     the Luxembourg
                            serving      short visit    Swiss area is one
                            French and   to the Lux-    of the most pic-
                            Luxembourg   embourg        turesque areas of
                            cuisine -    Swiss area.    the country.
                            the frog
                            legs and
                            Chateau-
                            briand are
                            highly re-
                            commended.

          Note:     It's advisable to bring some raingear on this tour.
                    Fall in Europe can be rather moist at times.  We
                    disclaim any responsibility for the weather, although
                    we'll be happy to take credit for it if it's sunny.

   Oct 25      Trier        Dorint       Porta Nigra;   Supposedly found-
                            Hotel        Cathedral      ed in 2000 B.C.,
                                         and Imperial   this small city
                                         Baths          became the capi-

        C:\WP50\QUENEW\PARALLEL                    Col 5 Doc 1 Pg 1 Ln 1.66" Pos 5.75"
```

To combine parallel columns with regular text, do the following:

1. Move the cursor to the end of the text in the right-hand column.

2. Press Math/Columns (Alt-F7).

3. Select Column On/Off (**3**).

4. Type your regular text.

5. When you have finished typing, press Math/Columns (Alt-F7) and select Column On/Off (**3**) to return to your columns.

Editing Parallel Columns

You edit in parallel columns just as you do in newspaper columns, but you must remember to create new columns by using Hard Page (Ctrl-Enter). Be careful when you use the Delete key as you edit; do not accidentally erase one of the hidden column codes.

If you do erase a code, leave the cursor in the position where you accidentally erased the code and go into Reveal Codes (Alt-F3, or F11). Then reinsert the code in its proper place by pressing Math/Columns (Alt-F7) and selecting **Column On/Off** (**3**). WordPerfect remembers which code should be there and inserts the correct one. To see how this procedure works, press Reveal Codes (Alt-F3, or F11), move the cursor to a **[Col Off]** code, and press Delete. Then press Math/Columns (Alt-F7), select **Column On/Off** (**3**), and watch the code reappear.

You can do your editing in Reveal Codes if you like, although you will have a very busy screen.

Unlike the cursor movement in newspaper columns, the cursor movement for parallel columns is the same as in regular text. The cursor movement keys function in the following manner:

- GoTo (Ctrl-Home), → moves the cursor to the column on the right.

- GoTo (Ctrl-Home), ← moves the cursor to the column on the left.

- Home, ↓ moves the cursor to the bottom of the screen.

- Home, ↑ moves the cursor to the top of the screen.

- The gray + and – keys move the cursor to the bottom or the top of the screen, respectively.

Moving Parallel Columns

If you decide to move one section of your parallel column text to another location in your document, you can move the section—carefully—but this maneuver is tricky and perhaps best done in Reveal Codes. You MUST include the **[Column On]** and **[Column Off]** codes in the move.

To move a section of a parallel column to another location in your document, do the following:

1. Move the cursor to the first column of the section you want to move.

2. Press Home, Home, ← to get to the left-hand margin.

3. Press Block (Alt-F4, or F12).

4. Press the sequence GoTo (Ctrl-Home), → four times.

5. Move the cursor down to include the last line of the right-hand column in your block.

6. Press Move (Ctrl-F4).

7. Select **Block** (**1**).

8. Select **Move** (**1**).

9. Move the cursor to the spot where you want to insert the block and press Enter.

   If the margins of your columns are wider than your regular document, you have to press Margin Release (Shift-Tab) before pressing Enter.

Changing Line Spacing

The ability to change line spacing between columns is a handy feature of WordPerfect. If you want to double-space the "Sightseeing" column, for example, WordPerfect allows you to do so (see fig. 16.17).

Fig. 16.17.

Line spacing changed in one parallel column.

Date	Location	Hotel	Sightseeing	Remarks
			Windy City Tour Schedule	
Oct 24	Luxembourg	Hotel Aerogolf– excellent restaurant serving French and Luxembourg cuisine – the frog legs and Chateau- briand are highly re- commended.	Tour of the Kasematten and if time permits, a short visit to the Lux- embourg Swiss area.	The Kasematten are an ancient fortification; the Luxembourg Swiss area is one of the most pic- turesque areas of the country.
Oct 25	Trier	Dorint Hotel	Porta Nigra; Cathedral and Imperial	Supposedly found- ed in 2000 B.C., this small city

C:\WP50\QUENEW\PARALLEL   Doc 1 Pg 1 Ln 1" Pos 1"

To change the line spacing in a parallel column, do the following:

1. Move the cursor to the beginning of the column where you want to start the spacing change.

   For this example, position your cursor on the "T" of the word "Tour."

2. Press Format (Shift-F8).

3. Select **Line** (**1**).

4. Select **S**pacing (**6**).

5. Type *2* for double-spacing and press Enter.

6. Press Exit (F7) twice to accept the spacing and return to your document.

Your text is now double-spaced in the column. If you also want the "Remarks" column double-spaced, simply move the cursor to the first letter of the first word in that column (the "T" in "The") and repeat Steps 2 through 6. If you want the text in a column single-spaced again, position the cursor at the beginning of the column, press Format (Shift-F8), select **L**ine (**1**), choose **S**pacing (**6**), type **1**, press Enter, and press Exit (F7) twice.

If you want just one section of one column double-spaced, you must insert a single-space code at the point where you want to return to single spacing. You do this by following the previous procedure and typing a *1*.

If you know in advance that you want the first two columns of your schedule to be single-spaced and the remainder of the columns double-spaced, you can change the line spacing as you type. When you get to the end of the last single-spaced column, just press Ctrl-Enter to go to the next column and continue with the steps for changing line spacing. The remainder of the text is double-spaced until you enter another code for a different line-spacing measurement.

A Macro To Define Parallel Columns

In parallel columns, as in newspaper columns, you can speed up the process of defining columns by using either macros or styles, particularly if you use the same setups on a regular basis. In this section, you learn how to create macros to set up your parallel columns. (For information on how you can use Styles to automate this process, see Chapter 12.)

Let's use the setup for the tour itinerary as an example for creating a macro.

To create a macro that speeds up the definition of parallel columns, do the following:

1. Press Macro Define (Ctrl-F10).

2. Press Alt-T to name the macro for "tour."

3. Type *Tour itinerary* for the definition and press Enter.

   The words Macro Def start flashing in the lower left corner of the screen.

4. Press Math/Columns (Alt-F7) to start your column definition.

5. Follow Steps 1 through 13 outlined previously in the "Defining Parallel Columns" section. Pressing **C**olumn On/Off (**3**) to turn the column on should be the last step in your definition.

6. Press Macro Define (Ctrl-F10) to end the macro definition.

If you frequently change the spacing within parallel columns, you can write a macro to change the spacing for you.

To create a macro to change the spacing within parallel columns, do the following:

1. Press Macro Define (Ctrl-F10).

2. Press Alt-S to name the macro for "spacing."

3. Type *Change to double-spacing* for the definition and press Enter.

4. Press Format (Shift-F8).

5. Select **Line** (**1**).

6. Select **S**pacing (**6**), type *2*, and press Enter.

7. Press Exit (F7).

8. Press Macro Define (Ctrl-F10) to end the macro definition.

WP 5 Summary

You will not need the Column format for everything you write, but when you do want to use columns, WordPerfect provides you with a powerful feature. The Columns feature is not the easiest concept to learn, but if you have worked your way through this chapter, you should have a good idea of the feature's capabilities.

In this chapter, you have learned to do the following:

- Define newspaper columns
- Define parallel columns
- Type in columns
- Edit in columns
- Mix columns with regular text
- Create macros for newspaper columns and parallel columns

WordPerfect columns are designed to help you write more simply and efficiently. With experience, columns will become just as easy for you to use as any other feature. And if you combine columns with WordPerfect's graphics capability, you have the makings of a good desktop publishing system. The quality of the printed piece, of course, depends also on the printer you are using, but even with a good dot-matrix printer, you can achieve excellent results.

17

Using Math

James McKeown, Ph.D.,
an accounting professor at
the University of Illinois at
Urbana, has worked with
computers for 25 years
and with WordPerfect
from version 3.0 to the
present. ∎

B y the time you reach this point in the book, you probably have decided that WordPerfect can do just about anything with words and letters, but you might wonder what WordPerfect can do with numbers. The Math feature of WordPerfect is intended to provide limited calculation capability for simple calculations, like preparing an income statement or an invoice.

This chapter shows you how to go through the various steps necessary to set up and use WordPerfect's Math feature. You learn the uses and features of the various types of Math columns and how to change your setup as the Math needs in your document change. Please read this entire chapter from start to finish. Skipping around in the chapter may cause some parts of the WordPerfect Math feature to seem confusing to you.

Creating Math Columns

WordPerfect supports two basic types of Math operation. The more commonly used (and simpler) operation calculates and displays the totals of numbers in columns. The more complex operation calculates and displays the results of computations involving numbers in different columns in the same line.

To use any type of Math operation in WordPerfect, the following six steps must be performed:

1. Set tabs for your columns.

2. Define the type and format of your columns.

3. Turn on the Math feature.

4. Enter the text (for captions) and numbers with appropriate math operators in the columns.

5. Calculate the results of your Math setup.

6. Turn off the Math feature.

Setting Tab Stops

The first step in using the Math feature is to set your tab stops so that your columns will be in the proper location. (The basic procedure for setting tab stops is described in Chapter 2.) If you are going to have headings for the columns, enter the headings before setting the tab stops so that you easily can place the tab stops in relation to the column heading positions.

To set the tab stops for columns, do the following:

1. Make sure the cursor is positioned after the headings (if any).

2. Press Format (Shift-F8).

3. Select Line (1).

4. Select Tab Set (8).

5. Press Home, Home, ← to move the cursor to the 0 position.

6. Remove the existing tab stops by doing Erase EOL (Control-End).

7. Move the cursor to the position where you want the decimal character to be aligned for the first column.

8. Press L (Left) to set the tab stop for the first column.

9. Repeat Steps 7 and 8 for the second and later columns.

10. Press Exit (F7) twice to return to the editing screen.

Because all numbers entered in the Math feature are aligned on the tab stop, you can set any type of tab you want (left, right, center, or decimal) for columns that contain figures. For columns that contain text, such as item descriptions, however, the text aligns according to the type of tab stop you set for that column. The text column is the only case in the WordPerfect Math feature where the type of tab stop you set affects the document.

Make sure that your columns are wide enough to contain the largest numbers you will put in them. If numbers extend outside their columns, your calculations will give incorrect results.

Setting the Math Definition

You are now ready to set your Math Definition. The WordPerfect Math Definition is your way to tell WordPerfect what calculations you want performed and how you want the results displayed. Let's explore the process of developing the document shown in figure 17.1.

Figure 17.1 shows a simple example of a letter that uses the WordPerfect Math feature. You learn how to use the Math feature to calculate and display the $1,808.15 for "Total expenses" and the $308.15 for "Reimbursement requested."

```
Dear Bob:

I enclose a copy of the receipts for my travel expenses last
month.  These included:

Airfare                           $746.55
Hotels                             843.18
Meals                              218.42
  Total expenses                 $1,808.15+

Less: Travel advance              Nt1500.00

Reimbursement requested           $308.15=




Math                            Doc 1 Pg 1 Ln 12 Pos 10
```

Fig. 17.1.
A letter using the WordPerfect Math feature.

To set your Math Definition, do the following:

1. Position the cursor after any heading for your Math area.

2. Press Math/Columns (Alt-F7).

    The following Math/Columns menu appears at the bottom of your screen:

    1 Math On; **2** Math Def; **3** Column On/Off; **4** Column Def: **0**

Selecting Math On (**1**) turns on the Math feature, and selecting Math Def (**2**) defines the Math columns you want. (You do not use menu options **3** and **4** in the Math feature.)

3. Select Math Def (**2**).

    The Math Definition screen appears (see fig. 17.2).

The Math Definition screen is divided into three parts. The top part allows you to specify certain characteristics about the columns. In the middle part, you can enter calculation formulas for up to four columns. The bottom part simply provides

Fig. 17.2.

The Math Definition screen with default settings.

Column characteristics →

Calculation formulas →

Code explanations →

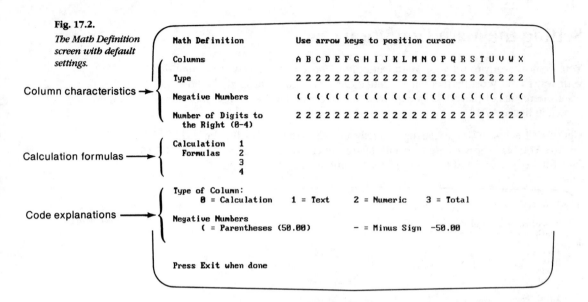

```
Math Definition              Use arrow keys to position cursor

Columns                      A B C D E F G H I J K L M N O P Q R S T U V W X

Type                         2 2 2 2 2 2 2 2 2 2 2 2 2 2 2 2 2 2 2 2 2 2 2 2

Negative Numbers             ( ( ( ( ( ( ( ( ( ( ( ( ( ( ( ( ( ( ( ( ( ( ( (

Number of Digits to          2 2 2 2 2 2 2 2 2 2 2 2 2 2 2 2 2 2 2 2 2 2 2 2
   the Right (0-4)

Calculation    1
   Formulas    2
               3
               4

Type of Column:
     0 = Calculation    1 = Text      2 = Numeric    3 = Total

Negative Numbers
     ( = Parentheses (50.00)        - = Minus Sign  -50.00


Press Exit when done
```

explanations of the codes used in the top part. You do not input or change any information in the bottom part. Let's look at the parts of the Math Definition screen.

Exploring the Math Definition Screen

WordPerfect uses the letters A through X to identify the columns. The letter A represents the column aligned on the first tab stop on the left; B represents the second tab stop from the left margin; and so on. The only time you actually need to use the column letter is to define a calculation formula for a calculation column (as described later in this chapter).

You may use *up to* 24 columns (represented by 24 letters of the alphabet—far more than you will use for most documents). However, the left margin cannot be defined as a column; therefore, WordPerfect cannot perform calculations on numbers entered at the left margin.

The next three lines on the Math Definition screen display the settings for each column. The first setting is the Type of column. This setting is set to 0 for calculation, 1 for text, 2 for numeric, or 3 for total. The most common type of column is the numeric column (type 2). Calculations are performed also in total columns and calculation columns (types 3 and 0, respectively).

Text columns (type 1) are simply used for entering captions. You can enter either numbers or text in text columns, but anything entered in text columns is interpreted as text and is not used in any calculations. You can enter text also in nontext columns, but the text can cause incorrect results in your calculations. If at all possible, enter text only at the left margin (which is not a Math column) and in columns defined as text columns. Numeric, total, and calculation columns are discussed in more detail later in this chapter.

The next setting indicates which format WordPerfect uses to display negative numbers that are the results of calculations. The program displays negative numbers either with a preceding minus sign, – 42.25, or in parentheses (42.25). Any number you enter into a column appears as you have typed it in the column, regardless of the negative-number format setting for that column. The format setting affects only the display of numbers that WordPerfect calculates.

The last setting for each column indicates the number of digits displayed to the right of the decimal point in calculated numbers. WordPerfect rounds the calculated numbers to the number of decimal places you specify in this setting. As in the negative number format, this setting affects only the number of digits displayed for numbers that WordPerfect calculates.

WordPerfect displays the numbers you enter in the columns exactly as you enter them. If you want each number that you enter or that WordPerfect calculates to be displayed with two digits after the decimal point, be sure that each number you enter has two digits after the decimal point.

Changing the Math Default Settings

The numeric column (type 2) is the default setting because the numeric column is the most common column used in Math functions. Type 2 appears for each column when you first access the Math Definition screen. If you want to change the Type code, use the arrow keys to move the cursor to the code you want to change and enter the new code. For example, if you want to change column A to a total column, move the cursor to the 2 under the A and type *3*.

The default setting for negative numbers is the use of parentheses, and the default for digits to the right of the decimal point is 2. Changing the default settings for these two column characteristics is similar to changing the default column type. Simply move the cursor to the code you want to change and enter the appropriate code or number.

If you want to use the default settings (numeric columns with negative numbers displayed in parentheses and two digits to the right of the decimal point), you do not need to define your Math columns: just go ahead and turn on Math.

You do not need to set all 24 columns (A through X) on the Math Definition screen. For example, if you intend to use only one calculation column, the settings for column A are the only ones that matter; if you intend to use two calculation columns, set columns A and B; and so on. Simply make sure that the settings are correct for the number of columns you intend to use.

When you have the codes set the way you want them, press Exit (F7) to leave the Math Definition screen and return to the Math/Columns menu.

Changing the Decimal and Thousands Separator Characters

In WordPerfect, the period is the default setting for the decimal character, and the comma is the default setting for the thousands separator. With the default settings in place, then, WordPerfect displays one million (with two digits to the right of the decimal) as 1,000,000.00—with the alignment based on the period.

If the default settings are unsatisfactory, you can change them by selecting Format (Shift-F8) and choosing Other (4) and then Decimal/Align Character (3). Simply enter the desired decimal character and thousands' separator character as indicated on that screen (see fig. 17.3) and then press F7 to exit to the editing screen. If you change the setting so that the comma is the decimal character and the period is the thousands' separator, WordPerfect would display one million as 1.000.000,00—with the alignment based on the comma.

Fig. 17.3.

The screen to change decimal align and thousands' separator characters.

```
Format: Other

    1 - Advance

    2 - Conditional End of Page

    3 - Decimal/Align Character      ,
        Thousands' Separator         ,

    4 - Language                     EN

    5 - Overstrike

    6 - Printer Functions

    7 - Underline - Spaces           Yes
                    Tabs             No




Selection: 0
```

Using Numeric Columns

Now that you know how to define your Math columns, let's look at how to enter the numbers into the columns. Before you enter any numbers or math operators, be sure to turn on the Math function.

To turn on the Math function, do the following:

1. Be sure that the cursor is positioned after the Math Definition (if needed) and before the part of your document that contains the math operations.

   You can use Reveal Codes (Alt-F3, or F11) to be sure of the placement of your cursor.

2. Press Math/Columns (Alt-F7) to display the Math/Columns menu.

3. Press **Math On** (**1**) to turn on the Math feature.

   The word Math appears in the lower left corner of your screen.

This Math indicator means the cursor is in a Math area of your document (between the Math On and the Math Off codes in your document—use Reveal Codes to see them). Make sure this indicator appears on-screen whenever you intend to enter numbers or operators into the WordPerfect Math feature.

As in other areas, the WordPerfect Math/Columns menu changes according to the situation in which you access the menu. Until you turn on Math, the Math/Columns menu appears as shown:

   1 Math On; **2** Math Def; **3** Column On/Off; **4** Column Def: **0**

However, after you turn on Math (when Math appears at the lower left of your screen), the Math/Columns menu changes to the following:

   1 Math Off; **2** Calculate; **3** Column On/Off; **4** Column Def: **0**

The first two choices have been changed. Once you have turned on Math, you naturally would not need to turn it on again; therefore, WordPerfect changes the item to allow you to turn off Math. Similarly, you cannot change your Math Definition when Math is on, so WordPerfect does not allow you that choice either. You discover later in the chapter that you use Calculate (**2**) to tell WordPerfect to perform the calculations you have specified.

Numbers in Numeric Columns

Now you are ready to enter numbers in the columns you have defined.

Use the following procedure to enter a number into a numeric column:

1. Press the Tab key or Tab Align (either one has the same effect) to position the cursor to the appropriate column.

2. Type the number.

3. After you have entered each number, press Tab again to proceed to the next column, or press Enter to go to the next line.

Be sure that the decimal point is in the appropriate position. (If you are entering a whole number, you need not enter the decimal point.) Use the desired number of digits after the decimal point. Negative numbers may be entered either with a preceding minus sign or enclosed in parentheses.

Remember, the number appears as *you* type it (with the number of decimal places and the negative number format that you enter), regardless of the Math Definition settings for this column.

Math Operators for Numeric Columns

You can use six Math operators in a numeric Math column (see table 17.1). Use the *Math operators* to tell WordPerfect what calculation should be performed and where to display the result. You enter a Math operator by using the Tab key to position the cursor at the location where the result should be displayed and by entering the appropriate operator.

Table 17.1
The Function of Math Operators

Symbol	Function	Description	Hierarchy Level
+	Subtotal	Add all numbers in the column above the + since the last total or subtotal was taken (or from the beginning of the column).	2
t	Extra subtotal	Treat the number immediately following this operator as a subtotal.	2
=	Total	Add all subtotals (+) and extra subtotals (numbers preceded by t operators) since the last total.	3
T	Extra total	Treat the number immediately after this operator as a total.	3
*	Grand total	Add all totals (=) and extra totals (numbers preceded by T operators) since the last grand total.	4
N	Negate	Reverse the sign of the result or number immediately following this operator for use in further calculations.	1, 2, or 3

The +, =, and * operators are *accumulation* operators because they cause WordPerfect to display an accumulated total. Accumulation operators appear by themselves. The t and T operators are *promotion* operators because they promote to a higher level the number that follows them. Promotion operators must be followed immediately by a number entered in the same column.

N is a *modifier* because it modifies the way WordPerfect interprets the value of the number that follows the operator. The effect of the N operator is to reverse the sign of the number that follows the N. For example, if the number is positive, it is treated in further calculations as a negative number. On the other hand, if a negative number is preceded by N, the number is treated in further calculations as a positive number. A modifier must be followed by a number or another operator in the same column.

The general structure of these Math operators is a four-level hierarchy. This hierarchy is useful as a basis to describe the relationship of numbers and operators in the WordPerfect Math feature. From the lowest to the highest level, the hierarchy works in the following manner:

- Level 1: Numbers entered without any accumulation or promotion operators

- Level 2: Subtotals (and numbers preceded by t operators)

- Level 3: Totals (and numbers preceded by T operators)

- Level 4: Grand totals

An operator at a particular level of the hierarchy deals only with items at the next lower level. Therefore, a subtotal (level 2) adds only numbers entered without operators or with the N operator (level 1); a total (level 3) adds only subtotals and numbers preceded by t operators (level 2); and a grand total (level 4) adds only totals and numbers preceded by T operators (level 3).

In each case, the program adds all the lower-level numbers that appear above the current line in the same column. This addition proceeds upward until an item of an equal or higher level is encountered. For example, a subtotal (level 2) adding the numbers above it would be stopped if it encountered a total (level 3) in the column. Therefore, the subtotal would add only the numbers in its own column between the total and its own line.

Because WordPerfect uses the t and T operators to promote numbers to level 2 or level 3 respectively, the "promoted" numbers are included in a higher-level calculation. Although WordPerfect usually accepts instructions without distinguishing between upper- and lowercase, you must make that distinction when you use the promotion operators. The uppercase T means something quite different to the program than the lowercase t. If you use the wrong case for your operator, your results will not be correct.

A Numeric Columns Example

To understand the process of the Math function in columns, let's look at the sample letter in figure 17.4. The first three amounts are entered as normal numbers with no operators. These amounts are at level 1 and are included only in a subtotal (level 2). The + sign in the "Total expenses" line is an operator telling WordPerfect to calculate a subtotal. Because the subtotal is level 2, the subtotal includes the three level-1 numbers above it.

After WordPerfect computes the "Total expenses" subtotal, the next step is to subtract the "Travel advance" from the subtotal. If you enter the "Travel advance" amount with no operators, however, that amount is not included in a computation with the subtotal because only items of equal level are added together. To solve the problem, use the t operator to tell WordPerfect to consider the 1500.00 to be the same level as a subtotal. Thus, when WordPerfect calculates the total (as instructed

Fig. 17.4.

A sample letter before calculation.

```
    Dear Bob:

    I enclose a copy of the receipts for my travel expenses last
    month.   These included:

    Airfare                               $746.55
    Hotels                                 843.18
    Meals                                  218.42
       Total expenses                       $+

    Less: Travel advance                 Nt1500.00

    Reimbursement requested                 $=




    Math                                        Doc 1 Pg 1 Ln 12 Pos 10
```

by the = sign in the "Reimbursement requested" line), the total includes the subtotal and the "Travel advance."

You use the N operator to tell WordPerfect to negate (change the sign of) the 1500.00 "Travel advance." The N operator causes the 1500.00 to be subtracted (or added as a negative number) from the preceding subtotal in computing the total.

The example also shows two ways of enhancing the appearance of your Math documents: using dollar signs and underlines. You can insert dollar signs ($) in the places where they should appear in the finished document. Insert the dollar signs ($) in front of any item, including operators (as was done with the + and = operators in the example).

You also can use the standard Underline key (F8) to tell WordPerfect to underline at the point where the program performs the calculations (see the lines under figures 218.42 and 1500.00).

The example shows the use of numbers and the +, t, N, and = operators. The T promotion operator is similar to t, and the * grand total operator is just another higher level of total. Although figure 17.4 displays the Math operators, it does not show any calculation results yet.

To display the results of specified calculations, you must tell WordPerfect to perform the calculation by doing the following:

1. Press Math/Columns (Alt-F7).

2. Select Calculate (2).

The calculations now appear (refer to fig.17.1). The program still displays the operators on-screen, but they will not appear in the printed document. (You can check the document by viewing it as described in Chapter 6.)

If you make any changes in the numbers or operators in a math area, remember to tell WordPerfect to perform the calculation again. Be sure that the cursor is in the Math area (between the Math On and Math Off codes) when you perform the calculation.

When you are satisfied that your Math computations are complete, place the cursor after the Math area and turn off the Math feature.

To turn off the Math feature, do the following:

1. Press Math/Columns (Alt-F7).

2. Select Math Off (**1**).

You can turn on Math as needed for other Math areas of your document. Any document can have any number of Math areas. You can tell whether the cursor is in a Math area by observing the Math indicator in the lower left of the screen.

Using Total Columns

In the preceding sections, you have learned about numeric columns and text columns. Another type of Math column is a total column, indicated by Type code 3 in the Math Definition. The difference between a numeric column and a total column is that the subtotal operators (+) in the total column add items in the column immediately to the left of the total column.

```
Math Definition          Use arrow keys to position cursor

Columns                  A B C D E F G H I J K L M N O P Q R S T U V W X

Type                     2 3 2 2 2 2 2 2 2 2 2 2 2 2 2 2 2 2 2 2 2 2 2 2

Negative Numbers         ( ( ( ( ( ( ( ( ( ( ( ( ( ( ( ( ( ( ( ( ( ( ( (

Number of Digits to      2 2 2 2 2 2 2 2 2 2 2 2 2 2 2 2 2 2 2 2 2 2 2 2
  the Right (0-4)

Calculation      1
  Formulas       2
                 3
                 4

Type of Column:
     0 = Calculation    1 = Text     2 = Numeric    3 = Total

Negative Numbers
     ( = Parentheses (50.00)       - = Minus Sign  -50.00


Press Exit when done
```

Fig. 17.5.

A Math Definition for a total column.

To help explain subtotal operators in total columns, assume that you have the Math Definition shown in figure 17.5. Column A is a numeric column (indicated by type 2), and column B is a total column (indicated by type 3). Insert numbers in your Math columns as follows:

A	B
15.0	
(22.)	
27.00	t25.00
80.	
–18.000	
40.	+

The A and B above the columns are headings to help you identify the columns. Column A looks sloppy because the user entered the amounts with a different number of zeros following the decimal points. Because the user entered these items, WordPerfect does not make the format conform to the settings in the Math Definition. WordPerfect uses these settings only for numbers that WordPerfect calculates (62.00, for example).

Now consider the subtotal operator at the bottom of column B. After you tell WordPerfect to perform the Math calculation—by pressing Math/Columns (Alt-F7) and selecting Calculate (2)—the + changes to 62.00 +. How does WordPerfect arrive at this figure?

Remember that the subtotal in column B, a total column, is the subtotal of the items from the column to the left (column A in the example). The addition starts in column A with the line *preceding* the subtotal operator in column B and continues upward until it reaches, but does not include, a line that contains another item of a level greater than 1 in column B.

In the example, the subtotal operation does not include 40 because it is on the same line as the subtotal operator (+). The operation also excludes the 27.00 and all numbers above it because those numbers are on the same line or above the line containing the promoted number t25.00. Remember that the subtotal operation stops when it reaches the line containing an item of a level greater than 1. The only numbers in column A above the subtotal line and below the promoted number are 80 and –18.000, so the subtotal is calculated and displayed as 62.00 +.

The 40 and 27.00 will never be included in any calculation in the total column. Unless you have a particular reason to do so, do not put an item in a total column on the same line as an item in the column to the left of the total column. If you violate this rule, the item in the column to the left will be ignored in all calculations in the total column.

A Total Columns Example

Total columns are particularly useful for such applications as entering simple accounting statements. Consider the simple income statement in figure 17.6. The Math Definition for this document is positioned just above the line starting with "Service revenue." Because the definition is the same as the Math Definition used for the example in figure 17.5, you do not need to go back into Math Def to change the definition. The first Math column is a numeric column, and the second Math column is a total column.

```
                        Sample Company
                        Income Statement
                    For the Month of June, 1988



     Service revenue                            t$10,000.00

     Expenses:
        Employee wages              $5,400.00
        Advertising                  1,250.00
        Insurance                    1,800.00
           Total Expenses                          N+

     Income for the month                          $=




  Math                                    Doc 1 Pg 1 Ln 14 Pos 10
```

Fig. 17.6.

The income statement before calculation.

By examining the document itself, you can see the individual expense amounts entered in the numeric column. The subtotal operator (+) in the total column instructs WordPerfect to add those items. The N preceding the + indicates that the "Total expenses" are to be subtracted from the "Service revenue" amount in the calculation of the total. The $10,000 received for service has the t operator so that it will be included in the total calculation indicated by the = in the "Income for the month" line. After the Math calculation has been ordered by pressing Math/Columns (Alt-F7) and selecting Calculate (**2**), the document appears as shown in figure 17.7.

```
                        Sample Company
                        Income Statement
                    For the Month of June, 1988



     Service revenue                            t$10,000.00

     Expenses:
        Employee wages              $5,400.00
        Advertising                  1,250.00
        Insurance                    1,800.00
           Total Expenses                      N8,450.00+

     Income for the month                      $1,550.00=




  Math                                    Doc 1 Pg 1 Ln 14 Pos 10
```

Fig. 17.7.

The income statement after calculation.

Guidelines for Using Total Columns

Total columns may seem complex, but they are easy to use. If you need a set of total columns to compute several levels of totals, you should have no trouble if you consider the following guidelines:

- The column to the left of the leftmost total column can be either a calculation column or a numeric column.

In either case, do not use any items in the numeric or calculation column other than simple numbers or calculation results, shown with an exclamation point (!). (WordPerfect uses ! to show that the calculation should be performed at that position.)

- In a total column, use *only* subtotal operators (+) when you want to add numbers from the column to the left.

(Although subtotal operators do not add subtotals in numeric columns, subtotal operators *will* add subtotals from the column to the left in this particular case.) When placing your subtotal operators, remember that an item immediately to the left of a subtotal operator is never included in any subtotal.

- You may include the t promotion operator in a total column so that it will be added to the subtotals in the same column.

Because the t operator has a level greater than 1, place the t so that it does not interfere with the operation of any subtotals in the same column below the t. (*Don't* do what was done in placing the t25.00 in the example. The t25.00 prevented the subtotal operator from including the numbers in the top three lines of the example.)

- In addition to the subtotal operators (+), you may include higher-level items (levels 3 or 4) in the rightmost total column.

In this case, the total (=) and grand total (˙) items operate in a vertical fashion, as if they were in a simple numeric column.

Using Calculation Columns

Numeric and total columns calculate vertical addition of numbers. The last type of Math column is calculation (type 0). Calculation columns calculate numbers within the same line of a WordPerfect document and are sometimes called horizontal calculations. Although using calculation columns can be more complex than using the calculations performed in numeric and total columns, the calculations allowed in calculation columns are still quite simple. Remember that the WordPerfect Math feature is not intended for complex calculations.

WordPerfect allows up to four calculation columns in a Math Definition. You use the Math Definition screen to specify a column as a calculation column by inserting the 0 code in the Type line as shown for column D in figure 17.8.

Fig. 17.8.

The Math Definition screen for a calculation column.

```
Math Definition          Use arrow keys to position cursor

Columns                  A B C D E F G H I J K L M N O P Q R S T U V W X

Type                     2 2 2 0 2 2 2 2 2 2 2 2 2 2 2 2 2 2 2 2 2 2 2 2

Negative Numbers         ( ( ( ( ( ( ( ( ( ( ( ( ( ( ( ( ( ( ( ( ( ( ( (

Number of Digits to      0 3 2 2 2 2 2 2 2 2 2 2 2 2 2 2 2 2 2 2 2 2 2 2
  the Right (0-4)

Calculation   1    D     _
  Formulas    2
              3
              4

Type of Column:
     0 = Calculation   1 = Text    2 = Numeric    3 = Total

Negative Numbers
     ( = Parentheses (50.00)       - = Minus Sign  -50.00


Press Exit when done
```

When you insert a 0 for the Type code, WordPerfect automatically moves the cursor down to the middle of the screen to allow you to enter the calculation formula for the calculation column. In figure 17.8, the cursor is sitting at Calculation Formula 1. WordPerfect has already set the D to the left of the cursor to indicate that this calculation formula gives instructions to calculate the result stored in column D.

Your calculation formula can include the following numbers:

- The numbers in other columns (either to the left or right of the calculation column) in the same line of your document

- The number appearing in the calculation column on the preceding line of your document

- Numbers you type explicitly into the formula

Your calculation formula can include also the following four standard arithmetic operators:

- \+ Add
- − Subtract
- * Multiply
- / Divide

(WordPerfect allows four other special operators, but they are not discussed here because you can achieve the same result by using the preceding operators.)

When you enter your calculation formula, use the standard arithmetic operators and use letters to refer to the columns (either other columns on the same line or the same column in the preceding line) and type your numeric constants explicitly.

When entering your calculation formula, do not include any spaces between the characters. Although formulas may be easier to read if you inserted spaces, WordPerfect does not allow spaces in calculation formulas. If you try to enter a space in the formula, the space has the same effect as pressing the Enter key: the space signals that you have completed entering the formula.

WordPerfect does its calculations from left to right, but you can modify this order by using parentheses in the calculation formula. Using parentheses to control the order of calculation is limited, however, because you are not allowed to put parentheses inside another set of parentheses.

Sample Calculation Formulas

Assume that you have a document which has the following four numeric columns (A, B, D, and E):

(A)	(B)	(C)	(D)	(E)
1.00	2.00		4.00	5.00
18.30	.05		0.00	3.00

The capital letters above the columns are simply to help you identify the columns. The letters are not necessary for the WordPerfect Math feature and have no effect on it.

You now want to enter a calculation formula for column C. Let's look at some possible calculation formulas as they relate to the figures in columns A, B, D, and E. The first grouping of numbers or letters represents the calculation formula. The second grouping of numbers represents the results of the calculation formula that would be displayed in the two lines of column C. The explanation of the formula follows the formula itself.

Formula	Results
3*2	6.00
	6.00

If you enter only numbers (with no letters to reference other columns) in your formula, each line displays the same result.

3−1/2	1.00
	1.00

The result may not be what you anticipated because the formula 3−1/2 does not mean 3 minus one-half. Remember that WordPerfect does not allow spaces between the math operators. The formula means 3 minus 1 divided by 2. Because WordPerfect performs each operation in sequence from left to right, the program first performs the subtraction, giving a result of 2. Then the result is divided by 2 to give the final result of 1.00 (which is equal to 2/2).

If you want to have the division performed first, however, use parentheses to instruct WordPerfect to perform the division function first. For example, the formula 3-(1/2) produces the result of 2.50.

A+B/D	0.75
	??

Again the result may be different from what you expected. Because the formula is given as A +B/D, WordPerfect calculates the addition first and then the division. Thus, the calculation for the first line takes place in the following manner: 1.00 + 2.00 = 3.00 divided by 4.00 = 0.75.

If you want to have the quotient given by dividing column B by column D, you should use the formula A +(B/D), which results in the number 1.50 (2.00 divided by 4.00 = 0.50; then 1.00 + 0.50 = 1.50).

If you have a formula for which the result cannot be calculated properly, WordPerfect displays the result with question marks. The question marks in the second line reflect WordPerfect's inability to divide the number 18.35 (the sum of columns A and B) by 0.

        A*B   2.00
                         0.92

In the Math Definition for the example, the default setting for decimal places is active. Therefore, when you have a formula that produces a number with more than two digits following the decimal point, WordPerfect rounds that number to the number of decimal places you have specified in your Math Definition. For example, in the second line, 18.30 multiplied by 0.05 results in the number 0.915. WordPerfect rounds the resulting number to 0.92.

        A*B +C   2.00
                         2.92

The last formula references the calculation column itself. In this case, the C in the formula instructs WordPerfect to use the number in the preceding line of column C. That number in the preceding column would normally be the result of the same calculation for the preceding line but could also be a number you have inserted manually (as described later).

In the particular case here, the formula is intended to compute a cumulative sum or running total of the product of column A multiplied by column B. Even though the formula is A*B +C, the result displayed in the first line of column C really reflects the result of the formula A*B because column C of the preceding line does not have a number or result in the line. A running total normally would be started in this way. The result displayed on the second line is A*B for the second line plus the result from the preceding line (0.92 + 2.00 = 2.92). If you were to add a third line to the Math area, the program would add A*B from the third line to the 2.92 result displayed in column C of the second line.

An important point to remember when you devise a calculation formula for running totals is to put at the end of the equation the calculation for adding the previous line. Putting the calculation for the previous line (C +A*B, for example) at the beginning of the equation would not work because the addition would be performed first. Performing the addition first would mean the previous total (from column C of the previous line) would be added to column A of this line and the sum of those two would be multiplied by B. Formula C +A*B would give a result quite different from the desired running total: the formula would give 2.00 on the first line, but a total of 1.02 on the second line (2.00 + 18.30 = 20.30; then 20.30 * .05 = 1.015 rounded up to 1.02).

A Calculation Column Example

To give a more complete illustration of the use of calculation, assume that you want to prepare an invoice similar to the one shown in figure 17.9, where each product's "Amount Billed" will be calculated by WordPerfect. The headings are typed before inserting the Math Definition. (The capital letters above the headings are there only to help you identify the columns. They have no effect on the calculations.) The Math Definition is the one shown in figure 17.8 with Calculation Formula 1 entered as $A^*B^*(-C/100+1)$.

Fig. 17.9.

The invoice before calculation.

```
                    (A)          (B)      (C)         (D)
                  Number        Unit               Amount
    Product      of units       Price   Discount    Billed

 1 inch springs     1000        5.305     15%         $!
 5 inch springs       32        8.001     35%          !
 Leaf springs         27       14.010     25%          !

 Total amount billed                                  $+



 Math                                         Doc 1 Pg 1 Ln 8 Pos 10
```

After you have entered the calculation formula, the middle part of the Math Definition screen looks like the following:

```
Calculation    1    D       A*B*(-C/100+1)
   Formulas    2
               3
               4
```

The formula looks strange, but it must be entered this way to describe the correct calculation without inserting parentheses within another set of parentheses—a shortcut WordPerfect does not allow. The next paragraph describes the formula's application to the first line of figure 17.9.

WordPerfect first takes the number entered in column C of the current line, changes the number's sign (because of the minus sign), then divides the number by 100 to convert the number to a decimal fraction equal to the discount percentage $(-15/100 = -.15)$. Though the percent symbol appears in column C, WordPerfect pays attention only to the number entered there. The result is then added to 1 ($-.15 + 1.00 = .85$).

WordPerfect first calculates the steps in parentheses—producing a *result* (.85 in this case)—before doing anything with columns A and B. After the expression inside the parentheses has been fully calculated, WordPerfect then calculates the formula from left to right as if the formula had been entered as $A^*B^*result$. The program first calculates A·B (1000 · 5.305 = 5305). Its product then is multiplied by the result of the calculation in parentheses (5305 · .85 = 4509.25). Figure 17.10 shows the result of this calculation.

```
          (A)         (B)      (C)        (D)
        Number      Unit               Amount
 Product      of units     Price    Discount    Billed

1 inch springs    1000    5.305     15%    $4,509.25!
5 inch springs      32    8.001     35%       166.42!
Leaf springs        27   14.010     25%       283.70!

Total amount billed                        $4,959.37+



 Math                              Doc 1 Pg 1 Ln 8 Pos 10
```

Fig. 17.10.
The invoice after calculation.

If the formula had been entered as A·B·(1–C/100), the full discount would have been subtracted before being converted to a percentage. Using the numbers from the previous example, this formula would produce the following results: The parentheses would give –.14 (1 – 15 = –14/100). The product would then be computed as 1000 · 5.305 · –.14 = –742.70 (not at all the result you want).

After you enter the Math Definition, turn on Math, and enter the numbers, the display should look like figure 17.9. Note that an exclamation point appears in column D on each product line. WordPerfect uses the ! to indicate that the defined calculation should be performed on that line with the result being displayed in column D.

WordPerfect inserts the ! only if you have tabbed over to the calculation column. The program does not insert the ! and does not perform the calculation for that line if you just enter the information up through the "Discount" column and press Enter to get a hard return without pressing the Tab key to move over to column D.

If you do not want the calculation formula to be calculated and displayed for a given line, simply delete the ! for that line. The last line ("Total amount billed") of column D should contain the sum of the "Amount Billed" column for the individual products rather than the result of the column C calculation. To achieve the proper calculation, delete the ! for the last line and replace the ! with a + operator, which indicates that the program should calculate and insert a subtotal for that column (refer to fig. 17.9).

After making the change and telling WordPerfect to perform the calculations by pressing Math/Columns (Alt-F7) and then Calculate (2), the display looks like the one in figure 17.10. The operators ! and + appear on the display, but do not appear on the printed document. (You can verify that the operators do not appear on the printed document by using View Document on the Print menu.)

Editing Your Math Definition

You may have occasions when you need to modify a Math Definition. For example, you may decide to alter the layout of the document, which then requires a change in the Math Definition. Or your Math Definition may not give you the desired results, so you must alter it.

If you want to change your Math Definition, do the following:

1. Place the cursor immediately after the Math Definition code you want to edit.

The easiest way to position the cursor is to switch into Reveal Codes mode (Alt-F3, or F11). The symbol **[Math Def]** is displayed to indicate the location of the Math Definition. Place the cursor so that the character or code following **[Math Def]** is highlighted in the Reveal Codes display.

2. Press Math/Columns (Alt-F7).

3. Select Math Def (**2**) to display the Math Definition screen as you have previously defined it.

4. Edit your Math Definition by simply moving the cursor to the specification(s) you want to change and typing in the new specification(s).

5. Press Exit (F7) to return to the Math/Columns menu.

Unless you have a good reason to save the old Math Definition, delete it. (If you keep old, unused codes in a document, they may cause confusion as you continue to edit the document.) Thus, you should complete the process of editing your Math Definition with the following actions:

6. Press 0 (or the space bar) to leave the Math/Columns menu.

7. Press ← to move past your edited Math Definition.

8. Press the Back space key to delete the old Math Definition.

You can change a calculation formula by reentering the 0 code for the appropriate column. The cursor then is placed in a position to edit the previously defined calculation formula for that column. The formula is edited in the same way that file names are edited. If the first character typed is a character, WordPerfect erases the previous formula because the program assumes that you want to replace the formula. You can edit the existing formula by either pressing Insert/Typeover (Ins) to go to Typeover mode or by moving the cursor to the right with the → key. If you want to insert something at the beginning of the previous formula, press Insert/Typeover twice, which places you in Insert mode at the beginning of the formula. Be warned that pressing Enter without doing any editing of the formula erases the formula.

When editing a Math Definition, remember that a calculation formula is erased if you press Enter without doing any editing. A calculation formula for a column is erased also if you enter a Type code other than 0 for that column. If you inadvertently enter an incorrect Type code in a calculation column, you can revert to your previous Math Definition by pressing Cancel (F1), which cancels the current edit of your Math Definition. You then can restart your Math Definition edit by selecting Math Def (**2**), because you are still in the Math/Columns menu.

If you want to adjust the position of one or more columns, position the cursor before the Math Definition code and change the tabs by selecting Format (Shift-F8), choosing **Line** (**1**), and then choosing **T**ab Set (**8**). Remember that numeric columns are aligned with the decimal character at the tab stop you specify. Insert new codes for the columns you wish to move. Before leaving the tab set display, be sure to delete the tab stop codes from the original locations for the columns you have moved.

Creating a Useful Macro for Math Columns

Most WordPerfect macros to be used with the Math columns feature are quite specific to your application, but one general purpose macro exists that you may find useful.

To understand the macro's usefulness, recall that WordPerfect does not do the Math calculation automatically. You need to tell WordPerfect to do the calculation after you have entered the numbers in a Math area. If you change any numbers in a Math area or change the settings in a Math Definition, you must tell WordPerfect to perform the calculation again to make sure that the program updates the Math area based on the new information. If you have more than one Math area in your document, you have to make sure that the update has been done separately for each Math area. (When you tell WordPerfect to do the calculation for one Math area, no other Math areas are affected.)

The easiest way to ensure that all Math areas are calculated properly before printing is to tell WordPerfect to perform the calculation in each Math area just before printing—a tedious task if you have several Math areas in your document. To avoid this task, the following general purpose macro performs this function for you.

You actually need two macros because you do not want to start from the top of the document after each calculation. The first macro sets up and calls the second macro, which then repeats itself.

Begin by creating the first macro in the following manner:

1. Press Macro Define (Ctrl-F10) to begin the macro definition.

2. Type *recalc* and press Enter to name the macro.

3. Type *To recalculate all Math areas in a doc* and press Enter to give the macro a description.

4. Press Home, Home, Home, ↑ to go to the top of the document in front of all format codes.

5. Press Macro (Alt-F10).

6. Type *recalc2* and press Enter to invoke the macro RECALC2.

7. Press Macro Define (Ctrl-F10) to end the definition of the first macro.

Now do the following procedure to create the second macro:

1. Press Macro Define (Ctrl-F10) to begin the second macro definition.

2. Type *recalc2* and press Enter to name the macro.

3. Type *To recalculate a Math area and loop* and press Enter to give the macro a description.

4. Press Forward Search (F2).

5. Press Math/Columns (Alt-F7).

6. Select Math Define (**2**) to search for Math On codes.

7. Press Forward Search (F2) to indicate the end of the search string.

8. Press the → to move across the Math On code.

9. Press Math/Columns (Alt-F7) to bring up the Math/Columns menu.

10. Select Calculate (**2**) to do the recalculation.

11. Press Macro (Alt-F10).

12. Type *recalc2* and press Enter.

This step causes WordPerfect to invoke the macro RECALC2 again until the search is unsuccessful (because all Math On codes have been processed).

13. Press Macro Define (Ctrl-F10) to end the second macro definition.

Then to invoke these macros, do the following:

1. Press Macro (Alt-F10).

2. Type *recalc* and press Enter.

When you invoke RECALC, it moves the cursor to the top of the document in front of all codes and then calls RECALC2. Then RECALC2 finds each Math area, tells WordPerfect to perform the calculation for that Math area, and then calls itself again. These repeated calls stop when no further Math areas are found.

WP 5 Summary

WordPerfect's Math features provide a limited facility for performing simple arithmetic calculations in a document. The Math features work nicely for documents where columns of numbers must be added or where simple calculations involving different columns in the same line are needed.

WordPerfect's Math features are not a substitute for a spreadsheet. If you need anything other than very simple calculations, you will find it easier to use a standard spreadsheet program such as Lotus 1-2-3 or SuperCalc® to perform the actual computations. You then can print the results to a disk file in text format and retrieve that file into WordPerfect using the techniques described in Chapter 15.

Another option for more complicated calculations is to use PlanPerfect®, another WordPerfect Corporation product, which is a spreadsheet with direct capability to transfer material into WordPerfect.

Remember the following points when using Math:

- Be sure to set your Math Definition before turning on Math (unless you are using the default settings).

- If your calculations do not appear to be working correctly (such as results appearing incorrectly or no results appearing), edit the Math Definition to be sure that it is defined correctly.

- When you want to edit or examine the Math Definition, be sure that you position the cursor immediately after the **[Math Def]** code for the existing Math Definition.

- Be sure to tell WordPerfect to perform the specified calculations in *each* Math area before you print your document, or you can create a macro to perform this function for you.

- If you have any difficulty changing numbers or operators in a Math area, delete the numbers and start over.

18

Customizing WordPerfect

Judy Housman, a WordPerfect trainer and consultant, leads the Boston Computer Society's Training and Documentation Group. She is a WordPerfect Certified Training Instructor based in Cambridge. ∎

E very office has different needs. As earlier chapters have demonstrated, WordPerfect allows you to adjust its features to your work habits. You can change the style of outlines, for example, to reflect the style you use in your documents. If your office customarily uses legal-size paper rather than letter-size, you can change WordPerfect's paper size setting. If your office stamps documents with the time as well as the date, you can change the format in which WordPerfect displays dates.

You can change many of WordPerfect's features either temporarily or permanently to meet your needs. Using the Format key (Shift-F8), you can change the paper size and many other formatting options temporarily for individual documents. With the Setup key (Shift-F1), you can change WordPerfect's formatting features permanently.

In addition to changing formatting features, you can change the way WordPerfect functions. For instance, you can change the location of special files, such as the dictionary and macro files. You even can change the action that is performed when you press a particular key or key combination.

Conservatively, several dozen options are available for customizing the way WordPerfect works. This chapter explains how to customize WordPerfect to work the way you do. The text gives you a brief description of the options for using Setup (Shift-F1) to change WordPerfect. (You can find more details on each of the available Setup menu options in Appendix A and in the WordPerfect manual.) This chapter devotes considerable attention to keyboard layout customization, a dramatic new addition to WordPerfect 5.

Not only does WordPerfect 5 offer more options for customization, but its approach to customization is somewhat different from version 4.2. If you are upgrading from 4.2, be sure to read the related section in Appendix B before you explore this chapter.

Making Global Changes with the Setup Menu

The Setup key (Shift-F1) is your door to changing how WordPerfect works. When you press Setup (Shift-F1), the menu shown in figure 18.1 appears. Each of the menu's options is described in the text that follows.

Fig. 18.1.

The Setup menu.

```
Setup

    1 - Backup

    2 - Cursor Speed              30 cps

    3 - Display

    4 - Fast Save (unformatted)   Yes

    5 - Initial Settings

    6 - Keyboard Layout

    7 - Location of Auxiliary Files

    8 - Units of Measure




    Selection: 0
```

The Backup (**1**) option lets you request one or both of two types of backups: *Timed Document Backups* and *Original Document Backups*. If you choose Timed Document Backups, you can request automatic backups at the intervals you specify, for instance, every 10 minutes. Use these backup files as insurance against system crashes. If you request Original Document Backups, WordPerfect automatically retains a copy of your previous version of a document when you save the current version. This option lets you keep a copy of both your current version and the previous version. (See Appendix A for more information on backups.)

WordPerfect keys, when held down, normally repeat at the rate of 10 times per second. Select the Cursor Speed (**2**) option to change this repetition rate. If you are a very fast typist, you may want to speed up the rate at which keys repeat. If you find that you are getting rows of letters (such as "aaaa") when you only want one, you may choose to slow down the repeat speed. With certain monitors, keys that repeat quickly can cause "snow" on the screen. In this case, as well, you will want to slow down the rate of repetition. (See Appendix A for more details.)

You can use the Display (**3**) option to change aspects of WordPerfect's on-screen display. You can specify whether comments are displayed or hidden and whether the file name is shown on the status line. Or you can change the graphic card WordPerfect expects, the colors (or brightness, if you have a monochrome monitor) used to distinguish various WordPerfect features, and other aspects of the display. (See Chapter 5 for more information on display attributes.)

Before you save a document, WordPerfect formats it. To save time, you can select the Fast Save (4) option so that WordPerfect skips the formatting process. Although you gain speed, a disadvantage of this option is that you cannot print a document from disk. If you press Home, Home, ↓ to move to the end of the file before saving, however, you can print a document from disk while the Fast Save option is active.

If you select Initial Settings (5), you can customize the following options:

- The circumstances under which WordPerfect beeps

- The format in which dates are displayed

- The creation of a document summary

- The initial codes contained in a document. This versatile and important option allows you to set the formatting codes that appear in every document. (See this chapter's "Changing the Default Initial Codes" section.)

- The number of times the repeat key (usually Esc) causes the next character or WordPerfect feature to repeat

- The formatting of the Table of Authorities

An extraordinary new option, Keyboard Layout (6), allows you to specify the effects of pressing any key or key combination used in WordPerfect. See the "Customizing Keyboard Layouts" section later in this chapter.

WordPerfect uses a variety of *auxiliary* files in its operation. Because these files do not have to be in the same directory as the main WordPerfect program files, you can use Location of Auxiliary Files (7) to specify where these key files are stored. See the "Changing the Location of Auxiliary Files" section later in this chapter.

The Units of Measure (8) option specifies whether measurement units are displayed in inches, centimeters, points, or WordPerfect 4.2 units. You can change the way the status line in your document appears, and you can change the measurements used for margins, tabs, and other settings. (See Chapter 5 for more information.)

Some changes under Setup are global: they affect the way WordPerfect works and acts without resulting in codes being embedded in any individual document. For example, you can specify where WordPerfect can find the auxiliary files that are vital to its operation. You can make changes in WordPerfect's formatting default settings that will affect all documents. You also can request automatic backups, change cursor speed, control aspects of the screen display, and decide the number of times the repeat key (usually the Esc key) causes an operation to repeat. This section shows an example of customizing a particular global setting: the location of auxiliary files.

Changing the Location of Auxiliary Files

Structuring your hard disk into directories is similar to organizing your papers into categories with folders. Most people agree that both activities are important, but some disagreement exists concerning the best way to go about these tasks. You can customize WordPerfect to fit whatever organization you choose. For instance, you can keep the auxiliary program files anywhere you decide—as long as you let the program know the location.

You can choose where you keep backup files, hyphenation modules, keyboard and macro files, main dictionary(s), printer files, library files, supplementary dictionary(s), and the thesaurus. You also can choose the name of the style library file and the directory in which it can be found. You may want to keep several types of files (such as the dictionary, hyphenation, and thesaurus files) in the same directory.

Note: Before you can assign your files to directories, you first must create those directories.

From the Setup menu, select Location of Auxiliary Files (7) to specify the location of your files. For instance, you can use the following steps to store the thesaurus in a directory called C:\LEX:

1. Press Setup (Shift-F1).

2. Choose Location of Auxiliary Files (7).

   A menu similar to the one shown in figure 18.2 appears. (Your menu may contain different file locations.)

Fig. 18.2.
Location of auxiliary files.

```
Setup: Location of Auxiliary Files

     1 - Backup Directory            C:\BACKUP

     2 - Hyphenation Module(s)       C:\LEX

     3 - Keyboard/Macro Files        C:\MACROS

     4 - Main Dictionary(s)          C:\LEX

     5 - Printer Files               C:\PRINTER

     6 - Style Library Filename      C:\STYLES\MASTER.LST

     7 - Supplementary Dictionary(s) C:\LEX

     8 - Thesaurus                   C:\LEX
```

3. Choose the file location you want to change.

   For example, to change the file location for Thesaurus, choose **Thesaurus (8)**.

4. Type the full path name of the directory, and then press Enter.

   For example, type

   C:\LEX

   and then press Enter.

5. Press Exit (F7) to return to your document.

You can organize your WordPerfect auxiliary files in many different ways. The following suggestions provide one useful way of setting up files:

- Place the backup files in their own separate directory called C:\BACKUP. Then you can easily find backup files when necessary.

- Place the following auxiliary files from the WordPerfect disks in a directory called C:\LEX: the Hyphenation Module, Main Dictionary(s), Supplementary Dictionary(s), and Thesaurus. These files are stored separately from program files.

- Place the keyboard\macro files in a directory called C:\MACROS.

- Place the printer files in their own directory called C:\PRINTER.

After you have determined the most effective organization for your files, use the Location of Auxiliary Files screen to implement your choices.

Changing the Default Initial Codes

WordPerfect makes certain assumptions concerning the paper size, left and right margin settings, justification of text, and many other formatting specifications that affect how a document looks on-screen and when it is printed. When you initially install the package, WordPerfect assumes that you use letter-size paper with left and right margins of one inch. For many people, WordPerfect's default settings match the choices they would make; WordPerfect sets the defaults for the most commonly used paper size, margins, date formats, and other specifications.

For convenience, you might want to change the assumed format and style for all documents. Initial Codes is a powerful option that enables you to decide which codes will appear in the Initial Codes screen of each and every subsequent document. Both Initial Codes under Setup (Shift-F1) and Initial Codes under Format (Shift-F8) are entered through screens that look like a document displaying reveal codes (see fig. 18.3). However, Initial Codes under Setup (Shift-F1) affects every subsequent document while Initial Codes under Format (Shift-F8) affects only the document you are currently working on. Any number of codes can be entered at this screen.

Press Exit when done   Ln 1" Pos 1"

Fig. 18.3.
The screen for entering initial codes.

Table 18.1 lists WordPerfect's default settings. You can change these defaults through the Initial Codes option on the Setup: Initial Settings menu.

Perhaps WordPerfect's default settings don't suit your needs. In Chapter 6, you learned how to change the paper size and other initial settings for an individual document with Format (Shift-F8). If you only occasionally produce a document with different format options, you can change the settings for individual documents. However, you may habitually use legal-size paper and always prefer 3/4-inch margins

Table 18.1
Default Settings

Feature	Default
Center Page (top to bottom)	No
Decimal/Align Character	. (period)
Display Pitch	Automatic =Yes
	Width =0.1″
Force Odd/Even Page	Off
Hyphenation	Off
Hyphenation Zone	Left =10%, Right =4%
Justification	Yes
Kerning	No
Language	English
Line Height	Auto
Line Numbering	No
Line Spacing	1 (Single)
Margins Left/Right	Left =1″, Right =1″
Margins Top/Bottom	Top =1″, Bottom =1″
New Page Number	1
Page Numbering	No page numbering
Paragraph Number Definition Style	Outline Style
Paper Size/Type	Size =8.5″ × 11″
	Type =Standard
Tab Set	Every .5″
Thousands' Separator	, (comma)
Underline	Spaces =Yes, Tabs =No
Widow/Orphan Protection	No
Word Spacing/Character Spacing	Word Spacing =Optimal
	Character Spacing =Optimal
Word Spacing Justification Limits	Compress =60%, Expand =400%

on each side. In that case, you save time by using Setup (Shift-F1) to change the defaults permanently. When you change the defaults, all future documents have the initial codes you specify.

Setting Up Your Standard Page

You can change any of the default initial codes to suit your preference. For example, you might use paper that has a fancy border on the left side and at the bottom of the page. For this reason, you want to have larger left and bottom margins. To change the default settings, complete the following steps:

1. Press Setup (Shift-F1).

2. Choose Initial Settings (5).

    The menu shown in figure 18.4 appears.

```
Setup: Initial Settings

      1 - Beep Options

      2 - Date Format               3 1, 4

      3 - Document Summary

      4 - Initial Codes

      5 - Repeat Value             8

      6 - Table of Authorities
```

Fig. 18.4.

The Setup: Initial Settings menu.

3. Choose Initial Codes (4).

   You see a split screen that looks like a document with reveal codes displayed. Notice that the status line does not contain a document number. If you have not made any other changes, both halves of the screen are empty.

4. Press Format (Shift-F8).

5. To change the margins, choose Line (1).

6. Choose Margins (7).

7. Type *1.5* for the left margin and press Enter. Then press Enter again to finish with margins.

8. Press Exit once to return to the Initial Codes screen.

   You now can enter the codes to change the bottom margin.

9. Press Format (Shift-F8).

10. To change the bottom margin, choose Page (2).

11. Choose Margins (5).

12. Use the ↓ to move the cursor to the setting for the bottom margin.

13. Type *2* for the bottom margin and press Enter. Then press Enter again to finish with margins.

14. Press Exit once to return to the Initial Codes screen.

    The Initial Codes screen now should look like figure 18.5.

15. Press Exit (F7) twice to return to your document.

Each time a new document is created with this copy of WordPerfect, the document will have an initial code that changes the left margin to 1.5″ and the bottom margin to 2″. To see this for yourself, try creating a new document. Then look under initial settings by pressing Format (Shift-F8) and choosing Document (3) followed by Initial Codes (2). The bottom half of the screen displays the following:

   [L/R Mar:1.5″,1″][T/B Mar:1″,2″]

Press Exit (F7) twice to return to your original document.

Fig. 18.5.
Codes for the margin settings.

```
Press Exit when done                                    Ln 1" Pos 1.5"
▲    {    ▲    ▲    ▲    ▲    ▲    ▲    ▲    ▲    ▲    }    ▲    ▲
[L/R Mar:1.5",1"][T/B Mar:1",2"]
```

By changing the initial codes, as illustrated in the preceding steps, you can modify WordPerfect's defaults to match your own standard page format. While in the initial codes screen, you can change the style of outlining, whether or not type is justified, or any of a number of features whose codes are inserted at the beginning of a document. You can change several of these features. Enter the initial codes screen through Setup (Shift-F1), followed by Initial Settings (5) and Initial Codes (4). After you press Format (Shift-F8), enter the codes in succession that change the format or the style of a function to match your preference.

CAUTION: Although WordPerfect 5 allows you to change many initial codes through Setup, certain formatting codes cannot be changed permanently in this way. These include any text, indents, tabs, comments, list definitions, fonts, attributes, styles, center page top to bottom, headers, footers, form size and type, and advance functions. Even though you can enter these code changes on-screen, they are not instituted. When you press Exit (F7), they disappear. To verify the codes, reopen the initial codes screen and check for the codes you entered. Place any that are missing at the top of the document.

Customizing Keyboard Layouts

An exciting and useful new feature of WordPerfect is the capability to change the actions performed by keys and key combinations. Moreover, you can create several *keyboard definitions* for different purposes.

With the Keyboard Layout feature, you can do the following:

- Learn WordPerfect more easily by making the keyboard emulate popular programs

- Assign frequently performed commands or combinations of commands to keys that are easy to reach

- Remap the Alt-*key*, Ctrl-*key*, or even regular keys for foreign or statistical typing (*key* can be a letter, numeral, or key)

- Make the keyboard function as a macro library for specialized tasks

With WordPerfect 5, you can define nearly every key and key combination on the keyboard, including the following:

- Key combinations, such as Alt-*key*, Ctrl-*key*, and Shift-*key*

- All the function keys, including F11 and F12 on the IBM Enhanced Keyboard, as well as function keys in combination with Alt, Ctrl, or Shift

- Any key that performs a function in WordPerfect

- Any key on the keyboard, such as R, r, 1, the Tab key, the question mark (?), and so on. You cannot, however, assign actions to keys for which DOS does not return anything (such as typing 5 on the numeric keypad without pressing Shift).

Selecting a Keyboard Definition

You can use WordPerfect's standard keyboard definition, or you can select another keyboard definition, create a keyboard definition from scratch, or alter an existing keyboard definition. For instance, you may choose to use the ALTRNAT keyboard. That keyboard definition makes the actions of the WordPerfect keyboard work like 1-2-3. With this keyboard definition, you use F1 to get help and Esc to cancel an action.

WordPerfect Corporation includes several alternate keyboard layout files on the Conversion disk. If you plan to use an alternate keyboard definition, be sure to copy the alternate keyboard files to the directory you indicated for Keyboard/Macro Files on the Setup: Location of Auxiliary Files screen. If you do not specify a directory, WordPerfect looks for keyboard definitions in the current directory. Suppose, for example, that you are keeping the Keyboard/Macro Files in C:\MACROS and you already have created a directory called C:\MACROS. Copy the files with the .WPK extension from the Conversion disk into your \MACROS directory.

The Keyboard Layout menu, accessed from the Setup menu, works in a manner similar to List Files. Suppose that you want to perform a menu action such as deleting or editing a keyboard definition. You use the cursor keys to highlight the desired keyboard definition, and then you choose the desired action from the menu displayed at the bottom of the screen.

To select a keyboard definition, complete the following steps:

1. Press Setup (Shift-F1).

2. Choose **K**eyboard Layout (**6**).

3. Use the cursor keys to highlight the keyboard definition you want to select (see fig. 18.6).

   For example, highlight ENHANCED.

Fig. 18.6.

The Setup: Keyboard Layout menu.

Setup: Keyboard Layout

ALTRNAT
ENHANCED
MACROS

1 Select; 2 Delete; 3 Rename; 4 Create; 5 Edit; 6 Original; N Name search: 1

    4. Choose **Select** (**1**) from the menu at the bottom of the screen:

    1 Select; **2** Delete; **3** Rename; **4** Create; **5** Edit; **6** Original; **N** Name Search: 1

    5. Press Exit (F7).

Now the keyboard definition defined by ENHANCED is in effect.

Using Other Keyboard Definition Options

You can perform other actions by first completing the preceding Steps 1–3 for selecting a keyboard definition and then choosing one of the other options from the menu at the bottom of the screen. This section describes the other available options.

Select **Delete** (**2**) to delete a keyboard definition.

Use **Rename** (**3**) to change the name of a keyboard definition.

Select **Create** (**4**) to design your own keyboard definition from scratch.

Use **Edit** (**5**) to change an existing keyboard definition.

Choose **Original** (**6**) to restore the keyboard to its original definition. For instance, if you create and select a keyboard definition that causes you problems, use this option. If you run into trouble, you may need to enter WordPerfect with the command WP/X. This option instructs WordPerfect to restore for the current session the Setup to the default settings with which the program shipped.

Name Search (**N**) works just as it does in List Files. Select Name Search (**N**) and then type the first letter (or first few letters) of the keyboard you want to select, edit, or perform some other action on.

Each keyboard definition is stored in a file with its given name and the extension *.WPK, for example, ALTRNAT.WPK. You can delete, rename, or copy keyboard definitions in WordPerfect's List Files (F5) or DOS. You can access keyboard definitions altered in this way from the Keyboard Layout menu, provided they have been given the extension .WPK.

Investigating Other WordPerfect Keyboard Definitions

WordPerfect 5 includes three useful alternate keyboard definitions: ALTRNAT, ENHANCED, and MACROS. Each of these are accessed from the Keyboard Layout menu.

ALTRNAT: This keyboard definition makes the actions of the WordPerfect keyboard work more like 1-2-3, dBASE, and many other programs for the IBM. With this keyboard definition, you use F1 to get help and Esc to cancel an action (see fig. 18.7).

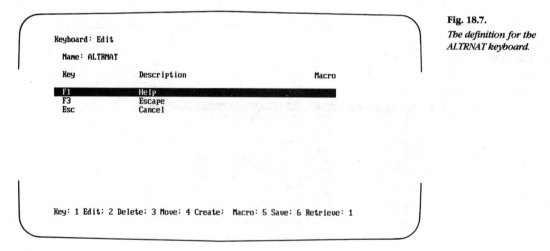

Fig. 18.7.
*The definition for the
ALTRNAT keyboard.*

ENHANCED: This keyboard definition takes advantage of the additional keys on the IBM Enhanced Keyboard (see fig. 18.8).

MACROS: This keyboard definition attaches a set of macros written by WordPerfect Corporation to various key combinations. Among the key definitions provided is Ctrl-E, which prints an address to an envelope, and Ctrl-G, which expands a glossary of abbreviations. To review the available macros, see figure 18.9.

The MACROS keyboard illustrates how a keyboard definition can be used to create a macro library (see this chapter's "Using the Keyboard as a Macro Library" section). Examine the techniques used in this keyboard layout to learn ways that you can use key definitions to create your own macro library.

Fig. 18.8.

The definition for the ENHANCED keyboard.

```
Keyboard: Edit

   Name: ENHANCED

   Key                 Description                        Macro

   Home                Home Home Home Left                5
   Num 5               Home
   Shft-F11            Italics                            6
   Shft-F12            Retrieve Block                     11
   Ctrl-F11            Large                              7
   Ctrl-F12            Move Block                         9
   Alt-F11             Very Large                         8
   Alt-F12             Copy Block                         10
   Ctrl-Up             Move Up by Sentence                2
   Ctrl-Num 5          Go To
   Ctrl-Down           Move Down by Sentence              4
   Alt-Up              Move Up by Paragraph               12
   Alt-Left            Move Left One Column               14
   Alt-Right           Move Right One Column              15
   Alt-Down            Move Down by Paragraph             13
   Ctrl-e Up           Move Up by Sentence                1
   Ctrl-e Down         Move Down by Sentence              3

   Key: 1 Edit; 2 Delete; 3 Move; 4 Create;  Macro: 5 Save; 6 Retrieve: 1
```

Fig. 18.9.

The definition for the MACROS keyboard.

```
Keyboard: Edit

   Name: MACROS

   Key                 Description                        Macro

   Alt-E               Get to Main Editing Screen         11
   Alt-T               Transpose 2 visible characters     7
   Alt-I               Insert a line                      2
   Alt-D               Delete a line                      3
   Alt-F               Find the Bookmark                  10
   Alt-G               Send GO to printer                 4
   Alt-C               Capitalize 1st letter of current word  8
   Alt-B               Restore the previous block         6
   Alt-N               Edit the Next or Previous Note     5
   Alt-M               Insert Bookmark                    9
   Ctrl-F8             Font Key                           17
   Alt-F9              List Files from Graphics Key       1
   Ctrl-C              Calculator                         13
   Ctrl-D              Generate Standard Documents        12
   Ctrl-E              Print Name & Address on an Envelope 19
   Ctrl-G              Glossary Macro - Expand Abbreviations  18

   Key: 1 Edit; 2 Delete; 3 Move; 4 Create;  Macro: 5 Save; 6 Retrieve: 1
```

Creating a Simple Keyboard Definition

If none of the supplied keyboard definitions meets your needs, you may choose to create your own. To create a keyboard definition, you first must specify a name for the definition. Then you need to define the keys and the key actions.

Perhaps the simplest type of keyboard definition assigns a frequently used keystroke or series of keystrokes to a conveniently accessible key combination. Suppose, for instance, that you have several shortcuts that you would like to make available from the keyboard. You could create a keyboard definition named SHORTCUT and define the keys and key combinations with your timesaving shortcut techniques.

Suppose that Ctrl-PgDn is one of the key combinations you want to redefine for your SHORTCUT keyboard definition. Normally, Ctrl-PgDn deletes text from the cursor through the rest of the page. Because you do not use that function, you decide to substitute the keystrokes for deleting a single block of text for the action that Ctrl-PgDn normally performs. In your definition, you want to eliminate the need to confirm the deletion by pressing *Y* because you find that extra step annoying. You therefore assign the series of keystrokes {DELETE}Y to the key combination Ctrl-PgDn.

To create a keyboard definition, complete the following steps:

1. Press Setup (Shift-F1).

2. Choose **Keyboard Layout (6)**.

   The Setup: Keyboard Layout screen is displayed.

3. Choose **Create (4)**.

4. When prompted for the Keyboard Filename, type the file name and press Enter.

   For the example, type *Shortcut* and press Enter (see fig. 18.10).

   After you name the keyboard, you must define the keys for this keyboard layout. The following menu appears at the bottom of the screen:

   Key: 1 Edit; 2 Delete; 3 Move; 4 Create; Macro: 5 Save; 6 Retrieve: 1

```
 Keyboard: Edit

   Name: SHORTCUT

   Key            Description                    Macro




   Key: 1 Edit; 2 Delete; 3 Move; 4 Create;  Macro: 5 Save; 6 Retrieve: 1
```

Fig. 18.10.
The Keyboard: Edit screen for the SHORTCUT keyboard definition.

5. Select **Create (4)**.

   At the bottom left corner of the screen, the word Key: appears.

6. Press the key or key combination you want to define.

   For this example, press Ctrl-PgDn.

   A screen similar to the macro editing screen appears (see fig. 18.11).

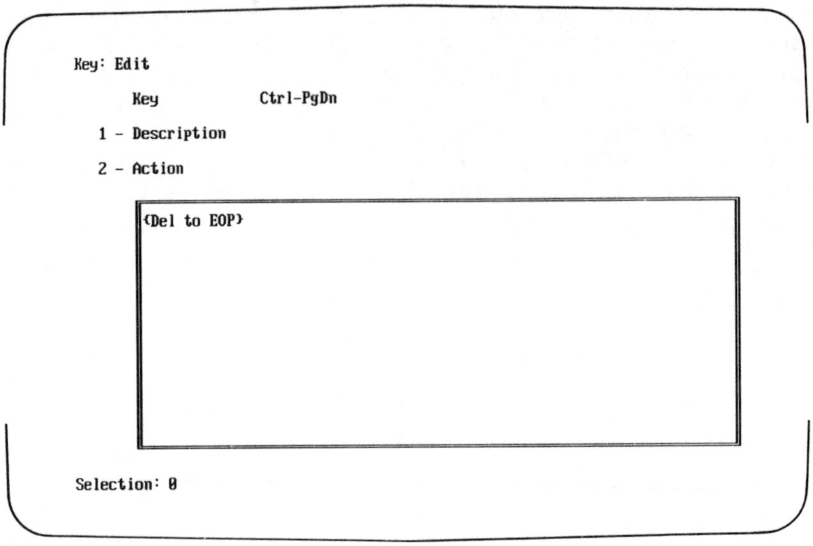

Fig. 18.11.

The Key: Edit screen.

```
Key: Edit

        Key           Ctrl-PgDn

    1 - Description

    2 - Action

    ┌─────────────────────────────────────────────────┐
    │ <Del to EOP>                                    │
    │                                                 │
    │                                                 │
    │                                                 │
    │                                                 │
    │                                                 │
    └─────────────────────────────────────────────────┘

    Selection: 0
```

7. Choose **Description** (**1**) to edit the description for the selected key.

8. Type a short description of the key action and press Enter.

    For example, type *Deletion without confirm* and press Enter.

9. Select **Action** (**2**).

10. Press the Del key to delete the action that is currently performed when you press this key.

11. Specify the new action that you want the key to perform.

    For the new definition of Ctrl-PgDn, press Ctrl-V, the Del key, and then *Y.*

    Within the macro editor, the Del key actually performs the function of deleting text. You therefore must press Ctrl-V before pressing the Del key to let WordPerfect know that you don't want to delete a character in the macro. Instead, you want to insert the deletion action in the definition.

12. To create other key definitions, press Exit (F7) twice to return to the Keyboard: Edit screen, and then repeat steps 5–11 to define other keys for this keyboard definition.

13. If you want to select this keyboard definition before exiting, press the Exit key (F7) once to go to the Keyboard Layout screen. Then use the cursor keys to highlight the keyboard name, for instance, SHORTCUT. Finally, choose **Select** (**1**). Then press Exit (F7) once to return to your document.

    or

    To return to your document without selecting this keyboard definition, press Exit (F7) twice.

Creating a Foreign Language Keyboard Definition

Typing in a foreign language can be a tedious task using the standard keyboard. In Spanish, for example, you must use several steps to compose frequently used characters such as ñ or é. At best, with the aid of a macro, you have to use a key combination such as Alt-N to create a foreign language character. To save time, you might want to create a special Spanish keyboard definition. You can assign foreign characters to specified keys. For instance, you could change the semicolon key (;) to ñ.

To create a foreign language keyboard definition, complete the following steps:

1. Press Setup (Shift-F1).

2. Choose **Keyboard Layout** (6).

3. Choose **Create** (4).

4. When prompted for the Keyboard Filename, type the file name and press Enter.

   For example, type *Spanish* and press Enter.

   You are now ready to define the keys for this keyboard layout. The following menu appears at the bottom of the screen:

   Key: 1 Edit; 2 Delete; 3 Move; 4 Create; Macro: 5 Save; 6 Retrieve: 1

5. Choose **Create** (4).

   At the bottom left corner of the screen, the word Key: appears.

6. Press the key or key combination you want to define.

   For this example, press ; to define the semicolon key as ñ.

7. Choose **Description** (1) to edit the description for the selected key.

8. Type a short description of the key action and press Enter.

   For this example, type *Spanish ene* and press Enter.

9. Select **Action** (2).

10. Press the Del key to delete the action that is currently performed when you press this key.

11. Enter the new action.

    For this example, use the compose feature to create an ñ: press Ctrl-2 followed by *n* and ~.

12. Create other key definitions.

    Press Exit (F7) twice to return to the Keyboard: Edit screen and define other keys.

13. If you want to select this keyboard definition before exiting, press the Exit key (F7) once to go to the Keyboard Layout screen. Then use the cursor keys to highlight the keyboard name, for instance, SPANISH. Finally, choose **Select (1)**. Then press Exit (F7) once to return to your document.

or

To return to your document without selecting this keyboard definition, press Exit (F7) twice.

Editing a Keyboard Definition

After creating a new keyboard definition, you may decide to add keys, edit keys, delete keys, move keys, change macros to keys, or change keys to macros. To perform any of these tasks, you must start at the Setup: Keyboard Layout screen and specify which keyboard definition you want to edit. Then, from the Keyboard: Edit screen, you can change the definitions of specific keys.

TIP: If you drastically change the way WordPerfect function keys work, you may find that getting help with your WordPerfect problems is difficult. If you work in a large company with a microcomputer support person, for instance, that person probably won't be able to help you if your keyboard definition is significantly different from the company standard.

To specify which keyboard definition you want to edit, complete the following steps:

1. Press Setup (Shift-F1).

2. Choose **Keyboard Layout (6)**.

3. Use the cursor keys to highlight the keyboard definition you want to edit.

4. From the menu at the bottom of the Setup: Keyboard Layout screen, select **Edit (5)**.

The Keyboard: Edit screen is displayed along with the following menu at the bottom of the screen:

Key: 1 Edit; 2 Delete; 3 Move; 4 Create; Macro: 5 Save; 6 Retrieve: 1

Notice the tasks that you can perform from this menu.

Editing a Key Definition

Sometimes you may need to edit a key, for instance, when the action performed is not correct. Complete the preceding steps for editing a keyboard definition, and then complete the following steps to edit the definition of a particular key:

1. At the Keyboard: Edit screen, use the cursor keys to highlight the key you want to edit.

2. Choose **Edit** (**1**).

3. Choose **Description** (**1**) to edit the description of the key definition, make the desired changes, and then press Enter

   or

   Choose **Action** (**2**) to edit the keystrokes of the key definition. To add a particular keystroke to the keyboard definition, position your cursor where you want to make the insertion and press the key. After you have made your changes, press Exit (F7).

   To include certain special keys, such as Cancel and Del, in a key definition, you need to press Ctrl-V before pressing the key. Pressing Ctrl-V tells WordPerfect that you want to include these keystrokes in the key definition rather than immediately perform the key actions. You also can insert commands into a key definition by pressing Ctrl-PgUp, highlighting the command you want to insert, and pressing Enter. You edit a key definition almost exactly as you edit a macro. For more information about how to edit in this screen, see Chapter 11.

4. Press Exit (F7) to return to the Keyboard: Edit screen.

5. Continue within the Keyboard: Edit screen to make other changes to the keyboard definition.

6. Press Exit (F7) to return to the Keyboard Layout screen.

7. To reselect your keyboard definition before exiting, highlight the keyboard name, and then choose **Select** (**1**).

8. Press Exit (F7) to return to the Keyboard: Edit screen.

   or

   Press Exit (F7) twice to your document without selecting the keyboard definition.

Note: If you make a change in your current keyboard definition, the change does not take effect until you leave and reenter WordPerfect or you reselect the current keyboard definition.

Deleting a Key Definition

If you want to return a key to its original definition, first perform the previous steps for editing a keyboard definition. Then complete the following steps to delete a new definition you have entered:

1. At the Keyboard: Edit screen, use the cursor keys to highlight the key whose new definition you want to delete.

2. Choose **Delete** (**2**).

   The key name appears along with a prompt asking you to confirm that you want to make the deletion.

3. To confirm the deletion, press *Y*.

4. Continue editing key definitions

or

Press Exit (F7) twice to return to your document.

Moving a Key Definition

Suppose that you have defined a particular key (Ctrl-PgDn, for example) in a key definition, and you decide that you want to move the definition to another key. Perhaps you think that another key combination, such as Ctrl-D, would be easier to press or easier to remember.

To change the key or key combination, first follow the previous steps for editing a keyboard definition, and then complete these steps to move the key definition:

1. At the Keyboard: Edit screen, use the cursor keys to highlight the key.

   For this example, highlight Ctrl-PgDn.

2. Choose **Move** (**3**).

   The word Key: appears at the bottom left corner of the screen.

3. Press the new key combination that you want for this definition.

   For this example, press Ctrl-D.

4. Continue within the Keyboard: Edit screen to make other changes to the keyboard definition

   or

   Press Exit (F7) twice to return to your document.

Using the Keyboard as a Macro Library

A keyboard definition can function as a library of macros for a particular task. Suppose that you want to use special shortcuts under certain circumstances—for example, when you are working with columns. You do not, however, want to tie up the easy-to-invoke Alt-*key* combinations. Under these circumstances, your needs would best be served by a keyboard layout definition specially designed to make working with columns easier.

To create such a keyboard definition for working with columns, begin by creating a set of macros. One macro could define the columns (for example, Alt-D). Another macro could turn the column feature on and off (for example, Alt-O). Still other macros could move one column to the right or left (Alt-L and Alt-R). After you create the macros, you can turn them into key definitions in a keyboard layout. Any set of macros that work well together can become a keyboard definition. Your imagination is the only limit.

Note: If you define a particular Alt-*key* combination both via the selected keyboard definition and by a macro, the keyboard definition takes precedence.

Making a Macro into a Key Definition

After you have created a macro and find you use it frequently, you may decide to change it into a key definition. Macros are usually easier to create than key definitions because you initially create macros through a learn mode. You start the macro and record the keystrokes as you perform the actions. As you enter the steps of the macro, you see the effects of your actions. You also can look at the menu choices available at a particular point in the macro's creation.

A key definition, on the other hand, is created "blind." You do not have immediate access to the effects of your actions or to the menus that are available at a particular point during creation. Under these conditions, you need to remember accurately the WordPerfect menu options. Fortunately, turning the commands associated with a macro into a key definition is easy.

Creating a Macro

The first step in creating a key definition from a macro is to create the macro. Use the following steps to create a macro that produces the French cedilla character (ç):

1. Press Macro Define (Ctrl-F10).

    The words Define Macro: appear in the bottom left corner of the screen.

2. Press the key or key combination to which you want to assign the macro.

    For this example, press Alt-C.

    The word Description: appears in the bottom left corner of the screen.

3. Type a description of the macro and press Enter.

    For this example, type *French cedilla* and press Enter.

    Notice the flashing Macro Def indicator in the lower left corner of the screen.

4. Perform the steps that you want the macro to execute.

    To create a French cedilla, press Ctrl-2, type *c* (the letter does not appear on-screen), and then type a comma (,). After you type both characters, the ç character appears.

5. To end the macro, press Macro Define (Ctrl-F10).

Retrieving a Macro

After you define a macro, you easily can turn it into a key definition. For instance, you can turn your Alt-C macro, which types a character, into the new definition for the apostrophe (').

To retrieve a macro you want to include in a keyboard definition, complete the following steps:

1. Press Setup (Shift-F1).

2. Choose **Keyboard Layout** (**6**).

3. Use the cursor keys to highlight the name of the keyboard definition you want to edit.

4. Select **Edit** (**5**).

5. From the Keyboard: Edit menu, choose **Retrieve** (**6**).

   The word Key: appears in the bottom left corner of the screen.

6. Press the key you want to define in this keyboard definition.

   For this example, press the apostrophe (').

   The word Macro: appears in the left corner of the screen.

7. Press the Alt-*key* or type the name of the macro.

   For this example, press Alt-C.

   You also can retrieve a temporary macro or a macro that has a 2- to 8-character file name. (Temporary macros are evoked by pressing Alt-F10 and then Enter or by pressing a single letter; see Chapter 11 for more details.)

8. Enter other key definitions

   or

   Press Exit (F7) twice to return to your document.

CAUTION: If the same key combination both calls a macro and is redefined in the selected keyboard definition, do not attempt to retrieve the macro version. Instead of retrieving the macro, the program will perform a runaway rendition of the keystrokes invoked by the key combination in the keyboard definition. To avoid this problem, you may want to create your new keyboard definition while using either the original WordPerfect layout or an alternate keyboard that has been tested thoroughly.

Making a Macro from a Key Definition

Not only can you change a macro into a key definition, but you also can change a key definition into a macro. After you define a particular key, for example, you might find that the routine it executes is so useful that you want it available no matter what keyboard definition you are using.

To turn a defined key into a macro, complete the following steps:

1. Press Setup (Shift-F1).

2. Choose **Keyboard Layout** (**6**).

3. Use the cursor keys to highlight the keyboard definition that contains the key you want to turn into a macro.

4. Press **Edit** (**5**).

5. At the Keyboard: Edit screen, use the cursor keys to highlight the key you want to turn into a macro.

6. Choose **Save** (**5**).

   Define macro: appears in the left corner of the screen.

7. Press the Alt-*key* combination or enter the name you want to assign to the macro.

8. Press Exit (F7) twice to return to your document.

Now this macro is available no matter what keyboard definition is in use. Note: A macro assigned to an Alt-*key* combination is available as long as you don't use the same Alt-*key* combination in your keyboard definition. If you do, the keyboard definition will override the action of the macro.

Copying a Key Definition

Suppose that you have defined a key and you want to modify the definition and use the modified version for another key definition. In effect, you want to copy the first key's definition to a second key and then modify it. Save the key definition to a macro—a temporary macro assigned to the Enter key or to a single letter would be best—and then retrieve the macro to the second key. Now you can modify the second key definition without affecting your original definition.

Summary

In this chapter, you have learned how to customize WordPerfect to meet your needs. You now should be able to use the Setup key (Shift-F1) to change many WordPerfect features, such as the following:

- Change the global aspects that control how WordPerfect works, such as where the program looks for auxiliary files and how many times the repeat key (Esc) repeats the next keystroke

- Control the initial codes that regulate document format for all documents

You also learned to customize your keyboard by creating and modifying keyboard definitions. After learning the basics presented in this chapter, you should be able to do the following:

- Remap the keyboard to make foreign language and statistical typing easier

- Use a keyboard definition to change WordPerfect combinations that you find awkward

- Use a keyboard definition as training wheels to make the WordPerfect command structure imitate the commands of a word processor with which you are familiar

- Set up different keyboard definitions to function as macro libraries containing sets of macros that work well together

Making WordPerfect work your way can save time and inconvenience. Customization ensures that when you sit down at the computer, WordPerfect is ready to go in the direction and manner you want it to go.

19

Using Special Characters and Typing Equations

*As as an independent computer consultant in the Boston area, **Marilyn Horn Claff** has exceptional knowledge of WordPerfect Corporation software and experience teaching advanced applications.* ■

As a general-purpose word processor, WordPerfect does not offer any features designed exclusively for technical typists. Nevertheless, its superb text-processing features, such as master documents, automatic referencing, footnotes, endnotes, and styles, make it a strong contender where light-to-moderate technical typing is required. If your technical typing needs are demanding, you still may be able to use WordPerfect with a dedicated equation-generating program, such as Exact™.

This chapter only introduces some of the issues, techniques, and problems involved in creating technical documents with WordPerfect. Because technical word processing is not a self-contained topic, like a Table of Authorities or the Thesaurus, this chapter refers to other discussions in this book. Technical typing includes many general features that are combined to create complex documents with extraordinary printed output. Technical typists need to know virtually everything from keyboard mapping and graphics boxes to such operations as changing the Tab Align character, using Advance, and moving tabular Columns.

Despite the difficulty of technical word processing, WordPerfect 5 should satisfy the technical word-processing requirements of most users. On the other hand, if you work with complex equations, frequently mix characters of different sizes in the same equations, or use proportional fonts for your equations, consider using a dedicated equation program with WordPerfect.

Using Special Characters in Equations

The chief difficulties involved with creating equations are handling special characters and aligning the characters on the printed page.

Another difficulty is that many special characters, such as sigmas, integrals, and radicals, often need to be in a font larger than the other characters in the equation.

WordPerfect 5 offers several ways to enter special characters. For simplicity, a *special character* is any character not displayed on a standard PC keyboard. Special characters include nonkeyboard characters in the IBM Extended Character set and characters in the WordPerfect character sets, as well as characters in printer fonts.

The Control/Alt key mapping in version 4.2 was replaced by WordPerfect's Keyboard Layout and Compose features. Using the Compose feature is discussed in this chapter; see Chapter 18 for a discussion of Keyboard Layout.

Using the IBM Extended Character Set

Every character that you see on your screen is represented internally by a number, called its *ASCII code*. The letter **A**, for example, is ASCII 65, **B** is ASCII 66, and **a** is ASCII 97.

The term *ASCII* is an acronym for the American Standard Code for Information Interchange. The original ASCII code, which consisted of 128 characters (0-127), was extended to 256 (128-255) characters when IBM introduced the IBM PC. The IBM PC's 256-character set is therefore referred to as the *IBM Extended Character Set* or the *Extended ASCII Character Set* (see table 19.1).

Table 19.1
The IBM Extended Character Set

Hex	Dec	Screen	Ctrl	Key	Hex	Dec	Screen	Ctrl	Key
00h	0		NUL	^@	11h	17	◄	DC1	^Q
01h	1	☺	SOH	^A	12h	18	↕	DC2	^R
02h	2	●	STX	^B	13h	19	‼	DC3	^S
03h	3	♥	ETX	^C	14h	20	¶	DC4	^T
04h	4	♦	EOT	^D	15h	21	§	NAK	^U
05h	5	♣	ENQ	^E	16h	22	▬	SYN	^V
06h	6	♠	ACK	^F	17h	23	↨	ETB	^W
07h	7	●	BEL	^G	18h	24	↑	CAN	^X
08h	8	◘	BS	^H	19h	25	↓	EM	^Y
09h	9	○	HT	^I	1Ah	26	→	SUB	^Z
0Ah	10	◙	LF	^J	1Bh	27	←	ESC	^[
0Bh	11	♂	VT	^K	1Ch	28	∟	FS	^\
0Ch	12	♀	FF	^L	1Dh	29	↔	GS	^]
0Dh	13	♪	CR	^M	1Eh	30	▲	RS	^^
0Eh	14	♫	SO	^N	1Fh	31	▼	US	^_
0Fh	15	☼	SI	^O	20h	32			
10h	16	►	DLE	^P					

Hex	Dec	Screen	Hex	Dec	Screen	Hex	Dec	Screen
21h	33	!	4Fh	79	O	7Dh	125	}
22h	34	"	50h	80	P	7Eh	126	~
23h	35	#	51h	81	Q	7Fh	127	⌂
24h	36	$	52h	82	R	80h	128	Ç
25h	37	%	53h	83	S	81h	129	ü
26h	38	&	54h	84	T	82h	130	é
27h	39	'	55h	85	U	83h	131	â
28h	40	(	56h	86	V	84h	132	ä
29h	41	)	57h	87	W	85h	133	à
2Ah	42	*	58h	88	X	86h	134	å
2Bh	43	+	59h	89	Y	87h	135	ç
2Ch	44	,	5Ah	90	Z	88h	136	ê
2Dh	45	-	5Bh	91	[	89h	137	ë
2Eh	46	.	5Ch	92	\	8Ah	138	è
2Fh	47	/	5Dh	93	]	8Bh	139	ï
30h	48	0	5Eh	94	^	8Ch	140	î
31h	49	1	5Fh	95		8Dh	141	ì
32h	50	2	60h	96	`	8Eh	142	Ä
33h	51	3	61h	97	a	8Fh	143	Å
34h	52	4	62h	98	b	90h	144	É
35h	53	5	63h	99	c	91h	145	æ
36h	54	6	64h	100	d	92h	146	Æ
37h	55	7	65h	101	e	93h	147	ô
38h	56	8	66h	102	f	94h	148	ö
39h	57	9	67h	103	g	95h	149	ò
3Ah	58	:	68h	104	h	96h	150	û
3Bh	59	;	69h	105	i	97h	151	ù
3Ch	60	<	6Ah	106	j	98h	152	ÿ
3Dh	61	=	6Bh	107	k	99h	153	Ö
3Eh	62	>	6Ch	108	l	9Ah	154	Ü
3Fh	63	?	6Dh	109	m	9Bh	155	¢
40h	64	@	6Eh	110	n	9Ch	156	£
41h	65	A	6Fh	111	o	9Dh	157	¥
42h	66	B	70h	112	p	9Eh	158	₧
43h	67	C	71h	113	q	9Fh	159	ƒ
44h	68	D	72h	114	r	A0h	160	á
45h	69	E	73h	115	s	A1h	161	í
46h	70	F	74h	116	t	A2h	162	ó
47h	71	G	75h	117	u	A3h	163	ú
48h	72	H	76h	118	v	A4h	164	ñ
49h	73	I	77h	119	w	A5h	165	Ñ
4Ah	74	J	78h	120	x	A6h	166	ª
4Bh	75	K	79h	121	y	A7h	167	º
4Ch	76	L	7Ah	122	z	A8h	168	¿
4Dh	77	M	7Bh	123	{	A9h	169	⌐
4Eh	78	N	7Ch	124			AAh	170	¬

Hex	Dec	Screen	Hex	Dec	Screen	Hex	Dec	Screen
ABh	171	½	C8h	200	╚	E4h	228	Σ
ACh	172	¼	C9h	201	╔	E5h	229	σ
ADh	173	¡	CAh	202	╩	E6h	230	µ
AEh	174	«	CBh	203	╦	E7h	231	τ
AFh	175	»	CCh	204	╠	E8h	232	Φ
B0h	176	░	CDh	205	═	E9h	233	θ
B1h	177	▒	CEh	206	╬	EAh	234	Ω
B2h	178	▓	CFh	207	╧	EBh	235	δ
B3h	179	│	D0h	208	╨	ECh	236	∞
B4h	180	┤	D1h	209	╤	EDh	237	φ
B5h	181	╡	D2h	210	╥	EEh	238	∈
B6h	182	╢	D3h	211	╙	EFh	239	∩
B7h	183	╖	D4h	212	╘	F0h	240	≡
B8h	184	╕	D5h	213	╒	F1h	241	±
B9h	185	╣	D6h	214	╓	F2h	242	≥
BAh	186	║	D7h	215	╫	F3h	243	≤
BBh	187	╗	D8h	216	╪	F4h	244	⌠
BCh	188	╝	D9h	217	┘	F5h	245	⌡
BDh	189	╜	DAh	218	┌	F6h	246	÷
BEh	190	╛	DBh	219	█	F7h	247	≈
BFh	191	┐	DCh	220	▄	F8h	248	°
C0h	192	└	DDh	221	▌	F9h	249	•
C1h	193	┴	DEh	222	▐	FAh	250	·
C2h	194	┬	DFh	223	▀	FBh	251	√
C3h	195	├	E0h	224	α	FCh	252	n
C4h	196	─	E1h	225	β	FDh	253	²
C5h	197	┼	E2h	226	Γ	FEh	254	■
C6h	198	╞	E3h	227	π	FFh	255	
C7h	199	╟						

The original ASCII character set includes the characters found on an English-language typewriter: upper- and lowercase letters, digits, and punctuation. The term *ASCII file* refers to a file consisting exclusively of characters from the original ASCII character set.

The upper ASCII character set added many foreign characters, mathematical symbols, and line-drawing characters. For foreign-language or technical typing, you must be able to access many of the characters in the IBM extension.

If you need to use a character in the IBM Extended Character set only occasionally, you may prefer to enter the character on the numeric keypad rather than to map it to a key or to use the Compose feature described later.

First, look up the number of the character you want in a chart of the IBM Extended Character set. To enter the character, hold down the Alt key, and type on the numeric keypad the ASCII number. The corresponding character appears on-screen when you release the Alt key. (You must type on the numeric keypad; you cannot use the numbers on the top row of your keyboard.)

For example, to insert the character ê, press and hold down the Alt key and type *136*. For the mathematical intersection symbol ∩, hold down Alt and type *239*.

Using WordPerfect's Character Sets

To facilitate foreign-language and scientific word processing, WordPerfect Corporation designed a number of its own character sets, consisting of 1,702 characters grouped by subject into 13 (0 through 12) font sets (see table 19.2). Each WordPerfect character is identified by a two-part number. The first part is the number of the character set in which the character is contained. The second part is the number of the character within that character set. Thus, the section symbol (§, or ASCII 21) is located in Character Set 4 (Typographic Symbols). The WordPerfect code for the section symbol is **4,6**.

Most video card-monitor combinations are limited to the 256 characters in the IBM Extended Character set. If you have a special display adapter, such as the Hercules Plus card, you will be able to display up to 512 different characters. The choice of WordPerfect characters is fixed.

Whenever you use a character your monitor cannot display, WordPerfect represents the character on your editing screen as a small solid box (■). If you have graphics capability *and* your printer is capable of printing that character, you will be able to see the character by using Print, View Document (Shift-F7, **6**). Remember that View Document shows you *exactly* how your document will be printed on the currently selected printer. If your printer cannot print a particular character, it will be invisible in View Document, and a blank space will be left when you print the document.

To determine the value of a nondisplayable-character box without leaving the main editing screen, press Reveal Codes (Alt-F3, or F11) and move the cursor to the character. When the cursor is directly on a special character, its WordPerfect code is visible in brackets. Figure 19.1 illustrates how the paragraph symbol (¶) appears in Reveal Codes when the cursor is on the character. When the cursor is not directly over a special character, the character appears the same in Reveal Codes as it does in the normal editing screen.

Because the characters in the WordPerfect character sets are grouped according to subject, you easily can locate the character you need. Simply refer to the appropriate character chart in the Appendix of the WordPerfect manual.

Two files on the Conversion disk provide additional information about the WordPerfect character sets. Retrieve or print CHARACTR.DOC to review a list of each character by name. Print CHARMAP.TST to see which characters your printer can print.

Table 19.2
The WordPerfect Character Sets

Character Set	Number	Contents
ASCII	0	ASCII space through tilde
Multinational 1	1	Common capitalizable multinational characters, diacriticals, and noncapitalizable multinational characters
Multinational 2	2	Rarely used noncapitalizable multinational characters and diacriticals
Box Drawing	3	All 81 double/single box drawing characters
Typographic Symbols	4	Common typographic symbols not found in ASCII
Iconic Symbols	5	Rarely used "picture" (icon) symbols
Math/Scientific	6	Nonextensible, nonoversized math/ scientific characters not found in ASCII sets
Math/Scientific	7	Extensible and oversized math/ scientific characters
Greek	8	Full Greek character set for ancient and modern applications
Hebrew	9	Hebrew character set
Cyrillic	10	Full Cyrillic character set for ancient and modern applications
Japanese Kana	11	Characters for Hiragana or Katakana (The type is determined by the typeface.)
User	12	255 user-definable characters

Creating WordPerfect Special Characters with Compose

WordPerfect's Compose feature, new to version 5, provides two ways to enter special characters.

To enter special characters with Compose, press the Compose key (Ctrl-2) and enter the number of the WordPerfect character, a comma, and the number of the

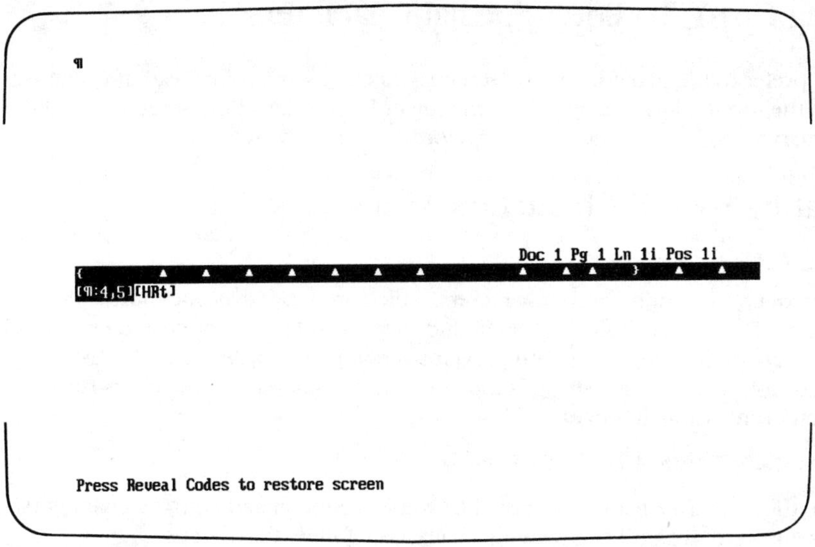

Fig. 19.1.
*The paragraph
symbol in Reveal
Codes.*

character itself. For example, to enter the copyright symbol, press Ctrl-2 and type *4,23* (the WordPerfect code for ©), and press Enter. (Remember that not all codes will display on-screen.)

CAUTION: Compose is *Ctrl-2*, not Ctrl-F2.

Using Compose To Create Other Special Characters

Compose allows you to enter certain characters if you can remember what they look like. If the character is a digraph (a combination of two characters) or a diacritical (a character plus a diacritical mark such as a circumflex), you probably can enter the character with Compose, without knowing its WordPerfect code.

Press Compose (Ctrl-2). Then type the two characters that you wish to combine. Only certain predefined pairs of characters work with Compose. The order in which you enter the characters is immaterial. For example, you could type either the comma , or the *c* first to compose the cedilla (ç).

You also can enter the fractions $1/_2$ and $1/_4$ by pressing Compose (Ctrl-2), the slash key, and 2 (or 4). Enter bullets by pressing Compose (Ctrl-2), an asterisk, and then one of the following characters:

period	small filled bullet
asterisk	medium filled bullet
lowercase o	small hollow bullet
uppercase O	large hollow bullet

Using Ctrl-V To Enter Special Characters

If you prefer to see prompts on the screen, you can use Ctrl-V instead of Compose. When the prompt Key = appears on the lower left corner of the screen, type the two characters, or enter the code of a WordPerfect character.

Creating Special Characters with Overstrike

Overstrike is still another technique for creating special characters. You can overstrike up to eight different characters, which are treated as one indivisible character. The Overstrike string can include super- and subscript characters, as well as automatic font changes. As with previous versions of WordPerfect, the last character of the overstrike string is the one that is displayed. All the overstruck characters are visible in Reveal Codes:

[Ovrstk:O[SUPRSCPT] _ [suprscpt]

To use the overstrike feature, access the Overstrike menu and type the characters. For example, to overstrike an O with a backslash, follow these steps:

1. Press Format (Shift-F8).

2. Select Other (**4**).

3. Select Overstrike (**5**).

4. Select Create (**1**).

5. At the [Ovrstk] prompt, type O\ and press Enter.

6. Press Exit (F7) to return to the editing screen.

Despite the number of keystrokes required to access it, WordPerfect 5's Overstrike feature is well-designed. The overstruck characters are melded together so that they act like a single character. No longer can you inadvertently delete part of an overstrike sequence. Separate menu choices for creating and editing overstrike characters make Overstrike more convenient, whereas the eight-character limit provides greater flexibility.

TIP: Create a macro for special characters that you use frequently, or assign them to a keyboard layout. See Chapter 11 and Chapter 16.

Changing Fonts

Font changes in WordPerfect 5 are intended to change typeface or font size. Changing to another font to access a particular character should not be necessary if your printer is defined correctly. When you use a character that is not available in your current font, WordPerfect's printer drivers look for that character in your other fonts.

The main reason for changing fonts in typing equations is to use oversized characters. You can use the oversized characters contained in WordPerfect's Character Set 7; simply use the Compose feature to insert these characters in your equation. Or, you can change the font size and appearance and the base font. See Chapter 5 for a discussion of changing fonts.

Combining Special Characters in Equations

Despite its capability to incorporate graphics files and to use a graphics preview mode, WordPerfect remains a text-based word processor. Therefore, whether you can create equations directly into WordPerfect depends on whether the special symbols you need are available in your printer. If your printer cannot print the required characters but is capable of printing graphics, consider creating equations with a separate graphics program and incorporating them into WordPerfect as graphics files.

Writing Equations in WordPerfect

Although you can use many techniques to create equations directly in WordPerfect, the method you choose should be determined by the structure of the equation and by what works best for your particular printer. For the sake of simplicity, equations can be divided into two groups. The first group comprises simple equations entered as regular text with super- and subscripts. Unfortunately, few real-world equations can be created this way. The second group is multiline equations that must be entered line by line. The equations in this group are best entered in graphics boxes to protect the extensive formatting they require.

Using Interlinear Equations

Interlinear equations are equations that can be entered on a single line, using no more than one level each of super- and subscripts. Interlinear equations do not require special techniques such as space fill and graphics boxes. Because they can be entered on a single line of text, interlinear equations flow with the text of the paragraph. If the equation has more than one level of super- or subscripts, you should use a graphics box (see "Using Graphic Boxes for Equations" later in this chapter).

Interlinear equations are easy to create. Just use WordPerfect's super- and subscript attributes. Keep the text from breaking by using hard spaces and minus signs.

TIP: When you create an interlinear equation in a paragraph, WordPerfect automatically adjusts the line spacing of the surrounding text so that the super- and subscripts do not overprint the lines above and below the equation.

Keeping an Equation on One Line

Two invaluable tools for keeping equations from dividing, if they fall at the end of the line, are hard spaces and minus signs. Use a *hard space* between words or in formulas to prevent text from breaking at that point. To insert a hard space, press the Home key, release it, and then press the space bar. (Do not press and hold down the Home key while you press the space bar.) A formula such as $(x + y)^2 = (x^2 + 2xy + y^2)$ will remain intact if you use hard spaces instead of regular spaces. If there is not enough room on the current line, the entire formula will be "wrapped" to the next line. Hard spaces appear in Reveal Codes as [ ].

If you use regular WordPerfect hyphens in formulas, your lines will "break" at the hyphen sign. Instead, use the key sequence Home, hyphen to create a nonbreaking *minus sign*. Again, press the Home key, release it, and then press the hyphen key. If your formulas are constructed with both hard spaces and minus signs, they will not wrap to the next line. Note: a regular WordPerfect hyphen appears as [-] in Reveal Codes; a minus sign appears as - (without brackets).

CAUTION: Don't use the minus key on the numeric keypad to insert the Home, hyphen combination.

Positioning the Text

You can use several WordPerfect capabilities to position text precisely on the printed page. One of these is Advance, which is one of WordPerfect's most sophisticated new features. With this feature, you insert a code which tells your printer to print text a specified distance up, down, left, or right. You can enter an absolute measurement (1 inch from the top of the page) or a relative measurement (1 inch from the current cursor position). Unfortunately, it is difficult to edit equations if you use the Advance feature. The distances are actual measurements, and if you change to a different point size, you must delete and reenter the advance commands because the distances are no longer correct.

You can use also superscripts and subscripts to position text. Press Font (Ctrl-F8), select Size (**1**), and choose from the Size menu either Suprscpt (**1**) or Subscpt (**2**). Like other font attributes, super- and subscripts stay on until you turn them off by returning to the Font submenu and pressing Normal (**3**).

If the text to be superscripted is already typed, mark it as a Block (Alt-F4, or F12), press Font (Ctrl-F8), select Size (**1**), and choose Suprscpt (**1**).

You should note that WordPerfect does not support simultaneous or multiple levels of super- and subscripts.

Using Tab Align

Tab Align (Ctrl-F6) allows you to align words or numbers on a character you designate; the default alignment character is a period. The decimal character makes it easy to line up columns of numbers on the decimal point. For technical word processing, the alignment character can be redefined as the equal sign so that equations can be aligned vertically. (Setting tabs and changing the alignment character are discussed in Chapter 5.)

To use Tab Align in an equation, follow these steps (the equal sign has been defined as the alignment character):

1. Press Tab Align (Ctrl-F6).

2. Type *Distance = Rate × Time* and press Enter.

3. Press Tab Align (Ctrl-F6).

4. Type *Work = Force × Distance* and press Enter.

5. Press Tab Align (Ctrl-F6).

6. Type *Y = AX + B* and press Enter.

   You will see:

   ```
   Distance = Rate × Time
       Work = Force × Distance
          Y = AX + B
   ```

Creating Equations with Space Fill and Half-line Spacing

To create more complex equations with additional levels of sub- and superscripts, use a combination of half-line spacing, space fill, and typeover to "paint" the equation on the screen, starting with the topmost line. (See Chapter 5 to review how to change line spacing.)

Even though half-line spacing cannot be represented on-screen, it affords a rough approximation of the spatial relationship among the components of the equations. With half-line spacing, superscripts and subscripts are placed on separate lines. Alternative techniques such as Advance, superscript, and subscript display the text on a single line, which is difficult to visualize.

Note: This technique works best if you are using a fixed-pitch font. If you are using a proportional font, you need to align characters vertically with the Advance feature.

The term *space fill* refers to a work space consisting of several rows of space characters. You *must* have a hard return at the end of each line of spaces. Simply press the space bar to create several lines of space characters. When you use typeover, you can move the cursor through the blank screen area and type the equation. If you insert or delete characters, the alignment will not be thrown off.

Using Graphics Boxes for Equations

Placing multiline equations in graphics boxes solves many of the problems of technical word processing. (Chapter 24 explains using graphics boxes in detail.) You can create boxes and type equations in the box, or you can import equations from a separate graphics program.

Graphics boxes eliminate the need for block-protect codes and make it easy to maintain the same amount of white space surrounding an equation. The size of the box adjusts if you edit the equation.

Graphics boxes are easy to move. If you create an equation manually, moving it to another point in the document can be very difficult.

Equations in graphics boxes are out of your way. Text wraps around the boxes. You do not have to worry about editing changes affecting your equation.

You can use one of WordPerfect's predefined graphics boxes (figure, table, text box, and user-defined box) or define your own boxes. For example, you might define Maps, Graphs, and Equations as separate graphics types, and use the fourth type to create blank space for pasting in photographs.

Graphics boxes are numbered automatically. You can have up to two levels of numbering (such as *I-a* or *A1*). WordPerfect numbers them consecutively within each type. You can move, delete, or add equations, and they are automatically renumbered.

If you use graphics boxes for your equations, you can generate a list of equations automatically, without marking each one individually. Just define the list at the point where you want the list to be generated. (Chapter 22 discusses generating lists.)

Importing Equations Created in Graphics Programs

When you incorporate a graphics file in a WordPerfect document, WordPerfect stores a compressed copy of the file in the document file header. Because the link is not dynamic, WordPerfect does not automatically update the graphic in your document if you edit the original graphics file. Once you have incorporated an external file in a WordPerfect graphic, modifying the external file has no effect whatsoever on your document.

Updating the graphic in your WordPerfect document is easy. Go to the Graphics Edit screen, delete the name of the graphics file, reenter the name (or the name of the new file), and save your document.

Let's suppose you want to update Equation 12, which you have imported in User-defined Box 12. The equation is contained in a MacPaint graphics file called **EQUA12.PIC**. Follow these steps:

1. Press Graphics (Alt-F9).

2. Select User-defined Box (**4**).

3. Select Edit (**2**).

4. At the User-defined Box number? prompt, type the number of the box containing the file you want to change and press Enter.

   For instance, type *12* and press Enter.

5. Select Filename (**1**) from the Definition menu.

6. When prompted for Enter Filename:, type the file name and press Enter.

7. When prompted Replace contents w/ (followed by the file name), press *Y.*

Your new file is inserted in the box.

WP 5 ▬▬▬ Summary

Creating technical documents in WordPerfect demands a solid knowledge of WordPerfect, a good understanding of your hardware, and a certain amount of ingenuity. If technical word processing is an important part of your work, you owe it to yourself to choose the best hardware you can afford. Experiment with the techniques described in this chapter until you find the ones that are easiest for you and work well with your particular hardware configuration.

20

Using Footnotes and Endnotes

Susan Hafer combines her knowledge of WordPerfect with her degree in Language Studies from Wellesley College to write this chapter on using footnotes and endnotes in WordPerfect 5. ■

Just about anyone writing academic papers needs to be able to do footnotes, endnotes, or a combination of the two in his or her documents. These notes provide a simple, standard way of referencing quotations as well as showing a reader additional parenthetical information. But be wary of putting *vital* information necessary to the reader's understanding of your overall text in a note because most readers tend to skim or totally ignore the contents of notes.

Footnotes are inserted at the bottom or *foot* of the page, whereas endnotes are grouped together at the *end* of your document or wherever you request them. Both types of notes are marked in the text either by numbers or by such special characters as asterisks (*). If you use both types of notes in one document, WordPerfect gives you the option of assigning the notes different numbering systems.

Fortunately, WordPerfect makes using footnotes and endnotes easy. The advantages of having the word processor control your footnotes are obvious if you ever have typed them by hand. For example, figuring out how much space to leave for footnotes at the bottom of a page is NOT fun, nor is renumbering footnotes that have been relocated in your document. However, these tasks are simple for a computer. WordPerfect has been designed to calculate automatically how much room you need at the bottom of each page for your footnotes and to renumber automatically your notes any time you add to, delete, or move them.

You also can use WordPerfect's new Automatic Referencing feature (see Chapter 22) if you will be referring to notes by their number in the context of your paragraphs. For example, you might include the following reference in your paragraph: (see explanation in endnote 6). You could simply type the note number, of course; but if the note numbers change in your final draft, then you would have to go back through your entire text to check all embedded references. Although notes are automatically renumbered for you, references to those notes are not renumbered if you type the numbers yourself. Automatic Referencing takes care of this updating for you.

Users of 4.2 will be happy to hear that the contents of the menus are now clearer and that distinguishing between footnotes and endnotes is easier. The notes are still on the same function key (Ctrl-F7) as they were in the past, however.

Because footnotes and endnotes are similar in WordPerfect, the discussion in this chapter concentrates on footnotes, with differences for endnotes highlighted and one or two of the basics covered so that you can see the similarity between the two notes. The menus (except for the Options menu) are identical for each type of note. When you select Create or Edit from the Footnote menu, for example, a footnote is created or edited; and if you do the same from the Endnote menu, an endnote is created or edited.

This chapter covers how you create notes, look at them, change existing ones, delete them, move them from one place to another in your text, and change their styles. You learn also how to put endnotes someplace other than at the end of your document and to change footnotes to endnotes (and vice versa).

Footnotes

A footnote is a reference or some other parenthetical text that appears at the bottom of a page. Creating and then editing footnotes in WordPerfect is easy, as you see in the next sections.

Creating Footnotes

Before creating a footnote, you naturally start with text that needs a note. For this example, type the text in italics—and don't forget to indent the long quotation by using Indent (F4):

In Charles Dickens's story of Nicholas Nickleby, one of the villains is Mr. Wackford Squeers:

> *Mr. Squeers's appearance was not prepossessing. He had but one eye, and the popular prejudice runs in favour of two. . . . The blank side of his face was much wrinkled and puckered up, which gave him a very sinister appearance, especially when he smiled, at which times his expression bordered closely on the villainous. . . . He wore . . . a suit of scholastic black, but his coat sleeves being a great deal too long, and his trousers a great deal too short, he appeared ill at ease in his clothes, and as if he were in a perpetual state of astonishment at finding himself so respectable.*

Compare this description with one of the hero, Nicholas himself, whose face was "open, handsome, and ingenuous," and whose eyes were "bright with the light of intelligence and spirit. His figure was somewhat slight, but manly and well-formed; and apart from all the grace of youth and comeliness, there was an emanation from the warm young heart in his look and bearing. . . ."

Once you have the text that needs footnoting, go ahead and create the note. To create a footnote, do the following:

1. Place the cursor in your text where you want a footnote number to appear.

   For this example, place the cursor after the period following "so respectable" at the end of the indented quotation.

2. Press the Footnote function key (Ctrl-F7).

   You see the Footnote/Endnote menu giving you the following three choices:

   1 Footnote; **2** Endnote; **3** Endnote Placement: **0**

Choose **Footnote** (**1**) to create, edit, change the style, and so on, for footnotes. Choose **Endnote Placement** (**3**) to tell WordPerfect to place endnotes where the cursor is located in your document (more on this option later). Select **Endnote** (**2**) to do everything else related to endnotes.

3. Select **Footnote** (**1**).

   The Footnote menu with the following choices appears at the bottom of the screen:

   Footnote: 1 Create; **2** Edit; **3** New Number; **4** Options: **0**

Create (**1**) lets you create a new footnote; **Edit** (**2**) lets you make changes to an existing footnote; **New Number** (**3**) starts numbering any footnotes after the cursor at whatever number you specify; and **Options** (**4**) lets you change how footnotes appear in your document.

4. Select **Create** (**1**) to create a footnote.

   The screen goes blank for a moment and then returns a footnote entry screen, which closely resembles the normal WordPerfect workspace.

Notice that a footnote number has already been typed for you. The number is not superscripted yet, but it is displayed in whatever way that superscripts have been designed to appear in the Setup menu. On your screen, for example, the number may be highlighted. The program positions the footnote number just before the cursor so that you immediately can begin typing to enter the text of the footnote that will be placed at the bottom of the page.

The footnote-entry screen is like the normal text-entry screen because you can use the function keys as well as enter and edit text. You even can use the spell-checker from within a note.

5. Type the text of the footnote.

For your first footnote, type the following:

Charles Dickens, The Life and Adventures of Nicholas Nickleby (Philadelphia: University of Pennsylvania Press, 1982), vol.1, p. 24.

When you finish typing, your screen should resemble the one in figure 20.1.

Fig. 20.1.

The footnote entry screen with a footnote.

```
        [Charles Dickens, The Life and Adventures of Nicholas Nickleby
     (Philadelphia: University of Pennsylvania Press, 1982), vol. 1, p.
     24.




     Press Exit when done                        Doc 1 Pg 1 Ln 19 Pos 13
```

6. Press Exit (F7), as instructed at the bottom of the screen, when you finish typing the text of the footnote.

Step 6 saves the note and puts you back in your document where you were when you began the footnote. Now, however, you see a superscripted or highlighted number representing the location of the footnote you just entered. Notice that you do not see the text of the footnote, just the number (see fig. 20.2), even if you were to move the cursor to the bottom of that page.

Sometimes people forget to press Exit and end up typing the rest of the normal text in the footnote-entry screen. If you make this mistake, block off the text that does not belong in the note, delete the block, press Exit to get back to the normal text, and undelete the block.

7. Repeat Steps 1 through 6 to enter any other footnotes.

For your example, you have two more footnotes to enter. Put footnote 2 after the quotation mark following "ingenuous" and type *Dickens, p. 19.* as its text. Put footnote 3 after the quotation mark following "bearing" and type the same text.

Fig. 20.2.
A footnote in the text.

```
Mr. Squeers's appearance was not prepossessing. He had but
one eye, and the popular prejudice runs in favour of
two.... The blank side of his face was much wrinkled and
puckered up, which gave him a very sinister appearance,
especially when he smiled, at which times his expression
bordered closely on the villainous.... He wore...a suit
of scholastic black, but his coat sleeves being a great
deal too long, and his trousers a great deal too short,
he appeared ill at ease in his clothes, and as if he were
in a perpetual state of astonishment at finding himself
so respectable.▮

Compare this description with one of the hero, Nicholas himself,
whose face was "open, handsome, and ingenuous," and whose eyes were
"bright with the light of intelligence and spirit. His figure was
somewhat slight, but manly and well-formed; and apart from all the
grace of youth and comeliness, there was an emanation from the warm
young heart in his look and bearing...."


                            Doc 1 Pg 1 Ln 15 Pos 21,76
```

TIP: To avoid separating the page number (24, for example) from its page reference (p.), as happens in figure 20.1, insert a hard space (Home, space bar) instead of a normal space between the "p." and the number that follows. Then the page number and the page reference (p. 24, for example) will appear on the next line.

Looking at Footnotes

Now that you have made a footnote, how do you examine it? When you created the footnote, you saw only the superscripted or highlighted number appear on-screen. With WordPerfect, you can use a variety of ways to view your footnotes: Reveal Codes, View or Print Document, or Footnote Edit.

Using Reveal Codes

Using Reveal Codes shows you the footnote code created earlier with the Footnote function key. You see the text surrounding the footnote and the information in the note itself; however, you cannot make changes to the note here.

The Reveal Codes method is useful if you want to see the beginning of the footnote in the context of the normal text because only the first few words of the footnote appear. If your note is long, it will end with an ellipsis (...), but do not think the rest of the note is gone. The entire note is there, but it cannot be seen in Reveal Codes. You can see an entire footnote by using other methods; however, the advantage of viewing only the beginning of a note in Reveal Codes is that the screen is less cluttered than it would be if all the text of a footnote were shown here.

To view a footnote by using the Reveal Codes method, do the following:

1. Place the cursor under a footnote number (the first one, for this example).

2. Press Reveal Codes (Alt-F3, or F11).

   Your screen should look similar to the one in figure 20.3 and should have the following code blocked in the text:

   `[Footnote:1;[Note Num]Charles Dickens, [UND]The Life and Adventures of Ni ... ]`

3. Press Reveal Codes (Alt-F3, or F11) again to exit back to your normal document.

Fig. 20.3.

Reveal Codes of a footnote in the text.

```
        but one eye, and the popular prejudice runs in favour of
        two.... The blank side of his face was much wrinkled and
        puckered up, which gave him a very sinister appearance,
        especially when he smiled, at which times his expression
        bordered closely on the villainous.... He wore...a suit
        of scholastic black, but his coat sleeves being a great
        deal too long, and his trousers a great deal too short,
        he appeared ill at ease in his clothes, and as if he were
        in a perpetual state of astonishment at finding himself
        so respectable.█

                                        Doc 1 Pg 1 Ln 14 Pos 30
[   ▲    ▲    ▲    ▲    ▲    ▲    ▲    ▲    ▲    ▲    }   ▲    ▲
he appeared ill at ease in his clothes, and as if he were[SRt]
in a perpetual state of astonishment at finding himself[SRt]
so respectable.[Footnote:1;[Note Num]Charles Dickens, [UND]The Life and Adventur
es of Ni ... ][HRt]
[HRt]
Compare this description with the hero, Nicholas himself, whose[SRt]
face was "open, handsome, and ingenuous," and whose eyes were[SRt]
"bright with the light of intelligence and spirit. His figure was[SRt]
somewhat slight, but manly and well[-]formed; and apart from all the[SRt]
grace of youth and comeliness, there was an emanation from the warm[SRt]

Press Reveal Codes to restore screen
```

The blocked text is the footnote code you created in the previous section of this chapter. The part of the footnote you see in the normal screen is represented by the word Footnote, which tells WordPerfect to superscript the number that follows, in this case a 1. After the semicolon is the part of the note that appears at the bottom of your printed page, represented by the Note Num notation followed by the beginning of the text of the footnote.

Using Reveal Codes to see your notes is a quick solution; however, because you see only part of the note, you may prefer to check your notes by using one of the methods covered in the next two sections.

Using Print

If you do not have a printer set up to print, skim through this section for future reference but do not follow the instructions.

To view your footnotes by using a printer, follow the normal procedures to print the document. You can print the entire document or only the part that contains the note(s) you are interested in viewing.

Compare the footnotes on the printout with those on-screen. Your printout should look something like the one in figure 20.4.

Fig. 20.4.
Sample document with footnotes.

> In Charles Dickens's story of Nicholas Nickleby, one of the villains is Mr. Wackford Squeers:
>
> > Mr. Squeers's appearance was not prepossessing. He had but one eye, and the popular prejudice runs in favour of two.... The blank side of his face was much wrinkled and puckered up, which gave him a very sinister appearance, especially when he smiled, at which times his expression bordered closely on the villainous.... He wore...a suit of scholastic black, but his coat sleeves being a great deal too long, and his trousers a great deal too short, he appeared ill at ease in his clothes, and as if he were in a perpetual state of astonishment at finding himself so respectable.[1]
>
> Compare this description with one of the hero, Nicholas himself, whose face was "open, handsome, and ingenuous,"[2] and whose eyes were "bright with the light of intelligence and spirit. His figure was somewhat slight, but manly and well-formed; and apart from all the grace of youth and comeliness, there was an emanation from the warm young heart in his look and bearing...."[3]

---

[1] Charles Dickens, The Life and adventures of Nicholas Nickleby (Philadelphia: University of Pennsylvania Press, 1982), vol. 1, p. 24.

[2] Dickens, p. 19.

[3] Dickens, p. 19.

Notice that you can see both the numbers in the text and the complete footnotes at the bottom of the page of the printout. On the normal screen, you see only the footnote numbers. If your printer is capable of doing so, the numbers in the text will be superscripted.

Using View Document

If you do not have a graphics card in your computer, View Document functions in the same way as it does in version 4.2. You do not have a Full Page option, and you see only such items as margins, headers and footers, page numbers, and foot- and endnotes. Again, you may wish to skim this section for future reference and then continue with the rest of the chapter.

If you feel that printing your document just to see your footnotes is a waste of paper, you might want to use View Document. As you learned in Chapter 6, this WordPerfect feature allows you to view your document as it appears when printed— with page numbers, spacing, headers and footers, footnotes, and so on.

To view your footnotes by using View Document, do the following:

1. Put the cursor on the same page as the footnote(s) to be viewed.

   In this example, the cursor still should be on a footnote and so does not need to be moved.

2. Press the Print function key (Shift-F7).

3. Select View Document (6) from the Print menu.

4. If you do not see the entire page on-screen, select Full Page (3) and look at the bottom of the page to be sure that the footnote is there (see fig. 20.5).

5. Select 100% (1) to zoom in more closely on the text (see fig 20.6).

6. If your footnote does not appear on-screen, move the cursor to the footnote number in the text to see what the number looks like. (The number should be superscripted.)

   For this example, all three footnote numbers do appear on-screen, so no movement is necessary.

7. Move the cursor to the bottom of the page with GoTo, ↓ (Ctrl-Home, ↓) to see the footnote as it will be printed at the bottom of the page.

8. Press Exit (F7) to return to your normal document.

The Print and View Document methods of looking at your notes are helpful because you can see the complete footnotes as your readers will—in context.

Using Footnote Edit

In the "Editing Footnotes" section, you see how to use the Footnote Edit feature to make changes to a note, but you also can use Footnote Edit to examine the note without making any changes. This method does not permit you to view both the note and the text that surrounds it at the same time, but Footnote Edit is the only

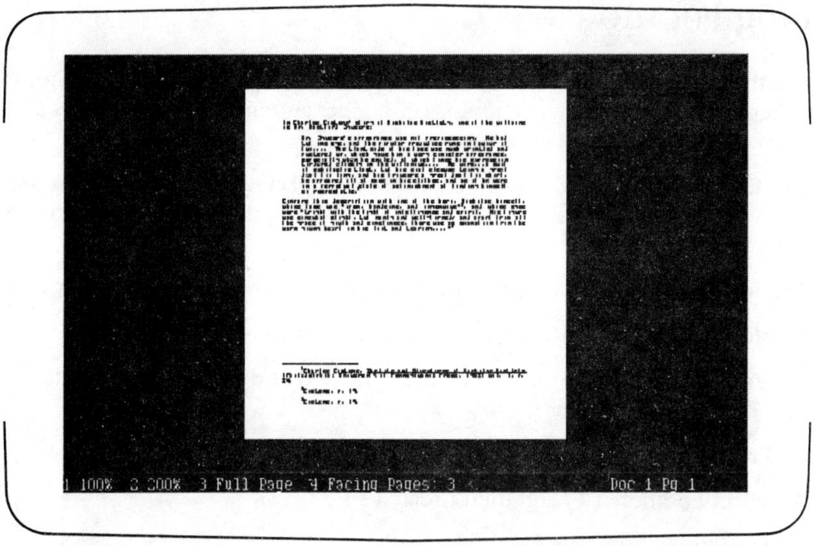

Fig. 20.5.
*A Full Page View
Document of text
with footnotes.*

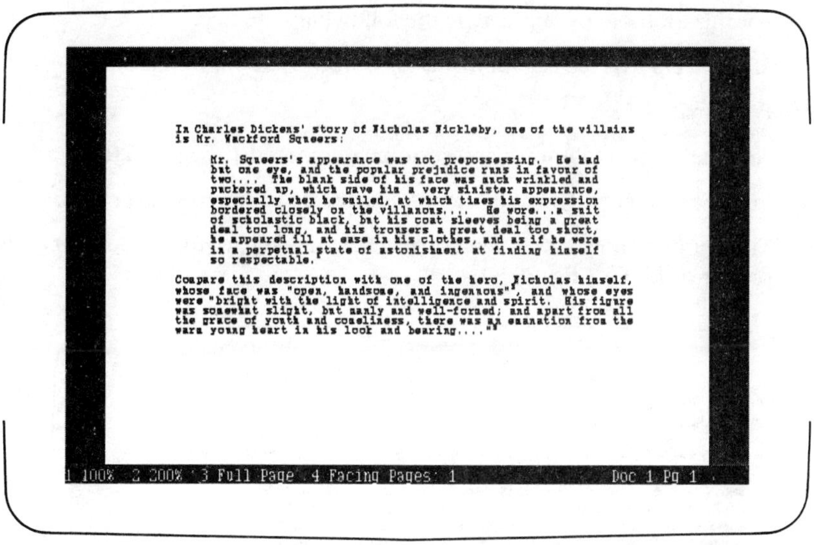

Fig. 20.6.
*100% View
Document of
footnotes.*

method that allows you to make changes in the note if you see something you do not like.

Enough of looking at notes—it's time to make some changes!

Adding Footnotes

Suppose that after entering several footnotes, you realize you need another footnote somewhere in the midst of the others. WordPerfect automatically renumbers all the footnotes after you enter the new note.

Let's say, for example, that you want to add some explanation of who Mr. Wackford Squeers is in *Nicholas Nickleby*. The information is parenthetical, not vital, so you put it in a footnote.

To add a new footnote to text previously containing footnotes, do the following:

1. Move the cursor to the place where you want to insert the footnote.

   For this example, move the cursor to the end of the first sentence, after "Mr. Wackford Squeers."

2. Press the Footnote key (Ctrl-F7).

3. Select **Footnote** (**1**) and then **Create** (**1**).

4. Type the text of your footnote.

   For this footnote example, type the following sentence:

   Mr. Squeers was the schoolmaster of Dotheboy's Hall in this story.

5. Press Exit (F7).

   Notice that two footnotes appear to be numbered 1 (see fig. 20.7).

6. Press Screen (Ctrl-F3) and select **Rewrite** (**0**) to rewrite the screen.

   The numbers now have been corrected, and you have four footnotes in the proper order (see fig. 20.8).

Fig. 20.7.

A new note added before WordPerfect renumbers the footnotes.

In Charles Dickens's story of Nicholas Nickleby, one of the villains is Mr. Wackford Squeers[]:

> Mr. Squeers's appearance was not prepossessing. He had but one eye, and the popular prejudice runs in favour of two.... The blank side of his face was much wrinkled and puckered up, which gave him a very sinister appearance, especially when he smiled, at which times his expression bordered closely on the villainous.... He wore...a suit of scholastic black, but his coat sleeves being a great deal too long, and his trousers a great deal too short, he appeared ill at ease in his clothes, and as if he were in a perpetual state of astonishment at finding himself so respectable.[]

> Compare this description with one of the hero, Nicholas himself, whose face was "open, handsome, and ingenuous,"[2] and whose eyes were "bright with the light of intelligence and spirit. His figure was somewhat slight, but manly and well-formed; and apart from all the grace of youth and comeliness, there was an emanation from the warm young heart in his look and bearing...."[3]

Doc 1 Pg 1 Ln 3 Pos 24.76

In Charles Dickens's story of Nicholas Nickleby, one of the villains
is Mr. Wackford Squeers▯:

> Mr. Squeers's appearance was not prepossessing. He had but
> one eye, and the popular prejudice runs in favour of
> two.... The blank side of his face was much wrinkled and
> puckered up, which gave him a very sinister appearance,
> especially when he smiled, at which times his expression
> bordered closely on the villainous.... He wore...a suit
> of scholastic black, but his coat sleeves being a great
> deal too long, and his trousers a great deal too short,
> he appeared ill at ease in his clothes, and as if he were
> in a perpetual state of astonishment at finding himself
> so respectable.▯

Compare this description with one of the hero, Nicholas himself,
whose face was "open, handsome, and ingenuous,"▯ and whose eyes were
"bright with the light of intelligence and spirit. His figure was
somewhat slight, but manly and well-formed; and apart from all the
grace of youth and comeliness, there was an emanation from the warm
young heart in his look and bearing...."▯

Doc 1 Pg 1 Ln 3 Pos 24.76

Fig. 20.8.

After Screen Rewrite,
WordPerfect
renumbers the
footnotes.

Deleting Footnotes

As you read earlier, the entire footnote (the number and the text) is in one code;
therefore, you can delete the footnote in the same way you delete any other code in
WordPerfect. You might, for example, decide that a note explaining part of the text
is not necessary because it interrupts the flow of the text.

To delete a footnote, do the following:

1. Put the cursor under the footnote to be deleted.

   In the example, put the cursor under the first footnote, the one you just
   added.

2. Press Del.

3. Answer **Y** for Yes when asked if you want to delete the footnote.

   The footnote numbers that follow the deleted footnote are rewritten
   when you press Screen (Ctrl-F3) and choose **Rewrite (0)**.

TIP: If you use Reveal Codes, the program does not ask whether you want to
delete the footnote, because WordPerfect assumes that you see the cursor on a
code and want to delete it. Use the method with which you feel the most
comfortable.

Moving Footnotes

When editing a paper, you may want to move or copy a footnote, with or without the normal text that surrounds it. To move just the footnote, you can delete the code as you have just seen and then undelete it elsewhere. (Keep in mind that when you use Undelete or Cancel (F1), you can undelete up to the last three deletions, cycling through them by selecting **Previous Deletion (2)** from the Undelete menu.)

If you want to copy the note rather than move it, you go through the same procedure, with a few exceptions. First undelete the note in its original location, leaving it just as it was, and then immediately move the cursor to the position where you want another copy of the same footnote to appear, and undelete it again.

Moving the Footnote and Its Normal Text

Normally when you want to move a footnote, you are more interested in moving the text that happens to contain the note. For example, you may want to move a block of text in your document and not realize that a footnote is in the block. If you move the text, the footnotes will be out of sequence, but WordPerfect automatically corrects the sequence for you. Moving text that contains a footnote is the same as moving text without footnotes, because a note is, after all, just another code in your text.

For this example, you decide that it would be more striking to the reader to present the hero before the villain in your discussion of Nicholas Nickleby. You need to move the first two paragraphs to the end of the discussion.

To move a footnote and its surrounding text, do the following:

1. Place the cursor at the beginning of the block of text to be deleted (moved).

   For this example, place the cursor at the beginning of the document.

2. Press the Block key (Alt-F4, or F12) to turn on Block.

3. Move the cursor to the end of the block of text to be deleted (moved).

   Move the cursor to the end of the indented quotation. Make sure that you include the footnote number in the block (see fig. 20.9).

4. Press the Del key and press *Y* for Yes when asked if you want to delete the block.

5. Move the cursor to the point where you want the deleted text to reappear.

   For this example, move the cursor to the end of the document.

6. Press Cancel (F1) for the Undelete menu.

7. Select **Restore (1)** to undelete what was last deleted.

   WordPerfect automatically renumbers the footnotes.

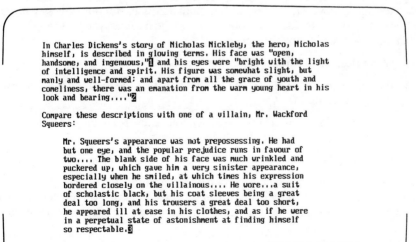

Fig. 20.9.
Blocking the text and footnote number to be deleted.

In Charles Dickens's story of Nicholas Nickleby, one of the villains is Mr. Wackford Squeers:

Mr. Squeers's appearance was not prepossessing. He had but one eye, and the popular prejudice runs in favour of two.... The blank side of his face was much wrinkled and puckered up, which gave him a very sinister appearance, especially when he smiled, at which times his expression bordered closely on the villainous.... He wore...a suit of scholastic black, but his coat sleeves being a great deal too long, and his trousers a great deal too short, he appeared ill at ease in his clothes, and as if he were in a perpetual state of astonishment at finding himself so respectable.1

Compare this description with one of the hero, Nicholas himself, whose face was "open, handsome, and ingenuous,"2 and whose eyes were "bright with the light of intelligence and spirit. His figure was somewhat slight, but manly and well-formed; and apart from all the grace of youth and comeliness, there was an emanation from the warm young heart in his look and bearing...."3

Block on   Doc 1 Pg 1 Ln 15 Pos 21.76

If this were a real document, you now would need to go in and change your text by inserting and deleting blank lines and rewording the first paragraph to be the introductory text (see fig. 20.10).

Fig. 20.10.
Edited text after moving the first two paragraphs.

In Charles Dickens's story of Nicholas Nickleby, the hero, Nicholas himself, is described in glowing terms. His face was "open, handsome, and ingenuous,"1 and his eyes were "bright with the light of intelligence and spirit. His figure was somewhat slight, but manly and well-formed; and apart from all the grace of youth and comeliness, there was an emanation from the warm young heart in his look and bearing...."2

Compare these descriptions with one of a villain, Mr. Wackford Squeers:

Mr. Squeers's appearance was not prepossessing. He had but one eye, and the popular prejudice runs in favour of two.... The blank side of his face was much wrinkled and puckered up, which gave him a very sinister appearance, especially when he smiled, at which times his expression bordered closely on the villainous.... He wore...a suit of scholastic black, but his coat sleeves being a great deal too long, and his trousers a great deal too short, he appeared ill at ease in his clothes, and as if he were in a perpetual state of astonishment at finding himself so respectable.3

                                    Doc 1 Pg 1 Ln 1 Pos 1

Moving Just the Footnote

Moving only the footnote code (the superscripted number with the text of the note itself) is just a matter of locating, deleting, and undeleting the code wherever you want it to reappear.

In the previous example, you changed the order of the footnotes, and now the first footnote no longer contains the complete reference information. You can delete the footnote and retype it, or you can move footnotes 1 and 3 and then correct the page number references.

To move a footnote number and the contents of the note to a different position in the text, do the following:

1. Follow the previous steps for deleting a footnote (see "Deleting Footnotes").

   In this case, you want to move the third note to the first footnote position, so delete footnote 3.

2. Move the cursor to the new position for the footnote.

   Place the cursor under the first footnote so that the undeleted note appears just in front of the current footnote number 1.

3. Press Cancel (F1) for the Undelete menu.

As usual, the last thing deleted is highlighted on-screen. Only the note number appears for notes, however, because the note number is all you normally see. If you want to see the text of the deleted note as well as the number, you first can go into Reveal Codes before pressing the Cancel key.

4. Select **Restore (1)** to undelete what was last deleted.

5. Press Reveal Codes (Alt-F3, or F11) to verify that the footnote is in its new location (see fig. 20.11).

   Notice that you now have two adjacent footnotes that appear as though you have a footnote "12" in the normal screen.

6. Press Reveal Codes (Alt-F3, or F11) again to return to your normal screen.

Repeat the instructions, moving the now-current footnote 2 to the end of the document after the word "respectable." You successfully have switched footnotes 1 and 3. To complete the process, you need to correct the page number references.

Editing Footnotes

You have seen how to create, view, delete, and move notes; but what do you do if you want to change a note you already have created? For example, suppose that you remembered only the title of a book and nothing else when you originally typed a footnote; now you want to enter the complete reference. Or perhaps the style of a

Fig. 20.11.

Reveal Codes of the footnote in its new location.

```
himself, is described in glowing terms. His face was "open,
handsome, and ingenuous"12, and his eyes were "bright with the light
of intelligence and spirit. His figure was somewhat slight, but
manly and well-formed; and apart from all the grace of youth and
comeliness, there was an emanation from the warm young heart in his
look and bearing...."3

Compare these descriptions with one of a villain, Mr. Wackford
Squeers:

     Mr. Squeers's appearance was not prepossessing.  He had
                              Doc 1 Pg 1 Ln 3 Pos 34.58
[    ▲    ▲    ▲    ▲    ▲    ▲    ▲    ▲    ▲    ▲    ▲    }   ▲ ]
In Charles Dickens' story of Nicholas Nickleby, the hero, Nicholas[SRt]
himself, is described in glowing terms. His face was "open,[SRt]
handsome, and ingenuous"[Footnote:1:[Note Num]Charles Dickens, [UND]The Life and
 Adventures of Ni ... ][Footnote:2:[Note Num]Dickens, p. 19,], and his eyes were
"bright with the light[SRt]
of intelligence and spirit. His figure was somewhat slight, but[SRt]
manly and well[-]formed; and apart from all the grace of youth and[SRt]
comeliness, there was an emanation from the warm young heart in his[SRt]
look and bearing...."[Footnote:3:[Note Num]Dickens, p. 19,][HRt]
[HRt]

Press Reveal Codes to restore screen
```

footnote does not fit the person or journal to which you are sending the text, and you have to change the style. You already have seen that your entire note is a single code, so you know you can't get into the note to make changes while you are in the normal text screen. Fortunately, WordPerfect provides an easy way to edit a footnote from the Footnote menu.

To edit a footnote from anywhere in your document, do the following:

1. Press the Footnote key (Ctrl-F7).

2. Select Footnote (**1**).

3. Select Edit (**2**).

   WordPerfect prompts you at the bottom of the screen with `Footnote number?` and then the number of the footnote that immediately follows the cursor. If the cursor is after the last footnote in the document, however, WordPerfect prompts you with a number for a footnote that does not exist! If you then press Enter to accept the number, WordPerfect displays the message `* Not found *` on-screen, and you must begin again. To avoid this waste of time, always verify the number with which WordPerfect prompts you.

4. Press Enter if the footnote number WordPerfect gives you matches the one you wish to edit, or type the correct number and then press Enter.

   For this example, type *3* and press Enter.

5. Because you are now in a footnote edit screen, use normal cursor movement and editing to change the footnote.

   In the example, change the page number from 19 to 24 (see fig. 20.12).

6. As instructed at the bottom of the screen, press Exit (F7) when you have finished editing the footnote.

Repeat these instructions for footnote 1 and change the page number from 24 to 19.

When you finish the footnote edit, your cursor is positioned just after the footnote in question. If you want to return the cursor to its original location, use the GoTo, GoTo (Ctrl-Home, Ctrl-Home) command.

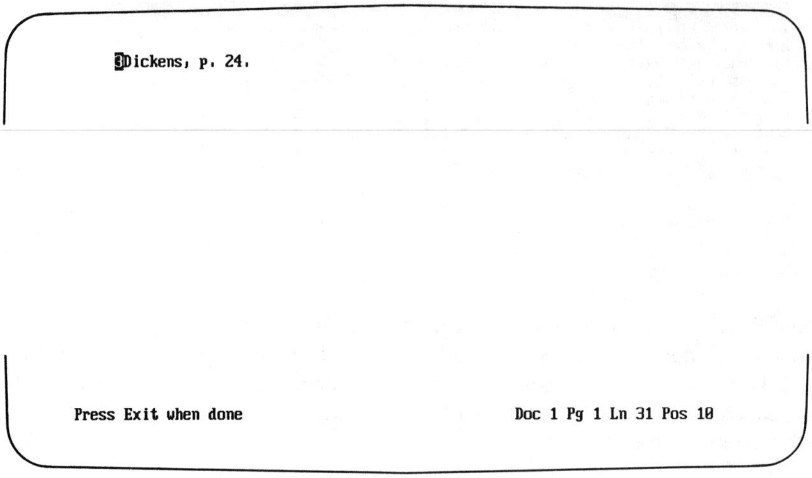

Fig. 20.12.
An edited footnote.

```
        Dickens, p. 24.




   Press Exit when done                    Doc 1 Pg 1 Ln 31 Pos 10
```

Changing Footnote Options

If you want to use footnotes but don't like the way WordPerfect formats them, you have some choices in the Options menu for changing the style. Just Press the Footnote key (Ctrl-F7), select Footnote (1), and choose Options (4) to bring up the Footnote Options menu, as shown in figure 20.13. Before you work on an example, let's look at the options available on the Footnote Options menu.

The first option, Spacing Within Footnotes and Between Footnotes (1) allows you to change the spacing *within* the footnotes (with the text of your notes single-spaced, the default) as well as *between* the notes (the space between one note and the next, if more than one note is on the page). Spacing Within Footnotes is shown in *lines*, while Spacing Between Footnotes is shown in inches (0.16″ being one line if you are using a standard font at six lines per inch).

The most common change in the default setting of Spacing Within Footnotes is from 1 to 2, which accommodates people printing drafts or printing an article for a publisher who wants all text double-spaced. You could change the setting to 3 or some other spacing as well.

```
Footnote Options

  1 - Spacing Within Footnotes          1
              Between Footnotes          0.16"

  2 - Amount of Note to Keep Together    0.5"

  3 - Style for Number in Text           [SUPRSCPT][Note Num][suprscpt]

  4 - Style for Number in Note                   [SUPRSCPT][Note Num][suprscp

  5 - Footnote Numbering Method          Numbers

  6 - Start Footnote Numbers each Page   No

  7 - Line Separating Text and Footnotes 2-inch Line

  8 - Print Continued Message            No

  9 - Footnotes at Bottom of Page        Yes


Selection: 0
```

Fig. 20.13.
The Footnote Options menu.

TIP: To change the spacing in the footnote, you also can use the Format function key (Shift-F7) from within the footnote entry screen, unlike in previous versions of WordPerfect. You now can have normal spacing for most notes but change to 1.5 line spacing within an individual note to use WordPerfect's *statistical typing* (equations). This spacing control is particularly useful for people doing scientific papers.

You also can change the amount of blank space between consecutive footnotes that appear on the same page. This feature is helpful if you need to squeeze more text on a page (reducing the space between footnotes) or spread text out (increasing the space between footnotes). If you prefer, you can enter the value in a unit other than inches (1 cm, for example), and WordPerfect converts the value for you.

You use the second option, Amount of Note to Keep Together (**2**), when you have a long footnote that may not fit at the bottom of the page. This option allows you to decide how much of a given footnote WordPerfect should keep together on one page before continuing the rest of the note on the bottom of the next page. You could change the default 0.5″ setting (one-half inch, or three lines at the normal six lines per inch) to 1″ (one inch), for example, if you want more than just 0.5 inch of a footnote to stay together.

Choosing this footnote option does not mean that every footnote longer than 0.5 inches is split across pages. Instead, the option means that if the footnote is over 0.5 inches long *and* the entire footnote will not fit at the bottom of the page because the reference is close to the bottom, then the footnote will be split. If *less than* 0.5 inches of the note will fit at the bottom of the page, however, WordPerfect moves both the text containing the footnote number and the entire footnote to the next page. If your footnote is long enough to split across pages, you will see a page break in the footnote as you type it.

If you don't like your footnote numbers superscripted in the text or if your printer doesn't handle superscripts well, choose Style for Number in Text (3) to change the appearance of the footnotes. For example, you can have your note numbers appear in brackets. Or, if your printer has the capability, you can use a new Font attribute that prints your footnotes in a smaller typeface than the regular text.

If you do replace the style, remember to include the **[Note Num]** code by pressing Footnote (Ctrl-F7), selecting Footnote (1), and then choosing Number Code (2).

If, for the same reasons, you want to change the style of the superscripted number in the footnote itself, choose Style for Number in Note (4). You could change the footnote to be just the number followed by a period and a Tab, or five spaces. The instructions for including the **[Note Num]** code are the same as for the third option.

(If you use option 3 or 4, be sure to look at the example in the Endnote section at the end of this chapter to see how to enter the proper codes.)

Choose Footnote Numbering Method (5) if you do not want to use numbers for your footnotes. You could set up the notes with letters (a, b, c instead of 1, 2, 3) by choosing Letters (2), or with different characters (*, **, *** instead of 1, 2, 3) by selecting Characters (3). You even can have more than one type of character by entering something like *#, for example, so that the order would be *, #, **, ##, and so on. By using multiple characters, you avoid long references (footnote 6, for example, would be ### instead of ******).

If you use both footnotes and endnotes in one document, you can use option 5 to give the notes different numbering systems. Use numbers for the endnotes at the end of the chapter (the majority of your references) and use special characters for the footnotes you may have at the bottom of the pages (to explain parenthetical information that must be close to its reference). By using different numbering methods, you help the reader to distinguish easily between footnotes and endnotes.

If you change the default numbers setting, remember that when you edit a footnote, you must enter the number of the note in the new style (for example, ** instead of 2).

The default setting for option 6, Start Footnote Numbers each Page (6), is No; therefore, WordPerfect numbers your footnotes consecutively throughout the document. If you have all your footnote numbers marked with asterisks instead of numbers, however, the footnotes start to take up space after just a few notes (footnote 6 would be ******). One way to avoid the long references is to start the footnotes at 1 on each page by setting this option to Yes.

Figure 20.4 shows an example of the default setting for the separator—a 2-inch line printed at the left margin—between text and footnotes. You can change the separator by selecting Line Separating Text and Footnotes (7). To have a line that stretches all the way across the page, choose Margin to Margin (3); or to have no line at all, choose No Line (1).

If you have long footnotes that WordPerfect breaks up from one page to the next, you might want the program to signal this break to the reader. If you set Print Continued Message (**8**) to **Yes**, WordPerfect prints a (...continued) message on both the last line of the footnote on the first page and on the first line of the footnote on the next page.

The last option, Footnotes at **B**ottom of Page (**9**), allows you to alter where on the page the footnotes are printed. In figure 20.4, the footnotes are printed at the very bottom of the page, leaving several inches of blank space between the text and the footnotes. If you would rather have the notes printed just below the text, leaving the blank space after the footnotes instead, set this option to **No**.

One option that the menu does not cover, however, is footnote margins. In version 4.2, all notes adopt the margins of your normal text. If some text on a page is set to different margins than other text on the same page, however, the footnotes for the different sections would have different margins from each other!

Now in version 5, both footnotes and endnotes are assigned one-inch left and right margins, regardless of the margins of your normal text. In future versions, WordPerfect perhaps will include a selection for margins in the note Options menus. In the meantime, if you want anything other than the default one-inch margins in your notes, you either must put a margin change in each note or change your default margins in the Setup menu by selecting Initial Settings (**5**) and then Initial Codes (**4**).

If you want all your notes to have the same margins (1.5 inches, for example), the easier process is to change the margins to 1.5″ in the Setup menu and then change the normal text margins for that document back to 1 inch or to whatever margins you want. Remember to change the margins back to 1 inch in the Setup menu when you finish. Keep in mind, too, that you must Exit (F7) WordPerfect before your new initial settings go into effect.

Now that you are familiar with the options in the Footnote Options menu, let's examine how easy it is to make adjustments in your footnote form by changing to asterisks the numbering scheme in the Dickens example.

To change the numbering style in footnotes, do the following:

1. Place the cursor before the point where you want the changes to take place.

   In this example, put the cursor at the beginning of the document.

2. Press the Footnote key (Ctrl-F7).

3. Select Footnote (**1**).

4. Select Options (**4**) for the Footnote Options menu.

5. Select Footnote Numbering Method (**5**).

6. Select Characters (**3**).

7. Type an asterisk (‘) and press Enter.

   Notice that the menu item you just changed now reads Characters, *.

8. Press Exit (F7) to return to your document.

9. Press Screen (Ctrl-F3) and then select **Rewrite (0)** in order to rewrite the screen to reflect the new footnote numbers (see fig. 20.14).

Fig. 20.14.

The footnote numbers changed to asterisks.

In Charles Dickens's story of Nicholas Nickleby, the hero, Nicholas himself, is described in glowing terms. His face was "open, handsome, and ingenuous,"* and his eyes were "bright with the light of intelligence and spirit. His figure was somewhat slight, but manly and well-formed; and apart from all the grace of youth and comeliness, there was an emanation from the warm young heart in his look and bearing...."*

Compare these descriptions with one of a villain, Mr. Wackford Squeers:

Mr. Squeers's appearance was not prepossessing. He had but one eye, and the popular prejudice runs in favour of two.... The blank side of his face was much wrinkled and puckered up, which gave him a very sinister appearance, especially when he smiled, at which times his expression bordered closely on the villainous.... He wore...a suit of scholastic black, but his coat sleeves being a great deal too long, and his trousers a great deal too short, he appeared ill at ease in his clothes, and as if he were in a perpetual state of astonishment at finding himself so respectable.***

Doc 1 Pg 1 Ln 1 Pos 1

Feel free to experiment with the various options, using View Document where necessary to see the results.

Endnotes

An endnote is a reference or some other parenthetical text that appears at the end of a document (or wherever you specify). WordPerfect puts your endnotes at the end of your text without a page break. You may, therefore, want to place a hard page at the very end of your document and add a title (NOTES, centered on the line) at the top of that last page.

Working with Endnotes

Working with endnotes is essentially the same as working with footnotes. You can create, view, edit, delete, and move endnotes just as you do footnotes.

When you are ready to enter an endnote, do the following:

1. Place the cursor where you want the endnote to appear.

2. Press the Footnote key (Ctrl-F7).

3. Select Endnote (**2**) for the Endnote menu, which contains the following choices (the same as the Footnote menu):

Endnote: 1 Create; **2 Edit; 3** New Number; **4** Options: **0**

4. Select **Create** (**1**) to create an endnote.

   The cursor appears in an endnote-entry screen, similar to a footnote-entry screen except that the number in the top left corner is not superscripted on-screen.

5. Tab once or press the space bar twice to separate the period after the number from the text you are about to enter.

6. Enter the text of the note.

7. When you have finished, press Exit (F7) to get back to your normal document.

This procedure, using the default endnote settings, produces an endnote that appears as follows at the end of a document:

1.   Charles Dickens, *The Life and Adventures of Nicholas Nickleby* (Philadelphia: University of Pennsylvania Press, 1982), vol. 1, p. 24.

Notice how the number is neither superscripted nor indented. Unfortunately, most style guides require endnotes to be in the same form as footnotes. You learn how to change the endnote options in the next section so that your endnotes conform to the same style as footnotes.

You can delete and undelete the endnote code (which looks the same as a footnote but begins with the word **[Endnote:...]**) in exactly the same way you would a footnote code.

Look at your text by pressing Print (Shift-F7) and selecting View Document (**6**) to see the endnotes. Remember to go to the end of the entire document to find the notes.

Changing Endnote Options

The Endnote Options menu is very much like the Footnote Options menu except that it has fewer options (see fig. 20.15). The Footnote Options menu has nine choices (refer to fig. 20.13), but the Endnote Options menu has only five. In addition, the Style for Numbers in Note (**4**) option simply has **[Note Num]** followed by a period instead of being surrounded by superscript notations.

As previously noted, a problem with the WordPerfect program is that it creates a different default form for its endnotes than for its footnotes. With a few simple changes in the Endnote Options menu, however, you can adjust the form so that it is the same as the footnote form.

```
Endnote Options

    1 - Spacing Within Endnotes              1
                 Between Endnotes            0.16"

    2 - Amount of Endnote to Keep Together   0.5"

    3 - Style for Numbers in Text            [SUPRSCPT][Note Num][suprscpt]

    4 - Style for Numbers in Note            [Note Num].

    5 - Endnote Numbering Method             Numbers




    Selection: 0
```

To achieve the proper form for your endnotes, do the following:

1. Place the cursor before the point where the first endnote appears in your document.

2. Press Footnote (Ctrl-F7).

3. Select Endnote (**2**).

4. Select **Options** (**4**) for the Endnote Options menu.

5. Select Style for Number in Note (**4**) to change the way the endnote numbers appear at the end of your document.

   You are prompted with Replace with: at the bottom of the screen.

6. Press the space bar five times so that each endnote is indented five spaces from the left margin.

7. Insert a superscript code by pressing the Font key (Ctrl-F8) and selecting Size (**1**) and then Superscript (**1**).

8. Insert a note number code by pressing Footnote (Ctrl-F7) and selecting Endnote (**2**) and then Number Code (**2**).

9. Press Enter to save your new endnote style for the numbers in notes.

   Notice that WordPerfect automatically inserts an end superscript code (**[suprscpt]**) for you.

10. Press Exit (F7) to save your new endnote options and to return to your document.

You then enter your endnotes following the steps outlined at the beginning of this section, but omitting Step 5. Your endnote numbers are superscripted, and you can begin typing the text of a note immediately after the note number without the intervening tab or spaces. **TIP:** You might want to use a macro to create your notes if you will be doing many of them (see Chapter 11).

Feel free to experiment with these endnote options and use View Document to see the results before moving on to the next section.

Positioning Endnotes

The one remaining difference between footnotes and endnotes is that you can tell WordPerfect to put endnotes anywhere in your document—at the end of each chapter, for example. If you don't select Endnote **P**lacement (**3**), however, the program automatically places the endnotes at the end of your document.

To insert a code that puts your endnotes at some place other than the end of your document, do the following:

1. Place the cursor where you want the program to compile the endnotes.

2. Press the Footnote key (Ctrl-F7).

3. Select Endnote **P**lacement (**3**).

   The prompt Restart endnote numbering? (Y/N) appears.

4. Select *Y* if you want the endnotes that follow to begin at 1 (or whatever number you specify); select *N* if you want the endnotes to continue with the same numbering.

   After making your choice, the following message appears on-screen:

   Endnote Placement
   It is not known how much space endnotes will occupy here.
   Generate to determine.

   This message shows up in Reveal Codes as **[Endnote Placement][HPg]**.

WordPerfect does not continually keep track of the space the endnotes occupy because you may be deleting, adding, or moving notes throughout the document. Because people usually work with page limitations for their writing, however, WordPerfect provides a way for you to see how many lines the endnotes use.

If you want to see how many pages the endnotes occupy, do the following:

1. Press Mark Text (Alt-F5).

2. Select **G**enerate (**6**).

3. Select **G**enerate Tables, Indexes, Automatic References, etc. (**5**).

4. Answer *Y* for Yes when asked if you want to continue.

After the generation process, you might expect to *see* your endnotes appear here. Instead, the boxed message changes to Endnote Placement, and you see the line count, in the status line at the bottom of the screen, that reflects how many lines the endnotes use.

If you want to add text *after* endnotes, be careful: you must enter the text after a hard return between the **[Endnote Placement]** and **[HPg]** codes, as in the following example:

> **[Endnote Placement][HRt]**
> **[HRt]**
> text**[HPg]**

You can erase the **[HPg]** that WordPerfect automatically gives you after the **[Endnote Placement]** code if you want to have additional text immediately after the notes with no page break in between.

Do NOT enter your text immediately after the Endnote Placement code because the text will print *before* the endnotes even if it appears to follow the Endnote Placement code in Reveal Codes. If you choose View Document, you see that the following example produces text that prints *before* the endnotes:

> **[Endnote Placement]**text**[HPg]**

A Macro

If you want to change footnotes to endnotes (or vice versa), WordPerfect provides no easy way to accomplish the task. Instead, you must create a macro. To change a footnote to an endnote, for example, you edit the footnote, move or cut its text, delete the footnote, create an endnote, and retrieve the cut block of text into the new endnote. If you have such a macro from version 4.2, you essentially do the same process in version 5, although the menu choices are different.

In your sample document, you will change all the footnotes to endnotes, so you will create a macro that accomplishes this purpose.

To create a macro to change footnotes to endnotes, do the following:

1. Go to the beginning of the document with Home, Home, ↑.

2. Press Macro Def (Ctrl-F10).

   WordPerfect prompts you with the message Define Macro:.

3. Type *FOOT-END* to name the macro; press Enter.

   WordPerfect prompts you with the message Description:.

4. Type *Changes all footnotes to endnotes* and press Enter.

5. Begin the macro with a Search (F2).

6. Have WordPerfect search for a footnote with Ctrl-F7, **Footnote (1)**, **Note (1)**, F2.

7. Move the cursor under the footnote just found by pressing ←.

8. Now that the cursor is under the footnote, you can go into the note with Ctrl-F7, **Footnote (1)**, **Edit (2)**. Press Enter to accept the number with which WordPerfect prompts you.

   Now that you are inside the footnote, you can extract its text and move it to an endnote.

9. Move to the right of the note number with → and then turn on Block (Alt-F4, or F12).

10. Move the cursor to the end of the note with Home, Home, ↓.

11. Press the Move key (Ctrl-F4), select **Block (1)**, and then select **Move (1)**.

TIP: Using the Move key at this point is better than just blocking and deleting. Because you are going to delete the footnote code in a moment, you can use the Move key to retrieve the deleted text instead of having to cycle through previous deletions.

---

12. Press Exit (F7) to return to the normal document.

13. Delete the footnote code by pressing Backspace and answering *Yes* when WordPerfect prompts you to delete the code.

14. Create an endnote by pressing Footnote (Ctrl-F7), selecting **Endnote (2)**, and then choosing **Create (1)**.

15. Retrieve the moved note text by pressing Enter.

16. Press Exit (F7) to return to the normal document.

17. Have the macro repeat itself until the original search fails by pressing Macro (Alt-F10), giving its own name *FOOT-END*, and pressing Enter.

18. End the macro definition by pressing Macro Def (Ctrl-F10).

19. Run the macro on the rest of your document by pressing Macro (Alt-F10), giving it the name *FOOT-END*, and pressing Enter.

Now all the notes in your document have been converted to endnotes. You can confirm the procedure with View Document. You may want to go back to the beginning of the document to change your endnote options at this point, if your newly converted endnotes don't look the way you want them to look.

If you want to change endnotes to footnotes, just use these instructions as a model, substituting a footnote selection for an endnote selection, and vice versa.

Summary

WP
5

In this chapter, you have seen how to do the following:

- Create a note by selecting Ctrl-F7, Footnote (**1**) or Endnote (**2**), and Create (**1**)

- Look at notes by using the following choices:

  Reveal Codes (Alt-F3, or F11)

  Print (Shift-F7) and choosing Full Document (**1**)

  Print (Shift-F7) and choosing View Document (**6**)

  Footnote (Ctrl-F7) and selecting Footnote (**1**) or Endnote (**2**), Edit (**2**), and "number"

- Delete and move notes, as you would any other WordPerfect code

- Edit notes by choosing Ctrl-F7, Footnote (**1**) or Endnote (**2**), Edit (**2**), and "number"

- Change note options by selecting Ctrl-F7, Footnote (**1**) or Endnote (**2**), and Options (**4**)

- Specify endnote placement by selecting Ctrl-F7 and Endnote Placement (**3**)

- Change footnotes to endnotes, or vice versa, by using a macro

21

Outlining, Paragraph Numbering, and Line Numbering

Susan Hafer, a microcomputer specialist for academic computing at Wellesley College, contributes to this chapter her knowledge of the various numbering methods in WordPerfect 5. ∎

I n this chapter you learn various numbering methods in WordPerfect: outlining, paragraph numbering, and line numbering. The features have been moved from their previous function keys in version 4.2 to new keys in version 5. All three of these features provide automatic numbering.

Why bother with an automatic numbering feature when you can type these numbers yourself? Use automatic numbering to create outlines without having to remember what number you should enter. Use automatic numbering also to go back and make changes easily. For example, if you number paragraphs and then delete, add, or change the order of the paragraphs, WordPerfect automatically renumbers them. Without this feature, you would have to renumber the paragraphs by hand.

Line Numbering is the simplest form of automatic numbering: it places numbers for each line along the left edge of your text. You can begin and end the numbering at any place you choose, and you can specify the interval for numbers to appear (for instance, every line or every five lines). The numbers do not appear on-screen while you edit your document, but you can see them when you print the document or when you use View Document.

With Outline and Paragraph Numbering options, paragraphs are numbered, using one of several numbering styles. Don't let the names of the options mislead you, however: the difference between these two features is only in the way the numbers are created. The Outline option is more automated and more restrictive than Paragraph Numbering.

With Outline, WordPerfect automatically generates a new paragraph number every time you press Enter. With Paragraph Numbering, the program inserts a paragraph number only when you ask for one.

WordPerfect also numbers sub-paragraphs or sub-levels. Tab stops determine the level number: at the left margin, a number is the top level; one tab stop to the right is the second level; two tab stops is the third level; and so on.

In this chapter you explore the following three automatic numbering features:

- Outline—to create an outline and generate paragraph numbers automatically

- Paragraph Numbering—to generate paragraph numbers when you choose

- Line Numbering—to number lines automatically

In addition, you learn how to do the following:

- Make editing changes to your outline

- Change the numbering style used for Outline and Paragraph Numbering

- Change the defaults for Line Numbering

TIP: Because the locations of these options have changed from the previous version, WordPerfect 4.2 users will find Help (F3) especially useful in locating the function keys for these features.

Outlining

Outlines in WordPerfect are simply normal text with **[Par Num]** codes where paragraph numbers appear. The Outline feature automatically generates and inserts these codes. The feature has moved from its previous 4.2 location of Alt-F5 to its new Shift-F5 location.

Turning On Outline

Use Outline when you want automatically generated paragraph numbers. Each time you press Enter, you create a new paragraph number. Within the line, each time you press Tab, you create a different level number. The style you select determines the characters used for different levels (I., A., 1., a., and so on). The default paragraph numbering style is Outline.

```
                    Care of 5.25" Floppy Disks

    I.  Formatting Disks

        A.  New disks (You must format new disks before you can use
            them.)
        B.  Old disks (Formatting erases everything on the old disk,
            so make a copy of the disk first.)

    II. Storage of Disks

        A.  Temperature range: 50-125 degrees F
        B.  Not near a possible magnetic field

            1.  Telephone
            2.  File drawer with magnetic closure
            3.  Paper clips

    III. Handling

        A.  Do not bend disks.
        B.  Do not touch magnetic surface of disk.
        C.  Write on disk label with soft felt tip markers, never
            hard ballpoint pens.
                                    Doc 1 Pg 1 Ln 1 Pos 10
```

Fig. 21.1.
A sample outline.

Refer to figure 21.1 to create a sample outline. To turn on Outline, complete the following steps:

1. Press Center (Shift-F6) if you want to center the title.

2. Type the title of the outline and press Enter.

   Because the title is not part of the outline, you need to type the title before turning Outline on.

   For your example, type *Care of 5.25" Floppy Disks* and press Enter.

3. Place the cursor where you want to begin your outline.

   For this example, press Enter to leave a blank line; start the outline on the next line.

4. Press Date/Outline (Shift-F5).

   The following menu appears:

   1 Date **T**ext; **2** Date Code; **3** Date Format; **4** Outline; **5** Para Num; **6** Define: **0**

5. From the Date/Outline menu, select **O**utline (4) to turn on the automatic outlining feature.

The word Outline appears at the bottom left-hand corner of the screen (see fig. 21.2) and replaces the name of your file if one was displayed. Turning on Outline does not insert a code in your document, but while Outline appears on-screen, the Enter and Tab keys perform specific functions (see the next section).

Outline (4) is a *toggle switch*: if you select this option when it is on, it is turned off, and vice versa.

Fig. 21.2.

A paragraph number created by pressing Enter.

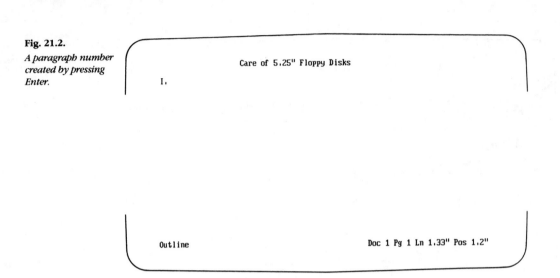

```
                                Care of 5.25" Floppy Disks


              I.




  Outline                                    Doc 1 Pg 1 Ln 1.33" Pos 1.2"
```

If you do not see Outline at the bottom of your screen, repeat Steps 4 and 5. Outline may already have been on when you selected it, effectively turning it off.

Creating Level Numbers with Enter and Tab

While Outline is on, the Enter and Tab keys have special functions. The Enter key, in addition to inserting a carriage return in your text, creates a new paragraph number [**Par Num:Auto**] on the new line. When the cursor is positioned just after this new code, the Tab key has another function. In addition to inserting a [**Tab**] and moving the cursor over one tab stop, pressing the Tab key pulls the paragraph number over with the cursor and changes the number's level.

For Outline style, levels are determined by tab stops in the following manner: numbers at the left margin (first level) are uppercase Roman numerals (I, II, III); numbers at the first tab stop (second level) are capital letters (A, B, C); numbers at the second tab stop (third level) are digits or Arabic numerals (1, 2, 3), and so on. Other styles have different level numbers. See "Defining the Numbering Style."

Once Outline is on, you can create the numbered paragraphs in the following manner:

1. Press Enter to create a paragraph number.

   Because Outline is on, WordPerfect generates a paragraph number at the left margin and places the cursor after the number. The default style determines the number (a Roman numeral one or "I." in the example in figure 21.2) for the levels.

If you press Enter again, you might expect the number to remain where it is and the cursor to move down a line, but because Outline is on, the number moves down with the cursor and leaves a blank line behind.

2. To place the number and move the cursor, press Indent (F4)

   or

Press the space bar

or

Press the space bar once and then Tab. You have to press the space bar before pressing Tab, or else the number moves with the cursor.

If you use Indent (F4), the text wraps so that any second line is aligned underneath the first character of the first line, creating a "hanging indent" and making a more appealing and readable outline.

3. Type the text for this level. (Remember that another paragraph number is created as soon as you press Enter again.)

   The text might be a short heading or a paragraph.

   For the example, type *Formatting Disks*.

4. Press Enter.

   WordPerfect generates the next paragraph number. In the default style, this number is "II."

5. Press Enter again to leave a blank line between paragraphs.

   Note that the number moves with the cursor.

6. Press Tab to move in one level.

   The number follows and changes, in this case to "A." (see fig. 21.3).

If you press Tab too many times, leave the cursor next to the paragraph number and press Margin Release (Shift-Tab) to move back one tab stop. No code is inserted, but the number moves back a tab stop and changes back one level.

```
                    Care of 5.25" Floppy Disks
        I.   Formatting Disks
             A.
```

Fig. 21.3.
Using Tab to change level numbers.

```
        Outline                      Doc 1 Pg 1 Ln 1.66" Pos 1.7"
```

With Outline on, the Tab key functions in a similar way to the Enter key: the number stays with the cursor as it moves. Unlike the Enter key, however, the Tab key determines the level number, changing the number and moving it forward.

7. Press Indent (F4) to leave the number, or press the space bar followed by an optional tab to place the number and move the cursor.

8. Type the text for this level.

   For the example, type the following:

   New disks (You must format new disks before you can use them.)

9. Repeat these steps to complete the outline in fig. 21.1.

Turning Off Outline

When you complete your outline and want to return to creating normal paragraphs, you need to turn off Outline in the following manner:

1. Press Date/Outline (Shift-F5).

2. Select **Outline** (4) to turn off Outline.

Remember that you use this toggle switch both to turn on and turn off Outline. If you aren't certain whether the switch is on or off, look at the bottom left corner of your document: if it says Outline, then the switch is on.

When you turn off Outline, the Enter and Tab keys revert back to their normal functions. You now can enter normal paragraphs after the outline or within the boundaries of the outline itself.

Defining the Numbering Style

Outline, the default numbering style, uses standard Roman numerals for its characters. You can choose another numbering style if you want. For instance, you can change the outline you just created to a paragraph numbering style.

To change the numbering style, complete the following steps:

1. Position the cursor at the beginning of the outline.

   For this example, the outline is at the beginning of the document, so press Home, Home, ↑.

2. Press Date/Outline (Shift-F5).

3. Select **Define** (6) from the menu.

   The Paragraph Number Definition menu appears (see fig. 21.4).

   The current definition appears in the center of the screen. Note that the numbering levels match those for Outline style, the default.

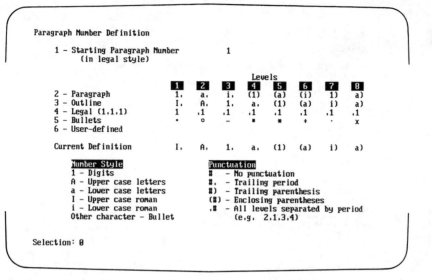

Fig. 21.4.

The Paragraph Number Definition menu.

4. Select the new style you want. (See "Investigating Numbering Styles" for a description of each option.)

   For this example, select **Paragraph** (**2**). Notice that the current definition in the center of the screen changes to reflect the new style.

5. Press Exit (F7) to save the current definition and return to the Date/Outline menu.

Whenever you Exit (F7) the Paragraph Number Definition menu, WordPerfect inserts a paragraph code into your document and begins numbering the subsequent paragraph with 1. If you notice your paragraphs being numbered with a "1, 2, 3, 1, 2" sequence rather than a "1, 2, 3, 4, 5" sequence, use Reveal Codes (Alt-F3, or F11) to find the **[Par Num Def]** code embedded in the middle of your outline and delete the code. If you do not want to save the settings in the Paragraph Number Definition menu, press Cancel (F1) instead of Exit (F7), and no code is inserted in your document.

6. Press Exit (F7) to return to your document from the Date/Outline menu.

7. Press Screen (Ctrl-F3) and select **Rewrite** (**0**) to redisplay your document so that you can make sure that the entire outline has been renumbered to match your new numbering style definition.

   The new outline should look like figure 21.5.

If the numbering did not change, check your procedure by doing the following:

1. Press Reveal Codes (Alt-F3, or F11).

2. Be sure that the **[Par Num Def]** code is at the beginning of your outline, not the end.

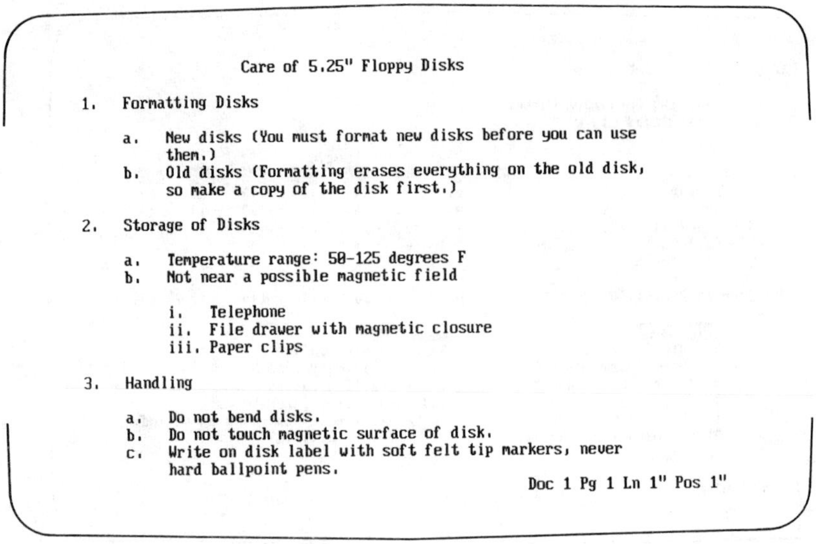

Fig. 21.5.

*Paragraph
numbering style.*

```
                          Care of 5.25" Floppy Disks

       1,   Formatting Disks

            a,   New disks (You must format new disks before you can use
                 them,)
            b,   Old disks (Formatting erases everything on the old disk,
                 so make a copy of the disk first,)

       2,   Storage of Disks

            a,   Temperature range: 50-125 degrees F
            b,   Not near a possible magnetic field

                 i,    Telephone
                 ii,   File drawer with magnetic closure
                 iii,  Paper clips

       3,   Handling

            a,   Do not bend disks,
            b,   Do not touch magnetic surface of disk,
            c,   Write on disk label with soft felt tip markers, never
                 hard ballpoint pens,
                                              Doc 1 Pg 1 Ln 1" Pos 1"
```

3. Check to be sure that your document has no other **[Par Num Def]** code canceling out the one you just entered.

   If you pressed Enter or Exit (F7) instead of Cancel (F1) from the Paragraph Number Definition menu, you might have inserted an additional code without intending to do so.

If you change frequently to one particular outline style, you can create a WordPerfect macro to speed up the process by following these steps:

1. Press Macro Def (Ctrl-F10).

2. Name the macro (for example, *PN-DEF* for "Paragraph Numbering Definition").

3. Type a brief description (such as *Paragraph Numbering Def*) and press Enter.

4. Follow Steps 2 through 6 or 7 in the procedure for selecting a new style.

5. Press Macro Def (Ctrl-F10) to end the definition.

Then to use the macro, do the following:

1. Place the cursor before the outline that will have this definition.

2. Press Macro (Alt-F10).

3. Type the macro name (*PN-DEF*, for example) and press Enter.

Investigating Numbering Styles

To view the Paragraph Number Definition menu, press Date/Outline (Shift-F5) and select **Define** (**6**). The first selection in the menu restarts paragraph numbering; the other five options are numbering styles (see fig. 21.4).

With **Starting Paragraph Number** (**1**), you can begin a new paragraph number by accepting the default 1, or you can choose another number. You might choose another number when you want to embed one outline in another, for example. Then you can continue the first outline's numbering scheme after you finish the embedded outline.

To enter another number, you must specify the number in legal style, as shown in option **4** of the menu. Enter the exact number of the paragraph you wish to begin with, not the level of the paragraph in the outline hierarchy. For instance, if the paragraph is at level 1 but is the third paragraph in the text, enter a 3 for its position in the text rather than a 1 for its level. Or if a paragraph is three paragraphs into the first level, four into the second level, and two into the third level (3.d.ii), you would enter 3.4.2 in legal style.

Paragraph (**2**) is the generic Paragraph Numbering style. Look to the right of the menu choice and note the eight defined levels for this style.

Outline (**3**) is the default style, as shown in figure 21.5. WordPerfect uses the default unless you specify another style. Again, note the eight defined levels for this style to the right of the menu choice.

Legal (1.1.1) (**4**) is the style used most often by law offices. See figure 21.6 for an example of this numbering style.

Fig. 21.6.
Legal numbering style.

```
                    Care of 5.25" Floppy Disks

        1   Formatting Disks

            1.1  New disks (You must format new disks before you can use
                 them.)
            1.2  Old disks (Formatting erases everything on the old disk,
                 so make a copy of the disk first.)

        2   Storage of Disks

            2.1  Temperature range: 50-125 degrees F
            2.2  Not near a possible magnetic field

                 2.2.1    Telephone
                 2.2.2    File drawer with magnetic closure
                 2.2.3    Paper clips

        3   Handling

            3.1  Do not bend disks.
            3.2  Do not touch magnetic surface of disk.
            3.3  Write on disk label with soft felt tip markers, never
                 hard ballpoint pens.
                                    Doc 1 Pg 1 Ln 1" Pos 1"
```

A new numbering style offered in version 5, **Bullets** (**5**) uses different characters to set off levels. Figure 21.7 shows an example of this numbering style. You should test on your printer a sample outline that uses this style, however, because not all printers can print all the characters.

Fig. 21.7.

Bullet numbering style.

```
                      Care of 5.25" Floppy Disks

        ·   Formatting Disks

            o   New disks (You must format new disks before you can use
                them.)
            o   Old disks (Formatting erases everything on the old disk,
                so make a copy of the disk first.)

        ·   Storage of Disks

            o   Temperature range: 50-125 degrees F
            o   Not near a possible magnetic field

                -   Telephone
                -   File drawer with magnetic closure
                -   Paper clips

        ·   Handling

            o   Do not bend disks.
            o   Do not touch magnetic surface of disk.
            o   Write on disk label with soft felt tip markers, never
                hard ballpoint pens.
                                        Doc 1 Pg 1 Ln 1" Pos 1"
```

If not all characters print, you might want to create your own numbering style by using similar characters that your printer can print. User-defined (**6**) allows you to create your own numbering style. For example, if you define the first level as (*1*), all top level numbers are surrounded by parentheses without a period.

To define your own numbering style, complete the following steps:

1. Press Date/Outline (Shift-F5), choose **Define** (**6**), and select User-defined (**6**).

   You move to the Current Definition in the center of the screen.

2. Type the character you want for the level.

   Use Number Style and Punctuation as guidelines for style. (For the example in figure 21.8, I typed (*1*) to have digits enclosed in parentheses for the first level.)

3. Press Enter to move to the next level.

4. After defining all the levels, press Exit (F7) three times to return to your document (once to exit the Current Definition level, once to exit the Paragraph Number Definition menu, and once to exit the Date/Outline menu).

Figure 21.8 shows an example of one type of user-defined numbering style.

```
                    Care of 5.25" Floppy Disks

    (1)  Formatting Disks

         A.   New disks (You must format new disks before you can use
              them.)
         B.   Old disks (Formatting erases everything on the old disk,
              so make a copy of the disk first.)

    (2)  Storage of Disks

         A.   Temperature range: 50-125 degrees F
         B.   Not near a possible magnetic field

              1.   Telephone
              2.   File drawer with magnetic closure
              3.   Paper clips

    (3)  Handling

         A.   Do not bend disks.
         B.   Do not touch magnetic surface of disk.
         C.   Write on disk label with soft felt tip markers, never
              hard ballpoint pens.
                                    Doc 1 Pg 1 Ln 1" Pos 1"
```

Fig. 21.8.
User-defined numbering style.

Editing an Outline

Once you have created your outline, you may want to go back to make structural changes: deleting, adding, or moving numbered paragraphs. The real advantage of using automatic numbering is the ease of editing and renumbering.

Deleting a Paragraph Number

Paragraph numbers are just another WordPerfect code in your document; therefore, you can delete the **[Par Num]** code the same way you delete any other code.

To delete a paragraph number, complete the following steps:

1. Press Reveal Codes (Alt-F3, or F11).

2. Move your cursor to the **[Par Num]** code that represents the number you want to delete.

3. Press Del.

4. Press Reveal Codes (Alt-F3, or F11).

Adding a Paragraph Number

If you accidentally delete a paragraph number or if you create an unnumbered paragraph and later decide to add a number, you easily can add a paragraph number.

To add a paragraph number, do the following:

1. Be sure that Outline is on (check lower left corner of screen); if it is not, press Date/Outline (Shift-F5) and then Outline (4).

2. Place the cursor at the beginning of the paragraph you want to number.

3. Press Enter to create a new number.

4. Press Tab (if necessary) to place the cursor where the number should appear on the line.

5. Press Indent (F4), the space bar, or a space followed by a Tab, to move the text over, if necessary.

6. Delete any extra hard returns to space your outline correctly.

To create another numbered paragraph immediately after this one, be sure to put the cursor at the end of the last line of this paragraph before continuing.

Changing a Paragraph Number

When reorganizing an outline, you may decide to change the level of a number ("1" to "a" for example) for a numbered paragraph. Remember that the position on the line determines the level of a number.

To change the level of a number, complete the following steps:

1. Place the cursor under the number you want to change; Outline may be on or off.

2. Press Tab to move the line to the right; the paragraph number changes to a lower level

   or

   Press Margin Release (Shift-Tab) to move the line to the left; the paragraph number changes to a higher level.

3. Press ↓ or press Screen (Ctrl-F3) and choose **Rewrite** (**0**) to redisplay and renumber the text.

Deleting a Numbered Paragraph

In editing your outline, you may want to delete an entire paragraph. For example, in the outline you created, you may decide to delete the "Storage of Disks" section (see fig. 21.9).

To delete a numbered paragraph, complete the following steps:

1. Place the cursor at the beginning of the paragraph or block you want to delete.

   For your example, place the cursor above the "2" at the beginning of the "Storage of Disks" section.

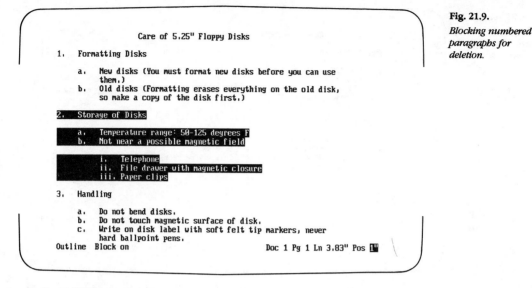

Fig. 21.9.

Blocking numbered paragraphs for deletion.

2. Press Block (Alt-F4, or F12) to turn on Block.

   Block on flashes at the bottom of the screen. Outline can be on or off.

3. Highlight the block you want to delete by moving the cursor to the end of that block.

   In your example, block to the blank line before the "3. Handling" section (see fig. 21.9).

Be sure that you delete the entire block. If you do not, information from one heading could be included with information in the preceding heading. For instance if you delete just "2. Storage of Disks," WordPerfect places the temperature and magnetic field headings under the "Formatting Disks" heading.

4. Press Del or Backspace.

5. Answer *Y* for Yes when asked Delete Block?

Note that the program renumbers the subsequent paragraphs (see fig. 21.10).

After deleting a block, you may need to tidy up the outline by adding or deleting extra carriage returns so that the spacing of the outline is correct. When you learn to begin and end the block wisely, however, this housekeeping maneuver should no longer be necessary.

Moving a Numbered Paragraph

In addition to deleting numbered paragraphs, you also can move them. For instance, instead of deleting the storage information, suppose that you decide to move the section so that it follows the section on handling disks. (After all, you handle disks

Fig. 21.10.

*Paragraphs
renumbered after
deleting the block.*

```
                        Care of 5.25" Floppy Disks

        1.  Formatting Disks

             a.  New disks (You must format new disks before you can use
                 them.)
             b.  Old disks (Formatting erases everything on the old disk,
                 so make a copy of the disk first.)


        2.  Handling

             a.  Do not bend disks.
             b.  Do not touch magnetic surface of disk.
             c.  Write on disk label with soft felt tip markers, never
                 hard ballpoint pens.




        Outline                                  Doc 1 Pg 1 Ln 2.5" Pos 1"
```

before you store them.) Begin by deleting the storage information section and then restoring it in its new location.

To move a numbered paragraph, do the following:

1. Delete the text by following the directions in "Deleting a Numbered Paragraph."

2. Place the cursor where you want to insert the deleted paragraph.

   For this example, place your cursor at the end of the document.

3. Press Cancel (F1).

   The following menu appears:

   Undelete: 1 Restore; **2** Previous Deletion: **0**

4. Select **Restore** (**1**).

WordPerfect inserts the block. Note that the paragraph numbers change again as soon as you undelete this numbered paragraph (see fig. 21.11).

Again, you may need to tidy up by adding or deleting extra carriage returns. If you do need to add a carriage return, you may want to turn off Outline first; otherwise, a paragraph number is created and you will need to delete it with Backspace.

Adding a Numbered Paragraph

In addition to deleting and moving paragraphs, you can add new paragraphs. For instance, in the outline you created, you may decide to include a section explaining how to help prevent a disaster to your disks.

```
                    Care of 5.25" Floppy Disks

    1.   Formatting Disks

         a.   New disks (You must format new disks before you can use
              them.)
         b.   Old disks (Formatting erases everything on the old disk,
              so make a copy of the disk first.)

    2.   Handling

         a.   Do not bend disks.
         b.   Do not touch magnetic surface of disk.
         c.   Write on disk label with soft felt tip markers, never
              hard ballpoint pens.

    3.   Storage of Disks

         a.   Temperature range: 50-125 degrees F
         b.   Not near a possible magnetic field

              i.    Telephone
              ii.   File drawer with magnetic closure
              iii.  Paper clips
    Outline                              Doc 1 Pg 1 Ln 4.83" Pos 1"
```

Fig. 21.11.

Paragraphs renumbered after restoring the block.

To add a paragraph or group of paragraphs, complete the following steps:

1. Make sure that Outline is on by pressing Date/Outline (Shift-F5) and then **Outline (4)**.

2. Place the cursor where you want to insert the text.

   In your example, place the cursor after the "Formatting Disks" section and before the "Handling" section.

3. Press Enter to create the new numbered paragraphs and press Tab, if necessary, to change the correct level for each paragraph.

   For your example, insert the paragraphs shown in figure 21.12.

Adding a Paragraph without a Number

In your outline, you may want to add some paragraphs, such as explanations under headings, that are not numbered. You can add unnumbered paragraphs by completing the following steps:

1. At the place where you want an unnumbered paragraph, press Date/Outline (Shift-F5).

2. Select **Outline (4)** to turn off Outline.

3. Type the paragraph.

4. Do Steps 1 and 2 again to turn on Outline when you want to start numbering paragraphs again.

If you do not want to keep turning Outline on and off (perhaps you have several unnumbered paragraphs within your outline), you can use the following second method to enter an unnumbered paragraph:

Fig. 21.12.

Adding numbered paragraphs.

```
                    a,   New disks (You must format new disks before you can use
                         them,)
                    b,   Old disks (Formatting erases everything on the old disk,
                         so make a copy of the disk first,)

              2,    Disaster Protection

                    a,   Make backup copies of all your work onto other disks,
                         i,   See the COPY command in the DOS manual for copying
                              files from one floppy disk to another,
                         ii,  See the BACKUP and RESTORE commands in the DOS
                              manual for copying files from a hard disk to a
                              floppy disk,
                    b,   Use the write-protect tabs (small stickers) to cover the
                         notch on the disk's side if you want to prevent anyone
                         from writing/modifying/erasing anything on the disk,
                    c,   Make files "Read-only" so that no one can erase or change
                         them,
                         i,   See the CHMOD command in some DOS manuals,
                         ii,  See the ATTRIB command in some DOS manuals,

              3,    Handling

                    A,   Do not bend disks,
        Outline                                           Doc 1 Pg 1 Ln 2,5" Pos 1"
```

1. Make sure that Outline is on by pressing Date/Outline (Shift-F5) and then Outline (4).

2. Place the cursor where you want the new paragraph to begin.

   For this example, place the cursor at the end of the paragraph that begins "Old disks" (see fig. 21.13).

Fig. 21.13.

Adding an unnumbered paragraph.

```
                         Care of 5,25" Floppy Disks

              1,    Formatting Disks

                    a,   New disks (You must format new disks before you can use
                         them,)
                    b,   Old disks (Formatting erases everything on the old disk,
                         so make a copy of the disk first,)

                         It's a good idea to format old disks (after copying
                         everything to another disk) because the format program
                         marks off any physically damaged parts ("bad sectors")
                         of a disk, and you can replace any damaged disks,

              2,    Disaster Protection

                    a,   Make backup copies of all your work onto other disks,
                         i,   See the COPY command in the DOS manual for copying
                              files from one floppy disk to another,
                         ii,  See the BACKUP and RESTORE commands in the DOS
                              manual for copying files from a hard disk to a
                              floppy disk,
                    b,   Use the write-protect tabs (small stickers) to cover the
                         notch on the disk's side if you want to prevent anyone
        Outline                                           Doc 1 Pg 1 Ln 2,5" Pos 1"
```

3. Press Enter twice to insert a blank line.

   You generate a number because Outline is on.

4. Press Backspace to get rid of the number.

5. Press Indent (F4) if you want to line up the paragraphs underneath preceding levels.

    Now that the number has been deleted, the Tab key reverts to its normal usage; therefore, you can use Tab instead of Indent (F4) if you prefer.

    In your example, press Indent (F4) twice so that the paragraph lines up with the text beginning "Old disks."

6. Type the new paragraph.

    Type the text shown in figure 21.13.

7. Press Enter to end the paragraph.

    Another paragraph number is created.

8. Press Backspace to delete the new paragraph number.

Numbering Paragraphs

You have seen that using Outline automatically creates numbered paragraphs. You also can use Paragraph Numbering to create numbered paragraphs. Both techniques use the same style of numbering; the options differ in the way the numbers are created.

When you use Outline to number paragraphs and you also want to include unnumbered paragraphs, you have to complete several steps. If you have many unnumbered paragraphs mixed in with the numbered ones, these extra steps can be cumbersome. If you choose Paragraph Numbering instead, the paragraph numbers have to be requested explicitly rather than generated automatically.

Defining the Numbering Style

Just as you can define a numbering style for Outline, you can select a numbering style for Paragraph Numbering as well. In fact, the **[Par Num Def]** code used by Outline is exactly the same code used by Paragraph Numbering. If you do not change the numbering style, the default style is Outline.

If you have changed the numbering style, do the following to change it back to Outline:

1. Position the cursor at the place where you want the new outline style to begin (at the beginning of the outline if you've already typed it or at the place you will start typing it).

    For this example, you will type a new outline (see fig. 21.14) at the end of your document, so press Home, Home, ↓.

2. Press Date/Outline (Shift-F5).

3. Select **Define** (6).

   The Paragraph Number Definition menu appears.

4. Select the style you want.

   For this example, select **Outline** (3) to choose the Roman numeral outline style.

5. Press Exit (F7) to save the Current Definition.

6. Press Exit (F7) to return to your document.

See "Investigating Numbering Styles" for more information on available styles.

Creating Numbered Paragraphs

After defining the style, you can begin typing your outline and specifying paragraph numbers by doing the following:

1. Press Enter.

   If a paragraph number is generated, Outline is on, and you should turn it off and delete the number. Otherwise you can continue.

2. Press Center (Shift-F6) to center the title.

3. Type the title and press Enter.

   For your example, type *Paragraph Numbering and Outlining in WordPerfect* and press Enter (see fig. 21.14) to end the title.

4. Press Enter to insert a blank line.

5. Be sure that the cursor is at the left-hand margin.

6. Press Date/Outline (Shift-F5).

7. Select **Para Num** (5) to insert a paragraph number.

8. When asked for Paragraph Level, press Enter for automatic numbering.

   WordPerfect chooses the appropriate number according to the cursor's position on the line. Because you are at the left margin, WordPerfect assigns the first level number a "I." Remember that the style you select determines the level numbers the program uses.

9. Press Indent (F4) (or press the space bar and Tab) and type the text for this numbered paragraph.

   For your example, press Indent (F4) and type *Defining the Style*.

If you use Indent (F4), text automatically wraps underneath the tab stop. As is the case when Outline is on, pressing Tab pulls the number with the cursor and changes its level.

10. Press Enter twice to begin a new paragraph and insert a blank line.

11. Press Tab to place the cursor for the next paragraph.

12. Follow Steps 6 through 11 to complete the outline from figure 21.14.

Fig. 21.14.
*Paragraph
Numbering.*

```
          Paragraph Numbering and Outlining in WordPerfect

     I.  Defining the Style

          A.  Make sure the cursor is positioned before the outline
              whose numbering style you're about to choose.
          B.  Press Date/Outline (Shift-F5) and select Define (6).
          C.  Make your selection.
          D.  Press Exit twice.

     II. Creating a Number

          A.  Paragraph Numbers

               1.  Press Date/Outline (Shift-F5).
               2.  Select Para Num (5).
               3.  Press Enter for an automatically selected level.

          B.  Outlining

               1.  Press Enter to create a number on the next line.
               2.  Press Tab to move the number in levels.


                              Doc 1 Pg 1 Ln 1" Pos 1"
```

Once you position the cursor (at the left margin or in one or more tab stops), you use the same keystrokes (Steps 6-9) to create a number. You can create a macro to save you these keystrokes, especially if you give the macro a short name like PN for paragraph number.

To create the macro, do the following:

1. Press Macro Def (Ctrl-F10).

2. Name the macro by typing *PN* for "paragraph number" and press Enter.

3. Type *paragraph number* for the description and press Enter.

4. Press Date/Outline (Shift-F5), select **Para Num (5)**, and press Enter.

5. Press Indent (F4).

6. End the macro by pressing Macro Def (Ctrl-F10).

Using Fixed Paragraph Levels

Normally WordPerfect automatically chooses what level a number should be by its position on a line: top level at the left margin, second level at one tab stop, third level at two tab stops, and so on. This numbering system makes reorganizing your material much easier: you just add or delete tabs before the number, and the level number is automatically adjusted.

You may want all your numbers, regardless of their levels, to line up at the left margin or in one tab stop, however. Or, you may want one number to stay at a particular level regardless of its position on the line. If so, you can force the level number to be whatever you request.

To "fix" a paragraph level, complete the following steps:

1. Position the cursor under the level number you want to fix.

   For instance, place the cursor under the "I." in your sample outline.

2. Press Tab to line the number up with the second level numbers beneath it.

3. Press Screen (Ctrl-F3) and select **Rewrite (0)**.

   Your number changes to "A."; the following paragraph numbers change as well (see fig. 21.15).

Fig. 21.15.

Moving the first paragraph number.

```
              Paragraph Numbering and Outlining in WordPerfect

          A.   Defining the Style

          B.   Make sure the cursor is positioned before the outline
               whose numbering style you're about to choose.
          C.   Press Date/Outline (Shift-F5) and select Define (6).
          D.   Make your selection.
          E.   Press Exit twice.

      I.   Creating a Number

          A.   Paragraph Numbers

               1.   Press Date/Outline (Shift-F5).
               2.   Select Para Num (5).
               3.   Press Enter for an automatically selected level.

          B.   Outlining

               1.   Press Enter to create a number on the next line.
               2.   Press Tab to move the number in levels.


      Outline                                    Doc 1 Pg 1 Ln 1" Pos 1"
```

4. Move the cursor back under the level number you want to force.

   For instance, place the cursor under the first "A."

5. Press Del to delete the **[Par Num:Auto]** code.

   You may want to do this step in Reveal Codes (Alt-F3, or F11).

   The number disappears and the other second level numbers revert back to their original order (see fig. 21.16).

6. Press Date/Outline (Shift-F5).

7. Select **Para Num (5)**, but do not press Enter.

8. Type the level number you want to assign and press Enter.

   For instance, type *1* and press Enter.

```
  Paragraph Numbering and Outlining in WordPerfect

     Defining the Style

  A.  Make sure the cursor is positioned before the outline
      whose numbering style you're about to choose.
  B.  Press Date/Outline (Shift-F5) and select Define (6).
  C.  Make your selection.
  D.  Press Exit twice.

I.  Creating a Number

  A.  Paragraph Numbers

      1.  Press Date/Outline (Shift-F5).
      2.  Select Para Num (5).
      3.  Press Enter for an automatically selected level.

  B.  Outlining

      1.  Press Enter to create a number on the next line.
      2.  Press Tab to move the number in levels.


Outline                                 Doc 1 Pg 1 Ln 1.33" Pos 1.5"
```

Fig. 21.16.
Deleting the first paragraph number.

WordPerfect ignores the cursor position and assigns "I." instead of "A." to this paragraph number (see fig. 21.17).

```
  Paragraph Numbering and Outlining in WordPerfect

  I.   Defining the Style

  A.  Make sure the cursor is positioned before the outline
      whose numbering style you're about to choose.
  B.  Press Date/Outline (Shift-F5) and select Define (6).
  C.  Make your selection.
  D.  Press Exit twice.

II.  Creating a Number

  A.  Paragraph Numbers

      1.  Press Date/Outline (Shift-F5).
      2.  Select Para Num (5).
      3.  Press Enter for an automatically selected level.

  B.  Outlining

      1.  Press Enter to create a number on the next line.
      2.  Press Tab to move the number in levels.


Outline                                 Doc 1 Pg 1 Ln 1.33" Pos 1.7"
```

Fig. 21.17.
Giving the first paragraph number a fixed level.

9. Press Screen (Ctrl-F3) and select **Rewrite (0)** to redisplay text.

10. Repeat this process for any other paragraph number levels you want to change.

   For instance, you can change the "II." in the outline. Remember to type *1* for its level number rather than *2* for the actual number.

If you know you want a number at a fixed level while you are typing the outline, enter the fixed level then. Type the level number instead of just pressing Enter at the Paragraph Level prompt.

Using Tab Align for Paragraph Numbers

In the paragraph numbering examples used in this chapter, the numbers are all flush left, as in the following example:

i.   Telephone
ii.   File drawer with magnetic closure
iii.   Paper clips

Flush left numbers, the automatic setting, are especially noticeable, possibly disturbing, when you use Roman numerals. Instead, you can align numbers at the period (.) after each number, as in the next example:

i.   Telephone
ii.   File drawer with magnetic closure
iii.   Paper clips

Because numbers are to the left of the tab stops, however, you have more white space between the period and the text that follows the number. To eliminate the white space, change your tab stops or use two spaces after each paragraph number.

To align tabs on a specific character, use Tab Align (Ctrl-F6). With this special Tab key, the cursor moves to the tab, and text moves left until you type the alignment character, usually a period (.). After you type the alignment character, text is pushed to the right, as usual.

To align paragraph numbers as you type an outline, do the following:

1. Press Tab Align (Ctrl-F6) before the Tab you want to align.

2. Press Date/Outline (Shift-F5).

3. Select **Para** Num (**5**).

4. Press Enter.

5. Press Indent (F4)

   or

   Type a period (.) to end the Tab Align, press Backspace to delete the extra period, and press the space bar once or twice. (The screen is not refreshed, and it appears as though the period is not deleted.)

6. Type the text for the numbered paragraph.

To align paragraph numbers you have already entered in an outline, complete the following steps:

1. Place the cursor at the paragraph number you want to align.

2. Press Tab Align (Ctrl-F6).

3. Press Screen (Ctrl-F3) and select **Rewrite** (**0**).

If you have several paragraph numbers to realign, you may want to create a macro that searches for the **[Par Num]** code and inserts Tab Align.

To create a macro that helps you realign your paragraph numbers, do the following:

1. Position the cursor before the outline(s) to be realigned.

   For your example, go to the beginning of the document with Home, Home, ↑.

2. Press Macro Def (Ctrl-F10) to begin defining the macro.

3. When the message Define macro: appears at the bottom of the screen, type *pn-align* for "paragraph number align" and press Enter.

4. When prompted for a description, type *Change Par Nums to Tab Aligned Par Nums* and press Enter.

5. Press Forward Search (F2).

6. Ask WordPerfect to search for a paragraph number code by pressing the Date/Outline key (Shift-F5) and selecting **Para Num** (**2**).

7. Press Forward Search (F2) to begin the search.

8. When the cursor stops at a paragraph number, press ←.

9. Press Tab Align (Ctrl-F6).

10. Press → to have Tab Align go into effect.

11. Press Macro (Alt-F10), type *pn-align*, and then press Enter.

   This step tells WordPerfect to end the macro by calling itself. Because a search is inside the macro, the macro repeats until the search fails.

12. Press Macro Def (Ctrl-F10) to end the macro definition.

To use the macro, press Macro (Alt-F10) and type *pn-align*; then press Enter to have the macro run repeatedly until it changes all the paragraph numbers in your document. Move the cursor back to the beginning of the "Telephone" line, where the effect of alignment is more striking and press Reveal Codes (Alt-F3, or F11) so that you can see the alignment codes mixed in with your numbers (see fig. 21.18).

The last point you should know about numbering paragraphs is how to edit them. You edit numbered paragraphs the same way you edit paragraphs created using Outline. See "Editing an Outline" in this chapter.

Fig. 21.18.

Reveal Codes of the outline after tab alignment.

```
         a.   Temperature range: 50-125 degrees F
            b.     Not near a possible magnetic field

                i.    Telephone
               ii.    File drawer with magnetic closure
              iii.    Paper clips


         Paragraph Numbering and Outlining in WordPerfect

Align char = .                                    Doc 1 Pg 1 Ln 8.33" Pos 2.3"
┌───▲─────▲─────▲─────▲─────▲─────▲─────▲─────▲─────▲─────▲───)───▲───────┐
[Tab][Align][Par Num:Auto][C/A/Flrt][+Indent]Not near a possible magnetic field[
HRt]
[HRt]
[Tab][Tab][Align][Par Num:Auto][C/A/Flrt][+Indent]Telephone[HRt]
[Tab][Tab][Align][Par Num:Auto][C/A/Flrt][+Indent]File drawer with magnetic clos
ure[HRt]
[Tab][Tab][Align][Par Num:Auto][C/A/Flrt][+Indent]Paper clips[HRt]
[HRt]
[Par Num Def][HRt]
[Cntr]Paragraph Numbering and Outlining in WordPerfect[C/A/Flrt][HRt]

Press Reveal Codes to restore screen
```

Line Numbering

In addition to numbering paragraphs, you also can number lines. You can use Line Numbering for legal documents, for example, or for any document where referencing a particular passage in the text would be easier with numbered lines. You can use Line Numbering also when several people edit the same document. In a group, you can discuss the work easily by referring, for example, to the word "cheap" on page 10, line 32.

If you used the Line Numbering feature in version 4.2, be aware that it has moved to the newly reorganized Format function key (Shift-F8) in the Line Format menu.

When you use Line Numbering, the program inserts a code into your document and begins numbering that line at 1. Remember to put the cursor at the point where you want the Line Numbering to begin (normally, the beginning of your text). The numbers are not displayed on-screen as you enter the text in your document, but you can check the numbers before printing by pressing Print (Shift-F7) and selecting View Document (6).

Turning On Line Numbering

To use Line Numbering, move to the line where you want numbering to begin. For this example, complete the following steps:

1. Press Home, Home, ↑ to place the cursor at the beginning of the document.

2. Press Format (Shift-F8).

    The Format menu appears (see fig. 21.19).

```
Format

    1 - Line
            Hyphenation              Line Spacing
            Justification            Margins Left/Right
            Line Height              Tab Set
            Line Numbering           Widow/Orphan Protection

    2 - Page
            Center Page (top to bottom)   New Page Number
            Force Odd/Even Page           Page Numbering
            Headers and Footers           Paper Size/Type
            Margins Top/Bottom            Suppress

    3 - Document
            Display Pitch            Redline Method
            Initial Codes/Font       Summary

    4 - Other
            Advance                  Overstrike
            Conditional End of Page  Printer Functions
            Decimal Characters       Underline Spaces/Tabs
            Language

Selection: 0
```

Fig. 21.19.
The Format menu.

3. Select **Line** (**1**).

   The Format: Line menu appears (see fig. 21.20).

```
Format: Line

    1 - Hyphenation                    Off

    2 - Hyphenation Zone - Left        10%
                          Right        4%

    3 - Justification                  Yes

    4 - Line Height                    Auto

    5 - Line Numbering                 No

    6 - Line Spacing                   1

    7 - Margins - Left                 1"
                  Right                1"

    8 - Tab Set                        0", every 0.5"

    9 - Widow/Orphan Protection        No


Selection: 0
```

Fig. 21.20.
The Format: Line menu.

4. Select Line **Numbering** (**5**).

5. Press *Y* (for Yes) to turn on Line Numbering.

   The Line Numbering menu appears. (See "Changing Line Numbering Settings" for details on each of the options.)

6. Press Enter to accept the default settings.

7. Press Exit (F7) to return to your document.

Checking Line Numbering with View Document

Remember that line numbers do not appear on-screen. You can use Reveal Codes (Alt-F3, or F11) to see the **[Ln Num:On]** code. To see the line numbers, you either can print the document or use View Document.

To view the document, complete the following steps:

1. Press Print (Shift-F7).

2. Select View Document (**6**).

3. Select 100 % (**1**) to see the numbers more clearly.

   Note the line numbers down the left margin (see fig. 21.21).

4. Press Exit (F7) after you have finished with View Document.

Fig. 21.21.

100% View Document with Line Numbering.

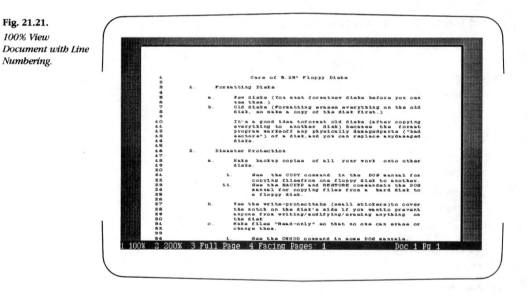

Turning Off Line Numbering

If you want to remove all line numbering from your document, delete the code inserted when you turned on Line Numbering.

To delete the Line Numbering code, do the following:

1. Press Reveal Codes (Alt-F3, or F11).

2. Move the cursor to the **[Ln Num:On]** code.

3. Press Del.

4. Press Reveal Codes (Alt-F3, or F11) to return to the normal screen or display.

If you entered more than one Line Numbering code, use Forward Search (F2) or Replace (Alt-F2) from the beginning of the document to make sure that you delete them all.

If you want only part of a document to contain line numbers, then turn off Line Numbering at the end of the numbered section.

To turn off Line Numbering, do the following:

1. Place the cursor where you want Line Numbering to stop.

2. Press Format (Shift-F8).

3. Select **Line** (**1**).

4. Select Line **Numbering** (**5**).

5. Press *N* (for No) to turn off Line Numbering.

6. Press Exit (F7) to return to your document.

You might want to use View Document to be sure that you turned off Line Numbering.

Changing Line Numbering Settings

Because the default settings for Line Numbering may not suit your preferences, you can change the defaults. For instance, you may prefer to number only every five lines instead of every line.

To change the default settings, complete the following steps:

1. Press Format (Shift-F8).

2. Select **Line** (**1**).

3. Select Line **Numbering** (**5**).

4. Press *Y* to turn on Line Numbering.

   The Format: Line Numbering menu appears on-screen (see fig. 21.22).

5. Select the item you want to change.

   For instance, select **Number Every n Lines** (**2**).

6. Enter the change.

   For this example, type *5* to number only every five lines and press Enter.

Fig. 21.22.

The Format: Line Numbering menu.

```
Format: Line Numbering

    1 - Count Blank Lines                          Yes

    2 - Number Every n Lines, where n is           1

    3 - Position of Number from Left Edge          0.6"

    4 - Starting Number                            1

    5 - Restart Numbering on Each Page             Yes
```

7. Press Exit (F7) to return to your document.

8. Follow the instructions for viewing your document to see the difference.

Let's look at the choices you can make.

If you want to alter whether blank lines are counted, select **Count Blank Lines (1)**. The default setting is *Y* (for Yes), which means that the blank lines are counted. If you want the program to skip blank lines so that they are not counted, press *N* (for No).

Choose **Number Every n Lines (2)** when you want to change the interval that WordPerfect uses to number lines. When you change the value of "n," WordPerfect still counts every line, but it prints the line number only at the interval you specify. For example, if you type a 5 and press Enter, the program prints numbers only every five lines.

Line numbers are printed six-tenths of an inch from the left edge of the paper. To change this measurement, select **Position of Number from Left Edge (3)**, type a new measurement, and press Enter. For instance, you may prefer to have numbers at the left edge of each page or closer to the text.

If you have a document with a left margin of only six-tenths of an inch, you must change this setting to something smaller than your margin, or WordPerfect will print the line numbers on top of your text. For example, if you have a left margin of one-half inch, set **Position of Number from left Edge (3)** to three-tenths of one inch.

Lines are numbered starting with number 1, regardless of the actual line number in the text. Use **Starting Number (4)** to specify a new starting number—for instance, line 25. The first line of the document after the **[Ln Num: On]** code will then be numbered 25. This feature is useful if you don't want the first half of a page to be numbered, but you want WordPerfect to number line 25 *as line 25* and not as line 1.

Normally line numbering begins over again at 1 on each page so that you can refer to something on page 12, line 22. If you don't have page numbers, though, you might want line numbering to continue unbroken from one page to the next so that you can refer to something on line 334 without using a page number. To print continuous numbers, select **Restart Numbering on Each Page (5)** and press *N*.

WP 5 ≡ Summary

You have explored in detail three of WordPerfect's automatic numbering systems: Outlining, Paragraph Numbering, and Line Numbering. With these options you can do the following:

- Turn on Outline to number paragraphs automatically

- Use Paragraph Numbering to number paragraphs only when you request a number

- Edit (delete, add, or move) both types of paragraph numbering and watch WordPerfect automatically renumber the paragraphs

- Change the numbering style used to number paragraphs

- Use Line Numbering to number each line on the page

- Change the default settings for line numbering to specify when and how WordPerfect numbers lines

- Check line numbering with View Document

22

Assembling Document References

Anders R. Sterner is a partner of Tanner Propp Fersko & Sterner, a Manhattan law firm. Besides practicing general business law and being the firm rhetorician, he does computer consulting for the firm's clients and for other law firms using microcomputer systems. He is a WordPerfect beta tester, having been addicted since version 3.0. He types like a banshee; he can make a keyboard sing. ∎

For many writing tasks, the main text is just the tip of the iceberg. Often you need tables of contents, indexes, and other document references to help a reader navigate through what you have written.

In the old days, writers had to stop editing days before a document was due and start combing through the main text to prepare the document references. One of WordPerfect 5's handiest features is that it speeds up that process. With a little foresight and planning, you can work on a document right down to a few hours before a deadline, confident that as your main text changes, the document references will keep up with it.

This chapter shows you how to create lists, tables of contents, tables of authorities, and indexes. You also learn to use automatic cross-referencing, which lets you change the structure of your document and automatically maintain accurate references to footnotes, pages, and sections. Finally, you learn to use the Document Compare feature so that you can show someone else what was omitted from, or added to, a document without having to mark all those changes yourself.

The central example in this chapter is a sample legal brief and an accompanying affidavit. Both are used to illustrate the principles for marking and generating document references. Indexing is illustrated with a partial index from a book chapter, and the Document Compare feature is demonstrated with successive versions of two paragraphs from this chapter.

Let's suppose that a lawyer's written argument to the judge consists of 75 pages of main text (a lawyer is a person who writes a 75-page document and calls it a brief). The brief cites 45 cases in 4 jurisdictions, 8 state and 4 federal statutes, and 2 treatises. Half the argument is found in 48 footnotes. The affidavit (a sworn statement providing factual basis for the brief's legal argument, to which the brief refers) consists of 92 numbered paragraphs and introduces Exhibits A through X (Exhibits are documents supporting the facts sworn to).

The lawyer needs to assemble the following document references to help the reader through this morass of convoluted logic:

- A table of contents showing the layout of the brief

- A table of authorities cited in the brief

- A list of exhibits in the affidavit

The reader can use the table of contents to skip to any particular part of the brief. With the table of authorities, the reader can locate cases cited in the argument. Using the numbered list of included exhibits, the reader can easily find the significance attached to a particular supporting document.

Indexes are not common in legal documents, so this chapter uses a nonlegal example of an index—a partial index for a book on database applications—to illustrate WordPerfect's indexing feature.

The chapter concludes with an illustration of the Document Compare feature, designed to let you show changes in successive drafts of a document.

Before you read about each type of document reference, keep in mind that these techniques require that you plan ahead. They work much better if you decide from the outset which document references you want and provide for them as you go along. Planning ahead is especially important for a function like Document Compare, which compares an edited version of your document with the original on disk and highlights additions and deletions. If you make changes in a document and save it periodically (as you should) without first saving the original under a different name, you can't use Document Compare because you have nothing to compare to.

When you know that you need document references, you can't afford the attitude, "Right now I just want to get it down on paper; I'll do the fancy stuff later." Later will come, and you'll pay in the form of anxious, high-pressure, catch-up work against an inexorable deadline.

It is therefore a good idea to *start* work on the document by creating first the preliminary pages, or front matter. In each major section of this chapter, you'll find instructions for setting up pages for the tables and lists described. Before you write the first word, then, you should

- Create a cover page with the caption and title, complete with a paragraph numbering scheme. End the cover page with a hard page-break (Ctrl-Enter).

- Start page numbering anew with roman numerals, put in the Table of Contents title, and put in your ToC definition. End this too with a hard page-break (Ctrl-Enter).

- On the next page, put in the Table of Authorities title and the subheadings you want for the Table of Authorities. End this page too with a hard page-break (Ctrl-Enter).

- On the next page, restart page numbering again in arabic numerals. Save the document (F10), and start writing.

If doing all this seems overwhelming, don't despair. Just read on, and you will learn to create all these reference aids, beginning with lists.

Creating Lists

WordPerfect's List function is the simplest "reference generation" feature. If you're creating a legal document, you may want a list of exhibits; a scientific paper may need a list of tables; a book chapter may need a list of figures. The List feature allows you to mark specific items in the text as you create a document. Then, when you finish editing the document, the program generates a list of the marked items, followed by page numbers or other identifying features. On the final list, items are shown in the order in which they appear in the document.

Starting with the model affidavit, you are introduced to a number of basic techniques for making lists. Frankly, the suggestions for automating list-marking do not save very much time, but the same techniques save a great deal of sweat and error when you get to Table of Contents and the other document reference functions.

You can create as many as nine lists per document. Each item must be marked for the list in which it is to be included, as well as for features (such as boldfacing) that you want to include with the items on that list. List references contain only what you mark. Unlike Table of Authorities, there is no way to specify a separate text to be reported in the list. Therefore, your writing style has to be consistent. You have to say "The lease is Exhibit B, and the notice is Exhibit C" instead of "The lease and notice are Exhibits B and C, respectively" so that "Exhibit B" and "Exhibit C" can be marked separately.

Let's suppose that an affidavit mentions several leases, referred to as Exhibit A, Exhibit B, and so forth. As you write the affidavit, you mark each Exhibit reference (at the point each Exhibit is introduced) for inclusion in the list. Then, no matter how many times you edit the document, WordPerfect is able to find the item and generate a list of all marked items, in the proper order, with correct page numbers.

Marking Text for Lists

When you mark text for lists, you mark an item to include any codes for features that you want to appear with that item on the list. WordPerfect lets you choose from two separate approaches to marking text for lists.

Once again, it's important to mark text for lists as you write. You can always go back and delete items you don't want, but it's time-consuming and risky to search for things to mark after you finish writing the document.

Marking Text the Hard Way (Manually)

We call the method in this section the "hard way" because it takes several keystrokes, and these are enough to disrupt the creative process. Furthermore, the keystrokes can't really be put into a macro that will mark text for you because the material to be included will vary from one case to another. (If you're not familiar with macros, see Chapter 11.)

Let's suppose that you want a list of all exhibits referred to in an affidavit, along with the page numbers on which they first appear. Let's suppose also that you just typed the first item, *Exhibit A*, on your screen.

To mark "Exhibit A" for inclusion in a list, you must first block the word or phrase. Move the cursor to the first character of a word or phrase you want to include in the list (for example, to the *E* of *Exhibit*) and press Block (Alt-F4). Now, move the cursor to the end of the last word in the phrase (*A*).

TIP: To mark a word or a phrase quickly, use the space bar rather than the → key after you press Block (Alt-F4). If the last word of the phrase has no space after it, you may have to use the → key to highlight the last word. Keep in mind the other shortcuts for highlighting a block after you press Alt-F4, such as pressing Enter to make the cursor jump to the next hard return or typing a comma to make the cursor jump to the next comma.

Now mark the blocked text for a particular list. Press Mark Text (Alt-F5) and select List (2) from the menu at the bottom of the screen:

Mark for: 1 ToC; **2** List; **3** Index; **4** ToA: **0**

You now see a List Number: prompt, which asks you for the number of the list (from 1 through 9) on which you want to include this marked block. Type *1* for List 1. The highlighting of the block disappears, and you return to your document.

Next you may want to view the codes (optional). If you want to see the codes marking this phrase for List 1, press Reveal Codes (Alt-F3, or press F11). The codes should appear on-screen and resemble those shown in figure 22.1.

Repeat Steps 1 and 2 for any other words or phrases you want to mark now for List 1.

TIP: If you have several lists in your document and want to avoid confusion, keep a written record of them. The best method is to define your lists before you start writing. That way, you can allocate marked text to different lists as you write. Lists may come before or after your main text.

```
     3,    Defendant had theretofore, daily and hourly,
harangued, pestered, screamed at, vilified, and subjected to
shrill contempt and contumely all her neighbors, including
me, Indeed, more than 40 people testified against her at
trial, See People v, Therblig, unreported, decision annexed
hereto as Exhibit A,
                                         Doc 1 Pg 1 Ln 9,25" Pos 2,2"
[   ▲   ▲   ▲   ▲   ▲   ▲   ▲   ▲   ▲   ▲   ▲   ▲   ▲   ▲   ]
me, Indeed, more than 40 people testified against her at[SRt]
trial, [UND]See[und] [Target(CONVICT)][UND]People v, Therblig[und], unreported,
decision annexed[SRt]
hereto as [Mark:List,1][BOLD]Exhibit A[End Mark:List,1][bold],



Press Reveal Codes to restore screen
```

Fig. 22.1.
*Reveal Codes of text
marked for inclusion
in List 1.*

WordPerfect offers specialized lists that already have dedicated functions. The following are dedicated lists, shown with features that appear automatically without a need for feature codes:

- List 6   Includes captions (if any) in graphics figure boxes
- List 7   Includes captions of table boxes
- List 8   Includes captions of text boxes
- List 9   Includes captions of user-defined boxes

Marking Text the Easy Way (Using Styles)

Don't confuse this discussion on marking text with the section "Define the Style" under "Lists" in the Reference portion of the WordPerfect manual. Styles, new with WordPerfect 5, give you a way to automate document formatting. The following section discusses the use of styles for marking text. (For an in-depth exploration of styles, see Chapter 12.)

Creating a Style

Before you write a document, you can create a style for marking text. It isn't necessary to use a style to mark text, but a style speeds up the process of marking text for a list. More important, the principles that follow are vital to Table of Contents. To create a style, perform the following steps:

First, press Style (Alt-F8). The Styles screen appears. If you already defined some styles and indicated their file in Setup, they are listed on this screen.

Next, select **Create (3)** from the menu. The Styles: Edit menu appears.

From the Styles: Edit menu, select **Name** (**1**), type *List 1* as the name for the list in this example, and press Enter. Leaving Paired as is for Type, select **Description** (**3**), type a descriptive phrase such as *Includes in Exhibit List*, and press Enter. Your screen should now look like the one in figure 22.2.

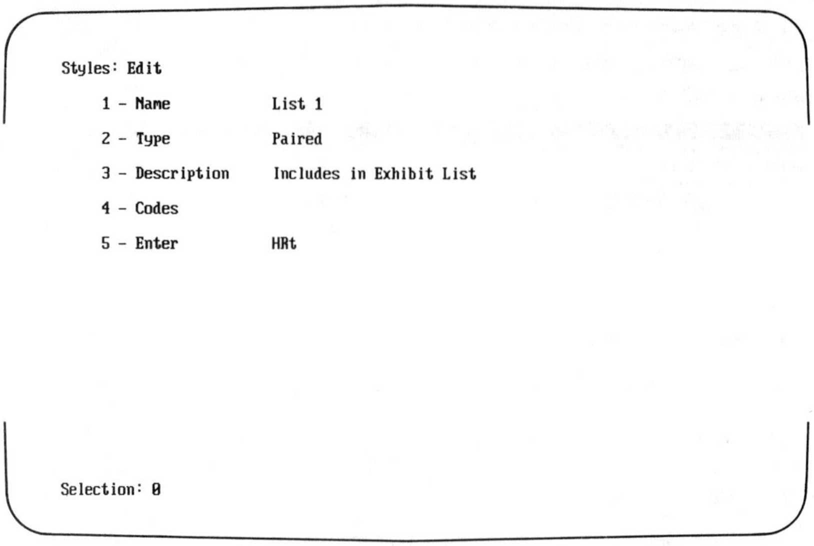

Fig. 22.2.

Styles: Edit menu with Name and Description defined.

```
Styles: Edit

    1 - Name          List 1

    2 - Type          Paired

    3 - Description   Includes in Exhibit List

    4 - Codes

    5 - Enter         HRt






    Selection: 0
```

Now Select **Codes** (**4**). You see what looks like a Reveal Codes screen with **[Comment]** at the left edge. **Comment** stands for the text that is inserted when the style is used.

Turn Block on by pressing Alt-F4. Then press Home, Home, and ↓ to move the cursor to a point just after the last item on the screen. Now mark the comment for inclusion in the list. Press Mark Text (Alt-F5), and a Mark for: prompt and a brief menu appear.

Select **List** (**2**) from the menu, and at the List Number: prompt that appears, type the list number. For this example, type *1*. The comment now becomes surrounded by list codes (see fig. 22.3).

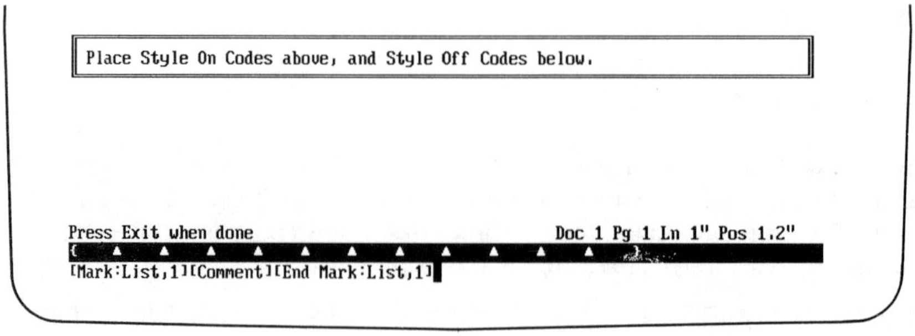

Fig. 22.3.

Mark and End Mark codes for List 1.

```
  Place Style On Codes above, and Style Off Codes below.




Press Exit when done                    Doc 1 Pg 1 Ln 1" Pos 1,2"
[Mark:List,1][Comment][End Mark:List,1]
```

Press Exit (**F7**) twice to return to the Styles screen and menu. List 1 and the brief description of it are now visible in the List of Styles. Select Save (**6**) from the menu along the bottom of the screen to save the style. At the prompt Filename:, give the full path name (for example, *C:\WP5\HEADINGS*) of your style library (if you're adding to existing styles) or a new file name (if you're creating a new style library).

If you're adding to your existing library, answer *Y* to the question whether to replace that file. If you give only a file name without the full path, your new heading is probably stored in a wrong and inaccessible subdirectory. Press Enter, and end the procedure by pressing Exit (F7).

Using a Created Style

Now that you defined this Style for marking text, you can use the following procedure to mark existing text—for example, text that you just wrote and now decide to mark.

To mark existing text, move the cursor to the beginning of the text you want to mark for a list and press Block (Alt-F4). Then move the cursor to the end of the block of text and press Style (Alt-F8). Now move the cursor to List 1 and turn the style **On** (**1**).

For our example, if you press Reveal Codes (Alt-F3 or F11) at this point, the screen should display the following codes surrounding the first list entry:

[Style On: List 1][BOLD]Exhibit A[bold].[StyleOff:List 1]

To mark text as you write it, do these steps instead. First, press Style (Alt-F8). Move the cursor to List 1 and turn the style **On** (**1**). Type the item to be included on the list. Press → to close the style, and you return to your document.

Creating Macros for a Style To Mark Text

You can simplify even more the process of marking text as you write it if you create for Steps 1, 2, and 3 a macro that turns style on and takes you to the point of typing the item. When you finish, press → once to end the style. The macro/style combination reduces the process of marking text to just a few extra keystrokes.

Note: If you aren't familiar with WordPerfect 5's macro capability, see Chapter 11.

To create a macro for marking text with Style, follow these steps. Press Macro Define (Ctrl-F10). At the Define Macro: prompt, type a name for the macro—something like *L1* (for List 1)—and press Enter. Use this name to invoke the macro when you want to run it. At the next prompt (Description:), type a descriptive title for the macro (such as *First List*) and press Enter. At the Macro Def prompt, press Style (Alt-F8). Now press Search (F2), type the exact name of your First List style (*List 1*, in our example), and press Enter. This directs WordPerfect to the style you created for marking text. Turn the style **On** (**1**), and you return to your document. Insert a {PAUSE} in the macro by pressing Ctrl-PgUp, 1, Enter. (This gives the user time to enter the text.) Press right arrow to get outside the style code. Press Macro Define (Ctrl-F10) again to stop recording the macro.

To use that macro to mark text as you type it, follow these steps. Press Macro (Alt-F10) to run a macro. At the Macro: prompt, type *L1* to invoke the macro and press Enter to mark text for List 1. Type the text you want to mark. Then press Enter to get outside the style and end the macro.

Defining a List

Defining means telling WordPerfect where you want it to place the list of marked items and how you want the list to look. You've been through the list of exhibits in the affidavit and are now ready to set up a page in the affidavit where you want the list to print. Usually, you place a list on a page by itself. To illustrate list definition, set up the page in the affidavit as described in the procedures that follow.

To create a List of Exhibits page, press Home, Home, ↓ to move the cursor to the end of the document and press Ctrl-Enter for a hard page-break. Do what you think is appropriate about page numbering. For instance, you may begin numbering again in roman because the list follows the main text. Or you may turn numbering off entirely.

Type *List of Exhibits* for a title. Now define the list of exhibits. First, place the cursor where you want the list to start. Press Mark Text (Alt-F5) and select **Define (5)** from the menu at the bottom of the screen. From the resulting Mark Text: Define menu (see fig. 22.4), select Define List (**2**).

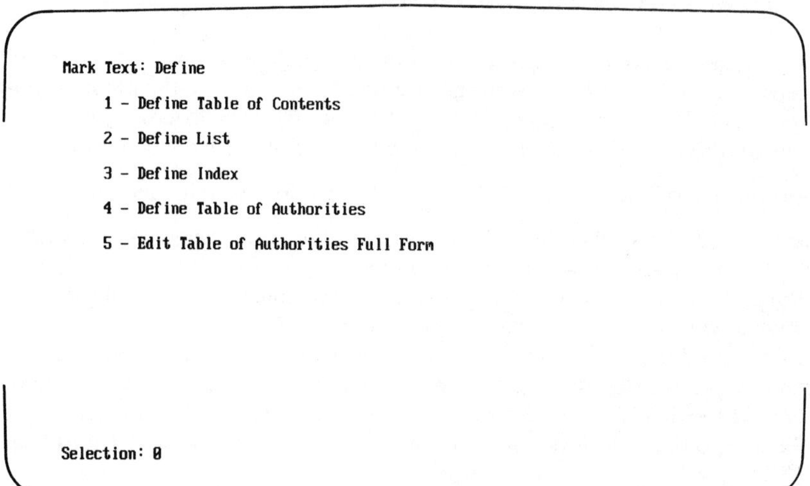

Fig. 22.4.

The Mark Text: Define menu.

```
Mark Text: Define

      1 - Define Table of Contents

      2 - Define List

      3 - Define Index

      4 - Define Table of Authorities

      5 - Edit Table of Authorities Full Form




   Selection: 0
```

At the prompt, type the number of the list. A List Definition menu appears, bearing the list number you just typed (see fig. 22.5). This menu offers five ways to handle page numbers, ranging from none to flush right with dot leaders.

```
List 1 Definition

    1 - No Page Numbers

    2 - Page Numbers Follow Entries

    3 - (Page Numbers) Follow Entries

    4 - Flush Right Page Numbers

    5 - Flush Right Page Numbers with Leaders




    Selection: 0
```

Fig. 22.5.
The List Definition menu.

Select the style you want. (This is the "style" the WordPerfect manual refers to under "'Lists" in the Reference section.) If you select **No Page Numbers** (**1**), the list is pointless. For most work, select Flush Right Page Numbers with **Leaders** (**5**), which is easiest to read. For the list of exhibits, in Reveal Codes you see [**Def Mark:List,1:5**] under the heading for the first list. End the page with a hard page-break (Ctrl-Enter). Save the document (F10) before you generate your list.

Generating Document References

All lists, as well as the Table of Contents, Table of Authorities, and cross-references, are generated in a single sweep, usually just before printing. As with all other functions in this chapter, you should plan to generate well ahead of the deadline for the document. Beware of long documents with several document references; the generating process can be quite slow, often requiring 45 minutes. Second, always plan to generate lists twice. The first time, you find your mistakes; the second time, you get it right.

CAUTION: Before you generate document references, be sure to save your document, and save an additional copy of it elsewhere. This advice is especially important when you are generating references from large documents. Long operations are more vulnerable to power disruptions, "bad spots" on a disk, and other calamities. If you carefully save your document and save a second copy elsewhere, your precious text is safe.

TIP: Except for the simplest, smallest tables, clear your second screen to free up as much RAM as possible before you start generating.

To generate a list, follow these steps. After saving, press Mark Text (Alt-F5). Then select **Generate** (6) from the menu at the bottom of the screen. A Mark Text: Generate menu appears (see fig. 22.6).

Fig. 22.6.

The Mark Text: Generate menu.

```
Mark Text: Generate

    1 - Remove Redline Markings and Strikeout Text from Document

    2 - Compare Screen and Disk Documents and Add Redline and Strikeout

    3 - Expand Master Document

    4 - Condense Master Document

    5 - Generate Tables, Indexes, Automatic References, etc.




    Selection: 0
```

Select **Generate Tables, Indexes, Automatic References, etc.** (5). WordPerfect issues the message Existing tables, lists, and indexes will be replaced. Continue? (Y/N). If you're sure that you want to go ahead, type *Y* to confirm your intention. WordPerfect begins generating, passing through the document several times, compiling document references, and reporting any irregularities it finds. When generating is done, your document appears on-screen with all tables and lists updated. Press Save (F10) to preserve the generated document.

The list of exhibits marked in the affidavit appears on-screen as shown in figure 22.7.

CAUTION: When you generate for the first time, WordPerfect inserts an **[EndDef]** code after each completed document reference. WordPerfect uses this code to determine what to delete when you generate again. Don't move or delete this code under any circumstances. WordPerfect is civilized enough not to delete anything, but it will report that it can't find the **[EndDef]** code and produce two tables, one after the other.

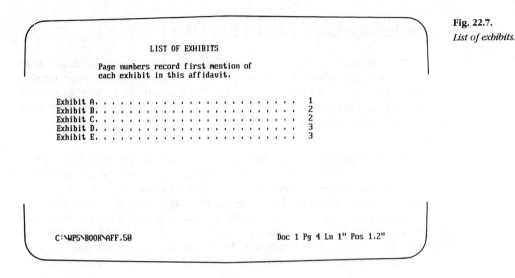

Fig. 22.7.
List of exhibits.

TIP: Some lists are better ordered alphabetically than by order of appearance. You can get that using an index, but you can have only one index in a document (or, indeed, in any collection of master and subdocuments). You can use a list to accomplish much the same thing, by generating once (to get the **[End Def]** code), and then putting a unique nonprintable ASCII code (such as ASCII 182) immediately *before* the List Definition and immediately *after* the **[End Def]** code for that list.

You then use a macro to cause the sort. That sounds easy, but there are some complications. First, because each entry in a list begins with [→**Indent** ←] **[Mar Rel]**, the sorter reads the text as being in Field 3. Second, unless you do something to prevent it, your **[List Def]** code will get swept up in the sort and perhaps end up in the middle of the list, producing weird results the next time you generate. Third, if you use Line Sort, but you have some multiline entries in the list, the sort will produce hash; so you have to use a Paragraph Sort—but paragraphs in single space are defined by *two* **[HRt]** codes, and a List has only a single **[HRt]** at the end of each item. Fourth, if you have multiline entries in your list, you may want them separated by an extra blank line.

LSTSRT.ARC, in DL0 (zero) of CompuServe's WordPerfect Support Group forum, contains a macro that deals with all those problems. This macro is fully documented. It works right out of the box, provided you mark your list with ASCII 182 codes (hold down Alt and press 1, 8, 2—without the commas—on the numeric keypad) as set forth above. If you want to use some other code, edit the macro to replace each instance of ASCII 182 with your own code. If you want to mark more than one list, you'll want to mark each list with a different unique ASCII code, and have a different macro—LSTSRT1, LSTSRT2, and so on—for each list. Teaching you to develop the macro yourself is beyond the scope of this chapter, requiring (as it does) use of the macro programming language.

Considering Other Uses for Lists

As you will see in the next chapter, WordPerfect now allows you to generate various tables, lists, and cross-references involving several otherwise separate but related documents. You may, for instance, have a brief that refers to an affidavit, which you want to generate together. Or you may have a dissertation or book spread out among any number of files. And what if the affidavit is so long that it has its own table of contents?

WordPerfect can handle only one table of contents for a set of related documents. The solution is to create a list in the affidavit and let the list masquerade as a table of contents. It must not bear the number of any other list in the set of related documents. Although lists don't have different heading levels, you can create artificial hierarchies within lists. You do this by enclosing within the list marks the formatting codes (L/R Indents, Indents, Tabs, Underlining, and the like) you use within the document itself to distinguish the level of headings. If you want the headings separated by a blank line, enclose a final hard return after each heading.

Creating a Table of Contents

This section assumes that you read and understood the preceding discussion of lists. Many of the procedures are identical or similar enough to be described by their differences.

Setting Up Automatic Paragraph Numbering

As you write, you may use automatic paragraph numbering to number paragraphs or headings and subheads in hierarchical material. Do this for two reasons: paragraph and outline numbers are necessary for cross-referencing, and the numbers are adjusted automatically if you move or delete any paragraphs or headings during editing.

Before you mark text for paragraph numbering, it's a good idea to define your paragraph numbering scheme. If you haven't already defined your system in Setup, or if you want to use a system different from the one you specified earlier, use the following procedures.

To view the current paragraph numbering scheme, follow these steps. First, press Date/Outline (Shift-F5). Select **Define** (**6**) from the menu at the bottom of the screen. You see the Paragraph Number Definition menu with the default settings (see fig. 22.8).

Select **Paragraph** (**2**). The current definition of paragraph levels is displayed. Now suppose that you want to use the following scheme of numbering paragraphs:

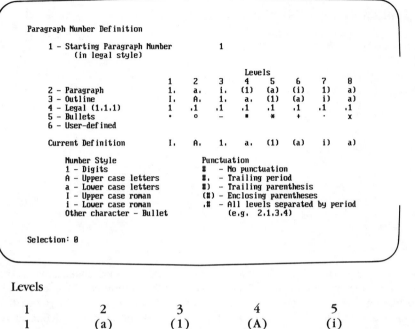

Fig. 22.8.
*Paragraph Number
Definition menu.*

Levels

1	2	3	4	5
1	(a)	(1)	(A)	(i)

To make this scheme the current definition, continue with these steps. Select User-defined (6). The cursor moves to the first column for you to define the number style and punctuation for Level 1 paragraphs. Type *1* and press Enter. (If 1 already exists, merely press Enter.) The cursor moves to the second column for definition of styles for Level 2 paragraphs. Type *(a)* and press Enter. The cursor jumps to the third column. Type *(1)* and press Enter. At the fourth column, type *(A)* and press Enter. At the fifth column, type *(i)* and press Enter. To delete the default styles for heading levels 6, 7, and 8, press space bar, Enter, space bar, Enter, space bar, Enter. Your screen should look like the one in figure 22.9.

TIP: The remaining three paragraph numbering definitions can be anything you like, particularly different kinds of bullets, inserted by using the Compose function (Ctrl-2). See the discussion of Compose in Chapters 18 and 19.

TIP: It's a good idea not to define the paragraph numbering definitions to include trailing periods, because they show up in automatic cross-referencing like this:

    See section 1.(a).(1).(B).(ii). above.

Instead, include trailing periods in the macro or style that invokes automatic numbering.

Fig. 22.9.

Paragraph Number Definition menu after changing the numbering scheme.

```
Paragraph Number Definition

    1 - Starting Paragraph Number         1
            (in legal style)

                                        Levels
                            1    2    3    4    5    6    7    8
    2 - Paragraph           1.   a.   i.   (1)  (a)  (i)  1)   a)
    3 - Outline             I.   A.   1.   a.   (1)  (a)  i)   a)
    4 - Legal (1.1.1)       1    .1   .1   .1   .1   .1   .1   .1
    5 - Bullets             •    o    -    ■    *    +    ·    x
    6 - User-defined

    Current Definition      1    (a)  (1)  (A)  (i)

        Number Style                Punctuation
        1 - Digits                  #   - No punctuation
        A - Upper case letters      #.  - Trailing period
        a - Lower case letters      #)  - Trailing parenthesis
        I - Upper case roman        (#) - Enclosing parentheses
        i - Lower case roman        .#  - All levels separated by period
        Other character - Bullet          (e.g. 2.1.3.4)


    Selection: 0
```

If you're writing something with numbered paragraphs, you can make a macro that ends one paragraph and begins the next by putting in the number. (For a complete explanation of macros, see Chapter 11.) And if, for instance, you ordinarily write in double-space and like three blank lines between paragraphs, you may define such a macro as follows. (Note: The remaining instructions assume that you have custom-defined your paragraph numbering scheme in the manner just recommended. If not, you must make appropriate adjustments in the macro. Putting the period in manually after the number, instead of including it in the paragraph numbering definition, has advantages when you come to automatic cross-referencing).

Here's how to do the macro. First, press Macro Define (Ctrl-F10). At the prompt Define Macro:, press Alt-Z. At the prompt Description:, enter *Paragraph Change*. Record the following keystrokes: press Format (Shift-F8), select **Line** (**1**), select **Line** Spacing (**6**), and type *1*. Now press Enter three times to get back to the screen.

Press Enter to create a third line between paragraphs. Press Format (Shift-F8) and select **Line** (**1**). Select **Line** Spacing (**6**) and type *2*. Press Enter three times to get back to the screen. Tab to the position for the paragraph number. Press Date/ Outline (Shift-F5); then select **Para Num** (**5**). Type *1* (for the paragraph level) and press Enter. Your automatic paragraph number appears on-screen.

Type a period after the number and press Tab to put you at the start of the text. End macro definition by pressing Macro Define (Ctrl-F10).

For guidelines on storing and managing macro files, see Chapter 11.

Marking Text for a Table of Contents (ToC)

In general, you mark text for the Table of Contents by blocking the text and any desired codes, then specifying to WordPerfect the level of that heading.

When you mark chapter or section headings for inclusion in the Table of Contents, you must make an initial decision about how you want the result to look. WordPerfect puts a blank line before all first-level Table of Contents entries, but subheads are not separated by blank lines:

> This is a first-level heading
> > This is a second-level subhead
> > This is a second-level subhead
> > This is a second-level subhead
>
> This is a first-level heading
> > This is a second-level subhead

This format is fine where the subheads are only one line long. But if you have subheads below the first level that wrap to the next line, you want to maintain a blank line between them:

> This is a first-level subhead
>
> > This is a long second-level subhead that wraps to the
> > next line
>
> > This is a second-level subhead
>
> > This is a second level subhead

With section titles (as opposed to headings of logical argument) you can choose how you want them to print—centered or flush left, for example—in the Table of Contents.

Marking ToC Entries the Hard Way

Let's suppose that you want the "Argument" title for your legal brief centered, with the first-level headings flush left and the second-level subheads indented.

To mark this title for the Table of Contents so that it appears centered, follow these steps. First press Reveal Codes (Alt-F3, or F11). Then place the cursor to the left of the first Center code, turn Block on (Alt-F4), and move the cursor to the right of the second center code. Press Mark Text (Alt-F5) and select ToC (**1**). At the prompt for ToC Level, type *1*. Note: if you want this title flush left, block the text so that the Center codes are excluded.

To mark the first-level heading, follow these steps. Press Reveal Codes (Alt-F3, or F11). Position the cursor on the **[Par Num:1]** code. Press Block (Alt-F4) and highlight the text up through the final period. Press Mark Text (Alt-F5) and select ToC (**1**). At the prompt for ToC Level, type *1*. The text appears as shown in figure 22.10.

To mark a second-level subhead, repeat the procedure, but in the next-to-last step specify the ToC Level as *2*. Go through the entire document, marking each level of heading.

Fig. 22.10.

Marking text for a first-level heading in the Table of Contents.

```
more appropriate method of fact-finding in this unusual

case.

                            Argument

1.   HISTORICALLY, TRIAL BY JURY AS WE KNOW IT IS A
     RECENT UPSTART, BY NO MEANS UNIVERSAL.

C:\WP5\BOOK\BRIEF.50                        Doc 1 Pg 2 Ln 3.5" Pos 5.5"
[  ▲   ▲    ▲    ▲    ▲    ▲    ▲    ▲    ▲    ▲   ▲   }
[HRt]
[Mark:ToC,1][Par Num:1],[→Indent←]HISTORICALLY, TRIAL BY JURY AS WE KNOW IT IS A
[SRt]
RECENT UPSTART, BY NO MEANS UNIVERSAL.[End Mark:ToC,1][HRt]
[HRt]
[HRt]
[Mark:ToC,1][→Indent←][Par Num:2][→Indent][UND]The Founding Fathers, When They G
uaranteed[SRt]
The Right to Trial By Jury, Did Not Mean To[SRt]
Exclude Older Forms of Trial[und].[End Mark:ToC,1][HRt]

Press Reveal Codes to restore screen
```

Although you haven't yet read how to generate a Table of Contents, you will now see what a partial, generated Table of Contents looks like. Don't worry about the steps for generating a Table of Contents. You will get to them further in the chapter. Note in figure 22.11 how no line separates first-level headings from second-level subheads.

Fig. 22.11.

Generated Table of Contents with no blank line between headings and subheads (partial ToC shown).

```
                      TABLE OF CONTENTS



Introduction . . . . . . . . . . . . . . . .   1

                 Argument . . . . . . . . . .   2

1.   HISTORICALLY, TRIAL BY JURY AS WE KNOW IT IS A
     RECENT UPSTART, BY NO MEANS UNIVERSAL.. . . . . . .   2
     (a)  The Founding Fathers, When They Guaranteed
          The Right to Trial By Jury, Did Not Mean To
          Exclude Older Forms of Trial.. . . . . . . . .   2
     (b)  The Laws of This State Do Not Expressly For-
          bid Trial by Alternative Means.. . . . . . . .   3

2.   TRIAL BY FIRE IS MORE APPROPRIATE THAN TRIAL BY
     JURY IN THIS CASE.. . . . . . . . . . . . . . . .   4
     (a)  The Offense Charged is Ancient, Venerable,
          and Ineluctably Associated with Trial by
          Alternative Means. . . . . . . . . . . . . . .   4

C:\WP5\BOOK\BRIEF.50                        Doc 1 Pg 1 Ln 4.83" Pos 1.2"
```

Now let's see how to mark text so that a blank line appears between all headings and subheads.

Marking All ToC Entries as Level 1 Headings

You have seen in figure 22.11 that WordPerfect always places a blank line before first-level headings. If your subheads tend to be long, however, your Table of Contents may end up looking crowded. You can go back through the Table after you generate it and manually place a blank line before each subhead, but this method is tedious. On the other hand, if you're resourceful and foresighted, you can tell WordPerfect that all headings are first-level, so they get blank lines between them, then differentiate the lower-level headings by some other means. What you want to end up with is a Table of Contents like the one shown in figure 22.12.

```
                    TABLE OF CONTENTS .


  Introduction . . . . . . . . . . . . . . . . . . . . . .   1

                    Argument . . . . . . . . . . .   2

  1.   HISTORICALLY, TRIAL BY JURY AS WE KNOW IT IS A
       RECENT UPSTART, BY NO MEANS UNIVERSAL.. . . . . . .   2

       (a)  The Founding Fathers, When They Guaranteed
            The Right to Trial By Jury, Did Not Mean To
            Exclude Older Forms of Trial. . . . . . . . .   2

       (b)  The Laws of This State Do Not Expressly For-
            bid Trial by Alternative Means.. . . . . . . .   3

  2.   TRIAL BY FIRE IS MORE APPROPRIATE THAN TRIAL BY
       JURY IN THIS CASE.. . . . . . . . . . . . . . . . .   4

       (a)  The Offense Charged is Ancient, Venerable,
  C:\WP5\BOOK\BRIEF.50                     Doc 1 Pg 1 Ln 1" Pos 1.2"
```

Fig. 22.12.

Table of Contents with blank lines inserted between headings and subheads (partial ToC shown).

For instance, if you mark text including the codes for indentation, underlining, and other format factors, your Table of Contents appears with these in place. Let's use the same legal brief example to demonstrate how to mark text for this appearance.

To mark this way for a Table of Contents, block each subhead separately, starting at the left margin and continuing until you capture all the codes for that level. Be sure to capture the code for underlining and indentation at the second level, or the second level will not appear subordinate to the first-level headings at the left margin. Mark all entries as ToC Level 1. Figure 22.13 shows a second-level subhead marked as a first-level heading. Note that the **[Mark:ToC,1]** code precedes the codes for [→Indent] and **[Par Num:2].**

Note that if you mark all subheads as first level, page numbers for all headings and subheadings appear in the final product, as shown in figure 22.12.

If your Table of Contents runs over several pages, you may be disappointed to find that headings and subheads are split between succeeding pages. You cannot avoid this split automatically, but you can correct it by going back through the Table of Contents after it is generated and using block protect to rejoin any split headings.

Fig. 22.13.

*Marking a subhead
as a first-level
heading for a table of
contents.*

```
                    .Argument

  1.   HISTORICALLY, TRIAL BY JURY AS WE KNOW IT IS A
       RECENT UPSTART, BY NO MEANS UNIVERSAL.


       (a)  The Founding Fathers, When They Guaranteed
            The Right to Trial By Jury, Did Not Mean To
            Exclude Older Forms of Trial.

  C:\WP5\BOOK\BRIEF.58                        Doc 1 Pg 2 Ln 4" Pos 1.2"
  [     ▲     ▲     ▲     ▲     ▲     ▲     ▲     ▲     ▲     }
  [HRt]
  [HRt]
  [Mark:ToC,1][→Indent←][Par Num:2][→Indent][UND]The Founding Fathers, When They G
  uaranteed[SRt]
  The Right to Trial By Jury, Did Not Mean To[SRt]
  Exclude Older Forms of Trial[und],[End Mark:ToC,1][HRt]
  [HRt]
  [HRt]
  [Ln Spacing:2][Tab]Common law long recognized the virtues of letting God[SRt]
  decide the rights and wrongs of a dispute.  In ancient[SRt]

  Press Reveal Codes to restore screen
```

(Block protect codes within the ToC codes do not survive into the Table of
Contents.)

Using Styles To Mark ToC Entries

So far, you've seen how to mark headings for inclusion in the Table of Contents,
using a method equivalent to that shown for Lists. (But marking headings is a lot
more important with ToC.) As with Lists, you can also define a paired style for every
level of the Table of Contents. Each style should contain all the formatting codes
(including the automatic paragraph numbering code manually set for the correct
level) that you use for the level of heading in question. (If you need a basic
understanding of WordPerfect Styles, see Chapter 12.)

With the Style method, you can not only save keystrokes but also change the way a
particular heading level is handled by using a single command. For example, you can
put a second indent in front of second-level subheads throughout the document just
by editing the Heading 2 style you created. Let's prepare a style for a second-level
subhead in another example like the one you just worked with:

(a) <u>The Offense Charged is Ancient, Venerable, and Ineluctably
    Associated with Trial by Alternative Means</u> 4

To prepare a style for marking ToC text, follow these steps. Press Styles (Alt-F8); if
you have indicated a Style library in setup by filename, it appears here. Select
Create (3). From the resulting menu, select **Name (1)**; type an appropriate name,
such as *Heading 2*. Leave the Paired choice as is; select **Description (3)** and enter
something like *Marks Heading for Level 2 ToC*. Next, select **Codes (4)** to bring up
the Codes screen with its comment section. To be on the safe side, change to
single-spacing: press Format (Shift-F8), select **Line (1)**, choose Line **Spacing (6)**,
type *1*, and press Enter. Press Exit (F7) to return to the Styles screen.

Press Left/Right indent (Shift-F4). Put in the automatic paragraph code by pressing Date/Outline (Shift-F5). Choose **P**ara Num (**5**), type *2* (or the level you chose), and press Enter. Now press Indent (F4); then press Underline (F8). Use the right arrow (→) to move the cursor to the other side of the comment. Press Underline (F8) to turn underlining off. Type a period to include the period in the ToC subhead but to prevent its being underlined. Press Home, Home, → to close the paired codes of the style.

Now press Enter two or more times for blank lines to separate the subhead from the text that will follow. Position the cursor immediately before the first [→**Indent** ←]. Turn on Block (Alt-F4) and move the cursor to a point immediately to the left of the first **[HRt]**. Mark the comment for inclusion in the ToC. Press Mark Text (Alt-F5). Select **T**oC (**1**) and type *2*. The comment and its associated codes to be transferred to the Table of Contents are now surrounded by the ToC codes (see fig. 22.14).

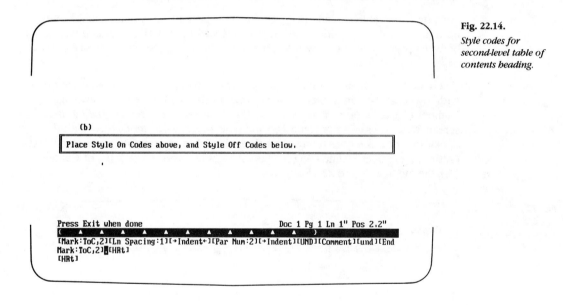

Fig. 22.14.
Style codes for second-level table of contents heading.

Press Exit (F7) twice and **S**ave (**6**). Then end with Exit (F7).

When you are ready to type a second-level heading, use the style you just created. Press Styles (Alt-F8) and move the cursor to Heading 2. Turn the style **O**n (**1**). Type the text for the heading and press →.

TIP: You can make the process even easier by adding a macro that duplicates Steps 1, 2, and 3. You can then type the heading, pause, and continue. To create these macros, see the procedures given for "Marking Text for Lists Using Style."

> **TIP:** For a ready-made and fully documented style library of headings and an Alt-H macro that runs them and also inserts single-spacing and conditional end-of-page codes as needed, download HEAD.ARC from Data Library 0 (zero) in CompuServe's WordPerfect Support Group. You can reach that special interest group (SIG) by logging into CompuServe and entering *G WPSG* at the prompt.

Defining the Table of Contents

Plan this page as part of your front matter before you start writing. The Table of Contents is generally placed just after the cover or title page.

First, start the Table of Contents page on a new page by moving the cursor to the bottom of the cover or title page and pressing Ctrl-Enter to insert a hard page-break between pages. The cursor is now at the top of what will be the Table of Contents page.

To create the Table of Contents page, follow these steps. To start page numbering with lowercase roman numerals, press Format (Shift-F8), **Page** (**2**), New Page Number (**6**) and type *i*. Press Enter and then Exit (F7) to return to the editing screen. Next, press Center (Shift-F6) and type *Table of Contents*. Now with the cursor two or three lines below the title of the Table of Contents, press Mark Text (Alt-F5) and select **Define** (**5**) (see fig. 22.4). When you select Table of Contents (**1**), the menu in figure 22.15 appears.

Fig. 22.15.
Table of Contents Definition menu.

```
Table of Contents Definition

    1 - Number of Levels            1

    2 - Display Last Level in       No
        Wrapped Format

    3 - Page Numbering - Level 1    Flush right with leader
                         Level 2
                         Level 3
                         Level 4
                         Level 5
                                            ⋮

    Selection: 0
```

Select **Number of Levels** (**1**) and type *5*. When you do this, Page Numbering Style option attaches the "'Flush right with leader" style option to all five levels. Just to see the other style options for your table of contents, select **Page Numbering** (**3**). The following menu is displayed along the bottom of the screen:

1 None; **2 Pg** # Follows; **3 (Pg** # Follows); **4** Flush Rt; **5** Flush Rt with **Leader**

Unless you want the last level wrapped, skip item 2; select the numbering style you want at item 3. Select Flush Rt with **Leader** (**5**) unless required otherwise; this is easiest for the reader to follow.

In Reveal Codes (Alt-F3, or F11), your screen should display

[Def Mark:ToC,5:5,5,5,5].

End the Table of Contents with a hard page-break (Ctrl-Enter).

Generating the Table of Contents

As you remember, all document references generate together. To generate a table of contents, follow the steps presented under "Generating Document References."

Figure 22.16 shows a printed Table of Contents.

Fig. 22.16.
Printed Table of Contents.

```
                        TABLE OF CONTENTS


     Introduction  . . . . . . . . . . . . . . . . . . . .    1

                          Argument  . . . . . . . . .    2

     1.   HISTORICALLY, TRIAL BY JURY AS WE KNOW IT IS A
          RECENT UPSTART, BY NO MEANS UNIVERSAL. . . . . .    2

          (a)  The Founding Fathers, When They Guaranteed
               The Right to Trial By Jury, Did Not Mean To
               Exclude Older Forms of Trial. . . . . . . .    2

          (b)  The Laws of This State Do Not Expressly For-
               bid Trial by Alternative Means. . . . . . .    3

     2.   TRIAL BY FIRE IS MORE APPROPRIATE THAN TRIAL BY
          JURY IN THIS CASE. . . . . . . . . . . . . . . .    4

          (a)  The Offense Charged is Ancient, Venerable,
               and Ineluctably Associated with Trial by
               Alternative Means. . . . . . . . . . . . .     4

          (b)  Of the Alternative Means Traditionally Em-
               ployed, Only Fire Is Available. . . . . . .    5

          (c)  Trial By Fire Serves The Interests of Judi-
               cial Economy. . . . . . . . . . . . . . . .    5

     Conclusion  . . . . . . . . . . . . . . . . . . . . .    5




                               i
```

Using Multiple Tables of Contents

For help with problems associated with generating Tables of Contents for two related documents, tables that must be generated simultaneously, see the earlier discussion, "Considering Other Uses for Lists."

Creating a Table of Authorities (ToA)

The Table of Authorities in a document provides long-form references to any authorities cited in the text. In our brief, a ToA includes the exact sources of cases cited in the argument. Once the long-form citation for a particular authority is established, the writer can later refer to that authority by a short-form abbreviation of the citation. In this section, you'll see how to mark the text temporarily as you write and how to go back into the edited document and use those marks and a macro to mark all items for the Table of Authorities in one sweep.

Adjusting Setup for the ToA

Before starting your document, you should first enter Setup to specify some features of your Table of Authorities. Decide whether you want underlining in the text marked for a Table of Authorities to be included in the actual table. If you don't want underlining to appear in the table, skip the following procedure. (Ordinarily you *do* want underlining to carry through; as it comes from the factory, WP5 is set to *exclude* it. This procedure changes that default—you should need to do it only one time.)

To maintain underlining on items to be included in a table of authorities, follow these steps. Press Setup (Shift-F1) and select Initial Settings (5). Select Table of Authorities (6). The menu in figure 22.17 is shown.

Select Underlining Allowed (2) and type *Y* to change the default setting to Yes. Press Exit (F7) twice to return to the screen.

Marking Text for the ToA

Unlike Table of Contents and List markings, most Table of Authorities markings are best done *not* as you go along, but when the document is nearly ready for the final printing—when you finish editing. Nothing is worse than going through the completed document and trying to find the cases you added during editing.

If an authority is cited several times, you may want to use a macro *after* you edit. On the other hand, you should fully mark treatises, statutes, and other authorities besides cases that are clearly going to be cited only once—it saves having to find them later, and the MARK macro system (described below) does not work well with them.

```
Setup: Table of Authorities

     1 - Dot Leaders                        Yes

     2 - Underlining Allowed                No

     3 - Blank Line between Authorities     Yes




     Selection: 0
```

Fig. 22.17.
*Setup: Table of
Authorities menu.*

It is virtually impossible to mark a brief for a Table of Authorities if you are not the author; and if you are the author, it is still hard if someone else does the typing for you. The person marking really has to know what to look for, such as the kinds of citations that may not fit the general rules outlined in the following discussion.

TIP: As you mark cases, keep a handwritten list (or a list in WordPerfect's second window) of those you already marked. Some appear more than once in long form, and it's easy to put in a second long-form Table of Authorities code by mistake.

When you refer to a case in the text, use either the long form of citation or a short form of citation not only unique to that case but also not duplicated elsewhere in the text. For instance, the short form for *United Airlines, Inc. v. AFL-CIO* is *United Airlines*, not *United*, because the word *united* can appear elsewhere in text not referring to the case.

If you refer to different decisions in the same case, use designations like *Tavoulareas (I)* and *Tavoulareas (II)*. Note that the parentheses are needed to differentiate between the two. If you search for *Tavoulareas I*, WordPerfect picks up *Tavoulareas II* as well. The parentheses make each case unique.

If at all possible, make the short form of reference to an item duplicate part of the long form so that a search for the short form finds the long-form citations as well. Cite each case the same way *every* time, and be absolutely consistent in your use of short references.

Marking Temporarily While You Write

To mark cases efficiently, you must observe a few rules in the course of creating the document. The process of creating a Table of Authorities works best when you mark temporarily as you write, then search for those marks at the end when you are ready to mark the cases for the Table of Authorities.

The best way to mark cases temporarily as you write is to place a backslash ($\backslash$) immediately before the *long-form* citation. Thus, in Reveal Codes, a citation looks like the following:

\[**UND**]U.S. v. Royall[**und**], 57 U.S. 427 (1837)

Don't bother marking short-form citations temporarily.

The backslash marking also works for the ancillary program CiteRite (JURISoft Corp., Cambridge, MA; at this writing not yet adapted to WP5, but great with WP4.2), a helpful program for correctly citing authorities. The backslash or any other character not used elsewhere in the document is easy to find when you are ready to mark it.

Leave the backslashes in the document as it goes through its several drafts. After you settle on a version of the text, run CiteRite or do your cite check by other means, and make all corrections to citations. At this point you should not have marked *any* case citations (that is, citations other than books, statutes, and the like) with anything other than the backslash.

Using the macro system described in this section, you can then mark text for the Table of Authorities in one sweep, *after* all the citations have been corrected.

Marking the Finished Document

To mark text for inclusion in the Table of Authorities, follow these steps. Find the first citation (which should be in long form). You can find it very easily by doing an Extended Search (Home, F2) for the backslash. If you didn't use the backslash, search for the underline code. Press Backspace to delete the backslash (if any), or use the left arrow to position the cursor left of the underline code. Then turn on Block (Alt-F4), and press Shift-0 (zero) to move the highlight to the right parenthesis at the end of the citation. This procedure should block the whole citation because most end in a parenthesis. In some cases, however, you may have to press Shift-0 (zero) once or twice more to get the whole thing in. (Citations for books, statutes, and similar items have to be blocked by eye. They vary, so you should mark them as you write.)

Now press Mark Text (Alt-F5) and select ToA (4). Enter the number of the Table of Authorities section where you want to place the citation. A screen appears showing what you've blocked; edit it so it looks as you want it to in the Table of Authorities. (In particular, remove any reference to a specific page—other than the first page—of a decision.) There is no wrapping in Table of Authorities, so you should end the first line about two inches from the left margin and tab in once for the second and subsequent lines, which also end two inches from the right margin (see fig. 22.18).

```
    Farhadi v. Anavian, 321 Misc.2d 194, 345 N.Y.S.2d
         229 (Sup. Ct., N.Y. County 1981)




    Press Exit when done                          Ln 1" Pos 1.2"
```

Fig. 22.18.
Editing screen for the full form of the authority.

When you finish editing, WordPerfect asks you for the unique short form that you'll use to refer to that authority. Type exactly the form you will use (or edit the string suggested on the prompt line).

For the example shown here, the status line would display the following:

Short Form: Farhadi v. Anavian, 321 Misc.2d 194, 345

Using cursor and delete keys, edit that to read

Short Form: Farhadi

To check that the short form also captures the long form in a search and to prepare for using the MARK macro, do a search for the short-form reference after you finish defining the long form. You should end at your first long-form reference to the case, which you just marked.

To mark all the other long- and short-form references to that case, now use the MARK macro described in the next section.

Creating the MARK Macro To Mark Text for ToA

Once you create the MARK macro, you can let WordPerfect find cases for you. This macro is absolutely the *best* way to go about marking for a Table of Authorities. (Note: WP5 comes with a factory-created MARK.WPM for inserting a bookmark. This MARK macro is not that MARK macro. Delete it.)

Note: Creating the MARK macro requires you to use WordPerfect 5's macro programming language. If you haven't read Chapter 11 on macros or Appendix C on the macro programming language, you are urged to do so before you proceed. At the very least, you should be familiar with the basics of macro creation in WordPerfect 5. Or you can download the MARK macro ready-made and ready to run, with complete documentation from CompuServe's WordPerfect Support Group. At the

CompuServe Prompt, enter *G WPSG* (see the discussion above regarding HEAD.ARC). MARK.WPM is in CASES.ARC in Data Library 0 (zero).

To create the MARK macro yourself, follow these steps. Press Macro Define (Ctrl-F10) and at the Define Macro: prompt enter *MARK*. For a description, type *Marks Cases for ToA*. At the flashing Define macro: prompt, hold down the Alt key and type *023* on the numeric keypad (not the number keys across the top). A funny-looking ASCII symbol (↕) appears on-screen when you release the Alt key. The symbol's purpose is to mark your starting point so that WordPerfect can return after marking the other references to the case. Now press Macro Define (Ctrl-F10) to end the macro.

Now that you created the first step of the MARK macro, you must get into the Macro Editor and modify MARK accordingly. You remember from Chapter 11 that you cannot use the editor to create a macro from scratch. You can get to the editor only from the menu that comes up when you try to create a macro with the same name as an existing macro.

So press Macro Define (Ctrl-F10) again, and at the Define macro: prompt, enter *MARK*. Because you gave the name of an existing macro, a menu appears that allows you to edit existing macros. Select Edit (**2**). The macro edit screen for MARK is displayed, showing {DISPLAY OFF} (the default) and the ASCII 023 code. Select Action (**2**) to place the cursor in the edit screen; move the cursor to the immediate left of the ASCII 023 code. Access WordPerfect's command language by pressing Ctrl-PgUp. (What follow are rote instructions. For an explanation of their significance, see Appendix C.)

A scrolling menu of macro commands appears on the upper right with the cursor highlighting the first term. Move the cursor to {ON NOT FOUND}action~ and press Enter. Now press Ctrl-PgUp again, move the cursor to {GO}label~, and press Enter. Type *B*; then press and hold down the Shift key as you press the tilde key (~) twice. Now your screen should look like this:

{DISPLAY OFF}{ON NOT FOUND}{GO}B~~ ↕

Move the cursor to the right of the ASCII 023 code. Press Ctrl-PgUp, move the cursor to {LABEL}label~, and press Enter. Type *A*; then press and hold down the Shift key as you press the tilde key (~) twice. Press Macro Define (Ctrl-F10). This procedure has the effect of toggling you out of the macro editing mode into a mode where every function you press is inserted into the macro, instead of being executed. Thus F7 inserts {EXIT} into the macro instead of exiting you from the edit screen.

Now press Home, Forward Search (F2), Forward Search (F2). Press Mark Text (Alt-F5), select ToA Short Form (**4**), and press Enter. Press Macro Define (Ctrl-F10) to toggle back to editing mode. Press Ctrl-PgUp to access the command language again. Move the cursor to {GO}label~ and press Enter. Type *A*; then press and hold down the Shift key as you press the tilde key (~) once. Press Ctrl-PgUp to display the list of macro commands. Move the cursor to {LABEL}label~ and press Enter. Type *B*; then press and hold down the Shift key as you press the tilde key (~) once.

The macro created up to this point finds what is in the search memory when the search starts (in our example, this is your short-form reference). At each instance, the macro inserts a short-form ToA reference. When WordPerfect finds no more references, the macro executes what you are about to put in following Label B.

Now you need to have the macro erase the ASCII 023 code at the starting point and let you continue to mark additional authorities. To finish the MARK macro, follow these steps. Press Macro Define (Ctrl-F10) to toggle back into entry mode. Press Home, Backward Search (Shift-F2). Hold down the Alt key; type *023* on the numeric keypad to insert the ASCII code; release the Alt key. Press Foward Search (F2), then press the back space key. Move back into editing mode with Macro Define (Ctrl-F10) and press Exit (F7) to save the macro and exit the macro editor.

The macro editor screen shown in figure 22.19 displays the contents of the MARK macro.

Fig. 22.19.
MARK macro in the macro editor.

```
Macro: Edit

        File        MARK.WPM

    1 - Description   Marks Cases for ToA

    2 - Action

    {DISPLAY OFF}{ON NOT FOUND}{GO}B~~‡{LABEL}A~~{Home}{Search}{Search}
    {Mark Text}4{Enter}{GO}A~{LABEL}B~{Home}{Search Left}‡{Search}
    {Backspace}

    Selection: 0
```

Use the MARK macro by pressing Macro (Alt-F10) and entering *MARK*. Once WordPerfect finds all occurrences of this case, you are ready to search for the next case, mark it, search for the short form, and invoke the MARK macro again. Do not run the MARK macro until you have searched for and found the first occurrence of the short-form reference of the case for which you are presently marking all other occurrences.

Correcting Mistaken References

Inevitably, you'll find mistakes or needed changes after you mark citations. If you have to change the way a citation is reported in the Table of Authorities, follow these steps. From the first page of the main text (to avoid previously generated ToA's) press Extended Search (Home-F2) for the short-form citation; the first reference you come to should contain the long-form code.

Using the example, from the top of page 1 press Extended Search (Home-F2), type *Farhadi*, and press Extended Search again. Move the cursor a little below it and press Mark Text (Alt-F5). Now select **Define** (**5**). Select Edit Table of Authorities Full Form (**5**) and make changes on the editing screen. When you've made corrections, press Exit (F7). At this point WordPerfect prompts you for the section number; change it if you marked it wrong in the first place.

TIP: Always remember that if there is a mistake in the original citation, you must edit both the citation and the full-form ToA code.

Marking a large brief can take a couple of hours, especially if you allow for a few dry runs before you get it right. Generating takes a *long* time; leave yourself plenty of time at the end.

Defining a Table of Authorities

You should define the Table of Authorities when you start to write the document. You can amend it if necessary, but you should at least try to get it right at the start.

As with all other tables, the Table of Authorities should be contained in a separately numbered part of the document. Specifically, there *must* be a hard page-break and a new page number code somewhere after the last Table of Authorities section definition and the first citation marked for inclusion.

Remember that the first page of the Table of Authorities usually follows the last page of the Table of Contents in a brief. Front matter for a brief usually consists of the following (in this order): cover page, Table of Contents, and Table of Authorities.

Make certain that you put a hard page-break (Ctrl-Enter) at the bottom of the ToC page. Next, to set up the Table of Authorities page, follow these steps. Type *Table of Authorities* (centered) and mark this title for inclusion in the Table of Contents. Press Enter three times, Center (Shift-F6), Underline (F8) and type the name of first section heading. In a legal brief, you may have separate sections labeled (for instance) "Decisions," "Statutes," and "Other Authorities." In the example used in this chapter, the first section is entitled "Decisions—State." Subsequent sections are entitled "Decisions—Federal," "Statutes," and "Other Authorities."

After the first section head, enter the Table of Authorities definition (see the next procedure for defining a Table of Authorities).

If you want, create a "Table of Authorities Continued" header for subsequent pages.

If you have more than one type of authority, repeat the above steps until you create a section for *each* one. You may have up to 16 different sections in the Table of Authorities.

TIP: You should keep a list handy showing the ToA section numbers you define so that you can correctly mark citations.

Next, press Ctrl-Enter to insert a hard page-break to end the ToA page. To define each section for the Table of Authorities, follow these steps. Move the cursor to a point below the corresponding section title where you want the first citation when you generate the document. Then press Mark Text (Alt-F5) and select **Define** (**5**). Choose Define Table of Authorities (**4**). Where WordPerfect requests the section number, type it in. For the example shown in this chapter, type *1* at this point to select the first section. A menu for defining the format of the first section of the Table of Authorities is displayed.

If you haven't yet changed the default to include underlining, do so now. (If you followed the steps for changing this default through Setup, you won't need to change this menu.) In most cases you select dot leaders, underlining, and a blank line, as shown in figure 22.20.

```
Definition for Table of Authorities 1

        1 - Dot Leaders                          Yes

        2 - Underlining Allowed                  Yes

        3 - Blank Line Between Authorities       Yes




    Selection: 0
```

Fig. 22.20.

Format defined for the first section of the Table of Authorities.

Now exit this menu by pressing Enter; this takes you back to the normal screen. Repeat this procedure for each section of the Table of Authorities.

Generating the Table of Authorities

To generate a Table of Authorities, follow the steps outlined under "Generating Document References."

Figure 22.21 shows the first page of a printed Table of Authorities. It was printed after ToA generation by moving the cursor to the generated ToA, selecting Print (Shift-F7), and selecting **Page** (**2**).

Fig. 22.21.
Printed Table of Authorities.

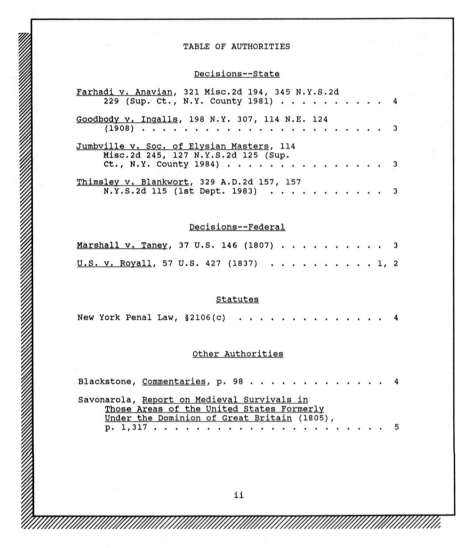

```
                        TABLE OF AUTHORITIES

                          Decisions--State

Farhadi v. Anavian, 321 Misc.2d 194, 345 N.Y.S.2d
        229 (Sup. Ct., N.Y. County 1981) . . . . . . . . .   4

Goodbody v. Ingalls, 198 N.Y. 307, 114 N.E. 124
        (1908) . . . . . . . . . . . . . . . . . . . . . .   3

Jumbville v. Soc. of Elysian Masters, 114
        Misc.2d 245, 127 N.Y.S.2d 125 (Sup.
        Ct., N.Y. County 1984) . . . . . . . . . . . . . .   3

Thimsley v. Blankwort, 329 A.D.2d 157, 157
        N.Y.S.2d 115 (1st Dept. 1983) . . . . . . . . . .    3


                         Decisions--Federal

Marshall v. Taney, 37 U.S. 146 (1807) . . . . . . . . . .    3

U.S. v. Royall, 57 U.S. 427 (1837) . . . . . . . . . . 1, 2


                             Statutes

New York Penal Law, §2106(c) . . . . . . . . . . . . . .     4


                         Other Authorities


Blackstone, Commentaries, p. 98 . . . . . . . . . . . .      4

Savonarola, Report on Medieval Survivals in
        Those Areas of the United States Formerly
        Under the Dominion of Great Britain (1805),
        p. 1,317 . . . . . . . . . . . . . . . . . . . . .   5




                                ii
```

Creating an Index

A good index anticipates the "search procedures" that readers use to find information in a document. WordPerfect's index feature creates an alphabetized list of index entries and subentries for a document. You can mark preexisting text in your document for inclusion in an index, or you can create entries manually.

Because an index is the least common reader aid in a legal document, indexes practically never show up in legal work. In this section you see how the index feature can be used to index part of a book.

Creating an index is similar to, although not quite the same as, creating a list or a table of contents. You mark each index entry, define the index format, and generate the index. You can omit page numbers or display them in any of several formats. The procedure for marking index entries is somewhat different from that for marking entries for a list or a table of contents. Moreover, an index *must* be defined and generated at the end of the document.

WordPerfect has tried to make the monumental job of preparing an index a little less daunting by providing the Concordance feature. Briefly, a *Concordance* file is a regular WordPerfect file into which you place a list of words or phrases repeated throughout a document. Somewhat like the MARK macro (see Table of Authorities), the Concordance then searches the document and notes each instance of words or phrases you have put in the Concordance file. Still, marking for an index must often be painstakingly done by hand to ensure accuracy. WordPerfect offers two levels of classification for items in an index: headings and subheadings. Proper use of these levels requires some planning and knowledge of your subject matter.

Marking Text for the Index

Marking text for lists and tables of contents involves pressing first the Block key (Alt-F4). Marking text for indexes is a bit different. When the index entry is a single word, you don't need to block the text first. When the index entry is two words or more, you need to mark the text as a block first.

Marking Text the Hard Way

To mark a one-word index entry, place the cursor anywhere in the word, press Mark Text (Alt-F5), and select Index (3). The prompt Index heading: appears on the status line, followed by the word you chose for the index. To have WordPerfect mark the word for the index, press Enter. WordPerfect enters the word as a major heading, then prompts you for a subheading. Type a subheading name, and press Enter. Or simply press Enter if you do not want a subheading.

To mark an index entry that is longer than one word, move the cursor to the beginning of the phrase and turn on Block (Alt-F4). Highlight the text you want to mark, press Mark Text (Alt-F5), and select Index (3). To accept the marked text as an index entry, press Enter. At the prompt for a subheading entry, either enter a subheading or press Enter.

Suppose, for example, that you are indexing a book of database applications. One of the applications can be used to keep track of product sales. You mark the first mention of *Sales-tracking system* as a major head. At the Subheading: prompt, you type *functions* and press Enter. If you press Reveal Codes (Alt-F3, or F11), you see the following hidden code embedded in the text:

   [**Index:** Sales-tracking system; functions]

Sales-tracking system is a major head. The word *functions*, which follows that head, is listed as a subhead when the index is generated.

WordPerfect automatically marks a word or phrase in the document for the index, but it also can create custom headings and subheadings. At the Index heading: prompt, type the heading that you want to include in the index and press Enter. Next, type a subheading, if you want one, and press Enter.

You can repeat this procedure hundreds of times throughout the document, or you can construct a macro (like MARK) for each word or phrase to be indexed. To mark for indexing, a macro should go to the top of the document, do a recursive extended search for the phrase in question, and mark it for the index each time the phrase is found. Even so, you have to construct many, many macros. If you are very fluent in macros, you can construct a macro that prompts you for the phrase to mark and how to mark it, does the marking, then goes to page 1 of the main text (using the GoTo command instead of Home, Home, ↑) and prompts you again. When the macro finishes, you just press F1.

Marking Text Using a Concordance

A concordance file is a regular WordPerfect file. In this file put any words and phrases to be included in the index. Be sure that you put each index entry on a separate line and that you press Enter after each entry to insert a hard return. Recall the preceding index entries. To create a concordance file for all the entries under *Sales-tracking system*, for example, enter these items in a file:

    block diagram
    file structures
    functions
    master files
    opening data files
    printing sales reports
    procedure files
    program development
    purging sales transactions
    system memory file
    transaction file

Note that the list does not have to be typed in alphabetical order; WordPerfect alphabetizes the items when it builds the index. If you type the Concordance with index codes embedded in the entries, the Concordance treats each occurrence in the way indicated by its associated code.

Save (F10) this file to the same subdirectory or disk where you store the document you are indexing.

When you instruct the program to generate the index, WordPerfect asks for the name of the concordance file. Enter the name of the file containing the list of words. WordPerfect considers the entries in the concordance file, treats each occurrence of these items in the main document as though it is marked, and includes the items in the index.

One problem with concordance files is that they place all entries in the index as main headings. If you want entries to appear as subheadings, you must mark them as such. As many users have discovered, the Concordance feature is a blunt instrument. If you use it, be sure you really want every instance of a word or phrase reported in the same place in the index.

Suppose that you want the entries in the concordance file example shown previously to be subheads under the main heading *Sales-tracking system*. With the concordance file on-screen, move the cursor to the first line of the file, press Block (Alt-F4), and highlight the entry. Next, press Mark Text (Alt-F5) and select Index (3). The following prompt is displayed:

```
Index heading: Block diagram
```

WordPerfect assumes that you want Block diagram to appear as a main heading. Instead, type *Sales-tracking system* for the main heading and press Enter. Press Enter at the Subheading: block diagram prompt to make that entry a subheading. Repeat this procedure for each item in the concordance file.

Remember that for all entries more than one word long, you must first press Block (Alt-F4) and highlight the entry before you press Mark Text (Alt-F5). For one-word entries such as *functions*, you won't need to block the entry first. Just press Mark Text (Alt-F5) and follow the steps as described.

If some of the concordance entries are under different main headings, type the appropriate headings at the prompt. If an entry should be its own main heading, you don't have to mark it at all. When WordPerfect generates the index, it treats such an entry as a main heading.

Marking Text Manually and with the Concordance

You can also mark for the index using the manual method in combination with a Concordance file. Just remember that if a word or phrase in the Concordance has also been marked in the main text, that word is reported twice: once with the associated code in the Concordance and once with the code in the main text.

In other words, the code in the main text does not override the code in the Concordance. You can't create an exception to the treatment of a word or phrase specified in the Concordance by embedding a conflicting code in the main text. Instead, you get two index entries, one of which you don't want. But if you use the Concordance wisely and mark other entries by hand, you should come up with a fairly sensitive index with a minimum of repetitious marking.

Be careful not to index the same word or phrase in too many different ways. If you put the word *exhibit* in the Concordance and mark one occurrence in the text as "Briefs, Exhibits in" and another as "Affidavits, Exhibits in", the Concordance has no way to tell which rule to follow for unmarked occurrences of the word *exhibit*. Your only solution is to leave *exhibit* out of the Concordance entirely and mark each occurrence appropriately by hand.

Defining the Index Format

Word Perfect gives you the same options for the format of page numbers in an index as are available for lists and tables of contents. The index must follow the text it is to analyze. To create an index page, follow these steps. Press Home, Home, ⌐ to move the cursor to the end of the document. Press Ctrl-Enter to place a hard page-break after the main text. Then type a title, such as *Index*. Press Enter twice or more to leave blank lines between the title and body of the index, and press Mark Text (Alt-F5). Select **Define** (**5**); then select Define Index (**3**). Enter the concordance file name you want to use (if any), and select the numbering style for the index. The numbering style choices are the same five as for Table of Contents, Table of Authorities, and Lists. Select the one that best suits your format for the index. You can omit page numbers or choose one of the following styles: page numbers following entries, in parentheses following entries, flush right, and flush right with dot leaders (see fig 22.22).

Fig. 22.22.
*Index Definition
menu.*

```
Index Definition

    1 - No Page Numbers

    2 - Page Numbers Follow Entries

    3 - (Page Numbers) Follow Entries

    4 - Flush Right Page Numbers

    5 - Flush Right Page Numbers with Leaders




    Selection: 0
```

In the most popular format for index entries, a comma is placed after each entry, followed by the page reference. (To see what this index format looks like, see the next section on generating an index.)

Generating the Index

You can find the steps for generating an index in the section on "Generating Document References" that appears earlier in this chapter. You can issue the command to generate a list or table of contents from any spot in a document. An index, however, must be generated at the end of the document. Before you generate the index, be sure that all entries are marked. Also, be sure that you defined the index format.

If you mark text within a document for an index, WordPerfect includes that text in the index as well as the text in the concordance file. If only the text in the concordance file has been marked for the index, only that text appears in the generated index. When the index is printed, all index entries are alphabetized. Main index entries are printed at the left margin, with subheads indented one tab stop.

CAUTION: If your concordance file is large, you may not have enough RAM to use all of it when you generate an index.

Whether you can use your entire concordance file depends on available RAM. If you run out of memory, WordPerfect prompts

`Not enough memory to use entire concordance file. Continue? (Y/N)`

Pressing *Y* at this point instructs WordPerfect to use only as much of the file as possible. If you tell it to continue, WordPerfect generates the Index as far as it has room in RAM and *drops the rest*, a result which can be dangerous if you don't realize that the Index is incomplete. Pressing *N* aborts index generation. Perhaps the best course is to watch the size of the concordance file if the amount of RAM memory you have is limited. And version 5 takes a lot more RAM than 4.2 did.

The entries under *Sales-tracking system* from the database applications book mentioned previously look like this when they are generated:

Sales-tracking system, 133-227
    block diagram, 136-139
    file structures, 134
    functions, 133-134
    master files, 135-136
    opening data files, 141
    printing sales reports, 179-186
    procedure files, 199
    program development, 140
    purging sales transactions, 194-195
    system memory file, 142
    transaction file, 142

Preparing Indexes and Multiple Related Documents

If you must include separate documents in the same file for cross-referencing purposes, you may have a problem with indexing. Let's assume that you have main text, which you want indexed, and three related documents, which you want cross-referenced. Even if you generate the index for the main text before you write the related documents, you have to mark index items manually. Otherwise, the

Concordance picks up all references found in the expanded document when you generate later. You can solve this problem by placing the related documents that you don't want indexed so that they *follow* the main text. Because the index must come after the material to which it refers, it picks up only the words and phrases preceding it. That may mean making the master a subdocument, and the subdocument the master.

Using Automatic Cross-Referencing (ACR)

This feature is essential for lawyers, academics, and anyone who writes using references to text located elsewhere in a document. Automatic cross-referencing helps writers keep track of where a topic is first discussed.

Until now, a phrase like *see discussion on page 25* could cause problems during editing. The writer had to be careful about reorganizing and maintaining proper references. Writers had three unsatisfactory choices for handling the problem of cross-referencing. They could

- Avoid cross-references containing the specific location of the discussion referred to.

- Find all references with locators before printing to see if the page number was still accurate.

- Leave locations blank during writing and try to find page numbers after editing. By this time, most writers forget what they were referring to.

With WordPerfect 5, cross-referencing encompasses page numbers, footnote numbers, and section numbers (if sections are numbered with outlining or automatic paragraph numbering). Cross-referencing also includes endnotes and graphics box numbers; and, as a breathtaking expansion, WordPerfect now handles cross-references across document boundaries with the Master Document feature (discussed in the next chapter).

Note: There is a bug in cross-referencing: although you can define your own system of automatic paragraph numbering (as suggested above), automatic cross-references to sections numbered that way are displayed in the default style for paragraph numbering.

Nevertheless, true WordPerfect aficionados are already demanding cross-references to line numbers, if line numbering is on, and some kind of directional sensor so that if the reference moves, *above* becomes *below* (or *supra* becomes *infra*) automatically.

TIP: If you still use WordPerfect 4.2, you have an external program that performs automatic cross-referencing with a few limitations. This program, WPXREF.EXE, is "shareware" (you're on your honor to pay a small fee if you use it). By David Seidman, WPXREF.EXE is available in the WordPerfect Support Group on CompuServe.

Marking Text for Automatic Cross-Referencing

Cross-referencing is easy; the only potential pitfall is in the terminology you use to refer to text. If you refer on page 50 to a discussion on page 21, you mark the text on page 50 as a *reference* and the text on page 21 as *target*. A target (the discussion referred to) can have any number of references made to it later in the document. For each target you also need a unique name or identifier that links target and reference.

When WordPerfect performs automatic cross-referencing, target and reference marks find each other using a unique short-form name. In a document with several targets and references, it's a good idea to keep a list of these unique names. A list helps you remember the names for all the different references and prevents duplicating names by mistake.

Depending on your preferred method, you can mark a target when you first write about it, knowing that you'll mark references to it later, or you can mark both target and reference at the same time. These marks identify references to footnotes and to sections of main text. You can even use them to set up page numbering in footers.

Marking References to Footnotes

Automatic referencing is particularly handy when you need to refer to a footnote. You can refer to a footnote even before you create the target footnote. You can also have one footnote refer to another. The following sections tell you how to mark footnote text as target or reference.

Marking Footnote References When the Footnote Doesn't Yet Exist

Here's how to make a footnote reference before you create the footnote. Type the phrase you usually use to introduce a reference, such as *see* discussion, fn. , *supra*. In this phrase, *fn.* is followed by the footnote reference code. (WordPerfect's manual says to type *up to* the point of the reference, but this example includes the phrase in which the footnote will be placed. It's easier to type the whole phrase and then go back and type in the reference.) Next, move the cursor back to the comma (or where you want the footnote number to appear). Press Mark Text (Alt-F5) and select AutoRef (1). The menu in figure 22.23 appears. Then select Mark **Reference** (1) and select Footnote Number (3). The menu in figure 22.24 appears. At the Target Name: prompt for the unique code, type it. Write down the code so that you remember to use it for the target footnote when you do create that footnote.

Fig. 22.23.

The Mark Text: Automatic Reference menu.

```
Mark Text: Automatic Reference

    1 - Mark Reference

    2 - Mark Target

    3 - Mark Both Reference and Target




















Selection: 0
```

Fig. 22.24.

Automatic reference submenu for identifying the target.

```
Tie Reference to:

    1 - Page Number

    2 - Paragraph/Outline Number

    3 - Footnote Number

    4 - Endnote Number

    5 - Graphics Box Number
```
```
Selection: 0
```

Now press Enter. Your marked reference appears as See discussion, fn. ?, supra. The question mark changes to the correct number once you identify the target footnote and generate.

Always make the target code first thing in the target footnote itself. Don't put it in the main text after the superscript. Even though a code placed after the superscript correctly records the preceding footnote, it's too easy to leave the code behind if you have to move the footnote. If this happens, code in the text reports the next preceding footnote and throws off numbering. If you form the habit of putting the code in the footnote itself, even before the **[Note Num]** code, you'll always know where to find it.

Marking Footnote References When the Footnote Already Exists

To generate a footnote reference, follow the procedure just given for marking text when the footnote doesn't yet exist. Select Mark **B**oth Reference and Target (**3**). Then select **F**ootnote Number (**3**).

You'll see a message Press Enter to select footnote.

CAUTION: This message sounds as if it wants you to press Enter right now. Don't!

Instead, press Footnote (Ctrl-F7), select **F**ootnote (**1**), and choose **E**dit (**2**). Enter the number of the footnote you are referring to (the target), and the target footnote appears. Press Enter. At the prompt, type the unique code and press Enter. Write the code down on your list in case you need to refer to that footnote again.

Press Enter to return to your reference, which correctly reports the footnote to which you referred. You can now continue typing.

Referring from One Footnote to Another

To refer to one footnote from another, follow the procedure just given for marking references to a footnote when the footnote already exists. Ignoring the temptation to press Enter, press Exit (F7) to get back to the main text. Then, select **F**ootnotes (**1**), then **E**dit (**2**). Enter the number of the footnote you are referring to (the target). The target footnote appears. Press Enter; then at the prompt, type the unique code and press Enter. Write the code down on your list in case you need to refer to that footnote again. Press Enter to return to your reference, which correctly reports the footnote to which you referred. You can now continue typing.

Marking Endnotes

Mark these the same way you do footnotes, but be sure to place the target codes for page references to endnotes in the endnotes themselves.

Marking a Reference to a Page

This procedure is essentially the same as the one for referring to a footnote. Press Mark Text (Alt-F5) and select AutoRef (**1**). Select Mark **B**oth Reference and Target (**3**); then select **P**age Number (**1**). Ignore the Press Enter to select page message. To move to the page that is the target reference, press GoTo (Ctrl-Home), type the page number, and press Enter. You still see a message Press Enter to select page. The Enter you pressed after GoTo just gets you to the page designated and doesn't plant the target code. Now move the cursor to the first text on that page to which you are actually referring; then press Enter to make the mark. It's a good idea to put the code within a key word so that if the text gets moved, the code moves with it. At the Target Name: prompt for a unique code, enter and note it.

Marking a Reference to a Paragraph or Section

With this function of automatic cross-referencing, you can give a precise address for a particular target using the subordination of paragraphs. Earlier in this chapter, you read about the importance of redefining the paragraph numbering scheme. Here is one place where it pays off.

You read that you could supply any periods needed after paragraph or outline section numbers; this means that those periods aren't carried into automatic cross referencing where trailing periods are not wanted. Suppose you want to refer to the material under the Last Level Heading below.

1. Primary Heading.
   (a)Secondary Heading the First.
   (b)Secondary Heading the Second.
     (1)Last Level Heading.

The cross-reference should appear as follows: *see section 1(b)(1), supra.* (See note at end of chapter.) You don't want the period after the main heading number to appear in the cross-reference.

Mark section references exactly as you would mark page references. You read about these procedures earlier.

The best place for the code is probably right after the heading itself or even inside it (the code isn't incorporated in the Table of Contents).

Marking Boxes

Place target codes for references to graphics boxes in their captions, inside the boxes themselves. If, however, you use user-defined text boxes, only reference codes are allowed inside. In this case, put target references immediately to the right of the box code in the main text. (See Chapter 24 for an explanation of how to create graphics boxes in WordPerfect 5.)

Creating "Page 2 of 20" Footers

The reference and target marking system can be used in headers and footers, finally making it possible to have a footer that automatically gives the present page and updates the last page. For this type of page numbering, follow these steps. Press Format (Shift-F8). Select **Page (2)** and select Page Number Position (**7**). Now type 9 to turn off ordinary page numbering. Select **Footers (4)**. Then select Footer **A (1)** and then Every **Page (2)**. Depending on the format you want, press Center (Shift

F6), type *Page*, and press Ctrl-N—in which case your screen then reads Page ^N. Type *of* and press Mark Text (Alt-F5). Select AutoRef (**1**). Select Mark **Reference** (**1**) and specify Tie Reference to **Page** Number (**1**). Where WordPerfect requests a target name, type a unique code, such as LASTPAGE. You then return to the Footer Screen, which now reads Page ^N of ?. Press Exit (F7) twice to return to the text.

After you finish the first draft of the document, when you are sure what the last page is (for example, at the bottom of a signature page), put the target code on that page with the unique code (LASTPAGE) that identifies it. You do this by moving to the bottom of the last page of your document (Home, Home, ↓), and pressing Mark Text (Alt-F5), 1, 2. At the Enter Target Name: prompt, type *lastpage* and press Enter. The number of pages adjusts to subsequent editing as long as that code in fact remains in the last page.

Unless the target has been identified, references appear as ? in the text. Once the target is identified, WordPerfect updates all cross-references every time you generate.

Generating Cross-References

Cross-references are generated in the same manner as lists, tables of contents, indexes, and tables of authority. See the section on "Generating Document References" that appears earlier in this chapter.

Using Automatic Document Comparison

Document Compare is extremely convenient to run.

But in Document Compare, more than any other area, foresight is necessary. Always keep a copy of the original document so that you have something with which to compare the new version of a document. You can compare documents only when the new version is on-screen and the old version is saved under another name.

When you start editing an old draft, ask yourself where there's the slightest possibility that someone may want to see exactly what the changes were.

Saving an Old Version Document for Comparison

To allow for automatic document comparisons, follow these steps. Select List Files (F5), press Enter, move the cursor to the document you want to edit, and press **Retrieve** (**1**). Enter List Files again (F5) and put the cursor on the same file name. Select **Move**/Rename (**3**) and change the file name to something else, such as MYDOC.OLD.

Now make changes to the on-screen file and save it using Save (F10). Don't forget to save your edits before you do the automatic comparison. You may find that some editing is necessary before you print a comparison document, particularly where text affected involves codes for automatic paragraph numbering and indents.

Comparing a New Version to an Old Version

To compare the new version on-screen with the old version on disk, follow these steps. Press Mark Text (Alt-F5) and select **Generate** (**6**). Then select **Compare** (**2**). WordPerfect asks for a file to compare to, giving the name of your screen file as a default. Type the name of the old version of the file and press Enter.

The new version of the document is redlined automatically, showing new material in redline and deleted material with strikeout. None of that means much as long as it stays on-screen, because neither redlining nor strikeout shows up much differently from ordinary text on most monitors. Next, print (Shift-F7), and select **Full Document** (**1**) to see the results (see fig. 22.25). Text shaded in gray represents redlined text; text marked for strikeout has a line running through it. These are the factory defaults, but you can use PTR.EXE to modify your .PRS file to change the way your printer indicates redline and strikeout.

Fig. 22.25.

Edited document compared to its original version.

```
In the old days, writers had to stop editing days before a
document was due and start combing through the main text to
prepare the document references. One of WordPerfect 5's handiest
features is that it speeds up that process. One of WordPerfect
5's handiest features is that it speeds up the process of
assembling document references. With a little foresight and
planning, you can work on a document right down to a few hours
before a deadline, confident that as your main text changes, the
document references will keep right up with it.

This chapter shows you how to create lists, tables of contents,
tables of authorities, and indexes. You also learn to use
automatic cross-referencing, which lets you change the structure
of your document and automatically maintain accurate references
to footnotes, pages and sections. which lets you change the
structure of your document and automatically maintain accurate
references to certain spots in a document. Finally, you learn to
use the Document Compare feature so that you can show someone
else what was omitted from, you learn to use the Document Compare
feature so that you can see what was omitted from, or added to, a
document, without having to mark all those changes yourself.
```

WordPerfect's Document Compare function works in phrases, defined as strings of words bounded by punctuation marks, tabs, or hard returns. If you change a single word in a phrase two lines long, Document Compare reports that change by printing the *entire* phrase with the changed word in redline, followed by the *entire* phrase as originally written, struck-through. If you move a chunk of material from one place to another, Document Compare brackets that material in its new location with an explanatory message in strikeout.

Purging Redlining from a Saved Document

When you're in a hurry, it's easy to make big mistakes. If you accidentally save the screen document with redlining over your edited file, you can retrieve it and get rid of the redlining and strikeout.

To purge a file of redlining, follow these steps. Press Mark Text (Alt-F5). Then select **Generate** (**6**) and select **Remove** (**1**).

All redlined text reverts to its normal state, and the strikeout marks disappear. Save the document again (F10). Unfortunately, Document Compare is one of the least successful innovations in WordPerfect 5. These problems become apparent with use:

- The user lacks control over the degree of resolution on the redlining.

- No option exists to indicate that something was taken out without saying what it was. Often, it is clearer just to indicate that something has been omitted.

- The user lacks control of how redlining is indicated.

- Redlining is as broad as the phrase in which the changed text is contained. This practice redlines more than the actual change, in many cases obscuring rather than highlighting the change.

TIP: By comparison, JURISoft's CompareRite™ is much more effective. Until CompareRite is adapted to WordPerfect 5, many offices may keep using WordPerfect 4.2 just for making comparisons. WordPerfect Corporation will undoubtedly polish this feature in the future because of the three degrees of resolution CompareRite offers (as opposed to WordPerfect's "phrase" approach) and the flexibility of display it gives the user. At the moment, though, at least for 4.2, CompareRite doesn't handle footnotes. If CompareRite (updated for WP5) doesn't handle footnotes as well as WP5, the choice of which method to use will probably depend on whether footnotes are in the document.

TIP: Use a macro to replace selected text marked for strikeout with a special symbol to indicate simply that something was deleted. The STRIKE.ARC file in DL0 (zero) in the WordPerfect Support Group forum on CompuServe contains the STRIKE.WPM macro and accompanying documentation.

If you invoke the macro STRIKE, the program goes to the top of the document and sequentially blocks and presents each bit of text marked for strikeout. It then asks whether you want to replace it with the strikeout code. If you type *Y*, it does it and goes on to the next bit. If you type *N*, it turns off the block and goes on to the next bit. The question is necessary because the messages indicating that a section was moved appear in strikeout, and you probably won't want to delete them. If you answer anything but what is permitted, a prompt appears telling you to type *Y* or *N*. My symbol that SOMETHING was deleted is a bold underlined bullet with a caret over it in braces. It's probably specific to my printer, a LaserJet 2686A running the A and F cartridges. You will easily identify the spot in the macro where the symbol is inserted, and can change it to anything else that suits your fancy.

Summary

In this chapter, you learned

- How to set up a list, a table of contents, and a table of authorities.

- How to mark text for a list, a table of contents, a table of authorities, and an index.

- How to make an index using a concordance file coupled with markings in the main text.

- How to use styles to mark titles and headings for inclusion in the table of contents.

- How to set up automatic paragraph numbering to get the most from WordPerfect's generating capabilities.

- How to make automatic cross-references.

- How to compare a document with one of its ancestors and print a document showing the differences between them.

The next chapter examines in greater detail the ways in which the foregoing techniques can (or cannot) be used across document boundaries through WordPerfect's Master Document feature.

CAUTION: No matter how you define your own system for paragraph numbering, cross references to paragraph/outline numbers will be reported using WordPerfect's factory-imposed numbering system—which is to say, wrongly. The default numbering system is useless for brief headings; hence, a suitable user-defined system, such as the one set forth in this chapter, cannot be used with automatic referencing until this limitation is removed. WordPerfect corporation has indicated that a future maintenance release of version 5.0 will address this problem.

23

Using the Master Document Feature for Large Projects

*In addition to being president of Documentation Systems, a private consulting firm, **Joel Shore** teaches a range of personal computing courses at Massachusetts Bay Community College and conducts private, corporate, in-house seminars. He participates in several of the Boston Computer Society's Special Interest Groups, including the Special Interest Group for WordPerfect.* ■

This chapter examines the techniques needed to create subdocuments and master documents and shows how to increase the power of other WordPerfect features through master documents. The Master Document feature, brand new for version 5, makes the handling of large documents much less of a chore than handling large documents with earlier versions of WordPerfect.

With Master Document you can manage large projects with the following cycle:

- Maintain and store the sections of a long document as individual files called *subdocuments*

- Build a skeleton or *master* document that includes the name of each subdocument

- Temporarily *expand* the master document and link the individual files to work with all the individual files simultaneously (generating a table of contents or printing the entire document, for example)

- Separate, or *condense,* the expanded document back into its component subdocument files

A master document consists of two kinds of files: master document files and subdocument files. An ordinary WordPerfect file, the master document contains codes that reference the subdocument files. In addition to these codes, the master document can contain anything else that you would put in a document like a table of contents definition code, styles, or text.

The second kind of file, the subdocument, contains the text for each section of the total document. You can include as many subdocuments as you need. Advantages to using subdocument files include saving memory and time retrieving and saving files. Remember that instead of one large file, you have several smaller files.

Before you begin working with master documents, you should be familiar with defining and generating tables of contents, lists, indexes, automatic references, and tables of authorities. These topics are covered in Chapter 22.

Creating Master and Subdocuments

To illustrate the techniques of creating and working with a master document, let's assume that you are working on your doctoral dissertation. Because the dissertation will be long and complex, you've developed a plan of attack that consists of two phases: first, you write the dissertation and save each section as a separate file; and second, after you finish writing, you create a master document. Within the master document, you identify and place all the subdocuments in the order they should appear in the printed version.

Adopt this approach to managing large projects for several reasons. First, creating each chapter as a separate file is natural: you can save each section of writing in its own file, you can work on the section of the document you want without having to worry about the order within a larger document, and you can concentrate on your writing. Second, you should create the subdocuments before the master document because you must enter actual file names to build a master document. Third, building a master document allows you to perform operations, such as spell-checking, much more efficiently.

Working with Subdocuments

You do not use a special feature to create a subdocument; any WordPerfect file can be used as a subdocument. WordPerfect imposes no limits on the number of subdocuments you can specify in a master document, so you can create as many individual files as you need to keep your project organized. These files can be as large or small as needed.

For instance, if you're writing a book, you'll probably want to maintain each chapter and appendix as a separate file. For this chapter's example, the dissertation is divided into 12 sections, each saved as a separate file. Some of the dissertation's subdocuments are less than a page long; others are over 50 pages.

CAUTION: Codes contained in a subdocument file override codes in the master document. You won't encounter a problem for codes to bold or underline specific blocks of text, but you should be careful about codes that affect document formatting like margins and base font. You should insert these codes near the beginning of the master document and omit them from the subdocuments. Inserting codes in only the master document ensures that all subdocuments are formatted with the same initial codes.

When you finish composing all the subdocuments, you can begin to build the master file. The subdocuments of the dissertation consist of 12 files (see fig. 23.1).

Fig. 23.1.
A List Files display showing the dissertation's individual files.

As you build your master document, you include the subdocuments in the order you choose. For the dissertation, the order is determined by guidelines published by the educational institution. For example, dissertations submitted to the University of Illinois at Urbana-Champaign must be assembled in the order shown in table 23.1.

Table 23.1
Order of Documents in Dissertation

Section Name	Page Numbering Requirements
Notice of Copyright	No page number
Title page	No page number
Abstract	Must be page iii if included
Dedication	Roman numerals
Acknowledgments	Roman numerals
Table of Contents	Roman numerals
List of Tables	Roman numerals
Text	Page 1
Endnotes	Arabic numerals
Appendixes	Arabic numerals
Works Cited	Arabic numerals
Vita	Arabic numerals

Remember that you won't have files for the table of contents, list of tables, and endnotes because you will, of course, use WordPerfect to generate these for you.

Building the Master Document

After you determine the order of your subdocuments, you can begin building your master document, adding the subdocuments in the order you want them. Clear the screen before beginning this procedure; remember that you are creating a *new* document.

For your example, the guidelines indicate that the copyright page must be the first page in the dissertation. The file COPYRITE contains the text for this page, so you want to include this file first in your master document.

To include a subdocument in a master document, complete the following steps:

1. Move the cursor to where you want the subdocument to appear.

   For your example, to place the copyright on the first page, press Home, Home, ↑ to move the cursor to the beginning of the document.

2. Press Mark Text (Alt-F5).

   The following menu appears:

   1 Auto Ref; **2** Subdoc; **3** Index; **4** ToA Short Form; **5** Define; **6** Generate: **0**

3. Select Subdoc (**2**).

   WordPerfect displays the prompt Subdoc filename:

4. Type the file name (including drive letter and path if necessary) of the subdocument and then press Enter.

   For your example, type *COPYRITE* and press Enter.

   WordPerfect draws a box on-screen labeled Subdoc: followed by the file name (see fig. 23.2).

Note that because you cannot use List Files (F5), you must know the name of the file before starting this procedure. Also, you are not prompted if a file does not exist.

5. Press Hard Page (Ctrl-Enter) to force the text following your subdocument to start on a new page

   or

   Omit the hard page break to make subsequent text continue immediately following the end of the subdocument.

6. Use the same procedure to include additional subdocuments.

7. After selecting all the subdocuments, name and save your document. See "Saving the Master Document" in this chapter.

```
┌──────────────────────────────────────────────────────────────╮
│                                                                 │
│    ┌────────────────────────────────────────────────────────┐  │
│    │ Subdoc: C:\WP50\DISSERTA\COPYRITE                       │  │
│    └────────────────────────────────────────────────────────┘  │
│                                                                 │
```

Fig. 23.2.
*A subdocument box
and its associated
code.*

```
                                    Doc 1 Pg 1 Ln 1" Pos 1"
{    ▲    ▲    ▲    ▲    ▲    ▲    ▲    ▲    ▲    }    ▲    ▲
[Subdoc:C:\WP50\DISSERTA\COPYRITE]
```

```
    Press Reveal Codes to restore screen
```

> For your example, name the master document MASTER.DOC.

Figure 23.3 shows the COPYRITE, TITLE.PG, and ABSTRACT files as subdocuments
in a master document named MASTER.DOC. The hard page breaks cause each
subdocument to print on a new sheet of paper. Figure 23.4 shows the same
information in Reveal Codes.

```
    ┌────────────────────────────────────────────────────────┐
    │ Subdoc: C:\WP50\DISSERTA\COPYRITE                       │
    └────────────────────────────────────────────────────────┘
    ==========================================================

    ┌────────────────────────────────────────────────────────┐
    │ Subdoc: C:\WP50\DISSERTA\TITLE.PG                       │
    └────────────────────────────────────────────────────────┘
    ==========================================================

    ┌────────────────────────────────────────────────────────┐
    │ Subdoc: C:\WP50\DISSERTA\ABSTRACT                       │
    └────────────────────────────────────────────────────────┘
    ==========================================================

                                    Doc 1 Pg 4 Ln 1" Pos 1"
```

Fig. 23.3.
*Three subdocuments
separated by hard
page breaks.*

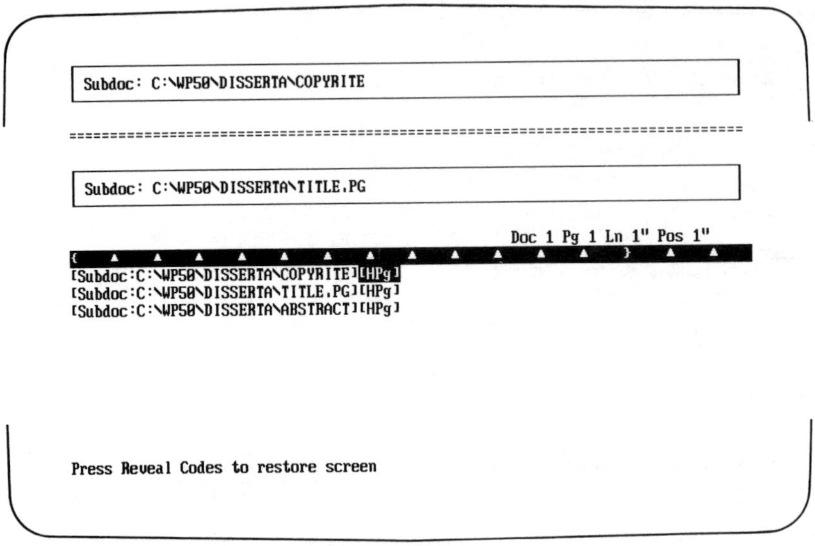

Fig. 23.4.
The same three documents shown in Reveal Codes.

Subdoc: C:\WP50\DISSERTA\COPYRITE

==

Subdoc: C:\WP50\DISSERTA\TITLE.PG

```
                                        Doc 1 Pg 1 Ln 1" Pos 1"
{   ▲   ▲   ▲   ▲   ▲   ▲   ▲   ▲   ▲   ▲   ▲   }   ▲   ▲
[Subdoc:C:\WP50\DISSERTA\COPYRITE][HPg]
[Subdoc:C:\WP50\DISSERTA\TITLE.PG][HPg]
[Subdoc:C:\WP50\DISSERTA\ABSTRACT][HPg]
```

Press Reveal Codes to restore screen

Deleting a Subdocument

As you can see from figure 23.4, subdocuments are simply WordPerfect codes—no different than a margin setting or an indent. To delete a subdocument, simply delete its corresponding code; subdocument codes include **[Subdoc:]** followed by the file name.

Expanding the Master Document

Expanding the master document lets you work with all of the subdocuments at the same time to perform WordPerfect operations like printing or spell-checking and generating tables of contents that affect the entire project. Working with all the files for tasks like printing and spell-checking saves you time.

Complete the following steps to expand the master document:

1. Make sure the master document is displayed on-screen.

2. Press Mark Text (Alt-F5).

    WordPerfect displays the Mark Text menu:

    1 Auto **Ref**; **2 Subdoc**; **3** Index; **4** ToA Short Form; **5** Define; **6 Generate**: **0**

3. Select **Generate** (**6**).

    WordPerfect displays the Mark Text: Generate menu (see fig. 23.5).

4. Select **Expand Master Document** (**3**).

```
Mark Text: Generate

    1 - Remove Redline Markings and Strikeout Text from Document

    2 - Compare Screen and Disk Documents and Add Redline and Strikeout

    3 - Expand Master Document

    4 - Condense Master Document

    5 - Generate Tables, Indexes, Automatic References, etc.




    Selection: 0
```

Fig. 23.5.
*The Mark Text:
Generate menu.*

WordPerfect begins combining all the specified subdocuments into the master document skeleton. If the subdocument file is found, then expansion continues uninterrupted. If WordPerfect can't locate the specified subdocument, you see the prompt Subdoc not found (Press Enter to skip): followed by the file name. You can press Enter to skip this subdocument and go on to the next, or you can edit the file name.

When WordPerfect expands the master document, each subdocument box is replaced with a pair of boxes: one to mark the beginning of that subdocument's text and another to mark the end. WordPerfect then inserts the entire subdocument between the beginning and ending codes. Figure 23.6 shows the copyright page in an expanded master document.

CAUTION: Never delete the [Subdoc Start] or [Subdoc End] codes. These codes are a matched set, and if you delete them, WordPerfect cannot keep track of each individual subdocument.

If you want to delete a subdocument, delete the subdocument code from the nonexpanded master document (see "Deleting a Subdocument" in this chapter).

When all subdocuments have been included, WordPerfect returns you to the expanded master document. You can edit the text of any of the subdocuments or perform any other WordPerfect operation—for example, spell-check. Remember that an expanded document is slightly larger than the sum of its parts because of the subdocument codes.

Fig. 23.6.

A portion of the expanded master document with Start and End boxes.

```
Subdoc Start: C:\WP50\DISSERTA\COPYRITE
                        c Copyright by
                     Noralyn Jean Masselink
                            1987
Subdoc End: C:\WP50\DISSERTA\COPYRITE


========================================================================

Subdoc Start: C:\WP50\DISSERTA\TITLE.PG
                     EXAMPLE AND RULE IN DONNE
                               BY
                     NORALYN JEAN MASSELINK
                    B.A., Calvin College, 1981
                  A.M., University of Illinois, 1983
                             THESIS
            Submitted in partial fulfillment of the requirements
             for the degree of Doctor of Philosophy of English
                      in the Graduate College of the
                                       Doc 1 Pg 2 Ln 7.27" Pos 1"
```

Creating a Table of Contents, List, Index, or Table of Authorities

The master document feature lets you generate tables of contents, lists, indexes, and tables of authorities that span all your subdocuments. (Chapter 22 discusses these features in detail.) In previous versions of WordPerfect, generating any of these items for an extremely large document would be difficult and slow at best or impossible at worst. Master document overcomes this shortcoming by pulling in each subdocument file one at a time to make generating the table of contents much more efficient.

This chapter illustrates how to generate a table of contents for a master document; to use other generating features for master documents, simply follow the same procedure. You create a table of contents in a master document and associated subdocuments almost exactly as you create a table of contents for an ordinary document. You follow three separate procedures: marking text for inclusion in the table of contents, defining the table of contents, and generating the table of contents.

Marking Text for the Table of Contents

Marking text tells WordPerfect what to include in the table of contents. The material that you want to include in the table of contents is contained in your subdocuments, not the master document.

To mark text for inclusion in the table of contents, complete the following steps:

1. Move the cursor to the beginning of the text you want to include in the table of contents.

2. Press Block (Alt-F4, or F12).

3. Move the cursor to the end of the text you want to include in the table of contents.

   WordPerfect highlights the block.

4. Press Mark Text (Alt-F5).

   WordPerfect displays the Mark Text menu:

   Mark for: 1 ToC; **2** List; **3** Index; **4** ToA: **0**

5. Select ToC (**1**).

   WordPerfect displays the prompt ToC Level:

6. Type the appropriate level number for this table of contents entry.

7. Repeat this procedure for all your subdocuments and the master document if you typed text that you want included in the table of contents.

Defining the Table of Contents

After marking the text for the table of contents, you define the style for the table of contents next. Defining a table of contents specifies where the table is to appear and how the table should be formatted.

Complete the following steps to define the table of contents in the master document:

1. Make sure the master document is displayed on-screen.

   If you are working with a subdocument, save it and clear the screen before retrieving the master document.

2. Move the cursor to the location in the master document where you want the table of contents to appear.

   You may want to insert a hard page break (Ctrl-Enter), so the table prints on a new page.

3. If you want, type and center the title of the table of contents.

   For your example, press Center (Shift-F6), type *Table of Contents*, and press Enter.

4. Press Enter several times to insert blank lines between the title and the actual table of contents.

5. Press Mark Text (Alt-F5).

   WordPerfect displays the Mark Text menu:

   1 Auto Ref; **2** Subdoc; **3** Index; **4** ToA Short Form; **5** Define; **6** Generate: **0**

6. Select **Define** (**5**).

   The Mark Text: Define menu appears.

7. Select Define Table of Contents (**1**).

   The Table of Contents Definition menu appears.

8. Define the number of levels you want to appear in the table of contents, the wrap option, and the numbering style.

   Even if you mark text for five levels, only the number of levels you enter here prints in the generated table of contents.

9. Press Enter to return to your document.

Figure 23.7 shows a table of contents definition in a master document in Reveal Codes.

Fig. 23.7.

The table of contents definition code in the master document.

```
    Subdoc: C:\WP50\DISSERTA\DEDICATE


    ===============================================================================


    Subdoc: C:\WP50\DISSERTA\ACKNOWL


    ===============================================================================
                             Table of Contents
                                                   Doc 1 Pg 4 Ln 1" Pos 1"
    [    ▲    ▲    ▲    ▲    ▲    ▲    ▲    ▲    ▲    ▲    }    ▲    ▲
    [Subdoc:C:\WP50\DISSERTA\TITLE.PG][HPg]
    [Subdoc:C:\WP50\DISSERTA\ABSTRACT][HPg]
    [Subdoc:C:\WP50\DISSERTA\DEDICATE][HPg]
    [Subdoc:C:\WP50\DISSERTA\ACKNOWL][HPg]
    [Cntr]Table of Contents[C/A/Flrt][HRt]
    [HRt]
    [Def Mark:ToC,5:5,5,5,5,5][HPg]



    Press Reveal Codes to restore screen
```

CAUTION: Don't define the table of contents in the subdocuments or you generate multiple copies of the table.

Generating the Table of Contents

After marking all the entries you want to include in the table of contents and defining the location and style of the table in the master document, you're ready to generate the actual table.

Complete the following steps to generate the table of contents:

1. Make sure the master document is displayed on-screen.

   If a subdocument is displayed, save it and clear the screen before retrieving the master document.

2. Press Mark Text (Alt-F5).

   WordPerfect displays the Mark Text menu:

   1 Auto Ref; **2** Subdoc; **3** Index; **4** ToA Short Form; **5** Define; **6** Generate: **0**

3. Select **Generate** (**6**).

   The Mark Text: Generate menu appears (see fig. 23.5).

4. Select **Generate** Tables, Indexes, Automatic References, etc. (**5**).

   You are prompted Existing tables, lists, and indexes will be replaced. Continue? (Y/N) Yes

5. Press *Y* or Enter to continue

   or

   Press *N* to stop.

When you answer yes, WordPerfect generates and displays on-screen the table of contents.

If the master file is not already expanded, WordPerfect first expands it before generating the table of contents and displays the prompt Update Subdocs (Y/N)? No. Press *Y* to direct WordPerfect to save each subdocument. Press *N*; the files are not saved. Remember that the subdocuments are already on the disk. You need answer yes only if the subdocument was changed (hyphenation prompts or document conversion, for example).

Figure 23.8 shows part of the generated table of contents.

Printing the Master Document

You can print either the complete expanded master document or the condensed skeleton master document. If you print the expanded master document, all text from the subdocuments and any text contained in the master document print. If you print the condensed document, only text contained in the master document prints; text from the subdocument does not print.

To print the entire master document, first expand it and then print. To print just the condensed master document, print the document without first expanding it, or condense the master document if it is already expanded.

Condensing the Master Document

When you finish working with the expanded master document, you can condense it back into its individual subdocument files.

Fig. 23.8.

A part of the master document's generated table of contents.

```
                        Table of Contents
     CHAPTER ONE     Introduction. . . . . . . . . . . . . . . 1

          Critical Background . . . . . . . . . . . . . . . 5
          Augustinian Versus Thomistic Epistemology . . . . . . 5

     CHAPTER TWO  Memory and Epistemology in Donne. . . . . . . .18

          Loci Et Imagines and Donne's Distrust of Memory . . .18
          "Remembring our selues": Thomistic Tendencies in
            Sermon on Psalm 38:3. . . . . . . . . . . . . . .23
          "Remember now thy Creator": "A Sermon of
            Valediction at my going into Germany" . . . . . . .31
          Knowing God: Memory, Faith, and Two Kinds of
            Reason  . . . . . . . . . . . . . . . . . . . . .39
          Seeing and Beholding God. . . . . . . . . . . . . .52

     CHAPTER THREE    Non-epistemological Reasons for Relying
       on Example to Teach Rule . . . . . . . . . . . . . . .69

          Example to Teach Rule . . . . . . . . . . . . . . .69
          Definition of Terms . . . . . . . . . . . . . . . .69
          The Rhetorical Tradition. . . . . . . . . . . . . .74
                                       Doc 1 Pg 1 Ln 1i Pos 1i
```

To condense an expanded master document, complete the following steps:

1. Press Mark Text (Alt-F5).

   The Mark Text menu appears:

   1 Auto **Ref; 2** Subdoc; **3** Index; **4** ToA Short Form; **5** Define; **6** Generate: **0**

2. Select **Generate (5).**

   The Mark Text: Generate menu appears (see fig. 23.5).

3. Select **Condense Master Document (4).**

   WordPerfect displays the prompt Save Subdocs (Y/N) Yes.

4. Press *Y* to save the individual subdocuments to disk

   or

   Press *N* to condense without saving the subdocuments.

   If you modified the subdocuments, you should press *Y.*

   If you choose to save the subdocuments, WordPerfect checks for duplicate file names. If you already created and named the files, WordPerfect displays the prompt Replace: followed by the file name and this menu:

   1 Yes; **2** No; **3** Replace all remaining.

5. Select **Yes (1)** to replace just the current subdocument

   or

   Select **No (2)** if you want to edit the file name before continuing

   or

Select **Replace All Remaining** (**3**) to replace all the subdocuments without being prompted.

Saving the Master Document

When you finish working with the master document, save it. You can save the master document in condensed or expanded form (although you don't gain anything and you waste disk space by saving an expanded master document). Condense the master document before saving unless you have special reasons for doing otherwise.

Complete the following steps to save the master document:

1. Press Exit (F7)

   WordPerfect prompts Save document? (Y/N) Yes.

2. Press Enter or press *Y* to save the document.

   WordPerfect prompts Document is expanded, condense it? (Y/N) Yes.

3. Press Enter or press *Y* to condense the master document.

   If you press *N* for Step 3, WordPerfect no longer displays this prompt when saving the master document. If, in the future, you want to save a condensed version, you must first condense the master document (see the section "Condensing the Master Document" in this chapter) and then save it.

   WordPerfect prompts Save Subdocs? (Y/N) Yes.

4. Press *N* if you saved the subdocuments when you condensed the master document or if you did not make any changes

   or

   Press Enter or *Y* if you made any changes; the updated subdocument files are saved.

   If you press Enter or *Y*, you are prompted Replace: for each subdocument. See the instructions in "Condensing the Master Document" to review your options.

   WordPerfect prompts: Document to be saved:

5. For a new file, type a document name and press Enter

   or

   For an existing file, confirm the name by pressing Enter, or edit the file name and then press Enter.

Using Other Features in a Master Document

Many of WordPerfect's features can be used with master documents—for instance, page numbering, searching and replacing, spell-checking, and automatic references with master documents.

Inserting a New Page Number

You can insert new page number codes in the master so that all pages from that point forward for all subdocuments are sequentially numbered. For example, in the dissertation, the numbering begins with the abstract as page iii in Roman numerals, and the text itself must begin with page 1 (see table 23.1). To control page numbering in the dissertation, insert two new page number codes in the master document: one at the beginning of the abstract file to start numbering with Roman numeral iii and another at the top of the first text page to start numbering with Arabic numeral 1.

To set a new page number, complete the following steps:

1. Move the cursor to where you want the new page number code to appear.

   For the dissertation example, the first two pages must be unnumbered and the abstract page must be page iii. Press GoTo (Ctrl-Home), type *3*, and press Enter to move to the abstract page.

2. Press Reveal Codes (Alt-F3, or F11) to make sure that you position the cursor before the subdocument code.

3. Press Format (Shift-F8).

   The Format menu appears.

4. From the Format menu, select **Page** (**2**).

5. From the Format: Page menu, select **New Page Number** (**6**).

6. Type the new page number and press Enter.

   For your dissertation, type *iii* for Roman numeral page three and press Enter.

7. Press Exit (F7) to return to the document.

To force the text section to start with page 1, repeat the same process, but move the cursor immediately before the subdocument code for the first chapter and type *1* for the new page number.

Using Search and Replace

You can use Search (F2 and Shift-F2) and Replace (Alt-F3) features in a master document to perform the operation across all the subdocument files simultaneously. (See Chapter 3 for more information about Search and Replace.)

Suppose, for example, that after completing work on the dissertation you discover that you've misspelled a name throughout the entire document. How can you fix this misspelling? You could retrieve the individual files one by one and perform a Replace on each, but this method would be time-consuming and tedious. After all, you would need to go to the List Files screen to retrieve each file, and then you would need to perform a separate Replace for each. Fortunately, you can perform

Replace in a better way. By first expanding the master document, you can perform the Replace just once.

To search and replace across all the subdocument files at once, complete the following:

1. Make sure the master document file is displayed on-screen.

   If you are working with a subdocument, save it and clear the screen before retrieving the master document.

2. Expand the master document.

3. Perform the Replace.

4. Condense the master document.

5. Press *Y* in response to the Save Subdocs? prompt.

Spell-Checking

Spell-checking is similar to Replace. You can spell-check an individual subdocument in the normal way, or you can spell-check all subdocuments at once. (See Chapter 7 for complete instructions on using the Speller.)

To spell-check all the subdocument files at once, complete the following steps:

1. Make sure the master document is displayed on-screen.

   If you are working with a subdocument, save it and clear the screen before retrieving the master document.

2. Expand the master document.

3. Spell-check the expanded master document.

4. Condense the master document.

5. Press *Y* in response to the Save Subdocs? prompt if you corrected any misspellings.

Adding Footnotes and Endnotes

You can use footnotes and endnotes with the master document. When you use these features, you need to consider the footnote and endnote options and footnote numbering. (Chapter 20 discusses footnote and endnotes in detail.)

If you use a footnote option code or an endnote option code, be sure that you have no more than one of each, and be sure to place these codes in the master document only. Remember that codes in the master document apply to all subdocuments unless overridden by codes placed in a subdocument. If you place footnote option codes in your subdocuments, and the option codes are slightly different, you end up with a different style of footnote in each chapter.

The best method is to place one footnote option code and one endnote option code at the beginning of the master document; don't place any option codes in any of the subdocuments.

Numbering Footnotes

You can number your footnotes consecutively throughout your dissertation, or you can begin footnotes for each chapter with 1.

To number footnotes consecutively, create your footnotes in each subdocument in the usual manner. You don't need to follow any special procedures.

When you work with an individual subdocument, the footnotes always begin with 1. When you expand the master document, all the dissertation's footnotes are numbered sequentially.

Instead of consecutively numbered footnotes, you might want each chapter's footnotes to start with number 1. To force each chapter's footnote to restart with number 1, you must place a Footnote: New Number code at the beginning of every subdocument. Restarting footnote numbering is one of the rare occasions when you want to override the codes in a master document.

To begin each chapter's footnotes with number 1, complete the following steps:

1. Make sure a subdocument is displayed on-screen.

    If the master document appears on-screen, save it and clear the screen before retrieving a subdocument file.

2. Press Home, Home, ↑ to go to the beginning of the subdocument.

3. Press Footnote (Ctrl-F7).

    WordPerfect displays the Footnote menu:

    1 Footnote; **2** Endnote; **3** Endnote **Placement: 0**

4. Select Footnote (**1**).

    The following menu appears:

    Footnote: 1 Create; **2** Edit; **3** New Number; **4** Options

5. Select New Number (**3**).

    WordPerfect prompts `Footnote Number?`

6. Type *1* and press Enter.

Repeat this procedure for every subdocument file. When you expand the master document, the footnotes for each chapter begin with number 1.

Placing Endnotes

Although you do not need to follow any special procedures for creating endnotes in a subdocument, you should consider carefully the endnote placement. If you want all endnotes gathered in one place, then insert a single endnote placement code at that point in the master document. In the dissertation example, the endnotes occur just before the appendix.

If you want the endnotes for each chapter to print at the end of the chapter, then you should insert an endnote placement code at the appropriate location in each subdocument file and override any option codes in the master document.

To place an endnote placement code in the master document, complete the following steps:

1. Make sure the master document is displayed on-screen.

   If you are working with a subdocument, be sure to save it and clear the screen before retrieving the master document.

2. Move the cursor to the desired location for the endnotes.

3. Press Footnote (Ctrl-F7).

   The following menu appears:

   Footnote; **2** Endnote; **3** Endnote Placement: **0**

4. Select Endnote Placement (**3**).

   WordPerfect prompts Restart endnote numbering? (Y/N) Yes

5. Press Enter or press *Y* to restart endnote numbering.

TIP: Place Hard Page Breaks before and after the endnote placement code to make sure the endnotes start on a new page and to keep text following the endnotes on its own page.

Using Automatic References

Master documents and automatic references work well together. You can create automatic references with the reference in one document and the target in another document. For example, in the dissertation you can mark references in several chapters that refer to a target contained in the appendix subdocument. Normally WordPerfect would not be able to match references and targets contained in different files; by expanding the master document, all references and targets are combined into one file.

When you choose **Generate** (4) to generate a table of contents, list, index, or table of authorities, WordPerfect updates any automatic references in your master or subdocuments also. When you condense the master document, be sure to save the updated subdocuments.

Creating Subdocuments within Subdocuments

You can make any document (including a subdocument file) into a master document by simply inserting a subdocument code. Imagine that Chapter 2 of the dissertation requires a table listing all the characters that appeared in a particular literary work. You can build this table right into the body of the chapter, or you can create the table as a separate file (called TABLE-3.1 for example) and, at the appropriate place, insert a subdocument code into the CHAPTER.3 file. By creating the files this way, CHAPTER.3 is both a subdocument (to the dissertation as a whole) and a master document (to the TABLE-3.1 file).

Finding Other Uses for Master Documents

Using master documents to manage a large dissertation or a book is a natural application. You can use this feature in other ways to improve the appearance of your document and to make your work easier.

Building Legal Contracts

If you've ever rented an apartment or bought a house, you know how complicated a contract can be. Preprinted contracts, because they must be all things to all people, usually include many sections and subsections that don't apply to your particular transaction. Usually these sections are crossed out by hand or stamped with the word delete.

Imagine now that you work in a law office preparing contracts of this type. With master document, you can save each section of a contract as individual files. Then, when you need to create a printed contract, you simply use the master document feature to pull together only those sections that you need. Every contract is a now a custom job!

Managing Group Writing

Many writers, for instance technical writers, frequently work in groups; each writer is assigned a specific group of tasks. Combining all these individual efforts into a single cohesive document is a time-consuming chore that takes away from the time available for researching and writing. Creating a master document saves time because you no longer have to combine manually the individual files for generating a table of contents or printing the final product.

WP
5 === Summary

This chapter illustrates how the Master Document feature helps you work more efficiently by separating a large document into small, easy-to-handle pieces. You can cut large jobs down to size with the Master Document feature by doing the following:

- Work with individual subdocument files, creating as many you need

- Build a master document, placing the subdocuments in the order you want them to appear

- Simplify editing tasks like spell-checking and replacing by performing these options on all the files at once

- Generate a table of contents, an index, lists, and a table of authorities for the entire project

- Print your complete, edited master document

Part

IV

Using WordPerfect
for Desktop Publishing

Includes

24

Integrating Text
and Graphics

*Karen Rose teaches
desktop publishing
courses at Sonoma State
University; she is also a
desktop publishing trainer
for businesses through Ron
Person & Co.* ∎

Desktop publishing means being able to create a publication-quality document using the computer on your desk. Because of WordPerfect 5's advanced formatting capabilities—such as working with columns, including different font sizes and styles, and creating and importing graphics—you no longer need a special desktop publishing program to publish an attractive document.

What distinguishes an ordinary document from a publication-quality document? For the most part, your document's graphical appearance makes a document publication-quality. In addition to presenting text in columns and varying the size and style of your text, you can improve the appearance of your document by including graphics.

With WordPerfect 5, you can include two types of graphics in your document. First, you can create graphics, such as lines, boxes, and shades. Second, you can import graphics created in graphics programs, such as PC Paintbrush®, Microsoft® Windows Paint, GEM Paint™, Dr. Halo, and many others. You also can import drawings from the popular drafting program AutoCAD®, and you can import graphs and spreadsheets from programs like Lotus 1-2-3 and Excel.

One major difference between a dedicated desktop publishing program and a word processing program is the appearance of your document on the computer screen. In a desktop publishing program like PageMaker®, what you see on-screen closely resembles what you see on your printed page. When editing with WordPerfect, graphics on-screen represent, but don't look like, what you'll see when you print your document. Figure 24.1 shows a figure with text as it appears on the WordPerfect screen; figure 24.2 shows the figure when it is printed.

Fig. 24.1.

A figure on-screen.

```
                    with  the knowledge, the money, and the time to
                    engage in a  complex process involving many players.
        ng          The process begins  with    ┌TXT 1──────────
                    an idea. It continues with   │
                    a writer, who originates     │
        t           the  material to be          │
                    published. An editor         │
                    modifies it for accuracy     │
        ,           and editorial slant; a       │
        sh          designer gives the           │
        te          publication its  shape; a    │
                    typesetter sets the words;   │
                    an illustrator enhances      │
                    ideas with pictures; and     │
        r           a pasteup artist             │
        r           assembles the                │
                    publication. A               │
                    commercial printer           │
                    completes the cycle.         │
        ts,         Each  one of these           │
                    skilled steps takes days     │
                    or weeks, and must be        │
                    precisely coordinated. Just managing that process can
                    be a  full-time job.
        C:\CH25\SAMPLNL3                       Col 2 Doc 1 Pg 1 Ln 5.27" Pos 4.37"
```

Fig. 24.2.

A printed figure.

Until now, publishing has belonged to the few: those with the knowledge, the money, and the time to engage in a complex process involving many players. The process begins with an idea. It continues with a writer, who originates the material to be published. An editor modifies it for accuracy and editorial slant; a designer gives the publication its shape; a typesetter sets the words; an illustrator enhances ideas with pictures; and a pasteup artist assembles the publication. A commercial printer completes the cycle. Each one of these skilled steps takes days or weeks, and must be precisely coordinated. Just managing that process can be a full-time job.

Johannes Gutenberg, the fifteenth-century inventor of movable type, brought the written word to the public. Today, personal computers bring a new generation of publishing to the individual.

In this chapter, you learn how to use graphics to enhance your document:

- Create figures, tables, text boxes, or user-defined boxes
- Select the options for each type of box: for instance, the borders of the box, the caption, and the spacing within the text
- Import graphics into boxes
- Edit the graphic image, making it smaller or larger, rotating it or inverting it
- Draw lines

Choosing the Type of Box

You can include boxes in your publication to highlight important text, such as a memorable quote; to separate a special type of text (a table of contents, for example) from the rest of the document; to frame a graphic; or to leave space for an illustration you'll add later.

To create a box, you complete three basic steps: first, you choose the type of box you want; second, you define the appearance of the box; and third, you create the box and define its contents.

WordPerfect offers you four different types of boxes: Figure, Table, Text Box, and User-defined Box. These four types of boxes are not really different. You follow the same steps to create each, and you can include text or graphics in any type of box. The distinction exists primarily for design convenience—you define each type of box as having specific design elements.

Figure 24.3 shows the default design for a Figure box; figure 24.4 shows the default design for a Table box. The default design for a Text Box is illustrated in figure 24.5, and figure 24.6 shows the default design for a User-defined Box. You can change the default design and change, for instance, the borders of the box, the caption, the spacing within the text, and other options for each type of box as you see fit.

Figure 1: A figure created with WordPerfect's default figure options. The WordPerfect graphic "BOOK.WPG" is included in the figure.

Fig. 24.3.
The default box for a figure.

Table I: A WordPerfect table, using default options.

	STAFF MEETING TIMES July, 1988		
	Dept. A	Dept. B	Dept. C
Week 1	9:00	10:00	1:30
Week 2	10:00	1:30	3:00
Week 3	9:00	10:00	1:30
Week 4	10:00	1:30	10:00

Fig. 24.4.
The default box for a table.

Fig. 24.5.

The default box for a text box.

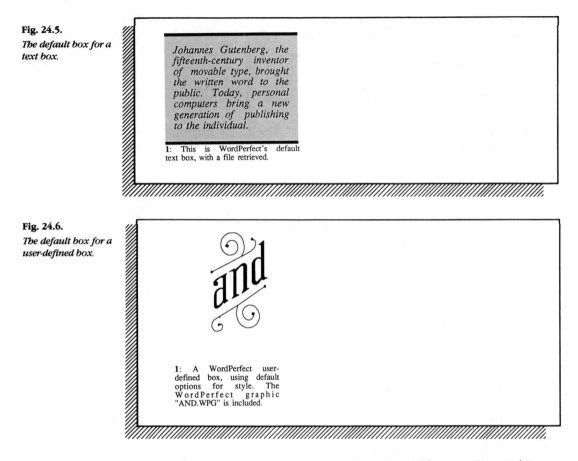

Johannes Gutenberg, the fifteenth-century inventor of movable type, brought the written word to the public. Today, personal computers bring a new generation of publishing to the individual.

1: This is WordPerfect's default text box, with a file retrieved.

Fig. 24.6.

The default box for a user-defined box.

and

1: A WordPerfect user-defined box, using default options for style. The WordPerfect graphic "AND.WPG" is included.

For example, if you publish a newsletter, such as the one shown in figure 24.7, you might have several types of items to include in boxes: nameplate, footer, quotes, and graphics. To manage the appearance of each, you can define the elements that make up each type of box and then assign each item to a type of box. For example, put the nameplate and footers in user-defined boxes, quotes in text boxes, and graphics in figures.

In addition to design convenience, assigning types of boxes also allows WordPerfect to keep track of each of the different box types. You can print lists of boxes. For example, you can create a list of all the figures and another list of all the tables. (See Chapter 22.)

To choose the type of box you want to create, complete the following steps:

1. Press Graphics (Alt-F9).

   The following menu appears:

   1 Figure; **2 T**able; **3 T**ext Box; **4 U**ser-defined Box; **5 L**ine: **0**

2. Select the type of box.

   For instance, select **F**igure (**1**).

Fig. 24.7.
A sample newsletter.

The following menu appears (the first word varies depending on the type of box you selected):

Figure: 1 Create; **2** Edit; **3** New Number **4** Options: **0**

Your next selection depends on which stage of the publication you're in:

- In the planning stages, select **Options** (**4**) to define the design of this type of box.

- If you have already set the options for the box type and are ready to create the box, select **Create** (**1**).

- In the later stages of production, you may need to edit or renumber a box. Select **Edit** (**4**) or New Number (**3**) for these cases.

Choosing Box Options

As you plan your publication, you should decide in advance what you'll use each of the different types of boxes for and how each will look.

For example, you may decide to use figures to import graphics created in another program, such as PC Paintbrush; therefore, you Define Figure as a box with double borders. You may decide to use text boxes to call out important text in your document. Define Text Box as a box with thick top and bottom borders and no side borders. Put the nameplate and footers in user-defined boxes that span the width of the page, and define User-defined box as having thick top and bottom borders, single left and right borders, and 10% gray shading.

When you define box options, those options remain in effect from that point forward in your document. Make sure that you define options before you draw the box. If you want to change the options after you've drawn the box, position the cursor before the box. Use Reveal Codes (Alt-F3, or F11) to check the cursor's position.

To choose box options, complete the following steps:

1. Select **Options** (**4**) from the command line.

   The Options: Figure menu appears (see fig. 24.8). (The name of the menu varies depending on the type of box you are defining.)

2. If you simply want to review and keep the pre-defined options, press Exit (F7)

   or

   Change the options.

You can change the border style, the space between the border and the text, the space between the border and the contents of the box, the caption (numbering and placement), and the shading. See the following sections on each option.

Choosing the Border Style

A box has four sides. You can define each side to appear the way you choose. The sides can all look the same, or they can all be different.

To choose a border style for your box, complete the following steps:

1. Select **Border** Style (**1**) from the Options menu.

```
Options:    Figure

        1 - Border Style
              Left                         Single
              Right                        Single
              Top                          Single
              Bottom                       Single
        2 - Outside Border Space
              Left                         0.16"
              Right                        0.16"
              Top                          0.16"
              Bottom                       0.16"
        3 - Inside Border Space
              Left                         0"
              Right                        0"
              Top                          0"
              Bottom                       0"
        4 - First Level Numbering Method   Numbers
        5 - Second Level Numbering Method  Off
        6 - Caption Number Style           [BOLD]Figure 1[bold]
        7 - Position of Caption            Below box, Outside borders
        8 - Minimum Offset from Paragraph  0"
        9 - Gray Shading (% of black)      0%

    Selection: 0
```

Fig. 24.8.
The Options: Figure menu.

The following menu appears:

1 None; **2** Single; **3** Double; **4** Dashed; **5** Dotted; **6** Thick; **7** Extra Thick: **0**

2. Select a border style for the Left border

   or

   Press Enter to leave style the same and move to the next choice.

   For example, to create the borders for the user-defined box containing the nameplate, select **Single** (**2**).

3. Select border styles for the Right, Top, and Bottom borders in the same way.

   For the user-defined box, select **Single** (**2**) for the Right border and **Thick** (**6**) for the Top and Bottom borders.

4. After entering the borders, select other options from the menu

   or

   Press Exit (F7) to return to your document.

Figure 24.9 shows some sample borders.

Setting Space between Border and Text

Because you don't want the text of your publication to run into the box, use Outside Border Space to specify how much space should be left between your box and the text that surrounds the box.

Fig. 24.9.
Different types of borders.

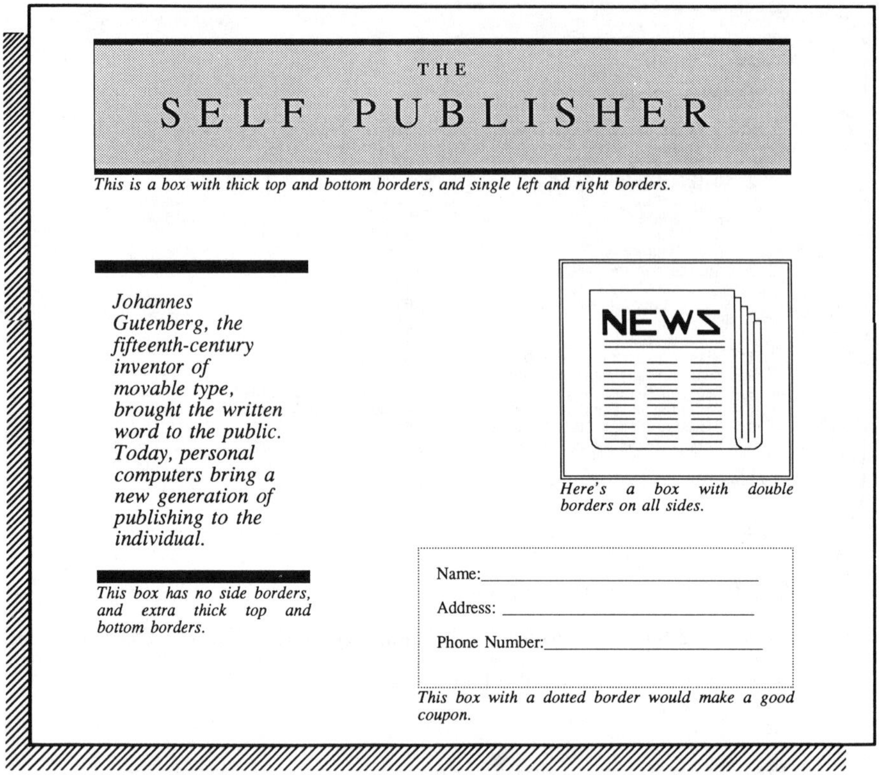

To choose an outside border space, complete the following steps:

1. Select **O**utside Border Space (**2**) from the Options menu.

2. Type a distance for the left outside border and press Enter

   or

   Press Enter to leave the measurement and move to the next border.

   If you're working in inches, type the distance as a decimal.

   For your example, type *.25* and press Enter.

3. Type distances for each of the three remaining outside border spaces and press Enter.

4. Select other options to change

   or

   Press Exit (F7) to return to your document.

The measurements you enter for border space and other options depend on your Initial Setup. WordPerfect's default unit of measurement is inches, and for the examples in this chapter, inches are used. You can change the measurement to picas, centimeters, or units (columns and rows) in Setup (see Appendix A); then enter measurements in these units.

Setting Space between Border and Contents

In addition to space between the text and the box, you probably want some distance between what's inside your box and the border of the box; you don't want the text to run into the side of the box. The Inside Border Space selection on the Options menu measures the distance between the contents of your box and the border.

To specify the space between the contents of the box and the border, complete the following steps:

1. Select Inside Border Space (3) from the Options menu.

2. Type a distance for the left inside border and press Enter

   or

   Press Enter to leave the distance and move to the next border.

   For your example, leave 1/8-inch by typing *.12* and pressing Enter.

3. Type inside border distances for the remaining three sides of your box; press Enter after each choice.

   For your example, type *.12* and press Enter three more times.

4. Select other options to change

   or

   Press Exit (F7) to return to your document.

Choosing the Caption Numbering Style

As you create individual boxes, you specify whether to include a caption. If you do include captions, you can elect to let WordPerfect number them automatically. With this menu, you select the style of caption numbering that will be used for the caption.

If you choose automatic numbering, WordPerfect numbers each of the four box types consecutively within type. For example, if you include three figures and two tables in your document, they are numbered Figure 1, Figure 2, Figure 3, Table I, and Table II (depending on which style of numbering you choose). You can create lists of these figures and tables automatically .

You can select two levels of numbering; each level can be written in numbers, letters, or Roman numerals. Letters and Roman numerals for first-level box numbering print in uppercase. Letters and Roman numerals for second-level box numbering print in lowercase.

To choose the numbering style, complete the following:

1. Select **First Level Numbering Method (4)** from the Options menu.

   The following menu appears:

   1 Off; **2** Numbers; **3** Letters; **4** Roman Numerals: **0**

2. Select the numbering style you want.

3. Select **Second Level Numbering Method (5)** from the Options menu if you want to include a second number in the caption.

4. Choose the numbering style you want.

5. Select other options to change

   or

   Press Exit (F7) to return to the document.

Selecting Text for Captions

In addition to defining caption numbering style, you also define the caption appearance and the text contained in the caption. Captions can include any text, formatted in any way. For example, WordPerfect's default caption number style for figures is [BOLD]Figure 1[bold]; the number 1 indicates first-level numbering. The caption appears as **Figure 1** when printed.

You can change the default to suit your preferences. For instance, you might want your figure captions to read Fig. 1.2 and to be underlined.

To specify the caption number style, complete the following steps:

1. Select **Caption Number Style (6)** from the Options menu.

   Replace with: appears, followed by the default numbering style.

2. If you want the text formatted a certain way, enter text formatting codes (bold, underline, or font size and appearance).

   For example, press Underline (F8).

3. Type the text of the caption.

   Type *1* to include first level caption numbering; type *2* for second level numbering. Also, include any punctuation between levels.

   For example, type *Fig. 1.2.*

4. Press ending formatting codes.

   For example, press Underline (F8).

5. Press Enter.

6. Select other options to change

or

Press Exit (F7) to return to your document.

Setting the Position for Captions

Captions appear either below or above boxes, and either inside or outside the border.

To choose the caption position, complete the following steps:

1. Select Position of Caption (7) from the Options menu.

   The following menu appears:

   Caption Position: 1 Below Box; **2** Above Box: **1**

2. Select **Below Box (1)** to position the caption below the box

   or

   Select Above Box (**2**) to position the caption above the box.

   The following menu appears:

   Caption: 1 Outside of Border; **2** Inside Border: **1**

3. Select **Outside of Border (1)** to position the caption outside the border of the box

   or

   Select Inside of Border (**2**) to position the caption inside the border of the box.

4. Select other options to change

   or

   Press Exit (F7) to return to your document.

Determining Offset from Paragraph

When you define a box as a paragraph (see "Anchoring a Box to the Text"), you attach the box to the paragraph, and the box stays with the paragraph. For instance, a box can contain a picture referred to in the paragraph. You want the paragraph and box to stay together, and they will unless the paragraph is at the bottom of the page. Then, it may be impossible for the box to fit exactly as you've specified.

When the box cannot fit on the page, WordPerfect first tries to fit the box on the page by reducing the distance between the top of the paragraph and the start of the box. With this option, you specify the distance this space can be reduced.

For example, you can specify that the box should be two inches from the top of the paragraph. With the Options menu, you specify that this two-inch space can be reduced to one inch if necessary. Then, if the box doesn't fit two inches from the paragraph, WordPerfect pushes the box up to within one inch of the top of the paragraph. If the box still won't fit, WordPerfect moves the box to the next page.

To set the minimum paragraph offset, complete the following steps:

1. Select Minimum Offset from Paragraph (**8**) from the Options menu.

2. Type the minimum offset distance and press Enter.

3. Select other options to change

   or

   Press Exit (F7) to return to your document.

Determining Percent of Gray Shading

If your printer supports gray shading, you can add shading to boxes. A light gray shading, for example, is like a screen or tint on a printed publication. Use shading to highlight text or add graphic interest to a page.

Gray shading is measured as a percent of black. Zero percent shading is no shading; 100 percent shading is black. Ten percent shading makes a good background for text. The nameplate and footers in figure 24.7 contain 10% shading.

To determine percent of gray shading, complete the following steps:

1. Select **Gray** Shading (% of black) (**9**) from the Options menu.

2. Type a number from 1 to 100 and press Enter.

3. Press Exit (F7) to return to the document.

Creating the Box

After you've selected options for each type of box, you're ready to create boxes. (You can create boxes without choosing options. WordPerfect will use its own initial box settings.)

To create a box, complete the following steps:

1. Press Graphics (Alt-F9).

2. Select a box type (Figure, Table, Text Box, or User-defined Box).

   For instance, select Figure (**1**) to create a figure.

3. Select **Create (1)**.

   The Definition: Figure menu appears (see fig. 24.10). The name varies depending on the type of box you select.

4. Press Enter to accept the defaults for the definitions

   or

   Select and enter the definitions you want.

```
Definition: Figure

      1 - Filename

      2 - Caption

      3 - Type                    Paragraph

      4 - Vertical Position       0"

      5 - Horizontal Position     Right

      6 - Size                    3.25" wide x 3.25" (high)

      7 - Wrap Text Around Box    Yes

      8 - Edit




   Selection: 0
```

Fig. 24.10.
The Definition: Figure menu.

You can enter a file name to import a graphics or text file, add a caption, select box type, position the box on the page, specify the size of the box, and edit the box.

Entering a File Name

When you create a box, it can be empty, filled with text, or filled with a graphic. If you want to retrieve a text file or graphics file, you can enter the file name, and the file is inserted in the box. Or, you can skip this option and create an empty box, or you can type the text to be included in the box as you create it. (Including text in the box is discussed in the section "Entering Text in a Box".)

To retrieve a file into your box, complete the following steps:

1. Select Filename (**1**) from the box Definition menu.

2. At the prompt Enter filename:, type the name of the file to retrieve and press Enter.

3. Select other options to define

or

Press Exit (F7) to return to your document.

WordPerfect retrieves many different types of graphics files, including AutoCAD, PC Paintbrush, Lotus 1-2-3, and others. For many other types of graphics, you can export files into another format that can be retrieved (see Chapter 25). WordPerfect also supplies several clip-art graphics on the Fonts/Graphics disk. (See "Importing Graphics.")

Entering a Caption

With this option, you choose whether to include a caption for each box and whether to add text to the caption. Remember that when you defined the options for this type of box, you specified the caption numbering style and the caption.

To enter a caption for a box, complete the following:

1. Select Caption (2) from the Definition menu.

   A screen appears with the default caption you have assigned.

2. Press Exit (F7) to leave the caption

   or

   Type additional text for the caption

   or

   Replace the caption by pressing Backspace, typing the new caption, and pressing Enter.

   If you change your mind about the replacement, press Graphics (Alt-F9) to restore the default caption.

3. Press Exit (F7).

You can use any character formatting commands to enhance the appearance of your text in the caption. Captions conform to the width of the box to which they're associated.

4. Select other definitions to change

   or

   Press Exit (F7) to return to your document.

Anchoring a Box to the Text

You can define a box to be one of three types of boxes: paragraph, page, or character. The box type determines the relationship between box and text.

A *Paragraph* box stays with its paragraph: if the paragraph moves, so does the box. The box can be offset from the top of the paragraph. Use this type of box when the box explains the text of the paragraph. In the sample newsletter, the quill illustration and the pull quote are contained in paragraph-type boxes (see fig. 24.7).

A *Page* box is anchored to the page and stays on the page regardless of changes to the surrounding text. You can use this type box for headlines, for instance. The headline should always appear on the first page no matter what the text of the page is. (Be sure that the box code falls before any text you want to wrap around the box.) In the sample newsletter, the nameplate is contained in a page-type box so that the nameplate always stays at the top of the page (see fig. 24.7).

A *Character* box is treated as a character, no matter how big the box is. If a character-type box is included in a line of text that wraps to the next line, the wrapped text appears below the box. (Only character-type boxes can be used in footnotes and endnotes.)

In the next section, "Aligning a Box," you learn how to position a box in relation to the paragraph, page, or character.

To determine the box type, complete the following steps:

1. Select **Type (3)** from the Definition menu.

   The following menu appears:

   Type: 1 Paragraph; **2** Page; **3** Character: **0**

2. Select the type of box you want.

3. Select other definitions

   or

   Press Exit (F7) to return to your document.

Aligning a Box

The box type determines how you align the box. Box alignment defines, simply, where the box appears on the page. Does the box align with the top of a paragraph, or with the right margin of the page, or with the top edge of a line of text? You specify two types of box alignment: vertical and horizontal.

Aligning a Paragraph Box

The vertical (top-to-bottom) alignment for a paragraph-type box is measured from the top of the paragraph. The horizontal (left-to-right) alignment for a paragraph-type box is measured from the margins of the paragraph.

To align a paragraph-type box, complete the following steps:

1. Select Vertical Position (4) from the Definition menu.

   The following message appears:

   ```
   Offset from top of paragraph: 0"
   ```

   The number following the prompt represents the current distance of the cursor from the top of the paragraph. Thus, if the number is 0 (zero), the cursor is in the top line of the paragraph.

2. To place the box where your cursor is currently located in the paragraph, press Enter to leave this number

   or

   Type the distance the box should be offset from the top of the paragraph and press Enter.

   To line up the box with the top of the paragraph, type *0* (zero) and press Enter. To place the box one-half inch below the top of the paragraph, type *.5* and press Enter.

   If the paragraph starts close to the bottom of the page, the box may move up in the paragraph in order to fit on the page (see "Determining Offset From Paragraph"). If the box still can't fit, it moves to the next page or column.

3. Select Horizontal Position (5) from the Definition menu.

   The following menu appears:

   Horizontal Position: 1 Left; 2 Right; 3 Center; 4 Both Left & Right: 0

4. Select **Left** (1) to align the box with the left margin

   or

   Select **Right** (2) to align the box with the right margin

   or

   Select **Center** (3) to center the box between the two margins

   or

   Select **Both Left & Right** (4) to extend the box from margin to margin.

Aligning a Page Box

You can specify a page-type box's position on the page. For instance, for a nameplate, you can specify that the box appear at the top of the page. If you want to insert a full-page picture, you can specify that the box fill the entire page.

To align a page-type box, complete the following:

1. Select Vertical Position (**4**) from the Definition menu.

   The following menu appears:

   Vertical Position: 1 Full Page; **2** Top; **3** Center; **4** Bottom; **5** Set Position: **0**

2. Select Full Page (**1**) to expand the box to fill the entire page

   or

   Select Top (**2**) to align the box with the top margin

   or

   Select Center (**3**) to center the box between the top and bottom margin

   or

   Select Bottom (**4**) to align the box with the bottom margin (above any footers or footnotes).

   To specify an exact position on the page, select Set Position (**5**). When prompted `Offset from top of paragraph:`, type the distance the box should be offset from the top of the page, and press Enter.

   The measurement that appears for Set Position (**5**) reflects the current distance of the cursor from the top of the page; if you want the box to be anchored at that point, don't change this distance.

3. Select Horizontal Position (**5**) from the Definition menu to specify the horizontal position of the box.

   The following menu appears:

   Horizontal Position: 1 Margins; **2** Columns; **3** Set Position: **0**

4. Select the placement you want.

To align the box with the margins, complete the following steps:

1. Select Margins (**1**).

   The following menu appears:

   Horizontal Position: 1 Left; **2** Right; **3** Center; **4** Both Left & Right: **0**

2. Select the placement: aligned with left margin, aligned with right margin, centered between margins, or extended between both margins.

If your document includes columns, you can align a page-type box inside the column you specify. To align the box within a column, do the following steps:

1. Select Columns (**2**).

2. When prompted `Enter column(s):1`, specify the column or columns in which you want the box aligned.

The following menu appears:

Horizontal Position: 1 Left; **2** Right; **3** Center; **4** Both Left & Right: **0**

3. Select the placement.

For instance, to center the box between columns 2 and 3, type *2-3* for columns and then select **Center** (**3**).

To specify an exact horizontal position, complete the following steps:

1. Select **Set Position** (**3**).

You are prompted: `Offset from left of page:`

2. Type the distance for the box to be offset from the left margin and press Enter.

Aligning a Character Box

Horizontally, the character-type box always aligns to the right of the character before the box. You can specify the vertical alignment of the text relative to the box (rather than choosing the alignment of the box relative to a margin or column).

To align a character box, complete the following steps:

1. Select **Vertical Position** (**4**) from the Definition menu.

The following menu appears:

Align Text with: 1 Top of Box; **2** Center of Box; **3** Bottom of Box: **0**

2. Select **Top of Box** (**1**) to align the text with the top of the box

or

Select **Center of Box** (**2**) to align the text with the center of the box

or

Select **Bottom of Box** (**3**) to align text with bottom of box.

Selecting the Box Size

After you specify the alignment of the box, you then select the size of the box. Boxes are measured in decimal inches (unless you change the units of measurement in the Setup menu).

You can set the box width and let WordPerfect calculate its height based on the size of the graphic or the amount of text the box contains. (WordPerfect automatically calculates the height of a box containing a retrieved text file.) For instance, you might want a text box to be three inches wide. Because you are not sure how much height the text will take when it is inserted in a three-inch box, let WordPerfect calculate the height.

As an alternative, you can set the box height and let WordPerfect calculate the width Or, you can set both width and height.

To select the size of the box, complete the following steps:

1. Select Size (**6**) from the Definition menu.

   The following menu appears:

   1 Width (auto height); **2** Height (auto width) **3** Both Width and Height: **0**

2. Select **Width** (**1**) to specify the width of the box; WordPerfect calculates the height based on the contents of the box

   or

   Select **Height** (**2**) to specify the height of the box; WordPerfect calculates the width based on the contents of the box

   or

   Select **Both Width and Height** (**3**) to specify both the width and height.

3. Type in the width, height, or both measurements (depending on your selection in Step 2) and press Enter.

4. Select other definitions to change

   or

   Press Exit (**F7**) to return to your document.

Wrapping Text around the Box

If you elect to wrap text around the boxes you create, then WordPerfect notes the position of the box. Any text you type goes around the box without touching its edges (see fig. 24.11). The Outside Border Space you select when you define the box determines how close the text comes to the box.

Johannes Gutenberg, the fifteenth-century inventor of movable type, brought the written word to the public, and thus is responsible for publishing as it has been known for five hundred years. In the last quarter century, Gutenberg's metal type has been replaced by electronic typesetting - faster, more flexible, but still very expensive, and still only part of the complex process of publishing. Today, personal computers bring a new generation of publishing to the individual.

The mighty quill has been replaced by a powerful desktop computer

Fig. 24.11.
Text wrapped around a box.

You can wrap text around 20 boxes on a page; if you include more than 20 boxes, text prints through them. Note that text wraps only to the left of a box created in the center of a page; if you want text to the right as well, use columns.

The default specifies text to be wrapped because more than likely you want text to wrap around the boxes. If you choose not to wrap text, text goes right through your box. You won't see an outline of your box on-screen with View Document.

To change the text wrap feature, complete the following:

1. Select **Wrap Text Around Box (7)** from the Definition menu.

2. Press *Y* to wrap text around the box

   or

   Press *N* if you want text to print through the box.

3. Select other definitions to change

   or

   Press Exit (F7) to return to your document.

Entering Text in a Box

You can include text in a box by retrieving a text file that you've already created, or you can include text directly in a box by using Edit (**8**). You can format the text while you type, or you can use the Block command to make formatting changes after you've typed the text. Formatting options include bold, underline, and font attributes such as size and appearance.

To enter text in a box, complete the following steps:

1. Select Edit (**8**) from the Definition menu.

   A special screen for entering text appears.

2. Type the text, using any of WordPerfect's text formatting capabilities.

3. Select **Graphics** (Alt-F9) to rotate your text

   or

   Press Exit (F7) to return to your document.

If you choose, you can rotate the text counterclockwise—a capability sorely missing from most dedicated desktop publishing programs! (However, your printer must be able to support rotated fonts if you plan to print rotated text. PostScript printers, such as the Apple LaserWriter, support rotated text.)

To rotate text, complete the following steps:

1. Press Graphics (Alt-F9) from the Edit (**8**) screen.

The following menu appears:

Rotate: 1 0°; **2** 90°; **3** 180°; **4** 270°: **1**

2. Select a degree of rotation.

3. Press Exit (F7) twice to return to the document.

The Edit command can be used to modify the appearance of a graphic (see "Editing a Graphic Image").

Remember that text in a box doesn't appear on-screen; you can see only the outline of the box. You can use View Document to see the contents of a box.

Note that any time you select **Create** (**1**) to create a figure, table, text box, or user-defined box, and then press Exit (F7) to leave that menu, you create a box. To exit without creating a box, press Esc.

Viewing the Document

Keep in mind that WordPerfect boxes look one way on-screen and another way when printed. The screen representation is just that—a representation. When you create a figure, on-screen for example, you see only an outline with the abbreviation FIG 1 at the top (FIG 2 if it's the second figure, and so forth). You don't see the contents of the figure. In fact, you don't even see the outline until you've moved the cursor past the place on-screen where the figure is placed.

To view the box, complete the following steps:

1. Press Print (Shift-F7).

2. Select View Document (**6**).

3. Select a display size.

For instance, select 200% (**2**).

100% displays the page in actual size; 200% displays the page in twice its actual size. Full Page shows you the entire page reduced to fit on-screen; Facing Pages displays a full page view of two pages.

Figure 24.12 shows the page in twice its actual size (200%).

As you're creating boxes, you should check your document's appearance frequently. You can use View Document fairly easily, but you can create a macro that lets you view your document even more quickly.

To create a quickview macro, complete the following:

1. Press Macro Define (Ctrl-F10).

2. Press Alt-V.

Fig. 24.12.
*Using View
Document.*

3. Type the description *quickview* and press Enter.

4. Press Print (Shift-F7).

5. Press View Document (**6**).

6. Press Macro Define (Ctrl-F10).

7. Press Exit (F7) to return to your document.

To view your document quickly, just press Alt-V, and then press Exit (F7) when you're ready to return to the document.

Editing a Box

Once you create a box, you then can edit the box, whether the box is a figure, a table, a text box, or a user-defined box, and whether the box is empty or contains text or a graphic.

Boxes are labeled and numbered on-screen. The first figure you create is called FIG 1; the first table is TAB 1. To edit a box, you must identify the box by type and number.

Follow these steps to edit a box:

1. Press Graphics (Alt-F9).

2. Select the type of box (Figure, Table, Text Box, User-defined Box).

3. Select Edit (**2**).

4. Type the box number and press Enter.

   The Definition menu appears.

5. Make any changes you like.

6. Press Exit (F7) to return to your document.

Changing the Box Type

Besides editing the contents, size, shape, and appearance of a box, you can change the box type also. For instance, you may decide Figure 1 should be a user-defined box.

To change the box type, complete the following steps:

1. Press Graphics (Alt-F9).

2. Select the type of box you want to change.

   For instance, select **Figure (1)**.

3. Select **Edit (2)**.

4. Type the number of the box you want to change and press Enter.

   For instance, type *1* to change Figure 1 and press Enter.

   The Definition menu appears.

5. Press Graphics (Alt-F9) again.

6. Select the new type of box you want.

   For example, select User-defined Box (**4**) to change the figure to a user-defined box.

7. Press Exit (F7) to return to the document.

The change doesn't appear immediately; move the cursor beyond the box you've changed to display the change.

Changing a Box Number

Box numbering begins with 1 (or I, or A) at the beginning of the document and continues consecutively through the document. You can change the numbering at any time. The new numbering remains in effect until you change it again. For example, if you include four figures in your document, they're probably numbered Figure 1, Figure 2, Figure 3, and Figure 4. Suppose you want to skip number 3 and continue with 4 and 5.

To change a box number, complete the following steps:

1. Move the cursor to the place in your document where you want numbering to change.

2. Press Graphics (Alt-F9).

3. Select the type of box to renumber.

4. Select New Number (3).

5. Type the new number and press Enter.

6. Press Exit (F7) to return to your document.

Move the cursor past the newly-numbered box to see the change.

You can enter the new number in any format—numeric, roman, or letter—and the number translates into the format being used for the selected box type. For example, if your figures are numbered 1, 2, 3, 4, and you enter the new number as "D," the number automatically translates to "4."

Importing Graphics

Importing graphics is an integral part of creating a box. WordPerfect supports many types of graphics files, either directly or indirectly. See Chapter 25 for a complete list of graphics files you can import.

WordPerfect also supplies clip-art graphics images on the Fonts/Graphics disk (see fig. 24.13). All of these files end in the extension .WPG.

Fig. 24.13.

A sampling of the graphic images supplied on Fonts/ Graphics disk.

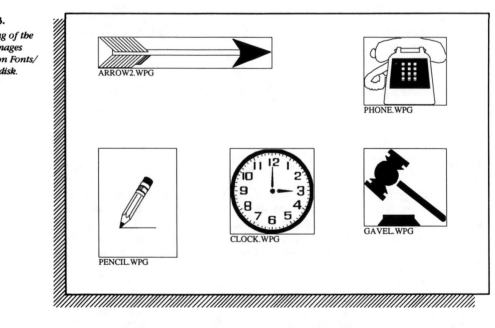

ARROW2.WPG

PHONE.WPG

PENCIL.WPG

CLOCK.WPG

GAVEL.WPG

To import a graphic into a box, complete the following steps:

1. Press Graphics (Alt-F9).

2. Select the type of box (Figure, Table, Text Box, or User-defined Box).

   For your example, select **Figure (1)**.

3. Select **Create (1)**.

4. Select **Filename (1)** from the Definition menu.

5. Type the name of the graphics file and press Enter.

   For your example, type *quill.wpg* and press Enter.

6. Select other items from the Definition menu

   or

   Press Exit (F7) to return to your document.

If you do not specify the box size, WordPerfect calculates the size of the box for you, based on the size of the file you're retrieving.

Editing a Graphic Image

Once you import a graphic, you can manipulate it to suit your preferences. You can use the Edit command to move the graphic to a different position inside the box, to make the graphic smaller or larger, to rotate the graphic, or to invert (switch) the graphic.

To edit a graphic, complete the following steps:

1. Press Graphics (Alt-F9).

2. Select the type of box to edit (Figure, Table, Text Box, or User-defined Box).

3. Select **Edit (2)**.

4. Type the box number and press Enter.

5. Select **Edit (8)** from the Definition menu.

The graphic appears on-screen (see fig. 24.14). The bottom of the screen shows the editing changes you can make; the top of the screen shows shortcuts to make the changes.

Moving an Image

When you move a graphic image, the graphic moves, but the box stays where it is. You can move or *crop* an image so that only part of the image is visible in the box. For instance, you may want to crop the feather from the quill (see fig. 24.15).

Fig. 24.14.
Editing a graphics image.

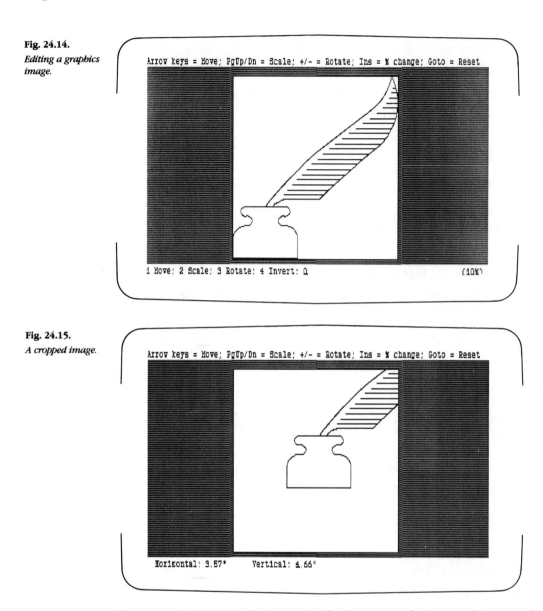

Arrow keys = Move; PgUp/Dn = Scale; +/- = Rotate; Ins = % change; Goto = Reset

1 Move; 2 Scale; 3 Rotate; 4 Invert; 0   (10%)

Fig. 24.15.
A cropped image.

Arrow keys = Move; PgUp/Dn = Scale; +/- = Rotate; Ins = % change; Goto = Reset

Horizontal: 3.57"   Vertical: 4.66"

To move an image inside the box using the shortcut method, press ↑ to move the image up, ↓ to move the image down, → to move the image to the right, or ← to move the image to the left. The image is moved the percent amount shown in the bottom right of your screen. (You can change this amount; simply press Ins until the amount you want appears: 1%, 5%, 10%, or 25%.)

To move an image by a specified distance, complete the following steps:

1. Select **Move (1)** from the menu bar.

2. Type the horizontal distance to move and press Enter.

Enter a positive number to move the image to the right; enter a negative number to move the image to the left.

For instance, type *1* and press Enter to move the quill to the right one inch.

3. Type the vertical distance to move and press Enter.

Enter a positive number to move the image up; enter a negative number to move the image down.

For instance, type *1* and press Enter to move the image up one inch.

4. Make other editing changes

or

Press Exit (F7) twice to return to your document.

Scaling an Image

Scaling an image means changing its size — making it larger or smaller. Only the graphic changes; the box size stays the same.

To scale an image using a shortcut, press PgUp to make the image larger, or press PgDn to make the image smaller. The image is scaled by the percentage amount shown at the bottom right corner of your screen.

To scale an image up or down by a specified percent, complete the following steps:

1. Select **Scale** (**2**) from the menu bar.

2. For **Scale X:**, type the percent to scale the image horizontally (from side to side) and press Enter.

For example, type *150* and press Enter.

3. For **Scale Y:**, type the percent to scale the image vertically (from top to bottom) and press Enter.

For example, type *150* and press Enter.

To make an image smaller, enter amounts less than 100 for Steps 2 and 3; to make an image larger, enter amounts larger than 100 for Steps 2 and 3.

4. Make other editing changes

or

Press Exit (F7) twice to return to your document.

Figure 24.16 shows the quill scaled 150 percent both horizontally and vertically.

Fig. 24.16.

An image scaled up.

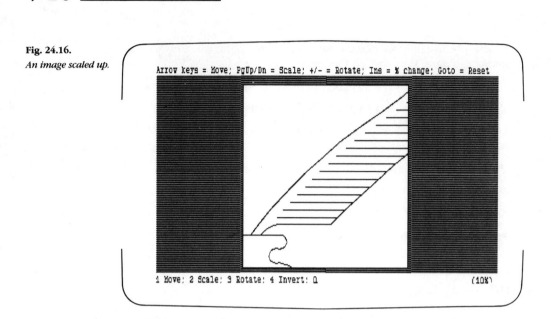

```
Arrow keys = Move; PgUp/Dn = Scale; +/- = Rotate; Ins = % change; Goto = Reset
```

```
1 Move; 2 Scale; 3 Rotate; 4 Invert: 0                              (10%)
```

Rotating and Mirroring an Image

In addition to moving or scaling an image, you also can rotate or mirror it. Rotating an image turns it clockwise or counter-clockwise inside the box; mirroring an image turns it to face in the opposite direction.

There are two types of graphic images: object and bitmap. An object-oriented graphic is made of lines, while a bitmapped image is made of dots. (See Chapter 25 for more information on types of images.) WordPerfect treats the two types of graphics differently: you can't rotate a bitmap image, but you can mirror it.

To rotate the image using a shortcut, press Screen Up (- on the numeric keypad) to rotate the image clockwise, or press Screen Down (+ on the numeric keypad) to rotate the image counter-clockwise.

To rotate an image by a specified amount, complete the following steps:

1. Select **R**otate (**3**) from the menu bar.

2. Type the number of degrees to rotate the image and press Enter.

    For example, type *90* and press Enter.

A full circle is 360 degrees. You can rotate an image counter-clockwise (to the left) only; to rotate clockwise (to the right), use the keyboard shortcut.

Figure 24.17 shows an image rotated 90 degrees.

    If you don't want to rotate the image, but want only to mirror the image, type 0 (zero) and press Enter.

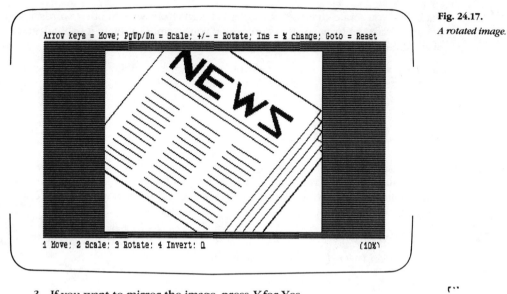

Fig. 24.17.
A rotated image.

3. If you want to mirror the image, press *Y* for Yes

   or

   Press *N* for No.

A mirrored image is flipped on the page (see fig. 24.18).

4. Make other editing changes

   or

   Press Exit (F7) twice to return to your document.

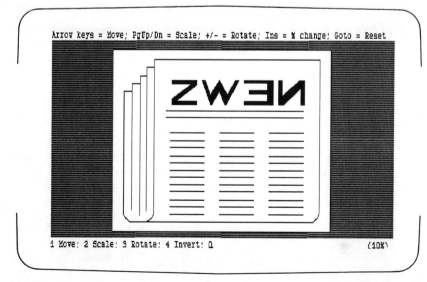

Fig. 24.18.
A mirrored image.

Each time you rotate an image, WordPerfect starts from zero. In other words, if you already rotated an image by 90 degrees, and you attempt to rotate it by 90 degrees again, the image is not rotated 180 degrees. The rotation remains 90.

Similarly, you mirror an image when you press *Y* for Yes for Step 3; the only way to restore the image to its original position is to press *N* for No.

Inverting an Image

If your graphic is a *bitmap image* (composed of dots) rather than an *object-oriented image* (made of lines), you can invert it. When you invert an image, each black dot turns white, and each white dot turns black. Or, put another way, each "on" dot turns off, while each "off" dot turns on.

To invert an image, complete the following steps:

1. Select Invert (4) from the menu bar.

2. Make other editing changes

   or

   Press Exit (F7) to return to your document.

Including an Image in a Header, Footer, Footnote, or Endnote

You can include any type of box as part of a header or footer, and the box appears on each page (or on the pages you choose as part of your header/footer definition).

To include an image in a header or footer, complete the following:

1. Create your header or footer (see Chapter 6).

2. At the header/footer editing screen, press Graphics (Alt-F9).

3. Create the box as usual.

4. Press Exit (F7) to return to the header/footer editing screen.

You can include text in the header or footer as well; type the text either before or after you create the box. There's only one restriction on including a box in a header or footer: you can't include a caption. Figure 24.19 shows how a user-defined box (containing text and automatic page numbering) is included in a footer; the footer repeats on every page of the newsletter.

If you're creating footnotes or endnotes, you may include only a character-type box.

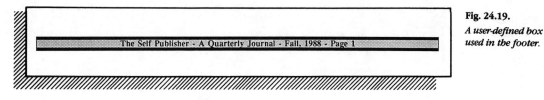

Fig. 24.19.
*A user-defined box
used in the footer.*

Creating Graphics Lines

You can draw lines and boxes by using Line Draw or by using Graphics. When you
use Graphics to create lines and boxes, they are objects that are separate from, yet
attached to, your text. Drawing graphics in this manner has many advantages. Most
important, the line or box remains intact when you make changes in the text. A
paragraph wraps around a figure, for example, and a column goes up to, but not
over, a line.

With Line Draw, the line or box is made up of characters in the text. You can't type
over or through lines drawn with Line Draw. Also, you can't use Line Draw with
proportionally spaced fonts such as Times Roman or Helvetica.

You create graphics lines in much the same way that you create graphics boxes, and
graphics lines offer similar options. For example, you can create lines in different
widths and different shades, and you can position them anywhere on the page. You
can't, however, edit a line. To change a line, use Reveal Codes (Alt-F3, or F11) to
delete the line code and create a new line. (The Reveal Code is either **[HLine]** or
[VLine] followed by the line specifications.)

You can draw two types of lines in WordPerfect: horizontal (from side to side on the
page), and vertical (up and down on the page). Actually, you don't draw the lines;
rather you describe how they look and then define where they should appear on the
page.

Creating Horizontal Lines

Use horizontal lines to set off text on the page. For example, the sample newsletter
contains a horizontal line below the the nameplate to separate it from the start of
the text (see fig. 24.7).

To draw a horizontal line, complete the following steps:

1. Press Graphics (Alt-F9).

   The following menu appears:

   1 Figure; **2** Table; **3** Text Box; **4** User-defined Box; **5** Line: 0

2. Select Line (**5**).

3. Select Horizontal Line (**1**).

   The Graphics: Horizontal Line menu appears (see fig. 24.20).

Fig. 24.20.

*The Graphics:
Horizontal Line
menu.*

```
Graphics: Horizontal Line

    1 - Horizontal Position          Left & Right

    2 - Length of Line

    3 - Width of Line                0.01"

    4 - Gray Shading (% of black)    100%
```

```
Selection: 0
```

4. Select **Horizontal Position** (**1**).

   This option determines where the line begins and ends; the following
   menu appears:

   Horizontal Pos: 1 Left; 2 Right; 3 Center; 4 Both Left & Right; 5 Set Position: 0

5. Select **Left** (**1**) to start the line at the left margin

   or

   Select **Right** (**2**) to start the line at the right margin

   or

   Select **Center** (**3**) to center the line between the margins

   or

   Select **Both Left & Right** (**4**) to extend the line from the left to the right
   margin

   or

   Select **Set Position** (**5**) to specify an exact location. When prompted
   Offset from left of page:, type the distance from the left edge of the
   paper that the line should begin, and press Enter.

6. Select **Length of Line** (**2**).

7. Enter the length of the line.

   You can specify a line length as precise as two decimal places, and you can
   specify a line of up to 54 inches in length. Most printers don't
   accommodate paper that wide, however. In any case, your line will be only
   as wide as the distance between the two margins.

Depending on the placement of the line, WordPerfect may have calculated the length for you. The length of the line is calculated as the distance between the cursor and the margin.

8. Select Width of Line (**3**).

9. Enter the width of the line.

   The width of a line is its thickness. You can choose a width up to two decimal points in precision, creating a line that's as narrow as .01 (one-hundredth of an inch) or as wide as 54 inches. Keep in mind that the precision of your printed line depends on your printer. A laser printer can produce a very fine line, while the thinnest line a dot matrix printer can print will be much coarser.

10. Select Gray Shading (% of black) (**4**).

11. Enter a value describing the shade of gray you want.

    Gray is calculated as a percentage of black. A 100% shade is black; 0% is white. Any value in between is a gray shade or screen.

12. Press Exit (F7) to return to your document.

You can't see a graphics line on-screen. Use the View Document command to see the lines you've created.

Creating Vertical Lines

Like defining a horizontal line, you define a vertical line by its position on the page, its length, its width, and its shading. You can position the line between specific columns, an additional feature for vertical lines. In the sample newsletter in figure 24.7, vertical lines separate the two columns of text.

To create a vertical line, complete the following steps:

1. Press Graphics (Alt-F9).

2. Select Line (**5**).

3. Select Vertical Line (**2**).

   The Graphics: Vertical Line menu appears (see fig. 24.21).

Fig. 24.21.
The Graphics: Vertical Line menu.

```
Graphics: Vertical Line

        1 - Horizontal Position        Left Margin

        2 - Vertical Position          Full Page

        3 - Length of Line

        4 - Width of Line              0.01"

        5 - Gray Shading (% of black)  100%
```

4. Select **Horizontal Position** (**1**).

The following menu appears:

Horizontal Position: 1 Left; **2** Right; **3** Between Columns; **4** Set Position: **0**

5. Select **Left** (**1**) to place the line on the left margin

or

Select **Right** (**2**) to place the line on the right margin

or

Select **Between** Columns (**3**) and specify the column the line should appear to the right of

or

Select **Set** Position (**4**), type the distance from the left edge of the paper that the line should appear, and press Enter.

An easy way to set the line's horizontal position is to move the cursor where you want the line to begin before you select **Set** Position (**4**). WordPerfect automatically calculates the cursor's horizontal position (how far it is from the left edge of the page) and enters that number for you.

6. Select **Vertical Position** (**2**).

The following menu appears:

Vertical Position: 1 Full Page; **2** Top; **3** Center; **4** Bottom; **5** Set Position: **0**

7. Select **Full Page** (**1**) to extend the line from the top margin to the bottom margin

or

Select **Top** (**2**) to start the line at the top margin

or

Select **Center** (**3**) to center the line between the top and bottom margins

or

Select **Bottom** (**4**) to start the line at the bottom margin

or

Select **Set** Position (**5**), type the distance from the top of the page that the line is to begin, and press Enter.

An easy way to set the line's vertical position is to move the cursor where you want the line to begin before you select **Set** Position (**4**). WordPerfect automatically calculates the cursor's vertical position (how far it is from the top edge of the page) and enters that number.

8. Select **Length of Line** (**3**).

9. Type the line length and press Enter.

   Notice that based on the line's positioning, WordPerfect may calculate a line length for you. For example, if your page is nine inches tall (an 11-inch page with one inch top and bottom margins), your cursor is on the top line, and your line is bottom-aligned, then the line is calculated as being nine inches long. Use the Length of Line selection only when you want to create a line of a specific length, overriding WordPerfect's calculated length.

10. Select Width of Line (**4**).

11. Type a line width and press Enter.

12. Select Gray Shading (% of black) (**5**).

13. Enter a percent gray shade.

   A 100% shade is black; 0% is white. All other percentages are shades of gray. A lower percentage creates a lighter shade of gray.

14. Press Exit (F7) to return to the document.

Using Line Draw

If you plan to edit your document, use Graphics to draw lines and boxes. If you want, though, you can use Line Draw to draw a line or box by just moving the cursor. Line Draw is quick and easy.

Lines and boxes drawn with the Line Draw tool are actually composed of characters and are part of the text. You can't type over them or around them without disturbing them. Be sure to experiment with line drawing before you plan a document using this tool.

To draw a line or box, complete the following steps:

1. Press Screen (Ctrl-F3).

   The following menu appears:

   0 Rewrite; **1** Window; **2** Line Draw: **0**

2. Select Line Draw (**2**).

   The following menu appears:

   1 |; **2** ‖; **3** *; **4** Change; **5** Erase; **6** Move: **1**

3. Select **1** for a single line, **2** for a double line, or **3** to draw a line composed of asterisks (like this: ****).

4. Use the cursor keys to draw the line or box.

5. Press Exit (F7) to quit Line Draw.

Changing the Line Style

You can change the style of the line to something other than single, double, or asterisk lines by selecting Change (4) from the Line Draw menu.

To change the line style from the Line Draw menu, complete the following steps:

1. Select Change (4) from the Line Draw menu.

2. Select any of the eight line styles shown

   or

   Press 9 and type the character you want for the lines.

   You return to the Line Draw menu; your new style is now selection **3**.

3. Use the cursor keys to draw the line.

4. Press Exit (F7) to quit Line Draw.

Erasing the Line

You can erase the line in the same way you drew it:

1. Choose Erase (5) from the Line Draw menu.

2. Use the cursor keys to trace over the line you want to erase.

To start drawing again after you've erased, select one of the line drawing tools (1, 2, or 3) again.

3. Press Exit (F7) to quit Line Draw.

To move the cursor without drawing, select Move (6) from the Line Draw menu and then use the cursor keys.

Note that if you use proportionally spaced type, lines and boxes drawn with Line Draw won't print correctly. For instance if you use a laser printer with fonts like Times or Helvetica or any of the Bitstream fonts, don't use Line Draw. In fact if you're doing laser-printed desktop publishing, you must avoid the line draw command altogether.

Assessing Hardware Limitations

WordPerfect offers many advanced formatting and graphics capabilities. With WordPerfect, you can create different font sizes, and you can create boxes, lines, and graphics. Not every computer is equipped to match WordPerfect's power; your hardware, specifically your graphics card and your printer, may limit your use of advanced formatting and graphics. If you have a graphics card, such as a Hercules or an InColor card, then graphics appear correctly on-screen. If you don't have a graphics card, they won't. You won't be able to see lines, boxes, shades, or imported graphics.

The second hardware limitation is your printer. If your printer won't support proportional fonts (like Times and Helvetica) or enhanced fonts (bold, italic, and reduced or enlarged text), then you can't print them. If you plan to use WordPerfect as a desktop publishing tool, consider your hardware carefully. It might be worth the investment in some extra equipment to get the capabilities you need.

WP 5 Summary

WordPerfect has powerful graphics capabilities. In this chapter, you've learned how to integrate text with graphics, such as lines, boxes, screens, and imported graphics images. You've experimented with the following options:

- Creating any of four types of boxes: Figure, Table, Text Box, or User-defined Box

- Defining the appearance of each type of box and specifying line style (single, double, dashed, dotted, thick, or thicker line), amount of space around the box, shading inside the box and captions (numbering, position, and style)

- Inserting a file (text or graphic) in a box

- Positioning the box on the page and specifying how the box is attached to the text (stays with paragraph or page)

- Creating graphics lines and defining each line in terms of its appearance (line style and width) and location on the page (on a margin, near a margin, between margins, between columns)

You've learned that although WordPerfect has powerful graphics capabilities, the results you get are dependent on the equipment you own. WordPerfect's powerful graphics capabilities, used in combination with formatting features like text columns, can turn you into a desktop publisher!

25

Producing Publications

O ver the past three years, a new wave of technology has swept the computer industry like a giant tsunami. Called "desktop publishing," it has made major changes in the way people produce and think about publications. Modern business people save time and money producing their own newsletters, magazines, reports, brochures, and ads. More than that, the way people think about the appearance of documents has changed. With desktop publishing, it's easy to create attractive and professional-looking pages, no matter what the subject. We've come to expect forms, flyers, press releases, résumés, reports, business presentations, and even letters and memos to look attractive.

Advanced programs, like PageMaker and Ventura Publisher, are complex and quite specialized. These programs are ideal for people whose primary task is publishing, but they aren't well-suited for people who simply want to produce attractive documents. WordPerfect 5, however, is.

WordPerfect 5 is one of a new breed of software programs that combine the power of desktop publishing with the simplicity of word processing. WordPerfect's desktop-publishing features—columns, different type sizes, graphics, and many more options—make it possible for you to produce a surprising variety of attractive publications. The results of your work can range from subtle to dramatic. The main ingredient that desktop publishing adds to word processing is graphic variety. By including graphics in your document's design, you can create a publication that is visually appealing, using simple WordPerfect techniques.

In Chapter 24 you had some hands-on experience integrating text and graphics. This chapter moves to creating entire publications, combining several WordPerfect features: columns, font changes, graphics boxes and lines, and others. Use this chapter as a primer on desktop publishing.

- Start by reading about some general desktop-publishing principles and design guidelines. Use these pointers on document appearance to help you plan your publication.

- Consider the desktop-publishing features WordPerfect offers. Decide which elements you will incorporate in your publication design.

- Look at the list of graphics programs that you can use with WordPerfect.

- Review a list of tips that will help you get the best results from Wordperfect's desktop-publishing features.

- Finally, study a series of specification sheets for sample publications: a newsletter, a brochure, a form, and an annual report. You can modify any of these specifications to meet your own desktop-publishing needs.

Realizing the Potential of Desktop Publishing

The difference between a plain document (see fig. 25.1) and a document carefully laid out (see fig. 25.2) can be subtle. Both contain the same information, maybe even in the same order. Both contain the same title, subtitles, and paragraphs of text.

One document is, however, more inviting to the reader, more visually appealing, and perhaps even easier to read. What's the difference?

The first document was prepared by a word-processing program using traditional typewriter-like techniques. Text enhancements are limited to tricks like underlining or bolding text, typing words in all uppercase letters, and centering lines. Text is printed margin to margin, and sections of the document are presented one after the other, with no indication of relative importance.

The second document is prepared using desktop-publishing techniques. The text is presented in easier-to-read columns; articles are carefully arranged to indicate relative importance and to show relationships between stories. The desktop-published document uses different type effects for headlines, subheads, and captions. Finally, the document prepared with page layout techniques includes graphics. A box encloses a table of contents; a gray shade calls attention to the sidebar of text; illustrations add interest to a story.

With WordPerfect 5, you have the software to step beyond word processing and into desktop publishing. Note that it isn't always appropriate to take that step. Does a simple memo benefit from large headlines, graphics, and fancy fonts? Probably not. Can an ad be improved with those attention-getting techniques? Yes! Does a three-page technical report intended for a small and highly interested audience merit the time it takes to arrange the text in columns and boxes? Maybe not. Will a promotional newsletter meant for customers and prospects be better received if it is spiced up with columns and graphics? Definitely!

Fig. 25.1.
A plain document.

```
                              THE
                         SELF PUBLISHER


A Quarterly Journal                              Fall, 1988
_____

DESKTOP PUBLISHING: NEW TECHNOLOGY FOR AN OLD ART

Johannes Gutenberg, the fifteenth-century inventor of  movable type,
brought the written word to the public, and  thus is responsible for
publishing as it has been known for  five hundred years. In the last
quarter century, Gutenberg's  metal type has been replaced by electronic
typesetting - faster, more flexible, but still very expensive,  and still
only part of the complex process of publishing.  Today, personal computers
bring a new generation of  publishing to the individual. The technology
is called "desktop publishing," and it represents a whole new approach to
a very old art.

Desktop publishing starts with a personal computer. It  may be an IBM AT
or compatible (such as a Compaq 286), or it  may be a Macintosh SE. Your
high-powered computer, along  with the right software, gives you all the
tools you need to  design and publish a variety of printed materials at
your  own desk. Write a press release or create a simple  letterhead with
a word processing program like WordPerfect  for IBM and compatible
computers. Design a logo or business  card with a graphics program like
Adobe Illustrator or Aldus  Freehand for the Macintosh. Create a
newsletter and  experiment with page layout with a page-design program
like   Aldus PageMaker for either IBM or Macintosh. Prepare graphs,
illustrations, forms, applications, stationery, brochures,  catalogs,
reports, and much more - easily - with desktop  publishing on a personal
computer.

There  are many software and hardware enhancements that can broaden  your
desktop publishing talents. Word processors give you  powerful editing and
document creation capabilities.  Page-design software lets you shape your
finished material  into blocks or columns of text, and it lets you insert
or  outline illustrations. Graphics packages guide you in  creating
detailed illustrations or charts that you can add  to a page you've
already created. A scanner, video or  optical, reproduces drawings or
photos for you by  electronically "reading" them with a camera or
digitizer.

The laser printer, whether it's a Hewlett-Packard  LaserJet or an Apple
LaserWriter, is the printing department  in your desktop publishing
office. It prints  near-typeset-quality text and graphics at a resolution
of  300 dots per inch. Using laser printing technology, the  laser printer
produces finished pages that can be used as  final copies or as originals
for the mass reproduction on a  printer's press.

Until now, publishing has belonged to the few: those with  the knowledge,
the money, and the time to engage in a  complex process involving many
players. The process begins  with an idea. It continues with a writer, who
originates the  material to be published. An editor modifies it for
accuracy   and editorial slant; a designer gives the publication its
_____

    The Self Publisher - A Quarterly Journal - Fall, 1988 - Page 1
```

Considering Design Guidelines

You can see that using desktop-publishing techniques can enhance the appearance of your publications. Before you start adding illustrations, drawing vertical rules, and varying font sizes, you should consider some basic design principles. These principles help you understand the importance of planning your publication and

Fig. 25.2.

A document enhanced with page layout techniques.

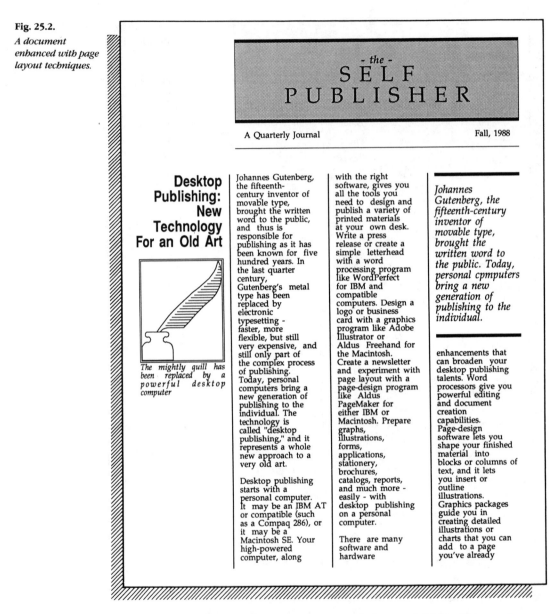

- the -

**S E L F
P U B L I S H E R**

A Quarterly Journal   Fall, 1988

Desktop Publishing: New Technology For an Old Art

The mightly quill has been replaced by a powerful desktop computer

Johannes Gutenberg, the fifteenth-century inventor of movable type, brought the written word to the public, and thus is responsible for publishing as it has been known for five hundred years. In the last quarter century, Gutenberg's metal type has been replaced by electronic typesetting - faster, more flexible, but still very expensive, and still only part of the complex process of publishing. Today, personal computers bring a new generation of publishing to the individual. The technology is called "desktop publishing," and it represents a whole new approach to a very old art.

Desktop publishing starts with a personal computer. It may be an IBM AT or compatible (such as a Compaq 286), or it may be a Macintosh SE. Your high-powered computer, along

with the right software, gives you all the tools you need to design and publish a variety of printed materials at your own desk. Write a press release or create a simple letterhead with a word processing program like WordPerfect for IBM and compatible computers. Design a logo or business card with a graphics program like Adobe Illustrator or Aldus Freehand for the Macintosh. Create a newsletter and experiment with page layout with a page-design program like Aldus PageMaker for either IBM or Macintosh. Prepare graphs, illustrations, forms, applications, stationery, brochures, catalogs, reports, and much more - easily - with desktop publishing on a personal computer.

There are many software and hardware

Johannes Gutenberg, the fifteenth-century inventor of movable type, brought the written word to the public. Today, personal cpmputers bring a new generation of publishing to the individual.

enhancements that can broaden your desktop publishing talents. Word processors give you powerful editing and document creation capabilities. Page-design software lets you shape your finished material into blocks or columns of text, and it lets you insert or outline illustrations. Graphics packages guide you in creating detailed illustrations or charts that you can add to a page you've already

help you decide when and how to incorporate desktop-publishing features. As you plan your publication, keep these points in mind:

Consistency—Establish a format for your publication, and stick with it! Decide on the features and formats you will use: the margins; number of columns; headers and footers; graphics boxes, lines, and captions; size and style typeface for text elements (headlines, subheads, and body copy); and colors for ink and paper. Design a strong and appropriate nameplate (masthead) for the publication.

Clarity—A page should not be confusing. Can you look at the page and immediately know where to begin reading? Do you immediately know what the publication is about? Do you know whom it's from? Is the message clear, obvious, and foremost?

Emphasis—Put important ideas first. Most designers agree that every page has four regions of importance. Top left is the most important and first to be read. Bottom right is least important and last to be read. Also, your publication should have only one title. If you need to say more than a single title permits, use a subtitle. Similarly, each article should have only one headline, and articles of equal importance should have headlines of equal size, type, and weight. Use type size to signal importance.

Unity—Keep text together. Remember that readers expect to read from left to right, top to bottom. Text itself is a graphic element, and scattering it over the page is confusing—the eye doesn't know where to go.

White space—Learn to love white space, the space on the page where nothing appears but paper. It's an important part of any design. Make white space work by including it deliberately in the design.

Balance—Surprisingly, a carefully imbalanced page can be more interesting than a perfectly balanced page. If you have two photos to use with a story, run the more important one larger, and the less important one smaller.

Proportion—Be sure that the elements on a page are proportioned appropriately. An unimportant illustration seems inappropriate if you run it too large; a major headline gets lost if you run it too small.

Drama—You can achieve a feeling of drama if one visual element dominates the page. It may be a graphic, a headline, or a block of copy.

Dimension—A page may be flat, but a publication usually isn't. A two-page spread (the two pages you see when you hold a magazine open, for example) isn't perceived as two separate pages. It's seen as one double-wide page. A book or magazine held in the hand has zones that are easily and quickly seen (the outside edges of the pages, for example) and zones that remain more hidden (the inside edges).

Experimentation—Be willing to experiment. Planning is imperative, and consistency is necessary, but plan some flexibility into your publication. Leave room for some experimentation. Have fun with it!

Above all, your publication should be clear and readable.

Enhancing Your Publication

Now that you have reviewed some general guidelines for page layout, think about the kinds of effects you can achieve with WordPerfect features. Using WordPerfect 5 as a publishing tool for your desktop, you can enhance your document with the following features.

Using Columns

Columns make text easier to read, add graphic interest to a page, and create areas of white space. When you plan your publication, decide how many columns it should contain. Remember that columns don't have to all start at the same place or end at the same place. Also, you can vary column width to add interest.

When you work with columns, remember a couple of rules to keep pages neat. First, avoid *widows* and *orphans*. A widow is the first line of a paragraph left alone at the bottom of a column. An orphan is the last line of a paragraph left alone at the top of a column. If possible, always keep three lines of a paragraph together at the top or bottom of a column. A second rule concerns column bottoms. For graphic interest, it's acceptable to leave the bottoms of columns widely uneven. If columns are *almost* even, make them *exactly* even at the bottom. Your work looks unfinished if column lengths differ by only half a line.

Varying Paragraphs

The paragraph is the basic building block of the document. You can find many ways to vary paragraphs to create an interesting texture. You can design paragraphs flush left; you can justify them, center them, or align them flush right for special effects. Creative indenting and paragraph spacing can add interest to a page, also. Figure 25.3 shows various paragraph alignments.

Fig. 25.3.

Varying paragraph styles.

Johannes Gutenberg, the fifteenth-century inventor of movable type, brought the written word to the public, and thus is responsible for publishing as it has been known for five hundred years.	Johannes Gutenberg, the fifteenth-century inventor of movable type, brought the written word to the public, and thus is responsible for publishing as it has been known for five hundred years.	Johannes Gutenberg, the fifteenth-century inventor of movable type, brought the written word to the public, and thus is responsible for publishing as it has been known for five hundred years.	Johannes Gutenberg, the fifteenth-century inventor of movable type, brought the written word to the public, and thus is responsible for publishing as it has been known for five hundred years.
JUSTIFIED	**FLUSH LEFT**	**FLUSH RIGHT**	**CENTERED**

Choosing Fonts

A font is simply a type style. You can use different fonts (though not too many different fonts!) in your publication, and you can vary their size and appearance. The printer you use dictates which fonts are available. (See Chapters 8 and 9 on printing.)

Large font sizes are perfect for headlines and even for the nameplate of a publication. Medium-sized fonts are useful for subtitles or subheadings, and regular-sized fonts (nine-, ten-, or eleven-point) are meant for text. Use small sizes only for the "fine print" that isn't crucial; don't ever use large blocks of fine print. Figure 25.4 shows some various font types, sizes, and appearances.

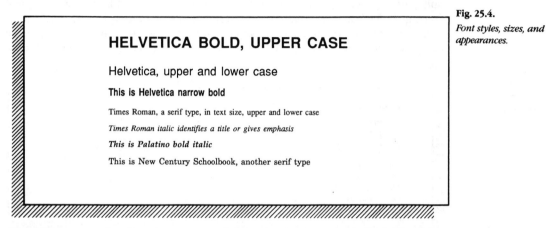

Fig. 25.4.
Font styles, sizes, and appearances.

Inside the box:

HELVETICA BOLD, UPPER CASE

Helvetica, upper and lower case

This is Helvetica narrow bold

Times Roman, a serif type, in text size, upper and lower case

Times Roman italic identifies a title or gives emphasis

This is Palatino bold italic

This is New Century Schoolbook, another serif type

In addition to varying font size, you can change the appearance of a font. Use Bold and Underline to enhance titles and subtitles, adding weight and emphasis. Avoid using these styles within the text because it can be distracting to the eye. Italics can take the place of both bold and underlining when you need emphasis within the text.

Use upper- and lowercase characters for text (it's easier to read); try uppercase for big, bold titles. Reserve appearances like shadow and outline for special effects.

Don't overuse font effects. They are probably most effective in an ad or flyer, but if you use them sparingly, they have a place in publications and brochures.

Adding Lines and Boxes

With just a little extra labor, you can add a lot of graphic impact to a publication by including lines, boxes, and shades.

One common use for vertical lines or *rules* is to separate columns of text. Use horizontal lines to mark the top and bottom edges of the page, to separate articles, or to border a special area of text. In Chapter 24, you learned how to create and incorporate lines in your publication.

Boxes add visual variety to a page and usually frame text or graphics. Use a box to set apart the contents of a box from the rest of the text, to emphasize important points (for instance, to highlight quotations or important messages), and to enclose certain types of text. The table of contents, for example, stands out as a separate block of text that's quickly recognized if it's inside a box. Chapter 24 shows the vast potential of using boxes in your publication.

Creating Special Effects

You can illustrate text subtly but very effectively just by using WordPerfect's built-in features of text enhancement, lines, and boxes. For instance, you can turn text into graphics several ways. One of the most widely used special effects is the *pull quote*; a pull quote is an enlarged excerpt from text, set apart for visual interest and emphasis (see fig. 25.5). You can call attention to a pull quote in a variety of ways: make it bold or italicized, stretch it across two or more columns, put it in a box or between bars. Use pull quotes to fill space when you have almost, but not quite, enough text for a page.

Fig. 25.5.
A pull quote.

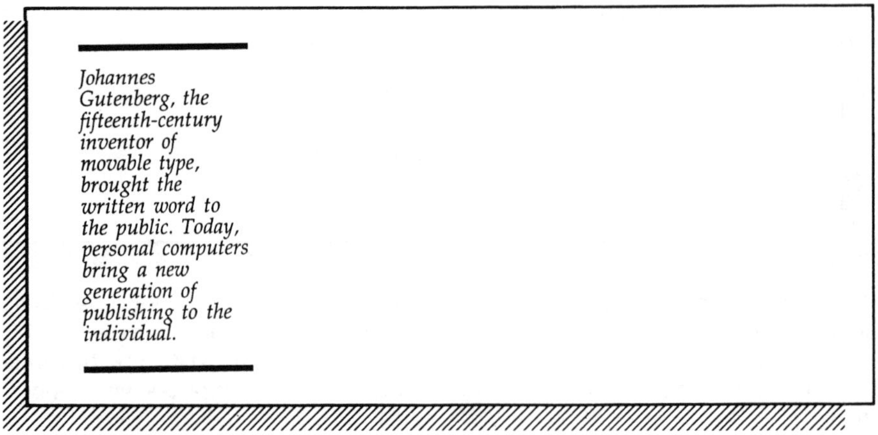

Johannes Gutenberg, the fifteenth-century inventor of movable type, brought the written word to the public. Today, personal computers bring a new generation of publishing to the individual.

Large initial caps are fun and graphical. (The brochure example later in this chapter contains a large initial cap.) Use your imagination and put a single giant letter at the beginning of an article or even at the start of a pull quote. Separated from the text, enlarged, bold, maybe shadowed, outlined, or italicized, the letter becomes a picture.

Including Illustrations

In addition to using WordPerfect's text enhancements, you can take your publication another step by adding illustrations. Chapter 24 discusses importing graphics files into your document.

Add illustrations to spice up text in one of two ways: include illustrations as part of your computer-generated page (for instance, import a graph from 1-2-3), or add them later, after you print your publication (for instance, paste in a photograph).

Computer art can come from several sources. Several graphics programs, like Windows Draw™, PC Paint™, GEM Paint, and many others, can be used to create drawings. Other programs, like the spreadsheet programs 1-2-3 and Microsoft® Excel, can generate graphs based on data. You can use these drawings and graphs in your publications.

Computer clip-art is another source of illustrations (see fig. 25.6). You can buy packages of computer clip-art from companies like Micrografx, Inc. or DeskTop Art. These images, like the clip-art images supplied by WordPerfect on the Fonts/ Graphics disk, are ready-to-use pictures of various subjects.

Figure 1: This Encapsulated PostScript clip art graphic is from a collection by T/Maker Company.

Figure 2: This Encapsulated PostScript clip art image is from T/Maker Company in Mountain View, California

Another source of graphics is a scanner or digitizer, a piece of equipment that "reads" a picture and converts it into a digital format which can be used by WordPerfect.

Understanding Types of Graphics

If you include illustrations as part of your computer-generated pages, you work with one of four file formats: two formats relate to graphics programs, one is for scanned images, and one is used with the page description language PostScript.

Object-oriented and Bit-mapped Images

Graphics programs create two types of images: object-oriented (sometimes called *vector* graphics) images and bit-mapped images. An object-oriented graphic is built from lines and shapes (see fig. 25.7); a bit-mapped image is composed of dots (see fig. 25.8).

Object-oriented graphics are composed of lines, boxes, and shapes, which can be either empty or filled. Once drawn, a box is forever a box, made up of sides, corners, and sometimes a fill. You can change the box's size or shape; you can change the

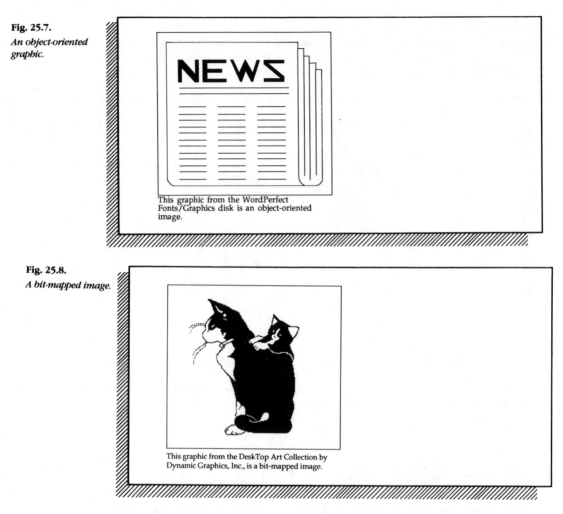

Fig. 25.7.

An object-oriented graphic.

This graphic from the WordPerfect Fonts/Graphics disk is an object-oriented image.

Fig. 25.8.

A bit-mapped image.

This graphic from the DeskTop Art Collection by Dynamic Graphics, Inc., is a bit-mapped image.

style of its lines; and you can change its fill. You cannot cut away the box's corner because the corner is part of the box's identity. The graphics supplied on your WordPerfect Fonts/Graphics disk are object-oriented images.

Files from AutoCAD, 1-2-3, Picture Pak, and Symphony ® are compatible with WordPerfect and can be imported directly. To use the other files with WordPerfect, you must export the file into the format indicated (see table 25.1).

Bit-mapped graphics are composed of dots on-screen. Although a bit-mapped box is drawn the same way and looks the same as an object-oriented box, it behaves differently. The bit-mapped box is not a whole object; rather, it is a series of dots that are arranged in the shape of a box. You can't change the size, shape, or border style of the box. If you want to change the box, you must erase it and draw a new box.

Table 25.1
Object-oriented Files

Program	Exported Format
CCS Designer	HPGL (Hewlett-Packard Graphics Language Plotter File)
ChartMaster	HPGL
Diagram Master	HPGL
Diagraph	HPGL
Freelance Plus	CGM (Computer Graphics Metafile)
Generic CAD	HPGL
Graph-in-the-Box	HPGL
GraphWriter	CGM
Harvard Graphics	HPGL, CGM, EPS
IBM CADAM	HPGL
IBM CATIA	HPGL
IBM CBDS	HPGL
IBM GDDM	HPGL
IBM GPG	HPGL
Microsoft ® Chart	HPGL
PlanPerfect	CGM
SignMaster	HPGL
SlideWrite Plus	HPGL, TIFF, PCX
Versacad	HPGL

The following bit-mapped graphics programs create files that you can import directly in WordPerfect documents:

Dr. Halo II
GEM Paint
GEM SCAN™
1-2-3
MacPaint ®
PC Paint Plus
PC Paintbrush
PicturePak
Professional Plan
Symphony
Windows Paint

Some files can be imported directly; others must be exported into a WordPerfect-compatible format (see table 25.2).

Once they are part of a WordPerfect file, both object-oriented and bit-mapped graphics can be edited. They can be scaled larger or smaller, and they can be moved around inside a box. Object-oriented images can also be rotated or mirrored, and bit-mapped graphics can be inverted. Chapter 24 shows you how to edit a graphics file.

Table 25.2
Bit-mapped Files

Program	Exported Format
Adobe Illustrator	EPS (Encapsulated PostScript)
Boeing Graph	IMG (GEM Paint IMG Format)
CIES (Compuscan)	TIFF (Tagged Image File Format)
DFI Handy Scanner	IMG, TIFF
ENERGRAPHICS	IMG, TIFF
Harvard Graphics	EPS, HPGL, EPS
HP Graphics Gallery®	TIFF, PCX (PC Paintbrush PCX Format)
HP Scanning Gallery®	TIFF, PCX
Quattro®	PIC, EPS
SlideWrite Plus	TIFF, PCX
SuperCalc 4	PIC (Lotus 1-2-3 PIC Format)
VP Planner	PIC
Words & Figures	PIC

TIFF Files

TIFF (tagged image file format) is used by most scanning equipment. It's a special format that allows the scanner to register gray scales on a photograph. TIFF files are usually extremely large; they can be slow and awkward to work with and extremely slow to print. For this reason, many desktop publishers prefer to treat photographs conventionally, leaving a space in the publication for the printer to add a prepared photograph.

EPS Files

EPS (encapsulated PostScript) files are produced by some advanced graphics programs like Adobe Illustrator—a professional-level illustration program. PostScript is a page description language used in some laser printers and typesetting machines. You can print an EPS graphic at very high resolution (up to 2400 dots per inch) on typesetting equipment that supports PostScript.

Using WordPerfect as a Desktop Publisher

Once you realize the types of available features, you next need to learn how to use the features. The most important guideline to remember when you use WordPerfect as a desktop publishing program is simplicity. You can use WordPerfect to create columns of text, different text sizes, and special text effects, and you can create a great variety of shaded figures, framed graphics, horizontal bars, and vertical rules. Although all these features are available, using them can be cumbersome.

Creating graphics can be awkward because it is not a visual process. You can't, for example, arbitrarily draw a line from one point on the page to another. You need to know beforehand exactly where you want that line to appear and how long and wide the line should be. It's critical, for this reason, to preplan your publication carefully. Using a desktop-publishing program like PageMaker, you can easily experiment with elements on a page, trying different effects. With WordPerfect, experimentation can be slow and awkward.

Once you decide the placement, you then begin the three-part creation process. As you saw in Chapter 24, to draw a box, you must enter the Graphics Definition menu and go through several steps to define the size, shape, location, and contents of the box. Then, you return to your document, and finally, you use View Document to see the box as it will appear when printed.

Another area of potential difficulty is in the way WordPerfect presents graphics on-screen. When you work on a document, you don't see the page as it appears when you print the page. Instead, you see a representation of the page. A graphics illustration, for example, appears on the working screen as an outline (and even the outline doesn't appear until you move the cursor beyond the place on the page where you placed the graphic). You can preview the page only by using a special command, and you can't edit the page while you're previewing it.

A final area of difficulty is in editing. Once you lay out a WordPerfect page, even minor changes can be difficult to make. To change a line, for example, you must use Reveal Codes, delete the code for the incorrect line, return to the document, and use Graphics to re-create the line. Finally, you should return to the document and use View Document to check the appearance of your new line. If the line still isn't right, you must repeat the process.

Getting the Most from WordPerfect as a Desktop Publisher

Because of these difficulties, desktop-publishing with WordPerfect can be a very slow process. Yet WordPerfect has desktop-publishing power, and you can use WordPerfect to produce very successful documents. If you understand WordPerfect well, know how codes work, and are pretty good at troubleshooting, give desktop publishing with WordPerfect a try. Keep in mind two guiding principles: simplicity and preplanning.

The following tips show how to get the most from WordPerfect when you're using it as a desktop-publishing tool:

- Practice using graphics, columns, and fonts before you begin a publishing project.

- Familiarize yourself with all the codes you plan to use. Understand how to apply codes and what codes look like. Use Reveal Codes to ferret out areas of trouble.

- Before you begin the design, look carefully at publications similar to the one you are planning. See what looks best, and try to evaluate why it works. Make a sketch of the page layout before you start. Figure 25.9 shows some thumbnail sketches of a newsletter.

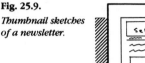

Fig. 25.9.

Thumbnail sketches of a newsletter.

- Keep your layout simple. Decide in advance how many pages your publication will contain, what regular features you will include, what types of illustrations (photos, clip-art, graphs) you will use.

- Design columns of text to extend the full length of the page. This layout is easier to create and edit than creating one three-column article on the top of the page and another three-column article on the bottom of the page.

- WordPerfect is a linear program. Think about working through your document step-by-step, and be careful to keep codes and graphics in the correct position on the page. For example, when you insert a code turning on a feature, the feature affects only the text following the code. Look for out-of-place codes when you run into difficulties.

- Plan graphics (lines and boxes) to line up with a margin or column or to be centered on the page. Placing graphics this way is easier than trying to place them a specific distance from some element on the page.

- Place the graphics first when you lay out a page and let text wrap around them.

- Set tabs from the left edge of the page for all columns if you're using tabbed paragraphs in a multicolumn layout.

- Use View Document frequently to check your progress. Don't assume your page will look the way you think it will.

- When you close a publication and reopen it to do further work, press Home, Home, ↓ to move the cursor to the very bottom of the document after any codes.

Creating a Template

Because some publications (for instance, a newsletter) are published periodically and have a consistent design, you can save time by developing a template to use with each issue. A template is like an issue stripped bare of its contents. For instance, a template for a newsletter can include the nameplate on page one, the columns for the text, headers and footers, box definitions, and anything else that repeats from issue to issue. A template saves you the time of reconstructing each of these elements every time you produce an issue.

Name your template something obvious, like NLTEMP. Then when you're ready to develop the summer issue, for example, retrieve the file NLTEMP, and immediately resave it as NLSUMMER. That way, your template remains intact for use with the next issue.

Placing Graphics

You should place graphics on your page before you type (or retrieve) text. That's especially true of page-type graphics, which are anchored to a margin or column and must stay in position on the page. You can create the graphics in the appropriate size and location on the page, and let text wrap around them automatically. Then, if you have too much material on the page, you can delete some text or reduce box size. Or, if you don't have enough material, you can enlarge a box or create a pull quote in a separate box.

A paragraph-type box, which is anchored to a paragraph, shouldn't be placed on the page first. Instead, create this type box when you type (or retrieve) the paragraph to which it belongs. Remember that the box may move on the page (to a different column or even a different page) if you add or delete text later.

Adding Text

You can add text to your publication in two ways: type text directly (after all, WordPerfect is a word-processing program) or retrieve a previously created file. You may find it easier to create the text files independently so that you can make most editing changes before placing text. Then you can assemble the text files as the final step in the production process. Remember that extensive editing can throw off the formatting.

If you choose to retrieve text files you've already created, do all your character formatting before you retrieve the files. You can even set up a subtemplate (containing font and formatting choices) that you can use for creating the individual files. If you decide to type the text, simply place your cursor and begin typing.

To move part of a text file to another page, use Block (Alt-F4, or F12) to highlight the text, append the text to a file with a new name, delete the text from the page, and retrieve the new file on the page you want it to appear.

Creating a Newsletter

A newsletter is a periodical publication issued monthly, bimonthly, quarterly, or at other intervals. A newsletter has an underlying theme or purpose and usually contains timely information. Many clubs and associations publish newsletters to make their members aware of past and upcoming events. Businesses use newsletters to keep in touch with clients or employees. Subscription newsletters often provide high-value information to subscribers who are willing to pay for the service.

Most newsletters are formatted with a large nameplate (sometimes known as the "masthead" or "banner") at the top of page one; with text arranged in at least two columns; and with graphic enhancements such as lines, boxes, illustrations, photographs, and special text treatments placed throughout. Newsletters commonly have a consistent design used for every issue, and most include repetitive text elements such as a table of contents, an editorial from the club president, a new product announcement section, or a monthly calendar. The majority of newsletters are printed on regular letter-size paper.

Figure 25.10 shows a sample newsletter. Note that these special graphic techniques are used to give *PC Productivity Pointers* greater visual appeal:

Fig. 25.10.
PC Productivity Pointers, a three-column newsletter.

Ron Person & Co. ————————————————————————————

PC Productivity Pointers

Produced monthly for the clients of Ron Person & Co., Software Training Consultants   Fall, 1988

STUDENTS LEARN USEFUL PC SKILLS

Ron Person & Co. instructors work hard to help our students learn PC application skills they can immediately apply to their work. The applications we currently teach are WordPerfect for PCs and minicomputers, Microsoft Excel for the PC or Macintosh, Lotus 1-2-3, and Aldus PageMaker. Our classes are hands-on, with a low student-teacher ratio of four to six students. Classes are usually held at a company's site using our equipment, but other arrangements can be made. Students return from class with the specific skills need for their work and with a support system that includes the best Que book on the application, a subscription to our **PC Productivity** newsletter, and telephone support.

Two Goals: Practicality and Learning to Learn

We have two primary goals for the people we teach. First, people should learn PC skills they can directly apply to specific tasks at their job. Second, we teach people how to find answers to their own PC related questions and how to learn more about applications by themselves.

Our beginning level courses start with a standardized three to four hour introduction to the software application. Other courses begin with a quick review of fundamentals. This review of fundamentals brings students to a common level and frequently presents the big picture that is often missed when people learn through trial and error.

We don't resort to "intermediate" or "advanced" courses that teach software features and skills that aren't needed in the workplace. Instead we use a modular course design and modular practice files to tailor instruction to the specific features and skills people need to get their jobs done.

Our Instructors Are Experienced

Our instructors are experienced as both teachers, consultants, and as business people using the applications we teach. Karen Rose, our desktop publishing instructor, was the marketing communications manager for Texas Instruments and owns Write On Target, a desktop publishing company that produces seven newsletters and an international quarterly. My experience includes a technical MS, an MBA, and seven years as an industry analyst for Texas Instruments.

My background includes having written ten computer books for Que Corporation and Osborne/McGraw-Hill. These books include rewriting **Using WordPerfect** (originally written by Beacham). The rewritten edition, **Using WordPerfect 3rd Edition**, has now sold over 300,000 copies making it the most popular word processing book sold. I've also written **1-2-3 QueCards** (quick reference cards that have just been released) and **1-2-3 Business Formula Handbook**. My most recent two books, **Using Excel: IBM Version** and **Using Microsoft Windows** cover the next generation

---

WordPerfect: The Most Popular Gets Better

WordPerfect 4.2 is the most widely sold word processing software. in the United States. It's speed, clutter-free screen, and large number of professional-level features have made it the word processor of choice for most businesses. But a competitor is out now that will take the place of WordPerfect 4.2.

It's WordPerfect 5! In WordPerfect 5 the menus are easier to follow, complex features such as printer and font selection have been simplified, and the power to incorporate graphics has been added.

- Title of the newsletter in Extra Large print across the top of page one

- Subtitle below the nameplate, which identifies the publisher and includes the date of the issue

- Horizontal bars used in nameplate and narrow rules used between columns

- Three-column format

- Text in Times Roman; pull quotes in Large Times Roman Italic; headlines in Very Large Helvetica Bold, Uppercase

- One or two articles on page one (articles can continue on page four); one illustration on page one

- A two-column shaded sidebar on page one

A template was created for *PC Productivity Pointers* that includes the format settings (margin, base font, binding offset), a nameplate, a subtitle, a title placeholder, newspaper-style text columns, and box definitions. Defining the boxes gives you a consistent set of graphic box styles to use in your publication. For the sample newsletter, figures are used for graphic illustrations; text boxes are used for text files; and user-defined boxes are used for pull quotes.

Table 25.3 shows the specifications for the sample newsletter.

Table 25.3
Newsletter

Element	Option		Setting
Format: Line	Hyphenation		Auto
	Justification		No
	Margins	Left	.75 inch
		Right	.75 inch
	Line Spacing		1
Printer: Options	Binding		.25 inch
Columns	Type		Newspaper
	Number		3
	Space Between Columns		.25 inch
Text	Files		
	Base Font		Times Roman, 10 pt.
Nameplate and Subtitle			
Format: Line	Line Spacing		1.2
Title	Font	Size	Extra Large
		Appearance	Bold
PC in Title	Font	Appearance	Shadow
Subtitle	Font	Appearance	Italic
Article Title	Font	Size	Very Large
	Base Font		Helvetica Bold, 10 pt.
Lines			
Horizontal Line 1	Horizontal Position		Right
	Length of Line		WP calculates
	Width of Line		.02 inch
Horizontal Line 2	Horizontal Position		Left & Right
	Width of Line		.02 inch

Horizontal Line 3	Horizontal Position		Left & Right
	Width of Line		.02 inch

Figure 1

Figure Options	Border Style		Single
Creation Options	Filename		PC.WPG
	Type		Page
	Vertical Position		Set Position
	Horizontal Position		Margins, Left

Text Box 1: Sidebar

Text Box Options	Border Style	Left	Single
		Right	Single
		Top	Thick
		Bottom	Thick
	Inside Border Space		.25 inch
	Gray Shading		10%
Creation Options	Filename		Text file
	Type		Page
	Vertical Position		Bottom
	Horizontal Position		Margins, Right
	Size		Width 4.5 inch

Vertical Lines

Vertical Lines	Horizontal Position	Between Columns
	Vertical Position	Set Position
	Length	Measure

Creating a Two-Fold Brochure

Like a newsletter, a brochure is designed to inform readers about a business, product, service, organization, program, or event. Unlike a newsletter, a brochure is short—usually not more than a single piece of paper printed on both sides. Because a brochure is brief, its message is concise and direct. A brochure is less time-sensitive than a periodical; typically it contains information, but not news. A brochure, usually a one-time-only publication, is intended to promote one idea one time.

A brochure can take many shapes. Most often, it is smaller than a single sheet of letter-size paper, and very often, the format for a brochure is some variation on that single sheet of paper. A common format is the two-fold brochure, which is simply a letter-size piece of paper printed horizontally and folded twice to form a three-panel piece that fits neatly into a standard business envelope.

You can use WordPerfect's desktop-publishing tools to produce a two-fold brochure such as the one shown in figure 25.11A and figure 25.11B.

Fig. 25.11A.

A brochure created on a standard letter-size piece of paper.

Learning How To Learn

We strive to teach people how to help themselves. This helps people learn new skills to cope with new tasks. It also reduces long-term PC support costs and overhead. We use multiple approaches to reach this goal,

* Every student receives a Que or Osborne/McGraw-Hill book. During class students learn how to solve problems using their books as the resource. When class is over, students keep their books to use on the job. The books we use are appropriate to the topic and level of instruction. Some of the titles we use are **Using WordPerfect 5, Using WordPerfect 3rd Edition, Using Excel: IBM Version, Using 1-2-3 Special Edition, 1-2-3 Tips, Tricks, and Traps, Using Microsoft Windows,** and **Using PageMaker on the IBM.**

* We call our students a week to ten days after a class to see if they have any additional questions. All students receive our phone number and we make an effort to have a timely response to their questions.

* Our newsletter, **PC Productivity Pointers,** is mailed regularly to students and contains helpful tips, tricks, and traps for the applications we teach.

* We work with new software as soon as it's released. This means that shortly after a new version of an application is available we can help you learn how to put it to work. For example, beginning in May we will offer a WordPerfect 4.2 to WordPerfect 5 cross-over course designed to teach students the ins and outs of this exciting new release.

Ron Person & Co.
243 Rabbit Lane
Memphis TN 23843

RON

PERSON

&

COMPANY

**Software
Training
Consultants**

Fig. 25.11B.

A brochure created on a standard letter-size piece of paper (second side).

Ron Person & Co. instructors work hard to help our students learn PC application skills they can immediately apply to their work. The applications we currently teach are WordPerfect for PCs and minicomputers, Microsoft Excel for the PC or Macintosh, Lotus 1-2-3, and Aldus PageMaker. Our classes are hands-on, with a low student-teacher ratio of four to six students. Classes are usually held at a company's site using our equipment, but other arrangements can be made. Students return from class with the specific skills need for their work and with a support system that includes the best Que book on the application, a subscription to our **PC Productivity** newsletter, and telephone support.

Two Goals: Practicality and Learning to Learn

We have two primary goals for the people we teach. First, people should learn PC skills they can directly apply to specific tasks at their job. Second, we teach people how to find answers to their own PC related questions and how to learn more about applications by themselves.

Our beginning level courses start with a standardized three to four hour introduction to the software application. Other courses begin with a quick review of fundamentals. This review of fundamentals brings students to a common level and frequently presents the big picture that is often missed when people learn through trial and error.

We don't resort to "intermediate" or "advanced" courses that teach software features and skills that aren't needed in the workplace. Instead we use a modular course design and modular practice files to tailor instruction to the specific features and skills people need to get their jobs done.

Our Instructors Are Experienced

Our instructors are experinced as both teachers, consultants, and as business people using the applications we teach. Karen Rose, our desktop publishing instructor, was the marketing communications manager for Texas Instruments and owns Write On Target, a desktop publishing company that produces seven newsletters and an international quarterly. My experience includes a technical MS, an MBA, and seven years as an industry analyst for Texas Instruments.

My background includes having written ten computer books for Que Corporation and Osborne/McGraw-Hill. These books include rewriting **Using WordPerfect** (originally written by Beacham). The rewritten edition, **Using WordPerfect 3rd Edition,** has now sold over 300,000 copies making it the most popular word processing book sold. I've also written **1-2-3 QueCards** (quick reference cards that have just been released) and **1-2-3 Business Formula Handbook.** My most recent two books, **Using Excel: IBM Version** and **Using Microsoft Windows** cover the next generation of Windows and OS/2 software being developed by Microsoft Corporation.

I currently teach two classes, **Business Applications of Personal Computers** and **Lotus 1-2-3 for Accounting and Finance,** for the **University of California,** Berkeley Extension and for **Sonoma State University,** Extension. With a co-instructor from the Palo Alto division of Hewlett-Packard I will be teaching a train-the-trainer class for UC Berkeley titled **Accelerated Learning Techniques for Data Trainers.** Our clients include Pacific Bell, Northern California Power Agency, and the City of Santa Rosa. I have taught people with backgrounds that range from entry level clerks to financial executives, and from writers to technical engineers.

WordPerfect: The Most Popular Gets Better

WordPerfect 4.2 is the most widely sold word processing software in the United States. It's speed, clutter-free screen, and large number of professional-level features have made it the word processor of choice for most businesses. But a competitor is out now that will take the place of WordPerfect 4.2.

It's WordPerfect 5! In WordPerfect 5 the menus are easier to follow, complex features such as printer and font selection have been simplified, and the power to incorporate graphics has been added.

My partner, Karen Rose, teaches desktop publishing on Aldus PageMaker for both PCs and Macintosh. Karen was the technical editor for the books, **Using PC PageMaker** and **Using WordPerfect 3rd Edition.** She is also the co-author of **Using Microsoft Windows** and the author of five chapters in **Using WordPerfect 5.** Karen teaches desktop publishing for Sonoma State University.

Remember that you fold the paper to create the brochure; notice the layout used. You use landscape mode to print the document sideways on the paper. (To be able to print in landscape, your printer must support rotated text.)

Each page has three columns, and each column makes up one panel of the brochure. When you fold the paper, the following occurs:

Column 1 becomes the Inside Panel.
Column 2 becomes the Back Panel with return address.
Column 3 becomes the Front Panel.
Columns 4, 5, and 6 on the second side become inside panels.

When you create a brochure, you should make a sketch to check the layout.

If you create many brochures, you can, as with the newsletter, create a template to use again.

Table 25.4 shows the specifications for the sample brochure.

Table 25.4
Brochure

Element	Option		Setting
Format: Line	Margins	Right	.25 inch
		Left	.25 inch
Format: Page	Margins	Top	.25 inch
		Bottom	.25 inch
	Size/Size		Standard/Landscape
Columns	Type		Newspaper
	Number		3
	Distance Between		.5 inch
Text	Text files		
Text for Title	Centered on line		
	Centered on page		
Subheads	Font	Size	Large
		Appearance	Italic

Horizontal Lines (Panels 1 and 3)

Horizontal Line 1	Horizontal Position	Left & Right
	Width of line	.02 inch
Horizontal Line 2	Horizontal Position	Left
	Length of line	.75 inch
	Width of line	.25 inch
Horizontal Line 3	Horizontal Position	Right
	Length of line	.75 inch
	Width of line	.25 inch
Horizontal Line 4	Horizontal Position	Left & Right
	Width of line	.02 inch

Panel 2: Figure 1 with Return Address

Figure Options	Border Style	All Single
	Inside Border Space	All .25 inch
Creation Options	Type	Page
	Vertical Position	Set Position, .25 inch
	Horizontal Position	Column 2, Left & Right
	Edit	Type text, Rotate 90°

Panel 4: User-defined Box 1 with Large R

User-defined	Border Style		None
	Outside Border Space		Zero
	Inside Border Space		Zero
Creation Options	Type		Character
	Vertical Position		Bottom
	Size		.25 x .26 inch
	Edit		Type text
	Font	Size	Extra Large
		Appearance	Bold

Panel 6: Text Box 1

Text Box Options	Border Style	Left	Single
		Right	Single
		Top	Thick
		Bottom	Thick
	Outside Border Space		0
	Inside Border Space		.16 inch
	Gray Shading		10%
Creation Options	Filename		Text file
	Type		Page
	Vertical Position		Place cursor Set Position
	Horizontal Position		Column 3, Left & Right

Creating a Form

Using a combination of WordPerfect's lines, boxes, and text, you can create forms useful in many business applications. Make forms such as membership applications, order forms, invoices, account statements, registration forms, and many more.

For instance, you can create the order form in figure 25.12 using WordPerfect.

To save copying costs, print the form twice, and cut and paste the second form to the bottom of the first sheet of paper. If your form is an invoice or a statement, you might want to take the form to a commercial printer and have it duplicated on multipart paper or onto pin-feed perforated paper that rolls through an impact printer.

You create the form with intersecting lines, rather than graphic boxes, because you cannot create a line inside a box. To match the lines up exactly, you must measure the lengths of some of the lines and create the lines to that precise length.

To create your own form, review the specifications used to create this form shown in table 25.5.

Table 25.5
Order Form

Element	Option		Setting
Format: Line	Margins	Left	.37 inch
		Right	.37 inch
Format: Page	Margins	Top	.37 inch
		Bottom	.37 inch
Text	Type, use tabs to space column headings		
Title	Font	Size	G's Extra Large
		Size	Other text Large
		Appearance	Underlined (except G's)

Figure 1: Logo

Figure Options	Border Style		None
	Outside Border Space		Zero
	Inside Border Space		Zero
Creation Options	Filename		PRESENT.WPG
	Type		Page
	Vertical Position		Top
	Horizontal Position		Margin, Left
	Size		Width 1 inch

Text Box 1: Satisfaction Guaranteed Box

Text Box Options	Border	Left	Single
		Right	Single
		Top	Thick
		Bottom	Thick
	Gray Shading		10%
Creation Options	Type		Page
	Horizontal Position		Margin, Right
	Size		Width 2 inch
	Edit		Type text

Lines

Horizontal Lines	Horizontal Position	Place cursor Left & Right
	Width of line	.01 inch
Vertical Lines	Horizontal Position	Place cursor, Set Position
	Vertical Position	Place cursor, Set Position
	Length	Place cursor, Set Position
Short Lines	Horizontal Position	Place cursor, Right

Creating an Annual Report

If you must create an annual report, a manual, or any other document that contains many pages broken up into several sections, you can use a number of WordPerfect features to make your job easier.

Figures 25.13A and 25.13B show the first two pages of an annual report created with WordPerfect. The specifications for this report are shown in table 25.6. Page one includes the company logo and the title of the report; the report includes figure boxes used for photographs (pasted in later) and table boxes used for charts (imported from a graphics program).

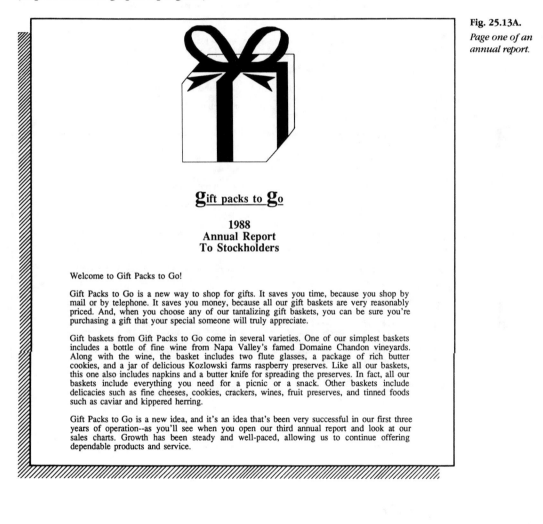

Fig. 25.13B.

Page two of an annual report.

Gift baskets from Gift Packs to Go come in several varieties. One of our simplest baskets includes a bottle of fine wine from Napa Valley's famed Domaine Chandon vineyards. Along with the wine, the basket includes two flute glasses, a package of rich butter cookies, and a jar of delicious Kozlowski farms raspberry preserves. Like all our baskets, this one also includes napkins and a butter knife for spreading the preserves. In fact, all our baskets include everything you need for a picnic or a snack. Other baskets include delicacies such as fine cheeses, cookies, crackers, wines, fruit preserves, and tinned foods such as caviar and kippered herring.

We ship our gift packs anywhere in the world. For continental deliveries, we guarantee three-day service, so you can be sure your gift pack arrives fresh and on time. Overseas deliveries are made within a week. Of course, if you like, we'll include a card from you.

A Successful New Idea

Gift Packs to Go is a new idea, and it's an idea that's been very successful in our first three years of operation--as you'll see when you open our third annual report and look at our sales charts. Growth has been steady and well-paced, allowing us to continue offering dependable products and service.

We thank you for your support, and look forward to sharing our success with you long into the future.

Gift Packs to Go is a new way to shop for gifts. It saves you time, because you shop by mail or by telephone. It saves you money, because all our gift baskets are very reasonably priced. And, when you choose any of our tantalizing gift baskets, you can be sure you're purchasing a gift that your special someone will truly appreciate.

Sales Have Increased Steadily in Our First Three Years

Gift Packs to Go is a new idea, and it's an idea that's been very successful in our first three years of operation--as you'll see when you open our third annual report and look at our sales charts. Growth has been steady and well-paced, allowing us to continue offering dependable products and service.

We thank you for your support, and look forward to sharing our success with you long into the future.

Gift baskets from Gift Packs to Go come in several varieties. One of our simplest baskets includes a bottle of fine wine from Napa Valley's famed Domaine Chandon vineyards. Along with the wine, the basket includes two flute glasses, a package of rich butter cookies, and a jar of delicious Kozlowski farms raspberry preserves. Like all our baskets, this one also includes napkins and a butter knife for spreading the preserves. In fact, all our baskets include everything you need for a picnic or a snack. Other baskets include delicacies such as fine cheeses, cookies, crackers, wines, fruit preserves, and tinned foods such as caviar and kippered herring.

Table 25.6
Annual Report

Element	Option		Setting
Format: Line	Hyphenation		No
	Justification		Yes
	Margins	Left	1.25 inch
		Right	1.25 inch
	Widow/Orphan		Yes
Format: Page	Margins	Top	1.5 inch
		Bottom	1.5 inch
Print: Options	Binding		.25 inch
Text	Text File		
G's in Title	Font	Size	Extra Large
		Appearance	Bold
Rest of Title	Font	Size	Large
		Appearance	Underlined
New sections	Start on odd-numbered page		
	Copy title		
Footnotes	Font	Appearance	Italic
	Even		Page,
			Flush Right, Logo
	Odd		Title,
			Flush Right, Page
Figure Options	Border Style		Single
	Outside Border Space		.16 inch
	Inside Border Space		.16 inch
	Caption		Italic, no numbering
Table Options	Border Style		Single
	Outside Border Space		.16 inch
	Inside Border Space		.16 inch
	Caption		Chart 1, numbering

User-defined Box 1: Logo

User-defined	Border Style	None
Options	Outside Border Space	None
	Inside Border Space	None
Creation	Filename	PRESENT.WPG
Options	Type	Page
	Vertical Position	Top
	Horizontal Position	Margin, Center
	Size	Width 2 inch

WP 5 Summary

Not long ago, desktop publishing—the ability to create publications using a desktop computer—revolutionized two major industries: the computer industry and the publishing industry. In its early days, desktop publishing stood alone. Word processing was a separate, but related, part of the publishing process. But today, with WordPerfect 5, word processing and desktop publishing have joined hands.

To use these tools effectively, remember the importance of planning the design. Planning not only makes the task of producing a publication easier, but also helps ensure that your publication shows consistency in design and layout. Remember one very important rule about design: Form follows function. Your design should always serve your primary purpose—to communicate a message clearly and effectively.

With WordPerfect's powerful desktop-publishing tools and a few simple rules about design and planning, you're on your way to a whole new approach to producing creative and attractive publications. With WordPerfect, you can be a desktop publisher!

A

WordPerfect 5 Installation, Setup, and Start-Up

Doug Hazen, Jr., is a computer programmer and ex-machinist who lives in the Boston area. He is a member of the Boston Computer Society WordPerfect Special Interest Group and has used WordPerfect for almost three years. He works for Intellution, Inc., in Norwood, Mass. ■

Wordperfect 5 has arrived, but before you can send those manuscripts, memos, and business letters flying, you must first install your program. This chapter details all the necessary steps you must complete before you can begin. The chapter includes the following:

- Installing WordPerfect 5 on both floppy and hard disk systems

- Using Setup to customize your system

- Starting WordPerfect 5

To get the most from this chapter, you need a basic understanding of DOS features, such as files, directories, wild cards, and some basic DOS commands. If you are not familiar with DOS, you may want to read and have for ready reference Que's best-selling publications on DOS: Chris DeVoney's *Using PC DOS*, 2nd Edition, or *MS-DOS User's Guide*, 3rd Edition, depending on the DOS your system uses; and Don Berliner's *Managing Your Hard Disk*, 2nd Edition. For an easy-to-use rapid reference, see also *DOS QueCards*™ by Glenn Larsen and Denise Slingsby.

Installing WordPerfect 5

To use WordPerfect, you must first install the program. The installation process prepares the program and your computer system for use. WordPerfect Corporation provides on the Learning disk an Install program that automatically installs the programs on hard disk systems.

When you use the Install program, you accept the preset disk organization determined by WordPerfect. Because you might want a different organization, you may want to install WordPerfect yourself instead of using the Install program. It isn't difficult. You can also use the Install program now and make any changes later.

However, you must use one method or the other. For your daily work, do *not* use the disks that came in your WordPerfect package.

Before you begin, you should complete the following steps:

For computer systems using 5 1/4-inch floppy disk drives:

1. Check to be sure that you have all the program disks. The WordPerfect 5 package includes 12 disks:

   WordPerfect 1 and *WordPerfect 2* contain the WordPerfect program itself, with one part of the program on each disk. *WordPerfect 1* contains also the Help files.

   Speller contains the Speller data file and the Spell program for modifying that file.

   Thesaurus includes the Thesaurus data file.

   Conversion contains the Convert program, the macro and graphics conversion programs, and miscellaneous sample keyboard definition and style files. It contains also a README.WP file that explains in more detail what the various files on the disk are.

   Fonts/Graphics includes sample graphics image files, font files, and the GRAB program.

   Learning contains the Tutor program and its files. It contains also files used in the lessons in the WordPerfect Workbook, plus the Install program.

   PTR Program contains the Printer program (for modifying printer definition files) and its Help file.

   Printer 1, *Printer 2*, *Printer 3*, and *Printer 4* contain the master printer definition files.

2. Put write-protect tabs over the small square cutout of each disk. Write-protect tabs are little black or silver stickers that prevent the disk drive from recording anything on, or deleting anything from, the disk. Using write-protect tabs is insurance in case you make a mistake during installation.

For PS/2 or other computers using 3 1/2-inch drives:

1. Check to be sure that you have all the program disks. The WordPerfect 5 package includes seven microfloppy disks:

   WordPerfect 1/WordPerfect 2, the master disk, which contains the WordPerfect program.

Speller/Thesaurus

Printer 1/Printer 2

Printer 3/PTR Program

Printer 4 for selected printer drivers. (When you order or upgrade to version 5, WordPerfect Corporation asks that you specify which printer(s) you use. You will be sent this disk if it is appropriate.)

Conversion

Learning/Fonts/Graphics

2. Write-protect each disk by sliding the little tab in the corner so that it *uncovers* the hole. Do this as insurance in case you make a mistake during installation.

Using the WordPerfect 5 Install Program

The WordPerfect INSTALL program is located on the Learning disk. *It is for use on hard disk systems only.* INSTALL copies the WordPerfect files onto your hard disk. This program is very simple to use, but also very simple-minded. It first makes two directories on your disk, \WP50 and \WP50\LEARN. Next it copies all the files from the WordPerfect 1, WordPerfect 2, Speller, Thesaurus, and Fonts/Graphics disks into \WP50, then copies the files on the Learning disk into \WP50\LEARN. Lastly, INSTALL will modify your DOS CONFIG.SYS file by adding the command FILES =20 to it. INSTALL will create a CONFIG.SYS file if you don't have one.

To use the INSTALL program:

1. Put the Learning disk into drive A:.

2. Change to drive A: by typing *A:* and pressing Enter.

3. Type *install* and press Enter.

4. Answer the questions and follow the instructions that INSTALL displays on your screen.

This disk organization works fine, but it creates a cluttered \WP50 directory. A more efficient organization for hard disk users is described in the section "Installing WordPerfect on a Hard Disk System."

Installing WordPerfect on a Floppy Disk System

WordPerfect 5 works on a floppy disk system, but you may find switching disks for different functions rather inconvenient. You may also not be able to use WordPerfect 5 to its full capability. For these reasons, you may want to consider buying a hard disk.

To install WordPerfect on a computer with two floppy disks, first make *working* copies of the disks in your WordPerfect package. You'll use these working copies and store the original disks in a safe place. If something should happen to your working copies, you can use the originals to make another set of copies.

(You need 10 formatted disks and 2 formatted system disks. If you don't already have formatted disks, begin with Steps 1 and 2. Otherwise, you can start at Step 3. The wording for your version of DOS may differ slightly.

1. Get out 10 new disks. Put your DOS disk in drive A: and the new disk in drive B:. Then with drive A: as the current drive, type:

   FORMAT B:

   After a moment, DOS will say:

   ```
   Insert new diskette for drive B:
   and strike ENTER when ready
   ```

   Press Enter and DOS will say:

   ```
   Formatting...
   ```

   After the disk is formatted, DOS will say:

   ```
   Formatting complete
   ```

   If you have 360K floppy drives, DOS will give you statistics about the disk:

   ```
   362496 bytes total disk space
   362496 bytes available on disk
   ```

   If you have different capacity disk drives, the numbers will be different. In any case, if the number in the second line doesn't match the number in the first line, you have bad spots on the disk. Throw the disk away. It's still usable, but there's no point in taking any chances.

   Finally, DOS will ask:

   ```
   Format another (Y/N)?
   ```

   Type *Y* and repeat the formatting process until you've finished all 10 disks.

2. Format two system disks, using the /s switch of the FORMAT command. Follow the procedure in Step 1, but type this command instead:

   FORMAT B: /S

   You need to use system disks for your copies of WordPerfect 1 and WordPerfect 2 disks. If you don't use system disks for *both* these copies, you won't be able to start your computer with the WordPerfect 1 disk, and you won't be able to use the Shell to DOS (Ctrl-F1) command in WordPerfect.

3. Label each formatted disk, using the titles on the original WordPerfect disks. That is, use the titles "WordPerfect 1" and "WordPerfect 2" to label your system disks.

4. Put the first WordPerfect disk in drive A: and the formatted disk labeled WordPerfect 1 in drive B:.

5. Type *A:* and press Enter to make drive A: your current drive. (You should see the A> prompt at the left edge of your screen.)

6. Type *COPY A:*.* B:* and press Enter to copy all the files on the disk in drive A: to the disk in drive B:.

7. Do this for each disk in the WordPerfect package, even the Printer 1, 2, 3, and 4 disks.

   Although you may use these disks only during installation, making a copy of each disk is good backup practice, particularly if you plan to upgrade your printer, change printers often, or need to alter your printer setup for some other reason.

8. Put the original WordPerfect disks in a safe place.

Installing WordPerfect on a Hard Disk System

To install WordPerfect on a computer system with a hard disk, you should first organize your hard disk by making subdirectories and then copy the files from the WordPerfect program disks into your subdirectories.

Making Directories

You can organize your WordPerfect files into subdirectories in many ways. Because there is no one right way, *you* must decide what organization best suits your needs.

The following example gives you some ideas and guidelines, but you do not have to follow this example. You can have more or fewer subdirectories, and you can name your subdirectories differently. Note that subdirectory names can be as long as eight characters, but each directory must have a unique name. Complete the following steps to create your WordPerfect directories:

1. Type *C:* and press Enter to switch to your hard disk drive.

2. Type *CD * to change to your root directory (if you are not already there).

3. Type *MD \WP* to make your main WordPerfect directory, which we have named (surprise!) WP.

   If you already have a WP directory for an earlier version of WordPerfect, you could name this new directory WP5 or WP50.

4. Type *CD \WP* to change to your new directory.

5. Type *MD MACROS* to make a subdirectory for macros.

   Unlike previous versions, WordPerfect 5 can store macros in a subdirectory you specify in Setup (Shift-F1).

6. Type *MD THDIC* to make a subdirectory for the Speller and Thesaurus files.

7. If you plan on having more than one printer definition, type *MD PRINTERS* to make a special subdirectory for printer definitions.

8. Finally, if you want, type *MD MISC* to make a miscellaneous subdirectory.

These subdirectories store program files. Where will you put your own documents? For most people, it is easiest to make document directories in the root directory. Make a directory for each type of document you compose: business letters, personal letters, cover letters, resumes, job applications, books, screenplays, etc. How you set up these directories and how many you set up depend on how you use WordPerfect.

Copying WordPerfect Program Disks to Your Hard Drive

After you've created your subdirectories, you need to copy the files from the WordPerfect program disks to your hard disk:

1. Put the WordPerfect 1 disk in your floppy drive and type the following command (If you have DOS 3.2 or later, you can use XCOPY in the following steps instead of COPY.):

   COPY A:*.* C:\WP

   This copies all the files on the disk into the WP subdirectory on the hard disk.

2. Do the same with the WordPerfect 2 disk.

3. If you made a Thesaurus/Speller subdirectory named THDIC (or whatever), copy the Speller and Thesaurus files to that subdirectory by inserting each disk in drive A: and typing the following command:

   COPY A:*.* C:\WP\THDIC

   If your subdirectory name is different, substitute its name for THDIC. If you have no Thesaurus/Speller subdirectory, copy all these disks into your \WP directory by typing:

   COPY A:*.* C:\WP

4. If you think you may need to use the PTR program to modify your printer drivers (which you should do only if you have to AND if you are comfortable with technical projects), copy the files from the PTR Program disk into your PRINTERS subdirectory by typing:

   COPY A:*.* C:\WP\PRINTERS

If you don't have a PRINTERS subdirectory, copy the PTR disk files into the subdirectory in which your printer definition files (which have a .PRS extension) are stored.

Making Working Copies of the Remaining Disks

You probably have no need to copy any of the remaining disks to the hard disk. You do not need most of these files, and the rest you may need only once. You can, of course, copy any or all of these disks to your hard disk if you want to, but in most cases, you'll just be wasting hard disk space.

One exception to this is the situation where a number of inexperienced people need to learn WordPerfect on your computer system. In this case, you probably want to make a Learning subdirectory and copy the Learning disk files into it.

Instead of copying the seven remaining disks to your hard disk, make and use working copies, as floppy disk system users do.

To make working copies of these disks on a hard disk system with *two* floppy drives, complete the following steps:

1. Make sure that write-protect tabs are on each of the seven remaining WordPerfect disks.

2. Put the first disk to be copied into your A: floppy drive.

3. Put a blank, *formatted* floppy disk in drive B:.

4. Type *A:* and press Enter to make drive A: your current drive.

5. If you have DOS 3.1 or *earlier,* type

    COPY A:.* B:*

    and press Enter to copy all the files on drive A: to drive B:.

    Or if you have DOS 3.2 or *later*, you can type

    XCOPY A: B:

    This command is much faster than COPY.

6. Take the original disk out of drive A: and store it with the other original WordPerfect program disks.

7. Put a write-protect tab on the new working disk from drive B: and label the disk, using the same name as is on the original disk.

If you have 3 1/2-inch floppy disk drives, the procedure for you is the same, except there aren't as many disks to copy.

To make these working copies on a hard disk system with *one* floppy drive, do these steps:

1. Make sure that write-protect tabs are on each of the remaining seven WordPerfect disks.

2. Put the disk to be copied into your floppy drive. Have a blank, *formatted* disk ready.

3. Type *A:* and press Enter to make drive A: your current drive.

4. Make sure your DOS directory is in your PATH command.

5. If you have DOS 3.1 or *earlier*, type

    DISKCOPY A: B:

    and press Enter, to copy all the files on the original disk in drive A: to the new disk.

    Even though you don't have a drive B:, DOS has to pretend that you do. It seems illogical, but it works.

CAUTION: The DISKCOPY command can be dangerous and can erase your whole floppy disk if you make a mistake. Make sure that you have write-protect tabs on all the *original* disks and *be careful*.

Or if you have DOS 3.2 or *later*, type

XCOPY A: B:

and press Enter.

Again, the command seems illogical without an actual drive B:, but the command works. The XCOPY command is much safer than DISKCOPY.

6. Follow the instructions you see on the screen, and change disks when prompted. You may have to swap disks more than once if you don't have enough memory in your computer. Be careful!

7. Put a write-protect tab on the new working disk and label the disk, using the same name as is on the original disk.

8. Put the original disk safely away with the other WordPerfect program disks.

If you have 3 1/2-inch floppy disk drives, the procedure for you is the same, except there aren't as many disks to copy.

There may be some files on the Fonts/Graphics and the Conversion disks that you want or need. If you have certain less common video displays, such as the Genius, IBM 8514/A, or Wyse 700, you need a special *display driver* file (all of which have a .WPD extension) that is on the Fonts/Graphics disk. There are also special *font resource* files (which have a .FRS extension) for the EGA and some other video displays that enable these displays to show fonts on-screen. If your video display type isn't on the Graphics Screen Type menu in Setup (see the section "Using WordPerfect's Setup Menu" in this appendix), check the Fonts/Graphics disk for a .WPD file named after your display adapter.

You may want a number of programs and files on the Conversion disk. The CONVERT program, which converts files of other programs into WordPerfect 5 format; the CURSOR program, which changes the shape of your cursor; and sample keyboard definitions and Style libraries are all on this disk. Read the README file on the disk for more information about these files.

Changing the CONFIG.SYS File

The last thing you need to do is to modify your CONFIG.SYS file if you have one. It will be located in your root directory. CONFIG.SYS is a plain text file, so you will have to use Text In/Out to bring it into WordPerfect for editing. To change CONFIG.SYS from within WordPerfect, follow these steps:

1. Press Text In/Out (Ctrl-F5).

2. Press DOS **Text (1)** and then select **Retrieve (2)** to bring the file into WordPerfect.

3. Type *CONFIG.SYS* at the Document to be retrieved: prompt; then press Enter.

If you get an ERROR: File not found message, make sure that you typed the name correctly and try again. If you still get the message, you haven't got a CONFIG.SYS file. Press Cancel (F1) to remove the Document to be retrieved: message and follow the remaining instructions.

If the file contains a line that starts FILES =, such as FILES =10, the number must be 20 or greater. If it isn't, move the cursor to the number and change it. If there is no such line, type *FILES =20* as the first line of the file.

An optional addition to this file will make your disk(s) work faster: add a line that starts BUFFERS =, such as BUFFERS =4. Make sure that the number is at least 20. If no such line exists, type *BUFFERS =20* after the FILES line you typed in Step 3.

Now, to save the file, follow these steps:

1. Press Text In/Out (Ctrl-F5).

2. Press DOS **Text (1)** and then **Save (1)**.

3. Because you want to use the same file name, press Enter at the Document to be saved prompt.

4. Answer *Y* to replace the original version of the file.

Using WordPerfect's Setup Menu

Once you've installed the programs, you can use WordPerfect's Setup menu to customize the system. By changing the *default settings* within this menu, you can select the way many of WordPerfect's features work. The choices you make are permanent: they will affect all documents every time you use WordPerfect, and the settings remain until you use this menu again to change them.

Many settings can be overridden for a specific document if you use the options on the Format key (Shift-F8) (see Chapter 6) and the Font key (Ctrl-F8) (see Chapter 5).

When you first install the program, you may not be sure of what defaults to select. A new feature of WordPerfect 5 is that you may use Setup at any time. After you have started WordPerfect by typing WP, pressing Enter, and waiting until the program has appeared on the screen, simply press Shift-F1 to display the Setup menu (see fig. A.1). WordPerfect 4.2 users have to start the program with the special command WP /S to reach Setup.

Fig. A.1.
The Setup menu.

```
Setup

    1 - Backup

    2 - Cursor Speed              Normal

    3 - Display

    4 - Fast Save (unformatted)   Yes

    5 - Initial Settings

    6 - Keyboard Layout

    7 - Location of Auxiliary Files

    8 - Units of Measure




    Selection: 0
```

Setup in WordPerfect 5 is quick and easy to use—an improvement over Setup in WordPerfect 4.2. Let's take a look at the available features.

Backup

For maximum safety, you can optionally make either of two types of *backups*, or copies, of your working file: timed document backups and original document backups.

Timed document backups are made at optional intervals (such as every 5 minutes or 30 minutes) you specify. As you work on a document, the Timed Document Backup option saves a copy of the document on-screen in its current state. The backup copy is then deleted as long as you Exit (F7) normally.

If you don't exit normally—for instance, if the power goes off or your computer crashes while you're working—you can retrieve the timed backup copy when you restart WordPerfect (assuming it's newer than your last save). You will be missing only what you added since the backup was made. The backup file is named WP{WP}.BK1 for Doc 1, and WP{WP}.BK2 for Doc 2.

CAUTION: You must still ALWAYS save your file before exiting. The timed backup copy is *only* for emergencies.

Original document backups can be requested when you want to keep a copy of the last saved version of your document. When you save a file with either Save (F10) or Exit (F7), WordPerfect normally records over the preceding version of the file, if one exists. If you select the Original Document Backup option, WordPerfect instead preserves the preceding version of the file and gives it a .BK! extension whenever you Save or Exit the file. This way, no matter how many times you save your document, you always have a copy of the version that was last saved.

You may choose either or both of these backup options by completing the following:

1. Press Setup (Shift-F1) to access the Setup menu.

2. Press **Backup (1)** from the Setup menu to display the Setup: Backup menu (see fig. A.2).

3. If you want to select timed backup, follow these steps:

   a. Select **Timed Document Backup (1)**.

   b. Type *Y* to turn on the feature. (Typing *N* turns it off.)

Fig. A.2.
The Setup: Backup menu.

```
Setup: Backup

    Timed backup files are deleted when you exit WP normally.  If you
    have a power or machine failure, you will find the backup file in the
    backup directory indicated in Setup: Location of Auxiliary Files.

    Backup Directory

    1 - Timed Document Backup          Yes
        Minutes Between Backups        8


    Original backup will save the original document with a .BK! extension
    whenever you replace it during a Save or Exit.

    2 - Original Document Backup       Yes




    Selection: 0
```

c. Enter the number of minutes for the interval you would like between each backup and press Enter. For example, type *15* and press Enter.

4. If you want WordPerfect to make a backup copy of the last saved version, follow these steps:

a. Select **Original Document Backup** (**2**).

b. Type *Y* to turn on the feature.

5. Press Enter to return to the Setup menu.

If you access the Setup menu from a document and want to return to the document, press Exit (F7) instead of Enter.

Cursor Speed

On the IBM PC and compatibles, if you hold down a key rather than press and release it, the key repeats its character as long as you hold down the key. The repeat rate is usually very slow, so you may want to increase it.

To change the cursor speed, following these steps:

1. Press Setup (Shift-F1) to access the Setup menu if it is not already visible on the screen.

2. Select **Cursor Speed** (**2**).

3. Set the cursor speed by choosing a rate in characters per second from the menu at the bottom of the screen (see fig. A.3). For example, press *3* if you prefer a rate of 30 characters per second.

4. Select another item from the Setup menu if you want, or press Exit (F7) to return to your document.

It's easy to change the rate, so experiment with different speeds until you find the one you like best.

Display

The **Display** (**3**) selection on the Setup menu controls many aspects of WordPerfect's screen display—for instance, how the text appears on-screen, how menu letters are displayed, etc. The general strategy for controlling the display is to follow these steps:

1. Press Setup (Shift-F1) to access the Setup menu if it is not already visible.

2. Select **Display** (**3**) to see the Setup: Display menu (see fig. A.4).

3. Select an item from this menu and take the appropriate step(s) for that item. (What you should do for each item is indicated in the following sections.)

4. Either select another item or press Exit (F7) to return to your document.

```
  Setup

      1 - Backup

      2 - Cursor Speed              Normal

      3 - Display

      4 - Fast Save (unformatted)   Yes

      5 - Initial Settings

      6 - Keyboard Layout

      7 - Location of Auxiliary Files

      8 - Units of Measure




  Characters Per Second: 1 15; 2 20; 3 30; 4 40; 5 50; 6 Normal: 0
```

```
  Setup: Display

      1 - Automatically Format and Rewrite   Yes

      2 - Colors/Fonts/Attributes

      3 - Display Document Comments           Yes

      4 - Filename on the Status Line         Yes

      5 - Graphics Screen Type                IBM CGA 640x200 mono

      6 - Hard Return Display Character       ◀

      7 - Menu Letter Display                 BOLD

      8 - Side-by-side Columns Display        Yes




  Selection: 0
```

Automatically Format and Rewrite

If you want WordPerfect to reformat your text and rewrite the screen as you edit,
turn on the **Automatically Format and Rewrite (1)** option from the Setup: Display
menu. To activate this feature, do the following steps:

1. Select **Display (3)** from the Setup menu to see the Setup: Display menu if it
   is not already visible (see fig. A.4).

2. Select **Automatically Format and Rewrite (1)**.

3. Press *Y* to turn on the feature.

   Pressing *N* turns off the feature if it is already on.

4. You either can select another item from the Setup: Display menu, press Enter to return to the Setup menu, or press Exit (F7) to return to your document.

If the automatic reformatting and rewriting feature is off, the text is reformatted line-by-line as you move the cursor downward. Most WordPerfect users will probably want this feature turned on for convenience.

Colors/Fonts/Attributes

The Colors/Fonts/Attributes (**2**) option on the Setup: Display menu controls the colors and fonts you can select to represent the many different text attributes you use (see Chapter 5). When you select this option, you may see a Setup: Colors/Fonts submenu (see fig. A.5) or a Setup: Colors submenu (see fig. A.6), depending on the kind of display your system has. This Setup: Colors submenu is for selecting Screen Colors or Fast Text and should not be confused with a second Setup: Colors submenu, which is for choosing colors for the text attributes (see fig. A.7).

Fig. A.5.

The Setup: Colors/Fonts submenu.

```
Setup: Colors/Fonts

     1 - Screen Colors

     2 - Italics Font, 8 Foreground Colors

     3 - Underline Font, 8 Foreground Colors

     4 - Small Caps Font, 8 Foreground Colors

     5 - 512 Characters, 8 Foreground Colors

    *6 - Normal Font Only, 16 Foreground Colors




     Selection: 0
```

What colors are available for your use also depends on the kind of video display your system has. Different types of video displays have different properties, and WordPerfect needs different information for each. Thus, WordPerfect displays different menus for this option, depending on your video display. Normally, WordPerfect can determine what type of display you have. Your task is to specify how you want text to look within the capabilities of your display.

```
Setup: Colors

     1 - Screen Colors

     2 - Fast Text                            Yes
         (may cause snow on screen)












     Selection: 0
```

Fig. A.6.
*The Setup: Colors
submenu.*

```
Setup: Colors          A B C D E F G H I J K L M N O P
                       A B C D E F G H I J K L M N O P
Attribute              Foreground  Background  Sample
Normal                 0           A           Sample
Blocked                L           D           Sample
Underline              L           A           Sample
Strikeout              I           C           Sample
Bold                   M           H           Sample
Double Underline       L           C           Sample
Redline                M           E           Sample
Shadow                 J           F           Sample
Italics                K           C           Sample
Small Caps             D           B           Sample
Outline                P           H           Sample
Subscript              J           B           Sample
Superscript            L           B           Sample
Fine Print             P           H           Sample
Small Print            K           H           Sample
Large Print            K           C           Sample
Very Large Print       0           C           Sample
Extra Large Print      M           C           Sample
Bold & Underline       0           E           Sample
Other Combinations     L           A           Sample

Switch to switch; Move to copy settings      Doc 1
```

Fig. A.7.
*The Setup: Colors
submenu (for text
attributes).*

If you are using a color monitor and want to alter colors or fonts, do the following:

1. Select Colors/Fonts/Attributes (**2**) from the Setup: Display menu.

   You soon see a Setup: Colors/Fonts submenu (fig. A.5) or a Setup: Colors submenu (fig. A.6), depending on the kind of display you use.

2. If you see the Setup: Colors/Fonts submenu, follow these steps:

   a. Select from the submenu the option whose colors you want to modify, if any. For example, select the **Screen Color** (**1**) option if you want to modify the foreground and background colors of text attributes, such as normal, blocked, underline, strikeout, bold, etc. (see fig. A.7).

b. When you are satisfied with any modifications and are ready to return to your document, press Exit (F7).

You will soon see the Setup: Colors/Fonts submenu again.

c. Press Enter to return to the Setup: Display menu (pressing Enter again takes you back to the Setup menu), or press Exit (F7) to go to a document.

3. If you see a Setup: Colors submenu (fig. A.6), follow these steps:

a. Select the **S**creen Colors (**1**) option if you want to modify the foreground and background colors of text attributes, such as normal, blocked, underline, strikeout, bold, etc.

You soon see a Setup: Colors submenu (fig. A.7).

b. Use the ↓ and ↑ keys to select a row—that is, the attribute you want to modify.

You can select any row you wish for whatever attribute you want to modify. For an example, move the cursor to the first row for Normal text if the cursor is not there already.

c. Use the → and ← keys to select a column—that is, to indicate whether a color you pick is to be for the foreground (text) or background.

You can modify any one or both. If you modify both foreground and background colors, it does not matter which one you alter first. For our example, move the cursor to the Foreground column.

d. When the cursor is at the appropriate row-and-column location, select a foreground color from the colors displayed at the top of the screen.

The first row of letters at the top of the screen indicates what key to press to choose a color evident in the corresponding row of letters below the first row. Sixteen foreground color options (black and seven dull colors; black and seven bright colors) are available, and these are displayed against a background currently selected for the attribute. (In figure A.7 the letter *A* is printed white against a black background so that you can see in the figure what you can't see on-screen: a black letter against a black background.)

For our example, to have bright yellow text characters, press the letter *O*.

Bright yellow letters should appear immediately in the word "Sample" on the same row but in the Sample column on the right.

e. Now move the cursor laterally to the Background column to select a background color for Normal text.

Eight background color options (black and seven colors) are available. To complete our example, press the letter *A* for a black background as a sharp contrast to our bright yellow letters.

The effect is evident immediately in the Sample column.

   f. Repeat Steps b through e as many times as you want until you are satisfied with your attribute colors.

   g. When you are through modifying attribute colors, press Exit (F7) to return to the Setup: Colors menu.

4. Press Enter if you want to return to the Setup: Display menu, or press Enter twice to return to the Setup menu. If instead you want to go directly to your document, press Exit (F7).

Display Document Comments

If you want WordPerfect to display document comments (see Chapter 3), select **Display Document Comments** (**3**) from the Setup: Display menu. Press *Y* to turn on the feature. Pressing *N* turns off the feature.

Filename on the Status Line

To have the name of your file displayed on the left of the status line (the bottom line of your screen) when you are working in a document, select **Filename on the Status Line** (**4**) from the Setup: Display menu. Press *Y* to activate the feature. Press *N* if you want the feature turned off.

Graphics Screen Type

The **Graphics Screen Type** (**5**) option on the Setup: Display menu records the type of video display you have. View the type indicated to make sure that the indication is correct. If it's not correct, select this option from the menu and use the cursor keys to pick your display type from the list (see fig. A.8). Follow these steps:

1. From the Setup: Display menu select **Graphics Screen Type** (**5**).

The last few displays in this list appear only if you copied the .WPD files from the Fonts/Graphics disk into your \WP directory.

2. Use the ↑ or ↓ keys to highlight your display type.

If you pick the first choice, Text (no graphics), you must have the STANDARD.PRS file (from the WordPerfect 2 disk) in your \WP directory. WordPerfect needs this file to know how to View in text mode.

3. Press Enter or Select (**1**) to select it and to return to the Setup: Display menu.

Fig. A.8.

The Setup: Graphics Screen Type menu.

```
Setup: Graphics Screen Type

* Text (no graphics)
  Hercules 720x348 mono
  Hercules InColor 720x348 16 color
  IBM CGA 640x200 mono
  IBM EGA 640x350 mono
  IBM EGA 640x200 16 color
  IBM EGA 640x350 4 color
  IBM EGA 640x350 16 color
  IBM VGA 640x480 mono
  IBM VGA 640x480 16 color
  IBM VGA 320x200 256 color
  AT&T 6300 640x400 mono
  Compaq Prtble plasma 640x400 mono
  IBM 8514/A 1024x768 256 color
  MDS Genius2 1280x1024 mono dual
  Multisync 800x560 16 color
  MDS Genius  736x1008 mono portrt
  WYSE Wy-700 1280X800 mono

  1 Select: 1
```

If your display is not on the menu list, call the WordPerfect toll-free support line and ask which display type you should use.

Hard Return Display Character

Hard returns do not normally appear on-screen (see Chapter 2). If you prefer to see hard returns, you can select the character you would like displayed for hard returns. To make the selection, do the following steps:

1. From the Setup: Display menu select Hard Return Display Character (**6**).

2. Enter the character number by holding down the ALT key and typing the number *on the numeric keypad*.

   For example, press the ALT key, and while still holding down the ALT key, type *17* to get the character ◄.

   The character appears when you release the Alt key.

3. Press Exit (F7) to return to your document.

To use this option, you must know the IBM character set. Check your DOS manual for a chart. Some characters you might want to use are numbers 27 (←), 254 (■), or 4 (◆).

Menu Letter Display

The Menu Letter Display (**7**) option on the Setup: Display menu controls how the emphasized letter of all menu selections is displayed. When you select this option, a submenu appears at the bottom of the screen for determining the size and appearance of the emphasized characters (see fig. A.9). If you select Size (**1**) from this submenu, another submenu appears along the bottom line (see fig. A.10). Selecting **Appearance** (**2**) produces a different submenu (see fig. A.11) at the bottom of the screen. On most monochrome monitors, the only real choices are **Normal** (**3**) (no emphasized letter) from the Menu Letter Display submenu, or **Bold** (**1**) or **Underline** (**2**) from the Appearance submenu. With Hercules Plus and color video displays, more choices are available.

```
Setup: Display

        1 - Automatically Format and Rewrite     Yes

        2 - Colors/Fonts/Attributes

        3 - Display Document Comments             Yes

        4 - Filename on the Status Line           Yes

        5 - Graphics Screen Type                  IBM CGA 640x200 mono

        6 - Hard Return Display Character         ◄

        7 - Menu Letter Display                   BOLD

        8 - Side-by-side Columns Display          Yes




    1 Size; 2 Appearance; 3 Normal: 0
```

Fig. A.9.
The Menu Letter Display submenu.

```
Setup: Display

        1 - Automatically Format and Rewrite     Yes

        2 - Colors/Fonts/Attributes

        3 - Display Document Comments             Yes

        4 - Filename on the Status Line           Yes

        5 - Graphics Screen Type                  IBM CGA 640x200 mono

        6 - Hard Return Display Character         ◄

        7 - Menu Letter Display                   BOLD

        8 - Side-by-side Columns Display          Yes




    1 Suprscpt; 2 Subscpt; 3 Fine; 4 Small; 5 Large; 6 Vry Large; 7 Ext Large: 0
```

Fig. A.10.
The Size submenu.

Fig. A.11.

The Appearance submenu.

```
Setup: Display

         1 - Automatically Format and Rewrite    Yes

         2 - Colors/Fonts/Attributes

         3 - Display Document Comments            Yes

         4 - Filename on the Status Line          Yes

         5 - Graphics Screen Type                 IBM CGA 640x200 mono

         6 - Hard Return Display Character         ◄

         7 - Menu Letter Display                  BOLD

         8 - Side-by-side Columns Display         Yes




    1 Bold 2 Undrln 3 Dbl Und 4 Italc 5 Outln 6 Shadw 7 Sm Cap 8 Redln 9 Stkout: 0
```

Side-by-Side Column Display

The last item on the Setup: Display menu is for columns. If you want to display columns side by side on-screen, do these steps:

1. Select Side-by-side Columns Display (**8**).

2. Type *Y* to have columns displayed side by side, or press *N* if you want columns to appear as if they were on separate pages (see Chapter 16).

   In either case, columns will be printed side by side.

3. Press Enter to return to the Setup menu, or press Exit (F7) if you want to return to a document.

Fast Save

WordPerfect 5 now has on the Setup menu an option to save files more quickly than in previous versions. This gain in speed has a cost, however. Unlike a normal save, a Fast Save saves files without preformatting. Thus, you can't print them from List Files (see Chapter 10). You must first Retrieve files onto your screen before printing. Unless you usually have very long files and don't print from List Files, turn Fast Save off so that files are saved formatted.

To change the Fast Save selection, follow these steps:

1. Press Setup (Shift-F1) to access the Setup menu.

2. Press Fast Save (**4**).

3. Press *Y* to turn Fast Save on, or *N* to turn it off.

Initial Settings

Selecting **Initial Settings** (**5**) from the Setup menu (fig. A.1) produces the Setup: Initial Settings menu (see fig. A.12). From this menu, you can turn off beeps, change date format, create document summaries, select initial codes, set the repeat value, and determine the format of a table of authorities.

Fig. A.12.
The Initial Settings menu.

```
Setup: Initial Settings

    1 - Beep Options

    2 - Date Format            3 1, 4

    3 - Document Summary

    4 - Initial Codes

    5 - Repeat Value           8

    6 - Table of Authorities




    Selection: 0
```

Beep Options

Beep Options (**1**) is the selection for controlling beep sounds. With it, you can specify whether you want to hear a beep when you've made an error, when a word needs to be hyphenated, or when no target is found during a Forward Search (F2). To select a beep option, do the following steps:

1. From the Setup: Initial Settings menu, select **Beep Options** (**1**).

2. From the Setup: Beep options menu (see fig. A.13), select the occasion(s) for which you want to hear a beep. For example, select Beep on **Error** (**1**) if you want a sound for an error.

3. Press *Y* to turn on that beep option, or press *N* to turn it off.

4. If you want to select another beep option, select Beep on **Hyphenation** (**2**) or Beep on **Search** Failure (**3**), and press *Y* to turn on the option.

5. Press Enter to return to the Setup: Initial Settings menu.

If you find beeps annoying, you may want to turn off all these beep options.

Fig. A.13.
The Setup: Beep options menu.

```
Setup: Beep options

    1 - Beep on Error              Yes

    2 - Beep on Hyphenation        Yes

    3 - Beep on Search Failure     No













    Selection: 0
```

Date Format

Date Format (2) on the Setup: Initial Settings menu determines the way dates and times are formatted (see Chapter 2). Selecting this option produces the Date Format menu (see fig. A.14). On this menu, characters in the Character column correspond to options for displaying date and time. Examples on the menu show you how to select and type after the `Date format:` prompt the characters you pick for the form you want.

Fig. A.14.
The Date Format menu.

```
Date Format

    Character   Meaning
        1       Day of the Month
        2       Month (number)
        3       Month (word)
        4       Year (all four digits)
        5       Year (last two digits)
        6       Day of the Week (word)
        7       Hour (24-hour clock)
        8       Hour (12-hour clock)
        9       Minute
        0       am / pm
        %       Used before a number, will:
                    Pad numbers less than 10 with a leading zero
                    Output only 3 letters for the month or day of the week


    Examples:  3 1, 4       = December 25, 1984
               %6 %3 1, 4   = Tue Dec 25, 1984
               %2/%1/5 (6)  = 01/01/85 (Tuesday)
               8:90         = 10:55am


    Date format: 3 1, 4
```

Document Summary

The Document Summary (3) selection on the Setup: Initial Settings menu governs whether a document summary is automatically created the first time you Save (F10) or Exit (F7) from a new document. This selection is also the one to use to specify Subject Search text (see the section on "Using Document Summaries" inChapter 6).

Initial Codes

With Initial Codes (4), you can select certain formatting commands—for example, margins, line spacing, and justification— that control the way your document looks. The codes you select here affect every new document unless you override them by using Document Format (see Chapters 6 and 18 for more information).

Repeat Value

Repeat Value (5) sets the value for the Repeat (Escape) Key when you first press it (see Chapter 2 for more information).

Table of Authorities

The Table of Authorities (6) selection produces a Setup: Table of Authorities menu for setting the default formatting style for WordPerfect's Table of Authorities feature. This menu controls whether dot leaders appear in the table, whether underlining is allowed, and whether a blank line is inserted between authorities (see Chapter 22).

Keyboard Layout

From the Setup menu (fig. A.1), select the Keyboard Layout (6) option to change the keyboard definition you normally use (see Chapter 18).

Location of Auxiliary Files

You can now specify separate paths for almost all of WordPerfect's auxiliary files. Select Location of Auxiliary Files (7) to display the Setup: Location of Auxiliary Files menu (see fig. A.15).

Select Backup Directory (1) to indicate the location of the directory that stores the Timed Document Backup files. (See "Backup" in this chapter's discussion of the Setup menu.) Use Hyphenation Module(s) (2) to specify where the Hyphenation

Fig. A.15.

The Setup: Location of Auxiliary Files menu.

```
Setup: Location of Auxiliary Files

     1 - Backup Directory              C:\WP

     2 - Hyphenation Module(s)         C:\WP\THDIC

     3 - Keyboard/Macro Files          C:\WP\MACROS

     4 - Main Dictionary(s)            C:\WP\THDIC

     5 - Printer Files                 C:\WP

     6 - Style Library Filename

     7 - Supplementary Dictionary(s)   C:\WP\THDIC

     8 - Thesaurus                     C:\WP\THDIC




     Selection: 0
```

information files are stored. Select **Keyboard/Macro Files (3)** to indicate the path for both macro files (files ending in .WPM) and keyboard definition files (files ending in .MRS). (See Chapter 11 for macros, and Chapter 18 for keyboard definitions.)

The **Main Dictionary(s) (4)** option on the Setup: Location of Auxiliary Files menu is for specifying where you keep the main spell check file WP{WP}EN.LEX. **Printer Files (5)** is for the location of the Printer definition files (files ending in .PRS). Use **Style Library File (6)** to specify the complete pathname of the file containing the default set of styles, and select **Supplementary Dictionary(s) (7)** for the path name to the Supplementary spell check file WP{WP}EN.SUP. The **Thesaurus (8)** option is for the Thesaurus file WP{WP}EN.THS.

Units of Measure

In WordPerfect 4.2, everything (margins, page lengths, etc.) is measured in lines or columns, which often makes it difficult to align text and characters exactly. With WordPerfect 5, you can specify many different units of measurement. You can control WordPerfect menu units that require entry of a measurement, such as margins and graphics boxes. You can also specify the units WordPerfect uses for the status line at the bottom of the main editing screen.

To set the units of measure, follow these steps:

1. Select **Units of Measure (8)** from the Setup menu to reach the Setup: Units of Measure menu (see fig. A.16).

   The possible units include inches (type " or *i*), centimeters (type *c*), points (a typesetter's measurement equal to 1/72", type *p*) or the original WordPerfect 4.2 units of lines and columns (type *u*).

2. Select **Display (1)** to change the units displayed on menus and the units you use to enter numbers.

3. Enter your selection, drawing from the column of characters below Legend: in the figure.

   For example, if you want menu units in centimeters, type *c*.

4. Select **Status (2)** if you want to change the status line display.

5. Enter your selection, again drawing from the same column of characters.

6. Press Enter if you want to return to the Setup menu, or press Exit (F7) to go to your document.

```
Setup: Units of Measure

    1 - Display and Entry of Numbers        "
            for Margins, Tabs, etc.

    2 - Status Line Display                 "


  Legend:

    " = inches
    i = inches
    c = centimeters
    p = points
    u = WordPerfect 4.2 Units (Lines/Columns)




  Selection: 0
```

Fig. A.16.

The Setup: Units of Measure menu.

Exit Setup

In many of the preceding sections on Setup procedures, you have seen that leaving Setup is easy: you just press Exit (F7). Leaving Setup is therefore no more difficult than launching it. You will recall that to access the Setup menu, you simply press Shift-F1. You can use Setup whenever you want, so don't be reluctant to experiment or change settings.

Starting WordPerfect 5

Starting WordPerfect can be done in many ways. This section shows first the simplest ways, then indicates some other ways to start WordPerfect. Although these other ways are more complex, they are more convenient.

Starting WordPerfect on a Floppy Disk System

To start and use WordPerfect on a floppy disk system, you must complete the following steps:

1. Boot DOS if you have not already done so.

2. Place in drive B: a formatted document disk—a disk on which you want to save the things you write.

3. Put in drive A: the disk you've labeled WordPerfect 1.

4. Type *B:* and press Enter, to change to drive B:.

5. You can now start WordPerfect from drive B: by typing *A:WP* and pressing Enter.

6. After a few seconds, WordPerfect's title screen appears with the message to Insert diskette labeled ``WordPerfect 2`` and press any key. Replace the disk in drive A: with your WordPerfect 2 disk and strike any key to finish starting up. You must leave the WordPerfect 2 disk in drive A: while you're using WordPerfect.

Any writing you save is recorded on the disk in drive B:. Remember that you will not be able to use conveniently WordPerfect's Help, Thesaurus, or Spell Check features because the necessary files for these features are on other disks.

Starting WordPerfect on a Hard Disk System

For hard disk system users, you can start WordPerfect in many ways. You can change into your document directory and then start WordPerfect, or you can start WordPerfect and then use List Files (F5) to change to your document directory. The best way for many people to start WordPerfect, though, is from a batch file.

Starting WordPerfect from a Batch File

Using batch files is one of the best ways to start WordPerfect on a hard disk system. (This method is rarely useful on floppy disk systems.) A *batch file* is a text file that contains only DOS commands. If you type the name of the batch file at the DOS prompt and press Enter, DOS executes each command in the file sequentially.

Batch files are especially useful if you keep different types of documents in different directories, as suggested in the section on "Making Directories." If different people use the computer and each person keeps document files in a separate directory on the hard disk, you can create a batch file, or a set of batch files, for each person.

You can use WordPerfect to make your batch files, but you *must* use Text In/Out (Ctrl-F5) and select DOS Text (**1**) and Save (**1**) to save the files. Batch files are text

(ASCII) files and don't work if you save them as WordPerfect files with Save (F10). Also, batch files *must* have the extension .BAT, as in JOE.BAT or LETTERS.BAT.

Making Batch Files with WordPerfect

Depending on how you use WordPerfect, you can create different batch files for special purposes. For example, you might create a batch file for each type of document you write: a batch file called BUSLTR.BAT for business letters, PERSLTR.BAT for personal letters, MISCDOC.BAT for miscellaneous documents, BOOK.BAT for chapters in a book, or SCHOOL.BAT for school assignments.

Each batch file changes into the appropriate directory and then starts WordPerfect. Because school assignments may require special formatting requirements, SCHOOL.BAT starts WordPerfect with a /m start-up option that runs automatically a macro to insert a special set of initial formatting codes.

1. Make a directory for all these batch files; type *MD\BAT.*

2. Change to your WordPerfect directory by typing *CD \WP* and pressing Enter.

3. Type *WP* and press Enter to start WordPerfect.

4. Press List Files (F5).

5. Type = to change the current directory.

6. Type *\BAT* and press Enter; then press Cancel (F1) to cancel the directory listing.

7. Now, the commands you use to start WordPerfect depend on which version of DOS you have. For the first batch file, type these commands for DOS 2:

    CD \BUSLTR
    WP

    For DOS 3, type these commands:

    CD \BUSLTR
    \WP\WP

8. In either case, save the document as a DOS Text file with the name BUSLTR.BAT.

    a. Press Text In/Out (Ctrl-F5).

    b. Select Dos Text (1) to get the DOS Text menu.

    c. Select Save (1) to save the file as a Text file.

    d. Type *BUSLTR.BAT* as the file name and press Enter.

    e. Press Exit (F7) and then type *N* twice to clear the screen.

9. Do the same for PERSLTR.BAT, MISCDOC.BAT, and BOOK.BAT, substituting the appropriate directory names.

10. Finally, to create SCHOOL.BAT for DOS 2, type the following:

    CD \SCHOOL
    WP /M-SCHLCODE

    For DOS 3, type these commands:

    CD \SCHOOL
    \WP\WP /M-SCHLCODE

11. Again, save the document as a DOS Text file.

Changing Your PATH Command

After creating your batch files, you also need to add your new \BAT directory to your existing PATH command so that you can start any of the batch files from any directory. Your PATH command is contained in your AUTOEXEC.BAT file. DOS automatically runs the AUTOEXEC.BAT file when you start or reboot. If your AUTOEXEC.BAT file has no PATH command, you'll have to add one. If you have an AUTOEXEC.BAT file, Retrieve it as a DOS Text file:

1. Press Text In/Out (Ctrl-F5).

2. Press DOS **Text** (**1**) to get the DOS Text menu.

3. Press **Retrieve** (**2**).

4. Type *\ AUTOEXEC.BAT* and press Enter.

5. If you already have a PATH command in your AUTOEXEC.BAT— for example, PATH C:\LOTUS;C:\DOS—just add a semicolon at the end of the command; then add the new subdirectory so that it looks like this: PATH C:\LOTUS;C:\DOS;C:\BAT.

   If you don't have a PATH command in your AUTOEXEC.BAT file, just type in this line at the beginning: *PATH C:\BAT.*

   If you don't have an AUTOEXEC.BAT, just type in this line: *PATH C:BAT.*

6. Additionally, if you use DOS 2, add your WordPerfect directory to the PATH in the following ways:

    PATH C:\ LOTUS;C:\ DOS;C:\ BAT;C:\ WP

   or

    PATH C:\ BAT;C:\ WP

When you're finished, save your AUTOEXEC.BAT file as a DOS text file:

7. Press **Text** In/Out (Ctrl-F5).

8. Press DOS **Text** (**1**) to get the DOS Text menu.

9. Press **Save** (**1**) to save the file as a text file.

10. Type the filename if it isn't already there: *AUTOEXEC.BAT* and press Enter.

11. Press Exit (F7) to leave WordPerfect.

12. Type *N* if you don't want to save a document (or *Y* if you do).

13. Type *Y* to confirm your intention to leave WordPerfect (or *N* if you change your mind and want to stay in the program).

Testing Your Batch Files

After creating your batch files and modifying your AUTOEXEC.BAT file, you should test your new batch files:

1. Reboot with Ctrl-Alt-Del so that your new PATH command takes effect.

2. Type any of the four batch file names you made, such as *BUSLTR* (but don't type the .BAT extension), and press Enter.

   You should be in WordPerfect in the proper subdirectory.

3. Press List Files (F5) and check the message at the bottom left of the screen to see whether you are in the right subdirectory.

4. Press Cancel (F1) because you don't want a file listing.

5. If your batch file does not work, carefully retrace these instructions and try again.

Starting WordPerfect with Parameters

You normally start WordPerfect from DOS, typing *WP* to launch the program. However, for greater convenience and efficiency, you can start WordPerfect, using two types of parameters.

Starting WordPerfect with a File Name

If you want to start WordPerfect and automatically retrieve a specified file, use the first type of parameter: the file name. Entering a file name parameter is more convenient and faster than retrieving a document by using either List Files (F5) (see Chapter 10) or Retrieve (Shift-F10).

For instance, type

WP MYFILE.MEM

to start editing MYFILE.MEM on a hard disk system, assuming that MYFILE.MEM is in the current directory.

With a document disk in drive B:, and with drive B: as the current drive, you would type

A:WP MYFILE.MEM

on a two-floppy system.

Note that you must enter the name of an *existing* file. If the file does not exist, you receive an error message.

Starting WordPerfect with a Command Line Option

Another type of parameter, the *command line option,* can be used for special circumstances. Each option begins with the slash character (/) and consists of one or two letters. Some options also need extra information, such as a name. In these cases, the option is followed by a hyphen and the extra data. Remember, all these commands can be typed in either upper- or lowercase.

If you need to use more than one option, you can combine them. The command

WP /B–10/M–START/X

is an example. (What these various options mean separately soon is explained.)

You can also start WordPerfect with both a file name and one or more start-up options. The command

WP BOOK.1 /B–15/NC

is an example.

/b–number

This option no longer works in WordPerfect 5.0.

/d– drive and/or directory

This option puts WordPerfect temporary files in the drive/directory you specify. Example:

WP /D– C:\WP5\TEMP

Because these files are deleted as long as you exit normally, few hard disk users need to use this option. Floppy system users also don't have much use for it because they have to keep the WordPerfect 2 disk in the floppy drive all the time.

/i

This option is applicable only in DOS 2, and then only rarely. If you run WordPerfect one or more times on a floppy disk and then decide to install the program on a hard disk, you may need to use this option the *first* time you start WordPerfect on the hard disk.

/m—name

When you use this option as you start WordPerfect, the program immediately executes a macro name you specify. Example:

WP /M—INITCODE

You could use this option, for instance, if you have a class of documents that you format with initial codes. Create a macro with the initial codes and then start WordPerfect with this command when you want to create a document in the specified format (see Chapter 11 on creating macros).

/nc

This option disables the keyboard speed-up feature in case it causes a conflict with your hardware or other software. (See the section on "Cursor Speed" near the beginning of this chapter's discussion of the Setup menu.) Example:

WP /NC

/ne

This option disallows the use of LIM-type expanded memory. Example:

WP /NE

/nf

Sometimes, especially if you use a windowing environment program like DESQView or Windows, the way characters are written onto the screen can cause problems. The /nf (nonfast) option should eliminate this problem.

/nk

Once in a while, the way the keyboard is read can cause a conflict with some memory-resident (TSR) programs and some not-quite-compatible computers. The /nk option should eliminate this problem.

/r

In WordPerfect 4.2, this option causes the entire WordPerfect program to load into memory. Example:

WP /R

Making WordPerfect work faster, this option in 4.2 is especially useful for floppy disk systems. Unfortunately, WordPerfect 5 takes too much memory to do this. This option now works only if you have LIM-type expanded memory.

/s

This option from WordPerfect 4.2 no longer exists in WordPerfect 5. The option has been replaced by Setup (Alt-F1).

/ss =rows,columns

This option allows you to adjust the screen size if, for some reason, WordPerfect can't automatically detect the screen size of your monitor. Find out the size information from your monitor manual. Example:

   WP /SS =80,150

/x

The /x option restores original default Setup values. Example:

   WP /X

This would be useful, for instance, if you wanted to restore temporarily the original keyboard layout.

These options can be used another way, by means of the DOS command SET. You can store information in DOS if you enter the command in the form

   SET name = data

where "name" is any word or character sequence you want, and "data" is the information you want to store. This information is then available for any program.

For example, you can give the command

   SET WP =/B

or

   SET WP =/M–START/SS = 80,150

and WordPerfect reads those options just as if you have typed them at the DOS prompt. Using the SET command means that you no longer have to type those options every time you start WordPerfect. Thus, you are able to start the program with just *WP*.

TIP: Put your SET command in your AUTOEXEC.BAT file so that the command is run automatically when you start your computer. For more on an AUTOEXEC.BAT file, see the earlier section "Changing Your PATH command."

WP
5 Summary

In this Appendix, you've learned about the following:

- Installing WordPerfect 5 on both floppy and hard disk systems

- Using Setup to change the way WordPerfect works and looks

- Starting WordPerfect:

  - with a file name or command line options

  - on both floppy disk and hard disk systems

  - more conveniently with batch files

There is more to Setup than we've covered here. The important thing to remember is that now you can use Setup as often as you want. Don't be afraid to experiment with different settings. Similarly, there are many other variations for batch files besides the examples in this appendix. Again, don't be afraid to experiment.

B

WordPerfect 5
for 4.2 Users

*As an independent computer consultant in the Boston area, **Marilyn Horn Claff**, has exceptional knowledge of WordPerfect Corporation software and experience teaching advanced applications.* ■

I f you are currently using WordPerfect 4.2, you may be wrestling with the question of whether to upgrade to WordPerfect 5. If you have already decided to upgrade, you may be wondering what upgrading involves and how you can make the transition easily. This appendix addresses questions about upgrading from previous versions of WordPerfect and consolidates information that will help you get off to a fast start with 5.

Deciding Whether To Upgrade

The wealth of new features in WordPerfect 5 makes the decision to upgrade an easy one for most users. In a few cases, however, sticking with WordPerfect 4.2 may make sense.

One reason for not upgrading might be that your computer system cannot run the new version. Two possible hardware limitations are insufficient memory and system incompatibility. WordPerfect 5 requires a minimum of 384K of free RAM. If you use memory-resident programs or edit large files, you may need more RAM. Although many users would gladly add memory to their computers to use WordPerfect 5, adding memory is not always feasible. If you have a laptop or a semicompatible computer, adding more RAM may be expensive or even impossible.

WordPerfect 5 runs on a narrower range of compatibles than WordPerfect 4.2. If your computer is not a true IBM-compatible, you may not be able to use WordPerfect 5. If you have any doubts, call WordPerfect Corporation and ask.

Another reason for not upgrading to version 5 is that your computer does not have a hard disk. Although WordPerfect 5 does not require a hard disk, it is strongly recommended. Without a hard disk, you may find WordPerfect 5 cumbersome because of the disk swapping required. Some computer novices may have trouble understanding when to change disks.

If you use WordPerfect 5 on a floppy system, you will need to use the /D start-up option to redirect the overflow files to drive B: because not enough room is available for them on the program disk. The presence of these files on your B: disk will reduce your usable disk space and limit the size of your documents. (If your floppy drives are 720K or higher, you will be able to manage just fine without a hard disk.)

A third reason for not upgrading is that you exchange files *regularly* with 4.2 users. Although you can retrieve 4.2 files directly into WordPerfect 5, not all formatting is converted automatically. Furthermore, you must remember to save version 5 files in 4.2 format before giving them to someone using 4.2. Without access to WordPerfect 5 or its external conversion program, there is no way to convert version 5 files to 4.2 format. (This appendix later gives detailed information about converting files.)

Unless you need to exchange files regularly, using different versions of WordPerfect in the same office should not pose a problem.

Making a Smooth Transition

If you are already comfortable with WordPerfect 4.2, you will find the transition to WordPerfect 5 relatively easy. Even so, you may be concerned about the two central issues of upgrading: learning the new version and converting your current WordPerfect files.

Learning WordPerfect 5

You can make the transition to WordPerfect 5 easier if you are aware of the program's new features. As you are learning the new program, you will want to keep the earlier version of the program available and learn the features that will save you the most time and effort first. This section tells you how to use both versions concurrently and how to ease into using WordPerfect 5. You also learn about the keystroke changes in the new version as well as about the many specific design changes and about a number of features that make the program now easier to use.

Using Both Versions Concurrently

While you are learning version 5, keep WordPerfect 4.2 available on your hard disk. If you run into a problem, you can fall back on 4.2. (If you are short on disk space, delete all the 4.2 files except WP.EXE; WP{SYS}.FIL; and the printer files: WPFONT.FIL, WPRINTER.FIL, and WPFEED.FIL.)

CAUTION: Be sure to install WordPerfect 5 in a new directory. Don't mix files from different versions in the same directory.

CAUTION: If you keep both versions of WordPerfect on your hard disk, put only *one* of the WordPerfect program directories on your path. Use a batch file to start the other program, or start it from its own directory. (If both directories are on the path, the WP.EXE file in the directory listed first will always be used. Listing the other directory merely slows down DOS's searches for other programs.)

Easing into Version 5

Don't be intimidated by the length of the feature list and the number of disks in the update package. As in previous versions, you can ignore features you don't need. Direct your initial learning effort to the features that will save you the most time and work. If you have been inserting cross-references by hand, investigate the auto-referencing feature. If you spend a lot of time looking for specific documents, focus on Document Summaries and the advanced Word Search feature in List Files. Learning to use even one new feature could dramatically reduce the amount of time you spend on a document. But don't try to learn everything in a single sitting; you won't remember much of what you learn.

Even though you are not a beginner, go through the on-disk tutorial included on the version 5 Learning disk. See Chapter 1 for a description of the new tutorial lessons.

Understanding Keystroke Differences

To make the transition easier for users of previous versions, WordPerfect Corporation retained as much as possible of the WordPerfect 4.2 keyboard layout so that you will be able to start producing documents with WordPerfect 5 right away. With the aid of the keyboard template and the on-line help, you will learn the new keystroke combinations without difficulty.

The Upgrade guide included in the WordPerfect 5 package describes the keyboard changes in detail. Only a few of the 40 function-key combinations have changed. The most significant difference is the F8 key. Previously, formatting was divided into Print Format (Ctrl-F8), Page Format (Alt-F8), and Line Format (Shift-F8). In version 5, all formatting is combined on the Shift-F8 key, freeing the Ctrl-F8 key for fonts, and the Alt-F8 for styles.

WordPerfect 5's keyboard layout may occasionally cost a few extra keystrokes, but in general, most features require fewer keystrokes than the corresponding features in

4.2. For example, setting left and right margins takes two more keystrokes in version 5 than in 4.2. However, design changes, such as absolute margins, automatic pitch adjustments, styles, and forms, eliminate many of the margin changes necessary in 4.2. Once you have set your margins at the beginning of the document, you rarely will need to change them, no matter how many different font sizes you use.

Learning Version 5's Design Changes

Although the keyboard is reassuringly familiar, you soon discover that more fundamental aspects of WordPerfect's design have changed. To use WordPerfect 5 productively, you must abandon your 4.2 way of thinking and learn to think in terms of version 5.

File Header

All version 5 documents have a *file header* that contains important information about the file. This file header, invisible when you are editing a document, was designed to eliminate many of the printing and conversion problems encountered in earlier versions of WordPerfect. The file header size varies greatly from document to document. The header can become quite large for documents that include graphics images, because a compressed version of each image is stored in the header. If you notice a discrepancy between the size of your document and the file size displayed in List Files, it is probably due to the size of the file header.

TIP: All WordPerfect 4.2 files will be larger when converted to version 5 format because of the overhead required for the file header.

Initial Codes

Previous versions of WordPerfect did not contain a file header. The only formatting codes in WordPerfect documents were the ones you inserted explicitly. If a document did not contain any formatting codes, WordPerfect formatted it according to your default settings. If your default margins were set at 12,89, WordPerfect assumed those margins when you retrieved a document, unless the program encountered a code for different margin settings. You generally did not need to include any formatting codes unless you wanted to format the document differently from your default settings.

This system worked well for individual users or for groups of users who shared the same default settings. Imagine what happened, however, when two users with different default settings needed to exchange files. Suppose, for example, that Lisa used a 12-pitch font, and she therefore had set her margins at 12,89. Betsy, on the other hand, used a 10-pitch font, and therefore she had not changed WordPerfect's defaults of margins at 10,74.

When Betsy retrieved Lisa's file, it appears completely jumbled because WordPerfect had reformatted the document to conform to Betsy's defaults. Because Lisa's line length was 77 characters, but Betsy's was only 64 characters, the line endings and page breaks were different. Tables (based on tab settings) were not aligned, and line drawings were impossible to decipher because the lines wrapped.

Documents created in previous versions of WordPerfect simply were not very portable because no information about what default settings were in effect when they were created was included in the documents themselves. Inserting formatting codes at the beginning of each document is only a partial solution for several reasons. First, the extra step cancels out the convenience of using defaults. Second, you may not even know that you later will need to give the document to someone else. Third, WordPerfect 4.x does not allow certain codes (such as Justification On or Justification Off) to be inserted in a document if those codes conform to the system default settings.

WordPerfect 5 solves the problem of "file portability" and file conversion by including in the document's file header the formatting codes that were in effect when the document was created. The initial codes in the document header can come from two sources: Initial Settings and Document Initial Codes.

Initial Settings

All file headers include a copy of the document's initial codes, which are the settings in effect when you create a document. If you did not change the Initial Settings when you set up WordPerfect 5 (Shift-F1, **5**, **4**), the Initial Codes contained in the file header are WordPerfect's factory defaults: one-inch margins on all sides, single-spacing, tabs set for every half-inch, right-justification on, no page numbering, underline spaces but not tabs, and so forth. If you *did* change the Initial Settings in the Setup menu, the settings you chose are your new default settings and will be included in the file header of every document you create, unless you override them with Document Initial Codes.

Document Initial Codes

Occasionally, you may want to create a document with initial settings that are different from your default settings. To avoid the nuisance of changing your default settings before you create the document and changing them back afterward, WordPerfect 5 provides an alternative way to insert initial settings in document headings: Document Initial Codes (Shift-F8, **3**, **2**).

Document Initial Codes act like default Initial Settings, which they override. Because they are part of the document header, Document Initial Codes are not visible within the document (although their effect is apparent).

Although you could just insert codes at the beginning of the document instead of using Document Initial Codes, placing formatting codes in the header has three advantages:

- The codes stay out of your way. When you use Reveal Codes, the codes will not clutter the screen.

- You cannot inadvertently delete codes in the header.

- You cannot inadvertently insert text in front of the codes.

Generally, you will find editing your documents much easier if you put as many of your formatting codes as possible in the document header.

CAUTION: If you have a document on-screen and retrieve another document, the file header of the retrieved file is stripped out. Thus, the initial codes of the first document affect the format of the retrieved text. To retain the format of a document even if it is retrieved into another document, use formatting codes in the body of the document, rather than as Document Initial Codes.

Printer-Specific Documents and Intelligent Printing

An unusual feature in WordPerfect 5 is its "intelligent printing" capability. To achieve the best possible output from a particular printer, WordPerfect takes the capabilities of that printer into account from the very beginning. When you create a document, WordPerfect formats it for the currently selected printer. When you change fonts in the document, WordPerfect lets you choose among only those fonts actually available for that printer, in the orientation of the form you are using. You cannot choose a landscape font if you are using a portrait orientation, and vice versa; fonts of the wrong orientation do not even appear on the list of available fonts.

Each version 5 document, therefore, is printer-specific. The name of the printer for which the document was formatted is stored in the document header, along with information about the fonts available for that printer. If you instruct WordPerfect to print the document on a different printer, WordPerfect reformats the document for the new printer. Reformatting involves substituting fonts and forms available to the new printer for the ones that were available to the original printer.

If you always use the same printer, you may not ever be aware of this reformatting. If you switch back and forth between two printers, however, you should get into the habit of first selecting the printer you plan to use, *before* you begin a new document, especially if you change fonts or paper sizes frequently. (You can write a simple macro to select each printer.)

Print Quality

One welcome enhancement in WordPerfect 5 is that you can select the print quality for text and graphics at the Print menu. In 4.2, you could sometimes accomplish this by changing fonts or by modifying your printer definitions, depending on your printer.

Unfortunately, there is no way to change your print-quality settings as defaults. Your changes to the print-quality settings remain in effect only for the rest of that session, or until you change them again. If you prefer print-quality settings that are different from the built-in ones (Text quality = high, Graphics quality = medium), your best option is to write a macro to change them.

When you save a document, the print-quality settings that are in effect are saved in the document header, along with the name of the printer, fonts, and other printing information. The advantage to saving the quality settings with the document is that whenever you print a document, the same quality settings will be used. You can therefore print a group of files from List Files, each with different settings, without having to answer a series of questions for each one.

The disadvantage of this method is that *the process of retrieving a document resets automatically the print quality to whatever settings had been saved in that document*. To illustrate, imagine that you have set both text and graphics quality to High. You retrieve a document that you previously saved with Draft text quality and Do Not Print for graphics quality. After making a few minor corrections, you issue the command to print the final copy.

Because you had just set text and graphics quality to High a few moments before, you expect the printout to conform to those settings. Instead, the text is printed as draft, and the graphics are not printed. When you look at the print control screen to determine why the file did not print as you expected, you see that the quality settings agree with your printout. Text quality is now set to Draft, and Graphics quality is set to Do Not Print.

You may suspect that a gremlin in your computer has arbitrarily changed your printer menu options. A more rational explanation, however, is that WordPerfect has simply used the print-quality settings that were saved with the document, instead of the settings that were in effect *before* you retrieved the document.

CAUTION: Every time you retrieve a document, you risk inadvertently resetting your print-quality settings.

To avoid this scenario, check the print-quality settings before printing a document that may have been created with different print-quality settings in effect. If you always use WordPerfect's default settings, this will not be a problem for you. If you tend however to print a draft document, modify it, and then print a higher-quality final version, pay special attention to the print-quality settings.

View Document

WordPerfect 5's View Document feature (Shift-F7, **6**) is far more powerful than the 4.2 Preview feature it replaces. If your printer has graphics capability, View Document lets you see *exactly* how your document will look when printed. You can even view a page at different magnifications. If you don't have graphics capability, your document will appear much as it would in 4.2's Preview, with margins, page numbering, headers, footers, footnotes, and endnotes displayed.

Unlike Preview, however, View Document displays *only what your printer is capable of printing*. For example, if you use WordPerfect's line-drawing feature in a document but your printer cannot print the line-drawing characters, they will be invisible when you view the document, even though they are displayed on the main editing screen. Before using View Document, therefore, be sure to select the printer with which you will print that document. Otherwise, View Document will not display an accurate image of the final document.

CAUTION: Because the preview is determined by the capabilities of your printer, the error message

    ERROR: Printer not selected

is displayed if you try to view a document without having selected a printer. Select a printer and try again.

CAUTION: If View Document (or Print) seems to ignore most of your formatting, check to make sure that you have selected the printer you actually plan to use, and not the Standard definition, which is a bare-bones definition limited to typewriter characters.

Fonts

WordPerfect 5's handling of font changes is different from that of previous versions. The limit of 8 fonts per printer definition has been removed, and fonts are chosen by name or attribute rather than by number. In version 5, you are limited only by the capability of your printer. For example, an HP LaserJet allows only 16 different fonts per page, and only 32 different fonts may be stored in the printer's memory at a time.

Base Font and Initial Font

In WordPerfect 5, selecting fonts by name is always printer-specific. When you select a printer, you must select one of the fonts available for that printer as your *initial font*. WordPerfect uses this initial font as your default font when that printer is selected. You cannot choose a default font in Setup, as you could in previous versions of WordPerfect. If you try, WordPerfect displays the following prompt:

    Use the Initial Font option to select a font.

You can, however, choose a different initial font in Document Initial Codes (Shift F8, **3, 3**). The initial font selection is saved in the document's file header, along with the name of the currently selected printer.

WordPerfect does not use the term *initial font* in the document proper, because the term would not be appropriate in documents with multiple fonts. The current font (which may or may not be the initial font) is called the *base font* because the current font is the basis for determining automatic (or relative) font changes, such as superscript, italic, and large fonts.

Relative versus Explicit Font Changes

WordPerfect 5 allows two types of font changes: relative and explicit. A *relative* font change is one that is determined by your base font. If your base font is a 12-point font, for example, then extra large may be a 24-point font. If your base font is a 10-point font, then extra large may be an 18-point font. An *explicit* font change is a change to a specific font or (in WordPerfect's terminology) a change to a new base font. You can, for example, choose explicitly to use Helvetica 18 point or Helvetica 24 point.

If you use a relative font change, you simply specify an attribute (such as bold or small caps) or a size (such as large, very large, or extra large) instead of choosing a font by name. WordPerfect selects an appropriate font automatically, using the automatic font changes defined in your printer driver.

Relative font changes have three distinct advantages over explicit fonts changes:

- *Simplicity*

  With relative fonts changes, you don't have to remember font names or combinations of fonts that work well together.

- *Ease of editing*

  Relative font changes adjust automatically if you change your base font. Suppose that you use a 12-point font for the text of a newsletter, but the captions, callouts, and headers are all in different point sizes. If you decide to change to a smaller 10-point font for your text, you also need to adjust the size of the other fonts, because they are no longer in proportion with your new font. If you use relative font changes, you merely need to change the base font and let WordPerfect make the other font changes automatically. If you use explicit font changes, you have to change all the fonts manually—a burdensome task because WordPerfect does not allow you to search and replace fonts.

- *Portability*

  Relative font changes provide more consistent results if you print the file on a different printer that does not have the same selection of fonts. If you choose fonts explicitly by name, WordPerfect must substitute an equivalent font individually from among those available to the new printer, according to a hierarchy of font properties including orientation, typeface, size, weight, and slant. If you use relative font changes, WordPerfect selects an appropriate base font and makes the relative font changes according to a table in your printer driver.

Units of Measure

Margins and tabs can now be specified in terms of absolute measurements, such as inches, centimeters, points (1/72″), and WordPerfect units (1/1200″). You can still use the 4.2 system of specifying measurements in terms of lines and characters, but the absolute measurements will make most word processing easier.

You can change the units of measure in Setup. You can use any unit you want at any point, no matter what unit you have selected for the screen display. For example, if you chose inches in Setup for displaying and entering margins and tabs, you still can use points when that is more convenient, without returning to Setup. You just follow the number with the letter *p*, the WordPerfect abbreviation for points. If you do not specify a unit of measure, WordPerfect uses your default unit of measure.

CAUTION: Don't confuse WordPerfect units (w) with WordPerfect 4.2 units (u).

TIP: Internally, WordPerfect stores all measurements in WordPerfect units (1/1200″) for greater precision. Although the option is undocumented, you can choose WordPerfect units (1/1200″) from the Units of Measure menu. To choose WordPerfect units, type *w* after a number of units and press Enter.

Printer Forms and Paper Size/Type

The use of absolute margins necessitated another design change: the use of forms. Because WordPerfect now calculates margins from the extremities of the page, it needs to know the dimensions of the page. The default page size is *Standard* (8.5″ x 11″). The available page sizes are determined by the capabilities of the currently selected printer.

You can change the paper size in a document at the Format Page menu (Shift-F8, **2**, **8**). To change your default paper size/type, mark a form as Initially Present in your printer definition in Select Printers (Shift-F7, **S**, **3**, **4**, **3**).

The concept of forms incorporates several 4.2 features, including printer bins and paper feeding options (continuous, manual, and sheet feeder). In addition, forms determine your printer orientation (portrait or landscape). You may choose only fonts whose orientation is consonant with the currently selected form. Thus, if you have selected a form defined as landscape, only landscape fonts will be displayed in the font menu.

Fast Save

A new option on the Setup menu is Fast Save. The Fast Save feature decreases the amount of time required to save documents. If you typically work on long documents (of 20 or more pages), you will appreciate Fast Save.

Be warned, however, that documents saved with Fast Save turned on are not fully formatted and therefore cannot be printed from disk. To print a document that has been Fast Saved, you must retrieve it to the screen. Because there is no way to tell whether Fast Save was on or off when you saved a document until you attempt to print it, using Fast Save is potentially inconvenient. If Fast Save was on when the document was saved, WordPerfect will display the following error message:

```
ERROR: Document was Fast Saved-Must be retrieved to print
```

If you are working on two documents and discover that you need to print a document that was Fast Saved, you must exit one of the documents, retrieve the Fast Saved document, print it, exit, and retrieve the original document. The time you may have saved by using Fast Save has been lost again, several times over.

Many users will therefore prefer to keep Fast Save turned Off (the default setting). The setting you choose will depend on many factors: the length of your document, whether you need to print page ranges, and your hardware (the speed of your printer, the speed of your computer, and whether you have a printer buffer).

TIP: If you want to leave Fast Save on and still be able to print from disk, move the cursor to the bottom of the file (Home, Home, ↓) before you save and exit the document. When you move the cursor down through the document, WordPerfect recalculates line endings and page breaks. If you save the document immediately after moving the cursor to the end of the document, it doesn't matter that Fast Save does not reformat the document. You will be able to print from disk, even though Fast Save was on.

Reveal Codes

Unlike WordPerfect 4.2, WordPerfect 5 allows full editing in Reveal Codes mode, which is now a toggle switch. After pressing Reveal Codes (Alt-F3, or F11) to turn on Reveal Codes, you must press Alt-F3, or F11 again to turn it off.

In version 5, Reveal Codes is a mode that affects *both* documents Doc 1 and Doc 2. If you turn on Reveal Codes in Doc 1 and switch to Doc 2, you will still be in Reveal Codes. (In 4.2, you could not switch documents while Reveal Codes was on.)

Spell Checking of Words with Numbers

WordPerfect 5 allows you to add words with numbers to the dictionary, a feature that many users have long requested. Unfortunately, the capability of skipping words with numbers was eliminated in the 5/5/88 release. If you have that release, call WordPerfect Corporation for an update. Note that your WordPerfect manual may not be accurate.

Deletable Soft Returns

One welcome change for veteran WordPerfect users is that you can finally turn hyphenation completely off. In 4.2, if a line was too long to fit within your margins, WordPerfect prompted you to hyphenate it, even if hyphenation was off. WordPerfect's beeping and incessant hyphenation requests could become quite annoying. If a line of text in 4.2 did not contain any spaces, there was no way to wrap it without hyphens.

To eliminate this problem, WordPerfect 5 added a Deletable Soft Return. If hyphenation is off and a line does not fit between your margins, WordPerfect will break the line for you without inserting any visible character on the screen. The break point will be indicated in Reveal Codes by a **[DSRt]** code. Deletable soft returns enable line drawings to wrap even when hyphenation is off.

Invisible Soft Returns

If you want to divide a word at a particular point without a hyphen, you can insert an Invisible Soft Return code **[ISRt]** by pressing Home, Enter. Invisible Soft Returns are handy if you want to break words at a virgule (slash).

Special Characters

The Ctrl/Alt key mapping in 4.2 was eliminated in WordPerfect 5. Instead, you can use two new features, Keyboard Layout and Compose, to enter special characters. Keyboard Layout lets you remap the keyboard any way you want. Although remapping the keyboard requires more effort than Ctrl/Alt key mapping in 4.2, it provides much more power and flexibility. Compose enables you to enter special characters such as á, â, and ñ without knowing their ASCII codes. See Chapter 18 for information about assigning special characters to a soft keyboard, and Chapter 19 for a description of the Compose feature.

As in previous versions, you can still insert a special character by depressing the Alt key and entering its ASCII code on the numeric keypad.

Overstrike has been improved in version 5 so that the overstruck characters act like a single indivisible character. Up to eight characters can be overstruck. Overstrike works differently in the new version. You now press the Overstrike key followed by the characters to be overstruck. In earlier versions, you typed the first character, entered the Overstrike code, and typed the second character.

Move

Move has been changed to cut down keystrokes and to clarify the screen prompts, which some 4.2 users found confusing. In version 5, after giving WordPerfect the command to move or copy text, you can retrieve the text at the cursor position by pressing Enter.

If you prefer not to retrieve the text immediately (for example, if you want to continue editing), press Cancel (F1). The text will remain in the Move buffer until you exit WordPerfect, or until you save more text to the Move buffer (thereby overwriting the buffer's previous contents).

As in WordPerfect 4.2, version 5 offers two ways to retrieve text from the Move buffer. The easier technique is to use the Retrieve command without specifying the name of a file (Shift-F10, Enter) to retrieve the contents of the Move buffer at the cursor position. A slightly longer technique is to go to the Move menu (Ctrl-F4) and choose **Retrieve** (**4**). At the Retrieve submenu, select **Block** (**1**), **Tabular Column** (**2**), or **Rectangle** (**3**).

The option to retrieve a block (Ctrl-F4, **4**, **1**) corresponds to Retrieve Text in 4.2 (Ctrl-F4, **5**) and is functionally equivalent to Shift-F10, Enter, in both programs. A Block in version 5 (or Text in 4.2) means a sentence, paragraph, page, or a marked block. In other words, by choosing Retrieve Block, you can retrieve any text except a tabular column or a rectangle, which WordPerfect considers special cases.

Block

Block now turns off immediately after you perform on the block an action, such as saving, deleting, or underlining. In 4.2, Block did not turn off automatically after all commands. Although the new Block is more consistent, it may seem inconvenient if you are accustomed to performing multiple operations on a single block (printing and deleting a block, for example) without rehighlighting it. If so, you can easily define a macro to rehighlight the block:

    {GoTo}{GoTo}{Block}{GoTo}{GoTo}

Retrieve and Text In Prompts

In earlier versions of WordPerfect, it was easy to combine files inadvertently by retrieving a copy of a document into an open document. To avoid this problem, WordPerfect now prompts for confirmation when you choose either **Retrieve** (**1**) or **Text In** (**5**) at the List Files screen if a document is already on the screen.

If you choose **Retrieve** (**1**), WordPerfect asks:

    Retrieve into current document? (Y/N) No

The prompt for **Text In** (**5**) is the following:

    (DOS) Retrieve [pathname]? (Y/N) No

If no document is open, no prompt is displayed. No prompt appears also if you choose either the alternative Retrieve command (Shift-F10) or one of the alternative Text In commands (Ctrl-F5, **1**, **2**, or **3**), because you are at the main editing screen and presumably know whether a document is open or not.

Setup

Setup, now incorporating many of the 4.2 Screen options, is conveniently accessible from inside WordPerfect. No longer do you have to start WordPerfect with the /S switch in order to change default values.

All of the Setup information is saved in a file called WP{WP}.SET. Previously, part of this information was saved in WP{SYS}.FIL. The remainder was saved in the WP.EXE file, which was self-modifying. One important advantage of the present method is that you can update your WP.EXE file without losing your default settings.

Codes

The representation of many codes has been made more self-explanatory in version 5. Underline, for example, changed from **[U]** and **[u]** to **[UND]** and **[und]**. For a list of codes, see the reference section of the WordPerfect manual or Chapter 3 of this book.

Search

You can now use the cursor keys to change the direction of Search or Replace. As soon as you see the Search prompt -> Srch: or <- Srch:, press the ↓ or the ↑ to change the direction of the search. (You can continue to use Forward and Backward Search as in earlier versions.)

Merge ^E

The merge code that indicates the end of a record in a secondary merge file is followed by a Hard Page code **[HPg]** instead of a Hard Return **[HRt]**, as in previous versions. Separating each record with a Hard Page code, represented by a broken double line, makes secondary merge files easier to read on-screen.

The Hard Page code also facilitates cursor movement in secondary files because each record is treated as a page. You can use the PgDn key to move to the beginning of a record, or use the Go To key to jump to a specific record (if you know the page number). If you need to print a copy of your secondary merge file, replace the **[HPg]** codes with a blank line or other delimiter. Otherwise, only one record will print per page.

Limitations Removed

In addition to the enhancements and new features offered by version 5, many limitations of the previous versions have been eliminated.

- *Search and replace codes.* While searching and replacing all codes is still not possible, you can now search and replace Indent, Left-Right Indent, Center, and Tab Align codes.

- *Endnote placement.* You can place endnotes anywhere in the document by inserting an Endnote Placement code. If you do not use an Endnote Placement code, the endnotes will print at the end of the document as in previous versions. The new Endnote Placement code enables you to place endnotes before a bibliography or index and to have endnotes at the end of each chapter in a long document.

- *Line spacing in endnotes and footnotes.* You can change line spacing in individual Endnotes and Footnotes, allowing equations that use half-line spacing in notes. In 4.2, all Endnotes and all Footnotes on a page used the same line spacing.

- *Parallel columns.* Parallel columns can extend over page breaks. WordPerfect now permits variable line spacing in parallel columns. For example, you can use single-spacing in column 1 and double-spacing in column 2.

- *Margins.* The design of 4.2 often caused text to be hidden off the left edge of the screen. Margins have been redesigned to avoid this problem, which made certain types of documents, such as scripts, difficult to edit.

Converting WordPerfect Files

Because of extensive changes in file formats, you may need to convert two categories of WordPerfect files to use them with version 5: regular documents; and special files, such as custom font tables, dictionaries, and macros. WordPerfect provides several utility programs to help you convert files in both categories.

WordPerfect Documents

Converting documents is a crucial issue for most users. Fortunately, WordPerfect offers two easy methods to convert documents created in previous versions. You can retrieve a document into version 5 and save it, or you can use a separate program called CONVERT.EXE, distributed on the Conversion disk (see Chapter 15).

CAUTION: Be sure to convert your secondary merge files to version 5 format before attempting to run a merge.

Converting by Retrieving

All versions of WordPerfect are upwardly compatible. This means that you can always retrieve a document created with one version directly into a later version of the program. If you need to use documents created under 4.1 or 4.2, just retrieve them into WordPerfect 5. You will see a message stating `Conversion in progress`. When you save the retrieved file, it becomes a version 5 document.

Because of design differences between the programs, not all 4.2 codes convert automatically. WordPerfect 5 inserts a comment whenever the program encounters a 4.2 code that it is unable to convert. You can then edit the file manually and delete the comments. These nonconvertible codes include primarily font and bin numbers.

Suppose, for example, that your 4.2 document contains a code to change to pitch 10, font 4. When you retrieve the document into version 5, the following comment is inserted in place of the font change code:

```
Note: The change to pitch (10) and font (4) must be converted
manually.
```

Creating a Conversion Resource File (.CRS)

If you have many font and bin changes in your 4.2 documents, or if you used nonstandard paper sizes, you can automate the conversion process by creating a conversion resource file. A *conversion resource file* is a WordPerfect 5 document that contains a table instructing WordPerfect how to convert specific codes. When you retrieve a document created in an earlier version of WordPerfect into version 5, WordPerfect looks in the program directory for a conversion table that corresponds to the printer you have selected. If the table exists, WordPerfect converts the codes automatically; if not, WordPerfect inserts comments to remind you that some codes were not converted. Unless you are using the STANDARD.PRS printer definition, for which WordPerfect provides a conversion resource file (STANDARD.CRS), you must create a conversion resource file for your printer.

The name of the conversion resource file must correspond to the name of the currently selected printer, or the file will be ignored. The first part the file name must be exactly the same as that of your printer definition file. The file name extension must be *.CRS*. For example, if your printer is a NEC Silentwriter™ LC-890, your printer definition file is named NESILC89.PRS. Your conversion resource file would therefore be named NESILC89.CRS.

The easiest way to create a conversion resource file for your printer is to modify the STANDARD.CRS file on the Conversion disk. Copy STANDARD.CRS to your WordPerfect program directory and rename the file as described in the preceding paragraph. Retrieve it into WordPerfect. In place of each comment, enter the WordPerfect code that you want to use. For example, if your Font 2 was a shadow font, insert the code to change the font appearance to Shadow **[SHADW]** in place of the comment

```
This was Font/Pitch 2,10 - On.
```

and the code to turn off shadow **[shadw]** in place of the comment

```
This was Font/Pitch 2,10 - Off.
```

In Reveal Codes, this section of your conversion file will appear as follows:

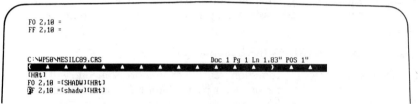

Do the same for all remaining fonts.

If your documents contained codes to change bins, insert a code for the appropriate paper size/type opposite the bin number. For example, if you used Bin 1 for legal paper, your document might look like this:

```
BN 1 =



C:\WP50\MESILC89.CRS                              Doc 1 Pg 1 Ln 1.83" POS 1"
[        ▲    ▲    ▲    ▲    ▲    ▲    ▲    ▲    ▲    ▲    }    ▲    ▲    ]
[HRt]
[HRt]
BN 1 =[Paper Sz/Typ:8.5" x 11",Standard]
```

If your 4.2 documents used a page size other than 8.5 x 11″ or if your margins were not set for one-inch top and bottom, you will also need to define a page size. Because you can have only a single page-size code for each conversion resource file, if your 4.2 documents used different margins, you will have to convert them in batches. Create a conversion resource file for one set of files, convert them, modify the conversion resource file, and convert another set.

Converting with CONVERT.EXE

To make the conversion process easier, the external conversion program CONVERT.EXE now has the capability of converting 4.2 files to version 5 format, permitting you to convert several files at once. If a conversion resource file is present in the same directory as CONVERT.EXE, the conversion program uses the conversion resource file to determine how to convert fonts, bin numbers, and margins. Otherwise, comments indicate the untranslatable 4.2 codes.

Font Conversion Program (FC.EXE)

If your copy of WordPerfect 5 is dated after 5/5/88, you have a font conversion utility program to convert 4.2 character tables to version 5 format. That utility program is provided on the Conversion disk for the convenience of users who created custom 4.2 font tables. Before investing time into converting your 4.2 font tables and writing a custom printer driver for version 5, check to make sure that you really need it. WordPerfect may have added support for the fonts you are using.

Although the font conversion program itself is simple to use, once you have converted your font table, you will need to use the new printer definition program, PTR.EXE, to integrate the new table into your printer driver. PTR.EXE is a powerful tool that all but the most advanced users will find daunting. Documentation for PTR.EXE is minimal. Trying to define your own printer driver is not recommended unless you are very knowledgeable about printers and there is no other way to get the driver you need.

Before you tackle PTR.EXE, try these alternatives:

1. Call WordPerfect Corporation's customer support. Someone will be able to check to see whether support for your printer fonts has been added in a more recent release. If so, you can request the new printer disk. (WordPerfect Corporation is constantly adding new printer drivers; unless your printer is either very new or very obscure, there is a good chance WordPerfect will support it.)

2. Contact the manufacturer of your printer or the designer of your fonts. Many companies will provide a pamphlet explaining how to use their products with major software programs such as WordPerfect 5.

3. Post a message in the printer section of the WPSG (WordPerfect Support Group) forum on CompuServe (GO WPSG). If one of the system operators can't help you, it is likely that a member of the Support Group will be able to answer your questions or even provide you with the custom definition you need. The odds are in your favor that someone else has already written or modified a driver for your printer.

Macro Conversion Program

Because macros from previous versions of WordPerfect are incompatible with version 5, WordPerfect Corporation has thoughtfully provided on the Conversion disk a macro conversion program called MACROCNV.EXE. It converts as much as possible from older macros and inserts comments for features that are not translatable. As with the conversion of WordPerfect documents (described earlier), several features, especially those relating to printing (fonts, pitch, printer number, and bin number) do not have unambiguous correspondents in version 5.

Many other 4.2 macros are no longer necessary because their functions have been built into version 5. For example, to work around 4.2's inability to replace a tab with an indent, many users wrote a repeating macro that searched for a tab, backspaced, and inserted an indent code. This macro is unnecessary in version 5 because you can now replace a tab with an indent.

The macro conversion program is especially useful for converting macros that consist primarily of text. Law and real estate offices that used macros to insert boilerplate paragraphs will appreciate not having to retype (and possibly introduce mistakes into) text macros.

The built-in macro editor in version 5 limits each macro to 5K (about 5,000 characters, or more than 2 typed pages). If you convert macros longer than 5K, the macro editor will divide them into smaller macros that are chained together, using the macro {CHAIN} command.

Converting Custom Dictionaries

If you customized your WordPerfect 4.2 dictionary by adding or deleting words, you can convert it to version 5 format with SPELL.EXE, a utility program that WordPerfect Corporation supplies on the SPELLER disk.

At the DOS level in the subdirectory where your WordPerfect Speller files are located, type *spell* to load the dictionary utility. If you have a floppy disk system, insert the Speller disk in drive A: and type *a:spell*. Choose option **9** from the main menu:

        Convert 4.2 Dictionary to 5.0

Enter the name of the 4.2 dictionary you want to convert and the name of the version 5 dictionary when you are prompted for them.

In 4.2, you could name your dictionaries anything you wanted. (The name of the main 4.2 dictionary supplied by WordPerfect Corporation was LEX.WP.) In version 5, the main dictionary for each language has an official name. When you install WordPerfect 5, you specify the directory where your main dictionary is kept, but (unlike 4.2) not the name of the dictionary file itself, which, for the American English version, is assumed to be WP{WP}US.LEX. If your converted dictionary replaces the main English dictionary, use this name.

CAUTION: Be sure to make a backup copy of the file you want to convert before continuing. Also, rename the version 5 dictionary supplied by WordPerfect Corporation so that you do not accidentally overwrite that dictionary with the converted file.

TIP: If you need to have more than one main English dictionary, copy them into separate directories. When you need to switch, change the path for the main dictionary file in Setup (Shift-F1, **7**, **4**) before spell-checking your document. (A simple macro makes switching almost automatic.)

If you saved the list of words you added to the main dictionary, you do not need to convert your main dictionary. Just use the SPELL.EXE program to add the list of words to your version 5 dictionary. (This solution is preferable to converting your old dictionary, because some misspellings have been eliminated from WordPerfect's own dictionary.) See Chapter 7 for more information.

TIP: Keep a list of the words you have added to the dictionary as well as the words you have deleted on a separate disk, for two reasons: (1) If your hard disk crashes or your spell disk goes bad, you can easily re-create your custom dictionary; (2) If WordPerfect ever changes its dictionary format again, you will avoid the need to translate your custom dictionary. You can just add the words to the new dictionary.

Conclusion

Now that you are up and running with WordPerfect 5, be sure to take the time to learn the program systematically. You will be amazed at how many new features have been added and how many others were present all along.

C

Macro Command Language

As a member of Boston Computer Society, **Marilyn Horn Claff** *leads the special interest group for WordPerfect. She also is an active participant in the WordPerfect forum on CompuServe; a columnist for* PC Report, *a Boston Computer Society newsletter; and a contributor to* The WordPerfectionist. ∎

This appendix serves as a brief overview of the commands in WordPerfect's macro language, a feature designed for advanced users. Before tackling the macro command language, be sure to read Chapter 11, which offers a general introduction to WordPerfect macros and to the built-in macro editor.

Note that you still can benefit from WordPerfect's macro capability without using the macro programming language. Simply record your keystrokes, as described in Chapter 11.

Note: Some macro commands require arguments. A *tilde* (~) character represents the end of the argument and separates a series of arguments. For example, the {PROMPT} command takes one argument, the message to be displayed on-screen. Use a tilde to indicate the end of the message. Without the tilde, the {PROMPT} command does not work properly. Forgetting to mark the end of an argument is a common mistake.

{PROMPT}Press·any·key·to·continue ~

Macro Command Reference List

{;}

Syntax: {;}*comment* ~

With the Comment command, you can embed your own remarks into a macro. Everything you type between {;} and ~ is ignored during execution of the macro.

833

{;}Go·to·top·of·doc·before·beginning·Search ~

Use comments to document your macro. You can place comments on the same line as macro commands or on a line by themselves. There are no limits to the length and to the number of comments you can use in a macro, provided that the total length of the macro does not exceed 5K (5,120 bytes).

{ASSIGN}

Syntax: {ASSIGN}*variable ~value ~*

Use this statement to assign a value to a variable in a macro (see "Variables"). The value can be a number, an expression that evaluates to a number, or a text string.

This macro assigns the value of 1,000 to {VAR 1}:

{ASSIGN}1 ~1000 ~

The following macro assigns the sum of the expression "2 + 3" to {VAR 1}:

{ASSIGN}1 ~2 +3 ~

In the following macro, the text string "YES" is assigned to {VAR 1}:

{ASSIGN}1 ~Y ~

{BELL}

The {BELL} command makes your computer beep. Use the beep to get your attention when you must enter something or to note when an error is encountered.

{BREAK}

Use the {BREAK} command to exit an {IF} structure.

{IF}{VAR 1}>5 ~
    {BREAK}
{END IF}

If you are not in an {IF} structure, use {BREAK} to move to the end of the macro. In this case, {BREAK} is equivalent to {RETURN}.

{ON ERROR}{BREAK}

{CALL}

Syntax: {CALL}*label ~*

{CALL} transfers control to a subroutine that begins at the designated label. After the subroutine ends, macro execution resumes at the statement following {CALL}.

{;}Call subroutine test next ~
{CALL}test ~

{CANCEL OFF}

{CANCEL OFF} prevents you from stopping macro execution by pressing Cancel (F1).

{CANCEL ON}

{CANCEL ON} allows you to stop the execution of a macro by pressing Cancel (F1). Because {CANCEL ON} is the default state, you need to use this command only if you used the {CANCEL OFF} command earlier in the macro.

{CASE}

Syntax: {CASE}*value ~case1 ~label1 ~case2 ~label2 ~* . . .

{CASE} lets you branch to a different point in a macro. After the {CASE} command, enter the *value* you want to test followed by a series of *cases* and associated *labels*. If the value matches one of the cases, the macro continues executing at the label associated with that particular case, and the statements following the {CASE} command do not execute. If the value does not match any of the cases, the macro falls through or continues executing at the statement following the {CASE} statement.

For example, if your macro asks you to choose between two options and assigns your answer to {VAR 1}, your case statement may look like the following:

{CASE}{VAR 1} ~1 ~Print_Doc ~2 ~Print_Page ~ ~

If you choose "1", the macro continues at the "Print_Doc" label. If you choose "2", the macro continues at the "Print_Page" label. If your answer does not match either of these cases, the macro continues with the next statement, and the {CASE} statement has no effect.

To test the {CASE} command, insert the following line after a case statement:

{PROMPT}This•tests•the•Case•command ~

If a match is found, the message is never displayed. If a match is not found, the message is displayed.

{CASE CALL}

Syntax: {CASE CALL}*value ~case1 ~label1 ~case2 ~label2 ~* . . .

{CASE CALL} combines the functions of a {CASE} statement and a {CALL} statement. The syntax for this command is exactly like that of {CASE}. The difference between the two commands is what happens *after* the statement.

A {CASE CALL} command transfers control to a subroutine, and when the subroutine finishes, the macro continues executing at the statement following the {CASE CALL} statement. The statement following the {CASE CALL} statement always executes, whether or not the value matches one of the cases. (The only exception, of course, is if the subroutine associated with the label causes the macro to end.)

{CASE CALL}{VAR 1} ~1 ~Print_Doc ~2 ~Print_Page ~ ~

{CHAIN}

Syntax: {CHAIN}*macro*

The {CHAIN} command transfers control to the designated macro after the current macro finishes executing. For instance, FIRST.WPM macro could chain to SECOND.WPM macro, which in turn could chain to THIRD.WPM. {CHAIN} is a one-way command: you cannot use this command to execute another macro and then continue with the first macro.

If you use the {CHAIN} command in a macro that includes {Search}, the chaining occurs only if the search is successful. If the search is unsuccessful, the {CHAIN} command is not executed because an unsuccessful search ends macro execution. The chaining does not occur in any case if the macro ends prematurely, as with {QUIT}.

Unless you enter more than one {CHAIN} command, the location of the {CHAIN} command in the macro does not matter. Chaining takes place only after the calling macro finishes executing. Also, note that no matter how many {CHAIN} statements you include in a macro, only the last one is executed.

To test the {CHAIN} command, write a simple macro called MASTER-1.WPM:

    {CHAIN}MACRO-A ~
    {CHAIN}MACRO-B ~
    {CHAIN}MACRO-C ~

MACRO-A consists of the following: This is MACRO-A.{Enter}
MACRO-B consists of the following: This is MACRO-B.{Enter}
MACRO-C consists of the following: This is MACRO-C.{Enter}

When you run MASTER-1, you should see This is MACRO-C, proving that only the last {CHAIN} command executes.

{CHAR}

Syntax: {CHAR}*variable ~message ~*

The {CHAR} command takes the single character you enter and assigns the character to a variable. You can specify a message to display on the status line.

In the following example, the macro displays the question Do you want to continue? (Y/N) on the status line and waits for you to press a single key (without pressing Enter). When you press the key, the macro assigns the value of the key to {VAR 1}, and the message disappears.

    {CHAR}1 ~Do you want to continue? (Y/N) ~

If you want to wait for a keystroke without displaying a message, just omit the message text:

{CHAR}1 ~ ~

Remember that you must type both tildes even if you do not enter a message prompt.

{DISPLAY OFF}

{DISPLAY OFF} makes the macro execute invisibly. Because {DISPLAY OFF} is the default state, you need to use this command only if you previously turned on the display.

{DISPLAY ON}

{DISPLAY ON} causes the macro to display on-screen as it executes. If your macro does not execute as you expect, you may be able to find your mistake by turning on the display. Macros execute somewhat faster if you turn on DISPLAY (contrary to your intuition).

{ELSE}

You can use {ELSE} with the {IF} and {IF EXISTS} commands. {ELSE} introduces an optional alternative action that will be taken only if the premise of the {IF} statement is untrue. If the first part of the {IF} statement is true, the statement following the {ELSE} statement has no effect. (See {IF} for a discussion of {IF} structures.)

{END IF}

{END IF} closes an {IF} or an {IF EXISTS} structure. Don't forget the {END IF}.

{Enter}

{Enter} represents the Hard Return function in a macro. If you record a macro and examine it in the Macro Editor, you see an {Enter} symbol at every point you pressed Enter.

The Macro Editor distinguishes between the Hard Returns that are part of the action of your macro and the Hard Returns that you use to format your macro. Press Ctrl-V, Enter to insert the {Enter} command. Press just Enter to insert a new line; the macro execution is unchanged.

{GO}

Syntax: {GO}*label* ~

The equivalent of GOTO in BASIC, {GO} lets you transfer program control to the designated label in the current macro. (You must define the label with the {LABEL} command.)

{IF}

{IF} introduces a conditional statement. {IF} tests a value and performs an action based on the outcome of the test. Optionally, an {ELSE} statement may introduce an alternative action to be taken if the value is zero or is a numeric string.

Syntax: {IF}*value ~action*{END IF}

Basic {IF} statement: If the value is not zero or is a non-numeric string, the action is performed. If the value is zero or if there is no value, the macro skips to the statement following the {END IF} statement.

Syntax: {IF}*value ~action*{ELSE}*action*{END IF}

{IF} statement with {ELSE}: If the value is not zero or is a non-numeric string, the first action is performed; otherwise, the action following the {ELSE} statement is performed.

{IF} structures may be nested.

{IF EXISTS}

Syntax: {IF EXISTS}*variable ~action*{END IF}
               {IF EXISTS}*variable ~action*{ELSE}*action*{END IF}

{IF EXISTS} tests the existence of a variable and performs an action based on the result. The syntax of this command is the same as the syntax of {IF}.

{LABEL}

Syntax: {LABEL}*name ~*

With the {LABEL} command, you can assign a name to a section of code, and then execute the commands in that section with the {CALL}, {CASE}, {CASE CALL}, and {GO} commands.

Labels have no length restrictions and are not case-sensitive. You can use any characters except a tilde in a label.

    {LABEL}START ~
    {LABEL}END ~

Make your labels meaningful: Choose labels like START, END, and ERROR instead of Label1, Label2, Label3, Label4.

{LOOK}

Syntax: {LOOK}*variable ~*

{LOOK} checks to see whether you typed a character; if so, the macro assigns the character to the variable named. {LOOK} is similar to {CHAR} except that {LOOK} does not wait for a keystroke.

The following statement assigns the keystroke (if there is one) to {VAR 1}:

    {LOOK}1 ~

{NEST}

Syntax: {NEST}*macro* ~

The {NEST} command causes the named macro to execute immediately. After the nested macro finishes executing, the calling macro resumes execution at the statement following the {NEST} command.

You can use as many {NEST} statements as you like in a macro. All of the nested macros execute unless the macro ends prematurely.

For example, each of the three nested macros in MASTER-2.WPM execute in sequence:

MASTER-2.WPM

{NEST}MACRO-1 ~
{NEST}MACRO-2 ~
{NEST}MACRO-3 ~

You also can nest macros within macros:

MASTER-2.WPM

{NEST}MACRO-1
{BELL}

MACRO-1.WPM

{NEST}MACRO-2

MACRO-2.WPM

{NEST}MACRO-3

In the preceding, MASTER-2.WPM executes MACRO-1, which in turn executes MACRO-2, which in turn executes MACRO-3. When MACRO-3 finishes, it returns to MACRO-2. MACRO-2 returns to MACRO-1, and MACRO-1 returns to MASTER-2, which executes the {BELL} command.

{ON CANCEL}

Syntax: {ON CANCEL}*command* ~

An exception handler, {ON CANCEL} instructs WordPerfect what to do if you press Cancel (F1) while the macro is executing. The default action is {RETURN CANCEL}.

You need to use the {ON CANCEL} command only if you want something different to happen when you press Cancel (F1). Place the {ON CANCEL} command before the point where Cancel (F1) might be pressed.

You can use the following commands after the {ON CANCEL} command: {BREAK}, {CALL}, {GO}, {QUIT}, {RESTART}, {RETURN}, {RETURN ERROR}, {RETURN NOT FOUND}. If you do not specify a command, the default {RETURN CANCEL} command executes.

{ON CANCEL}{RETURN ERROR} ~

Note that you must enter two tildes if you use the {GO} or {CALL} commands: one tilde is required by the {GO} or {CALL} command, and one is required by {ON CANCEL}.

{ON CANCEL}{GO}END ~ ~

{ON ERROR}

Syntax: {ON ERROR}*command* ~

An exception handler like {ON CANCEL}, {ON ERROR} instructs WordPerfect what to do if an error condition is encountered while the macro is executing. The default action for {ON ERROR} is {RETURN ERROR}.

Examples of common errors that can occur during a macro are attempting to retrieve a nonexistent file, to change to a nonexistent directory, to print a Fast Saved file from the disk, to save a file with insufficient disk space, and to use the Speller or the Thesaurus if they are not installed correctly.

Insert the {ON ERROR} command before the error condition. You can use {ON ERROR} with the following commands: {BREAK}, {CALL}, {GO}, {QUIT}, {RESTART}, {RETURN}, {RETURN CANCEL}, {RETURN NOT FOUND}.

{ON NOT FOUND}

Syntax: {ON NOT FOUND}*command* ~

The third exception handler, {ON NOT FOUND} instructs WordPerfect what to do if a condition is not found. (The program reports the not found condition as a result of an unsuccessful Search or Replace.)

The default action for {ON NOT FOUND} is {RETURN NOT FOUND}. When a macro encounters {RETURN NOT FOUND}, macro execution stops, and the statements after the search do not execute. If you want your macro to continue regardless of whether the not found condition is encountered, you can specify a different action. The {ON NOT FOUND} command must precede the not found condition. You can use {ON NOT FOUND} with the following commands: {BREAK}, {CALL}, {GO}, {QUIT}, {RESTART}, {RETURN}, {RETURN CANCEL}, {RETURN ERROR}.

The following statement instructs the macro to go to the Get_New_String label when a search fails:

{ON NOT FOUND}{GO}Get_New_String ~ ~

Note that because both the {ON NOT FOUND} and the {GO} commands require terminating tildes, the statement ends with a double tilde.

{ORIGINAL KEY}

{ORIGINAL KEY} provides a way to determine and use the original meaning of the last key pressed. If no other key has been pressed during the execution of the macro, {ORIGINAL KEY} has the original value of the key that started the macro.

For example, you could use WordPerfect's key remapping to redefine the F6 key so that (instead of turning on Bold) this key inserts your name and address at the cursor position, unless Block is on. If Block is on, pressing F6 makes the block bold:

```
{;}If·Block·is·ON,·Bold·it;·otherwise,·your·name·&·address. ~
{IF}{STATE}&128 ~
    {ORIGINAL KEY}
{ELSE}
    Your·Name{Enter}
    Your·Address{Enter}
{END IF}
```

{PAUSE}

Use {PAUSE} to pause the macro for input. A message does not appear, and the macro continues when you press Enter.

Unlike the other interactive commands ({CHAR}, {LOOK}, and {TEXT}), {PAUSE} does not capture your input.

{PROMPT}

Syntax: {PROMPT}*message* ~

{PROMPT} displays a user-defined prompt on the status line. Because the {PROMPT} is erased immediately, you need to follow the {PROMPT} statement with a {WAIT} statement to display the message long enough to read it.

```
{PROMPT}Press·any·key·to·continue ~
```

{QUIT}

Use {QUIT} to stop the macro.

```
{IF}{VAR 1}>5 ~
    {QUIT}
{END IF}
```

{RESTART}

{RESTART} terminates all macro execution at the end of the current subroutine or macro. Use {RESTART} with {IF} structures and after error trapping commands ({ON CANCEL}, {ON ERROR}, and {ON NOT FOUND}).

```
{ON CANCEL}{RESTART}
```

{RETURN}

Use {RETURN} to exit {CALL} or {CASE CALL} subroutines or leave the macro. If you are not in a subroutine, {RETURN} ends the macro.

{RETURN CANCEL}

{RETURN CANCEL} returns from the currently executing subroutine of macro, indicating cancel to the higher level.

{RETURN ERROR}

{RETURN ERROR} returns from a macro or a subroutine, indicating an error to the higher level.

{RETURN NOT FOUND}

{RETURN NOT FOUND} returns from a macro or subroutine, indicating a "not found" condition to the higher level.

{SPEED}

Syntax: {SPEED}*100th's seconds* ~

{SPEED} enables you to control the speed of the macro. Use this command to slow down your macros so that you can read messages on-screen. Also, you can use {SPEED} to help debug macros. {SPEED} stays in effect until you change the speed again or the macro finishes.

{SPEED}10 ~

{SPEED} causes the macro to pause for the specified amount of time between each step. Each character counts as a separate step, so even a very low value can cause your macro to execute too slowly if the macro includes text. To avoid executing too slowly, change the speed of the macro back to normal before any text strings.

{SPEED}10 ~
{Your Commands Here}
{SPEED}0 ~
your text here

{STATE}

Syntax: {STATE}&*[code]*

{STATE} provides a way for you to test the currently executing state of WordPerfect from within a macro. For example, you can determine if you are at the main editing screen or in a submenu, or if Reveal Codes or Merge is active. WordPerfect assigns numeric codes to each of the states for which you can test (see table C.1).

Table C.1
States of WordPerfect

Number	State
3	Document
4	Main Editing Screen
8	Editing Structure Other than Main Menu
16	Macro Definition Active
32	Macro Execution (always set)
64	Merge Active
128	Block Active
256	Typeover Active
512	Reveal Codes Active
1024	Yes/No Question Active

To determine any single item, use {STATE}, followed by &, then the numeric code. If the result is the code, the condition is true; if the result is 0, the condition is not true. This command uses a programming technique called *ANDing* and can be used in {ASSIGN}, {CASE}, {CASE CALL}, and {IF} statements.

For example, suppose you want to perform an action only if Block is on; if not, no action should be taken:

```
{IF}{STATE}&128 ~
    {your command}
{END IF}
```

{STEP OFF}

{STEP OFF} turns off the step mode.

{STEP ON}

A debugging tool, {STEP ON} executes the macro one step at a time. After each step, the macro pauses for you to press Enter. Isolate the portion of the macro that works incorrectly, if possible. Place a {STEP ON} command at the beginning of the trouble spot and a {STEP OFF} command at the end.

When you step through a macro, information appears on the status line about the next step to be executed. Printable characters are displayed normally. Macro commands are represented by two decimal numbers. The first number indicates the command type; the second number is the command, macro, or variable number. Four macro command types are possible:

```
128 = Normal Command Originally Assigned to a Key
252 = Specific Macro Command
254 = Alt-Macro Execution
255 = Variable Execution
```

{Tab}

{Tab} represents the tab function. To insert a {Tab} function, press Ctrl-V; then Tab. If you press just Tab (without Ctrl-V), the text is indented, and the Tab is not interpreted as a tab function.

{TEXT}

Syntax:　　　{TEXT}*variable ~message ~*

{TEXT} prompts you for a text string of up to 120 characters. You can display a message on the status line; when you enter the specified information, the program assigns the text string to the variable specified.

The macro assigns your name to {VAR 1} in the following macro:

　　{TEXT}1 ~Type·your·full·name·and·press·Enter. ~

{WAIT}

Syntax:　　　{WAIT}*10th's second ~*

{WAIT} causes the macro to pause for the specified amount of time. Use {WAIT} with screen prompts which would otherwise flash by too quickly to read.

Variables

A *variable* is a name given to a place in the computer's memory where a value is stored. Use variables to store a text string for reuse or to store your response to questions for conditional branching.

The value of a variable in WordPerfect can be an integer (a whole number) or a text string of up to 120 characters. You can have up to ten variables, named {VAR 1} through {VAR 0}. When you assign a value to a variable, it retains that value until you assign the variable a new value or exit WordPerfect.

For example, a macro could ask for your name and assign the answer to a variable. The macro could then address you by name:

　　{TEXT}1 ~Type·your·name·and·press·Enter. ~
　　{PROMPT}Hello,·{VAR 1}.·How·are·you·today? ~

Or the macro could ask a yes/no question:

　　{CHAR}1 ~Do·you·want·to·continue?·(Y/N) ~

Entering the Name of Variables

To insert the name of a variable in a macro, use the Macro Editor. In the macro editing screen, press Ctrl-V or press Macro Define (Ctrl-F10); then hold down the Alt key and press a digit from 1 to 0, corresponding to the number of the variable.

For example, to insert the variable name {VAR 9}, press Alt-9. If you pressed Macro Define (Ctrl-F10) to start, press Macro Define (Ctrl-F10) again.

The macro language uses two conventions to refer to each variable. In some cases, the macro language requires {VAR} followed by the digit—for instance, {VAR 8}. In others you can use just the digit—for instance, 8. To determine which form to use, follow these simple rules:

If the syntax of a command *requires* a variable, use just the digit (0 to 9). Examples:

    {ASSIGN}1 ~TRUE ~

    {CHAR}5 ~(Y/N) ~

If either a variable or a regular digit is acceptable in the command, use {VAR} followed by the digit. Examples:

    Dear {VAR 6}:

    {PROMPT}Hello, {VAR 3}!

CAUTION: These two forms are not interchangeable.

Assigning a Value to a Variable in a Macro

To assign a variable within the Macro Editor, use the {ASSIGN} command, or use one of the prompts for input, such as {CHAR}, {LOOK}, or {TEXT}. Examples:

    {ASSIGN}6 ~$2,067 ~

    {LOOK}5 ~

You also can assign a variable in the main editing screen as you record a macro. Press Ctrl-PgUp at the point where you wish to assign a value to a variable. From the menu that appears on the status line, select Assign (3). When prompted for the Variable:, type any of the digits 1-0 on the top row of your keyboard. When prompted for Value:, type anything you want, up to 120 characters.

Assigning a Value to a Variable outside a Macro

To assign a variable when you are not recording or editing a macro, press Ctrl-PgUp. When prompted for Variable:, type any of the digits 1 to 0 on the top row of your keyboard. When prompted for Value:, type anything you want, up to 120 characters.

To assign a block to a variable, Press Block (Alt-F4, or F12), block the text that you want to assign to a variable, press Ctrl-PgUp, and press a digit from 1-0.

The macro assigns only the text to the variable; attributes such as bold and underlining are lost.

CAUTION: Do not attempt to assign a block longer than 120 characters to a variable.

To insert the value of a variable at the cursor position, press Alt and the number of the variable (1 to 0 on the top row of your keyboard). The Alt-digit keys function as primitive, text-only macros. For example, if you assigned the value "Ann Arbor, Michigan" to {VAR 3}, pressing Alt-3 inserts these words at the cursor position.

D

List of WordPerfect Commands

Feature	Keystrokes	Feature	Keystrokes
Advance.......................	Shift-F8, 4, 1	Columns (Text and Parallel)......	Alt-F7
Appearance Attributes...........	Ctrl-F8, 2	Compose......................	Ctrl-2
Automatic Reference............	Alt-F5, 1	Concordance..................	Alt-F5, 5, 3
Automatically Format &		Conditional End of Page.........	Shift-F8, 4, 2
Rewrite	Shift-F1, 3, 1	Control Printer.................	Shift-F7, 4
Auxiliary Files Location..........	Shift-F1, 7	Copy File.....................	F5, Enter, 8
Back space....................	Back space	Create Directory................	F5, =
Backup.......................	Shift-F1, 1	Cursor Movement	
Base Font.....................	Ctrl-F8, 4	Beginning of Document	Home, Home, ↑
Binding	Shift-F7, B	Beginning of Line	
Block	Alt-F4	(before codes)...........	Home, Home,
Block Append (Block On).....	Ctrl-F4, 1, 4		Home, ←
Block Center (Block On)......	Shift-F6	Beginning of Line	
Delete (Block On)...........	Del	(after codes).............	Home, Home, ←
Move (Block On)............	Ctrl-F4	Character Left...............	←
Print (Block On)............	Shift-F7	Character Right	→
Protect (Block On)...........	Shift-F8	End of Document............	Home, Home, ↓
Save (Block On).............	F10	End of Line	Home, Home, →
Bold.........................	F6 or Ctrl-F8, 2, 1		or End
Cancel	F1	Left Edge of Screen	Home, ←
Print Job(s).................	Shift-F7, 4, 1	Right Edge of Screen..........	Home, →
Cartridges and Fonts............	Shift-F7, S, 3, 5	Line Down..................	↓
Case Conversion (Block On)......	Shift-F3	Line Up	↑
Center	Shift-F6	Page Down	PgDn
Center Page Top to Bottom.......	Shift-F8, 2, 1	Page Up....................	PgUp
Change Default Directory........	F5, Enter, 7	Screen Down	Home, ↓ or gray
Colors/Fonts/Attributes	Shift-F1, 3, 2		plus (+)

Feature	Keystrokes	Feature	Keystrokes
Screen Up	Home, ↑ or gray minus (–)	Force Odd/Even Page	Shift-F8, 2, 2
Word Left	Ctrl, ←	Format	Shift-F8
Word Right	Ctrl, →	Forms	Shift-F7, S, 3, 4
End of Document	Home, Home, ↓	Generate Tables, Indexes, etc.	Alt-F5, 6, 5
Date Code	Shift-F5, 2	Generic Word Processor	
Date Format	Shift-F5, 3	Format	Ctrl-F5, 3
Date Text	Shift-F5, 1	"Go" (Start Printer)	Shift-F7, 4, 4
Date/Outline	Shift-F5	GoTo	Ctrl-Home
Decimal/Align Character	Shift-F8, 4, 3	Go to DOS	Ctrl-F1, 1
Define (Mark Text)	Alt-F5, 5	Graphics	Alt-F9
Delete Character Left	Back space	Graphics Quality	Shift-F7, G
Delete Character Right	Del	Graphics Screen Type	Shift-F1, 3, 5
Delete Directory	F5, Enter, 2	Hard Page	Ctrl-Enter
Delete File	F5, Enter, 2	Hard Return	Enter
Delete to End of Line (EOL)	Ctrl-End	Hard Return Display Character	Shift-F1, 3, 6
Delete to End of Page (EOP)	Ctrl-PgDn	Hard Space	Home, space bar
Delete Word	Ctrl-Back space	Headers	Shift-F8, 1, 1
Delete Word Left	Home, Back space	Help	F3
Delete Word Right	Home, Delete	Horizontal Lines (Graphics)	Alt-F9, 5, 1
Directory	F5	Hyphenation	Shift-F8, 1, 1
Display All Print Jobs	Shift-F7, 4, 3	Hyphenation Zone	Shift-F8, 1, 2
Display Pitch	Shift-F8, 3, 1	Left Indent	F4
Display Setup	Shift-F1, 3	Left/Right Indent	Shift-F4
Document Comments	Ctrl-F5, 5	Index	
Document Compare	Alt-F5, 6, 2	Define	Alt-F5, 5, 3
Document Format	Shift-F8, 3	Mark	Alt-F5, 3
Document Summary	Shift-F8, 3, 4	Initial Codes (Format)	Shift-F8, 3, 2
DOS Text File		Initial Settings (Setup)	Shift-F1, 5
Retrieve (CR/LF to [HRt])	Ctrl-F5, 1, 2	Insert	Ins
Retrieve (CR.LF to [SRt])	Ctrl-F5, 1, 3	Italics	Ctrl-F8, 2, 4
Save	Ctrl-F5, 1, 1	Justifications	Shift-F8, 1, 3
Double Underline	Ctrl-F8, 2, 3	Kerning	Shift-F8, 4, 6, 1
Edit Table of Authorities		Keyboard Layout	Shift-F1, 6
Full Form	Alt-F5, 5, 5	Language	Shift-F8, 4, 4
Endnote	Ctrl-F7, 2	Large Print	Ctrl-F8, 1, 5
Endnote Placement Code	Ctrl-F7, 3	Line Draw	Ctrl-F3, 2
Exit	F7	Line Format	Shift-F8, 1
Extra Large Print	Ctrl-F8, 1, 7	Line Height	Shift-F8, 1, 4
Fast Save	Shift-F1, 4	Line Numbering	Shift-F8, 1, 5
Figure Box (Graphics)	Alt-F9, 1	Line Spacing	Shift-F8, 1, 6
Filename on Status Line	Shift-F1, 3, 4	List	
Fine Print	Ctrl-F8, 1, 3	Define	Alt-F5, 5, 2
Flush Right	Alt-F6	Mark (Block On)	Alt-F5, 2
Footers	Shift-F8, 2, 4	List Files	F5, Enter
Footnote	Ctrl-F7, 1	Location of Auxiliary Files	Shift-F1, 7
		Look	F5, Enter, 6

Feature	Keystrokes	Feature	Keystrokes
Macro	Alt-F10	Remove Redline/Strikeout	Alt-F5, 6, 1
Macro Define	Ctrl-F10	Repeat Value	Esc
Left Margin Release	Shift-Tab	Replace	Alt-F2
Margins		Replace, Extended	Home, Alt-F2
Left/Right	Shift-F8, 1, 7	Retrieve Block (Move)	Ctrl-F4, 4, 1
Top/Bottom	Shift-F8, 2, 5	Retrieve Document	Shift-F10
Mark Text	Alt-F5	Retrieve, List Files	F5, Enter, 1
Master Document		Retrieve Rectangle (Move)	Ctrl-F4, 4, 3
Condense	Alt-F5, 6, 4	Retrieve Tabular	
Expand	Alt-F5, 6, 3	Column (Move)	Ctrl-F4, 4, 4
Subdocument	Alt-F5, 2	Reveal Codes	Alt-F3
Math/Columns	Alt-F7	Rewrite Screen	Ctrl-F3, 0
Merge	Ctrl-F9, 1	Rush Print Job	Shift-F7, 4, 2
Codes	Shift-F9	Save	F10
Move	Ctrl-F4	Screen	Ctrl-F3
Block (Block On)	Ctrl-F4, 1	Forward Search	F2
Page	Ctrl-F4, 3	Forward Search, Extended	Home, F2
Paragraph	Ctrl-F4, 2	Backward Search	Shift, F2
/Rename (List Files)	F5, Enter, 3	Backward Search	
Sentence	Ctrl-F4, 1	Extended	Home, Shift-F2
Tabular Column (Block On)	Ctrl-F4, 2	Select Printer	Shift-F7, S
Name Search (List Files)	F5, Enter, N	Setup	Shift-F1
New Page Number	Shift-F8, 2, 6	Shadow Print	Ctrl-F8, 2, 6
Normal Font (Turn off Attrib.)	Ctrl-F8, 3	Shell	Ctrl-F1
Number of Copies	Shift-F7, N	Side-by-side Column	
Outline	Shift-F5, 4	Display	Shift-F1, 3, 8
Outline (Attribute)	Ctrl-F8, 2, 5	Size Attribute	Ctrl-F8, 1
Overstrike	Shift-F8, 4, 5	Small Caps	Ctrl-F8, 2, 7
Page Format	Shift-F8, 2	Small Print	Ctrl-F8, 1, 4
Page Numbering	Shift-F8, 2, 7	Sort	Ctrl-F9, 2
Paragraph Number	Shift-F5, 5	Spell	Ctrl-F2
Paragraph Numbering		Split Screen	Ctrl-F3, 1
Definition	Shift-F5, 6	Stop Printing	Shift-F7, 4, 5
Paper Size/Type	Shift-F8, 2, 8	Strikeout	Ctrl-F8, 2, 9
Password	Ctrl-F5, 2	Style	Alt-F8
Print	Shift-F7	Subscript	Ctrl-F8, 1, 2
Block (Block On)	Shift-F7, Y	Superscript	Ctrl-F8, 1, 1
Color	Ctrl-F8, 5	Suppress (Page Format)	Shift-F8, 2, 9
Full Document	Shift-F7, 1	Switch	Shift-F3
List Files	F5, Enter, 4	Tab Align	Ctrl-F6
Page	Shift-F7, 2	Tab Set	Shift-F8, 1, 8
Printer Command	Shift-F8, 4, 6, 2	Table (Graphics)	Alt-F9, 2
Printer Settings	Shift-F7, S, 3	Table of Authorities	
Redline	Ctrl-F8, 2, 8	Define	Alt-F5, 5, 4
Redline Method	Shift-F8, 3, 3	Edit Full Form	Alt-F5, 5, 5

Feature	Keystrokes
Full Form (Block On).........	Alt-F5, 4
Short Form	Alt-F5, 4
Table of Contents	
Define	Alt-F5, 5, 4
Mark (Block On).............	Alt-F5, 1
Text Box (Graphics).............	Alt-F9, 3
Text In (List Files)	F5, Enter, 5
Text In/Out	Ctrl-F5
Text Quality	Shift-F7, T
Thesaurus	Alt-F1
Thousand's Separator............	Shift-F8, 4, 3
Type Through..................	Shift-F7, 5
Typeover	Ins
Undelete	F1
Underline......................	F8 or Ctrl-F8, 2, 2
Underline Spaces/Tabs	Shift-F8, 4, 7
Units of Measure	Shift-F1, 8
User-Defined Box (Graphics)	Alt-F9, 4
Vertical Line (Graphics)..........	Alt-F9, 5, 2
Very Large Print	Ctrl-F8, 1, 6
View Document	Shift-F7, 6
Widow/Orphan Protection........	Shift-F8, 1, 9
Window.......................	Ctrl-F3, 1
Word/Letter Spacing	Shift-F8, 4, 6, 3
Word Search...................	F5, Enter, 9
Word Spacing Justification	
Limits......................	Shift-F8, 4, 6, 4
WordPerfect 4.2 Format	Ctrl-F5, 4

Index

X-Y-Z

More Computer Knowledge from Que

LOTUS SOFTWARE TITLES

DATABASE TITLES

MACINTOSH AND APPLE II TITLES

APPLICATIONS SOFTWARE TITLES

WORD-PROCESSING AND DESKTOP PUBLISHING TITLES

HARDWARE AND SYSTEMS TITLES

PROGRAMMING AND TECHNICAL TITLES

Que Order Line: **1-800-428-5331**

REGISTRATION CARD

Register your copy of *Using WordPerfect 5* and receive information about Que's newest products. Complete this registration card and return it to Que Corporation, P.O. Box 90, Carmel, IN 46032.

Name _____ Phone _____

Company _____ Title _____

Address _____

City _____ State _____ ZIP _____

Please check the appropriate answers:

Where did you buy *Using WordPerfect 5*?
- ☐ Bookstore (name: _____)
- ☐ Computer store (name: _____)
- ☐ Catalog (name: _____)
- ☐ Direct from Que _____
- ☐ Other: _____

How many computer books do you buy a year?
- ☐ 1 or less
- ☐ 2-5
- ☐ 6-10
- ☐ More than 10

How many Que books do you own?
- ☐ 1
- ☐ 2-5
- ☐ 6-10
- ☐ More than 10

How long have you been Using WordPerfect?
- ☐ Less than 6 months
- ☐ 6 months to 1 year
- ☐ 1-3 years
- ☐ More than 3 years

What influenced your purchase of *Using WordPerfect 5*?
- ☐ Personal recommendation
- ☐ Advertisement
- ☐ In-store display
- ☐ Price
- ☐ Other: _____
- ☐ Que catalog
- ☐ Que mailing
- ☐ Que reputation

How would you rate the overall content of *Using WordPerfect 5*?
- ☐ Very good
- ☐ Good
- ☐ Satisfactory
- ☐ Poor

How would you rate the chapters on *using laser printers*?
- ☐ Very good
- ☐ Good
- ☐ Satisfactory
- ☐ Poor

How would you rate the information on *WordPerfect macros*?
- ☐ Very good
- ☐ Good
- ☐ Satisfactory
- ☐ Poor

How would you rate the appendix titled *WordPerfect 5 for 4.2 Users*?
- ☐ Very good
- ☐ Satisfactory
- ☐ Good
- ☐ Poor

What do you like *best* about *Using WordPerfect 5*?

What do you like *least* about *Using WordPerfect 5*?

How do you use *Using WordPerfect 5*?

What other Que products do you own?

For what other programs would a Que book be helpful?

Please feel free to list any other comments you may have about *Using WordPerfect 5*.

_____

_____

_____

_____

_____

_____

FOLD HERE

Place
Stamp
Here

Que Corporation
P.O. Box 90
Carmel, IN 46032

ORDER FROM QUE TODAY

Item	Title	Price	Quantity	Extension
807	Using PC DOS, 2nd Edition	$22.95		
805	Using 1-2-3, Special Edition	24.95		
838	MS-DOS User's Guide, 3rd Edition	22.95		
74	WordPerfect QueCards	21.95		

Book Subtotal _____
Shipping & Handling ($2.50 per item) _____
Indiana Residents Add 5% Sales Tax _____
GRAND TOTAL _____

Method of Payment

☐ Check   ☐ VISA   ☐ MasterCard   ☐ American Express

Card Number _____ Exp. Date _____

Cardholder's Name _____

Ship to _____

Address _____

City _____ State _____ ZIP _____

If you can't wait, call **1-800-428-5331** and order TODAY.
All prices subject to change without notice.

FOLD HERE

_____

_____

_____

_____

Que Corporation
P.O. Box 90
Carmel, IN 46032

USING
WORDPERFECT® 5

Keyboard Command Map for the IBM PC, PC/XT, and look-alikes
featuring Version 5

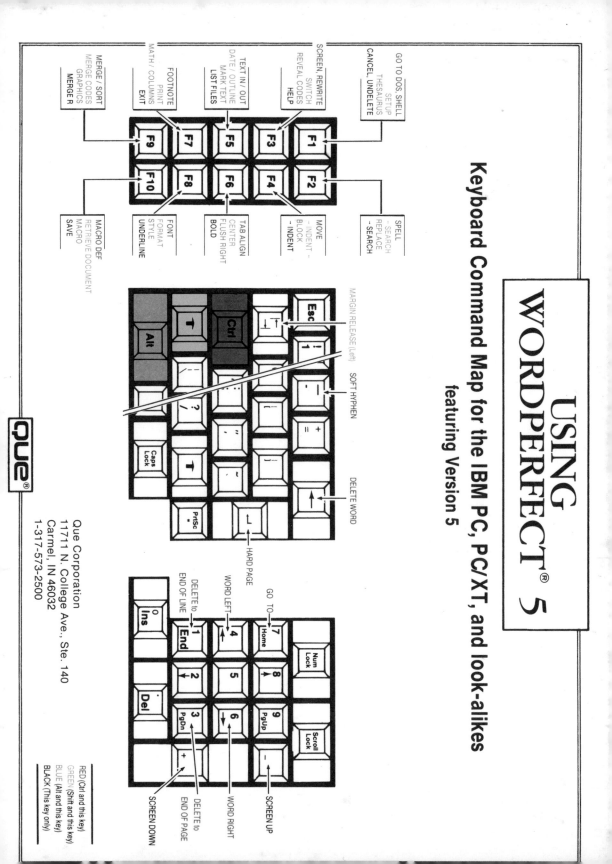

Que Corporation
11711 N. College Ave., Ste. 140
Carmel, IN 46032
1-317-573-2500

RED (Ctrl and this key)
GREEN (Shift and this key)
BLUE (Alt and this key)
BLACK (This key only)

USING
WORDPERFECT® 5

Keyboard Command Map for the IBM AT and look-alikes
featuring Version 5

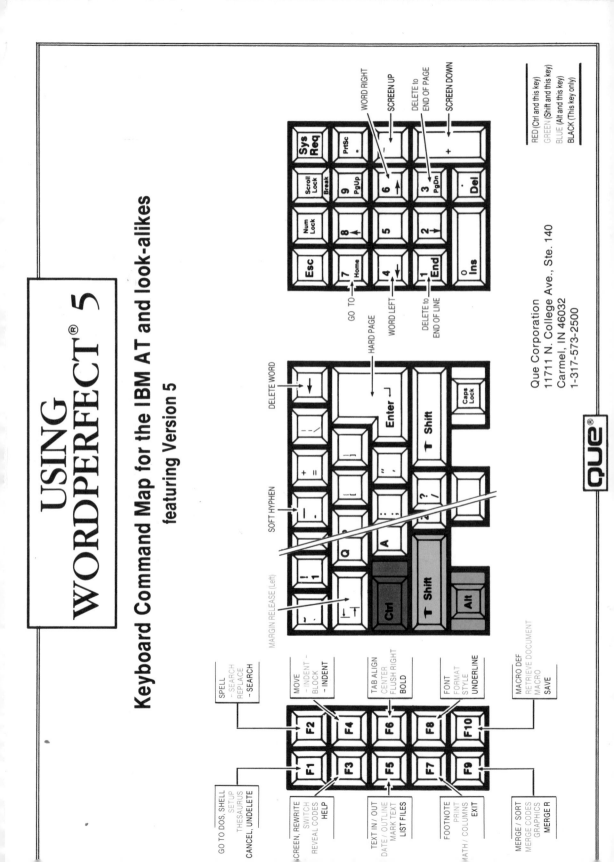

SPELL
- SEARCH
REPLACE
- SEARCH

MOVE
- INDENT -
BLOCK
- INDENT

TAB ALIGN
CENTER
FLUSH RIGHT
BOLD

FONT
FORMAT
STYLE
UNDERLINE

MACRO DEF
RETRIEVE DOCUMENT
MACRO
SAVE

GO TO DOS, SHELL
SETUP
THESAURUS
CANCEL, UNDELETE

SCREEN, REWRITE
SWITCH
REVEAL CODES
HELP

TEXT IN / OUT
DATE / OUTLINE
MARK TEXT
LIST FILES

FOOTNOTE
PRINT
MATH / COLUMNS
EXIT

MERGE / SORT
MERGE CODES
GRAPHICS
MERGE R

DELETE WORD

SOFT HYPHEN

MARGIN RELEASE (Left)

HARD PAGE

GO TO

WORD LEFT

DELETE to
END OF LINE

WORD RIGHT

SCREEN UP

DELETE to
END OF PAGE

SCREEN DOWN

RED (Ctrl and this key)
GREEN (Shift and this key)
BLUE (Alt and this key)
BLACK (This key only)

Que Corporation
11711 N. College Ave., Ste. 140
Carmel, IN 46032
1-317-573-2500

Que®

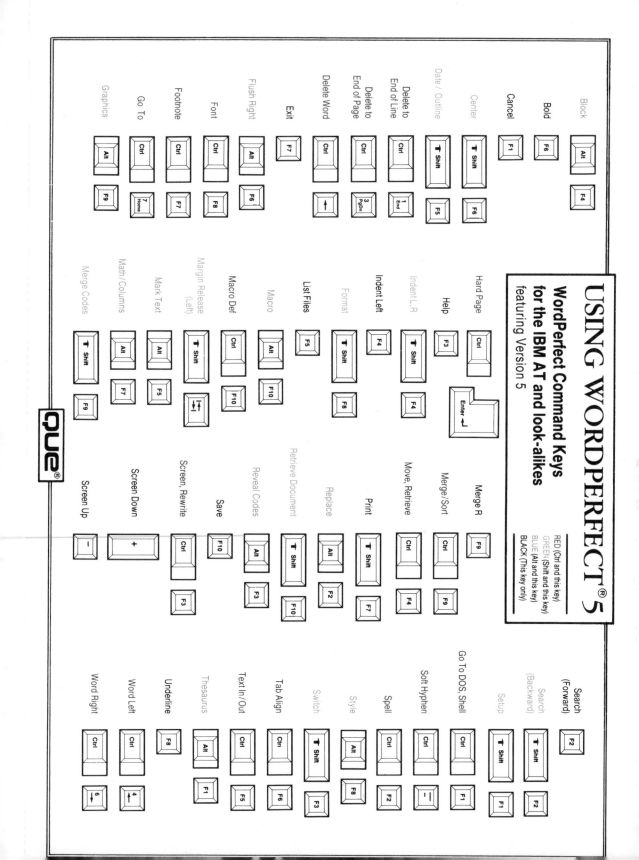

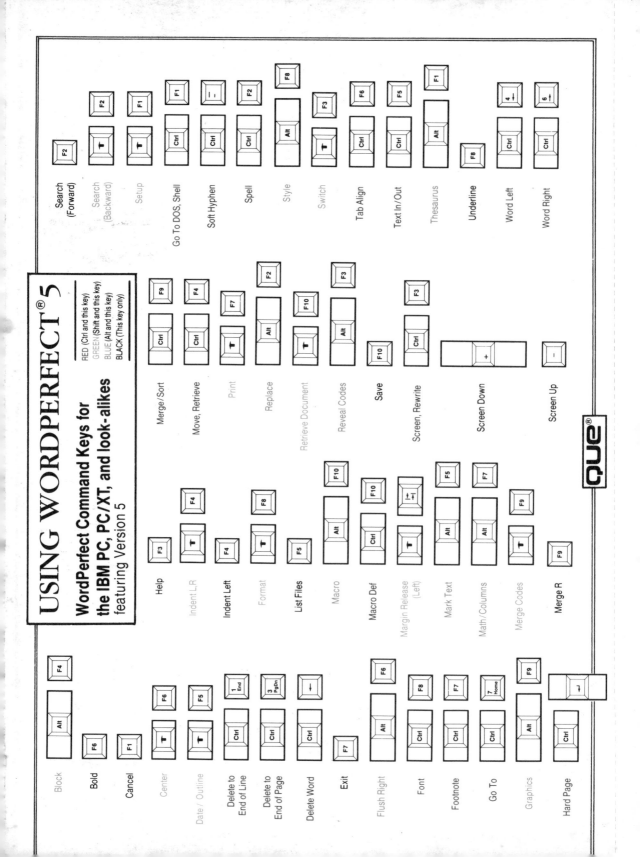

USING WORDPERFECT® 5

WordPerfect Command Keys for the IBM PC, PC/XT, and look-alikes

featuring Version 5

RED (Ctrl and this key)
GREEN (Shift and this key)
BLUE (Alt and this key)
BLACK (This key only)

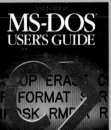

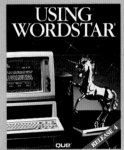
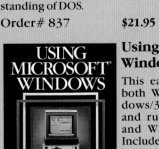

Introducing...

Que Quick Reference Series

When you need a convenient reference to your favorite applications, choose the Que **Quick Reference** series. Each Que **Quick Reference** is a low-priced, easy-to-use reference to common program commands and functions, and contains the high-quality information you expect from Que. Essential information in a compact format—the Que **Quick Reference** series.

Look for the following **Quick Reference** titles: *1-2-3 Quick Reference, MS-DOS Quick Reference, WordPerfect Quick Reference, C Quick Reference, QuickBASIC Quick Reference,* and *dBASE IV Quick Reference.* **Just $6.95 each, available this fall.**

and

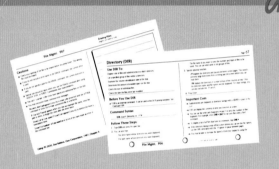

QueCards—The Comprehensive, Easy-To-Use Reference

For detailed reference information in an easy-to-use format, choose **QueCards**. **QueCards** are removable 5″ × 8″ cards, housed in a sturdy 3-ring binder. The cards can be used with the built-in easel or removed and placed next to your keyboard. Each **QueCard** contains detailed information about a particular command, function, or application. When you need a comprehensive, easy-to-use reference, you need **QueCards!**

Look for these **QueCards** titles: *1-2-3 QueCards, DOS QueCards, WordPerfect QueCards,* and *dBASE IV QueCards.* **Just $21.95 each.**

Que QuickStart Series— The Graphics Approach

If you believe that "a picture paints a thousand words," then the Que **QuickStart** series is for you! **QuickStarts** help you learn your applications quickly, using a unique new graphics-based presentation. Each book contains more than 100 two-page illustrations—accompanied by easy-to-follow text—that lead you step-by-step through program basics. Learn your applications the **QuickStart** way with the Que **QuickStart** series!

HyperCard QuickStart is currently available; the following **QuickStarts** will be available this fall: *1-2-3 QuickStart, MS-DOS QuickStart, WordPerfect QuickStart,* and *dBASE IV QuickStart.* **Just $21.95 each.**

LOOK FOR THESE OTHER INFORMATIVE QUE BOOKS:

All prices subject to change without notice.

Que books can be found in your local bookstore or computer store.

Prices and charges are for domestic orders only. Non-U.S. prices might be